SHOW TUNES

SHOW TUNES

1905–1991

*The Songs, Shows and Careers of
Broadway's Major Composers*

STEVEN SUSKIN

Revised and Expanded

Limelight Editions

NEW YORK

First Limelight Edition May 1992

Library of Congress Cataloging-in-Publication Data
Suskin, Steven
    Show Tunes, 1905-1991 : the songs, shows and careers of Broadway's major composers / Steven Suskin.–Rev. and updated.
    1st Limelight ed:
        p. cm.
    Includes bibliographical references (p.   ) and indexes.
    ISBN 0-87910-146-6 :
        1. Composers–United States. 2. Musicals–United States–History and criticism.
I. Title
ML390.S983   1992
782.1'4'0922–dc20
    [B]   91-23643
                                                                           CIP
                                                                           MN

Contents

PART 3

PART 4

PART 5

APPENDIX 1

APPENDIX 2

APPENDIX 3

Foreword

One of the happiest memories of my second Broadway engagement (in October of 1988) was the gift of a book from the property master of the Booth Theatre, Leo Herbert. Leo (a descendant of Victor Herbert) has been around the theater scene for a long time and describes himself as "an old guy who usually smiles and pisses ice water." But he was moved enough by my performance of well-known and lesser known Broadway and Hollywood songs to give me a copy of Steven Suskin's book *Show Tunes*. It was a perfect gift. The book had a very personal effect on me. Let me explain why.

I have spent most of my life not as a performer but as an archivist . . . someone who spends hours on end burrowing through stacks of musty papers and manuscripts in libraries and private collections (and sometimes other locales too exotic to mention). One's hope, of course, is to expand the general knowledge of the golden age of popular music and also to find some unknown treasure adding to the somewhat limited storehouse of knowledge about show music. We do know a lot, but there is also a lot that we don't know. Many songs are lost forever because of carelessness or simply lack of foresight.

During my six-year stint as assistant to Ira Gershwin, I gained a better perspective on why many songs created only a few decades ago no longer survive. Ira explained that theater songs enjoyed a limited shelf life. They were written for a show that, if it was lucky, might run for a couple of hundred performances—and that was the end of it. Nobody thought about preserving the music and no one was particularly concerned about what happened to original orchestrations after a show died. The orchestral parts were useless—dead weight that took up space. Ira told me that if a show failed, after the last performance all the musicians in the pit would gleefully tear up the music. Good riddance! Sometimes a successful show would go on tour, but when the tour was over, the music would again fall into oblivion.

Authors of songs don't always have copies of their own work, either.

When I first went to work for Ira Gershwin, I was amazed at what he had in his private archive, but also at what he didn't have. On the plus side, there were lyric sheets for most of his works, including extra words for some of the famous ones. He also had a caché of manuscripts of some unpublished songs in his brother George's own hand. There were, however, many holes in Ira's collection. Where were the original first edition copies of some of these songs? What happened to all the music written for several hundred of those lyric sheets? What happened to the lyrics not penciled in on some of the copies of George's mansucripts? Where were the copies of Ira's earliest songs written with Gus Edwards and Al Sherman?

Sometimes I would find a lyric sheet and a separate copy of the music for a particular song and "marry" the two, as I did with "Gather Ye Rosebuds." One time I found the music for an earlier version of the title song "Strike Up The Band," but I never found the lyrics. Ditto with a song called "Leave It To Love," cut from *Lady Be Good.* Ira would ask me once every couple of months if I had located the lyrics for that one—he couldn't believe that he didn't have the text for one of his favorite songs—but it never turned up.

Of course, sometimes treasures *do* turn up, as they did in 1982 at the Warner Brothers Music warehouse in Secausus, New Jersey. Boxes and boxes of "lost" songs and orchestrations by the Broadway greats and not-so-greats turned up—over 80 boxes, as I recall. Ira sent me to see what material written by the brothers Gershwin might have surfaced, not thinking that anything of consequence would be there. When I called to tell him that, for starters, I had counted 37 manuscripts in George's hand, he truly did not believe it, and it took a couple of months for the discovery to really sink in.

But the Lord giveth and the Lord taketh away. Shortly after the discovery in Secausus, I learned that many boxes of unique and irreplaceable musical theater scores housed in an old theater basement in London had been destroyed. The theater had been taken over by Andrew Lloyd Webber, and somebody had cleaned out the "useless" stuff taking up so much space in the basement. They saved the scores of all the old warhorses like *Annie Get Your Gun* (those might be of use, they thought) but destroyed the obscure material—including several complete Gershwin scores and orchestrations!

So in view of the above, if you want to find out what is available in the way of songs from a particular Broadway show, where do you look?

Most Broadway songs live on in two primary forms, sheet music or on record. Before the publication of *Show Tunes,* it was very hard to determine exactly what material exists in either of those formats. Thanks to Steven's meticulous research, we now have a complete chronicle of what is out there, combined with much pertinent information about the shows and their creators. His book is the first of its kind and is obviously a labor of love. It will only become more valuable through the years, as more of our Broadway heritage disappears. Many of the songs listed in *Show Tunes* are so obscure that many of their publishers do not even possess a copy of them. (EMI Music Publishers, for example, can only supply you with a blurry microfilm copy of many of their old songs. They didn't bother to save any of the originals.) *Show Tunes* also directs the reader to various archives to help locate a particular song, an especially valuable feature of the book.

Steven's magnum opus gives me a burst of adrenaline every time I open it. It is clearly and thoughtfully organized, and a pleasure to read. I also get a burst of adrenaline when I read some of his comments about various songwriters. I certainly don't agree with all of his opinions. For example, how can I possibly agree with his final paragraph in the section about George Gershwin? But I do respect his commentary.

I'm sure you will enjoy this revised edition of *Show Tunes.* I am very flattered to be a tiny part of it, and you can bet that I am going to send a copy to my friend Leo Herbert over at the Booth. After all, if it weren't for him I might never have found this treasure trove in the first place.

MICHAEL FEINSTEIN
July 1991

Preface

It's probably true that a few people are *not* interested in show tunes. This book isn't for them.

A veritable mountain of material has been written about Broadway musicals. Some volumes focus on individual creators or performers; others discuss shows in general or certain selected shows. Distinct musical theatre forms have been examined, as has the total work of an era. There are biographies—some excellent, some not—of specific composers, or groups of composers, or composers and their lyricists. All concentrate on the hit shows, with summaries of plots, excerpts from reviews, etc.

But the Broadway musical is built on show tunes.

Song soothes the soul. Personal favorites express our feelings better than we can in our own words. Truths captured in music and lyric by the Messrs. Rodgers and Hart, or Gershwin and Gershwin, or Arlen (and on) remain constant. Their songs are on our lips, or in our ears, or at the touch of our fingers whenever we want them, whenever we need them. *Dancing In The Dark* at twilight, *Time On My Hands* at dawn. The plaintive *Someone To Watch Over Me*, the importunate *I Can't Get Started*. *All The Things You Are* in times rhapsodic, *Spring Is Here* in times unrequited, and *I've Got The World On A String* any old time at all.

This book grew from the assumption that for every well-known Kern or Duke or Youmans treasure, there were two or three unknown gems hidden from view. (An assumption that proved, for the most part, to be correct!) It was quickly discovered that there was no accurate list of *what* to look for. The works of Gershwin and Porter have been fairly well catalogued; information on other composers is inconsistent, haphazard, or simply nonexistent. Shows which closed out of town and "plays with music," particularly, have heretofore been ignored.

The search grew into a quest. Pursuit of accuracy eventually led to a piece-by-piece search through the copyright deposits at the Library of Congress. The Library's vast collection of uncatalogued material inconveniently mixes together all theatre, vaudeville, and motion picture music from America, England, France, Austria, Germany, Italy, Mexico, etc. registered since the turn of the century. In the interests of providing a fairly complete guide to important musical theatre, the number of examined composers trebled.

A list of song titles, though, is ultimately of limited interest, no matter how extensive. Personal involvement in and enthusiasm for the musical theatre led to an investigation of *why* these composers wrote what they did. *How* did they come to work with their various collaborators? Did the songs work in the theatre? What were the effects of success and failure on future work (and the work of others)? The Broadway musical has been examined from the perspective of scholars and musicologists, but rarely from a *theatrical* viewpoint; this book does so.

Show Tunes is my personal paean to (and investigation of) the music that makes me, figuratively, dance on the ceiling. I was born in a trunk full of original cast albums, and I have spent many a night and day— vocationally and avocationally—in the Broadway theatre. I have examined some 7,000 songs for this book, listening with a highly analytical musical ear. Shows by the hundreds (800 or so) were researched in my guise as musical-comedy detective, discovering coincidences, contradictions, surprises and curiosities. Finally, I liberally laced my accounts of songs, shows, and careers with random observations accumulated during my long years as a Broadway production manager. (Editor's note: the author appears to have been born sometime between WISH YOU WERE HERE and WONDERFUL TOWN).

The reader will find favorite and (nonfavorite) composers within, perhaps even a few unknowns. For one discriminating individual to enjoy all their songs is virtually impossible. Tastes, even among drama critics, vary. Whether you agree with my comments or not, I trust you will find them provocative and informative.

My reward has been the discovery of hundreds of good songs. The reader's rewards will be a better acquaintance with the show tunes he or she already enjoys, and a guide to new favorites.

STEVEN SUSKIN
New York
June 1985

Preface to the Second Edition

I'm somewhat surprised to find how much new material has crept into this "updated and expanded" edition. There has been a surprising increase in musical theatre activity over the last few years. Sixteen of the thirty composers discussed in this book are still around, although five are no longer active. New musicals by *all* of the others (except, oddly enough, Jerry Herman) have been produced since 1985! Only two of the shows had any success, alas. Several obscure, early productions by these composers have also come to my attention.

The section of "Notable Scores by Other Composers"—which was added to the First Edition as an afterthought—received so much favorable comment that it has been expanded; some worthy shows which were omitted from the first edition due to space constraints are now deservedly recognized. A section of "Notable Imported Scores" has also been added, recognizing the importance of these musicals, fifteen in all, going back to 1954. (No, they were not all composed by Andrew Lloyd Webber; and there are some excellent scores among them, too!)

Finally—and importantly—it will be seen that quite a few never-before-available songs have recently been published or recorded. Let us hope this practice continues, as there are still many long-lost treasures waiting to be "discovered."

New York
July 1991

How to Use This Book

Thirty major composers have been selected for discussion. They are divided into three generational groups, with each career discussed separately. Two groups of shows follow: notable scores by other composers, and notable imported scores.

The Composers

This study of the musical theatre starts at the very beginning, with Jerome Kern. Kern entered a theatre dominated by operetta and made radical changes. Other successful American composers chose to remain in operetta: Victor Herbert, Rudolf Friml, and Sigmund Romberg all retain a measure of popularity today. But they wrote operetta and light opera, not show tunes, and therefore are not included. The one early composer who *did* try to create a primitive American musical comedy was George M. Cohan, but his work was rather primitive.

Hundreds of American composers have been represented on Broadway since Kern discovered musical comedy in 1915. Selecting thirty out of the pack has not been all that difficult, though; most of the choices are obvious. The major criteria are importance of work, in terms of quality or popular success, and a sustained concentration on the musical stage. The lack of a theatre career does not signify the inability to write important musical theatre work, of course. The sections of "Notable Scores" have been added to represent such composers and their shows.

For purposes of chronology, composers are arranged by date of their first *important* work. Cole Porter was born just two years after Irving Berlin, and his initial Broadway hearing came in 1915; but the younger George Gershwin, Vincent Youmans, and Richard Rodgers were all firmly established before Porter achieved recognition in 1928.

The individual work of each composer is examined show by show, from the earliest interpolation by Kern through July, 1991. Each production is discussed in three parts: Show Data, Song Information, and (usually) Commentary.

Show Data

THE SHOWS

All stage productions from which songs were published or recorded are listed. This includes shows that closed during pre-Broadway tryouts, and others written specifically for production in London. Also included are shows that weren't intended for Broadway presentation. The majority are musicals and revues, but *any* organized stage production for which the composer wrote specific material is included. In addition, many productions for which *no* songs were published are included. Movie and television work is not discussed, except for material written for adaptations of theatrical productions. Revivals are mentioned when the show included previously unheard material. Amateur shows, unproduced musicals, and workshops are included when songs were published; much of the better material, of course, was reused in other productions and published at that time. Following show titles in some cases are subtitles or colorful, descriptive slogans ("A Bubbling Satirical Musical Revue of Plays, Problems and Persons") taken from original advertising material.

DATE

The date of the official Broadway (or London) opening is used. For shows which closed during tryout or were not intended to play Broadway or London, date of the opening or first public performance is given in [brackets]. Where exact date is unknown, month and year are given in [brackets].

THEATRE AND CITY

The theatre where the show officially opened is listed. All shows were produced in New York City unless otherwise indicated. Complete information is sometimes unknown, particularly for shows that did not play Broadway. This applies to credits and other data as well. In such cases, the listings herein are necessarily incomplete.

PERFORMANCES

The "official" number of performances is given. Published figures are, unfortunately, often contradictory. The most accurate-seeming number has been listed, usually from the earliest reliable reference source.

CREDITS

Composers

The composer under discussion wrote all music unless specifically noted. In the Gershwin chapter, for example: "Music also by Sigmund Romberg" means that Gershwin and Romberg each wrote substantial parts of the score. "Music mostly by Sigmund Romberg" means that Gershwin supplied interpolated song(s) to a Romberg score. "Music mostly by Gershwin" means that other composers provided interpolations. Where numerous composers were involved, the word "others" is usually used.

Lyricists

The overall lyricist for the production is named in the credit section; exceptions for specific songs are noted in the song listing. In cases of partial scores, the principal composer and lyricist are named; but only songs written by the composer under discussion are listed. Some of the composers wrote their own lyrics; this is mentioned at the beginning of their chapters, with specific exceptions noted. Songs for which the composer wrote lyrics *only* are included, but collaboration with another composer in this book is discussed under the career of the composer (and cross-referenced).

Others

Librettists, directors, and producers are listed where information is available. Choreographers are listed for productions in which dance was an important creative element. Certain cast members are listed: stars, supporting performers, and others of interest. Future stars in the chorus are specifically *not* included. Standardized terms are used: "directed" rather than "staged," "choreographed" rather than "dances by," "with" rather than "starring."

"Pre-Broadway Title"

When a show underwent a name change during tryouts, songs were sometimes issued using both titles. In such cases, the original title is mentioned. Songs cut from these shows might, in fact, have been issued using the earlier title only.

Song Listings

Song listings include all material from each production which was published or recorded. Information is given on lyricists, other uses of the same material, and related details. The purpose of the section is to provide a complete guide to all songs that *exist,* and that the reader can *find.* (Not all are found easily, sad to say; if only someone would gather all this rare material in one place!)

Other reference books are available with titles of published *and* unpublished songs, usually without any differentiation. Unfortunately, most unpublished manuscripts have long since disappeared and cannot be checked. These "unpublished" titles are sometimes songs that actually *were* published—with a different lyric, or merely a different title. Theatre programs can provide unreliable information, as shows-in-crisis make changes faster than a good press agent can keep track of (or wants to). Sometimes proposed titles for never-written songs find their way onto these lists. Accurate information and authorship of unpublished material is simply not verifiable. We have chosen to concentrate only on what is *real.* (Any unpublished manuscripts unearthed in research have been examined, and relevant findings are noted.)

Many of the composers discussed also wrote songs for motion pictures. A few wrote as carefully for film assignments as for theatre. It is regretted that these songs cannot be discussed in this book; but including the important songs would necessitate including them all, and there are hundreds.

Classification of Publications

Many songs were printed in more than one method: an individually published song was also included in the score (if any), etc. These listings are cumulative, the key phrase being "additional songs." Only songs written by the composer under discussion are included; contributions by other composers in the book are cross-referenced.

Nonsong material is listed where it is a separate composition: *Overture To Candide* as opposed to song-medley overtures, *Slaughter On Tenth Avenue* as opposed to dance music arrangements.

Certain songs were published with subtitles: *The Impossible Dream (The Quest).* In other cases, familiar subtitles follow official title for identification purposes: *He Dances On My Ceiling (Dancing On The Ceiling).* Vocal scores sometimes neglected to print song titles in favor of "Opening Act Two," "Scene And Song," or "Entrance Of Cowgirls." Where necessary, a suitable title or subtitle has been taken from the lyric. Where composer wrote different songs with the same title, they are referred to as [1st] and [2nd]; this does not apply to similarly titled songs by different composers.

PUBLISHED SONGS
Sheet music of individual songs, for sale in stores and theatre lobbies.

ADDITIONAL SONGS PUBLISHED IN VOCAL SCORE
Collections of all musical material needed for performance: songs, dances, underscoring, etc.

ADDITIONAL SONGS PUBLISHED IN VOCAL SELECTION
Collections of selected songs, sometimes including titles not published individually. In some cases revised editions have been issued with different contents.

ADDITIONAL SONGS PUBLISHED (NO LYRIC) IN PIANO SELECTION
Medleys of songs issued without lyrics, sometimes piano reductions of the overtures. Dozens of believed-to-be-vanished songs by Gershwin, Rodgers, Kern, etc. were published in this manner (and are here catalogued for the first time). In some cases American and British editions have different contents.

ADDITIONAL SONGS PUBLISHED
Otherwise unpublished material contained in songbooks, collections, scripts, or other publications. So-called "fakebooks" containing lyrics and melody lines (only) are not included.

ADDITIONAL SONGS RECORDED
Otherwise unpublished songs that were made available on recordings.

A Word About The Inclusion Of Recorded Material

In olden days, before the Depression, the publisher usually issued the "best" (i.e., most likely to sell) songs even before the tryout began. More numbers were added as demand was shown—if the show ran long enough. Leftover songs appeared only in the vocal score, if any; otherwise they were forgotten or eventually reused in another show. Since the advent of the original cast album, many such songs have been recorded. Others can be heard on "songwriter anthologies."

While this book is not about recorded theatre music, songs preserved only in this method are certainly to the point. Therefore, at the end of the song listings are unpublished-but-recorded songs, which appear on original (or studio) cast albums, "songwriter anthologies," pirated albums, and other special collections. Live tapes and noncommercial demonstration records are sometimes obtainable: imaginative readers interested in this material can easily track down sources. Due to space and the desire to concentrate on musical theatre matters, label and number information on unpublished-but-recorded songs is not given; most of them can be found on cast albums.

Song Explanations

Cut Songs

Material cut from shows before or after the opening. As these cases were not accurately chronicled in programs or anywhere else, such listings cannot be complete. By definition, cut material includes songs dropped during rehearsals—and therefore never actually performed.

Reused Songs

Material used in different productions, usually songs cut from their initial show. In some cases an absolutely identical song reappeared with a different title.

New (or Revised) Lyrics

Identical music reused with different lyrics.

Revised Music

At the least, basically similar music reworked. The same song in a different tempo with a new bridge, for example. At the most, virtually new music containing a recognizable theme from the composer's earlier work. (And why not? A good musical idea is well worth rescuing from ignominious obscurity.)

Advertised But Not Published

These might better be labeled *"believed to exist* but not published." Many were advertised by the publishers; other titles first appeared in reference books or song indexes. Nonexistence has been verified by all possible means; the names are included in hopes of ending confusion. Not listed are certain "advertised" titles which have indeed been found—and discovered to be interpolations by other composers.

Issued as Professional Copy (Only)

These were copies distributed for noncommercial use; usually printed without covers, sometimes on poor-quality paper. They were given to singers and recording companies in hopes of arranging performances outside the theatre. For any number of reasons—premature closing of the show, song cut on the road, etc.—some songs were never actually issued for sale, and exist only as professional copies.

"Initial Publication"

Certain songs were not published until long after the production had closed, usually in connection with a successful movie version or revival. These are listed as such. Because the individually published sheet is our primary source, "initial individual publication" supersedes an earlier printing in a vocal score or selection. It is regretted that current availability is impossible to indicate; please note that certain long-out-of-print individual sheets are now available in selections and collections.

"Additional Songs"

Songs by the composer *not* from the original production are sometimes interpolated into revivals or movie versions. These are listed only when specifically written by the composer for that purpose, or where use resulted in initial publication or recording of previously unpublished material.

Commentary

Pertinent—and sometimes impertinent—comments are given on the shows, songs, and careers. Other publications can be consulted for plot summaries and the like; my concern is with the *composers*. *What* they wrote and *whom* they wrote with; *why* and *how* they came to be involved with their chosen projects. All were influenced and/or affected by their counterparts/competitors. They shared the same collaborators and producers, wrote for the same performers. And, the shows were performed in the same theatres for the same audience (and the same reviewers).

Critical comments on contemporary shows come from actual viewing. Opinions on older productions have been derived from analysis of existing material, reviews, and first-hand reports. Certain critics, one finds, can be relied upon for generally insightful comments. Statements of commercial success/failure are derived from financial records.

Show Tunes is not meant to be a total history of the American musical theatre, but rather a look at the more important composers and their work, with incidental miscellania of curiosity and interest included.

Cross-Referencing

Reference to any of the productions discussed in this book is printed with the show title in boldface capitals, followed by composer and date:

SHOW BOAT [Kern: December 27, 1927]

This refers to the chapter on Kern, where the listing can be found chronologically. When reference is to a show written by the composer being discussed, his name will not be given:

(in chapter on Jerome Kern)

SHOW BOAT [December 27, 1927]

When reference is to a show included in the "Notable Scores" section, "PART 4" will be used for composer's name:

A CHORUS LINE [PART 4: April 15, 1975]

When more than one composer wrote for the same production contributions are discussed in each chapter. This is indicated in the "Show Data" section by naming the other composer in boldface; show title and date are not repeated:

(in chapter on Richard Rodgers)

BETSY

DECEMBER 28, 1926   NEW AMSTERDAM THEATRE   39 PERFORMANCES

Music mostly by Rodgers (see **Berlin**)
Lyrics mostly by Lorenz Hart

It will not always be necessary to check the reference, of course; often the date alone is the relevant factor. Finding the location of the most-referred-to chapters might take some getting used to. Specific page numbers for cross-referenced productions can be found in the Chronological Listing Of Productions (Appendix 1).

Sources and Contradictions

Standard reference sources—often compiled from earlier standard sources—can contain contradictory information. Titles and names with different spelling or punctuation; different dates, varying "official" numbers of performances; different facts, different facts about the same facts, and more.

Wherever possible, information has been taken directly from published music, theatre programs, reviews, and advertising material. Even primary source materials are often in disagreement. One piece of music can have different titles (or authors) listed on the cover and inside.

Obvious misspellings and errors have been corrected; alternate spellings have been standardized. In dealing with contradictions, the most likely information—usually from the earliest source—has been used. It will be noted that certain experts in the field are consistently reliable, while others are consistently not.

To verify song existence and to provide complete-as-practical reuse information, virtually all individual sheets, scores, selections, etc. have been personally examined and in most cases played. Copyright records and registration deposit copies have been checked to insure the greatest possible accuracy. Even so, we are fairly certain that this volume will contain an error or two.

Exact titles and composer/lyricist information are taken from the published song, as given at the top of the page with the copyright notice. Where reason exists to doubt authorship as credited, copyright and performing-rights organization records have been consulted. Such discrepancies have been included in the interests of completeness and accuracy, and only, of course, where documentation exists.

Acknowledgments

There are many existing sources for statistics, facts, and the like. Songs, though, could not be examined until they were found. The following people were of help in locating materials and clarifying information.

As representatives of the composers: Louis Abend of the Welk Music Group (T. B. Harms), Bob Baumgart, Eric Colodne of Notable Music, Michael Feinstein, John Fearnley, Jack Gottlieb of Amberson Productions, Michael Kerker of ASCAP, Dr. Leonard Lehrman, Paul McKibbins of the Tommy Valando Publishing Group, Dave Olsen of Columbia Pictures Publishing, Lys Simonette and David Farneth of the Kurt Weill Foundation, Allen Whitehead of Music Theatre International, Joseph Weiss of Eastman and Eastman (Edwin H. Morris), and Allen Whitehead of Music Theatre International. Early support came from Theodore S. Chapin of the Rodgers and Hammerstein (and Hart) Organization, and Mrs. Ceciley Youmans Collins. Jule Styne, Harold Rome, Jerry Herman, Bob Merrill, and Charles Strouse were all gracious and helpful. Stanley Green, Edward Jablonski, and Alfred Simon—biographers and friends of several of the composers—were generous with their time and knowledge.

A number of advanced music collectors have shared their knowledge of the field and helped track down obscure material: Don Stubblebine, Vi Foerster, Stan White, Bill Simon, the late Lawrence Jay Taylor, Joe Friedman, and Irv Gerst. James J. Fuld provided helpful suggestions and was responsible for the unexpected discovery of certain important items. Special thanks go to Don Stubblebine, who continually offered access to his extensive collections.

Much of the research was done at the following institutions: the Music Division and the Billy Rose Theatre Collection of The Performing Arts Research Center at Lincoln Center (thanks to the late Thor E. Wood and Richard Buck), the Music Reference Collection of The New York Public Library at Lincoln Center, and the Music Division of the Library of Congress in Washington, D.C.; also the now-defunct

Songwriters Hall of Fame Museum (where Frankie MacCormack was of great help), and other private collections that wish to remain private.

Quite a few readers of the first edition took the time to send in suggestions, comments, and corrections, which have resulted in some changes, additions, and clarifications. I thank all of them for their efforts and kind words. If *Show Tunes* has provided critical song information unavailable elsewhere, I can only say that that's precisely why I went to the trouble of writing it in the first place!

For all sorts of assistance, support, and encouragement, the following are gratefully acknowledged: Mitchell Erickson, Marion Finkler, Kate Glasner, Arlene Grayson, Kathleen Griffin, Leo and Janice Herbert, Carol Patella, Skipp Porteous, Stephanie Ross, Kim Sellon, Mark Sendroff, Dr. Barbara Ann Simon, Mary Jo Slater, Eugene V. Wolsk, Max Woodward, and Kee Young.

Much credit for the existence of this book goes to the enthusiasm and care of Jerry Gross and Jonathan Dodd of the now departed Dodd, Mead & Company. (In business since 1839, publishers of G. B. Shaw, A. Christie, and S. Sondheim, they publish my first book and proceed to disappear in a sea of red ink. Oh, well.) Jerry's ideas and suggestions helped make this book as comprehensive and usable as it is; he also encouraged me to "personalize" it into something more interesting and entertaining (hopefully) than a mere book of lists.

Finally, William W. Appleton has been an enthusiastic part of this project since its inception. A discerning theatregoer since 1925, he has graciously spent many hours double-checking song listings and consulting on commentary. His efforts are deeply appreciated.

PART 1

INTRODUCTION

The century began with American musical theatre dominated by European operettas—English, German, and Austrian. This held firm until 1914, when the Great War quickly ended popularity of things foreign. Jerome Kern, a practiced hand at "Americanizing" imports, finally had a chance to explore his own style; the result was the "modern musical comedy" form. (Actually, the first of many "modern musical comedy" forms.) Irving Berlin, already known to Broadway for pop song hits, tried his hand at complete scores; he was less adventurous than Kern, but highly successful. The postwar years brought three young Kern protégés: George Gershwin, Vincent Youmans, and Richard Rodgers. They surpassed the master with a newer "modern musical comedy" built on dance rhythms; Kern, meanwhile, began development of "musical drama." Cole Porter, of the Kern/Berlin generation, was next to make his mark on Broadway after a long, unapplied apprenticeship. Then came Arthur Schwartz, establishing himself in the months just before the stock market crash. 1930 saw the entrance of three talented protégés of Gershwin: Harold Arlen, Vernon Duke, and Burton Lane. But the worsening depression brought Broadway musical opportunity to a near halt.

Jerome Kern

BORN: January 27, 1885   New York, New York
DIED: November 11, 1945   New York, New York

Jerome Kern was raised in Newark, New Jersey, where his father was a merchant. By 1901 Kern was writing songs for amateur groups, leaving high school to work as a song plugger for Edward B. Marks' Lyceum Publishing Company. Lyceum issued Kern's first published piece, the 1902 piano solo *At The Casino*. Kern was already set on writing for the theatre; realizing the importance of the publisher in those Tin Pan Alley days, he became firmly established with the T. B. Harms firm late in 1903 and eventually bought into the company. Running the house was the remarkable Max Dreyfus: when Kern's fame began attracting novice composers, Dreyfus selected the most promising and convinced producers to hire the untried Gershwin, Youmans, Porter, Rodgers, Schwartz, etc. At the time, Dreyfus printed American editions of many of the imported British operettas. Interpolations were often needed to "Americanize" the material, so Dreyfus went about getting Kern these assignments.

AN ENGLISH DAISY

JANUARY 18, 1904   CASINO THEATRE   41 PERFORMANCES

Music mostly by A. M. Norden
Lyrics to Kern songs by Edgar Smith
Book by Seymour Hicks and Walter Slaughter
Directed by Ben Teal
Produced by Weber and Fields

Published songs:
The Downcast Eye—added to post-Broadway tour
Wine, Wine! (Champagne Song)

MR. WIX OF WICKHAM

SEPTEMBER 19, 1904   BIJOU THEATRE   41 PERFORMANCES

Music mostly by Herbert Darnley and George Everard
Lyrics mostly by John H. Wagner
Book by Herbert Darnley and John H. Wagner
Directed and produced by Edward E. Rice
With Julian Eltinge

Published songs:
Angling By The Babbling Brook (lyric by Kern)
From Saturday to Monday
Susan (lyric by Kern)
Waiting For You

Broadway heard a Kern sampler of four tunes in MR. WIX OF WICKHAM. Broadway was not impressed. Far more successful was Julian Eltinge, beginning his highly respectable career as the most popular female impersonator on the American stage (see COUSIN LUCY [August 27, 1915]).

THE SILVER SLIPPER

[CIRCA APRIL 1905]; POST-BROADWAY TOUR

Music mostly by Leslie Stuart
Lyrics by W. H. Risqué
Book by Clay M. Greene
(Based on the British book by Owen Hall)
Directed by Cyril Scott
Produced by John C. Fisher
With Samuel Collins, Ben Lodge, and George Tennery

Published song:
My Celia (by John Golden and Kern)—added during tour

THE CATCH OF THE SEASON

AUGUST 28, 1905   DALY'S THEATRE   104 PERFORMANCES

Music mostly by W. T. Francis and others
Book by Seymour Hicks and Cosmo Hamilton
Directed by Ben Teal
Produced by Charles Frohman
With Edna May

Published songs:
Frolic Of A Breeze (lyric by Clifford Harris)—see **The Beauty of Bath**
     [March 19, 1906]
Molly O'Hallerhan (Edna May's Irish Song) (lyric by Kern)
Oh, Mr. Chamberlain (lyric by Charles H. Taylor)—see **The Beauty of
     Bath**
Raining (lyric by Harris)
Take Me On The Merry-Go-Round (lyric by Kern)
Tulips (Two Lips) (lyric by Kern)
Won't You Kiss Me Once Before I Go? (lyric by Fred W. Leigh)

Charles Frohman revolutionized the haphazard American theatre business
with innovations still in effect today. By 1900 he was equally active in London,
mounting his hits on both sides of the Atlantic. Specializing in British plays
and operettas, he regularly refused Kern's offered interpolations until he met
the composer in England (and assumed he was English). Kern was soon
Frohman's favorite interpolator and good friend—but he never gave Kern a
chance at a complete score.

THE BABES AND THE BARON

October 14, 1905   < London >

Music mostly by H. E. Haines
Lyrics mostly by Charles H. Taylor
Book by A. M. Thompson and Robert Courtneidge
NOTE: **Babes in the Wood**, post-Broadway title

Published song:
Farewell, Dear Toys (March) [instrumental with partial lyric by Kern]

THE EARL AND THE GIRL

November 4, 1905   Casino Theatre   148 performances

Music mostly by Ivan Caryll
Lyrics mostly by Percy Greenbank
Book by Seymour Hicks
Directed by R. H. Burnside
Produced by Sam S. and Lee Shubert, Inc.
With Eddie Foy

Published songs:
How'd You Like To Spoon With Me? (lyric by Edward Laska)—also used
     in **The Rich Mr. Hoggenheimer** [October 22, 1906]
My Southern Belle (music by Max Eugene, lyric by Kern)

How'd You Like To Spoon With Me? was Kern's first hit song. Composer "Max Eugene" was Max Dreyfus, who had started as a songwriter. The Shubert Brothers (Sam S., Lee, and J. J.) came to Broadway in 1901. Sam, the unanimous favorite, died May 12, 1905 in a train crash en route from THE EARL AND THE GIRL tryout in Cincinnati. Lee opted to keep Sam billed for the next few years as coproducer, rather than credit J. J.; this greatly annoyed Jake, which was the intention.

THE BEAUTY OF BATH

MARCH 19, 1906   ALDWYCH THEATRE < LONDON >   287
  PERFORMANCES

Music mostly by H. E. Haines
Book by Seymour Hicks and Cosmo Hamilton
Choreographed by Edward Royce
Produced by Charles Frohman
With Hicks and Ellaline Terriss (Hicks)

Published song:
Mr. Chamberlain (lyric by P. G. Wodehouse and Kern)—revised lyric for
    Oh, Mr. Chamberlain from CATCH OF THE SEASON [August 28,
    1905]

Additional song published in vocal score:
The Frolic Of A Breeze (lyric by Wodehouse and Charles H.
    Taylor)—revised lyric for song from CATCH OF THE SEASON

Astute British showman Seymour Hicks brought Kern and Pelham Grenville Wodehouse together for these interpolations. The young humorist was working as a newspaper columnist; his contributions here indicated lyrical skill, but it wasn't till after the war began that the two resumed collaboration—with revolutionary (for the musical theatre) results. THE BEAUTY OF BATH was choreographed by Edward Royce, later to direct a number of important Kern (and non-Kern) American musicals.

THE SPRING CHICKEN

[CIRCA MARCH 1906]   GAIETY THEATRE < LONDON >   401
    PERFORMANCES

Music mostly by Ivan Caryll and Lionel Monckton
Lyrics mostly by Adrian Ross and Percy Greenbank
Book by George Grossmith
(Based on *Coquin de Printemps* [play] by Jaime and Duval)
With Richard Carle

Published song:
Rosalie (lyric by Grossmith)—added after London opening; see THE
   LAUGHING HUSBAND [February 2, 1914]

Although THE SPRING CHICKEN opened May 30, 1905, Kern's contribution
wasn't written until the following year. For purposes of song chronology, the
show listing uses the date *Rosalie* was interpolated.

THE LITTLE CHERUB

AUGUST 6, 1906   CRITERION THEATRE   155 PERFORMANCES

Music mostly by Ivan Caryll
Lyrics mostly by Adrian Ross
Book by Owen Hall
Directed by Ben Teal
Produced by Charles Frohman
With Hattie Williams

Published songs:
Meet Me At Twilight (lyric by F. Clifford Harris)
A Plain Rustic Ride ('Neath The Silv'ry Moon) (music by Jackson
   Gouraud and Kern, lyric by Kern)
Under The Linden Tree (lyric by M. E. Rourke)

Michael Elder Rourke, an England-born Irishman, began his Broadway career
as a press agent before moving on to lyric writing. He was to be Kern's major
collaborator until the Wodehouse partnership resumed in 1916.

MY LADY'S MAID

SEPTEMBER 20, 1906   CASINO THEATRE   44 PERFORMANCES

Music mostly by Paul Rubens
Lyrics by Rubens and Percy Greenbank
Book by Edward Paulton and R. H. Burnside
(Based on the British musical by Rubens and N. Newnham Davis)
Directed by Burnside
Produced by Sam S. and Lee Shubert
With Madge Crichton

Published song:
All I Want Is You (lyric by Paul West)

THE RICH MR. HOGGENHEIMER

October 22, 1906   Wallack's Theatre   187 performances

Music mostly by Ludwig Englander
Book and lyrics mostly by Harry B. Smith
(Based on a character from *The Girl from Kay's* [musical] by Owen Hall
Directed by Ben Teal
Produced by Charles Frohman
With Sam Bernard

Published songs:
Bagpipe Serenade (lyric by Kern)
Blue, Blue (lyric by Paul West)
Don't You Want A Paper Dearie? (lyric by West)
How'd You Like To Spoon With Me? (lyric by Edward Laska)—originally
    used in The Earl and the Girl [November 4, 1905]
I've a Little Favor (lyric by M. E. Rourke)
My Hungarian Irish Girl (lyric by West)
Poker Love (Card Duet) (lyric by West and Kern)
A Recipe (lyric by Kern and West)—added after opening; also used in
    The Orchid [April 8, 1907]

THE WHITE CHRYSANTHEMUM

[March 25, 1907]   Garrick Theatre < Philadelphia,
    Pennsylvania >; closed during pre-Broadway tryout

Music mostly by Howard Talbot
Lyrics mostly by Arthur Anderson
Book by Leedham Hantock and Anderson
With Edna Wallace Hopper and Lawrence Grossmith

Published songs:
Bill's A Liar (lyric by M. E. Rourke)
I Just Couldn't Do Without You (lyric by Paul West)

THE ORCHID

April 8, 1907   Herald Square Theatre   178 performances

Music mostly by Ivan Caryll and Lionel Monckton
Lyrics mostly by Adrian Ross and Percy Greenbank
Book by James T. Tanner and Joseph W. Herbert
Directed by Frank Smithson

Produced by Sam S. and Lee Shubert, Inc.
With Eddie Foy

Published songs:
Come Around On Our Veranda (lyric by Paul West and Kern)
I'm Well Known (lyric by Kern)
A Recipe (lyric by Kern and West)—originally used in THE RICH MR.
　　HOGGENHEIMER [October 22, 1906]

FASCINATING FLORA

MAY 20, 1907　CASINO THEATRE　113 PERFORMANCES

Music mostly by Gustave Kerker
Book by R. H. Burnside and Joseph W. Herbert
Staged by Burnside
Produced by Burnside and Comstock, Inc.

Published songs:
Ballooning (lyric by Paul West)
Katy Was A Business Girl (lyric by West)
The Little Church Around the Corner (lyric by M. E. Rourke)
Right Now (music by Fred Fisher, lyric by Kern)
The Subway Express (lyric by James O'Dea)

Producer F. Ray Comstock, an early Kern fan, was to devise the "Princess Theatre Show" series—and give Kern the assignment that would quickly establish him as Broadway's leading composer (see NOBODY HOME [April 20, 1915]).

THE DAIRYMAIDS

AUGUST 26, 1907　CRITERION THEATRE　86 PERFORMANCES

Music mostly by Paul A. Rubens and Frank A. Tours
Lyrics to Kern songs by M. E. Rourke
Book by A. M. Thompson and Robert Courtneidge
Directed by A. E. Dodson
Produced by Charles Frohman
With Julia Sanderson

Published songs:
Cheer Up Girls
The Hay Ride
I'd Like To Meet Your Father
I've A Million Reasons Why I Love You

Little Eva
Mary McGee
Never Marry A Girl With Cold Feet

Julia Sanderson was one of the top American musical comedy heroines of her day. She was to star in a number of Kern musicals.

THE GAY WHITE WAY

OCTOBER 7, 1907   CASINO THEATRE   105 PERFORMANCES

Music mostly by Ludwig Englander
Book by Sydney Rosenfeld and J. Clarence Harvey
Directed by R. H. Burnside
Produced by Sam S. and Lee Shubert, Inc.
With Melville Ellis

Published song:
Without The Girl—Inside! (lyric by M. E. Rourke and Kern)

THE MORALS OF MARCUS

NOVEMBER 18, 1907   CRITERION THEATRE   44 PERFORMANCES

Play by William J. Locke
Produced by Charles Frohman
With Marie Doro

Published song:
Eastern Moon (lyric by M. E. Rourke)

PETER PAN
Or, The Boy Who Wouldn't Grow Up
< First Version >

[CIRCA DECEMBER 1907]; POST-BROADWAY TOUR

Play by J. M. Barrie
Produced by Charles Frohman
With Maude Adams and Ernest Lawford

Published song:
Won't You Have A Little Feather? (lyric by Paul West)—added during
     tour

The eccentrics Frohman, Maude Adams, and J. M. Barrie formed an unlikely but enduring personal relationship. Written for Adams, PETER PAN cast something of a spell over each of their lives (see **Rosy Rapture** [**March 22, 1915**]). Adams' debut in the role had been November 6, 1905; she toured in the play for years. Kern later wrote a song for Broadway's first non-Adams production of the play, Marilyn Miller's unsuccessful version [**November 6, 1924**].

A WALTZ DREAM

January 27, 1908   Broadway Theatre   111 performances

Music mostly by Oscar Straus
Lyrics mostly by Joseph W. Herbert
Book by Felix Doermann and Leopold Jacobson
(Based on the Austrian musical by Hans Mueller)
Directed by Herbert Gresham
Produced by The Inter-State Amusement Co., Inc.

Published songs:
The Gay Lothario (lyric by C. H. Bovill)
I'd Much Rather Stay At Home (lyric by Bovill)
Vienna (lyric by Adrian Ross)

The course of the musical theatre changed abruptly on June 8, 1907 in London (October 21, 1907 in New York) when Franz Lehar's **Merry Widow** waltzed in. Kern's "Americanized" interpolations were attracting interest, and he was ready for his break; but now audiences only wanted Viennese operetta. So Kern began a new round of interpolations.

THE GIRLS OF GOTTENBERG

September 2, 1908   Knickerbocker Theatre   103 performances

Music mostly by Ivan Caryll and Lionel Monckton
Lyrics mostly by C. H. Bovill
Book by George Grossmith and L. E. Berman
Directed by J.A.E. Malone
Produced by Charles Frohman
With Gertie Millar

Published songs:
Freida (lyric by M. E. Rourke)
I Can't Say You're The Only One
Nothing At All (lyric by Rourke)

FLUFFY RUFFLES

SEPTEMBER 7, 1908   CRITERION THEATRE   48 PERFORMANCES

Music mostly by W. T. Francis
Lyrics mostly by Wallace Irwin
Lyrics to Kern songs mostly by C. H. Bovill
Book by John J. McNally
Directed by Ben Teal
Produced by Charles Frohman
With Hattie Williams

Published songs:
Aida McCluskie
Dining Out (lyric by George Grossmith)
Meet Her With A Taximeter
Mrs. Cockatoo
Sweetest Girl, Silly Boy, I Love You (lyric by Irwin)
Take Care
There's Something Rather Odd About Augustus
Won't You Let Me Carry Your Parcel?

KITTIE GREY

JANUARY 25, 1909   NEW AMSTERDAM THEATRE   48 PERFORMANCES

Music mostly by Augustus Barratt, Howard Talbot, and Lionel Monckton
Lyrics to Kern songs by M. E. Rourke
Book by J. Smyth Pigott
(Based on *Les Fetards* [play] by Mars and Hennequin)
Directed by Austin Hurgon
Produced by Charles Frohman
With Julia Sanderson and G. P. Huntley

Published songs:
Eulalie
If The Girl Wants You (Never Mind The Color Of Her Eyes)
Just Good Friends

THE GAY HUSSARS

JULY 29, 1909   KNICKERBOCKER THEATRE   44 PERFORMANCES

Music by Emmerich Kalman
English lyrics by Grant Stewart

Book by Maurice Browne Kirby
(Based on the Austrian musical by Karl Von Bakonyi and Robert
Bodansky)
Directed by George Marion
Produced by Henry W. Savage

Published song:
Shine Out All You Little Stars (lyric by M. E. Rourke)

THE DOLLAR PRINCESS

SEPTEMBER 6, 1909   KNICKERBOCKER THEATRE   288 PERFORMANCES

Music mostly by Leo Fall
Book by George Grossmith
(Based on the Austrian musical by Willner and Grunbaum)
Directed by J. A. E. Malone
Produced by Charles Frohman
With Donald Brian and Valli Valli

Published songs:
A Boat Sails on Wednesday [*Quartet*] (lyric by Adrian Ross and
    Grossmith)—written for London production [September 25, 1909]
Not Here! Not Here! (lyric by M. E. Rourke)—see THE GIRL FROM
    UTAH [**August 24, 1914**]
Red, White and Blue (lyric by Ross)—written for London production

Prima donna Valli Valli was married to Max Dreyfus's brother Louis, who ran
the London branch of the publishing house.

THE GIRL AND THE WIZARD

SEPTEMBER 27, 1909   CASINO THEATRE   96 PERFORMANCES

Music mostly by Julian Edwards (see **Berlin**)
Lyrics mostly by Robert B. Smith and Edward Madden
Lyrics to Kern songs by Percival Knight
Book by J. Hartley Manners
Directed by Ned Wayburn
Produced by the Messrs. Shubert
With Sam Bernard

Published songs:
By the Blue Lagoon
Frantzi
Suzette And Her Pet

THE GOLDEN WIDOW

[OCTOBER 26, 1909]   BELASCO THEATRE < WASHINGTON, D.C. >
CLOSED DURING PRE-BROADWAY TRYOUT

Music mostly by Melville Gideon and Louis Hirsch
Lyrics mostly by Edward Madden
Book by Joseph Herbert
Produced by Sam S. and Lee Shubert
With Louise Dresser

Published song:
Howdy! How D'You Do? (lyric by M. E. Rourke)

KING OF CADONIA

JANUARY 10, 1910   DALY'S THEATRE   16 PERFORMANCES

Music also by Sidney Jones
Lyrics to Kern songs by M. E. Rourke
Book by Frederick Lonsdale
Directed by Joseph Herbert
Produced by the Messrs. Shubert
With Marguerite Clark

Published songs:
The Blue Bulgarian Band
Catamarang (lyric by Percival Knight)—see SALLY [December 21, 1920]
Come Along, Pretty Girl—also used in THE GIRL AND THE DRUMMER
        [Circa August 1910]
Coo-coo Coo-coo (Marie) (lyric by Maurice Stonehill)
Every Girl I Meet (lyric by Percival Knight)
Hippopotamus
Lena, Lena
Mother And Father

THE ECHO

AUGUST 17, 1910   GLOBE THEATRE   53 PERFORMANCES

Music mostly by Deems Taylor
Book by William Le Baron
Directed by Fred G. Latham
Produced by Charles Dillingham
With John E. Hazzard, Bessie McCoy, and George White

Published song:
Whistle When You're Lonely (lyric by M. E. Rourke)

Dillingham, former aide to Charles Frohman, began his producing career in 1903 with a series of Victor Herbert musicals (including THE RED MILL [September 24, 1906]). Through the mid-Twenties he was the most respected producer of American musicals, often in competition with sometime partner (and comanager of the New Amsterdam Theatre) Florenz Ziegfeld, Jr.

OUR MISS GIBBS

AUGUST 29, 1910   KNICKERBOCKER THEATRE   64 PERFORMANCES

Music mostly by Ivan Caryll and Lionel Monckton
Book by James T. Tanner
Directed by Thomas Reynolds
Produced by Charles Frohman
With Pauline Chase

Published songs:
Come Tiny Goldfish To Me (music by Harry Marlow, lyric by Kern)
Eight Little Girls (lyric by M. E. Rourke)
I Don't Want You To Be A Sister To Me (lyric by Frederick Day)

THE GIRL AND THE DRUMMER

[CIRCA AUGUST 1910]; CLOSED DURING PRE-BROADWAY TRYOUT

Music mostly by Augustus Barratt (see **Berlin**)
Book and lyrics mostly by George Broadhurst
(Based on *What Happened to Jones* [play] by Broadhurst)
Produced by Wm. A. Brady, Ltd.
With Herbert Corthell and Belle Gold

Published song:
Come Along, Pretty Girl (lyric by M. E. Rourke)—originally used in KING
   OF CADONIA [January 10, 1910]

THE HENPECKS

FEBRUARY 4, 1911   BROADWAY THEATRE   137 PERFORMANCES

"Notes" mostly by A. Baldwin Sloane
"Rhymes" mostly by E. Ray Goetz
"Words" by Glen MacDonough
Directed by Ned Wayburn

Produced by Lew Fields
With Mr. and Mrs. Sam Watson and Gertrude Quinlan

Published song:
The Manicure Girl (lyric by Frederick Day)

LA BELLE PAREE

A Jumble of Jollity

MARCH 20, 1911   WINTER GARDEN THEATRE   104 PERFORMANCES

Music also by Frank Tours
Lyrics by Edward Madden
Book by Edgar Smith
Produced by the Messrs. Shubert
With Stella Mayhew, Kitty Gordon, Al Jolson, and Mitzi Hajos

Published songs:
De Goblin's Glide (lyric by Frederick Day)
The Edinboro Wriggle (lyric by M. E. Rourke)—originally printed in a
      newspaper supplement as *The Edinboro Jig*
I'm The Human Brush (That Paints The Crimson On Paree)
Look Me Over Dearie—added after opening
Paris Is A Paradise For Coons
Sing Trovatore
That's All Right For McGilligan (lyric by Rourke)—added after opening

The Shuberts opened their lavish new musical showplace—formerly a stable—with a vaudeville show featuring the two-act revue LA BELLE PAREE. The hit of the evening was Shubert discovery Al Jolson (singing, needless to say, *Paris Is A Paradise For Coons*). He was soon elevated to stardom and became a Winter Garden fixture.

LITTLE MISS FIX-IT

APRIL 3, 1911   GLOBE THEATRE   56 PERFORMANCES

Music and lyrics mostly by Jack Norworth
Book by William J. Hurlbut and Harry B. Smith
Directed by Gustav von Seyfferitz
Produced by Louis F. Werba and Mark A. Luescher
With Nora Bayes and Jack Norworth

Published songs:
There Is A Happy Land (Tale of Woe) (lyric by Norworth)
Turkey Trot [instrumental] (music by Kern and Dave Stamper)

ZIEGFELD FOLLIES OF 1911

June 26, 1911   Jardin de Paris   80 performances

Music mostly by Maurice Levi and Raymond Hubbell (see **Berlin**)
Book and lyrics mostly by George V. Hobart
Staged by Julian Mitchell
Produced by Florenz Ziegfeld, Jr.
With Bessie McCoy

Published song:
I'm A Crazy Daffydil (lyric by Bessie McCoy)

This fifth edition of the series marked Kern's first association with Ziegfeld; despite the producer's indifferent musical ear, he was later responsible for mounting Kern's finest work.

THE SIREN

August 28, 1911   Knickerbocker Theatre   136 performances

Music mostly by Leo Fall
Book and lyrics mostly by Harry B. Smith
(Based on the Austrian musical by Leo Stein and A. M. Willner)
Produced by Charles Frohman
With Donald Brian and Julia Sanderson

Published songs:
Follow Me Round (music by Fall, lyric by Adrian Ross and Kern)
In the Valley Of Montbijou (lyric by Rourke)
I Want To Sing In Opera (music and lyric by Morton David, George
        Arthurs, and Kern)
My Heart I Cannot Give To You (lyric by Matthew Woodward)

Donald Brian—star of the American **Merry Widow** [October 21, 1907]—and Julia Sanderson played together in several Kern shows he was to introduce Kern's biggest early hit, *They Didn't Believe Me,* in **The Girl From Utah** [August 24, 1914].

THE KISS WALTZ

September 18, 1911   Casino Theatre   88 performances

Music mostly by C. M. Ziehrer
Lyrics by Matthew Woodward
Book by Edgar Smith

Directed by J. C. Huffman
Produced by the Messrs. Shubert
With Adele Rowland

Published songs:
Fan Me With A Movement Slow
Love Is Like A Rubber Band (Hoop Song)
Love's Charming Art
Ta-Ta, Little Girl
There's A Resting Place For Every Girl (Sun Chair Song)

THE OPERA BALL

FEBRUARY 12, 1912   LIBERTY THEATRE   32 PERFORMANCES

Music mostly by Richard Heuberger
Book by Sydney Rosenfeld
(Based on the Austrian musical by Victor Leon and H. von Waldbaum)
With Marie Cahill

Published songs:
Nurses Are We—advertised but not published except in piano selection
Sergeant Philip Of The Dancers—advertised but not published except in
    piano selection

Additional song published (no lyric) in piano selection:
Marie-Louise

A WINSOME WIDOW

APRIL 11, 1912   MOULIN ROUGE THEATRE   172 PERFORMANCES

Music mostly by Raymond Hubbell
Lyrics mostly by Harry B. and Robert B. Smith
(Based on *A Trip to Chinatown* [musical] by Charles Hoyt)
Directed by Julian Mitchell
Produced by Florenz Ziegfeld, Jr.

Published song:
Call Me Flo (words and music by John Golden and Kern)

"Flo" was Ziegfeld's nickname, but the lyric dealt with a Florence; Kern
didn't call Ziegfeld "Flo" until their Twenties hits together.

THE GIRL FROM MONTMARTRE

AUGUST 5, 1912   CRITERION THEATRE   64 PERFORMANCES

Music mostly by Henry Bereny and Jerome Kern
Book and lyrics mostly by Harry B. and Robert B. Smith
(Based on the French musical by Bereny and Rodolph Schanzer, from *La Dame de Chez Maxim* [farce] by Georges Feydeau)
Directed by Tom Reynolds
Produced by Charles Frohman
With Hattie Williams and Richard Carle

Published songs:
Bohemia (lyric by Robert B. Smith)
Don't Turn My Picture To The Wall (lyric by Smith)
Hoop-La-La, Papa! (lyric by M. E. Rourke)
I'll Be Waiting 'Neath Your Window (written and composed by James Duffy and Kern)
I've Taken Such A Fancy To You (lyric by Clifford Harris)
Ooo, Ooo, Lena! (written and composed by John Golden and Kern)

A POLISH WEDDING

A Fascinating Farce With Dainty Music

[AUGUST 31, 1912]   EMPIRE THEATRE <SYRACUSE, NEW YORK>
    CLOSED DURING PRE-BROADWAY TRYOUT

Music mostly by Jean Gilbert
Book and lyrics mostly by George V. Hobart
(Based on *Die Polnische Wirtschaft* [musical] by Kraatz and Okonkowski)
Produced by George M. Cohan and Sam H. Harris
With Valli Valli, Ann Pennington, and Genevieve Tobin

Published songs:
Bygone Days (lyric by Kern)
He Must Be Nice To Mother
Let Us Build A Little Nest (lyric by Kern and Hobart)—see HEAD OVER HEELS [August 29, 1918]
You're The Only Girl He Loves—see OH, LADY! LADY!! [February 1, 1918]

THE "MIND-THE-PAINT" GIRL

SEPTEMBER 9, 1912   LYCEUM THEATRE   136 PERFORMANCES

Play by Sir Arthur Wing Pinero
Directed by Dion G. Boucicault
Produced by Charles Frohman
With Billie Burke

Published songs:
If You Would Only Love Me (words and music by John Crook and Kern)
Mind the Paint (lyric by Pinero)

Billie Burke was a major Frohman star. The producer demanded his leading ladies live secluded, scandal-free lives; he never for Burke when she clandestinely married Ziegfeld in 1914.

THE WOMAN HATERS

OCTOBER 7, 1912   ASTOR THEATRE   32 PERFORMANCES

Music mostly by Edmund Eysler
Book and lyrics by George V. Hobart
(Based on *Die Frauenfresser* [musical] by Leo Stein and Karl Lindau)
Directed by George Marion
Produced by A. H. Woods
With Dolly Castles

Published song:
Come On Over Here (music by Walter Kollo, lyric by Kern and
    Hobart)—also used in THE DOLL GIRL [August 25, 1913]

THE RED PETTICOAT

NOVEMBER 13, 1912   DALY'S THEATRE   61 PERFORMANCES

Lyrics by Paul West
Book by Rida Johnson Young
(Based on *Next* [play] by Young)
Directed by Joseph W. Herbert
Produced by Sam S. and Lee Shubert, Inc.
With Helen Lowell
NOTE: LOOK WHO'S HERE, pre-Broadway title

Published songs:
I Wonder
Little Golden Maid

My Peaches And Cream
Oh, You Beautiful Spring (lyric by M. E. Rourke)
The Ragtime Restaurant
Since The Days of Grandmama

After eight years Kern finally got his chance to write a complete score; not successfully, though. Kern had heretofore cloaked his individual style with English and Viennese overtones. Now, as the developing political situation ended the popularity of things Continental and English imports were halted, Kern's originality launched him into Broadway prominence.

THE SUNSHINE GIRL

FEBRUARY 3, 1913   KNICKERBOCKER THEATRE   160 PERFORMANCES

Music mostly by Paul A. Rubens
Lyrics mostly by Arthur Wimperis and Rubens
Book by Rubens and Cecil Raleigh
Directed by J.A.E. Malone
Produced by Charles Frohman
With Julia Sanderson and Joseph Cawthorn

Published song:
Honeymoon Lane (lyric by M. E. Rourke)

THE AMAZONS

APRIL 28, 1913   EMPIRE THEATRE   48 PERFORMANCES

Play by Sir Arthur Wing Pinero
Directed by William Seymour
Produced by Charles Frohman
With Billie Burke

Published song:
My Otaheitee Lady (lyric by Charles Taylor)

THE DOLL GIRL

AUGUST 25, 1913   GLOBE THEATRE   88 PERFORMANCES

Music mostly by Leo Fall
Book and lyrics mostly by Harry B. Smith
(Based on the Austrian musical by Leo Stein and A. M. Willner from
Riquette et sa Mere [play] by Caillavert and deFlers)
Produced by Charles Frohman
With Hattie Williams and Richard Carle

Published songs:

Come On Over Here (music by Walter Kollo, lyric by Smith and
Kern)—revised lyric for song of same title from THE WOMAN
HATERS [October 7, 1912]
If We Were On Our Honeymoon (Railway Duet)
A Little Thing Like A Kiss—see OH LADY! LADY!! [February 1, 1918]
When Three Is Company (Cupid Song) (lyric by M. E. Rourke)—see
ZIEGFELD FOLLIES OF 1917 [April 13, 1917]
Will It All End In Smoke?

Additional songs published (no lyric) in piano selection:
I'm Going Away
Opening Act Two (Russian Dance)

Harry Bache Smith was the most prolific writer in American musical history,
with lyrics and librettos for over three hundred shows. His early collaboration
with Reginald DeKoven (THE BEGUM [November 21, 1887]) is considered by
many the first American comic operetta. In the course of his long career he
also did important work with Victor Herbert. Smith's close friendship with
Kern included a shared passion for collecting antique books. Kern auctioned
off most of his collection early in 1929 for an unheard of $1.7 million . . . which
he immediately invested in the stock market!

LIEBER AUGUSTIN

SEPTEMBER 3, 1913   CASINO THEATRE   37 PERFORMANCES

Music mostly by Leo Fall
Book by Edgar Smith
(Based on the Austrian musical by Welisch and Bernauer)
Directed by Al Holbrook and Julian Alfred
Produced by Sam S. and Lee Shubert, Inc.
With DeWolf Hopper and George MacFarlane
NOTE: MISS CAPRICE, post-opening Broadway title

Published song:
Look In Her Eyes (lyric by Herbert Reynolds [M. E. Rourke])—also used
(as *Look In His Eyes*) in HAVE A HEART [January 11, 1917]

In 1913, Irish Mike Rourke anglicized his name to Herbert Reynolds. The
Shuberts anglicized LIEBER AUGUSTIN's name after the opening, but to no
avail.

THE MARRIAGE MARKET

SEPTEMBER 22, 1913   KNICKERBOCKER THEATRE   80 PERFORMANCES

Music mostly by Victor Jacobi
Lyrics to Kern songs by M. E. Rourke
Book by Gladys Unger
(Based on the Austrian musical by M. Brody and F. Martos)
Directed by Edward Royce
Produced by Charles Frohman
With Donald Brian

Published songs:
By The Country Stile (lyric by Kern)
I'm Looking for An Irish Husband—cut after opening
I've Got Money In The Bank
A Little Bit Of Silk—cut after opening
You're Here And I'm Here (lyric by Harry B. Smith)—added to
post-Broadway tour; originally used in THE LAUGHING HUSBAND
[February 2, 1914]

DIE BALLKÖNIGIN

Operette in 2 Akten

[CIRCA SEPTEMBER 1913]   < VIENNA, AUSTRIA >

Music mostly by [H.] E. Haines and Evelyn Baker
Book and lyrics by Fritz Luner and Karl Tuschl
(Based on a libretto by Seymour Hicks and Cosmo Hamilton)

Published song:
Die Süsse Pariserin (Fraulein de Loraine) (lyric by Luner)—see THE
STEPPING STONES [November 6, 1923] and LADY MARY [February
23, 1928]

Die Süsse Pariserin—The Sweet Parisian—seems to be one of Kern's early
British interpolations; it's highly unlikely that he wrote it specifically for this
Viennese operetta. DIE BALLKÖNIGIN (THE KING'S BALL) could well have
been an adaptation of THE BEAUTY OF BATH [March 19, 1906]. However,
Die Süsse Pariserin is not revised from either of the published Kern songs from
that show.

OH, I SAY!

A Riotous Musical Comedy

OCTOBER 30, 1913   CASINO THEATRE   68 PERFORMANCES

Music mostly by Kern
Lyrics mostly by Harry B. Smith
Book by Sydney Blowe and Douglas Hoare
(Based on a play by Keroul and Barré)
Directed by J. C. Huffman
Produced by the Messrs. Shubert
With Joseph W. Herbert and Cecil Cunningham
NOTE: THE WEDDING NIGHT, post-Broadway title

Published songs:
Alone At Last [1st]—different than song with same title from VERY
    GOOD EDDIE [December 23, 1915]; also see BLUE EYES [April 27,
    1928]
Each Pearl A Thought
I Can't Forget Your Eyes—see SUNNY [September 22, 1925] and
    CRISS-CROSS [October 12, 1926]
I Know And She Knows
Katy-did
A Wifie Of Your Own

Kern's second complete score—again for the Shuberts—was more successful
than THE RED PETTICOAT [November 13, 1912], if not particularly special.

THE LAUGHING HUSBAND

FEBRUARY 2, 1914   KNICKERBOCKER THEATRE   48 PERFORMANCES

Music mostly by Edmund Eysler
Lyrics to Kern songs by Harry B. Smith
Book by Arthur Wimperis
(Based on the Austrian musical by Julius Brammer and Alfred Grunwald)
Directed by Edward Royce
Produced by Charles Frohman
With Courtice Pounds

Published songs:
Bought And Paid For—see SUNNY [September 22, 1925] and
    CRISS-CROSS [October 12, 1926]
Love Is Like A Violin
Take A Step With Me—new lyric for *Rosalie* from THE SPRING CHICKEN
    [Circa March 1906]

You're Here And I'm Here—also used in THE MARRIAGE MARKET
[September 22, 1913]

You're Here And I'm Here was another Kern hit song. As the show had a brief
life, the song was inserted into the successfully touring MARRIAGE MARKET
to help sell tickets (and music sheets).

WHEN CLAUDIA SMILES

FEBRUARY 2, 1914   KNICKERBOCKER THEATRE   56 PERFORMANCES

Play by Anne Caldwell
(Based on a play by Leo Ditrichstein)
Produced by Frederic McKay
With Blanche Ring

Published song:
Ssh . . . You'll Waken Mister Doyle (music by John L. Golden, lyric by
    E. W. Rogers, Golden, and Kern)

THE GIRL FROM UTAH
The Acme Of Musical Comedy

AUGUST 24, 1914   KNICKERBOCKER THEATRE   120 PERFORMANCES

Music mostly by Paul Rubens and Sydney Jones
Lyrics to Kern songs by Harry B. Smith
Book by James T. Tanner
Directed by J.A.E. Malone
Produced by Charles Frohman
With Donald Brian, Julia Sanderson, and Joseph Cawthorn

Published songs:
Alice In Wonderland
The Land Of 'Let's Pretend'—revised version of *Not Here! Not Here!*
    from THE DOLLAR PRINCESS [September 6, 1909]
The Same Sort Of Girl—see ROSY RAPTURE [March 22, 1915]
They Didn't Believe Me (lyric by Herbert Reynolds)—also used in
    TONIGHT'S THE NIGHT! [April 28, 1915]
We'll Take Care Of You All—cut; also used in FADS AND FANCIES
    [March 8, 1915]
Why Don't They Dance The Polka Anymore?
You Never Can Tell—cut

Kern's best work thus far included the immensely popular *They Didn't Believe Me*. Already well known to theatre audiences, within the year Kern was established as Broadway's leading "modern" composer.

NINETY IN THE SHADE

JANUARY 25, 1915   KNICKERBOCKER THEATRE   40 PERFORMANCES

Music and lyrics also by Clare Kummer
Lyrics to Kern songs by Harry B. Smith
Book by Guy Bolton
Directed by Robert Milton
Produced by Daniel V. Arthur
With Marie Cahill and Richard Carle

Published songs:
Can't You See I Mean You? (lyric by Herbert Reynolds)—see VERY
    GOOD EDDIE [December 23, 1915] and THEODORE AND CO.
    [September 19, 1916]
It Isn't Your Fault (lyric by Reynolds)—initial publication upon reuse in
    LOVE O' MIKE [January 15, 1917]
Love Blossoms—advertised but not published
A Package Of Seeds—initial publication upon reuse in OH, BOY!
    [February 20, 1917]
The Triangle [musical scene] (lyric by Bolton)—initial publication upon
    reuse in VERY GOOD EDDIE
Where's The Girl For Me?—advertised but not published; initial
    publication upon reuse in THE LADY IN RED [May 12, 1919]
Whistling Dan—advertised but not published; see LEAVE IT TO JANE
    [August 28, 1917]

The thirty-year-old Kern entered the second phase of his career, divorcing himself from all European influences (except Arthur Sullivan). At the same time, his collaborators—led by librettist Guy Bolton—began using more realistic situations and contemporary American locales and characters. Bolton, born in England of American parents, followed his father into architecture before entering the theatre in 1912. NINETY IN THE SHADE was a failure; but Kern and Bolton were already at work on the first "Princess Theatre Show."

A GIRL OF TODAY

[FEBRUARY 8, 1915]   < WASHINGTON, D.C. > ; CLOSED DURING
    PRE-BROADWAY TRYOUT

Play by Porter Emerson Browne
Produced by Charles Frohman
With Ann Murdock

Published song:
You Know And I Know (lyric by Schuyler Greene)—see NOBODY HOME
    [**April 20, 1915**]

FADS AND FANCIES

MARCH 8, 1915   KNICKERBOCKER THEATRE   48 PERFORMANCES

Music mostly by Raymond Hubbell
Book and lyrics mostly by Glen MacDonough

Published song:
We'll Take Care Of You All (Refugee Song) (lyric by Harry B.
    Smith)—originally used (cut) in THE GIRL FROM UTAH [**August 24,
    1914**]

ROSY RAPTURE, THE PRIDE OF THE BEAUTY CHORUS

MARCH 22, 1915   DUKE OF YORK'S THEATRE < LONDON >

A burlesque by J. M. Barrie
Produced by Charles Frohman
With Gaby Deslys and Jack Norworth

Published song:
Best Sort Of Mother, Best Sort Of Child (lyric by F. W. Mark)—new
    lyric for *The Same Sort Of Girl* from THE GIRL FROM UTAH
    [**August 24, 1914**]

A legendary (but unconfirmable) story says that Frohman and Kern booked
passage to sail together to England. Kern overslept and missed the departure.
On May 7, 1915 the *Lusitania* was sunk by a German torpedo; the gentle
Frohman paraphrased his friend Barrie's PETER PAN [**Circa 1907**]—"Why
fear Death? It is the most beautiful adventure of Life"—as the ship went
down.

NOBODY HOME

APRIL 20, 1915   PRINCESS THEATRE   135 PERFORMANCES

Lyrics mostly by Schuyler Greene
Book by Guy Bolton
(Based on *Mr. Popple (of Ippleton)* [musical] by Paul Rubens)
Directed by J. H. Benrimo
Produced by F. Ray Comstock
With Adele Rowland

Published songs:
Another Little Girl (lyric by Herbert Reynolds)
Any Old Night (Is A Wonderful Night) (music by Otto Motzan and
    Kern, lyric by Greene and Harry B. Smith)—also used in TONIGHT'S
    THE NIGHT! [April 28, 1915]
At That San Francisco Fair (music by Ford Dabney, James Reese Europe,
    and Kern)
The Chaplin Walk (music by Motzan and Kern)
In Arcady (lyric by Reynolds)
The Magic Melody
That Peculiar Tune (music by Kern and Motzan, lyric by Greene and
    Reynolds)—cut; initial publication as 1916 nonshow song
Wedding Bells Are Calling Me (lyric by Smith)—added after opening;
    also used in VERY GOOD EDDIE [December 23, 1915]
You Know And I Know—originally used in A GIRL OF TODAY [February
    8, 1915]

F. Ray Comstock managed the 299-seat Princess for the Shuberts, who
opened the house in 1913. Having been unable to find suitable attractions for
the jewel-box theatre, Comstock and play agent Elisabeth Marbury (see SEE
AMERICA FIRST [Porter: March 28, 1916]) decided to try a moderately sized,
sophisticated musical comedy. NOBODY HOME, adapted from a 1905 British
musical, was not successful; but the concept worked. The series was quickly
established with the second "Princess Theatre Show," the very good VERY
GOOD EDDIE [December 23, 1915].

TONIGHT'S THE NIGHT!

APRIL 28, 1915   GAIETY THEATRE < LONDON >   460 PERFORMANCES

Music mostly by Paul A. Rubens
Lyrics mostly by Rubens and Percy Greenbank
Book by Fred Thompson
(Based on *The Pink Dominos* [play] by James Albery)

Produced by George Grossmith and Edward Laurillard
With Grossmith and Madge Saunders

Published songs:
Any Old Night (Is A Wonderful Night) (music by Otto Motzan and
    Kern, lyric by Schuyler Greene and Harry B. Smith)—originally used
    in NOBODY HOME [April 20, 1915]
They Didn't Believe Me (lyric by Herbert Reynolds)—originally used in
    THE GIRL FROM UTAH [August 24, 1914]

A MODERN EVE

MAY 3, 1915   CASINO THEATRE   56 PERFORMANCES

Music mostly by Jean Gilbert and Victor Hollaender
Lyrics to Kern songs by Harry B. Smith
Book by Will M. Hough and Benjamin Hapgood Burt
(Based on the German musical by Okonkowsky and Schoenfeld)
Directed by Frank Smithson
Produced by Mort H. Singer

Published songs:
I'd Love To Dance Through Life With You
I've Just Been Waiting For You

COUSIN LUCY

AUGUST 27, 1915   GEORGE M. COHAN THEATRE   43 PERFORMANCES

Play by Charles Klein
Lyrics by Schuyler Greene
Directed by Robert Milton
Produced by A. H. Woods
With Julian Eltinge

Published songs:
Society
Those 'Come Hither' Eyes—see THEODORE AND Co. [September 19,
    1916]
Two Heads Are Better Than One (lyric by Kern and Greene)—see
    ROCK-A-BYE BABY [May 22, 1918]

Eltinge was Broadway's finest female impersonator, immensely popular with
the family trade. In 1912 he became only the second performer to have a
Broadway theatre built in his honor; Maxine Elliott, a Lee Shubert mistress,
was the first. The charming Eltinge, now called the Empire, has endured more
than fifty years of 42nd Street abuse and still survives.

MISS INFORMATION

A Little Comedy with a Little Music

OCTOBER 5, 1915   GEORGE M. COHAN THEATRE   47 PERFORMANCES

Play by Paul Dickey and Charles W. Goddard
Music mostly by Jerome Kern (see **Porter**)
Lyrics mostly by Elsie Janis
Book by Paul Dickey and Charles W. Goddard
Directed by Robert Milton
Produced by Charles Dillingham
With Elsie Janis and Irene Bordoni

Published songs:
A Little Love (But Not For Me)
On The Sands of Wa-Ki-Ki (music by Henry Kailimai and Kern)
Some Sort of Somebody
NOTE: All reused in **VERY GOOD EDDIE** [December 23, 1915]

Cole Porter—the first of the Gershwin/Youmans/Rodgers group to reach Broadway—had his second interpolation in this little comedy, with little success. Eldest of the new generation, Porter was the only one *not* particularly influenced by Kern. (Nevertheless, Max Dreyfus was quick to sign him up.)

VERY GOOD EDDIE

DECEMBER 23, 1915   PRINCESS THEATRE   341 PERFORMANCES

Lyrics mostly by Schuyler Greene and Herbert Reynolds [M. E. Rourke]
(also see **Porter** [May 18, 1918])
Book by Philip Bartholomae and Guy Bolton
(Based on *Over Night* [play] by Bartholomae)
Directed by Frank McCormick
Produced by the Marbury-Comstock Co.
With Ernest Truex, Alice Dovey, and John E. Hazzard

Published songs:
Babes In The Wood (lyric by Kern and Greene)
Babes In The Wood ('Fox-Trot')—nonshow dance version
I'd Like To Have A Million In The Bank (lyric by Reynolds)
If I Find The Girl (lyric by John E. Hazzard and Reynolds)
Isn't It Great To Be Married? (lyric by Greene)—new lyric for *Can't You
    See I Mean You* from **NINETY IN THE SHADE** [January 25, 1915];
    also see **THEODORE AND CO.** [September 19, 1916]
I've Got To Dance (lyric by Greene)—cut

Nodding Roses (lyric by Greene and Reynolds)
Old Bill Baker (The Undertaker) (lyric by Ring Lardner)—added after
> opening
Old Boy Neutral (lyric by Greene)—music revised from *A Little Love*
> from Miss Information [October 5, 1915]
On The Shore At Le Lei Wi (music by Henry Kailimai and Kern, lyric by
> Reynolds)—new lyric for *On The Sands Of Wa-Ki-Ki* from Miss
> Information
Some Sort Of Somebody (All Of The Time) (lyric by Elsie
> Janis)—originally used in Miss Information
Thirteen Collar (lyric by Greene)
Wedding Bells Are Calling Me (lyric by Harry B. Smith)—originally used
> in Nobody Home [April 20, 1915]

Additional songs published in vocal score:
Alone At Last [2nd] (lyric by Reynolds)—different than song with same
> title from Oh, I Say! [October 30, 1913]
Buffo Dance [instrumental]
Dance Trio [instrumental]
The Triangle [musical scene] (lyric by Bolton)—originally used
> (unpublished) in Ninety In The Shade
We're On Our Way (lyric by Greene)

The first "Princess Theatre Show" had been an Americanized import. Beginning with Very Good Eddie, Kern and Bolton (soon joined by Wodehouse) concentrated on making comedy and song spring directly from situation and character. The practice at the time was to find a loose framework and insert whatever jokes and songs turned up. The difference was immediately noted, and Kern and company went on to continue working out the form. *Babes In The Wood* was Kern's second major song hit in his blossoming style.

ZIEGFELD FOLLIES OF 1916

June 12, 1916   New Amsterdam Theatre   112 performances

Music mostly by Louis Hirsch and Dave Stamper (see **Berlin**)
Book and lyrics mostly by George V. Hobart and Gene Buck
Lyrics to Kern songs by Gene Buck
Directed by Ned Wayburn
Produced by Florenz Ziegfeld, Jr.

Published songs:
Ain't It Funny What A Difference Just A Few Drinks Make?
Have A Heart [1st]—different than song from Have A Heart [January
> 11, 1917]

My Lady Of The Nile
When The Lights Are Low

THEODORE AND CO.

SEPTEMBER 19, 1916   GAIETY THEATRE <LONDON>   503
    PERFORMANCES

Music mostly by Ivor Novello
Lyrics by Clifford Grey
Book by H.M. Harwood and George Grossmith
Produced by Grossmith and Edward Laurillard

Published song:
Isn't There A Crowd Everywhere? (music by Kern and Novello, lyric by
    Grey and Adrian Ross)

Additional songs published in vocal score:
All That I Want Is Somebody To Love Me—new lyric for *Can't You See
    I Mean You?* from NINETY IN THE SHADE [January 25, 1915] and
    Isn't It Great To Be Married? from VERY GOOD EDDIE [December
    23, 1915]
The Casino Music Hall
That 'Come Hither' Look—new lyric for *Those 'Come Hither' Eyes* from
    COUSIN LUCY [August 27, 1915]
365 Days

MISS SPRINGTIME

SEPTEMBER 25, 1916   NEW AMSTERDAM THEATRE   224
    PERFORMANCES

Music mostly by Emmerich Kalman
Lyrics by P. G. Wodehouse
Book by Guy Bolton
Directed by Herbert Gresham
Produced by Klaw and Erlanger
NOTE: LITTLE MISS SPRINGTIME, pre-Broadway title

Published songs:
All Full Of Talk
My Castle In The Air
Saturday Night
Some One (lyric by Herbert Reynolds)

At the opening night party for NOBODY HOME [April 20, 1915] Kern ran into
Wodehouse and introduced him to Bolton. Wodehouse had been writing

stories and plays since THE BEAUTY OF BATH [March 19, 1906]. Bolton's next musical was this Kalman operetta; Wodehouse got the lyric assignment and Kern, suddenly very popular, helped out with a few songs.

GO TO IT

OCTOBER 24, 1916   PRINCESS THEATRE   23 PERFORMANCES

Music, lyrics and book mostly by John L. Golden, John E. Hazzard, and Anne Caldwell
(Based on *A Milk White Flag* [play] by Charles Hoyt)
Directed by William H. Post
Produced by the Comstock-Elliott Co.

Published song:
When You're In Love You'll Know (music by Golden and Kern, lyric by
    Golden)

The third *Princess Theatre Show.* Kern and Bolton disliked the idea and turned down the offer; the song contributed was presumably adapted from prior work with Golden. Go To It was a quick flop; Kern, Bolton and Wodehouse—already working together on a full-scale musical—agreed to ready something for the Princess.

HAVE A HEART

The Up-To-The-Minute Musical Comedy

JANUARY 11, 1917   LIBERTY THEATRE   76 PERFORMANCES

Lyrics by P. G. Wodehouse
Book by Guy Bolton and Wodehouse
Directed by Edward Royce
Produced by Henry W. Savage
With Louise Dresser

Published songs:
And I Am All Alone (lyric by Kern and Wodehouse)
Daisy
Have A Heart [2nd]—different than song from ZIEGFELD FOLLIES OF 1916
    [June 12, 1916]
Honeymoon Inn
I'm So Busy (lyric by Schuyler Greene and Wodehouse)
Look In His Eyes (lyric by Herbert Reynolds)—same song as *Look In Her
    Eyes* from LIEBER AUGUSTIN [September 3, 1913]
Napoleon

Polly Believed In Preparedness—cut
The Road That Lies Before
They All Look Alike
You Said Something (lyric by Kern and Wodehouse)

Additional songs published in vocal score:
Bright Lights
Finale Act One
I'm Here, Little Girls, I'm Here
It's A Sure Sign (by R. P. Weston and Kern)
The Nightingale (Turk's Song)
Opening Act Two
Reminiscences [instrumental]
Shop

The Kern and Wodehouse collaboration burst on the scene. The lyricist's humor and crisp language perfectly matched the composer's sprightliness, a modern-day equivalent to Gilbert and Sullivan of the 1880s. The run of **HAVE A HEART** was disappointingly short, but other shows were well underway.

LOVE O' MIKE

JANUARY 15, 1917   SHUBERT THEATRE   192 PERFORMANCES

Lyrics by Harry B. Smith
Book by Thomas Sydney
Directed by J. H. Benrimo
Produced by Elisabeth Marbury and Lee Shubert
With Peggy Wood, Luella Gear, and Clifton Webb
NOTE: **FOR LOVE OF MIKE** and **GIRLS WILL BE GIRLS**, pre-Broadway titles

Published songs:
The Baby Vampire
Don't Tempt Me
Drift With Me
I Wonder Why
It Can't Be Done—cut
It Wasn't My Fault (lyric by Herbert Reynolds)—same song as *It Isn't Your Fault* (unpublished) from **NINETY IN THE SHADE** [January 25, 1915]
Simple Little Tune
We'll See
Who Cares?—cut

Additional songs published (no lyric) in piano selection:
Life's A Dance
Look In The Book

While the Princess formula called for intimacy, **Love O' Mike** was a full-scale piece which had to play large houses (1,500 seats instead of 300). The show was not particularly memorable, but with a great deal of pre-Broadway revision and care it managed to do well enough.

OH, BOY!

February 20, 1917   **Princess Theatre**   463 **performances**

Lyrics by P. G. Wodehouse
Book by Guy Bolton and Wodehouse
Directed by Edward Royce and Robert Milton
Produced by Comstock and Elliott Co.
With Anna Wheaton, Edna May Oliver, and Dorothy Dickson

Published songs:
Ain't It A Grand And Glorious Feeling?—cut
Be A Little Sunbeam
The First Day Of May—written for British production, retitled **Oh, Joy!** [January 27, 1919]
Nesting Time In Flatbush [1st]
Nesting Time In Flatbush [2nd] (lyric by Wodehouse and Kern)—version with extended lyric
An Old Fashioned Wife
A Package Of Seeds (lyric by Herbert Reynolds and Wodehouse)—revised lyric for song with same title (unpublished) from **Ninety in the Shade** [January 25, 1915]
A Pal Like You—originally issued as *We're Going To Be Pals*
Rolled Into One
Till The Clouds Roll By (lyric by Kern and Wodehouse)
Words Are Not Needed—originally issued as *Every Day*
You Never Knew About Me

Additional songs published (no lyric) in piano selection:
Flubby Dub
Opening Act One

The most successful of the "Princess Theatre Shows." **Oh, Boy!** set the standard for early musical comedy, with the songs reasonably interpolated into entertainingly humorous (though often slight) stories. *Till The Clouds Roll*

By joined *They Didn't Believe Me* and *Babes In The Woods* as Kern's three biggest pre-Twenties hits.

ZIEGFELD FOLLIES OF 1917

JUNE 12, 1917   NEW AMSTERDAM THEATRE   111 PERFORMANCES

Music mostly by Raymond Hubbell and Dave Stamper
Lyrics mostly by Gene Buck
Book by Buck and George V. Hobart
Directed by Ned Wayburn
Produced by Florenz Ziegfeld, Jr.

Published song:
Just Because You're You—new lyric for *When Three Is Company* from
    THE DOLL GIRL [August 25, 1913]

LEAVE IT TO JANE

AUGUST 28, 1917   LONGACRE THEATRE   167 PERFORMANCES

Lyrics by P. G. Wodehouse
Book by Guy Bolton and Wodehouse
(Based on *The College Widow* [play] by George Ade)
Directed by Edward Royce
Produced by William Elliott, F. Ray Comstock, and Morris Gest
With Edith Hallor and Oscar Shaw

Published songs:
Cleopatterer
The Crickets Are Calling
I'm Going To Find A Girl—song version of *Little Billie* [instrumental], a
    theme for the 1916 film "Gloria's Romance"
It's A Great Big Land
Just You Watch My Step
Leave It To Jane—revised version of *Whistling Dan* (unpublished) from
    NINETY IN THE SHADE [January 25, 1915]
A Peach Of A Life
Poor Prune—cut
Sir Galahad
The Siren's Song
The Sun Shines Brighter
There It Is Again (When Your Favorite Girl's Not There)
What I'm Longing To Say
Why?—cut

Additional song published in vocal selection:
Wait Till Tomorrow—initial publication upon reuse in 1959 revival

Additional songs recorded:
Football Song (Opening Act Two)
Good Old Atwater

With the tremendously successful **OH, BOY!** [February 20, 1917] still strong at the Princess, this next show in the series was booked into a standard-sized, 1,000-seat theatre (which accounts for the considerably shorter run). Model for the college-football musicals of the future—specifically **GOOD NEWS!** [Part 4: September 6, 1927], **TOO MANY GIRLS** [Rodgers: October 18, 1939] and **BEST FOOT FORWARD** [Martin: October 1, 1941], **LEAVE IT TO JANE** was successfully revived off-Broadway [May 25, 1959] for a 928-performance run.

THE RIVIERA GIRL

SEPTEMBER 24, 1917   NEW AMSTERDAM THEATRE   78 PERFORMANCES

Music mostly by Emmerich Kalman
Lyrics by P. G. Wodehouse
Book by Guy Bolton and Wodehouse
Produced by Klaw and Erlanger

Published song:
Bungalow In Quogue

MISS 1917

NOVEMBER 5, 1917   CENTURY THEATRE   48 PERFORMANCES

Music also by Victor Herbert
Lyrics by P. G. Wodehouse
Book by Guy Bolton and Wodehouse
Directed by Ned Wayburn
Produced by Charles Dillingham and Florenz Ziegfeld, Jr.
With Lew Fields, Vivienne Segal, Bessie McCoy Davis, and Irene Castle

Published songs:
Go Little Boat—cut; also used in **OH, MY DEAR!** [November 27, 1918]
I'm The Old Man In The Moon
The Land Where The Good Songs Go
Peaches
The Picture I Want To See—also used in **OH LADY! LADY!!** [February 1, 1918]
Tell Me All Your Troubles, Cutie
We're Crooks

Dillingham and Ziegfeld had successfully taken over the Century Theatre with THE CENTURY GIRL [Berlin: November 6, 1916]. For their second presentation they kept Victor Herbert on and substituted Kern for Berlin. Kern and Herbert fought. Kern and star Vivienne Segal fought (when she sang Herbert's unauthorized interpolation of *Kiss Me Again* from MLLE. MODISTE [December 25, 1905], which didn't prevent her from getting the lead in Kern's very next show). MISS 1917 wasn't very good, and Dillingham and Ziegfeld let go of the Century. Rehearsal pianist was nineteen-year-old George Gershwin; Harry Askins, company manager, was impressed and sent him over to Max Dreyfus.

OH LADY! LADY!!

FEBRUARY 1, 1918   PRINCESS THEATRE   219 PERFORMANCES

Lyrics by P. G. Wodehouse
Book by Guy Bolton and Wodehouse
Directed by Robert Milton and Edward Royce
Produced by F. Ray Comstock and William Elliott
With Vivienne Segal and Carl Randall

Published songs:
Before I Met You
Bill—cut; see ZIP, GOES A MILLION [December 8, 1919] and SHOW
        BOAT [December 27, 1927]
Dear Old Prison Days
Greenwich Village—revised version of *A Little Thing Like A Kiss* from
        THE DOLL GIRL [August 25, 1913]
It's A Hard Hard World
Moon Song
Not Yet—revised version of *You're The Only Girl He Loves* from A
        POLISH WEDDING [August 31, 1912]
Oh Lady! Lady!!
Our Little Nest
The Picture I Want To See—originally used in MISS 1917 [November 5,
        1917]
The Sun Starts To Shine Again
Waiting Around The Corner—initially issued as *Some Little Girl*
Wheatless Day
When The Ships Come Home
You Found Me And I Found You

Additional songs published in vocal score:
Do It Now
Do Look At Him

Finale Act One
Opening Chorus Act One (Wedding Day)

Despite their enormous success, major disagreements—centering on money
and credit—developed between Kern and Wodehouse, and the precedent-
setting partnership suddenly ended. Both continued to work individually with
Bolton (and were to reunite briefly for unimportant work). The Kern, Bolton,
and Wodehouse collaboration made its remarkable contributions to the musical theatre in a period of just sixteen months.

TOOT-TOOT!

A Train Of Mirth And Melody

MARCH 11, 1918   GEORGE M. COHAN THEATRE   40 PERFORMANCES

Lyrics by Berton Braley
Book by Edgar Allan Woolf
(Based on *Excuse Me* [play] by Rupert Hughes)
Directed by Woolf and Edward Rose
Produced by Henry W. Savage
With Louise Groody and William Kent

Published songs:
Every Girl In All America
Girlie
Honeymoon Land—cut; see THE NIGHT BOAT [February 1920]
I Will Knit A Suit O' Dreams—cut; originally issued as *Teepee*
If (There's Anything You Want)—cut
If You Only Care Enough—revised lyric for *If (There's Anything You
    Want)*
Let's Go
When You Wake Up Dancing

Additional songs published (no lyric) in piano selection:
It's Greek To Me
Yankee Doodle On The Line

ROCK-A-BYE BABY

MAY 22, 1918   ASTOR THEATRE   85 PERFORMANCES

Lyrics by Herbert Reynolds
Book by Edgar Allan Woolf and Margaret Mayo
(Based on *Baby Mine* [play] by Mayo)
Directed by Edward Royce

Produced by Selwyn and Co.
With Louise Dresser, Frank Morgan, and Dorothy Dickson

Published songs:
The Big Spring Drive
I Believed All They Said
I Never Thought
The Kettle Song
Little Tune, Go Away
Lullaby
My Boy
Not You—cut
Nursery Fanfare
One, Two, Three
There's No Better Use For Time Than Kissing—revised version of *Two
        Heads Are Better Than One* from COUSIN LUCY [August 27, 1915]

Following his first book musical successes in 1915, Kern finally found himself
in great demand. After ten frustrating years of interpolation chores, he composed an unprecedented seven-and-a-half full scores for shows opening within
eighteen months. Some of his best early work was done in this period; a
considerable portion was rather weak, though.

HEAD OVER HEELS

AUGUST 29, 1918   GEORGE M. COHAN THEATRE   100 PERFORMANCES

Book and lyrics by Edgar Allan Woolf
(Based on *Shadows* [play] by Lee Arthur and [story] by Nalbro Bartley)
Directed by George Marion
Produced by Henry W. Savage
With Mitzi [Hajos], "The Little Human Dynamo"

Published songs:
All The World Is Swaying
The Big Show
Funny Little Something
Head Over Heels
Head Over Heels (Fox Trot)—nonshow dance version
I Was Lonely
Let's Build A Little Nest (lyric by Kern and Woolf)—cut; revised lyric for
        song from A POLISH WEDDING [August 31, 1912]
Mitzi's Lullaby
Moments Of The Dance

Additional song published (no lyric) in piano selection:
Spring

THE CANARY

November 4, 1918   Globe Theatre   152 performances

Music mostly by Ivan Caryll (see **Berlin**)
Book and lyrics mostly by Harry B. Smith
(Based on a play by Georges Barr and Louis Vermeuil)
Directed by Fred C. Latham and Edward Royce
Produced by Charles Dillingham
With Julia Sanderson and Joseph Cawthorn

Published songs:
Oh Promise Me You'll Write To Him Today (lyric by Harry Clarke)—cut;
     see She's A Good Fellow [May 5, 1919]
Take A Chance (Little Girl And Learn To Dance)

OH, MY DEAR!

November 27, 1918   Princess Theatre   189 performances

Music mostly by Louis Hirsch
Lyrics by P. G. Wodehouse
Book by Guy Bolton and Wodehouse
Directed by Robert Milton and Edward Royce
Produced by F. Ray Comstock and William Elliott
With Joseph Santley and Ivy Sawyer (Santley)

Published song:
Go Little Boat—originally used (cut) in **Miss 1917 [November 5, 1917]**

A non-Kern Princess show, reusing a Kern/Wodehouse song.

SHE'S A GOOD FELLOW

May 5, 1919   Globe Theatre   120 performances

Book and lyrics by Anne Caldwell
Directed by Fred G. Latham and Edward Royce
Produced by Charles Dillingham
With Joseph Santley and Ivy Sawyer (Santley)
NOTE: A New Girl, pre-Broadway title

Published songs:
The Bull Frog Patrol
First Rose Of Summer—see THE CABARET GIRL [September 19, 1921]
Ginger Town—cut
A Happy Wedding Day
Home Sweet Home
I Want My Little Gob
I've Been Waiting For You All The Time—new lyric for Oh Promise Me
　　You'll Write To Him Today from THE CANARY [November 4, 1918]
Jubilo (refrain from Kingdom Comin' by Henry Clay Work)
Just A Little Line
Letter Song—cut
Oh! You Beautiful Person
Some Party
Teacher, Teacher

Kern began a series of more-lavish-than-the-Princess shows for Charles Dilling-ham: six of eight were hits, albeit with undistinguished scores. Kern's new lyricist/librettist was Anne Caldwell, the first and (to this day) most successful woman writer in Broadway musical history.

THE LADY IN RED

MAY 12, 1919　　LYRIC THEATRE　　48 PERFORMANCES

Music mostly by Robert Winterberg (see **Gershwin**)
Book and lyrics mostly by Anne Caldwell
Directed by Frank Smithson
Produced by John P. Slocum

Published song:
Where's The Girl For Me? (lyric by Harry B. Smith)—originally used
　　(unpublished) in NINETY IN THE SHADE [January 25, 1915]

ZIP, GOES A MILLION

[DECEMBER 8, 1919]　　WORCESTER THEATRE < WORCESTER,
　　MASSACHUSETTS > ; CLOSED DURING PRE-BROADWAY TRYOUT

Lyrics by Bud (B. G.) DeSylva
Book by Guy Bolton
(Based on Brewster's Millions [play] by Winchell Smith and Byron Ongley, from the novel by George Barr McCutcheon)
Directed by Oscar Eagle
Produced by F. Ray Comstock and Morris Gest
With Harry Fox

Published songs:
Bill—unpublished; new lyric for song originally used (cut) in OH LADY!
    LADY!! [February 1, 1918]; also see SHOW BOAT [December 27,
    1927]
A Business Of Our Own
Forget Me Not
Give A Little Thought To Me
The Language Of Love
The Little Back-Yard Band
Look For The Silver Lining—initial publication upon reuse in SALLY
    [December 21, 1920]
A Man Around The House
Telephone Girls
Whip-Poor-Will—cut; also used in SALLY
You Tell 'Em

The final "Princess Theatre Show" closed before reaching the Princess. The series had included eight shows (with LEAVE IT TO JANE [August 28, 1917] and ZIP, GOES A MILLION, which did not actually play the Princess) in only four years. But the innovative work accomplished—introducing contemporary sounds and themes into the heretofore make-believe terrain of musical comedy—had immediate and far-reaching effects. Composers George Gershwin, Vincent Youmans, and Richard Rodgers (along with lyricists Ira Gershwin and Lorenz Hart) were just beginning their Broadway careers. Each had been excited and highly stimulated by the "Princess Theatre Shows," and their early work was to show an admitted indebtedness to Kern and Wodehouse.

THE NIGHT BOAT

FEBRUARY 2, 1920   LIBERTY THEATRE   313 PERFORMANCES

Book and lyrics by Anne Caldwell
Directed by Fred G. Latham
Produced by Charles Dillingham
With Louise Groody and John E. Hazzard

Published songs:
Bob White—cut
Chick! Chick! Chick!—cut; also used in HITCHY-KOO 1920 (Fourth
    Edition) [October 19, 1920]
Don't You Want To Take Me?
Good-Night Boat (lyric by Caldwell and Frank Craven)
A Heart For Sale

I'd Like A Lighthouse—new lyric for *Honeymoon Land* (cut) from
    TOOT-TOOT! [MARCH 11, 1918]
I Love The Lassies (I Love 'Em All)
Left All Alone Again Blues
The Lorelei—cut; initial publication upon reuse in SALLY [December 21,
    1920]
Rip Van Winkle And His Little Men—cut
Whose Baby Are You?

Additional song published [no lyric] in piano selection:
Some Fine Day

THE CHARM SCHOOL

AUGUST 2, 1920   BIJOU THEATRE   87 PERFORMANCES

Play by Alice Duer Miller and Robert Milton
"With A Wee Bit Of Music By Jerome Kern"
Produced and directed by Milton
With Sam Hardy and James Gleason

Published song:
When I Discover My Man (lyric by Miller)

HITCHY-KOO 1920
Fourth Edition

OCTOBER 19, 1920   NEW AMSTERDAM THEATRE   71 PERFORMANCES

Lyrics by Anne Caldwell
Book by Glen MacDonough
Directed by Ned Wayburn
Produced by Raymond Hitchcock
With Hitchcock and Julia Sanderson

Published songs:
Bring 'Em Back—see SHOW BOAT [December 27, 1927]
Buggy Riding
Chick! Chick! Chick!—cut; originally used in THE NIGHT BOAT [February
    2, 1920]
Cupid, The Winner
Ding Dong, It's Kissing Time
Girls In The Sea
Moon Of Love
The Old Town

The Star Of Hitchy Koo
Sweetie

SALLY

DECEMBER 21, 1920   NEW AMSTERDAM THEATRE   570
    PERFORMANCES

Lyrics mostly by Clifford Grey
Book by Guy Bolton
Directed by Edward Royce
Produced by Florenz Ziegfeld, Jr.
With Marilynn Miller, Leon Errol, and Walter Catlett

Published songs:
The Church 'Round The Corner (lyric by P. G. Wodehouse and Grey)
Look For The Silver Lining (lyric by B. G. DeSylva)—originally used
    (cut/unpublished) in ZIP, GOES A MILLION [December 8, 1919]
The Lorelei (lyric by Anne Caldwell)—originally used (cut/unpublished)
    in THE NIGHT BOAT [February 2, 1920]
On With The Dance
Sally—revised version of *Catamarang* from KING OF CADONIA [January
    10, 1910]
The Schnitza Komisski
Whip-Poor-Will (lyric by B. G. DeSylva)—originally used (cut) in ZIP,
    GOES A MILLION
Wild Rose
You Can't Keep A Good Girl Down (Joan Of Arc) (lyric by Wodehouse
    and Grey)

Additional songs published in British vocal score:
The Night Time
Opening Act Two (In Society)

Ziegfeld, king of the revue, wanted to attain a similar position in the world
of musical comedy: he determined to produce the most lavish, successful
musical comedy to date. Taking advantage of his FOLLIES talent, facilities, and
money, he did just that with SALLY. At the same time, he established his
favorite mistress as Broadway's favorite musical comedy star. Marilynn Miller
(originally Mary Ellen; soon to be further contracted to Marilyn, creating the
now popular name) had been discovered in a Winter Garden Revue by none
other than Mrs. Billie Burke Ziegfeld. Flo stole her from the Shuberts and
placed her in the FOLLIES OF 1918 [Berlin: June 18, 1918]. Miller turned on
Ziegfeld by marrying costar Frank Carter; Ziegfeld retaliated by sending
husband Carter on the road. When Carter was killed in a car crash on May

9, 1920, Ziegfeld made up with Miller and built SALLY around her. For Kern, the success of SALLY was deceptive: the better parts of the score were discards from earlier shows (including the hit *Look For The Silver Lining* and the entrancing *Whip-Poor-Will*).

ZIEGFELD FOLLIES OF 1921

JUNE 21, 1921   GLOBE THEATRE   119 PERFORMANCES

Music mostly by Victor Herbert, Rudolf Friml, and Dave Stamper
Lyrics mostly by Gene Buck
Directed by Edward Royce
Produced by Florenz Ziegfeld, Jr.

Published song:
You Must Come Over (lyric by B. G. DeSylva)

THE CABARET GIRL

SEPTEMBER 19, 1921   WINTER GARDEN THEATRE < LONDON >   361
      PERFORMANCES

Lyrics mostly by P. G. Wodehouse
Book by George Grossmith and Wodehouse
Directed by Grossmith
Produced by Grossmith and J.A.E. Malone
With Dorothy Dickson, Grossmith, and Heather Thatcher

Published songs:
Dancing Time (lyric by Grossmith)
First Rose Of Summer (lyric by Wodehouse and Anne Caldwell)—new
      lyric for song of same title from SHE'S A GOOD FELLOW [May 5,
      1919]
Journey's End—also used in THE CITY CHAP [October 26, 1925]
Ka-Lu-A (lyric by Anne Caldwell)—added after opening; originally used in
      GOOD MORNING DEARIE [NOVEMBER 1, 1921]
Looking All Over For You
Oriental Dreams (lyric by Grossmith)
Shimmy With Me

Additional songs published in vocal score:
At The Ball (lyric by Grossmith)—alternate lyric for *Dancing Time*
Chopin Ad Lib (Opening Chorus)
Finaletto Act One
Finale Act Two (Vicar Song)

London, Dear Old London
Mr. Gravvins—Mr. Gripps
Nerves
The Pergola Patrol—see SITTING PRETTY [April 8, 1924]
Those Days Are Gone Forever
Whoop-De-Oodle-Do!
You Want The Best Seats, We Have 'Em

Producers Grossmith and Malone decided to follow the 387-performance run of their London production [September 10, 1921] of SALLY [December 21, 1920] with an original Kern musical. Wodehouse proved amendable, so THE CABARET GIRL was written for the local SALLY stars—American Dorothy Dickson, who had been featured in OH, BOY! [February 20, 1917] and ROCK-A-BYE BABY [May 22, 1918], and author/director/producer Grossmith. The success of the venture paved the way for future London musicals by Kern, Gershwin, Rodgers, and Schwartz.

GOOD MORNING DEARIE

NOVEMBER 1, 1921   GLOBE THEATRE   347 PERFORMANCES

Book and lyrics by Anne Caldwell
Directed by Edward Royce
Produced by Charles Dillingham
With Louise Groody and Oscar Shaw

Published songs:
Blue Danube Blues
Didn't You Believe?
Easy Pickin's
Good Morning Dearie
Ka-Lu-A—also used in THE CABARET GIRL [September 19, 1921]
My Lady's Dress—cut
Niagara Falls
Rose Marie
Sing-Song Girl
Toddle
Way Down Town

Another Kern/Caldwell hit for Dillingham. Though Kern was writing successful shows, the music was generally stale and uninteresting. At the same time, younger Harms composers George Gershwin and Vincent Youmans were attracting notice with their first Broadway hits; Richard Rodgers was soon to join them. Kern didn't recover from his fallow period until SHOW BOAT [December 27, 1927]—when he once again led his contemporaries onto new musical theatre ground. *Ka-Lu-A*—Kern's most popular song between *Look For The Silver Lining* [ZIP, GOES A MILLION: December 8, 1919] and *Who?* [SUNNY: SEPTEMBER 22, 1925]—caused the composer to be sued on plagiarism charges. Publisher/songwriter (and one-time Kern collaborator) Fred Fisher claimed infringement on his 1919 hit *Dardanella*. The songs were determined similar enough for Kern to be ruled technically (though unconsciously) guilty, and he was fined a token $250 rather than the million sought by Fisher.

THE BUNCH AND JUDY

NOVEMBER 28, 1922   GLOBE THEATRE   65 PERFORMANCES

Book and lyrics by Anne Caldwell
Staged by Fred G. Latham and Edward Royce
Produced by Charles Dillingham
With Fred and Adele Astaire

Published songs:
Every Day In Every Way
'Have You Forgotten Me?' Blues
Hot Dog!—cut
How Do You Do, Katinka?
Morning Glory
The Pale Venetian Moon
Peach Girl

Dillingham had found Fred and Adele Astaire in vaudeville and nurtured them towards stardom, hoping to create a successor to his team of David Montgomery and Fred Stone. But THE BUNCH AND JUDY didn't work, and the aging Dillingham let the Astaires get away—to immediate success with George Gershwin and producer Alex Aarons (see FOR GOODNESS SAKE [Gershwin: February 20, 1922]).

ROSE BRIAR

DECEMBER 25, 1922   EMPIRE THEATRE   89 PERFORMANCES

Play by Booth Tarkington
Produced by Florenz Ziegfeld, Jr.
With Billie Burke

Published song:
Love And The Moon (lyric by Tarkington)

THE BEAUTY PRIZE

<small>SEPTEMBER 5, 1923   WINTER GARDEN THEATRE <LONDON>   213
PERFORMANCES</small>

Book and lyrics by George Grossmith and P. G. Wodehouse
Directed by Grossmith
Produced by Grossmith and J.A.E. Malone
With Dorothy Dickson, Leslie Henson, and Grossmith

Published songs:
Honeymoon Isle
I'm A Prize
It's A Long, Long Day
Meet Me Down On Main Street
Moon Love
Non-Stop Dancing (lyric by Wodehouse)
When You Take The Road With Me (lyric by Wodehouse)
You Can't Make Love By Wireless—see BLUE EYES [April 27, 1928]

Additional songs published in vocal score:
A Cottage In Kent
For The Man I Love
Joy Bells (lyric by Wodehouse)
We Will Take The Road Together (Finale)
You'll Find Me Playing Mah-Jongg (lyric by Wodehouse)

Another London success for the CABARET GIRL [September 19, 1922] group.
Grossmith, as can be seen above, was a versatile man of the theatre. He had
been associated with Kern on numerous London shows since 1906.

THE STEPPING STONES

<small>NOVEMBER 6, 1923   GLOBE THEATRE   241 PERFORMANCES</small>

Lyrics by Anne Caldwell
Book by Caldwell and R. H. Burnside
Directed by Burnside
Produced by Charles Dillingham
With Fred Stone (and introducing Dorothy Stone)

Published songs:
Everybody Calls Me Little Red Riding Hood
I Saw The Roses And Remembered You (lyric by Herbert Reynolds)
In Love With Love—revised version of *Die Süsse Pariserin* from DIE
    BALLKÖNIGIN [Circa September 1913]; also see LADY MARY
    [February 23, 1928]

Once In A Blue Moon
Our Lovely Rose
Pie
Raggedy Ann
Stepping Stones
Wonderful Dad

Additional songs included in published vocal score:
Babbling Babette
Because You Love The Singer
Cane Dance [instrumental]
Dear Little Peter Pan
Little Angel Cake
Nursery Clock
Palace Dance [instrumental]
Prelude

The title was a pun, as the show was built around the talents of dancing Fred Stone, with daughter Dorothy and wife Aileen Crater. Stone and his partner Dave Montgomery (who died in 1917) had been major family-trade stars for Dillingham since Victor Herbert's THE RED MILL [September 24, 1906]. Ivan Caryll was Caldwell's collaborator on the later Stone shows; when he died in 1921, Kern was the logical replacement. One of the STEPPING STONES songs, *Raggedy Ann,* is an especially infectious rag.

SITTING PRETTY

APRIL 8, 1924   FULTON THEATRE   95 PERFORMANCES

Lyrics by P. G. Wodehouse
Book by Guy Bolton and Wodehouse
Directed by Fred G. Latham and Julian Alfred
Produced by F. Ray Comstock and Morris Gest
With Queenie Smith and Gertrude Bryan

Published songs:
All You Need Is A Girl
Bongo On The Congo
The Enchanted Train
Mr. And Mrs. Rorer
On A Desert Island With You
Shadow Of The Moon
Shufflin' Sam
Sitting Pretty (lyric by Kern and Wodehouse)
Tulip Time In Sing-Sing

Worries
A Year From Today

Additional songs recorded:
All The World Is Dancing Mad—cut; music recorded only
Days Gone By
I'm Wise—cut; music recorded only
Is This Not A Lovely Spot?—new lyric for *The Pergola Patrol* from THE
    CABARET GIRL [September 19, 1921]
Just Wait—cut
Opening Act One (Coaching)—cut; music recorded with partial lyric
Opening Act Two (Ancient Tunes)
There Isn't One Girl
You Alone Would Do (I'd Want Only You)

What was to have been a happy return to the "Princess Theatre Show" fell short of expectations. This reunion of Kern, Wodehouse, and Bolton (with producer Comstock) was poorly received, despite a clever and amusing score. The highly polished set of lyrics was Wodehouse's final work with Kern; he soon gave up songwriting altogether.

DEAR SIR

SEPTEMBER 23, 1924   TIMES SQUARE THEATRE   15 PERFORMANCES

Lyrics by Howard Dietz
Book by Edgar Selwyn
Directed by David Burton
Produced by Philip Goodman
With Genevieve Tobin, Walter Catlett, and Oscar Shaw

Published songs:
All Lanes Must Reach A Turning—see BLUE EYES [April 27, 1928]
Gypsy Caravan
If You Think It's Love You're Right
I Want To Be There
Weeping Willow Tree—see BLUE EYES

Kern seems to have sensed that he needed to start working with younger collaborators (Wodehouse, Rourke, Smith, and Caldwell were all his seniors). Max Dreyfus matched him with a movie publicist who displayed a knack for wordplay, Howard Dietz. Dietz debuted with a more than respectable set of lyrics, but the poorly produced DEAR SIR proved a quick fiasco. Prior to DEAR SIR, Kern tried a few songs with the young Noël Coward, apparently while in London working on THE BEAUTY PRIZE [September 5, 1923]). These included *If You Will Be My Morganatic Wife,* which was rewritten by Dietz as *If We Could Lead A Merry Mormon Life* (both unpublished), and an early version of the song we know as *Where's The Mate For Me?* from SHOW BOAT [DECEMBER 27, 1927]. DeSylva, Coward, and Dietz were followed by a fourth youngster who was to become Kern's most frequent (and perhaps most complementary) collaborator, Oscar Hammerstein 2nd. Dietz, meanwhile, faced several bleak years until THE LITTLE SHOW [SCHWARTZ: APRIL 30, 1929] came along.

PETER PAN

< Second Version >

NOVEMBER 6, 1924   KNICKERBOCKER THEATRE   120 PERFORMANCES

Revival of play by J. M. Barrie
Directed by Basil Dean
Produced by Charles Dillingham
With Marilyn Miller

Published song:
The Sweetest Thing In Life (lyric by B. G. DeSylva)—new lyric for *When Three Is Company* from THE DOLL GIRL [August 25, 1913] and *Just Because You're You* from ZIEGFELD FOLLIES OF 1917 [June 12, 1917]

Marilyn Miller temporarily deserted Ziegfeld—star and producer were spatting—and signed with the competition. Dillingham worked with Kern to devise another SALLY [December 21, 1920], meanwhile placing his new star in this revival. Kern had written a PETER PAN song for the (**First Version**) [**Circa December 1907**]; he got DeSylva to reset an old tune for this one. Miller was somewhat out of place in Maude Adams' old role of the boy who wouldn't grow up, but the musical in preparation made up for that.

SUNNY

SEPTEMBER 22, 1925   NEW AMSTERDAM THEATRE   517
    PERFORMANCES

Book and lyrics by Otto Harbach and Oscar Hammerstein 2nd
Directed by Hassard Short
Produced by Charles Dillingham
With Marilyn Miller and Jack Donahue

Published songs:
D'ye Love Me?
Dream A Dream—cut
I Might Grow Fond Of You (lyric by Desmond Carter)—written for
      London production [October 7, 1926]
I Was Alone—written for 1930 movie version
I've Looked For Trouble (lyric by Carter)—written for London
      production; revised version of *Bought And Paid For* from THE
      LAUGHING HUSBAND [February 2, 1914]; also see CRISS-CROSS
      [October 12, 1926]
Let's Say Good-night—initial publication upon use in London production
Sunny
Sunshine—revised version of *I Can't Forget Your Eyes* from OH, I SAY!
      [October 30, 1913]; also see CRISS-CROSS
Two Little Bluebirds
When We Get Our Divorce—initial publication upon use in London
      production
Who?

Additional songs published in British vocal score:
The Chase
The Fox Has Left His Lair—written for London production
Here We Are Together Again (Opening Act One)
The Hunt Ball [instrumental]
It Won't Mean A Thing
So's Your Old Man
We're Gymnastic
Wedding Knell
Wedding Scene (Finale Act One)

Dillingham succeeded in out-Ziegfelding Ziegfeld with this extravaganza.
Hiring the Harbach and Hammerstein team on the heels of two long-running
hits—WILDFLOWER [Youmans: February 7, 1923] and the Friml/Stothart
ROSE MARIE [September 2, 1924]—Dillingham joined Kern with his two most
important future collaborators. Everything about SUNNY was spectacular except the score: nothing but the immense hit *Who?*.

THE CITY CHAP

OCTOBER 26, 1925   LIBERTY THEATRE   72 PERFORMANCES

Lyrics by Anne Caldwell
Book by James Montgomery

(Based on *The Fortune Hunter* [play] by Winchell Smith)
Directed by R. H. Burnside
Produced by Charles Dillingham
With Richard "Skeet" Gallagher, Irene Dunne, and George Raft

Published songs:
He Is The Type
Journey's End (lyric by P. G. Wodehouse)—originally used in THE
    CABARET GIRL [September 19, 1922]
No One Knows (How Much I'm In Love)
Sympathetic Someone
Walking Home With Josie
When I Fell In Love With You—cut after opening

CRISS-CROSS

OCTOBER 12, 1926   GLOBE THEATRE   206 PERFORMANCES

Book and lyrics by Otto Harbach and Anne Caldwell
Directed by R. H. Burnside
Produced by Charles Dillingham
With Fred and Dorothy Stone

Published songs:
Bread And Butter—cut
Cinderella Girl
In Araby With You—new lyric for *Sunshine* from SUNNY [September 22,
    1925], a revised version of *I Can't Forget Your Eyes* from OH, I
    SAY! [October 30, 1913]
Kiss A Four Leaf Clover—cut
Susie (Camel Song) (lyric by Caldwell)
That Little Something (lyric by Bert Kalmar and Harry Ruby)—added to
    post-Broadway tour; originally used in LUCKY [March 22, 1927]
You Will—Won't You?—new lyric for *I've Looked For Trouble* from
    London production of SUNNY, a revised version of *Bought And Paid*
    For from THE LAUGHING HUSBAND [February 2, 1914]

LUCKY

MARCH 22, 1927   NEW AMSTERDAM THEATRE   71 PERFORMANCES

Music mostly by Bert Kalmar and Harry Ruby
Lyrics by Kalmar and Ruby
Book by Otto Harbach, Kalmar and Ruby

Directed by Hassard Short
Produced by Charles Dillingham
With Mary Eaton, Walter Catlett, Ruby Keeler, and Paul Whiteman

Published songs:
That Little Something—see CRISS-CROSS [October 12, 1926]
When The Bo-Tree Blossoms Again

Additional songs published (no lyric) in piano selection (probably by Kern):
Ballet (Pearl of Ceylon)
Cingalese Village

SHOW BOAT

DECEMBER 27, 1927   ZIEGFELD THEATRE   575 PERFORMANCES

Music mostly by Kern
Book and lyrics by Oscar Hammerstein 2nd
(Based on the novel by Edna Ferber)
Directed by Zeke Colvan
Produced by Florenz Ziegfeld, Jr.
With Charles Winninger, Helen Morgan, Norma Terris, Howard Marsh,
Edna May Oliver, and Jules Bledsoe

Published songs:
Bill (lyric by P. G. Wodehouse and Hammerstein)—revised version of
      Bill (cut) from OH LADY! LADY!! [February 1, 1918] (lyric by
      Wodehouse), also used (unpublished, lyric by B. G. DeSylva) in ZIP,
      GOES A MILLION [December 8, 1919]
Can't Help Lovin' Dat Man
Dance Away The Night—written for London production [May 3, 1928]
I Have The Room Above—written for 1936 movie version
I Might Fall Back On You—initial individual publication upon use in
      1936 movie version
I Still Suits Me—written for 1936 movie version
Life Upon The Wicked Stage—initial individual publication upon use in
      1936 movie version
Make Believe
Nobody Else But Me—written for revival [January 5, 1946]; revised
      version of *Dream Of A Ladies Cloak Room Attendant*
      [instrumental] (unpublished) from unproduced 1935 movie "The
      Flame Within"
Ol' Man River

Why Do I Love You?—see THE CAT AND THE FIDDLE [OCTOBER 15,
    1931]
You Are Love

Additional songs published in vocal scores (several different editions):
Captain Andy's Entrance And Ballyhoo
Cotton Blossom
Dahomey—revised (fourth) version of *Bring 'Em Back* from HITCHY-KOO
    1920 [October 19, 1920]
Dandies On Parade (The Sports Of Gay Chicago)
Finale Act I (Wedding)
Hey, Fellah!
Mis'ry's Comin Aroun' (Act One, Scene IV)
Queenie's Ballyhoo (C'mon Folks, We'se Rarin' To Go)
'Til Good Luck Comes My Way
Villain Dance [instrumental]
When We Tell Them About It All (Opening Act II)
Where's The Mate For Me?

Additional songs recorded:
The Creole Love Song—cut
Gallivantin' Aroun'—written for 1936 movie version
I Would Like To Play A Lover's Part—cut
It's Getting Hotter In The North—cut
Out There In An Orchard (possibly by Kern and Hammerstein)—cut
A Pack Of Cards (possibly by Kern and Hammerstein)—cut
Pantry Scene—cut
Trocadero Opening Chorus (New Year Song)—cut
Yes, Ma'am! (You're From The Show Boat)—cut

Kern and Hammerstein knew they were onto something monumental with
SHOW BOAT. In the musical theatre of the day, other hands—or Kern and
Hammerstein two years earlier—might have woven Ferber's setting and ro-
mances into a moldy operetta, excising the miscegenation, prejudice, unhappy
marriages, etc. (As it was, the authors opted for a weak happy ending.) But
Kern and Hammerstein stayed close to the novel, and created a new musico-
dramatic form. In a period when shows were quickly written and put together,
Kern dedicated a full year to SHOW BOAT; Hammerstein also lavished an
uncommon amount of care on the project, for the first time in his heretofore
successful (but hacklike) career displaying his unique theatrical talents. The
score was incredibly rich, with Kern developing his highly melodic operetta
style in *Make Believe* and *You Are Love*. *Can't Help Lovin' Dat Man* and
Life Upon The Wicked Stage were perfect in their genre, while *Bill* finally

found a home (on the third try). With *Ol' Man River*, Hammerstein wasn't trying to make a far-reaching social statement: his primary concern was to bring the action downstage while the massive "Cotton Blossom" set was being struck. (Kern wasn't interested in the spot at all—he suggested merely taking the already written *Cotton Blossom* theme and inverting it.) Ziegfeld's lavishness was evident in the physical production, but director-in-fact Hammerstein kept the show boat from overwhelming the powerful material.

LADY MARY

FEBRUARY 23, 1928   DALY'S THEATRE < LONDON >   181
    PERFORMANCES

Music mostly by Albert Sirmay and Philip Charig
Lyrics by Harry Graham
Book by Frederick Lonsdale and John Hastings Turner

Published song:
If You're A Friend Of Mine—new lyric for *In Love With Love* from THE
    STEPPING STONES [November 6, 1923], revised from *Die Süsse
    Pariserin (Fraulein de Loraine)* from DIE BALLKÖNIGIN [Circa
    September 1913]

Composer Albert Sirmay apparently remembered *Die Süsse Pariserin* and had it interpolated here in revised form. He had also been a contributor to the score of DIE BALLKÖNIGIN, as Albert Szirmai. After emigrating to America, he became an important editor for Chappell & Co., publisher of Gershwin, Rodgers, Porter, and others.

BLUE EYES

APRIL 27, 1928   PICCADILLY THEATRE < LONDON >   276
    PERFORMANCES

Lyrics by Graham John
Book by Guy Bolton and John
Directed by John Harwood
Produced by Lee Ephraim
With Evelyn Laye

Published songs:
Back To The Heather
Blue Eyes—revised version of *All Lanes Must Reach A Turning* from
    DEAR SIR [September 23, 1924]

Bow Belles—revised version of *You Can't Make Love by Wireless* from
    THE BEAUTY PRIZE [September 5, 1923]
Do I Do Wrong—see ROBERTA [NOVEMBER 18, 1933]
Henry
In Love—revised version of *Alone At Last* from OH, I SAY! [October 30,
    1913]
No One Else But You

Additional songs published in vocal score:
Charlie (Opening Act One)
The Curtsey—revised version of *Weeping Willow Tree* from DEAR SIR
A Fair Lady (Opening Act Two)
Finale Act One
His Majesty's Dragoons
Long Live Nancy
Praise The Day
Romeo And Juliet
Someone
Trouble About The Drama

A British historical romance, which was moderately successful but nonexporta-
ble to Broadway.

SWEET ADELINE

Musical Romance Of The Gay Nineties

SEPTEMBER 3, 1929   HAMMERSTEIN'S THEATRE   34 PERFORMANCES

Book and lyrics by Oscar Hammerstein 2nd
Directed by Reginald Hammerstein
Produced by Arthur Hammerstein
With Helen Morgan and Charles Butterworth

Published songs:
Don't Ever Leave Me
Here Am I
Lonely Feet—added to 1955 movie version; originally used in THREE
    SISTERS [April 19, 1934]
Out Of The Blue
The Sun About To Rise
'Twas Not So Long Ago
We Were So Young—written for movie version
Why Was I Born?

Additional song published (no lyric) in piano selection:
Some Girl Is On Your Mind

Kern and Hammerstein followed their precedent-breaking SHOW BOAT [December 27, 1927] with this nostalgic look at the Nineties. (1890s, that is.) Written for the torch-singing Helen Morgan (of SHOW BOAT), the lovely score was particularly plaintive; but the favorably received SWEET ADELINE ran headlong into the stock market crash and could not survive. Producer Arthur Hammerstein, responsible for some of Broadway's most successful operettas (see WILDFLOWER [Youmans: February 7, 1923]), was bankrupt within a year. The family theatre on Broadway at 53rd Street was lost; it's now the Ed Sullivan. More importantly, the lucrative rights to the Hammerstein operettas—including NAUGHTY MARIETTA [November 7, 1910], THE FIREFLY [December 2, 1912], and ROSE-MARIE [September 2, 1924]—were auctioned off. (The sole bidder at the auction, which nobody else seems to have known about, was a fellow named Shubert—who got the lot for $684.)

RIPPLES

The New Musical Extravaganza

FEBRUARY 11, 1930   NEW AMSTERDAM THEATRE   55 PERFORMANCES

Music mostly by Oscar Levant and Albert Sirmay
Lyrics by Irving Caesar and Graham John
Book and direction by William Anthony McGuire
Produced by Charles Dillingham
With Fred, Dorothy, and (introducing) Paula Stone

Published song:
Anything May Happen Any Day (lyric by John)

A circus acrobat in his youth, Fred Stone's appearances always featured a daredevil stunt—like his entrance in THE RED MILL [October 24, 1906], falling backwards down an eighteen-foot ladder. In his midfifties, Stone and neighbor/friend Will Rogers took up the daredevil hobby of flying. A crash landing crushed Stone's legs, forcing him to miss the next scheduled show, the Raymond Hubbell/Roy Henderson THREE CHEERS [October 15, 1928] Daughter Dorothy proved star material on her own, and Rogers—who was to be killed in a 1935 plane crash—stepped into Fred's role. Stone returned to the stage with RIPPLES, bringing along Dorothy and his other dancing daughter, Paula. But the accident had aged the ageless Stone, and the times had made the innocent Stone shows obsolete. There was to be one last unsuccessful attempt, Harry Revel and Mack Gordon's SMILING FACES [August 30, 1932].

THE CAT AND THE FIDDLE
A Musical Love Story

OCTOBER 15, 1931   GLOBE THEATRE   395 PERFORMANCES

Book and lyrics by Otto Harbach
Directed by José Ruben
Produced by Max Gordon
With Bettina Hall, Georges Metaxa, and José Ruben

Published songs:
Don't Ask Me Not To Sing—cut; also used in ROBERTA [NOVEMBER 18, 1933]
I Watch The Love Parade
Misunderstood—advertised but not published (apparently a misprint)
A New Love Is Old
The Night Was Made For Love
One Moment Alone
Poor Pierrot
She Didn't Say 'Yes' "
Try To Forget

Additional songs published in vocal score:
The Breeze Kissed Your Hair
Hh! Cha Cha!—countermelody for *Why Do I Love You?* from SHOW BOAT [DECEMBER 27, 1927]
Opening Act One (Street Vendors)

Kern was joined by Otto Harbach in this successful integrated-score experiment, song arising naturally from the action. (The leading characters, conveniently, were composers, singers, and street musicians.) A new producer was found for CAT AND THE FIDDLE: Max Gordon, who had overwhelmed the depressed Broadway scene with the Schwartz and Dietz THREE'S A CROWD [Schwartz: October 15, 1930] and THE BAND WAGON [Schwartz: June 3, 1931]. An unhappy footnote: the financially bereft Charles Dillingham, crushed by the Depression, retained only his beloved (mortgaged) Globe Theatre. In May of 1932 he unaccountably absconded with the box office receipts and fled; his well-deserved reputation was such that Broadway pitied rather than censured him. He existed on charity from still-solvent former associates (including Kern) until his death on August 30, 1934.

MUSIC IN THE AIR

November 8, 1932   Alvin Theatre   342 performances

Book and lyrics by Oscar Hammerstein 2nd
Directed by Kern and Hammerstein
Produced by Peggy Fears
With Natalie Hall, Walter Slezak, Katherine Carrington, and Al Shean

Published songs:
And Love Was Born
I Am So Eager
I'm Alone
In Egern On The Tegern Sea
I've Told Ev'ry Little Star
One More Dance
The Song Is You
There's A Hill Beyond A Hill
We Belong Together
When The Spring Is In The Air

Additional songs published in vocal score:
At Stony Brook
Hold Your Head Up High [hymn]
Melodies Of May (music by Beethoven, arranged by Kern)
Prayer

Working again with Hammerstein, Kern turned out one of his richest scores for this charming Bavarian tale. As in Cat And The Fiddle [October 15, 1931], the European setting and musical subject matter enabled close integration of score and book. The authors felt they needed Ziegfeld for the show, but he was in hopeless financial/physical shape and died July 22, 1932. Dillingham and Arthur Hammerstein were bankrupt; even the Shuberts were bankrupt; and Kern had fought with Max Gordon on Cat and the Fiddle. Along came former Follies girl Peggy Fears with rich husband A. C. Blumenthal, who had kept Ziegfeld afloat during his final production (the May 19, 1932 revival of Show Boat [December 27, 1927]). Fears—with Blumenthal's money—presented Music in the Air, with Hammerstein and Kern doing the actual producing. Hammerstein followed this hit with a ten-year string of flops, until Dick Rodgers called looking to replace Larry Hart for the project that became Oklahoma! [Rodgers: March 31, 1943].

ROBERTA

November 18, 1933   New Amsterdam Theatre   295
PERFORMANCES

Book and lyrics by Otto Harbach
(Based on *Gowns by Roberta* [novel] by Alice Duer Miller)
Produced by Max Gordon
With Lyda Roberti, Fay Templeton, Tamara, Sydney Greenstreet, and
Bob Hope
NOTE: Gowns by Roberta, pre-Broadway title

Published songs:
Armful Of Trouble—cut
I Won't Dance (lyric by Oscar Hammerstein 2nd, Harbach, Dorothy
    Fields, and Jimmy McHugh)—added to 1935 movie version; new
    lyric for song from Three Sisters [April 19, 1934]
I'll Be Hard To Handle (lyric by Bernard Dougall)
Let's Begin
Lovely To Look At (lyric by Fields and McHugh)—written for 1935
    movie version
Smoke Gets In Your Eyes
Something Had To Happen
The Touch Of Your Hand
Yesterdays
You're Devastating—new lyric for *Do I Do Wrong* from Blue Eyes
    [April 27, 1927]

Additional songs published in vocal score:
Don't Ask Me Not To Sing—originally used (cut) in The Cat and The
    Fiddle [October 15, 1931]
Hot Spot
Madrigal

A dreary fashion show with many problems and few attributes. Gordon temporarily patched his shaky relationship with Kern by allowing the composer to
direct the show; then he fired Kern out of town and brought in Hassard Short.
(No one ultimately received director billing.) Roberta managed a fair run,
with minimal competition, drastically cut-rate tickets, and the song hit *Smoke
Gets In Your Eyes.*

THREE SISTERS

APRIL 19, 1934   THEATRE ROYAL, DRURY LANE <LONDON>   72
PERFORMANCES

Book and lyrics by Oscar Hammerstein 2nd
Directed and produced by Kern and Hammerstein
With Charlotte Greenwood, Adele Dixon, and Stanley Holloway

Published songs:
Hand In Hand
I Won't Dance—see ROBERTA [November 18, 1933]
Funny Old House
Keep Smiling
Lonely Feet—also used in 1935 motion picture version of SWEET ADELINE
    [September 3, 1929]
Roll On, Rolling Road
What Good Are Words?
You Are Doing Very Well

Additional songs published (no lyric) in piano selection:
Circus Queen
Here It Comes
Now That I Have Springtime
Somebody Wants To Go To Sleep

An original musical written for the Drury Lane, London home of Hammerstein's hit Twenties operettas. The score contained some particularly lovely
work, including *Lonely Feet* and *Hand In Hand*; but the disappointing failure of THREE SISTERS sent Kern to Hollywood for (almost) the rest of his
life.

GENTLEMEN UNAFRAID

[JUNE 3, 1938]   MUNICIPAL OPERA <ST. LOUIS, MISSOURI>   6
    PERFORMANCES; SUMMER STOCK TRYOUT

Book and lyrics by Oscar Hammerstein 2nd and Otto Harbach
(Based on a story by Edward Boykin)
Directed by Zeke Colvan
Produced by St. Louis Municipal Opera
With Ronald Graham, Vicki Cummings, Hope Manning, Avon Long, and
Richard (Red) Skelton
Note: HAYFOOT, STRAWFOOT, stock and amateur title

Published songs:

Abe Lincoln Had Just One Country—added to 1942 stock and amateur
    version, retitled **HAYFOOT, STRAWFOOT**; original publication as 1941
    nonshow song for War Bond drive

Cantabile (Song Without Words)—cut; for initial publication see **VERY
    WARM FOR MAY**

When A New Star (lyric by Harbach)—initial publication upon release of
    HAYFOOT, STRAWFOOT

Your Dream (Is The Same As My Dream)—only publication upon reuse in
    1940 movie "One Night in the Tropics"

This Civil War operetta never got further than its one-week tryout: no one
was interested in taking it to Broadway. **GENTLEMEN UNAFRAID** was yet
another theatrical disappointment for Kern. **HAYFOOT, STRAWFOOT,** a revised
1942 version released for stock and amateur groups, didn't create much more
interest. (The score, let it be added, is surprisingly bland.)

MAMBA'S DAUGHTERS

JANUARY 3, 1939   EMPIRE THEATRE   162 PERFORMANCES

Play by Dorothy and DuBose Heyward
(Based on the novel by DuBose Heyward)
Produced and directed by Guthrie McClintic
With Ethel Waters

Published songs:
Lonesome Walls (lyric by DuBose Heyward)

Kern and Hammerstein had expressed interest in musicalizing Heyward's
earlier novel "Porgy" (as an Al Jolson vehicle). By the time **MAMBA'S DAUGH-
TERS** was produced, Gershwin was no longer alive. Kern was asked to write the
one original song for the play and came up with the highly effective *Lonesome
Walls*, a companion to Ethel Waters' *Supper Time* from **AS THOUSANDS
CHEER** [Berlin: September 30, 1933].

VERY WARM FOR MAY

MAY 17, 1939   ALVIN THEATRE   59 PERFORMANCES

Book and lyrics by Oscar Hammerstein 2nd
Production staged by Vincente Minnelli
Book staged by Hammerstein
Produced by Max Gordon
With Grace McDonald, Jack Whiting, Eve Arden, Hiram Sherman, Avon
Long, and Donald Brian

Published songs:
All In Fun
All The Things You Are—revised version of *Cantabile (Song Without Words)* (cut/unpublished) from GENTLEMEN UNAFRAID [JUNE 3, 1938]
Heaven In My Arms (Music In My Heart)
In Other Words, Seventeen
In The Heart Of The Dark
That Lucky Fellow

With no Broadway opportunity since ROBERTA [November 18, 1933], Kern was in no position to hold out when Max Gordon called again. Things went even worse than on the previous show. Gordon was in Hollywood during the production period; he arrived at the tryout and panicked, demanding radical changes and once again calling Hassard Short for help. VERY WARM FOR MAY arrived on Broadway in dismal shape and quickly closed. Gordon still had major hits ahead of him, including the comedies *My Sister Eileen* [December 26, 1940] and *Born Yesterday* [February 4, 1946], but his future musicals were all troubled failures. Kern's final theatre score contained some fine work, although only *All The Things You Are*—one of the very best musical theatre songs—managed to escape the wreckage. In the mostly youthful cast, incidentally, was early Kern star Donald Brian—who had introduced *They Didn't Believe Me* in THE GIRL FROM UTAH [August 24, 1914]. Kern returned to Hollywood where he wrote a number of successful motion picture scores, collaborating with Hammerstein, Ira Gershwin, Dorothy Fields, Johnny Mercer and others. He won two Oscars, with Fields for *The Way You Look Tonight* (1936) and Hammerstein for *The Last Time I Saw Paris* (1941). By 1945 Hammerstein and Richard Rodgers had branched into producing. They commissioned Kern and Dorothy Fields to write a musical comedy biography of sharpshooter Annie Oakley for Ethel Merman (see ANNIE GET YOUR GUN [Berlin: May 16, 1946]). Simultaneously, Kern and Hammerstein planned to revive SHOW BOAT [December 27, 1927] and wrote a new song for the finale, *Nobody Else But Me*. Arriving in New York for SHOW BOAT auditions, Kern suffered a cerebral hemorrhage and collapsed in the street; with no identification, he was taken to the derelict ward on Welfare Island. Jerome Kern died on November 11, 1945.

Kern entered a musical theatre dominated by foreign operettas. During his thirty-five-year career, the American musical theatre first stood on its own during World War One, with the Kern, Bolton, and Wodehouse "Princess Theatre Shows." The early Twenties saw the arrival of the more sophisticated, jazz-influenced Gershwin and Youmans. Then, Kern (with Hammerstein) discovered the dramatic potential of musical theatre with SHOW BOAT [De-

cember 27, 1927] and succeeding scores. If Kern's early work—with a very few exceptions—is hopelessly dated, it is a case of the experimental being out-moded by the perfected. After sixty years, the best of Kern's songs remain high among the very best songs of the American musical theatre.

Irving Berlin

BORN: May 11, 1888   Mohilev, Russia
DIED: September 22, 1989   New York, New York

Irving Berlin's family fled from religious persecution and came to New York in 1892. The son of a part-time cantor, Berlin took to the streets as a singing panhandler and went on to become a singing waiter at a Chinatown saloon. It was here, at "Nigger Mike's", that he wrote his first published song, *Marie From Sunny Italy* (music by Nick Nicholson), issued in 1907 by Joseph W. Stern and Company. In 1908 came his first composer/lyricist effort, *Best Of Friends Must Part*. Berlin went to work as a staff lyricist (and occasional composer) for publisher/songwriter Ted Snyder and was soon a partner in the firm. As it was then common practice to interpolate songs in Broadway shows, Berlin found a natural showcase for a portion of his increasingly enormous output.

[all music and lyrics by Irving Berlin unless indicated]

THE BOYS AND BETTY

NOVEMBER 2, 1908   WALLACK'S THEATRE   112 PERFORMANCES

Music mostly by Silvio Hein
Book and lyrics mostly by George V. Hobart
Directed by George Marion
Produced by Daniel V. Arthur
With Marie Cahill

Published songs:
She Was A Dear Little Girl (music by Ted Snyder, lyric by Berlin)

THE GIRL AND THE WIZARD

SEPTEMBER 27, 1909   CASINO THEATRE   96 PERFORMANCES

Music mostly by Julian Edwards (see **Kern**)
Lyrics mostly by Robert B. Smith and Edward Madden

Book by J. Hartley Manners
Directed by Ned Wayburn
Produced by the Messrs. Shubert
With Sam Bernard

Published song:
Oh, How That German Could Love (music by Ted Snyder, lyric by
    Berlin)

THE JOLLY BACHELORS

JANUARY 6, 1910   BROADWAY THEATRE   84 PERFORMANCES

Music mostly by Raymond Hubbell
Music to Berlin lyrics by Ted Snyder
Book and lyrics mostly by Glen MacDonough
Directed by Ned Wayburn
Produced by Lew Fields
With Stella Mayhew, Nora Bayes (Norworth), Jack Norworth, and Emma
Carus

Published Berlin/Snyder songs:
If The Managers Only Thought The Same As Mother
Oh, That Beautiful Rag—also used in UP AND DOWN BROADWAY [July
    18, 1910]
Stop That Rag (Keep On Playing, Honey)
Sweet Marie, Make-A Rag-A-Time Dance Wid Me

ARE YOU A MASON?

[CIRCA APRIL 1910]; CLOSED DURING PRE-BROADWAY TOUR

Play by Leo Ditrichstein
Produced by Rich and Harris
With Ditrichstein and Beth Tate

Published song:
I'm Going On A Long Vacation (music by Ted Snyder)

ZIEGFELD FOLLIES OF 1910

JUNE 20, 1910   JARDIN DE PARIS THEATRE   88 PERFORMANCES

Music mostly by others
Book and lyrics mostly by Harry B. Smith and Gus Edwards

Directed by Julian Mitchell
Produced by Florenz Ziegfeld, Jr.
With Bert Williams, Lillian Lorraine, and Fanny Brice

Published song:
The Dance Of The Grizzly Bear (music by George Botsford)
Good-Bye Becky Cohen—advertised but not published (not by Berlin)

Florenz Ziegfeld, Jr. began his Broadway career in 1896 by importing and featuring (and marrying) Parisian star Anna Held in a series of musicals. He came up with his successful revue format with FOLLIES OF 1907 [July 8, 1907]. The editions became more lavish as competition developed in the mid-Teens. The scores were generally contributed by a throng of songwriters, the only exception being Berlin's ZIEGFELD FOLLIES OF 1927 [August 16, 1927].

UP AND DOWN BROADWAY

JULY 18, 1910   CASINO THEATRE   72 PERFORMANCES

Music mostly by Jean Schwartz
Lyrics mostly by William Jerome
Music to Berlin lyrics by Ted Snyder
Book by Edgar Smith
Directed by William J. Wilson
Produced by Messrs. Shubert
With Eddie Foy, Snyder, and Berlin

Published Berlin/Snyder songs:
Sweet Italian Love
Oh, That Beautiful Rag—originally used in THE JOLLY BACHELORS
     [January 6, 1910]

The popularity of the early Snyder and Berlin songs was such that the writers were hired to perform some of their work in this Shubert revue.

THE GIRL AND THE DRUMMER

[CIRCA AUGUST 1910]; CLOSED DURING PRE-BROADWAY TRYOUT

Music mostly by Augustus Barrett (see **Kern**)
Music to Berlin lyrics by Ted Snyder
Book and lyrics mostly by George Broadhurst
(Based on *What Happened to Jones* [play] by Broadhurst)
Produced by William A. Brady, Ltd.
With Herbert Corthell and Belle Gold

Published Berlin/Snyder songs:
Herman, Let's Dance That Beautiful Waltz—also used in TWO MEN AND
    A GIRL [Circa December 1910]
Wishing

HE CAME FROM MILWAUKEE

SEPTEMBER 21, 1910   CASINO THEATRE   117 PERFORMANCES

Music mostly by Ben M. Jerome and Louis A. Hirsch
Lyrics mostly by Edward Madden
Book by Mark Swan
Directed by Sidney Ellison
Produced by the Messrs. Shubert
With Sam Bernard

Published song:
Bring Back My Lena To Me (music and lyric by Berlin and Ted Snyder)

GETTING A POLISH

NOVEMBER 7, 1910   WALLACK'S THEATRE   48 PERFORMANCES

Play by Booth Tarkington and Harry Leon Wilson
Music by Ted Snyder
Lyrics by Irving Berlin
Directed by Hugh Ford
Produced by Liebler and Company
With May Irwin
NOTE: MRS. JIM, pre-Broadway title

Published Berlin/Snyder songs:
He Sympathized With Me
My Wife Bridget (music and lyric by Berlin)
That Opera Rag

TWO MEN AND A GIRL

[CIRCA DECEMBER 1910]; CLOSED DURING PRE-BROADWAY TRYOUT

Music mostly by Julian Edwards
Book and lyrics mostly by Charles Campbell and Ralph Skinner
With Fred Bailey, Ralph Austin, and Belle Gold

Published song:
Herman, Let's Dance That Beautiful Waltz (music by Ted Snyder, lyric
by Berlin)—originally used in THE GIRL AND THE DRUMMER [Circa
August 1910]

JUMPING JUPITER

MARCH 6, 1911   NEW YORK THEATRE   24 PERFORMANCES

Music mostly by Karl Hoschna
Lyrics mostly by Richard Carle
Music to Berlin lyrics by Ted Snyder
Book by Carle and Sydney Rosenfeld
Directed by Carle
Produced by H. H. Frazee and George W. Lederer
With Carle and Edna Wallace Hopper

Published Berlin/Snyder songs:
Angelo
It Can't Be Did
'Thank You Kind Sir!' Said She

GABY

Folies Bergère Revue

APRIL 27, 1911   FOLIES BERGÈRE THEATRE   92 PERFORMANCES

Music and lyrics by Vincent Bryan, Irving Berlin, and Ted Snyder; also by
others
Book by Harry B. and Robert B. Smith
Directed by George Marion
Produced by Henry B. Harris and Jesse L. Lasky
With Ethel Levey and Otis Harlan

Published Berlin/Bryan/Snyder songs:
Answer Me—advertised but not published
Down To The Folies Bergère
I Beg Your Pardon, Dear Old Broadway (music and lyric by Berlin)
Keep a Taxi Waiting Dear
Spanish Love

The Folies Bergère opened as a dinner theatre featuring a vaudeville show.
Within five months the house was closed and transformed into a legitimate
theatre, the Fulton (later renamed the Helen Hayes; demolished in 1981).
Ethel Levey was the former Mrs. George M. Cohan.

FRIARS' FROLIC OF 1911

Benefit Show

MAY 28, 1911   NEW AMSTERDAM THEATRE   1 PERFORMANCE

Music and lyrics mostly by others
Directed by George M. Cohan
Produced by A. L. Erlanger
With Cohan, Berlin, Julian Eltinge, and William Collier

Published song:
Alexander's Ragtime Band—published as 1911 nonshow song; see
    HOKEY-POKEY [February 8, 1912]

Berlin himself sang his one-month-old hit, which ushered a new sound into popular music. (Not ragtime, though, as it's *not* a rag.) Throughout his career, Berlin had the uncanny ability to express in song what the public was about to feel—just ahead of the competition.

ZIEGFELD FOLLIES OF 1911

JUNE 26, 1911   JARDIN DE PARIS THEATRE   80 PERFORMANCES

Music mostly by Maurice Levi and Raymond Hubbell (see **Kern**)
Book and lyrics mostly by George V. Hobart
Directed by Julian Mitchell
Produced by Florenz Ziegfeld, Jr.
With Bessie McCoy, Bert Williams, and Fanny Brice

Published songs:
Dog Gone That Chilly Man
Ephraham Played Upon The Piano (by Berlin and Vincent Bryan)
Woodman, Woodman, Spare That Tree! (by Berlin and Bryan)
You've Built A Fire Down In My Heart—also used in THE FASCINATING
    WIDOW [September 11, 1911]

THE FASCINATING WIDOW

SEPTEMBER 11, 1911   LIBERTY THEATRE   56 PERFORMANCES

Music mostly by others
Book and lyrics mostly by Otto Hauerbach (Harbach)
Directed by George Marion
Produced by A. H. Woods
With Julian Eltinge

Published songs:
Don't Take Your Beau To The Seashore (by E. Ray Goetz and Berlin)
You've Built A Fire Down In My Heart—originally used in ZIEGFELD
FOLLIES OF 1911 [June 26, 1911]

Songwriter/producer E. Ray Goetz was an early collaborator with Berlin, Gershwin and Porter. Goetz's sister Dorothy became Berlin's bride in 1912. Tragically, she contracted typhoid fever on the honeymoon and died—an event memorialized in the top-selling tear-jerker *When I Lost You.* (An ad features the smiling, tuxedoed tunesmith pointing to a copy, with the caption "Irving Berlin, song genius of the world, says this is the best song I ever wrote.")

THE LITTLE MILLIONAIRE

SEPTEMBER 25, 1911   GEORGE M. COHAN THEATRE   192
    PERFORMANCES

Book, music and lyrics mostly by George M. Cohan
Directed by Cohan
Produced by Cohan and Sam H. Harris
With Cohan, Jerry Cohan and Donald Crisp

Published song:
Down In My Heart

Cohan, recognizing Berlin as his natural successor in the popular music field, befriended and encouraged him. Sam H. Harris, who began his career producing melodramas, joined Cohan on the hit LITTLE JOHNNY JONES [November 7, 1904]. They became a major producing firm, presenting not only Cohan's plays and musicals, but others as well. After breaking up in 1919, Harris formed similar partnerships with Berlin and, later, George S. Kaufman.

THE NEVER HOMES

OCTOBER 5, 1911   BROADWAY THEATRE   92 PERFORMANCES

Music mostly by A. Baldwin Sloane
"Rhymes" mostly by E. Ray Goetz
"Words" by Glen MacDonough
Directed by Ned Wayburn
Produced by Lew Fields

Published song:
There's A Girl In Havana (by Goetz, Berlin, and Ted Snyder)

REAL GIRL

[Circa October 1911]; closed during pre-Broadway tryout

Music and lyrics also by others
Produced by Bonita Amusement Co.
With Bonita and Lew Hearn

Published songs:
Cuddle Up
One O'Clock In The Morning
That Mysterious Rag (by Berlin and Snyder)
When You're In Town

WINTER GARDEN VAUDEVILLE

[Circa November 1911]   Winter Garden Theatre

Music and lyrics mostly by others
Produced by the Messrs. Shubert
With Dolly Jardon

Published song:
Sombrero Land (by E. Ray Goetz, Berlin and Ted Snyder)

SHE KNOWS BETTER NOW

[January 15, 1912]   Plymouth Theatre < Chicago, Illinois >;
    closed during pre-Broadway tryout

Play by Agnes L. Crimmins
Music also by others
Directed by William Collier
Produced by Eisfeldt and Anhalt
With May Irwin and Arthur Byron

Published songs:
I'm Going Back To Dixie (music and lyrics by Berlin and Ted Snyder)
The Ragtime Mocking Bird

HOKEY-POKEY;
AND BUNTY, BULLS AND STRINGS

A Potpourri In Two Acts

FEBRUARY 8, 1912   BROADWAY THEATRE   108 PERFORMANCES

Music mostly by John Stromberg and A. Baldwin Sloane
Lyrics mostly by E. Ray Goetz
Sketches by Edgar Smith
Directed by Gus Sohlke
Produced by Weber and Fields
With Joe Weber, Lew Fields, William Collier, Lillian Russell, and Fay
Templeton

Published song:
Alexander's Bag-Pipe Band (by Goetz, Berlin, and Sloane)—revised
    version (take-off) of *Alexander's Ragtime Band* from FRIARS' FROLIC
    [**May 28, 1911**]

The famous comic acting/producing team of Weber and Fields had broken
up in 1904 after twenty-four years of partnership. Both continued successfully
on their own, and with HOKEY-POKEY began occasional "all-star" reunions of
their famous music-hall company. Fields remained a major musical theatre
force into the Twenties, when he discovered and nurtured his son Herbert's
colleagues Richard Rodgers and Lorenz Hart (see A LONELY ROMEO [**Rodgers: June 10, 1919**]).

THE WHIRL OF SOCIETY

MARCH 5, 1912   WINTER GARDEN THEATRE   136 PERFORMANCES

Music mostly by Louis A. Hirsch
Lyrics mostly by Harold Atteridge
Book by Harrison Rhodes
Directed by J. C. Huffman
Produced by Winter Garden Co. (Messrs. Shubert)
With Stella Mayhew and Al Jolson

Published songs:
I Want To Be In Dixie (by Berlin and Ted Snyder)—also used in HULLO,
    RAGTIME [**December 23, 1912**]
Opera Burlesque (On The Sextette From Lucia de Lammermoor)—initial
    publication upon reuse in HANKY PANKY [**August 5, 1912**]
That Society Bear

COHAN AND HARRIS MINSTRELS

[Circa April 1912]; post-Broadway tour

Music and lyrics mostly by others
Produced by George M. Cohan and Sam H. Harris
With Happy Lambert

Published song:
Lead Me To That Beautiful Band (lyric by E. Ray Goetz)

THE PASSING SHOW OF 1912

July 22, 1912   Winter Garden Theatre   136 performances

Produced by the Messrs. Shubert
With Eugene and Willie Howard, Charlotte Greenwood, and Trixie Fraganza

Published song:
The Ragtime Jockey Man

HANKY PANKY

A Jumble of Follification

August 5, 1912   Broadway Theatre   104 performances

Music mostly by A. Baldwin Sloane
Lyrics mostly by E. Ray Goetz
Book by Edgar Smith
Directed by Gus Sohlke
Produced by Lew Fields
With Carter De Haven, Myrtle Gilbert, and Bobby North

Published songs:
The Million Dollar Ball (by Goetz and Berlin)
*Opera Burlesque (On The Sextette From Lucia de
    Lammermoor)*—originally used (unpublished) in The Whirl of
    Society [March 8, 1912]

MY BEST GIRL

September 12, 1912   Park Theatre   68 performances

Music mostly by Clifton Crawford and Augustus Barratt
Book and lyrics mostly by Channing Pollock and Rennold Wolf

Directed by Sidney Ellison
Produced by Henry B. Harris
With Crawford

Published song:
Follow Me Around

ZIEGFELD FOLLIES OF 1912

OCTOBER 21, 1912   MOULIN ROUGE THEATRE   88 PERFORMANCES

Music mostly by Raymond Hubbell
Lyrics mostly by Harry B. Smith
Directed by Julian Mitchell
Produced by Florenz Ziegfeld, Jr.

Published song:
A Little Bit Of Everything

THE SUN DODGERS
Fanfare Of Frivolity

NOVEMBER 30, 1912   BROADWAY THEATRE   29 PERFORMANCES

Music mostly by A. Baldwin Sloane
Lyrics mostly by E. Ray Goetz
Book by Edgar Smith and Mark Swan
Directed by Ned Wayburn
Produced by Lew Fields
With Eva Tanguay and George Monroe

Published songs:
At The Picture Show (by Goetz and Berlin; issued as by Goetz and
     Sloane)
Hiram's Band (music by Goetz and Sloane, lyric by Berlin; issued as by
     Goetz and Sloane)

Exact authorship of a number of early Berlin songs is uncertain, as Berlin did
not take public credit. He wrote these two with his brother-in-law, Ray Goetz.
Baldwin Sloane, the composer of the show, allowed them to be interpolated
but insisted on taking sole credit for all the music in the score.

HULLO, RAGTIME!

DECEMBER 23, 1912   HIPPODROME < LONDON >   451 PERFORMANCES

Music mostly by Louis Hirsch
Sketches by Max Pemberton and Albert P. De Courville
Directed by Austen Hurgon
Produced by De Courville
With Ethel Levey, Bonita, and Lew Hearn

Published songs:
I Want To Be In Dixie (by Berlin and Ted Snyder)—originally used in
    THE WHIRL OF SOCIETY [**March 5, 1912**]
The Ragtime Soldier Man—initial publication as 1912 nonshow song

ALL ABOARD!

JUNE 5, 1913   44TH STREET ROOF GARDEN THEATRE   108
    PERFORMANCES

Music mostly by E. Ray Goetz and Malvin Franklin
Lyrics mostly by Goetz
Book by Mark Swan
Directed by Wm. J. Wilson and W. H. Post
Produced by Lew Fields
With Fields, Carter De Haven, and Claire Rochester

Published songs:
The Monkey Doodle Doo [1st]—different than song from THE
    COCOANUTS [**December 8, 1925**]
Somebody's Coming To My House
Take Me Back

THE TRAINED NURSES
Vaudeville Act
Jesse L. Lasky's Most Pretentious Production

[CIRCA SEPTEMBER 1913]

Produced by Lasky
With Gladys Clark and Henry Bergman

Published song:
If You Don't Want Me (Why Do You Hang Around?)

THE QUEEN OF THE MOVIES

JANUARY 12, 1914   GLOBE THEATRE   104 PERFORMANCES

Music mostly by Jean Gilbert
Book and lyrics mostly by Glen MacDonough
(Based on the German musical by Freund and Okonowski)
Directed by Herbert Gresham
Produced by Thomas W. Ryley

Published song:
Follow The Crowd

ALONG CAME RUTH

FEBRUARY 23, 1914   GAIETY THEATRE   56 PERFORMANCES

Play by Holman Day
(Based on the French of Fonson and Wicheler)
Directed by George Marion
Produced by Henry W. Savage
With Irene Fenwick

Published song:
Along Came Ruth

THE SOCIETY BUDS

Vaudeville Act

[CIRCA OCTOBER 1914]

Produced by Jesse L. Lasky
With Gladys Clark and Henry Bergman

Published songs:
Furnishing A House For Two
That's My Idea of Paradise

WATCH YOUR STEP

DECEMBER 8, 1914   GLOBE THEATRE   175 PERFORMANCES

Book by Harry B. Smith
Directed by R. H. Burnside
Produced by Charles Dillingham
With Irene and Vernon Castle, and Frank Tinney

Published songs:
Come To The Land Of The Argentine
Homeward Bound
I Hate You
I Love To Have The Boys Around Me
I'm A Dancing Teacher Now—advertised but not published
I've Got A Go Back To Texas
Lead Me To Love (music by Ted Snyder)
Let's Go 'Round The Town
Lock Me In Your Harem And Throw Away The Key
The Minstrel Parade
Move Over
Ragtime Opera Medley—published in separate edition
Settle Down In A One-Horse Town
Show Us How To Do The Fox Trot
Simple Melody
The Syncopated Walk
They Always Follow Me Around
Watch Your Step—published in separate edition
What Is Love?
When I Discovered You
When It's Night Time In Dixie Land

Additional songs published in vocal score:
Metropolitan Nights
Opening Chorus (Office Hours)
Polka (Mr. and Mrs. Castle's Specialty) [instrumental]

Berlin wrote his first full score for this "syncopated musical," which successfully brought new pop rhythms into the theatre. Berlin took the opportunity to break with partners Ted Snyder and Henry Waterson and start his own highly profitable publishing house. Producer Charles Dillingham began his career a decade earlier with hit Victor Herbert operettas; he was to play an important part in the Broadway musical field until the stock market crash.

WINTER GARDEN VAUDEVILLE

Did You Ever?

[Circa April 1915]   Winter Garden Theatre

Music and lyrics mostly by others
Produced by the Messrs. Shubert
With Blossom Seeley

Published song:
My Bird Of Paradise (My Honolulu Girl)

STOP! LOOK! LISTEN!

DECEMBER 25, 1915   GLOBE THEATRE   105 PERFORMANCES

Book by Harry B. Smith
Directed by R. H. Burnside
Produced by Charles Dillingham
With Gaby Deslys, Harry Fox, and Justine Johnstone

Published songs:
And Father Wanted Me To Learn A Trade
Blow Your Horn
England Every Time For Me—written for London version, FOLLOW THE
      CROWD [February 19, 1916]
Everything In America Is Ragtime
The Girl On The Magazine
I Love A Piano
I Love To Dance—advertised but not published
The Law Must Be Obeyed
A Pair Of Ordinary Coons—published in separate edition
Sailor Song
Skating Song—advertised but not published
Stop! Look! Listen!
Take Off A Little Bit
Teach Me How To Love
That Hula Hula
Until I Fell In Love With You
When I Get Back To The U.S.A.
When I'm Out With You
Why Don't They Give Us A Chance?—advertised but not published

Additional song published (no lyric) in piano selection:
I Love To Dance—initial publication in FOLLOW THE CROWD selection

A follow-up to WATCH YOUR STEP [December 8, 1914], not quite as successful
but with a more satisfying score (including the jaunty *I Love A Piano*).

FRIARS' FROLIC OF 1916
Benefit Show

MAY 28, 1916   NEW AMSTERDAM THEATRE   1 PERFORMANCE

Music and lyrics mostly by others
Directed by George M. Cohan
Produced by Sam H. Harris and A. L. Erlanger
With Cohan, Berlin, William Collier, Frank Tinney, and Harrison Fisher

Published song:
Friars' Parade

STEP THIS WAY

MAY 29, 1916   SHUBERT THEATRE   88 PERFORMANCES

Music mostly by E. Ray Goetz and Bert Grant
Lyrics mostly by Goetz
Book by Edgar Smith
(Based on *The Girl Behind the Counter* [musical] by Smith)
Directed by Frank McCormack
Produced by Lew Fields
With Fields, Gladys Clark, and Henry Bergman

Published songs:
I've Got A Sweet Tooth Bothering Me
In Florida Among The Palms—also used in ZIEGFELD FOLLIES OF 1916
    [June 12, 1916]
Step This Way (not by Berlin)

ZIEGFELD FOLLIES OF 1916

JUNE 12, 1916   NEW AMSTERDAM THEATRE   112 PERFORMANCES

Music mostly by Louis Hirsch and Dave Stamper (see **Kern**)
Book and lyrics mostly by George V. Hobart and Gene Buck
Directed by Ned Wayburn
Produced by Florenz Ziegfeld, Jr.

Published song:
In Florida Among The Palms—originally used in STEP THIS WAY [May
    29, 1916]

THE CENTURY GIRL

NOVEMBER 6, 1916   CENTURY THEATRE   200 PERFORMANCES

Music also by Victor Herbert
Lyrics also by Henry Blossom
Produced by Charles Dillingham and Florenz Ziegfeld, Jr.
With Elsie Janis, Hazel Dawn, Frank Tinney, and Sam Bernard

Published songs:
Alice In Wonderland [1st]—different than song from MUSIC BOX REVUE
    (Fourth) [December 1, 1924]
The Chicken Walk
It Takes An Irishman To Make Love (lyric by Janis and Berlin)

Dillingham and Ziegfeld took the lease on the New Theatre, a white elephant built to house the short-lived dramatic equivalent to the Metropolitan Opera. Renamed the Century, it opened with this successful wartime extravaganza. But with the failure of MISS 1917 [Kern: November 5, 1917] they gave up on the theatre. The Shuberts eventually bought and demolished the house, replacing it with their Century Apartments at 25 Central Park West. During the Depression, Shubert employees were "encouraged" to lease apartments.

DANCE AND GROW THIN
Nightclub Show

[CIRCA APRIL 1917]   COCOANUT GROVE (ATOP CENTURY THEATRE)

Music and lyrics mostly by others
Directed by Ned Wayburn
Produced by Charles Dillingham and Florenz Ziegfeld, Jr.

Published songs:
Dance And Grow Thin (music by George W. Meyer)
There's Something Nice About The South

RAMBLER ROSE

SEPTEMBER 10, 1917   EMPIRE THEATRE   72 PERFORMANCES

Music mostly by Victor Jacobi
Book and lyrics mostly by Harry B. Smith
Produced by Charles Frohman, Inc.
With Julia Sanderson and Joseph Cawthorn

Published song:
Poor Little Rich Girl's Dog

JACK O'LANTERN

OCTOBER 16, 1917   GLOBE THEATRE   265 PERFORMANCES

Music mostly by Ivan Caryll
Lyrics mostly by Anne Caldwell
Book by Caldwell and R. H. Burnside
Directed by Burnside
Produced by Charles Dillingham
With Fred Stone

Published song:
I'll Take You Back To Italy

GOING UP

DECEMBER 25, 1917   LIBERTY THEATRE   351 PERFORMANCES

Music mostly by Louis A. Hirsch
Book and lyrics mostly by Otto Harbach
(Based on *The Aviator* [play] by James Montgomery)
Directed by Edward Royce and Montgomery
Produced by George M. Cohan and Sam H. Harris
With Frank Craven and Edith Day

Published songs:
Come Along To Toy Town—also used in EVERYTHING [August 22, 1918]
When The Curtain Falls

THE COHAN REVUE OF 1918
A Hit And Run Play

DECEMBER 31, 1917   NEW AMSTERDAM THEATRE   96 PERFORMANCES

"Some of the Songs by Irving Berlin, Others by George M. Cohan"
Book "Batted Out by George M. Cohan"
Directed by Cohan
Produced by Cohan and Sam H. Harris
With Nora Bayes and Charles Winninger

Published songs:
Down Where The Jack O'Lanterns Grow
The Eyes Of Youth See The Truth (music by Cohan and Berlin, lyric by
    Cohan; issued as by Cohan)
Polly Pretty Polly (Polly With A Past) (lyric by Cohan)
Spanish (music by Cohan and Berlin, lyric by Cohan; issued as by Cohan)
Wedding Of Words And Music—advertised but not published

ZIEGFELD FOLLIES OF 1918

JUNE 18, 1918   NEW AMSTERDAM THEATRE   151 PERFORMANCES

Music mostly by Louis A. Hirsch
"Lines and lyrics" mostly by Rennold Wolf and Gene Buck
Directed by Ned Wayburn
Produced by Florenz Ziegfeld, Jr.
With Eddie Cantor, Frank Carter, Marilynn Miller, and W. C. Fields

Published songs:
The Blue Devils Of France (by Private Irving Berlin)
I'm Gonna Pin A Medal On The Girl I Left Behind
Oh, How I Hate To Get Up In The Morning—added three months after
    opening; originally used in YIP-YIP-YAPHANK [August 19, 1918]

YIP-YIP-YAPHANK

*A Military Musical "Mess" Cooked Up By The Boys Of
Camp Upton*

AUGUST 19, 1918   CENTURY THEATRE   32 PERFORMANCES

Words and music by Sergeant Irving Berlin
Directed by Private William Smith
Produced by Uncle Sam
With Danny Healy, Sammy Lee and Berlin

Published songs:
Bevo—also used in ZIEGFELD FOLLIES OF 1919 [June 23, 1919]
Ding Dong—also used in THE CANARY [November 4, 1918]
Dream On Little Soldier Boy (lyric by Jean Havez)
Ever Since I Put On A Uniform—advertised but not published
I Can Always Find A Little Sunshine In The Y.M.C.A.
Kitchen Police (Poor Little Me)
Mandy—also used in ZIEGFELD FOLLIES OF 1919; originally issued as
    Sterling Silver Moon

Oh, How I Hate To Get Up In The Morning—also used in Ziegfeld
     Follies of 1918 [June 18, 1918] and This Is The Army [July 4,
     1942]
Ragtime Razor Brigade
Send A Lot Of Jazz Bands Over There
We're On Our Way To France

Additional song published in This Is The Army [July 4, 1942] **"Special
edition" vocal selection:**
Ladies Of The Chorus

Berlin's contribution to the war effort was this successful service show (which
ended its run with the cast marching out of the theatre to be transported
overseas). Berlin appeared, introducing *Oh, How I Hate To Get Up In The
Morning* himself—which he was to revive for the next war in This Is The
Army [July 4, 1942].

EVERYTHING

August 22, 1918   Hippodrome Theatre   461 performances

Music mostly by John Philip Sousa and others
Lyrics mostly by John Golden and others
Book and direction by R. H. Burnside
Produced by Charles Dillingham
With De Wolf Hopper

Published songs:
The Circus Is Coming To Town
Come Along To Toy Town—originally used in Going Up [December 25,
     1917]

THE CANARY

November 4, 1918   Globe Theatre   152 performances

Music mostly by Ivan Caryll (see **Kern**)
Book and lyrics mostly by Harry B. Smith
(Based on the French play by George Barr and Louis Vermeuil)
Directed by Fred C. Latham and Edward Royce
Produced by Charles Dillingham
With Julia Sanderson and Joseph Cawthorn

Published songs:
Ding Dong—cut; originally used in Yip-Yip-Yaphank [August 19, 1918]
I Have Just One Heart For Just One Boy

I Wouldn't Give That For The Man Who Couldn't Dance
It's The Little Bit Of Irish—cut
You're So Beautiful

THE ROYAL VAGABOND

Opera Comique

FEBRUARY 17, 1919   COHAN AND HARRIS THEATRE   208
PERFORMANCES

Music mostly by Anselm Goetzl and George M. Cohan
Lyrics mostly by William Cary Duncan and Cohan
Book by Stephen Ivor Szinnyey and Duncan
Directed by Cohan
Produced by Cohan and Sam H. Harris

Published song:
That Revolutionary Rag

Berlin's musical secretary for a very brief time was George Gershwin, who
wrote the arrangement for *That Revolutionary Rag*. Berlin suggested Gershwin might be better off composing on his own (but did not offer to publish
him).

ZIEGFELD FOLLIES OF 1919

JUNE 23, 1919   NEW AMSTERDAM THEATRE   171 PERFORMANCES

Music and lyrics also by others
Sketches by Rennold Wolf, Gene Buck, and others
Directed by Ned Wayburn
Produced by Florenz Ziegfeld, Jr.
With Bert Williams, Eddie Cantor, Marilynn Miller, and Eddie Dowling

Published songs:
Bevo—originally used in YIP-YIP-YAPHANK [August 19, 1918]
Harem Life (Outside Of That Every Little Thing's All Right)
I'd Rather See A Minstrel Show
I'm The Guy That Guards The Harem (And My Heart's In My Work)
Look Out For The Bolsheviki Man—published in separate edition
Mandy—originally used in YIP-YIP-YAPHANK
My Tambourine Girl
A Pretty Girl Is Like A Melody
A Syncopated Cocktail

You Cannot Make Your Shimmy Shake On Tea (lyric by Wolf and
   Berlin)
You'd Be Surprised—added after opening; published in separate edition

Considered the best edition of the series, Berlin contributed a significant
amount of the score—including the most famous FOLLIES song, *A Pretty Girl
Is Like A Melody.*

ZIEGFELD MIDNIGHT FROLIC

OCTOBER 2, 1919   NEW AMSTERDAM ROOF   171 PERFORMANCES

Music mostly by Dave Stamper
Book and lyrics mostly by Gene Buck
Directed by Ned Wayburn
Produced by Florenz Ziegfeld, Jr.
With Fanny Brice, Ted Lewis, and W. C. Fields

Published song:
I'll See You In C-U-B-A

THE PASSION FLOWER

JANUARY 13, 1920   GREENWICH VILLAGE THEATRE
   (OFF-BROADWAY)   144 PERFORMANCES

Play by Jacinto Benavente, as translated by John Garrett Underhill
With Nance O'Neil

Published song:
The Passion Flower

ZIEGFELD GIRLS OF 1920
A 9 O'Clock Revue

MARCH 8, 1920   NEW AMSTERDAM ROOF   78 PERFORMANCES

Music mostly by Dave Stamper
Book and lyrics mostly by Gene Buck
Directed by Ned Wayburn
Produced by Florenz Ziegfeld, Jr.
With Fanny Brice, Lillian Lorraine, and W. C. Fields

Published song:
Metropolitan Ladies—advertised but not published

ZIEGFELD FOLLIES OF 1920

JUNE 22, 1920   NEW AMSTERDAM THEATRE   123 PERFORMANCES

Music and lyrics also by others
Sketches by George V. Hobart, James Montgomery, and W. C. Fields
Directed by Edward Royce
Produced by Florenz Ziegfeld, Jr.
With Fanny Brice, W. C. Fields, Mary Eaton, and Charles Winninger

Published songs:
Bells
Chinese Firecrackers
Come Along Sextette
The Girls Of My Dreams
The Leg Of Nations
The Syncopated Vamp
Tell Me Little Gypsy

BROADWAY BREVITIES OF 1920

SEPTEMBER 29, 1920   WINTER GARDEN THEATRE   105 PERFORMANCES

Music mostly by Archie Gottler (see **Gershwin**)
Lyrics mostly by Blair Treynor
Book by George LeMaire
Produced by Rufus LeMaire
With George LeMaire, Eddie Cantor, Edith Hallor, and Bert Williams

Published song:
Beautiful Faces

MUSIC BOX REVUE

First Edition

SEPTEMBER 22, 1921   MUSIC BOX THEATRE   440 PERFORMANCES

Sketches by William Collier, George V. Hobart, and others
Directed by Hassard Short
Produced by Sam H. Harris
With Collier, Sam Bernard, and Berlin

Published songs:
At The Court Around The Corner
Behind The Fan

Everybody Step
I'm A Dumb-Bell—advertised but not published
In A Cozy Kitchenette Apartment
Legend Of The Pearls
My Little Book Of Poetry
Say It With Music
The Schoolhouse Blues
Tell Me With A Melody—written for London version [May 15, 1923]
They Call It Dancing

Harris (see THE LITTLE MILLIONAIRE [September 25, 1911]) and Berlin began their partnership by building the intimate Music Box Theatre and starting their own revue series named after the theatre. Both ventures proved successful. The MUSIC BOX REVUES headed away from the overblown, lavish productions of Ziegfeld, White, and Carroll, opting for style and sophistication (and leading to the Thirties revue form of Arthur Schwartz and others). Guiding the MUSIC BOX REVUES, THE BAND WAGON [Schwartz: June 3, 1931], and AS THOUSANDS CHEER [September 30, 1933] was innovative director/designer Hassard Short, whose taste and talent were first demonstrated here.

MUSIC BOX REVUE

Second Edition

OCTOBER 23, 1922   MUSIC BOX THEATRE   330 PERFORMANCES

Sketches by George V. Hobart, Walter Catlett, and others
Directed by Hassard Short
Produced by Sam H. Harris
With William Gaxton, Charlotte Greenwood, and Bobby Clark and Paul McCullough

Published songs:
Bring On The Pepper
Crinoline Days
Dancing Honeymoon
Diamond Horseshoe
I'm Looking For A Daddy Long Legs
Lady Of The Evening
The Little Red Lacquer Cage
Mont Martre
Pack Up Your Sins And Go To The Devil
Porcelain Maid
Take A Little Wife

Three Cheers For The Red, White, And Blue—advertised but not
published
Will She Come From The East? (East-North-West or South)

Vaudevillians William Gaxton and Bobby Clark were to become major musical comedy stars by the end of the decade.

MUSIC BOX REVUE
Third Edition

SEPTEMBER 22, 1923   MUSIC BOX THEATRE   273 PERFORMANCES

Sketches by George S. Kaufman, Robert Benchley, and others
Directed by Hassard Short
Produced by Sam H. Harris
With Frank Tinney, Grace Moore, and Benchley

Published songs:
Climbing Up The Scale
Learn To Do The Strut
Little Butterfly
Maid Of Mesh
One Girl
An Orange Grove In California
Tell Me A Bedtime Story
Too Many Sweethearts—cut; for initial publication see THE COCOANUTS
[**December 8, 1925**]
A Waltz Of Long Ago
What'll I Do?—added after opening; initial publication as 1924 nonshow
song

As the series continued, a marked improvement was noticeable in the quality of the sketches. George S. Kaufman had already collaborated with Marc Connelly on two successful comedies; his first musical, with Connelly, Kalmar, and Ruby, had been the unsuccessful HELEN OF TROY, N.Y. [June 19, 1923]. To the MUSIC BOX REVUE he contributed the legendary sketch "If Men Played Cards As Women Do." Soprano Grace Moore went on to stardom; popular Irish song-and-dance man Tinney went on to obscurity, his career destroyed in Broadway's equivalent to the Fatty Arbuckle sex scandal. Charles Chaplin used Tinney as inspiration for his classic film "Limelight."

THE PUNCH BOWL

MAY 21, 1924   DUKE OF YORK'S THEATRE < LONDON >
565 PERFORMANCES

Music and lyrics mostly by others
Produced by Archibald De Bears
With Norah Blaney

Published song:
All Alone—added after opening; initial publication as 1924 non-show
   song; also used in MUSIC BOX REVUE (Fourth) [December 1, 1924]

The romance of immigrant Berlin and socialite heiress Ellin Mackay created
international headlines until their elopement in 1926. *Always, What'll I Do,*
and *All Alone* were courtship songs—and popular hits. Berlin interpolated the
last two in his then-running revues.

MUSIC BOX REVUE

Fourth Edition

DECEMBER 1, 1924   MUSIC BOX THEATRE   184 PERFORMANCES

Sketches by Bert Kalmar, Harry Ruby, and others
Directed by John Murray Anderson
Produced by Sam H. Harris
With Fanny Brice, Bobby Clark and Paul McCullough, Grace Moore,
and Oscar Shaw

Published songs:
Alice In Wonderland [2nd]—different than song from THE CENTURY
   GIRL [November 6, 1916]
All Alone—see THE PUNCH BOWL [May 21, 1924]
The Call Of The South
Don't Send Me Back (To Petrograd)
Don't Wait Too Long
I Want To Be A Ballet Dancer—advertised but not published
In The Shade Of A Sheltering Tree
Listening
Rockabye Baby
Tell Her In The Springtime
Tokio Blues
Unlucky In Love
Where Is My Little Old New York?
Who

The Music Box Revues had been expensively and tastefully produced, but with the length of runs (and size of profits) decreasing, Harris and Berlin decided to end the series. This jewel box of a theatre has been unable to support large, costly musicals. Except for a brief period in the Depression (including the most famous Music Box tenant, Harris and Kaufman's Of Thee I Sing [Gershwin: December 26, 1931]), it has usually been booked for straight plays. The theatre is still co-owned by the Berlin Estate, in partnership with the Shuberts.

THE COCOANUTS

December 8, 1925   Lyric Theatre   377 performances

Book by George S. Kaufman
Directed by Oscar Eagle
Produced by Sam H. Harris
With The Marx Brothers and Margaret Dumont

Published song:
Can't You Tell?—advertised but not published
Everyone In The World Is Doing The Charleston—added to 'New
        Summer Edition' (1926); issued as professional copy only
Five O'Clock Tea
Florida By The Sea
Gentlemen Prefer Blondes—added to 'New Summer Edition'; issued as
        professional copy only
A Hit With The Ladies—advertised but not published
A Little Bungalow
Lucky Boy
Minstrel Days—advertised but not published
The Monkey Doodle-Doo [2nd]—different than song from All Aboard
        [June 5, 1913]
Take 'Im Away (He's Breakin' My Heart)—advertised but not published
Tango Melody
Ting-A-Ling, The Bells'll Ring—added to 'New Summer Edition'
Too Many Sweethearts—issued as professional copy only; originally used
        (unpublished) in Music Box Revue (Third) [September 22, 1923]
We Should Care (Let The Lazy Sun Refuse To Care) [1st]—cut
We Should Care (Let The Sky Start To Cry) [2nd]
What's There About Me?—advertised but not published
When My Dreams Come True—written for 1929 movie version
When We're Running A Little Hotel Of Our Own—advertised but not
        published

Why Do You Want To Know Why?—added to 'New Summer Edition'
With A Family Reputation—issued as professional copy only

An unlikely project for Berlin, an early Marx Brothers fan who brought them together with Harris and Kaufman. Berlin's score was uninspired, except for the raggy *Monkey Doodle-Doo.*

BETSY

DECEMBER 28, 1926   NEW AMSTERDAM THEATRE   39 PERFORMANCES

Music mostly by Richard **Rodgers**
Lyrics mostly by Lorenz Hart
Book by Irving Caesar and David Freedman
Directed by Wm. Anthony McGuire
Produced by Florenz Ziegfeld, Jr.
With Belle Baker and Al Shean

Published song:
Blue Skies

Blue Skies was one of Berlin's biggest hits. He wanted belter Belle Baker to introduce it. She was in rehearsal for **BETSY**, so Berlin gave the song to Ziegfeld for interpolation—to Rodgers and Hart's great displeasure. The show flopped—but the song sure didn't.

ZIEGFELD FOLLIES OF 1927

AUGUST 16, 1927   NEW AMSTERDAM THEATRE   167 PERFORMANCES

Sketches by Harold Atteridge and Eddie Cantor
Directed by Zeke Colvan
Produced by Florenz Ziegfeld, Jr.
With Cantor, Ruth Etting, and Dan Healy

Published songs:
It—advertised but not published (probably a misprint)
It All Belongs To Me
It's Up To The Band
Jimmy
Jungle Jingle—advertised but not published
Learn To Sing A Love Song
My New York
Ooh, Maybe It's You
Rainbow Of Girls
Ribbons And Bows—advertised but not published

Shaking The Blues Away
What Makes Me Love You?—advertised but not published

Additional song recorded:
Tickling The Ivories

For the first time in the history of the series, Ziegfeld assigned the entire score to only one songwriter. The strategy backfired, as Berlin's work was mediocre. Cantor was featured as the sole star, also a departure from FOLLIES tradition. The show was very expensive and far from the best of the series; Ziegfeld was only able to mount one more edition [July 1, 1931]. Berlin, meanwhile, was in the midst of a creative drought, and the Depression left him terribly depressed. He earned some quick money in motion pictures—the talkies began with a brief flurry of movie musicals—but things didn't pick up for him until he turned his attention back to Broadway.

SHOOT THE WORKS

JULY 21, 1931   GEORGE M. COHAN THEATRE   87 PERFORMANCES

Music and lyrics mostly by others (see **Duke**)
Sketches by Nunnally Johnson, Heywood Broun and others
Directed by Ted Hammerstein
Produced by Broun, with Milton Raison
With Broun, George Murphy, and Imogene Coca

Published song:
Begging For Love—published in separate edition

FACE THE MUSIC

FEBRUARY 17, 1932   NEW AMSTERDAM THEATRE   165 PERFORMANCES

Book by Moss Hart
Book directed by George S. Kaufman
Production staged by Hassard Short
Produced by Sam H. Harris
With Mary Boland, J. Harold Murray, and Katherine Carrington

Published songs:
I Say It's Spinach
Let's Have Another Cup Of Coffee
Manhattan Madness
My Rhinestone Girl—advertised but not published
On A Roof In Manhattan
Soft Lights And Sweet Music

Berlin's career picked up with this mildly satirical success, produced concurrently with Kaufman and Harris's highly satirical smash OF THEE I SING [Gershwin: December 26, 1931]. Moss Hart, collaborator with Kaufman on the 1930 comedy *Once In A Lifetime,* provided the book; like Kaufman, he went on to important musical theatre work as librettist and director. Berlin once again exhibited his ability to sense the public's mood with *Let's Have Another Cup Of Coffee.*

AS THOUSANDS CHEER

SEPTEMBER 30, 1933   MUSIC BOX THEATRE   400 PERFORMANCES

Sketches by Moss Hart
Choreographed by Charles Weidman
Directed by Hassard Short
Produced by Sam H. Harris
With Marilyn Miller, Clifton Webb, Helen Broderick, and Ethel Waters

Published songs:
Easter Parade—revised version of 1917 nonshow song *Smile And Show Your Dimple*
The Funnies
Harlem On My Mind
Heat Wave
How's Chances
Lonely Heart
Not For All The Rice In China
Supper Time

Additional song published (no lyric) in piano selection:
Revolt In Cuba [instrumental]—initial publication upon reuse in London revue STOP PRESS [February 21, 1935]

A high point in Berlin's theatrical career, AS THOUSANDS CHEER was a socially conscious revue which succeeded on many levels. Along with his usual gifts, Berlin displayed a poignant, tragic voice in *Supper Time;* he never was to explore this vein further, though. Ethel Waters triumphed in her first non-black Broadway show, singing that song and the tropical *Heat Wave.* For Marilyn Miller, Broadway's favorite (and highest paid) star of the Twenties, it was the beginning of the end. Convinced she was washed up (at thirty-five), she left the show and married Chester ("Chet") O'Brien, a twenty-four-year old dancer/stage manager from CHEER. The star turned producer, backing FOOLS RUSH IN [December 25, 1934]; the Leonard Sillman revue, choreographed by O'Brien, ran a mere 14 performances. Miller died mysteriously on April 7, 1936, as a result of some questionable medical treatment. (O'Brien, now in his eighties, has been stage manager of "Sesame Street" since it first aired in 1969 and appears on it occasionally as Mr. Mackintosh, a dancing greengrocer.) MORE CHEERS, a sequel to As THOUSANDS CHEER, was announced for early 1935 but never produced; Berlin issued a professional copy of the song *Moon Over Napoli.* STOP PRESS was a Hassard Short/Moss Hart British revue, using the As THOUSANDS CHEER format and several of the songs. Berlin spent the rest of the Thirties writing movie scores.

LOUISIANA PURCHASE

MAY 28, 1940   IMPERIAL THEATRE   444 PERFORMANCES

Book by Morrie Ryskind
(Based on a story by B. G. DeSylva)
Choreographed by George Balanchine and Carl Randall
Directed by Edgar MacGregor
Produced by DeSylva
With William Gaxton, Vera Zorina, Victor Moore, and Irene Bordoni

Published songs:
Dance With Me (Tonight At The Mardi Gras)—originally issued as
     Tonight At The Mardi Gras
Fools Fall In Love
I'd Love To Be Shot Out Of A Cannon With You—cut; issued as
     professional copy
It'll Come To You
It's A Lovely Day Tomorrow
Latins Know How
The Lord Done Fixed Up My Soul
Louisiana Purchase
Outside Of That I Love You
Sex Marches On—issued as professional copy
What Chance Have I With Love?
Wild About You
You Can't Brush Me Off
You're Lonely And I'm Lonely

Additional songs published in "special edition" vocal selection:
Opening Chorus
Opening Letter

An entertaining hit loosely satirizing Louisiana governor Huey Long. Gaxton and Moore appeared in their final hit as a team, ably supported by Balanchine's wife Vera Zorina and Irene Bordoni, the former Mrs. E. Ray Goetz, Berlin's one-time sister-in-law.

THIS IS THE ARMY

JULY 4, 1942   BROADWAY THEATRE   113 PERFORMANCES

Directed by Ezra Stone
Produced by Uncle Sam
With Stone, Julie Oshins, Anthony Ross, and Berlin

Published songs:
American Eagles
The Army's Made A Man Out Of Me
How About A Cheer For The Navy
I Left My Heart At The Stage Door Canteen
I'm Getting Tired So I Can Sleep
Jap-German Sextet—issued as porfessional copy
My Sergeant And I Are Buddies
Oh, How I Hate To Get Up In The Morning—originally used in
    YIP-YIP-YAPHANK [August 19, 1918]
That Russian Winter
That's What The Well-Dressed Man In Harlem Will Wear
This Is The Army, Mr. Jones
What Does He Look Like—written for 1943 movie version
With My Head In The Clouds

Additional songs published in "special edition" vocal selection:
Closing
Ladies Of The Chorus—initial publication of song from YIP-YIP-YAPHANK
Opening (The Army And The Shuberts Depend On You)
Opening Chorus (Some Dough For The Army Relief)
Opening Of Second Act (Jane Cowl Number)
This Time—initial publication as 1942 nonshow song
Yip-Yip-Yaphanker's Introduction

Additional published songs added to Overseas Touring Productions:
The Fifth Army's Where My Heart Is (1944)—issued as professional copy
    only
The Kick In The Pants (1943)—issued as professional copy only
I Get Along With The Aussies (1945)—issued as professional copy only
My British Buddy (1943)
There Are No Wings On A Foxhole (1944)
Ve Don't Like It (1943)—issued as professional copy only
What Are We Going To Do With All The Jeeps? (1944)

The ultimate wartime service show, successor to YIP-YIP-YAPHANK [August
19, 1918]. Berlin kept things topical with an endless supply of good material.

The show toured for the duration, providing rousing entertainment and millions of dollars for the Army Emergency Relief.

ANNIE GET YOUR GUN

MAY 16, 1946   IMPERIAL THEATRE   1,147 PERFORMANCES

Book by Herbert and Dorothy Fields
Choreographed by Helen Tamiris
Directed by Joshua Logan
Produced by Rodgers and Hammerstein
With Ethel Merman and Ray Middleton

Published songs:
Anything You Can Do
Colonel Buffalo Bill
Doin' What Comes Natur'lly
The Girl That I Marry
I Got Lost In His Arms
I Got The Sun In The Morning
I'll Share It All With You
I'm A Bad, Bad Man
I'm An Indian Too
Let's Go West Again—written for 1950 movie version (cut); issued as
      professional copy and in orchestral arrangement only
Moonshine Lullaby
My Defenses Are Down
An Old Fashioned Wedding—written for revival [September 21, 1966: 77
      performances]
Take It In Your Stride—cut; advertised but not published
There's No Business Like Show Business
They Say It's Wonderful
Who Do You Love, I Hope
You Can't Get A Man With A Gun

Berlin wrote his best score (by far) for this entertaining, highly professional musical bull's-eye, one of the most hit-filled shows in Broadway history. Rodgers and Hammerstein had begun their producing career in 1944 (see **HAPPY BIRTHDAY** [Rodgers: October 31, 1949]). For their first musical they hired Jerome Kern and Dorothy Fields (see **VERY WARM FOR MAY** [Kern: November 17, 1939]). Following Kern's death, Berlin was asked to take on the score. Fields agreed to withdraw from the lyric assignment and provided the book with brother Herbert, Rodgers' original librettist. Rodgers brought along Joshua Logan, frequent associate since **I MARRIED AN ANGEL** [Rodgers: May

11, 1938], to direct. To all these professionals was added Merman—the show was initially conceived by Dorothy Fields as a vehicle for her pal Ethel—and a rip-roarin' time was had by all.

MISS LIBERTY

JULY 15, 1949   IMPERIAL THEATRE   308 PERFORMANCES

Book by Robert E. Sherwood
Choreographed by Jerome Robbins
Directed by Moss Hart
Produced by Berlin, Sherwood and Hart
With Allyn McLerie, Eddie Albert, and Mary McCarty

Published songs:
Business For A Good Girl Is Bad—cut; issued as professional copy only
Extra! Extra!
Falling Out Of Love Can Be Fun
Give Me Your Tired, Your Poor (poem by Emma Lazarus)
Homework
The Hon'rable Profession Of The Fourth Estate—cut
I'd Like My Picture Took
Just One Way To Say I Love You
Let's Take An Old-Fashioned Walk
Little Fish In A Big Pond
Me An' My Bundle
Miss Liberty
Mr. Monotony—cut; subsequently used in JEROME ROBBINS' BROADWAY
    [February 26, 1989]; initially issued as *Mrs. Monotony*
The Most Expensive Statue In The World
Only For Americans
Paris Wakes Up And Smiles
The Policeman's Ball
The Pulitzer Prize—cut; advertised but not published
What Do I Have To Do To Get My Picture In The Paper?—cut
You Can Have Him

A patriotic musical comedy about the Statue of Liberty by Berlin, Hart, and Pulitzer Prize-winning dramatist/Roosevelt speechwriter Robert E. Sherwood. The idea sounded a whole lot better than MISS LIBERTY turned out to be. One of Broadway's most disappointing musicals ever.

CALL ME MADAM

OCTOBER 12, 1950   IMPERIAL THEATRE   644 PERFORMANCES

Book by Howard Lindsay and Russel Crouse
Choreographed by Jerome Robbins
Directed by George Abbott
Produced by Leland Hayward
With Ethel Merman, Paul Lukas, and Russell Nype

Published songs:
Anthem For Presentation—cut; advertised but not published
The Best Thing For You
Can You Use Any Money Today?—initial individual publication upon use
       in 1953 movie version
Free—cut; revised for 1954 movie "White Christmas" with new lyric, as
       Snow
The Hostess With The Mostes' On The Ball
It's A Lovely Day Today
Lichtenburg—advertised but not published (except in vocal score)
Marrying For Love
Mrs. Sally Adams—advertised but not published (except in vocal score)
(Dance To The Music Of) The Ocarina
Once Upon A Time Today
Our Day Of Independence—cut; advertised but not published
Something To Dance About
They Like Ike
Washington Square Dance
You're Just In Love (I Wonder Why?)

This slick entertainment was Berlin's final Broadway hit, carried by Merman's
performance and the eleven-o'clock duet *You're Just In Love*. After some final
motion picture work, Berlin went into virtual retirement—which for him
meant writing (outdated) pop songs and continuing his publishing activities.
He wrote some additional MADAM material—including a title song—for a
proposed 1967 television version, but he was unable to get it produced.

MR. PRESIDENT

OCTOBER 20, 1962   ST. JAMES THEATRE   265 PERFORMANCES

Book by Howard Lindsay and Russel Crouse
Choreographed by Peter Gennaro
Directed by Joshua Logan

Produced by Leland Hayward
With Robert Ryan, Nanette Fabray, and Anita Gillette

Published songs:
Don't Be Afraid Of Romance
Empty Pockets Filled With Love
The First Lady
Glad To Be Home
I'm Gonna Get Him
I've Got To Be Around
In Our Hide-Away
Is He The Only Man In The World?—revised version of *Where Is The
      Song of Songs For Me?* from 1929 movie "Lady Of The
      Pavements"; lyric revised from the 1954 nonshow song, *Is She The
      Only Girl In The World?*
It Gets Lonely In The White House
Laugh It Up
Let's Go Back To The Waltz
Meat And Potatoes
Once Every Four Years—cut
Pigtails And Freckles
Poor Joe—cut
The Secret Service
Song For Belly Dancer (The Only Dance I Know)
They Love Me
This Is A Great Country
The Washington Twist

Additional song recorded:
You Need A Hobby

Berlin returned to Broadway with another mild political musical. With a weak
score and no support from any of his colleagues, **Mr. President** stayed around
just long enough to run through a substantial advance sale. The only bright
spot: Nanette Fabray as *The First Lady*. Berlin himself received a critical
drubbing, and the supersensitive songsmith went into virtual seclusion for the
rest of his long life. He resurfaced once with a final semi-hit, *An Old-Fashioned Wedding*, for the 1966 revival of **Annie Get Your Gun** [May 16,
1946]. Irving Berlin died on September 22, 1989, at the age of 101.

Berlin remains America's most popular composer, with handfuls of all-time
hits to his credit. His contributions to Broadway were often entertaining and
usually profitable—not a bad combination. But Berlin rarely attempted well-
rounded musical theatre scores; he always seemed more interested in parades

of song hits, which kept his publisher (i.e., himself) happy. An exception was ANNIE GET YOUR GUN, where he was no doubt motivated by the presence of producers Rodgers and Hammerstein. In 1914 Kern and Berlin had led Broadway into a new era. While Kern made musico-dramatic innovation his lifelong quest, Berlin seemed content just writing song hit after song hit.

George Gershwin

BORN: September 26, 1898   Brooklyn, New York
DIED: July 11, 1937   Beverly Hills, California

George Gershwin grew up in Manhattan, where his Russian immigrant father attempted a succession of unsuccessful businesses. At the age of eleven, Gershwin suddenly displayed an unexpected musical aptitude; at fifteen he quit school to work as song plugger for Tin Pan Alley publisher Jerome H. Remick. Supplementing his income by making player-piano rolls, he began writing songs of his own: *When You Want 'Em, You Can't Get 'Em (When You've Got 'Em, You Don't Want 'Em)* (lyric by Murray Roth) was published in 1916. Gershwin felt ready for Broadway, and made his debut at the age of seventeen.

PASSING SHOW OF 1916
The Annual Summer Review

JUNE 22, 1916   WINTER GARDEN THEATRE   140 PERFORMANCES

Music mostly by Sigmund Romberg and Otto Motzan
Book and lyrics mostly by Harold Atteridge
Directed by J. C. Huffman
Produced by The Winter Garden Company (Messrs. Shubert)

Published song:
The Making Of A Girl (music by Romberg and Gershwin)

Shubert staff composer Sigmund Romberg offered to listen to some of Gershwin's material. He liked one tune enough to use it and had Atteridge write a lyric—taking cocomposer credit for himself. Gershwin remained friendly with Romberg despite their divergent musical styles. Leaving song plugging, Gershwin was hired as rehearsal pianist for MISS 1917 [**Kern: November 5, 1917**]. Gershwin had been deeply influenced by Kern's "Princess Theatre" shows. Kern, on his part, was impressed with the youngster. Gershwin was sent to Max Dreyfus, who signed the eighteen-year-old and began placing his work.

HITCHY-KOO OF 1918

Second Edition

JUNE 6, 1918   GLOBE THEATRE   68 PERFORMANCES

Music mostly by Raymond Hubbell
Book and lyrics mostly by Glen MacDonough
Directed by Leon Errol
Produced by Raymond Hitchcock
With Hitchcock, Errol, and Irene Bordoni

Published song:
You-oo Just You (lyric by Irving Caesar)—initially published as 1918
     nonshow song

Gershwin had accompanied MISS 1917 [Kern: November 5, 1917] star Vivienne Segal at concerts. She introduced *You-oo Just You*, which soon found its way into HITCHY-KOO OF 1918. Gershwin and childhood friend Irving Caesar collaborated on several early songs, including their first major hit *Swanee* [CAPITOL REVUE: October 24, 1919].

LADIES FIRST

OCTOBER 24, 1918   BROADHURST THEATRE   164 PERFORMANCES

Music mostly by A. Baldwin Sloane
Book and lyrics mostly by Harry B. Smith
(Based on *A Contented Woman* [play] by Charles Hoyt)
Directed by Frank Smithson
Produced by H. H. Frazee
With Nora Bayes
NOTE: LOOK WHO'S HERE, pre-Broadway title

Published songs:
The Real American Folk Song (Is A Rag) (lyric by Arthur Francis [Ira
     Gershwin])—initial publication as 1959 nonshow song
Some Wonderful Sort Of Someone (lyric by Schuyler Greene)—see THE
     LADY IN RED [May 12, 1919]

Gershwin began an occasional collaboration with his older brother Ira. Not wishing to infringe on his brother's reputation—although George was by no means established yet—Ira chose to combine the names of his younger brother and sister for a pseudonym. After dropping out of college, Ira drifted through a series of odd jobs in the same unsuccessful manner as his father had until his first break, TWO LITTLE GIRLS IN BLUE [Youmans: May 3, 1921].

HALF PAST EIGHT

[DECEMBER 9, 1918]   EMPIRE THEATRE <SYRACUSE, NEW YORK>;
CLOSED DURING PRE-BROADWAY TRYOUT

Music mostly by Gershwin
Lyrics by Fred Caryll [Edward B. Perkins]
Produced by Perkins
With Joe Cook, Sybil Vane, and the Famous Original Clef Club Band

Published songs:
None

Gershwin wrote his first full score for this ill-assembled revue. Things went
so badly that at one of the six performances Gershwin himself was sent on
stage to play a medley of his "hits." Producer Perkins borrowed the title from
a Paul Rubens revue [August 19, 1916], claiming his show was direct from a
nine-month London run; he even billed the lyricist (himself) as "Fred Caryll"
(brother of popular British composer Ivan Caryll, perhaps?). Some of the songs
resurfaced with new lyrics in LA, LA LUCILLE [May 26, 1919].

GOOD MORNING JUDGE

FEBRUARY 6, 1919   SHUBERT THEATRE   140 PERFORMANCES

Music mostly by Lionel Monckton and Howard Talbot
Book by Fred Thompson
(Based on *The Magistrate* [play] by Sir Arthur Wing Pinero)
Directed by Wybert Stamford
Produced by the Messrs. Shubert
With Mollie King and Charles King

Published songs:
I Was So Young (You Were So Beautiful) (lyric by Irving Caesar and
    Alfred Bryan)
There's More To The Kiss Than The X-X-X (lyric by Caesar)—see LA, LA
    LUCILLE [May 26, 1919]

THE LADY IN RED

MAY 12, 1919   LYRIC THEATRE   48 PERFORMANCES

Music mostly by Robert Winterberg (see **Kern**)
Book and lyrics mostly by Anne Caldwell
Directed by Frank Smithson
Produced by John P. Slocum
With Adele Rowland

Published songs:
Something About Love (lyric by Lou Paley)—also used in London
    production [April 14, 1926] of LADY, BE GOOD! [December 1,
    1924]
Some Wonderful Sort Of Someone (lyric by Schuyler Greene)—revised
    version of song from LADIES FIRST [October 24, 1918]

LA, LA LUCILLE
*A New, Up-To-The-Minute Musical Comedy Of Class And
Distinction*

MAY 26, 1919   HENRY MILLER'S THEATRE   104 PERFORMANCES

Lyrics by Arthur J. Jackson and B. G. DeSylva
Book by Fred Jackson
Directed by Herbert Gresham and Julian Alfred
Produced by Alfred E. Aarons
With Janet Velie and John E. Hazzard

Published songs:
The Best Of Everything—see FOR GOODNESS SAKE [February 20, 1922]
From Now On
The Love Of A Wife—cut
Nobody But You—added after opening
Somehow It Seldom Comes True
Tee-Oodle-Um-Bum-Bo
There's More To The Kiss Than The Sound (lyric by Irving
    Caesar)—issued in separate edition; revised lyric for *There's More
    To The Kiss Than The X-X-X* from GOOD MORNING JUDGE
    [February 6, 1919]

Gershwin's first complete Broadway score was for this moderately successful
"modern" musical. Twenty-four-year-old B. G. DeSylva had already written
several Al Jolson hits; he was Gershwin's primary lyricist for the next few years.
Turn-of-the-century composer Alfred E. Aarons had become general manager
to (and sometime producer for) theatre owner A. L. Erlanger. Aarons' twenty-
nine-year-old son Alex was one of the first to praise Gershwin's work: he
convinced his father to choose Gershwin over Victor Herbert for this project.
Alex produced the post-Broadway tour of LA, LA LUCILLE and, beginning in
1924, joined with Vinton Freedley to produce a successful string of hit Gershwin musicals.

CAPITOL REVUE—"DEMI-TASSE"

Vaudeville Revue

OCTOBER 24, 1919   CAPITOL THEATRE

Directed and produced by Ned Wayburn
With Paul Frawley and Muriel DeForrest

Published songs:
Come To The Moon (lyric by Ned Wayburn and Lou Paley)—see THE
    RAINBOW [April 3, 1923]
Swanee (lyric by Irving Caesar)—also used in SINBAD [Circa December
    1919]

The opening bill for this movie palace included this quickly forgotten stage
show; but Al Jolson heard *Swanee* and wanted to sing it. . . . His recording
was spectacularly successful and Gershwin had his first hit.

MORRIS GEST'S MIDNIGHT WHIRL

DECEMBER 27, 1919   CENTURY GROVE THEATRE   110 PERFORMANCES

Book and lyrics by Bud (B. G.) DeSylva and John Henry Mears
Directed by Julian Mitchell and Dave Bennett
Produced by Morris Gest
With Bessie McCoy Davis and Bernard Granville

Published songs:
Limehouse Nights
Poppyland

SINBAD

The Winter Garden's Latest Extravaganza

[CIRCA DECEMBER 1919]; POST-BROADWAY TOUR

Music mostly by Sigmund Romberg
Book and lyrics mostly by Harold Atteridge
Directed by J. C. Huffman
Produced by Messrs. Shubert
With Al Jolson

Published songs:
Swanee (lyric by Irving Caesar)—originally used in CAPITOL REVUE
    [October 24, 1919]

Swanee Rose (lyric by Caesar and B. G. DeSylva)—published in nonshow
edition; originally issued as *Dixie Rose*

With *Swanee* a hit Jolson record, the singer inserted it into his current show
(to help sell more records).

DERE MABLE

[FEBRUARY 2, 1920]   ACADEMY OF MUSIC < BALTIMORE, MARYLAND > ;
    CLOSED DURING PRE-BROADWAY TRYOUT

Music mostly by Rosamond Hodges
Lyrics mostly by John Hodges
Book by Edward Streeter and John Hodges
(Based on the books by Streeter)
Directed by George Marion
Produced by Marc Klaw
With Louis Bennison

Published song:
We're Pals (lyric by Irving Caesar)

THE ED WYNN CARNIVAL

APRIL 5, 1920   NEW AMSTERDAM THEATRE   150 PERFORMANCES

Book and songs mostly by Ed Wynn
Directed by Ned Wayburn
Produced by B. C. Whitney
With Ed Wynn

Published song:
Oo, How I Love To Be Loved By You (lyric by Lou Paley)

GEORGE WHITE'S SCANDALS
Second Annual Event

JUNE 7, 1920   GLOBE THEATRE   134 PERFORMANCES

Lyrics by Arthur Jackson
Book by Andy Rice and George White
Directed by White and Willie Collier
Produced by White
With Ann Pennington, Lou Holtz, and White

Published songs:
Idle Dreams
My Lady
My Old Love Is My New Love—advertised but not published
On My Mind The Whole Night Long
Queen Isabella—advertised but not published
Scandal Walk
The Songs Of Long Ago
Tum On And Tiss Me

George White, a featured dancer in the ZIEGFELD FOLLIES, went into competition with his former boss: stealing Ziegfeld star Ann Pennington he produced the first SCANDALS [June 2, 1919], with a Richard Whiting/Arthur Jackson score. The SCANDALS ran neck and neck with the FOLLIES until the Depression effectively ended both series. While Ziegfeld was lavish, star-laden and traditional, White could be counted on for better music and exciting, modern-dance innovations.

THE SWEETHEART SHOP
The Fascinating Musical Play

AUGUST 31, 1920   KNICKERBOCKER THEATRE   55 PERFORMANCES

Music mostly by Hugo Felix
Book and lyrics mostly by Anne Caldwell
Directed by Herbert Gresham
Produced by Edgar J. MacGregor and William Moore Patch
Starring Helen Ford

Published song:
Waiting For The Sun To Come Out (lyric by Arthur Francis [Ira
    Gershwin])

This moderately successful interpolation was Ira Gershwin's first published song.

PICCADILLY TO BROADWAY
All Anglo-American Musical Review

[SEPTEMBER 27, 1920]   GLOBE THEATRE <ATLANTIC CITY, NEW
    JERSEY>; CLOSED DURING PRE-BROADWAY TRYOUT

Music also by William Daly, Vincent **Youmans**, and others
Sketches and lyrics mostly by Glen MacDonough and E. Ray Goetz

Directed by George Marion and Julian Alfred
Produced by Goetz
With Johnny Dooley, Anna Wheaton, Clifton Webb, and Helen
Broderick

Published songs:
None

Gershwin collaborated with Goetz on two songs: *On The Brim Of Her Old-
Fashioned Bonnet* and *Baby Blues* (both unpublished, also used in SNAPSHOTS
OF 1921 [June 2, 1921]). Among the other songwriters on PICCADILLY TO
BROADWAY were William Daly, an important future Gershwin associate; and
the new team of Vincent Youmans and Arthur Francis [Ira Gershwin].

BROADWAY BREVITIES OF 1920

SEPTEMBER 29, 1920   WINTER GARDEN THEATRE   105 PERFORMANCES

Music mostly by Archie Gottler (see **Berlin**)
Lyrics mostly by Blair Treynor
Book by George LeMaire
Produced by Rufus LeMaire
With George LeMaire, Eddie Cantor, Edith Hallor, and Bert Williams

Published songs:
Lu Lu (lyric by Arthur Jackson)
Snow Flakes (lyric by Jackson)
Spanish Love (lyric by Irving Caesar)

A DANGEROUS MAID
A New TNT Laugh Fest

[MARCH 21, 1921]   NIXON'S APOLLO THEATRE < ATLANTIC CITY, NEW
     JERSEY > ; CLOSED DURING PRE-BROADWAY TRYOUT

Lyrics by Arthur Francis [Ira Gershwin]
Book by Charles W. Bell
(Based on *A Dislocated Honeymoon* [play] by Bell)
Produced by Edgar MacGregor
With Vivienne Segal, Amelia Bingham, and Vinton Freedley

Published songs:
Boy Wanted—see PRIMROSE [September 11, 1924]
Dancing Shoes
Just To Know You Are Mine

The Simple Life
Some Rain Must Fall

The first complete score written by the brothers Gershwin was for this quick failure. Ira soon had a Broadway hit on his own, though, Two LITTLE GIRLS IN BLUE [Youmans: May 3, 1921].

SNAPSHOTS OF 1921

JUNE 2, 1921   SELWYN THEATRE   44 PERFORMANCES

Music mostly by others
Gershwin lyrics by E. Ray Goetz
Directed by Leon Errol
Produced by The Selwyns and Lew Fields
With Nora Bayes, Fields, and DeWolf Hopper

Published songs:
None

Goetz interpolated the leftovers from PICCADILLY TO BROADWAY [September 27, 1920], which remained unexceptional and unpublished. For the post-Broadway tour, Lew Fields assigned the job of conductor to his nineteen-year-old discovery Richard Rodgers.

GEORGE WHITE'S SCANDALS
Third Annual Edition

JULY 11, 1921   LIBERTY THEATRE   97 PERFORMANCES

Lyrics by Arthur Jackson
Book by Arthur "Bugs" Baer and White
Directed by White and John Meehan
Produced by White
With Ann Pennington, Lester Allen, and White

Published songs:
Drifting Along With The Tide
I Love You
She's Just A Baby
South Sea Isles
Where East Meets West

Additional song published (no lyric) in piano selection:
Russian Dance [instrumental]

THE PERFECT FOOL

NOVEMBER 7, 1921   GEORGE M. COHAN THEATRE   256
    PERFORMANCES

Book, music, and lyrics mostly by Ed Wynn
Directed by Julian Alfred
Produced by B. C. Whitney
Presented by A. L. Erlanger
With Ed Wynn and Janet Velie

Published songs:
My Log-Cabin Home (lyric by Irving Caesar and B. G. DeSylva)
No One Else But That Girl Of Mine (lyric by Caesar)—see THE
    DANCING GIRL [January 24, 1923]

FOR GOODNESS SAKE

FEBRUARY 20, 1922   LYRIC THEATRE   103 PERFORMANCES

Music mostly by William Daly and Paul Lannin
Lyrics mostly by Arthur Jackson
Lyrics to Gershwin songs by Arthur Francis [Ira Gershwin]
Book by Fred Jackson
Directed by Priestly Morrison
Produced by Alex A. Aarons
With Helen Ford, Vinton Freedley, and Fred and Adele Astaire
NOTE: STOP FLIRTING!, London title

Published songs:
The Best Of Everything (lyric by Arthur J. Jackson and B. G.
    DeSylva)—added to London production; revised lyric for song
    originally used in LA, LA LUCILLE [May 26, 1919]
I'll Build A Stairway To Paradise (lyric by DeSylva and Arthur Francis
    [Ira Gershwin])—added to London production; originally used in
    GEORGE WHITE'S SCANDALS (Fourth) [August 28, 1922]
Someone
Tra-La-La

Additional songs published (no lyrics) in piano selection:
All By Myself—written for London production
Opening Chorus Act One—written for London production

Aarons' second musical featured the Astaires, on loan from Charles Dillingham (see THE BUNCH AND JUDY [Kern: November 28, 1922]). Unsuccessful
on Broadway, the show was revamped for London with more Gershwin mate-

rial for the Astaires. Retitled **STOP FLIRTING!** [May 30, 1923], it ran an impressive 418 performances. The Nebraskan-born dance team suddenly found themselves major British stage stars, and spent the rest of their theatrical career shuttling across the Atlantic.

THE FRENCH DOLL

FEBRUARY 20, 1922   LYCEUM THEATRE   120 PERFORMANCES

Play by A. E. Thomas
(Based on a play by Armont and Germedon)
Produced by E. Ray Goetz
With Irene Bordoni (Goetz)

Published song:
Do It Again (lyric by B. G. DeSylva)

SPICE OF 1922

JULY 6, 1922   WINTER GARDEN THEATRE   73 PERFORMANCES

"Lyrics and Music by Everybody"
Book by Jack Lait
Directed by Allan K. Foster
Produced by Arman Kaliz
With Georgie Price

Published song:
The Yankee Doodle Blues (lyric by Irving Caesar and B. G. DeSylva)

GEORGE WHITE'S SCANDALS
Fourth Annual Production

AUGUST 28, 1922   GLOBE THEATRE   88 PERFORMANCES

Lyrics by B. G. DeSylva and E. Ray Goetz
Book by Andy Rice and White
Directed and produced by White
With W. C. Fields, Jack MacGowan, White, and Paul Whiteman and His Orchestra

Published songs:
Across The Sea
Argentina (lyric by DeSylva)
Cinderelatives (lyric by DeSylva)

I Found A Four Leaf Clover (lyric by DeSylva)
I'll Build A Stairway To Paradise (lyric by DeSylva and Arthur Francis
   [Ira Gershwin])—see **FOR GOODNESS SAKE** [February 20, 1922]
She Hangs Out In Our Alley—initially published as *Oh, What She Hangs
   Out*
Where Is The Man Of My Dreams?

Additional songs recorded:
Blue Monday Blues
Has Anyone Seen My Joe—revised version of 1919 string quartet *Lullaby*
   (published 1968)
I'm Gonna See My Mother

I'll Build A Stairway To Paradise was Gershwin's second hit song. The one-act
opera "Blue Monday" was withdrawn after the opening night performance.
A primitive forerunner of **PORGY AND BESS** [October 10, 1935], the work
marked Gershwin's first attempt at the extended musical form (and included
the lovely *Blue Monday Blues*). In 1925 the work was unsuccessfully revised
for the concert hall as "135th Street." Fragments of the score are published
in Isaac Goldberg's biography of Gershwin.

OUR NELL

A Musical Mellow Drayma

DECEMBER 4, 1922   NORA BAYES THEATRE   40 PERFORMANCES

Music also by William Daly
Lyrics by Brian Hooker
Book by A. E. Thomas and Hooker
Directed by W. H. Gilmore
Produced by Hayseed Productions (Ed Davidow and Rufus LeMaire)
NOTE: **HAYSEED**, pre-Broadway title

Published songs:
By And By
Innocent Ingenue Baby (music by Gershwin and Daly)—see **THE
   RAINBOW** [April 3, 1923]
Walking Home With Angeline

Daly, principal composer of **FOR GOODNESS SAKE** [February 20, 1922], became Gershwin's close friend and musical colleague. He was to conduct most
of Gershwin's future work. They collaborated here on the playfully chromatic
Innocent Ingenue Baby.

THE DANCING GIRL

January 24, 1923   Winter Garden Theatre   126 performances

Music mostly by Sigmund Romberg and Alfred Goodman
Book and lyrics mostly by Harold Atteridge
Directed by J. C. Huffman
Produced by Messrs. Shubert
With Trini, Marie Dressler, and Jack Pearl

Published songs:
That American Boy Of Mine (lyric by Irving Caesar)—revised lyric for *No
   One Else But That Girl Of Mine* from The Perfect Fool
   [November 7, 1921]

THE RAINBOW

April 3, 1923   Empire Theatre <London>   113 performances

Lyrics mostly by Clifford Grey
Book by Albert De Courville, Edgar Wallace, and Noel Scott
Directed by Allan K. Foster
Produced by De Courville
With Grace Hayes

Published songs:
All Over Town (lyric by Lou Paley and Grey)—cut; new lyric for *Come
   To The Moon* from Capitol Revue [October 24, 1919]
Any Little Tune—advertised but not published
Beneath The Eastern Moon
Give Me My Mammy—advertised but not published
Good-Night, My Dear
In The Rain
Innocent Lonesome Blue Baby (music by Gershwin and William Daly;
   lyric by Brian Hooker and Grey)—revised lyric for *Innocent Ingenue
   Baby* from Our Nell [December 4, 1922]
Moonlight In Versailles
Oh! Nina
Strut Lady With Me
Sunday In London Town—cut
Sweetheart, I'm So Glad That I Met You—see Tell Me More! [April
   13, 1925]

Gershwin wrote one of his blandest scores for this uninspired, unsuccessful
revue.

GEORGE WHITE'S SCANDALS

Fifth Annual Production

JUNE 18, 1923   GLOBE THEATRE   168 PERFORMANCES

Music mostly by Gershwin
Lyrics mostly by B. G. DeSylva
Book by George White and William K. Wells
Directed and produced by White
With Winnie Lightner and Lester Allen

Published songs:
Let's Be Lonesome Together (lyric by DeSylva and E. Ray Goetz)
The Life Of A Rose
Lo-La-Lo
(On The Beach At) How You've Been
There Is Nothing Too Good For You (lyric by DeSylva and Goetz)
Throw 'Er In High! (lyric by DeSylva and Goetz)
Where Is She?
You And I (In Old Versailles) (music by Gershwin and Jack Green)

Jack Green, brother of serious composer Louis Gruenberg, was rehearsal pianist; he presumably fashioned a Gershwin dance routine into *You and I*, meriting shared credit. In early 1924 he worked as a music copyist on the rush preparation of 'Rhapsody In Blue'—and tried to sue Gershwin, claiming coauthorship.

LITTLE MISS BLUEBEARD

AUGUST 28, 1923   LYCEUM THEATRE   175 PERFORMANCES

Play by Avery Hopwood
Produced by Charles Frohman [Inc.] in association with E. Ray Goetz
With Irene Bordoni (Goetz)

Published song:
I Won't Say I Will (But I Won't Say I Won't) (lyric by B. G. DeSylva
    and Arthur Francis [Ira Gershwin])

NIFTIES OF 1923

SEPTEMBER 25, 1923   FULTON THEATRE   47 PERFORMANCES

Music mostly by others
Produced by Charles Dillingham
With Sam Bernard and William Collier

Published songs:

At Half Past Seven (lyric by B. G. DeSylva)—see **Primrose** [September 11, 1924]

Nashville Nightingale (lyric by Irving Caesar)

SWEET LITTLE DEVIL

The Gayest Of Musical Comedies

January 21, 1924   Astor Theatre   120 performances

Lyrics by B. G. DeSylva
Book by Frank Mandel and Laurence Schwab
Directed by Edgar MacGregor
Produced by Schwab
With Constance Binney
note: **A Perfect Lady,** pre-Broadway title

Published songs:
Hey! Hey! Let 'Er Go!
The Jijibo
Mah-Jongg—cut; also used in **George White's Scandals** (Sixth) [June 30, 1924]
Pepita—cut; new lyric and verse for 1921 nonshow song *Tomale* (lyric by DeSylva)
Someone Believes In You
Under A One-Man Top
Virginia (Don't Go Too Far)

Gershwin's music had only hinted at the modern rhythms and colorings which soon distinguished him (and Vincent Youmans) from his contemporaries. Then came the 'Rhapsody In Blue,' introduced on February 12, 1924. The personal renown and radical reputation which followed this "assault by jazz on the concert hall" helped ease Gershwin away from his often hacklike early work.

GEORGE WHITE'S SCANDALS

Sixth Annual Edition

June 30, 1924   Apollo Theatre   192 performances

Lyrics mostly by B. G. DeSylva
Book by White and William K. Wells
Directed and produced by White
With Winnie Lightner and Lester Allen

Published songs:
I Need A Garden
Kongo Kate
Mah-Jongg—originally used (cut) in SWEET LITTLE DEVIL [January 21,
     1924]
Night Time In Araby
Rose Of Madrid
Somebody Loves Me (lyric by DeSylva and Ballard MacDonald)
Tune In To Station J.O.Y.
Year After Year

With increasing fame and more lucrative offers, Gershwin made this edition
of the SCANDALS his final revue; his work for the series had never been more
than adequate, with *Somebody Loves Me* only his second song hit in five
scores. Gershwin began to concentrate on contemporary musical comedy—although some of the properties chosen were to be exceedingly thin.

PRIMROSE

SEPTEMBER 11, 1924   WINTER GARDEN THEATRE < LONDON >
     225 PERFORMANCES

Lyrics mostly by Desmond Carter
Book by George Grossmith and Guy Bolton
Directed by Charles A. Maynard
Produced by Grossmith and J.A.E. Malone
With Heather Thatcher and Leslie Henson

Published songs:
Boy Wanted (lyric by Ira Gershwin and Carter)—revised lyric for song of
     same name from A DANGEROUS MAID [March 21, 1921]
The Country Side (This Is The Life For A Man)
Isn't It Wonderful (lyric by Ira Gershwin and Carter)
Naughty Baby (lyric by Ira Gershwin and Carter)
Some Far-Away Someone (lyric by Ira Gershwin and B. G.
     DeSylva)—new Gershwin lyric for *At Half Past Seven* from NIFTIES
     OF 1923 [September 25, 1923]
That New-Fangled Mother Of Mine
Wait A Bit, Susie (lyric by Ira Gershwin and Carter)—see ROSALIE
     [January 10, 1928]

Additional songs published in vocal score:
Beau Brummel
Berkeley Square And Kew
Can We Do Anything? (lyric by Ira Gershwin and Carter)

Four Sirens (lyric by Ira Gershwin)
I Make Hay While The Moon Shines
It Is The Fourteenth Of July
Leaving Town While We May
The Mophams
Roses of France
Till I Meet Someone Like You
When Toby Is Out Of Town

Additional song recorded:
Isn't It Terrible What They Did To Mary Queen Of Scots?

Gershwin was already extremely popular in England. **Primrose** was the first of a string of Gershwin musicals (the others being remountings of New York work) to achieve great success in London. Ira began writing under his own name. For the sake of clarity, "lyric by Ira" will be used in some cases hereafter.

LADY, BE GOOD!

December 1, 1924   Liberty Theatre   330 performances

Lyrics by Ira Gershwin
Book by Guy Bolton and Fred Thompson
Directed by Felix Edwardes
Produced by Alex A. Aarons and Vinton Freedley
With Fred and Adele Astaire, Walter Catlett, and Cliff Edwards

Published songs:
Fascinating Rhythm
The 'Half Of It, Dearie' Blues
Hang On To Me
I'd Rather Charleston (lyric by Desmond Carter)—written for London
        production [April 14, 1926; 326 performances]
Little Jazz Bird
The Man I Love—cut; also used in **Strike Up The Band** (First) [August
        29, 1927]
Oh, Lady Be Good
So Am I
Something About Love (lyric by Lou Paley)—added to London
        production; originally used in **The Lady In Red** [May 12, 1919]
Swiss Miss (The Cab-Horse Trot) (lyric by Ira and Arthur Jackson)—only
        publication (no lyric) upon use in London production

Additional song published (no lyric) in piano selection:
Evening Star—cut; for initial publication see **Tell Me More!** [April 13,
        1925]

Aarons was joined by Vinton Freedley—who had danced in A DANGEROUS MAID [March 21, 1921] and FOR GOODNESS SAKE [February 20, 1922]—in a producing partnership. They commissioned this musical for the Astaires, who were returning as stars from the London production of the latter show. LADY, BE GOOD! was Gershwin's biggest success to date, with his fascinating rhythms, jazzy harmonies, and lively melodies (with a touch of humor) consistent throughout the score.

TELL ME MORE!

APRIL 13, 1925   GAIETY THEATRE   100 PERFORMANCES

Lyrics by B. G. DeSylva and Ira Gershwin
Book by Fred Thompson and William K. Wells
Directed by John Harwood
Produced by Alfred E. Aarons
With Phyllis Cleveland, Alexander Gray, and Lou Holtz
NOTE: MY FAIR LADY, pre-Broadway title

Published songs:
Baby! [1st]—new lyric for *Sweetheart, I'm So Glad That I Met You* from
     THE RAINBOW [April 3, 1923]
Baby! [2nd]—written for London production; revised music for lyric of
     Baby! [1st]
Kickin' The Clouds Away
Murderous Monty (And Light-Fingered Jane) (lyric by Desmond
     Carter)—written for London production
My Fair Lady
Tell Me More
Three Times A Day
Why Do I Love You?

Additional songs published (no lyric) in piano selections:
Love I Never Knew (lyric by Carter)—London lyric for *Evening Star* (cut)
     from LADY, BE GOOD! [December 1, 1924]
Opening Chorus Act One
Where The Delicatessen Flows (In Sardinia)

Alex Aarons' father Alfred (see LA, LA LUCILLE [May 26, 1919]) produced this tame musical, which couldn't compare with LADY BE GOOD! [December 1, 1924]. But London had not yet seen the Astaire show; the British Gershwin craze made TELL ME MORE a London [May 6, 1925] hit, running 263 performances. The original title was changed on the road not because they felt MY FAIR LADY wouldn't sell, but because audiences turned down the anticipated hit title song in favor of "Tell Me More." (Shows are occasionally renamed for songs that work well during tryouts, OKLAHOMA [Rodgers: March

31, 1943] being a famous example.) There has been confusion as to the proper credits of father and son Aarons, not helped by some programs reading "Al. Aarons presents." For the record, Alfred was responsible for giving Gershwin and Youmans their first Broadway opportunities (upon advice from his son). Alex took over **La, La Lucille** for its tour and produced **For Goodness Sake** [February 20, 1922], with Gershwin interpolations. Then he joined dancer Vinton Freedley to produce five George and Ira hits, beginning with **Lady, Be Good!**

TIP-TOES

December 28, 1925   Liberty Theatre   194 performances

Lyrics by Ira Gershwin
Book by Guy Bolton and Fred Thompson
Directed by John Harwood
Produced by Alex A. Aarons and Vinton Freedley
With Queenie Smith and Allen Kearns

Published songs:
It's A Great Little World—cut
Harlem River Chanty—initial publication in 1968 nonshow choral
        arrangement
Looking For A Boy
Nice Baby
Nightie-Night
Sweet And Low-Down
That Certain Feeling
These Charming People
When Do We Dance?

Additional song published (no lyric) in piano selection:
Opening Act One

Another hit for the Gershwins, Aarons, and Freedley. Like **Lady, Be Good!** [December 1, 1924] and **Oh, Kay!** [November 8, 1926], **Tip-Toes** had a mindless but fast-paced book coauthored by Guy Bolton—as well as *Sweet And Low-Down* and *That Certain Feeling*. During the tryout, Gershwin's "Concerto In F" premiered at Carnegie Hall on December 3, 1925.

SONG OF THE FLAME

December 30, 1925   44th Street Theatre   219 performances

Music by George Gershwin and Herbert Stothart
Book and lyrics by Otto Harbach and Oscar Hammerstein 2nd
Directed by Frank Reicher
Produced by Arthur Hammerstein
With Tessa Kosta and Guy Robertson

Published songs:
Cossack Love Song
Midnight Bells (music by Gershwin only)
The Signal (music by Gershwin only)
Song Of The Flame
Vodka
You Are You—cut

Additional song published (no lyric) in piano selection:
Tartar

Arthur Hammerstein had met continued success teaming major composers with his house staff of Stothart, Harbach, and nephew Hammerstein for operettas (including **Wildflower** [Youmans: February 7, 1923] and **Rose-Marie** [Friml: September 2, 1924]). Gershwin was chosen for this Russian operetta, which opened just two days after **Tip-Toes** [December 28, 1925]. The result was successful but pedestrian.

AMERICANA

First Edition

July 26, 1926   Belmont Theatre   224 performances

Music mostly by Con Conrad and Henry Souvaine
Book by J. P. McEvoy
Directed by Allan Dinehart
Produced by Richard Herndon
With Lew Brice and Roy Atwell

Published song:
That Lost Barber Shop Chord (lyric by Ira Gershwin)

OH, KAY!

NOVEMBER 8, 1926   IMPERIAL THEATRE   256 PERFORMANCES

Lyrics by Ira Gershwin
Book by Guy Bolton and P. G. Wodehouse
Directed by John Harwood
Produced by Alex A. Aarons and Vinton Freedley
With Gertrude Lawrence, Oscar Shaw, and Victor Moore

Published songs:
Ask Me Again—added to 1990 revival; initial publication of nonshow
    song (written circa 1929)
Clap Yo' Hands
Dear Little Girl—initial publication upon reuse in 1968 movie "Star"
Do-Do-Do
Fidgety Feet
Heaven On Earth (lyric by Ira and Howard Dietz)—see ROSALIE [January
    10, 1928]
Maybe
Oh, Kay (lyric by Ira and Dietz)
Show Me The Town—cut; also used in ROSALIE
Someone To Watch Over Me

Additional songs published in vocal selection:
Bride And Groom
Don't Ask
A Woman's Touch

Gertrude Lawrence had conquered New York with Beatrice Lillie and Jack
Buchanan in CHARLOT'S REVUE [January 9, 1924]; with OH, KAY! she became
a star on her own, introducing "Do-Do-Do," "Maybe," and the unforgettable
"Someone To Watch Over Me." Comedian Victor Moore—whose last important Broadway role had been in George M. Cohan's THE TALK OF NEW
YORK [December 3, 1907]—began a profitable association with the Gershwins
and Vinton Freedley.

STRIKE UP THE BAND

The Gershwin-Kaufman Musical Play
((First Version—also see January 14, 1930)

[AUGUST 29, 1927]   BROADWAY THEATRE   < LONG BRANCH, NEW
    JERSEY > ; CLOSED DURING PRE-BROADWAY TRYOUT

Lyrics by Ira Gershwin
Book by George S. Kaufman
Directed by R. H. Burnside
Produced by Edgar Selwyn
With Jimmy Savo, Morton Downey, and Edna May Oliver

Published songs:
The Man I Love—originally used (cut) in **LADY, BE GOOD!** [December 1,
    1924]
Military Dancing Drill—also used in (**Second Version**)
Seventeen And Twenty-One
Strike Up The Band—also used in (**Second Version**)
Yankee Doodle Rhythm—also used in **ROSALIE** [January 10, 1928]

Additional song recorded:
Meadow Serenade—cut

This bitter antiwar satire met a stony reception and quickly closed "for re-
pairs." *The Man I Love* never made it back to Broadway, although Marilyn
Miller briefly gave it a try in **ROSALIE** [January 10, 1928]. Fortunately, it found
a well-deserved life of its own outside the theatre.

FUNNY FACE

NOVEMBER 22, 1927   ALVIN THEATRE   244 PERFORMANCES

Lyrics by Ira Gershwin
Book by Fred Thompson and Paul Gerard Smith
Directed by Edgar MacGregor
Produced by Alex A. Aarons and Vinton Freedley
With Fred and Adele Astaire, William Kent, Victor Moore, and Allen
Kearns
NOTE: **SMARTY,** pre-Broadway title

Published songs:
The Babbitt And The Bromide
Dance Alone With You—cut; see **ROSALIE** [January 10, 1928]
Funny Face

He Loves And She Loves
High Hat
How Long Has This Been Going On?—cut; also used in ROSALIE
Let's Kiss And Make Up
My One And Only—originally published as *What Am I Gonna Do?*
'S Wonderful
Tell The Doc—issued in vocal arrangement; initial publication upon use
    in London production
The World Is Mine—cut; see NINE-FIFTEEN REVUE [February 11, 1930]

Additional song published in vocal selection:
In The Swim—initial publication upon reuse in 1983 production MY ONE
    AND ONLY

"Al" Aarons and "Vin" Freedley built the Alvin Theatre with profits from
their three Gershwin musicals, and determined to open it grandly with another Astaire hit. But SMARTY started its pre-Broadway tryout—immediately
after the STRIKE UP THE BAND (First Version) [August 29, 1927] debacle—with grave problems. Drastic measures were taken as half the score was
discarded, colibrettist Robert Benchley was replaced, and Victor Moore (from
the cast of OH, KAY! [November 8, 1926]) was hurriedly added. The miracle
was achieved, and FUNNY FACE came in for a long run, followed by an even
longer run in London [November 8, 1928; 263 performances].

ROSALIE

JANUARY 10, 1928   NEW AMSTERDAM THEATRE   335 PERFORMANCES

Music also by Sigmund Romberg
Lyrics by P. G. Wodehouse and Ira Gershwin
Lyrics to Gershwin songs by Ira Gershwin
Book by Wm. Anthony McGuire and Guy Bolton
Directed by McGuire
Produced by Florenz Ziegfeld, Jr.
With Marilyn Miller, Jack Donahue, and Frank Morgan

Published songs:
Beautiful Gypsy—cut; new lyric for *Wait A Bit, Susie* from PRIMROSE
    [September 11, 1924]
Ev'rybody Knows I Love Somebody—added after opening; new lyric for
    Dance Alone With You from FUNNY FACE [November 22, 1927]
How Long Has This Been Going On?—originally cut from FUNNY FACE
Oh Gee! Oh Joy! (lyric by Ira and Wodehouse)
Rosalie—cut
Say So! (lyric by Ira and Wodehouse)

Setting Up Exercises [instrumental]—initial publication in 1967 as
    nonshow piano solo *Merry Andrew*
Show Me The Town—originally used in (cut) and only published as from
    Oh, Kay! [November 8, 1926]
Yankee Doodle Rhythm—cut; originally used in STRIKE UP THE BAND
    (First Version) [August 29, 1927]

Additional song published (no lyric) in piano selection:
Follow The Drum—added after opening; revised version of *Heaven On
    Earth* from Oh, Kay!

With Marilyn Miller returning to his management after three Dillingham
years (see PETER PAN (Second Version) [Kern: November 6, 1924]), Ziegfeld
combined Romberg (who had three other shows that fall) and Gershwin (with
two) for this modern-day fairy-tale romance. The result was nonmemorable
but successful, as Miller was second only to Al Jolson in Twenties musical
comedy stardom.

TREASURE GIRL

NOVEMBER 8, 1928   ALVIN THEATRE   68 PERFORMANCES

Lyrics by Ira Gershwin
Book by Fred Thompson and Vincent Lawrence
Directed by Bertram Harrison
Produced by Alex A. Aarons and Vinton Freedley
With Gertrude Lawrence, Paul Frawley, and Walter Catlett

Published songs:
Feeling I'm Falling
Got A Rainbow
I Don't Think I'll Fall In Love Today
I've Got A Crush On You—initial publication upon reuse in STRIKE UP
    THE BAND (Second Version) [January 14, 1930]
K-ra-zy For You
Oh, So Nice
What Are We Here For?
Where's The Boy? Here's The Girl

Additional song recorded:
What Causes That?

Closely copying the Oh, Kay! [November 8, 1926] formula, this "sure thing"
was a resounding failure despite of a nice score. Gershwin's third major
symphonic work, the tone poem "An American in Paris," premiered on
December 13, 1928.

SHOW GIRL

July 2, 1929   Ziegfeld Theatre   111 performances

Music mostly by Gershwin (see **Youmans**)
Lyrics mostly by Gus Kahn and Ira Gershwin
Book and direction by Wm. Anthony McGuire
(Based on the novel by J. P. McEvoy)
Produced by Florenz Ziegfeld, Jr.
With Ruby Keeler Jolson and Clayton, Jackson, and Durante

Published songs:
Do What You Do!
Feeling Sentimental—cut
Harlem Serenade
I Must Be Home By Twelve O'Clock
Liza (All The Clouds'll Roll Away)
So Are You! (The Rose Is Red—Violets Are Blue)

Additional song recorded:
Home Blues—lyric for *Blues Theme* from "An American In Paris"

Virtually all the great stage performers of the Twenties—Miller, Cantor, Williams, Fields, Rogers, Brice—starred for Ziegfeld. The sole exception was Jolson, who had been discovered by the Shuberts and stayed with them (as long as they paid him regally). So Ziegfeld decided to make a star out of Jolson's new wife, nineteen-year-old Ruby Keeler. He didn't succeed; Show Girl was poor, and if there had been a "Ziegfeld touch" it was by now lost. But he did manage to finally get hold of Jolson, who dropped in (gratis) to serenade his bride as she descended the full-stage staircase to Gershwin's *Liza.* She was, it seems, afraid of heights.

STRIKE UP THE BAND

<Second Version—also see August 29, 1927>

January 14, 1930   Times Square Theatre   191 performances

Lyrics by Ira Gershwin
Book by Morrie Ryskind
(Based on a libretto by George S. Kaufman)
Directed by Alexander Leftwich
Produced by Edgar Selwyn
With Bobby Clark and Paul McCullough

Published songs:
Hangin' Around With You
I Mean To Say

I Want To Be A War Bride
I've Got A Crush On You—originally used (unpublished) in TREASURE
    GIRL [November 8, 1928]
Mademoiselle In New Rochelle
Soon
Strike Up The Band—originally used in (**First Version**)

Additional songs published in vocal score:
Ding Dong
Fletcher's American Chocolate Choral Society (Opening Act One)
He Knows Milk
How About A Boy Like Me?—also published in piano selection (no lyric)
    as *How About A Man*
If I Became The President
In The Rattle Of The Battle
A Man Of High Degree
Military Dancing Drill (Opening Act Two)—originally used (with different
    verse) in (**First Version**)
Official Resume (First There Was Fletcher)
Soldiers' March
This Could Go On For Years
Three Cheers For The Union!
A Typical Self-Made American
The Unofficial Spokesman

Kaufman was unable to solve the problems discovered during the 1927 tryout;
he agreed to let Ryskind (with whom he'd scripted the Marx Brothers' ANI-
MAL CRACKERS [October 23, 1928]) come in to write a new book. Ryskind
toned down the bitterness of the satire, changing the source of the plot's
international dispute from bad cheese to grade-B chocolate, and post-stock
market crash audiences seemed more receptive. With a new cast and heavily
revised score, STRIKE UP THE BAND was the first hit of the Thirties. More
importantly, the Gershwins, Kaufman, and Ryskind were pointed in a new
musical theatre direction.

NINE-FIFTEEN REVUE

FEBRUARY 11, 1930   GEORGE M. COHAN THEATRE   7 PERFORMANCES

Music mostly by others (see **Arlen**)
Lyric to Gershwin song by Ira Gershwin
Directed by Alexander Leftwich
Produced by Ruth Selwyn
With Ruth Etting

Published song:
Toddlin' Along—published (cut) only as from **FUNNY FACE** [**November 22, 1927**] with original title *The World Is Mine*

GIRL CRAZY

OCTOBER 14, 1930   ALVIN THEATRE   272 PERFORMANCES

Lyrics by Ira Gershwin
Book by Guy Bolton and John McGowan
Directed by Alexander Leftwich
Produced by Alex A. Aarons and Vinton Freedley
With Ginger Rogers, Allen Kearns, Willie Howard, Ethel Merman, and William Kent

Published songs:
Bidin' My Time
Boy! What Love Has Done To Me!
But Not For Me!
Could You Use Me?
Embraceable You
I Got Rhythm
Sam And Delilah
Treat Me Rough!—initial publication upon reuse in 1943 movie version
You've Got What Gets Me—written for 1932 movie version

Additional songs published in vocal score:
Barbary Coast
Broncho Busters
Goldfarb, That's I'm
Land Of The Gay Caballero
The Lonesome Cowboy
When It's Cactus Time In Arizona

The last of the great Gershwin/Aarons and Freedley hits, enhanced by the strong score and stronger singing voice of Ethel Merman (on *I Got Rhythm* and *Sam And Delilah*). Ginger Rogers, in her second and final Broadway musical, introduced *But Not For Me* and *Embraceable You*. When help was needed to stage the dance for the latter song, Gershwin/Aarons and Freedley alumnus Fred Astaire stopped by to show Ginger what to do.

OF THEE I SING

DECEMBER 26, 1931   MUSIC BOX THEATRE   441 PERFORMANCES

Lyrics by Ira Gershwin
Book by George S. Kaufman and Morrie Ryskind
Directed by Kaufman
Produced by Sam H. Harris
With William Gaxton, Lois Moran, and Victor Moore

Published songs:
Because, Because
The Illegitimate Daughter
Love Is Sweeping The Country
Of Thee I Sing
Who Cares?
Wintergreen For President—initial individual publication upon revival
      [May 5, 1952; 72 performances]

Additional songs published in vocal score:
The Dimple On My Knee
Garçon, S'il Vous Plait
Hello, Good Morning
I Was The Most Beautiful Blossom
Jilted, Jilted!
A Kiss For Cinderella
Never Was There A Girl So Fair
On That Matter No One Budges
Prosperity Is Just Around The Corner
The Senatorial Roll Call
Some Girls Can Bake A Pie (Corn Muffins)
Trumpeter, Blow Your Golden Horn!
Who Is The Lucky Girl To Be?

Having forged new ground in musical satire with STRIKE UP THE BAND **(Second Version)** [January 14, 1930], Kaufman and Ryskind joined the Gershwins on this epochal piece of musical theatre. Being the first election year of the Depression, the choice target for satire was the Presidency. The score was remarkably cohesive, with the brothers working in extended musical scenes of rhymed dialogue as opposed to songs. Ira—at his very best—paid tribute to his idol, supreme social satirist W. S. Gilbert. All elements combined to make OF THEE I SING the most important musical of its time and the first to win the Pulitzer Prize (which went to the librettists and Ira—but not George). Kaufman made his musical directing debut. Several months after the opening he sent his famous telegram to star William Gaxton: "Watching show from back of house stop wish you were here."

PARDON MY ENGLISH

January 20, 1933   Majestic Theatre   46 performances

Lyrics by Ira Gershwin
Book by Herbert Fields
Directed by Vinton Freedley
Produced by Alex A. Aarons and Freedley
With Jack Pearl, Lyda Roberti, and George Givot

Published songs:
Isn't It A Pity?
I've Got To Be There
The Lorelei
The Luckiest Man In The World
My Cousin In Milwaukee
So What?
Tonight—initial publication as 1971 nonshow instrumental, retitled *Two Waltzes In C*
Where You Go, I Go

Additional song recorded:
Watch Your Head (Finaletto Act Two)—see Let 'Em Eat Cake [October 21, 1933]

A disaster produced by the financially desperate Aarons and Freedley, who had already lost their Alvin Theatre. Pardon My English's tryout troubles saw the departure of star Jack Buchanan and colibrettist Morrie Ryskind. Gershwin, busy with concert works, provided *My Cousin In Milwaukee* and the lovely *Isn't It A Pity*. As for the producers, Aarons never recovered from his bankruptcy; Freedley, though, rebounded with some of the biggest hits of the next ten years—starting with Anything Goes [Porter: November 21, 1934].

LET 'EM EAT CAKE

October 21, 1933   Imperial Theatre   90 performances

Lyrics by Ira Gershwin
Book by George S. Kaufman and Morrie Ryskind
(Based on characters from Of Thee I Sing [December 26, 1931])
Directed by Kaufman
Produced by Sam H. Harris
With William Gaxton, Lois Moran, and Victor Moore

Published songs:
Blue, Blue, Blue
Let 'Em Eat Cake

Mine
On And On And On
Union Square

Additional songs recorded:
Climb Up The Social Ladder
Comes The Revolution—new lyric for *Watch Your Head (Finaletto Act*
  Two) from PARDON MY ENGLISH [January 20, 1933]
First Lady And First Gent
The General's Gone To A Party
Hanging Throttlebottom In The Morning
I Know A Foul Ball
Introduction To Finale Act One (Dignitary's Song)
It Isn't What You Did (It's What You Didn't Do)
I've Brushed My Teeth
The League Of Nations
Mothers Of The Nation
No Comprenez, No Capish, No Versteh!
Shirts By The Millions
That's What He Did
Throttle Throttlebottom
Tweedledee For President—countermelody to *Wintergreen For President*
  from OF THEE I SING [December 26, 1931]
The Union League
Up And At 'Em
When Nations Get Together
Who's The Greatest?
Why Speak Of Money?

This eagerly awaited sequel to OF THEE I SING [December 26, 1931] proved
a great disappointment. More bitter than comic, the satire was forced; by the
time the authors realized the fundamental creative problems, it was too late
to cancel the production. Ironically, the LET 'EM EAT CAKE score contains
some of the best and most intricate work by the Gershwins. The beautifully
chromatic *Comes The Revolution* and *Blue, Blue, Blue,* along with the rest,
had all but disappeared—until 1987, when the entire score was finally and
happily recorded.

PORGY AND BESS

OCTOBER 10, 1935   ALVIN THEATRE   124 PERFORMANCES

Lyrics by DuBose Heyward and Ira Gershwin
Libretto by DuBose Heyward
(Based on *Porgy* [novel] by DuBose Heyward and [play] by DuBose and
Dorothy Heyward)

Directed by Rouben Mamoulian
Produced by The Theatre Guild
With Todd Duncan, Anne Brown, John W. Bubbles, and Warren
Coleman

Published songs:
Bess, You Is My Woman
I Got Plenty O' Nuttin'
I Loves You Porgy—initial individual publication upon use in 1959 movie
    version
It Ain't Necessarily So (lyric by Ira)
My Man's Gone Now (lyric by Heyward)
Oh Bess, Oh Where's My Bess? (lyric by Ira)
Summertime (lyric by Heyward)
There's A Boat Dat's Leavin' Soon For New York (lyric by Ira)
A Woman Is A Sometime Thing (lyric by Heyward)

Additional songs published in vocal score:
Buzzard Song (lyric by Heyward)—cut
Clara, Clara (lyric by Heyward)
Crap Game (lyric by Heyward)
Gone, Gone, Gone (lyric by Heyward)
I Ain't Got No Shame (lyric by Ira)
It Takes A Long Pull To Get There (lyric by Heyward)
Lawyer Frazier Scene (lyric by Heyward)
Leavin' Fo' De Promise' Lan' (lyric by Heyward)
Oh De Lawd Shake De Heavens (lyric by Heyward)
Oh, Doctor Jesus (lyric by Heyward)
Oh, I Can't Sit Down (lyric by Ira)
Oh Lawd, I'm On My Way (lyric by Heyward)
Overflow (lyric by Heyward)
A Red Headed Woman (lyric by Ira)
Storm Prayers (lyric by Heyward)
Street Cries (lyric by Heyward)
They Pass By Singin' (lyric by Heyward)
What You Want Wid Bess? (lyric by Heyward)

Gershwin was interested in "Porgy" upon its publication in 1926, but the
Theatre Guild's play version was already underway. Over the years, Gershwin
had experimented on near-operatic theatre pieces, including "Blue Monday"
(see GEORGE WHITE'S SCANDALS (Fourth) [August 28, 1922]) and a proposed
version of *The Dybbuk* for the Metropolitan Opera. When "Porgy" finally
became available, Gershwin was ready. The one-time song plugger had been
constantly learning, training, and experimenting since his early days on Tin

Pan Alley, reaching important plateaus with "Rhapsody in Blue" (1924), "Concerto in F" (1925), "An American in Paris" (1928), STRIKE UP THE BAND [January 14, 1930] and OF THEE I SING [December 26, 1931]. Now he immersed himself in the world of Catfish Row, writing an unparalleled score which is unlike anything he—or, I think it safe to say, anyone else—ever wrote. Mamoulian, director of the play version, made a remarkable musical debut. Demanding an exacting control over all production elements, his strong theatricality and sense of movement took Broadway in new directions—as did his next musical, OKLAHOMA! [Rodgers: March 31, 1943]. The initial commercial failure of PORGY AND BESS was due partially to the overuse of operatic conventions. The piece has been continually successful since Cheryl Crawford's revival [January 22, 1942; 286 performances], which cut the recitatives and presented the piece as more of a book musical. Broadway has enjoyed subsequent PORGY visits by two highly successful touring companies: the Robert Breen/Blevins Davis production [March 10, 1953; 312 performances], with a cast including Leontyne Price and Cab Calloway (playing Sportin' Life—not Porgy!); and a mounting by the Houston Grand Opera [September 25, 1976; 124 performances]. Gershwin finally made it to the Met—in 1985, when PORGY AND BESS entered the repertory. (The Met imprimatur doesn't matter to some of us, perhaps, but it probably would have mattered to Gershwin.)

THE SHOW IS ON

DECEMBER 25, 1936   WINTER GARDEN THEATRE   237 PERFORMANCES

Music mostly by Vernon Duke (also see Arlen, Rodgers, and Schwartz)
Lyric to Gershwin song by Ira Gershwin
Sketches mostly by David Freedman and Moss Hart
Directed by Vincente Minnelli
Produced by Lee Shubert
With Beatrice Lillie and Bert Lahr

Published song:
By Strauss

Gershwin contributed his final theatre song to this revue devised by his close friend Vernon Duke. Following PORGY AND BESS [October 10, 1935], Gershwin moved to Hollywood. After writing two complete film scores for Fred Astaire, Gershwin suddenly fell ill. A brain tumor was diagnosed, but it was too late. George Gershwin died on July 11, 1937 in Beverly Hills. He was thirty-eight years old.

LET ME HEAR THE MELODY

[MARCH 9, 1951] PLAYHOUSE THEATRE < WILMINGTON,
DELAWARE > ; CLOSED DURING PRE-BROADWAY TRYOUT

Play by S. N. Behrman
Incidental music by George Gershwin
Lyric by Ira Gershwin
Directed by Burgess Meredith
Produced by Harold Clurman and Walter Fried
With Melvyn Douglas, Anthony Quinn, Mike Kellin, and Morris
Carnovsky

Published song:
Hi-Ho!—initial publication as 1967 nonshow song

LET ME HEAR THE MELODY, about a songwriter in Hollywood, made use of
a considerable amount of Gershwin material. The jaunty *Hi-Ho!* was the only
never-before-heard song; it had been written for (but unused in) the 1937 Fred
Astaire movie "Shall We Dance."

The Gershwin section in the first edition of *Show Tunes* ended with the
statement: "With familiarity and increased exposure to Arlen, Youmans,
Duke, and Weill, Gershwin love diminishes to Gershwin respect. But Gershwin respect never diminishes"—for which I seem to have been drummed out
of the Gershwin lovers society. I repeat here that Gershwin respect never
diminishes. (I'll also add that I grow more and more impressed with Ira's later
work, much of which is unpublished; had he not withdrawn after LADY IN THE
DARK [Weill: January 23, 1941] and THE FIREBRAND OF FLORENCE [Weill:
March 22, 1945], he might have done for the comic musical what Oscar
Hammerstein did for the serious musical.) George brought new rhythms and
colors into the musical theatre, a significant and far-reaching contribution
without which we might never have been able to appreciate the work of his
followers. Gershwin's distinctive trademarks were jazz-influenced syncopation
and "blue-note" chromaticism, marvelous devices developed during his apprentice years (1919-1923) and showcased to the musical world's astonishment
in "Rhapsody In Blue" (1924). As wonderful as Gershwin's great songs are,
though, I'm constantly reminded that the devices are *conscious*—the delicious
parts are caused by an unexpected blue note here or a fascinating rhythmic
figure there. Out-of-key notes in musical terminology are called *accidentals.*
To Gershwin, they always were accidental—deliberately used to jar our ear and
create the desired effect. To Arlen and Weill, these seemed not to be atten-
tion-getting accidentals but a natural part of the musical fabric. (This can be
explained to some extent by the fact that both men were sons of cantors, the

improvisatory melodists of the Jewish faith.) My favorite Gershwin songs simply don't enthrall me the way the best of Arlen, Kern, or Rodgers does. *Fascinating Rhythm, Someone To Watch Over Me,* and *Isn't It A Pity?* are among my favorites by Gershwin or anyone; but I don't think he could ever have written a song like *Stormy Weather, Spring Is Here,* or *All The Things You Are*—he would have had to break too many "rules." Where did Gershwin ever display such a pure stream of melodic freeness? (In the stunning *Summertime,* that's where, but nowhere else; and it is my theory that here he was consciously emulating the style of his young friend Arlen.) It is pointless to ponder what might have happened had Gershwin continued working past PORGY. As it is, he left us with dozens of *'s wonderful* songs to be forever cherished.

Vincent Youmans

BORN: September 27, 1898   New York, New York
DIED: April 5, 1946   Denver, Colorado

Vincent Youmans was born the day after George Gershwin. Both played an important part in developing the new 1920s musical comedy, both tried to move into more serious theatre work, and both were struck by fatal illness in their mid-thirties. Unlike Gershwin, Youmans was born on the right side of the New York City tracks. His father, a prosperous hat manufacturer, moved the family to upper-class Larchmont, New York. After wartime Navy service, Youmans became a song plugger at Remick's—where civilian Gershwin had started three years earlier—and wrote his first published song, the 1920 *Country Cousin* (lyric by Alfred Bryan). Youmans moved on to play rehearsal piano for Victor Herbert's 1920 out-of-town failure OUI MADAME, produced by Alfred E. Aarons. Aarons had intended Herbert for his previous musical, but son-and-associate Alex convinced him to gamble on novice Gershwin (see LA, LA LUCILLE [Gershwin: May 26, 1919]). Youmans was to be next. Meanwhile, the ever-alert-for-talent Max Dreyfus signed Youmans at the same time Richard Rodgers was told "come back in a few years." Unlike Gershwin, Rodgers, and Kern, Youmans was established with a Broadway success within the year.

PICCADILLY TO BROADWAY

All Anglo-American Musical Review

[SEPTEMBER 27, 1920]   GLOBE THEATRE   < ATLANTIC CITY, NEW
    JERSEY > ; CLOSED DURING PRE-BROADWAY TOUR

Music also by William Daly, George **Gershwin,** and others
Sketches and lyrics mostly by Glen MacDonough and E. Ray Goetz
Lyrics to Youmans songs by Arthur Francis [Ira Gershwin]
Directed by George Marion and Julian Alfred
Produced by Goetz
With Johnny Dooley, Anna Wheaton, Clifton Webb, and Helen Broderick

Published song:

Who's Who With You?—initial publication upon reuse in Two LITTLE
  GIRLS IN BLUE [May 3, 1921]

Max Dreyfus placed interpolations by his two young composers into this
thrown-together revue. Youmans was paired with Gershwin's lyric-writing
older brother Ira, already briefly heard on Broadway (using the pseudonym
Arthur Francis). After the PICCADILLY TO BROADWAY failure, Dreyfus held the
two Youmans/Francis songs—the playfully catchy *Who's Who With You?*
and *Now That We're Mr. And Mrs.* (unpublished)—as bait while scouting
another opportunity.

TWO LITTLE GIRLS IN BLUE

MAY 3, 1921   GEORGE M. COHAN THEATRE   135 PERFORMANCES

Music also by Paul Lannin
Lyrics mostly by Arthur Francis [Ira Gershwin]
Book by Fred Jackson
Directed by Ned Wayburn
Produced by A. L. Erlanger
With The Fairbanks Twins (Madeline and Marion) and Oscar Shaw

Published songs:

Dolly (lyric by Francis and Schuyler Greene)
Oh Me! Oh My!
Orienta (lyric by Irving Caesar and Greene)
Rice and Shoes (lyric by Francis and Greene)
Who's Who With You?—originally used (unpublished) in PICCADILLY TO
        BROADWAY [September 27, 1920]
You Started Something—see No, No, NANETTE [September 16, 1925]

Producer Alfred Aarons, having done fairly well with LA, LA LUCILLE [Gersh-
win: May 26, 1919], offered the composer his next show. Gershwin, already
contracted for two complete scores, turned it down but recommended his
brother and Youmans for the job. Max Dreyfus sold the team on the strength
of the PICCADILLY TO BROADWAY [September 27, 1920] songs. Prior to the
tryout, tyrannical theatre-czar A. L. Erlanger took over the production. Aarons
was Erlanger's general manager, and it's probable that Aarons' shows were
actually owned by A. L. (for Abraham Lincoln, of course). Youmans and Ira
contributed the better portion of the score and came up with a moderate
success—far more popular than LA, LA LUCILLE—and two hit songs, the
adequate if undistinguished *Oh Me! Oh My!* and *Dolly.*

WILDFLOWER

FEBRUARY 7, 1923   CASINO THEATRE   477 PERFORMANCES

Music also by Herbert Stothart
Book and lyrics by Otto Harbach and Oscar Hammerstein 2nd
Directed by Oscar Eagle
Produced by Arthur Hammerstein
With Edith Day and Guy Robertson
NOTE: All songs issued as by Youmans and Stothart although written separately. Those listed below were Youmans' actual contributions.

Published songs:
Bambalina
I Can Always Find Another Partner
If I Told You—cut; see RAINBOW [November 21, 1928]
I Love You I Love You I Love You
Wildflower
You Never Can Blame A Girl For Dreaming—added after opening

Additional songs published in vocal score:
The Chase (Opening Act II) (probably by Youmans)
Come Let's Dance Through The Night (probably by Stothart)
'Course I Will (probably by Youmans)

The competent but unoriginal Stothart had collaborated with Harbach, Hammerstein, and Hammerstein on four competent but unoriginal musicals since 1920. The producer decided to bring in a more inventive cocomposer, resulting in the first of several immensely successful operettas. Broadway discovered Youmans' unconventional rhythmic style in *Bambalina,* a top song hit of the early Twenties; the less dynamic *Wildflower* was also enormously popular. For several seasons Gershwin had been intriguing Broadway audiences, but the long-running WILDFLOWER established Youmans as the leader of the new breed of composers. Otto Harbach had collaborated with Rudolf Friml on several hit operettas, including Arthur Hammerstein's first production THE FIREFLY [December 2, 1912]. Oscar Greeley Clendenning Hammerstein 2nd—for that was his name—began with his uncle as a stage manager in 1917; Arthur produced Oscar's first play in 1919 (it closed out of town). Then the veteran and the novice lyricist/librettist joined together and began to explore a new musical theatre form.

HAMMERSTEIN'S NINE O'CLOCK REVUE

OCTOBER 4, 1923   CENTURY ROOF THEATRE   12 PERFORMANCES

Music and lyrics mostly by Harold Simpson and Morris Harvey
Produced by Arthur Hammerstein

Published song:
Flannel Petticoat Girl (lyric by Oscar Hammerstein 2nd and Wm. Cary
    Duncan)—initial publication upon reuse in MARY JANE MCKANE
    [December 25, 1923]

MARY JANE MCKANE

DECEMBER 25, 1923   IMPERIAL THEATRE   151 PERFORMANCES

Music also by Herbert Stothart
Book and lyrics by Oscar Hammerstein 2nd and Wm. Cary Duncan
Directed by Alonzo Price
Produced by Arthur Hammerstein
With Mary Hay and Hal Skelly

Published songs:
Come On And Pet Me—see A NIGHT OUT [September 7, 1925]
Flannel Petticoat Girl—originally used (unpublished) in HAMMERSTEIN'S
    NINE O'CLOCK REVUE [October 4, 1923]
My Boy And I—see NO, NO, NANETTE [September 16, 1925]
Toodle-Oo

This moderate success opened the new Imperial Theatre. Youmans began to
constantly revise songs and reuse them in future shows. While a standard
practice of the day, Youmans came up with a noticeably high proportion of
hits in this manner.

LOLLIPOP

JANUARY 21, 1924   KNICKERBOCKER THEATRE   152 PERFORMANCES

Book and lyrics by Zelda Sears
Directed by Ira Hards
Produced by Henry W. Savage
With Ada May (Weeks), Harry Puck, and Sears
NOTE: THE LEFT OVER, pre-Broadway title

Published songs:
Deep In My Heart
Going Rowing

Honey-Bun
It Must Be Love—cut; see A NIGHT OUT [September 7, 1925]
Take A Little One-Step
Tie A String Around Your Finger

Additional songs published (no lyric) in piano selection:
Orphan Girl
Spanish [instrumental]

An old-fashioned, mediocre musical, LOLLIPOP drew on family trade for a moderately successful run.

CHARLOT'S REVUE

SEPTEMBER 23, 1924   PRINCE OF WALES'S THEATRE   <LONDON>
    518 PERFORMANCES

Music mostly by others
Book by Ronald Jeans
Produced by André Charlot

Published song:
That Forgotten Melody (lyric by Douglas Furber)

A NIGHT OUT

[SEPTEMBER 7, 1925]   GARRICK THEATRE <PHILADELPHIA,
    PENNSYLVANIA>; CLOSED DURING PRE-BROADWAY TRYOUT

Lyrics mostly by Clifford Grey and Irving Caesar
Book by George Grossmith and Arthur Miller
(Based on the British musical by Willie Redstone, Grossmith, and Miller
[see **Porter: September 18, 1920**])
Directed by Thomas Reynolds
Produced by Alfred E. Aarons in association with Edward Laurillard

Published songs:
I Want A Yes Man (lyric by Grey, Caesar, and Ira Gershwin)
Kissing—revised version of *It Must Be Love* from LOLLIPOP [January 21,
    1924]
Like A Bird On The Wing
Sometimes I'm Happy (lyric by Caesar)—revised version of *Come On And
    Pet Me* from MARY JANE McKANE [December 25, 1923]; also used
    in HIT THE DECK [April 25, 1927]

In 1924 Youmans had his greatest success, with two of Broadway's biggest
song hits ever; but a prolonged tryout kept No, No, NANETTE [September 16,

1925] from New York for a while. A NIGHT OUT added an American score to a British book and died aborning. It was produced by Alfred Aarons, who had discovered both Gershwin and Youmans. Son Alex had his first major Broadway hit in LADY, BE GOOD! [Gershwin: December 1, 1924]; Alfred produced 1925 flops by both composers. Ira, now collaborating full-time with brother George, received colyricist credit for *I Want A Yes Man.* This was a leftover reworked from the unused Youmans-Arthur Francis *Robbing Your Father* (probably intended for TWO LITTLE GIRLS IN BLUE [May 3, 1921]). Ira wasn't consulted or even aware of the new use until after A NIGHT OUT closed. The genial Ira Gershwin was a hard man to alienate, but Youmans managed to do it.

NO, NO, NANETTE

SEPTEMBER 16, 1925   GLOBE THEATRE   321 PERFORMANCES

Lyrics mostly by Irving Caesar
Book by Otto Harbach and Frank Mandel
(Based on *My Lady Friends* [play] by Emil Nyitray and Mandel)
Produced and directed by H. H. Frazee
With Louise Groody, Charles Winninger, and Georgia O'Ramey

Published songs:
The Boy Next Door (lyric by Schuyler Greene and Harbach)—cut
I Don't Want A Girlie (lyric by B. G. DeSylva)—cut
I Want To Be Happy
I've Confessed To The Breeze (lyric by Harbach)—cut
No, No, Nanette! (lyric by Harbach)—revised version of *My Boy And I*
        from MARY JANE MCKANE [December 25, 1923]
Santa Claus (lyric by Harbach)—cut
Tea For Two
Too Many Rings Around Rosie
'Where Has My Hubby Gone?' Blues
You Can Dance With Any Girl At All

Additional songs published in British vocal score:
Call Of The Sea
Fight Over Me
Flappers Are We (Opening Act I)
Peach On The Beach (lyric by Harbach)
Telephone Girlie (lyric by Harbach)
Waiting For You—new lyric for *You Started Something* from TWO
        LITTLE GIRLS IN BLUE [May 3, 1921]
We're All Of Us Excited (Finale Act II)
When You're Sad

No, No, NANETTE played a short tryout in Detroit [beginning April 23, 1924] before moving on to phenomenal success in Chicago. Nevertheless, the show underwent major changes: Irving Caesar was brought in to replace half of Harbach's lyrics, and producer Harry Frazee—best known as the man who sold Babe Ruth (he owned the Boston Red Sox)—fired director Edward Royce after all the work was done and took credit himself. By the time NANETTE reached Broadway there were two road companies, plus a London production [March 11, 1925] which ran an unprecedented 665 performances. As in WILDFLOWER [February 7, 1923], Youmans provided two smash hit songs, *Tea For Two* and *I Want To Be Happy*. A stylish Broadway revival opened January 19, 1971 and played 861 performances.

OH, PLEASE!

DECEMBER 17, 1926   FULTON THEATRE   75 PERFORMANCES

Lyrics by Anne Caldwell
Book by Otto Harbach and Caldwell
(Based on a play by Maurice Hennequin and Pierre Veber)
Directed by Hassard Short
Produced by Charles Dillingham
With Beatrice Lillie, Charles Winninger, and Charles Purcell

Published songs:
I Know That You Know
I'm Waiting For A Wonderful Girl
Like He Loves Me
Nicodemus

Having taken New York by storm in CHARLOT'S REVUE [January 29, 1924], Beatrice Lillie and Gertrude Lawrence signed with New York managements Dillingham and Aarons & Freedley, respectively. While Lawrence met immediate success (see OH, KAY! [Gershwin: November 8, 1926]), the Canadian-born Lillie suffered from inappropriate vehicles until the Thirties revue format caught up with her. Youmans had a difficult time dealing with Lillie, as did Richard Rodgers on SHE'S MY BABY [Rodgers: January 3, 1928]. Both of Youmans' future wives, incidentally, were in the OH, PLEASE! chorus.

HIT THE DECK
A Nautical Musical Comedy

APRIL 25, 1927   BELASCO THEATRE   352 PERFORMANCES

Lyrics by Leo Robin and Clifford Grey
Book by Herbert Fields
(Based on *Shore Leave* [play] by Hubert Osborne)
Directed by Alexander Leftwich
Produced by Vincent Youmans
With Louise Groody, Charles King, and Stella Mayhew

Published songs:
Armful Of You—cut
Hallelujah!—revised version of a 1918 march (unpublished) written for
     John Philip Sousa's U.S. Navy Band
Harbor Of My Heart
Join The Navy!
Keepin' Myself For You (lyric by Sidney Clare)—written for 1929 movie
     version
Loo-Loo
Lucky Bird
Nothing Could Be Sweeter—cut; see *Why, Oh Why?*
Sometimes I'm Happy (lyric by Irving Caesar)—see A NIGHT OUT
     [September 7, 1925]
Why, Oh Why?—new lyric for *Nothing Could Be Sweeter*

Having suffered from several indifferently mounted productions—and having
seen the financial returns generated by his mother's substantial investment in
No, No, NANETTE [September 16, 1925]—Youmans resolved to present his
own shows. For experienced advice, librettist Herb Fields' father Lew was
invited to coproduce HIT THE DECK; Youmans bought him out immediately
after the opening. This enormously successful producing debut proved to be
the disastrous turning point in Youmans' career: still to write his greatest
songs, HIT THE DECK was his last successful production. Keeping his eye on
Gershwin, Youmans—with new hits *Sometimes I'm Happy* and *Hallelujah!*—was still ahead. But 'Rhapsody In Blue' had startled the musical
world in 1924, and Gershwin was composing a string of popular hits; Richard
Rodgers burst on the scene in 1925; and Kern and Berlin were still very much
in evidence. Youmans felt self-conscious as the only "real" American among
this talented group of Jewish immigrants (and sons of immigrants). Competition prodded him to move away from his reliance on catchy, rhythmic phrases
and develop his new style of soaring melodies and complexly colored harmonies, initially heard in *Nothing Could Be Sweeter* and *Keepin' Myself For You.*

RAINBOW

NOVEMBER 21, 1928   GALLO THEATRE   29 PERFORMANCES

Lyrics and direction by Oscar Hammerstein 2nd
Book by Laurence Stallings and Hammerstein
Produced by Philip Goodman
With Libby Holman, Brian Donlevy, and Charles Ruggles

Published songs:
The Bride Was Dressed In White—initial publication upon use in 1929
     movie version *(Song of the West)*
Faded Rose—advertised but not published
Hay, Straw
I Like You As You Are
I Look For Love—advertised but not published
I Want A Man
Let Me Give All My Love To Thee—initial publication upon use in
     movie version
My Mother Told Me Not To Trust A Soldier—initial publication upon use
     in movie version
The One Girl
Virginia—unpublished; new lyric for *If I Told You* (cut) from
      WILDFLOWER [February 7, 1923]
West Wind (lyric by J. Russel Robinson)—written for movie version
Who Am I (That You Should Care For Me?) (lyric by Gus Kahn)—cut

Following the enormous breakthroughs of SHOW BOAT [Kern: February 27, 1927], Hammerstein rejoined with Youmans for the ambitious RAINBOW. Disastrously underrehearsed, the entire premiere was a shambles (highlighted by the legendary opening-night contribution of Fanny the donkey!). Surprisingly patient critics saw the piece as a successor to SHOW BOAT, and hoped RAINBOW could run long enough to be put into shape. It didn't. The failure of RAINBOW sent Hammerstein—ideal collaborator for perfectionist Youmans—back to other composers and (after one last hit) thirteen years of unrelieved failure. This was a crucial loss for Youmans. Unable to sustain relationships with Ira Gershwin, Hammerstein, or Harbach, the rest of his career was spent with uninspired pop-song lyricists. The haphazard production of RAINBOW unquestionably killed a potentially important piece, and Youmans became even more determined to produce his own work. Unhappy and insecure with Max Dreyfus (in the company of Kern, Gershwin, Rodgers, et al) at Harms, he also set up his own publishing company. Distrustful of everyone, Youmans took personal control of everything—and everything began to self-destruct.

SHOW GIRL

JULY 2, 1929   ZIEGFELD THEATRE   111 PERFORMANCES

Music mostly by George **Gershwin**
Lyrics mostly by Gus Kahn and Ira Gershwin
Book and direction by Wm. Anthony McGuire
(Based on the novel by J. P. McEvoy)
Produced by Florenz Ziegfeld, Jr.
With Ruby Keeler Jolson and Clayton, Jackson, and Durante

Published song:
Mississippi Dry (lyric by J. Russel Robinson)—added after opening

Faced with major troubles during the tryout of **GREAT DAY!** [October 17, 1929], Youmans arranged a badly needed cash advance from Ziegfeld against the promise of a future musical. More as a slap in the face to Gershwin than an improvement to the mediocre **SHOW GIRL**, Ziegfeld requested an interpolation from Youmans—who was to receive his own Ziegfeldian slaps in the face when **SMILES** [November 18, 1930] came along.

GREAT DAY!

A Musical Play of The Southland

OCTOBER 17, 1929   COSMOPOLITAN THEATRE   36 PERFORMANCES

Lyrics by William Rose and Edward Eliscu
Book by John Wells and Wm. Cary Duncan
Directed by R. H. Burnside and Frank M. Gillespie
Conceived and produced by Vincent Youmans
With Mayo Methot, Allen Prior, Lois Deppe, and Miller and Lyles

Published songs:
Great Day!
Happy Because I'm In Love
More Than You Know
One Love—cut; advertised but not published
Open Up Your Heart
Without A Song

Over a half dozen librettists and directors came and went, along with scores of actors (Harold Arlen among the departees) as Youmans prepared his **GREAT DAY!** But the show, anonymously redubbed "Great Delay!", retained its problems and quickly closed. Three songs escaped the shambles and became all-time standards: the rhythmic, spiritualistic *Great Day!*; the moving *With-*

out A Song; and the first of four great Youmans ballads, *More Than You Know* (sung by Mayo Methot, the penultimate Mrs. Humphrey Bogart). Lyricists were Edward Eliscu, who had helped on RAINBOW [November 21, 1928], and Billy Rose. Publisher Youmans thought the pop songwriter's name undignified for serious theatre music, hence "William" Rose.

SMILES

NOVEMBER 18, 1930   ZIEGFELD THEATRE   63 PERFORMANCES

Lyrics mostly by Harold Adamson
Book and direction by Wm. Anthony McGuire
(Based on a story by Noël Coward)
Produced by Florenz Ziegfeld, Jr.
With Marilyn Miller and Fred and Adele Astaire

Published songs:
Be Good To Me (lyric by Ring Lardner)
Blue Bowery—initial publication upon reuse in TAKE A CHANCE
        [November 26, 1932] with new lyric *My Lover*
Carry On, Keep Smiling
He Came Along—cut; initial publication as 1965 nonshow song
If I Were You, Love (I'd Jump Right In The Lake) (lyric by Lardner)
I'm Glad I Waited (lyric by Adamson and Clifford Grey)
More Than Ever—cut; advertised but not published
Time On My Hands (lyric by Adamson and Mack Gordon)

Additional songs recorded:
More Than Ever—cut
Say, Young Man Of Manhattan

With three enormous stars and a typically lavish Ziegfeld production, SMILES was sure-fire; Ziegfeld, devastated by the stock market crash, certainly hoped so. But the material wasn't there. And Ziegfeld, Youmans, and McGuire— leading names in Twenties musical comedy—were each on their last professional legs. Occasional-lyricist Lardner, a close Youmans friend on a similar self-destructive course, stepped in to help with some of his unique songwords. Youmans' consistent failures since HIT THE DECK [April 25, 1927] combined with financial pressures and emotional problems to transform the difficult perfectionist into an impossible-to-deal-with alcoholic. Remarkably, his music was not affected by this. The forgetable SMILES contained the unforgettable *Time On My Hands* (which Marilyn Miller refused to sing) and the rhythmically experimental but fascinating *Be Good To Me* and *Carry On, Keep Smiling*.

THROUGH THE YEARS

JANUARY 28, 1932   MANHATTAN THEATRE   20 PERFORMANCES

Lyrics by Edward Heyman
Book by Brian Hooker
(Based on *Smilin' Through* [play] by Allan Langdon Martin)
Directed by Edgar MacGregor
Produced by Vincent Youmans
With Natalie Hall and Charles Winninger
NOTE: SMILIN' THROUGH, pre-Broadway title

Published songs:
Drums In My Heart
It's Every Girl's Ambition
Kathleen Mine
Kinda Like You
Through The Years
You're Everywhere

Youmans once more displayed his inability to assemble the elements needed to produce a successful show: THROUGH THE YEARS was a much-doctored shambles. Again Youmans managed two hits—*Drums In My Heart* and one of his very best, *Through The Years.* The failure took Youmans out of the producing business, and his difficult reputation made him virtually unemployable.

TAKE A CHANCE

NOVEMBER 26, 1932   APOLLO THEATRE   243 PERFORMANCES

Music mostly by Richard A. Whiting and "Herb Brown Nacio"
Lyrics by B. G. DeSylva
Book by DeSylva and Lawrence Schwab
Directed by Edgar MacGregor
Produced by Schwab and DeSylva
With Ethel Merman, Jack Haley, and Jack Whiting
Note: HUMPTY DUMPTY, pre-Broadway title

Published songs:
I Want To Be With You—cut
My Lover—cut; new lyric for *Blue Bowery* (unpublished) from SMILES
       [November 18, 1930]
Oh, How I Long To Belong To You
Rise 'N Shine

Should I Be Sweet?
So Do I

When **Humpty Dumpty** [September 12, 1932] met with disastrous pre-Broadway notices, Schwab and DeSylva decided to take a chance and totally overhaul the piece. Merman remained, while Lou Holtz and Eddie Foy, Jr. were replaced; and DeSylva took an even bigger chance by bringing Youmans in to supplement the score. **Take A Chance** turned into a hit, though Youmans' contributions (except the spiritualistic *Rise 'N Shine*) were overshadowed by **Humpty Dumpty** leftover *Eadie Was A Lady*. Youmans' last great ballad, *I Want To Be With You*, was cut and remains neglected to this day. Youmans left Broadway for Hollywood, where he wrote the 1933 "Flying Down to Rio" (which introduced the Astaire/Rogers team). Despite three hit songs, the composer quickly alienated himself from future movie work. Years of heavy drinking and living had resulted in a weakened physical state. Youmans contracted tuberculosis and was forced into a long, discouraging retirement at the age of thirty-four.

VINCENT YOUMANS' BALLET REVUE

[January 27, 1944]   Lyric Theatre < Baltimore, Maryland > ;
  closed during pre-Broadway tour

Music by Rimsky-Korsakov, Maurice Ravel, and Ernesto Lecuona
Lyrics by Maria Shelton and Gladys Shelley
Choreographed by Leonide Massine and Eugene von Groza
Directed by Eric Hatch
Produced by Vincent Youmans
With Glenn Anders, Deems Taylor, Mason Adams, and Herbert Ross

Published songs:
None

Youmans had spent the stronger periods of his illness studying composition and experimenting. During a period of remission, Youmans briefly came back into view with this curious dance program featuring music by Mexican Lecuona and others (but no Youmans!). The amateurishly assembled fiasco lasted three weeks and Youmans went back to his sickbed. After another two years of illness, Vincent Youmans succumbed and died on April 5, 1946 in Denver, Colorado.

Vincent Youmans arrived on Broadway in the early Twenties, experimenting with the same "hot" music as the up-and-coming George Gershwin. Early success came via **Wildflower** [February 7, 1923], a mild operetta with a difference: one highly syncopated song hit. Within two years, jazz-based dance rhythms were dominating entire scores, with **No, No, Nanette** [September 16, 1925] in the vanguard. Then Youmans' myriad self-inflicted problems—physical, emotional, financial—began to overtake his career. His remaining projects were all hopelessly troubled and ended in failure. In the midst of this, Youmans developed an incredibly rich melodic style and wrote some of the most beautiful songs of the musical theatre. And then his career was over, after just a dozen years.

Richard Rodgers

BORN: June 28, 1902   New York, New York
DIED: December 30, 1979   New York, New York

Richard Rodgers' early years were filled with show tunes: his parents were operetta enthusiasts. From the age of seven his ambition was clearly set on musical theatre. In 1916 Rodgers discovered Kern—via a subway-circuit production of VERY GOOD EDDIE [Kern: December 23, 1915]—and began writing songs. In May of 1917, Rodgers' older brother took him to the annual Columbia Varsity Show; young Rodgers was impressed by the lyrics, so Mortimer introduced him to fraternity brother Oscar Hammerstein 2nd. The fifteen-year-old decided he was going to go to Columbia and write varsity shows (which he did). Meanwhile, Rodgers himself published his first song in June 1917: *Auto Show Girl* (lyric by David Dyrenforth).

ONE MINUTE PLEASE

Benefit Revue

DECEMBER 29, 1917   PLAZA HOTEL GRAND BALLROOM
     1 PERFORMANCE

Lyrics mostly by Richard C. Rodgers and Ralph G. Engelsman
Book by Engelsman
Directed by Milton Bender
Produced by Bender for The Akron Club

Published songs:
Auto Show Girl (lyric by David Dyrenforth)
Whispers (lyric by Engelsman and Rodgers)

Mortimer Rodgers was a member of the Akron Club, just then preparing a benefit for funds to send tobacco overseas. As there was no member-composer, Mortimer volunteered his brother; Richard Rodgers was to continue writing musicals for sixty-two years. *Auto Show Girl,* which had not yet created a stir, was used, as was Rodgers' second self-published effort, *Whispers.* Milton "Doc" Bender, a Broadway dentist, directed and produced. Bender enjoyed one of Broadway's less savory reputations. He was to become Lorenz Hart's agent, "man Friday," and all-around bad influence. Surprisingly, it was through Rodgers—who loathed Bender even more than everyone else did—that Hart first came together with his Svengali.

UP STAGE AND DOWN

Benefit Revue

MARCH 8, 1919   WALDORF ASTORIA GRAND BALLROOM
    1 PERFORMANCE

Lyrics mostly by Richard C. Rodgers
Book by Myron D. Rosenthal
Directed by Dr. Harry A. Goldberg
Produced by Infants Relief Society
With Phillip Leavitt, Ralph Engelsman, and Rosenthal

Published songs:
Asiatic Angles
Butterfly Love
Love Is Not In Vain
Love Me By Parcel Post (lyric by Mortimer W. Rodgers)
There's Room For One More (lyric by Oscar Hammerstein 2nd)—initial
    publication upon reuse in FLY WITH ME [March 24, 1920]
Twinkling Eyes

The Infants needed Relief, so Rodgers obliged with his second score. He also wrote most of the lyrics, with assists from his brother and Oscar Hammerstein, whose first Broadway show was about to go into rehearsal. (Uncle Arthur Hammerstein presented the drama *The Light* [May 21, 1919], which went out after only four New Haven performances. UP STAGE AND DOWN at least made it to Broadway with a second benefit performance. Retitled TWINKLING EYES [May 18, 1919], Rodgers—and, for that matter, Hammerstein—played a second benefit performance at the 44th Street Theatre.) Yet another collaborator lined up by Mortimer was theatrical lawyer Benjamin M. Kaye; the Rodgers-Kaye effort was *Prisms, Plums And Prunes* (unpublished).

A LONELY ROMEO

JUNE 10, 1919   SHUBERT THEATRE   87 PERFORMANCES

Music mostly by Malvin M. Franklin and Robert Hood Bowers
Lyrics mostly by Robert B. Smith
Book by Harry B. Smith and Lew Fields

Directed and produced by Fields
With Lew Fields

Published song:
Any Old Place With You (lyric by Lorenz Hart)—added after opening

Following UP STAGE AND DOWN [March 8, 1919], Rodgers began looking for a full-time collaborator. Phillip Leavitt, classmate and friend of Mortimer (and actor in UP STAGE AND DOWN), introduced high school student Rodgers to yet another Columbia man who was looking for a composer. Would-be lyricist Lorenz Hart had made little professional headway since graduation. Hart's first theatrical assignment was to provide translations for the German-language DIE TÖLLE DOLLY [October 23, 1916], which played in the Yorkville section of Manhattan. The strangely matched pair shared an admiration for the "Princess Theatre Shows" of Kern, Bolton, and Wodehouse and decided to get together for a few songs. Leavitt took songs and songwriters to his neighbor, Broadway star-producer-director Lew Fields (see HOKEY-POKEY [Berlin: February 8, 1912]). Fields liked *Any Old Place With You* and added it to A LONELY ROMEO (which had moved to the Casino Theatre) on August 26, 1919. It was Rodgers' first commercially published song. Three of Hart's Dolly songs had been published—including *Meyer, Your Tights Are Tight* (music by Walter Kollo).

YOU'D BE SURPRISED

An Atrocious Musical Comedy

MARCH 6, 1920   PLAZA HOTEL GRAND BALLROOM   1 PERFORMANCE

Lyrics mostly by Lorenz Hart and Milton G. Bender
Book and direction by Bender
Produced by The Akron Club
With Dorothy Fields, Ralph Engelsman, and Phillip Leavitt

Published songs:
A Breath of Springtime (lyric by Hart)
Don't Love Me Like Othello (lyric by Hart)—initial publication upon
        reuse in FLY WITH ME [March 24, 1920]
Mary, Queen Of Scots (lyric by Herbert Fields)—initial publication upon
        reuse in POOR LITTLE RITZ GIRL [July 28, 1920]
Princess Of The Willow Tree (lyric by Bender)—see POOR LITTLE RITZ
        GIRL
When We Are Married (lyric by Bender)

Broadway composer Rodgers entered Columbia in the fall of 1919, even though he hadn't finished high school. YOU'D BE SURPRISED was a second amateur show for the Akron Club. Rodgers wrote not only with Hart (and Milton Bender) but with Lew Fields' son Herbert, who had played a small role in A LONELY ROMEO [June 10, 1919]. Herbert Fields was to become librettist to the successful Rodgers and Hart team; during the five years of struggle before Broadway success, Herbert filled in as occasional lyricist, choreographer, whatever. YOU'D BE SURPRISED also made use of Lew Fields' fifteen-year-old daughter Dorothy, whom producer Rodgers eventually hired as lyricist (see ANNIE GET YOUR GUN [Berlin: May 16, 1946]).

FLY WITH ME
A Futurist Musical Comedy

MARCH 24, 1920   HOTEL ASTOR GRAND BALLROOM   4 PERFORMANCES

Lyrics mostly by Lorenz Hart
Book by Milton Kroopf and Phillip Leavitt
Choreographed by Herbert Fields
Directed by Ralph Bunker
Produced by The Columbia University Players

Songs published in vocal score:
Another Melody In F
A College On Broadway
Don't Love Me Like Othello—originally used in YOU'D BE SURPRISED
    [March 6, 1920]; also see POOR LITTLE RITZ GIRL [July 28, 1920]
Dreaming True—see POOR LITTLE RITZ GIRL
Gone Are The Days
Gunga Din
If You Were You—different than *If I Were You* from BETSY [December
    28, 1926]
Inspiration
Peek In Pekin—see POOR LITTLE RITZ GIRL
A Penny For Your Thoughts
There's Room For One More (lyric by Oscar Hammerstein 2nd)—initial
    publication of song originally used in UP STAGE AND DOWN [March
    8, 1919]
Working For The Government

Additional songs recorded:
Kid, I Love You
Moonlight and You
The Third Degree Of Love

Freshman Rodgers was selected to write the Columbia Varsity Show in his first year of eligibility. One of the three-judge panel which accepted FLY WITH

ME was alumnus Hammerstein, whose first Broadway show (**ALWAYS YOU** [January 5, 1920]; music by Herbert Stothart) had just closed after 66 performances. Lew Fields, father of choreographer Herbert, attended—and hired Rodgers and Hart to write his next show.

POOR LITTLE RITZ GIRL

JULY 28, 1920   CENTRAL THEATRE   119 PERFORMANCES

Music also by Sigmund Romberg
Lyrics to Rodgers songs by Lorenz Hart
Book by George Campbell and Lew Fields
Directed by Ned Wayburn
Produced by Fields
With Charles Purcell and Lulu McConnell

Published songs:
Boomerang—cut; advertised but not published
Lady Raffles Behave—cut
Let Me Drink In Your Eyes—cut; advertised but not published; see
    YOU'LL NEVER KNOW [April 20, 1921]
Love Will Call—new lyric for *Dreaming True* from **FLY WITH ME**
    [March 24, 1920]
Love's Intense In Tents—new lyric for *Peek In Pekin* from **FLY WITH ME**
Mary, Queen Of Scots (lyric by Herbert Fields)—originally used
    (unpublished) in **YOU'D BE SURPRISED** [March 6, 1920]
Will You Forgive Me?—cut; advertised but not published; new lyric for
    Princess Of The Willow Tree from **YOU'D BE SURPRISED**; also see
    YOU'LL NEVER KNOW
You Can't Fool Your Dreams—new lyric for *Don't Love Me Like Othello*
    from **YOU'D BE SURPRISED**

POOR LITTLE RITZ GIRL tried out in Boston, where it was the opening attraction at the Wilbur Theatre. Rodgers spent the tryout period as a counselor at summer camp. Back in Boston, Fields threw out half the score and brought in Sigmund Romberg. Rodgers didn't discover this until he arrived for the Broadway opening; thereafter he paid more attention to the proper use of his work. It was to be five years before Rodgers and Hart had another Broadway musical opportunity. It might be added that Rodgers' very early work was not overwhelming. Of course, he was still only eighteen.

YOU'LL NEVER KNOW

Columbia 15th Anniversary Varsity Show

APRIL 20, 1921   HOTEL ASTOR GRAND BALLROOM   4 PERFORMANCES

Lyrics by Lorenz Hart
Choreographed by Herbert Fields
Directed by Oscar Hammerstein 2nd and others
Produced by Players' Club of Columbia University

Songs published in vocal score:
Chorus Girl Blues
I'm Broke
Jumping Jack
Just A Little Lie
Let Me Drink In Your Eyes—originally used (cut, unpublished) in POOR
    LITTLE RITZ GIRL [July 28, 1920]
Virtue Wins The Day
Watch Yourself
When I Go On The Stage [1st]—different than song from SHE'S MY
    BABY [January 3, 1928]
Will You Forgive Me?—originally used (cut, unpublished) in POOR LITTLE
    RITZ GIRL
You'll Never Know
Your Lullaby

Rodgers wrote his second consecutive Columbia Varsity Show and then left
college, entering the Institute of Musical Art (Juilliard). The benefit-show
career continued (with no further efforts published) while Rodgers, Hart, and
Fields wrote musicals for—and were ignored by—Broadway. Meanwhile,
Rodgers went on the road with Papa Fields to conduct the post-Broadway tour
of SNAPSHOTS OF 1921 [Gershwin: June 2, 1921].

THE MELODY MAN

MAY 13, 1924   CENTRAL THEATRE   56 PERFORMANCES

Play with songs by "Herbert Richard Lorenz"
Directed by Lawrence Marston and Alexander Leftwich
Produced by Lew Fields
With Fields, Frederic Bickel (March), Eva Puck, and Sammy White
NOTE: THE JAZZ KING, pre-Broadway title

Published songs:
I'd Like To Poison Ivy (Because She Clings To Me)
Moonlight Mama

Unable to raise enthusiasm with any of their musicals, Herbert, Richard, and Lorenz combined to create this hackneyed comedy; not unwisely, they kept their names off it. Another year of nonproductive collaboration followed THE MELODY MAN. Things for the pair were bad: Hart managed a few assignments with other composers, and the discouraged Rodgers was on the verge of going into babies' underwear.

GARRICK GAIETIES

First Edition

A Bubbling Satirical Musical Revue Of Plays, Problems and Persons

MAY 17, 1925   GARRICK THEATRE   161 PERFORMANCES

Music mostly by Rodgers
Lyrics mostly by Lorenz Hart
Sketches by Benjamin M. Kaye, Morrie Ryskind, and others
Choreographed by Herbert Fields
Directed by Philip Loeb
Produced by The Theatre Guild
With Sterling Holloway, Edith Meiser, Romney Brent, and June Cochrane

Published songs:
April Fool
Do You Love Me? (I Wonder)
Manhattan
Old Fashioned Girl (lyric by Edith Meiser)
On With The Dance
Sentimental Me (And Romantic You)
The Three Musketeers—advertised but not published

Additional song published in "Rodgers and Hart Song Book":
Opening (Gilding The Guild)

Benjamin Kaye, lyricist of *Prisms, Plums and Prunes* (in UP STAGE AND DOWN [March 8, 1919]), asked Rodgers to write another benefit, this time to raise money for drapes in the new Guild (now the Virginia) Theatre; Kaye was lawyer for the Theatre Guild. Rodgers and Hart put together a bright and inventive score, including *Manhattan* from the unproduced 1923 WINKLE

Town. The two-performance run was such a success that the GARRICK GAIE-
TIES quickly reopened. With *Manhattan* an enormous hit, Rodgers and Hart
were no longer in the amateur show market.

JUNE DAYS

AUGUST 6, 1925   ASTOR THEATRE   84 PERFORMANCES

Music mostly by J. Fred Coots
Lyrics mostly by Clifford Grey
Book by Cyrus Wood
(Based on *The Charm School* [Kern: August 2, 1920])
Directed by J. J. Shubert
Produced by Lee and J. J. Shubert

Published songs:
None

Rodgers and Hart contributed one song, *Anytime, Anywhere, Anyhow.*

DEAREST ENEMY

SEPTEMBER 18, 1925   KNICKERBOCKER THEATRE   286 PERFORMANCES

Lyrics by Lorenz Hart
Book by Herbert Fields
Directed by John Murray Anderson
Produced by George Ford
With Helen Ford and Charles Purcell

Published songs:
Bye And Bye
Cheerio!
Here In My Arms—also used in LIDO LADY [December 1, 1926]
Here's A Kiss
Sweet Peter

Additional songs recorded:
Full-Blown Roses
Gavotte
Heigh-Ho, Lackaday
The Hermits
I Beg Your Pardon
I'd Like To Hide It
Old Enough To Love
War Is War
Where The Hudson River Flows

With an established hit playing, Rodgers, Hart, and Fields were finally able to get on one of their already written musicals. Musical-comedy star Helen Ford had long been interested in DEAREST ENEMY; with Rodgers and Hart now bankable, Ford's husband was able to raise the money. Revue director John Murray Anderson joined in, and the result was a fresh, unpretentious hit. *Here In My Arms* joined *Manhattan* as a popular 1925 song success.

FIFTH AVENUE FOLLIES

A Revue Superb

[CIRCA JANUARY 1926]   FIFTH AVENUE NIGHTCLUB

Lyrics by Lorenz Hart
Directed by Seymour Felix
Produced by Billy Rose
With Cecil Cunningham and Bert Hanlon

Published songs:
Maybe It's Me—see COCHRAN'S 1926 REVUE [April 29, 1926] and
     PEGGY-ANN [December 27, 1926]
Where's That Little Girl (In The Little Green Hat)—see LIDO LADY
     [December 1, 1926]

Rose's first nightclub venture was unsuccessful and short-lived. During his early pop-lyricist days, Rose occasionally used the slightly older (and taller) Hart as ghostwriter. Was it Hart—lyricist of *I'd Love To Poison Ivy (Because She Clings To Me)* (1923)—who first asked *Does The Spearmint Lose Its Flavor On The Bedpost Overnight?* (1924)? The *Green Hat* song, incidentally, was suggested by Michael Arlen's best seller, just then a hit Katharine Cornell vehicle.

THE GIRL FRIEND

MARCH 17, 1926   VANDERBILT THEATRE   301 PERFORMANCES

Lyrics by Lorenz Hart
Book by Herbert Fields
Directed by John Harwood
Produced by Lew Fields
With Eva Puck, Sammy White, and June Cochrane

Published songs:
The Blue Room
The Girl Friend
Good Fellow Mine

Sleepyhead—cut; also used in GARRICK GAIETIES (Second) [May 10, 1926]
Why Do I?

Additional songs published (no lyric) in piano selection:
Look For The Damsel
What Is It?

1926 was a time when Broadway gladly accepted musicals about six-day bicycle races and such. This second hit firmly established the Rodgers, Hart, and Fields team, with Lew Fields once again producing. THE GIRL FRIEND was written for husband-and-wife dance team Puck and White, who had been featured in THE MELODY MAN [May 13, 1924]. Their biggest success came as "Frank and Ellie," the husband-and-wife dance team in SHOW BOAT [Kern: December 27, 1927]. *The Blue Room* was yet another big song hit; the superb *Sleepyhead* wasn't.

COCHRAN'S 1926 REVUE

APRIL 29, 1926   LONDON PAVILION < LONDON >   149 PERFORMANCES

Music mostly by others
Book by Ronald Jeans
Produced by Charles B. Cochran

Published song:
I'm Crazy 'bout The Charleston (lyric by Donovan Parsons)—new lyric for *Maybe It's Me* from FIFTH AVENUE FOLLIES [Circa January 1926] and PEGGY-ANN [December 27, 1926]

In an era when song revisions and reuses were not exactly uncommon practices, *Maybe It's Me* stands out. It was initially performed and published in January 1926. When reused in London with a non-Hart lyric, the published sheet also included a second Hart version of the first lyric. In December a *third* Hart version of *Maybe It's Me* appeared. All four were similarly unsuccessful.

GARRICK GAIETIES
Second Edition

MAY 10, 1926   GARRICK THEATRE   174 PERFORMANCES

Music mostly by Rodgers
Lyrics mostly by Lorenz Hart
Sketches by Herbert Fields, Benjamin M. Kaye, and others

Choreographed by Fields
Directed by Philip Loeb
Produced by The Theatre Guild
With Sterling Holloway, Romney Brent, Edith Meiser, and Betty Starbuck

Published songs:
Idles Of The King—for initial publication see **London Pavilion Revue** [May 20, 1927]
Keys To Heaven
A Little Souvenir
Mountain Greenery
Queen Elizabeth
Sleepyhead—originally used (cut) in **The Girl Friend** [March 17, 1926]
What's The Use of Talking

Additional songs published in USO/Camp Shows "AT EASE" (Volume 4):
The Rose of Arizona, including:
Back To Nature
Davey Crockett
It May Rain
Say It With Flowers

A second successful edition of this revue, with *Mountain Greenery* a hit on the level of *Manhattan.* Rodgers, Hart, and Fields also contributed the classic one-act operetta spoof, "The Rose of Arizona." The first edition had also included a mock-operetta, "The Joy Spreader," which was unpublished.

LIDO LADY

December 1, 1926   Gaiety Theatre < London >
    529 performances

Lyrics by Lorenz Hart
Book by Guy Bolton, Kalmar and Ruby, and Ronald Jeans
Directed by Herbert M. Darsey
Produced by Jack Hulbert and Paul Murray
With Hulbert, Cicely Courtneidge (Hulbert), and Phyllis Dare

Published songs:
Atlantic Blues—see **Present Arms** [April 26, 1928]
Here In My Arms—originally used in **Dearest Enemy** [September 18, 1925]
I Want A Man—also used in **America's Sweetheart** [February 10, 1931]

Lido Lady
Morning Is Midnight—also used in SHE's MY BABY [January 3, 1928]
A Tiny Flat Near Soho Square—see SHE's MY BABY
Try Again To-morrow
What's The Use?—new lyric for *Where's That Little Girl (In The Little*
     Green Hat) from FIFTH AVENUE FOLLIES [Circa January 1926]
You're On The Lido Now

Additional songs published (no lyric) in piano selection:
I Must Be Going
My Heart Is Sheba Bound

Rodgers and Hart went to London to write this hit. As with Kern and (especially) Gershwin, Rodgers became immensely popular with British audiences through the early Thirties.

PEGGY-ANN

The Utterly Different Musical Comedy

DECEMBER 27, 1926   VANDERBILT THEATRE   333 PERFORMANCES

Lyrics by Lorenz Hart
Book by Herbert Fields
(Based on *Tillie's Nightmare* [musical] by Edgar Smith)
Directed by Robert Milton
Produced by Lew Fields and Lyle D. Andrews
With Helen Ford, Lulu McConnell, Edith Meiser, and Betty Starbuck

Published songs:
The Country Mouse (lyric by Desmond Carter)—written for London
     production [July 29, 1927]; new lyric for *A Little Birdie Told Me*
     So
Give That Little Girl A Hand—initial publication (as professional copy)
     upon use in London production
Hello—initial publication upon use in London production
Howdy To Broadway—initial publication (as professional copy) upon use
     in London production
A Little Birdie Told Me So
Maybe It's Me—revised lyric for song originally used in FIFTH AVENUE
     FOLLIES [Circa January 1926]; also see COCHRAN's 1926 REVUE
     [April 29, 1926]
A Tree In The Park
Where's That Rainbow?

Additional songs published (no lyric) in piano selection:
Chuck It!
Havana

A somewhat expressionistic musical, with Helen Ford (of DEAREST ENEMY [September 18, 1925]) starring in another Rodgers and Hart hit.

BETSY

DECEMBER 28, 1926   NEW AMSTERDAM THEATRE   39 PERFORMANCES

Music mostly by Rodgers (see **Berlin**)
Lyrics mostly by Lorenz Hart
Book by Irving Caesar and David Freedman
Revised and directed by Wm. Anthony McGuire
Produced by Florenz Ziegfeld, Jr.
With Belle Baker, Al Shean, and Dan Healy

Published songs:
Come And Tell Me—cut
If I Were You—different than *If You Were You* from FLY WITH ME
    [March 24, 1920]; also used in LADY LUCK [April 27, 1927] and
    SHE'S MY BABY [January 3, 1928]
Sing—also used in LADY LUCK and LADY FINGERS [January 31, 1929]   •
Stonewall Moscowitz March (by Caesar, Hart, and Rodgers)
This Funny World
You're The Mother Type

After six quick hits in eighteen months, Rodgers and Hart met failure the night after PEGGY-ANN [December 27, 1926] opened with this Ziegfeldian showcase for vaudeville balladeer Baker. The songwriters were rudely surprised opening night when Ziegfeld slipped in Irving Berlin's new *Blue Skies*; the song didn't help BETSY any, but it did all right by Berlin. Rodgers and Hart's contributions included one of their finest forgotten songs, *This Funny World*. The drawing on the sheet music cover shows Baker tying strings around three slightly embarrassed gentlemen. The first two look very much like the composer and lyricist.

LADY LUCK

APRIL 27, 1927   CARLTON THEATRE < LONDON >   324 PERFORMANCES

Music mostly by H. B. Hedley
Lyrics mostly by Greatrex Newman
Lyrics to Rodgers songs by Lorenz Hart

Book by Firth Shepherd
With Laddie Cliff and Leslie Henson

Published songs:
If I Were You—originally used in BETSY [December 28, 1926]; also used
in SHE'S MY BABY [January 3, 1928]
Sing—originally used in BETSY; also used in LADY FINGERS [January 31,
1929]

LONDON PAVILION REVUE
"One Dam Thing After Another"

MAY 20, 1927   LONDON PAVILION < LONDON >   237 PERFORMANCES

Lyrics by Lorenz Hart
Book by Ronald Jeans
Directed by Frank Collins
Produced by Charles B. Cochran
With Jessie Matthews, Sonnie Hale, and Melville Cooper

Published songs:
I Need Some Cooling Off—also used (unpublished) in SHE'S MY BABY
[January 3, 1928]
My Heart Stood Still—also used in A CONNECTICUT YANKEE [November
3, 1927]
My Lucky Star—also used (unpublished) in SHE'S MY BABY

Additional songs published (no lyric) in piano selection:
Danse Grotesque A La Nègre [instrumental]
Idles Of The King—originally used in GARRICK GAIETIES (Second) [May
10, 1976]
Make Hey! Make Hey! While The Sun Shines
One Dam Thing After Another
Sandwich Girls
Shuffle

A second London hit, memorable for establishing Jessie Matthews as a star.
Matthews introduced the soon-to-be-imported *My Heart Stood Still*, inspired
by the near-collision of a Paris taxicab containing the songwriters.

A CONNECTICUT YANKEE

< First Version—also see November 17, 1943 >

NOVEMBER 3, 1927   VANDERBILT THEATRE   418 PERFORMANCES

Lyrics by Lorenz Hart
Book by Herbert Fields
(Based on *A Connecticut Yankee in King Arthur's Court* [novel] by Mark Twain)
Directed by Alexander Leftwich
Produced by Lew Fields and Lyle D. Andrews
With William Gaxton, Constance Carpenter, and June Cochrane

Published songs:
I Blush—cut
I Feel At Home With You
My Heart Stood Still—originally used in LONDON PAVILION REVUE [May 20, 1927]
On A Desert Island With Thee!
Someone Should Tell Them—cut; see AMERICA'S SWEETHEART [February 10, 1931]
Thou Swell

Additional songs published (no lyric) in piano selection:
Here's A Toast
Nothing's Wrong

Another smash for Rodgers, Hart, and Fields. Song hits were the transatlantic *My Heart Stood Still* and the anachronistically slangy *Thou Swell.* Hart, who had displayed skill since THE GARRICK GAIETIES [May 17, 1925], began to exercise his talent for sustained comedy lyrics with *I Feel At Home With You* and *On A Desert Island With Thee!* Rodgers, meanwhile, wrote the first of his breathtaking waltzes, *Nothing's Wrong,* (only the music for the refrain of this stunner has been found; it is hoped that the verse and entire lyric will turn up someday, somewhere). The modern rhythms of Gershwin, Youmans, and Rodgers, combined with the decline of operetta, ended the popularity of the waltz. Rodgers, however, developed a distinctive, nonhackneyed waltz style, resulting in a dozen classics: *Lover, The Most Beautiful Girl In The World, Out Of My Dreams, Hello, Young Lovers,* and more. Surprisingly, no other theatre composer has made use of the waltz as effectively. A CONNECTICUT YANKEE was Rodgers and Hart's eighth hit in three years; unforeseeably, they were to be without further Broadway success until 1936.

SHE'S MY BABY

JANUARY 3, 1928 · GLOBE THEATRE 71 PERFORMANCES

Lyrics by Lorenz Hart
Book by Guy Bolton, Bert Kalmar, and Harry Ruby
Directed by Edward Royce
Produced by Charles Dillingham
With Beatrice Lillie, Clifton Webb, Jack Whiting, and Irene Dunne

Published songs:
A Baby's Best Friend
How Was I To Know?—cut; see HEADS UP! [November 11, 1929]
I Need Some Cooling Off—originally used in (and only published as from)
    LONDON PAVILION REVUE [May 29, 1927]
If I Were You—cut; originally used in BETSY [December 28, 1926] and
    LADY LUCK [April 27, 1927]
A Little House in Soho—revised lyric for *A Tiny Flat Near Soho Square*
    from LIDO LADY [December 1, 1926]
Morning Is Midnight—cut; originally used in LIDO LADY
My Lucky Star—originally used in (and only published as from) LONDON
    PAVILION REVUE
When I Go On The Stage [2nd]—different than song from YOU'LL
    NEVER KNOW [April 20, 1921]
Whoopsie!
You're What I Need

Rodgers and Hart were no more successful with Lillie than Vincent Youmans
had been on OH, PLEASE! [Youmans: December 17, 1926]); both composers
found her difficult to please and were unable to suit her special performing
style. Rodgers and Hart eventually did come up with a Lillie gem: *Rhythm*
(in the British revue PLEASE! [November 16, 1933]), which seems to have
been revised from unused SHE'S MY BABY material.

PRESENT ARMS!

APRIL 26, 1928 MANSFIELD THEATRE 155 PERFORMANCES

Lyrics by Lorenz Hart
Book by Herbert Fields
Directed by Alexander Leftwich
Produced by Lew Fields
With Charles King, Flora LeBreton, Busby Berkeley, and Joyce Barbour

Published songs:
Blue Ocean Blues—new lyric for *Atlantic Blues* from LIDO LADY
    [December 1, 1926]
Crazy Elbows
Do I Hear You Saying (I Love You?)
Down By The Sea
I'm A Fool, Little One
A Kiss For Cinderella
You Took Advantage Of Me

Additional song published (no lyric) in piano selection:
Tell It To The Marines

Herb Fields' first non-Rodgers and Hart show had been the monumental hit
HIT THE DECK [Youmans: April 25, 1927]. That musical had a Navy motif;
PRESENT ARMS! tried the Marines. Nothing from the score attracted attention
except *You Took Advantage Of Me*, a distant relative of *You're The Mother
Type* from BETSY [December 28, 1926].

CHEE-CHEE

SEPTEMBER 25, 1928   MANSFIELD THEATRE   31 PERFORMANCES

Lyrics by Lorenz Hart
Book by Herbert Fields
(Based on *The Son of the Grand Eunuch* [novel] by Charles Petit)
Directed by Alexander Leftwich
Produced by Lew Fields
With Helen Ford, Betty Starbuck, Philip Loeb, and William Williams

Published songs:
Better Be Good To Me
Dear, Oh Dear!
I Must Love You—see SIMPLE SIMON [February 18, 1930]
Moon Of My Delight
Singing A Love Song—see SIMPLE SIMON
The Tartar Song

Rodgers, Hart, and Fields decided to try something new, and CHEE-CHEE
certainly was: Broadway's first Chinese castration musical. After a stony reaction it was withdrawn, and the two Fieldses parted company with Rodgers and
Hart. Herbert soon joined Cole Porter for FIFTY MILLION FRENCHMEN [Por-
ter: November 27, 1929], the first of seven-out-of-seven hits. Lew's final book
musical was the aptly titled HELLO, DADDY! [December 26, 1928]—written
by Herbert and Dorothy (with Jimmy McHugh).

LADY FINGERS

JANUARY 31, 1929   VANDERBILT THEATRE   132 PERFORMANCES

Music mostly by Joseph Meyers
Lyrics mostly by Edward Eliscu
Lyrics to Rodgers songs by Lorenz Hart
Book by Eddie Buzzell
(Based on *Easy Come, Easy Go* [play] by Owen Davis)
Directed by Lew Levenson
Produced by Lyle D. Andrews
With Buzzell and John Price Jones

Published songs:
I Love You More Than Yesterday
Sing—originally used in **BETSY** [December 28, 1926]; also used in **LADY LUCK** [April 27, 1927]

SPRING IS HERE

MARCH 11, 1929   ALVIN THEATRE   104 PERFORMANCES

Lyrics by Lorenz Hart
Book by Owen Davis
(Based on *Shotgun Wedding* [play] by Davis)
Directed by Alexander Leftwich
Produced by Alex A. Aarons and Vinton Freedley
With Glenn Hunter, Lillian Taiz, and Charles Ruggles

Published songs:
Baby's Awake Now
The Color Of Her Eyes—cut; for initial publication see **EVER GREEN** [December 3, 1930]
Rich Man, Poor Man
Why Can't I?
With A Song In My Heart
You Never Say Yes
Yours Sincerely

Rodgers and Hart moved from producer Lew Fields to the Gershwins' Aarons and Freedley; the association was mutually unprofitable. **SPRING IS HERE** had two lovely songs—*Baby's Awake Now* and *Why Can't I?*—and one popular hit, *With A Song In My Heart.* The title song (unpublished) was *not* the superb *Spring Is Here*; that came later, in **I MARRIED AN ANGEL** [May 11, 1938].

HEADS UP!

NOVEMBER 11, 1929   ALVIN THEATRE   144 PERFORMANCES

Lyrics by Lorenz Hart
Book by John McGowan and Paul Gerard Smith
Produced by Alex A. Aarons and Vinton Freedley
With Jack Whiting, Barbara Newberry, Victor Moore, Betty Starbuck, and Ray Bolger
NOTE: ME FOR YOU, pre-Broadway title

Published songs:
As Though You Were There—cut; initial publication in 1940 as non-show
     song
I Can Do Wonders With You—cut; also used in SIMPLE SIMON
     [February 18, 1930]
It Must Be Heaven
Me For You!
My Man Is On The Make
A Ship Without A Sail
Sky City—cut
Why Do You Suppose?—new lyric for *How Was I To Know* (cut) from
     SHE'S MY BABY [January 3, 1928]

Additional songs published (no lyric) in British piano selection:
Daughter Grows Older
Knees

As with Aarons and Freedley's SMARTY [Gershwin: November 22, 1927], ME
FOR YOU—with an Owen Davis book—had grave tryout problems. Drastic
surgery was performed; but HEADS UP!, unlike FUNNY FACE, did not re-
spond—even with funny man Victor Moore in attendance.

SIMPLE SIMON

FEBRUARY 18, 1930   ZIEGFELD THEATRE   135 PERFORMANCES

Lyrics by Lorenz Hart
Book by Ed Wynn and Guy Bolton
Directed by Zeke Colvan
Produced by Florenz Ziegfeld, Jr.
With Wynn, Ruth Etting, Bobbe Arnst, and Harriet Hoctor

Published songs:
Don't Tell Your Folks
He Dances On My Ceiling (Dancing On The Ceiling)—cut; also used in
     EVER GREEN [December 3, 1930]

He Was Too Good To Me—cut
I Can Do Wonders With You—cut; originally used (cut) in **Heads Up!**
[November 11, 1929]
I Still Believe In You—cut; new lyric for *Singing A Love Song* from
Chee-Chee [September 25, 1928]
Send For Me—new lyric for *I Must Love You* from **Chee-Chee**
Sweetenheart
Ten Cents A Dance

With the Depression in progress and five consecutive failures, Rodgers and
Hart could not afford to turn down Ziegfeld's offer (despite their troubles with
Betsy [December 28, 1926]) and prepared this Ed Wynn vehicle. Matters
turned out little better. The score included three very good songs: *He Dances
On My Ceiling*, which was cut and found a better life; *He Was Too Good
To Me*, which was cut and didn't; and *Ten Cents A Dance*, a truly superb
song which can be examined alongside *Love For Sale* (from **The New Yorkers** (Second Version) [Porter: December 8, 1930]). Porter wails, while Hart
philosophizes; Hart's downtrodden girl is so very much more *real*, with
touches of irony, humor, and sympathy. (In an earlier version, *Hands*, she was
a manicurist, pawed by her male customers.) Porter's music, too, is syntheti-
cally dramatic, resting firmly on his oriental scale. Rodgers is weary-but-honest,
the unorthodox song structure (A-B-A/B; C-D-A/B) especially fitting the
exceptional lyric. Drama is reserved for the remarkable climax, (D into A/B),
resulting in a so much more effective song.

EVER GREEN

December 3, 1930   Adelphi Theatre < London >
254 performances

Lyrics by Lorenz Hart
Book by Benn W. Levy
(Based on an idea by Rodgers and Hart)
Directed by Frank Collins
Produced by Charles B. Cochran
With Jessie Matthews, Sonny Hale, and Joyce Barbour

Published songs:
The Colour of Her Eyes—issued as professional copy; revised lyric for *The
Color Of Her Eyes* (cut; unpublished) from **Spring Is Here** [March
11, 1929]
Dear! Dear!
Harlemania—issued as professional copy
He Dances On My Ceiling (Dancing On The Ceiling)—originally used
(cut) in **Simple Simon** [February 18, 1930]

If I Give In To You
In The Cool Of The Evening
No Place But Home

Additional song published (no lyric) in piano selection:
When The Old World Was New

This British hit was Rodgers and Hart's only theatrical oasis over a long dry spell. Of particular interest are the enthrallingly romantic *No Place But Home* and, for zealous Hart enthusiasts, *The Colour Of Her Eyes,* one of the first of his tart "battle-of-the-sexes" comedy duets. Rodgers and Hart spent much of the early Thirties in Hollywood, their output including the 1932 "Love Me Tonight" (where Rodgers first worked with Rouben Mamoulian) and the 1933 "Hallelujah, I'm a Bum." Both films are notable for Rodgers' first experiments in the close integration of music and dialogue (and songs like *Mimi, Lover,* and *You Are Too Beautiful*).

AMERICA'S SWEETHEART

FEBRUARY 10, 1931   BROADHURST THEATRE   135 PERFORMANCES

Lyrics by Lorenz Hart
Book by Herbert Fields
Directed by Monty Woolley
Produced by Lawrence Schwab and Frank Mandel
With Harriette Lake (Ann Southern), Jack Whiting, and Jean Aubert

Published songs:
How About It?
I've Got Five Dollars
I Want A Man—originally used in LIDO LADY [December 1, 1926]
A Lady Must Live
There's So Much More—revised lyric for *Someone Should Tell Them*
        from A CONNECTICUT YANKEE (First Version) [November 3, 1927]
We'll Be The Same

Rodgers, Hart, and Fields met up in Hollywood and returned to Broadway with this satire on Hollywood, and quickly returned to Hollywood. The trip was worth the visit, though, with the carefree, Depression-less *I've Got Five Dollars* and *A Lady Must Live.*

CRAZY QUILT

MAY 19, 1931   44TH STREET THEATRE   79 PERFORMANCES

Music mostly by Harry Warren
Lyrics mostly by Mort Dixon, Billy Rose, and others
Sketches by David Freedman
Produced and directed by Billy Rose
With Fanny Brice (Rose), Phil Baker, and Ted Healy

Published songs:
None

For *Second-Hand* Fanny Brice Rose *of Washington Square*, Rodgers and Hart supplied *Rest-Room Rose*. (Cole Porter tried *Hot-House Rose*, but Brice didn't like it.)

PLEASE!

NOVEMBER 16, 1933   SAVOY THEATRE <LONDON>   108
     PERFORMANCES

Music mostly by Vivian Ellis and Austin Croom-Johnson
Lyrics mostly by Dion Titheradge
Lyric to Rodgers song by Lorenz Hart
Book by Titheradge and Robert Macgunigle
Directed by Titheradge
Produced by André Charlot
With Beatrice Lillie and Lupino Lane

Recorded song:
Rhythm—also used in THE SHOW IS ON [December 25, 1936]

Rodgers and Hart supplied this very special material for the special Lillie, a minimedley of rhythm songs (see SHE'S MY BABY [January 3, 1928]).

SOMETHING GAY

APRIL 29, 1935   MOROSCO THEATRE   72 PERFORMANCES

Play by Adelaide Heilbron
Lyric by Lorenz Hart
Directed by Thomas Mitchell
Produced by the Messrs. Shubert
With Tallulah Bankhead and Walter Pidgeon

Published song:
You Are So Lovely And I'm So Lonely

JUMBO

NOVEMBER 16, 1935   HIPPODROME THEATRE   233 PERFORMANCES

Lyrics by Lorenz Hart
Book by Ben Hecht and Charles MacArthur
Book directed by George Abbott
Directed by John Murray Anderson
Produced by Billy Rose
With Jimmy Durante, Gloria Grafton, Donald Novis, and Paul Whiteman

Published songs:
The Circus On Parade
Diavolo
Little Girl Blue
The Most Beautiful Girl In The World
My Romance
Over And Over Again—song version of *Party Waltz* [instrumental] (cut, unpublished) from 1934 movie "Hollywood Party"

Additional song recorded:
Women

Rodgers and Hart returned to New York with a ballet-vs-jazz dance show, a proposed movie project Fred Astaire had turned down. In the meantime, Billy Rose approached the pair to write songs for his jumbo circus extravaganza. John Murray Anderson, director of **DEAREST ENEMY** [September 18, 1925], was the musical comedy veteran on hand. Hecht and MacArthur were writing their first (and only) musical, and farce playwright/director George Abbott was hired to stage the book (*his* first musical assignment). Everything about **JUMBO** was gargantuan, including Durante's costar "Big Rosie"—the title role—and the costs that ultimately overtook the show and closed it. (The 4 month run was shorter than the number of performances indicate, as **JUMBO** played 12 performances a week.) Rodgers provided a very beautiful waltz, *The Most Beautiful Girl In The World,* and a very beautiful nonwaltz, *Little Girl Blue*—which, come to think of it, includes a waltz interlude (during which the girls on the flying trapezes flew in).

ON YOUR TOES

APRIL 11, 1936   IMPERIAL THEATRE   315 PERFORMANCES

Lyrics by Lorenz Hart
Book by Rodgers and Hart and George Abbott
Choreography by George Balanchine
Directed by Worthington Minor
Produced by Dwight Deere Wiman
With Ray Bolger, Tamara Geva (Balanchine), Monty Woolley, and Doris Carson

Published songs:
Glad To Be Unhappy
The Heart Is Quicker Than The Eye
It's Got To Be Love
On Your Toes
Quiet Night
Slaughter On Tenth Avenue [ballet]—issued in separate edition
There's A Small Hotel
Too Good For The Average Man

Additional songs published in vocal score:
Princess Zenobia Ballet
The Three 'B's
Two-A-Day For Keith

The non-Fred Astaire project turned into one of the finer Rodgers and Hart shows, with Ray Bolger memorable in the lead. (Marilyn Miller was announced to costar, but withdrew.) With the success of ON YOUR TOES, Rodgers and Hart began a series of musicals with a new creative team. Producer Wiman (see THE LITTLE SHOW [Schwartz: April 30, 1929]) presented five Rodgers and Hart "spring" musicals over the next seven years; colibrettist Abbott wrote, directed, and produced four hits; and Wiman's set designer Jo Mielziner became one of Rodgers' most frequent associates. Diaghilev-trained George Balanchine made his musical comedy debut with two integrally plotted ballets, including the legendary *Slaughter On Tenth Avenue*; he choreographed four Rodgers and Hart hits. (Hart took Balanchine, Geva, Zorina, et al to agent "Doc" Bender.) Besides *Slaughter,* Rodgers and Hart sparkled with *Glad To Be Unhappy, There's A Small Hotel, The Heart Is Quicker Than The Eye,* and *It's Got To Be Love.* ON YOUR TOES was to have two Broadway revivals, in 1954 and 1982. Abbott directed both, the second at the age of ninety-two.

THE SHOW IS ON

December 25, 1936   Winter Garden Theatre   237 performances

Music mostly by Vernon **Duke** (see **Arlen, Gershwin,** and **Schwartz**)
Lyric to Rodgers song by Lorenz Hart
Sketches mostly by David Freedman and Moss Hart
Directed by Vincente Minnelli
Produced by Lee Shubert
With Beatrice Lillie and Bert Lahr

Recorded song:
Rhythm—originally used in Please! [November 16, 1933]

BABES IN ARMS

April 14, 1937   Shubert Theatre   289 performances

Lyrics by Lorenz Hart
Book by Rodgers and Hart
Choreography by George Balanchine
Directed by Robert Sinclair
Produced by Dwight Deere Wiman
With Mitzi Green, Ray Heatherton, Wynn Murray, Alfred Drake, and
The Nicholas Brothers

Published songs:
All At Once
All Dark People
Babes In Arms
I Wish I Were In Love Again
Johnny One Note
The Lady Is A Tramp
My Funny Valentine
Way Out West
Where Or When

Additional song published in vocal score:
Imagine

Additional song recorded:
You Are So Fair

Coming off the very good On Your Toes, Rodgers and Hart wrote their most hit-laden score. Rodgers was to have other charmed periods in his career, but the late Thirties showed Hart at the very top of his form with *Where Or*

177 / Richard Rodgers

When? and *My Funny Valentine* (Ray Heatherton—father of Joey—played Val), *I Wish I Were In Love Again,* and the twin knockouts *Johnny One Note* and *The Lady Is A Tramp.* That score is good even by *today's* standards. Rodgers and Hart also provided their first libretto, the one about the group of kids getting together to put on a show; somebody's father had a barn.

I'D RATHER BE RIGHT

November 2, 1937   Alvin Theatre   290 performances

Lyrics by Lorenz Hart
Book by George S. Kaufman and Moss Hart
Directed by Kaufman
Produced by Sam H. Harris
With George M. Cohan, Joy Hodges, and Austin Marshall

Published songs:
Ev'rybody Loves You—issued as professional copy only; subsequently
    published in "Rodgers and Hart: A Musical Anthology"
Have You Met Miss Jones?
I'd Rather Be Right (Don't Have To Know Much) [1st]—cut; see Two
    Weeks With Pay [June 24, 1940]
I'd Rather Be Right (Than Influential) [2nd]
Sweet Sixty-Five
Take And Take And Take

Additional song recorded:
Off The Record

Kaufman and producer Sam Harris decided to attempt another political satire along the lines of Of Thee I Sing [Gershwin: December 26, 1931] and the unsuccessful Bring On The Girls [Schwartz: October 22, 1934]. Kaufman worked extremely well with Gershwin, Berlin, Schwartz, and Loesser; but not Rodgers. The casting of George M. Cohan as Franklin D. Roosevelt made I'd Rather Be Right a highly awaited event: the "Yankee Doodle Boy" had been absent from the musical stage for a decade, and was performing his first non-Cohan score. However, Cohan *hated* Rodgers and Hart; "Gilbert and Sullivan" he called them; what he called Roosevelt in private is unknown, but the outspoken Cohan interpolated pro-Al Smith lyrics while G. & S. weren't listening. (Cohan was high on Broadway's most-hated list. When donations were sought for his Times Square statue, few professionals contributed—except for Oscar Hammerstein 2nd, who spearheaded the drive.) I'd Rather Be Right was weak in book, music, and satire, but the package sold enough tickets for success. Three fine songs were included: the moderate hit *Have You Met Miss Jones?* and two cuts, neither of which ever found favor: *I'd Rather*

Be Right [1st] is melodic and lovely; and *Ev'rybody Loves You* is the team's second tender lullaby, in a class with the equally obscure *Sleepyhead*.

I MARRIED AN ANGEL

MAY 11, 1938   SHUBERT THEATRE   338 PERFORMANCES

Lyrics by Lorenz Hart
Book by Rodgers and Hart
(Based on a play by John Vaszary)
Choreography by George Balanchine
Directed by Joshua Logan
Produced by Dwight Deere Wiman
With Dennis King, Vera Zorina (Balanchine), Vivienne Segal, and Walter Slezak

Published songs:
At The Roxy Music Hall—issued as professional copy only; subsequently
      published in "Rodgers and Hart: A Musical Anthology"
Did You Ever Get Stung?
How To Win Friends And Influence People
I Married An Angel
I'll Tell The Man In The Street
Spring Is Here—different than song (unpublished) from SPRING IS HERE
      [March 11, 1929]
A Twinkle In Your Eye

Additional song recorded:
Angel Without Wings

The angelic Zorina charmed Broadway in this happy, comic-fantasy hit. Zorina had played the lead in the London production [February 5, 1937] of ON YOUR TOES [April 11, 1936] and won Tamara Geva's part in the 1939 film version (and husband Balanchine, too). I MARRIED AN ANGEL originated as a 1933 Rodgers, Hart, and Hart (Moss) movie project for Jeanette Mac-Donald. Rodgers and Hart (Larry) wrote the stage book themselves, with the score including the lovely, lonely *Spring Is Here*. Operetta stars Dennis King and Vivienne Segal, of Friml's THE THREE MUSKETEERS [March 13, 1928], were reunited; the surprise was Segal, now a first-rate musical comedienne. Rodgers and Hart took note. The Wiman production team included not only Balanchine and Jo Mielziner, but also up-and-coming director Joshua Logan. P.S.: Jeanette MacDonald eventually starred in ANGEL'S 1942 movie version.

THE BOYS FROM SYRACUSE

NOVEMBER 23, 1938   ALVIN THEATRE   235 PERFORMANCES

Lyrics by Lorenz Hart
Book by George Abbott
(Based on *The Comedy of Errors* [play] by William Shakespeare)
Choreography by George Balanchine
Directed and produced by Abbott
With Eddie Albert, Ronald Graham, Teddy Hart, Jimmy Savo, Wynn Murray, and Marcy Westcott

Published songs:
Falling In Love With Love
Oh, Diogenes!
The Shortest Day Of The Year
Sing For Your Supper
This Can't Be Love
Who Are You?—written for 1940 movie version
You Have Cast Your Shadow On The Sea

Additional songs published in vocal score:
Big Brother
Come With Me
Dear Old Syracuse
He And She
I Had Twins
Ladies' Choice [ballet]
Ladies Of The Evening
Twins' Dance [ballet]
What Can You Do With A Man?

One of the finest musical comedies of the pre-Rodgers and Hammerstein era. Hart's brother Teddy bore a striking resemblance to burlesque comic Jimmy Savo; when the collaborators began looking at Shakespeare for source material, this potentially perfect casting made *The Comedy of Errors* (about two sets of twins) the obvious choice. Rodgers and Hart continued their association with George Abbott, Broadway's top farce man: the result was a perfect BOYS FROM SYRACUSE. Abbott's less-than-satisfying experiences with dilettante producers had led to his presenting his own work. He now entered the musical field (and was soon joined by Rodgers). The excellent score included *This Can't Be Love, Sing For Your Supper, Falling In Love With Love,* and *Dear Old Syracuse.*

TOO MANY GIRLS

OCTOBER 18, 1939   IMPERIAL THEATRE   249 PERFORMANCES

Lyrics by Lorenz Hart
Book by George Marion, Jr.
Choreographed by Robert Alton
Directed and produced by George Abbott
With Marcy Westcott, Richard Kollmar, Desi Arnaz, Eddie Bracken, and
Mary Jane Walsh

Published Songs:
All Dressed Up, Spic And Spanish
Give It Back To The Indians
I Didn't Know What Time It Was
I Like To Recognize The Tune
Love Never Went To College
She Could Shake The Maracas
You're Nearer—written for 1940 movie version

*Additional song published in "Rodgers And Hart: A Musical
Anthology":*
'Cause We Got Cake

Additional songs recorded:
Heroes In The Fall
Look Out
My Prince
Pottawatomie
Sweethearts Of The Team
Tempt Me Not
Too Many Girls

Abbott earned a reputation for fast-paced, youthful entertainments like this
college football musical. **TOO MANY GIRLS** was not up to the high Rodgers
and Hart caliber, but enjoyable enough to achieve hit status. Hart's years of
drinking and dissipation had begun to catch up with him, and he was growing
increasingly unreliable; Rodgers occasionally had to fill in during the lyricist's
absences. But Hart could still write intricately, as in *Give It Back To The
Indians* and *I Like To Recognize The Tune*. The score also contained the
gentler *I Didn't Know What Time It Was, My Prince,* and *Love Never Went
To College*. For the movie version, the pair added the tender *You're Nearer.*
Abbott took most of his youthful cast (including Desi Arnaz) to Hollywood,
but lead Marcy Westcott—who introduced the three ballads as well as the
earlier *This Can't Be Love*—was replaced by nonsinging starlet Lucille Ball.

HIGHER AND HIGHER

APRIL 4, 1940   SHUBERT THEATRE   108 PERFORMANCES

Lyrics by Lorenz Hart
Book by Gladys Hurlbut and Joshua Logan
(Based on an idea by Irvin Pincus)
Directed by Logan
Produced by Dwight Deere Wiman
With Jack Haley, Shirley Ross, Marta Eggerth, Leif Erickson, and Lee Dixon

Published songs:
Ev'ry Sunday Afternoon
From Another World
It Never Entered My Mind
Nothing But You

Additional songs published in "Rodgers And Hart: A Musical Anthology":
Disgustingly Rich
It's A Lovely Day For A Murder—different than *What A Lovely Day For A Wedding* from ALLEGRO [October 10, 1947]

Additional songs recorded:
A Barking Baby Never Bites
Blue Monday
How's Your Health?
I'm Afraid
Life! Liberty!—cut
Morning's At Seven
Pretty In The City—cut

HIGHER AND HIGHER was written for "Angel" Vera Zorina; she wisely opted for LOUISIANA PURCHASE [Berlin: May 28, 1940], and played opposite Gaxton and Moore instead of Sharkey, the scene-stealing seal. One of the very loveliest Rodgers and Hart songs was included, *It Never Entered My Mind,* but very little else. The song title *Morning's At Seven* was suggested by Wiman's simultaneous production of Paul Osborn's identically named play.

TWO WEEKS WITH PAY

[JUNE 24, 1940] RIDGEWAY THEATRE <WHITE PLAINS, NEW YORK>;
SUMMER STOCK TRYOUT

Music and lyrics mostly by others
Lyrics to Rodgers song by Lorenz Hart
Sketches by Charles Sherman and others
Created and conceived by Ted Fetter and Richard Lewine
Choreography by Gene Kelly
Directed by Felix Jacoves
Produced by Dorothy and Julien Olney
With Bill Johnson, Marie Nash, Hiram Sherman, and Pat Harrington

Recorded Song:
Now That I Know You—new lyric for *I'd Rather Be Right (Don't Have
    To Know Much)* [1st] (cut) from **I'D RATHER BE RIGHT** [November
    2, 1937]

This revue featured interpolations by several composers, compiled by cousins
of Porter (Fetter) and Rodgers (Lewine), including the unpublished *Will You
Love Me Monday Morning?* (from **LIFE BEGINS AT 8:40** [Arlen: August 27,
1934]) and *Just Another Page From Your Diary* (cut) from **LEAVE IT TO ME**
[Porter: November 9, 1938]). The weak **TWO WEEKS WITH PAY** played two
weeks in stock and folded. Gene Kelly, from the chorus of **LEAVE IT TO ME**,
had already been chosen for the lead in the next Rodgers and Hart musical;
in the meantime, he tried his hand at choreography in White Plains.

PAL JOEY

A Gaily Sophisticated Musical Comedy

DECEMBER 25, 1940   ETHEL BARRYMORE THEATRE
    374 PERFORMANCES

Lyrics by Lorenz Hart
Book by John O'Hara
Choreography by Robert Alton
Directed and produced by George Abbott
With Vivienne Segal, Gene Kelly, June Havoc, and Jack Durant

Published songs:
Bewitched
Do It The Hard Way
Happy Hunting Horn—initial individual publication upon use in 1952
    revival

I Could Write A Book
Plant You Now, Dig You Later
Take Him—initial individual publication upon use in revival
What Is A Man?—initial individual publication upon use in revival
You Mustn't Kick It Around
Zip—initial publication upon use in 1962 movie version

Additional song published in "Intimate Songs":
Den Of Iniquity

Additional songs published in vocal score:
The Flower Garden Of My Heart
A Great Big Town (Chicago)
Pal Joey (What Do I Care For A Dame?)
Pal Joey Ballet [instrumental]
That Terrific Rainbow

Additional song recorded:
I'm Talking To My Pal—cut

Rodgers, Hart, O'Hara, and producer/director/book doctor Abbott brought a new level of realism to the musical theatre with **PAL JOEY**. (Abbott was no doubt influenced by his classic melodrama *Broadway* [September 16, 1926], which had a similar setting and a similar effect.) Reaction was cautious, with a considerable segment of the audience alienated by the heel of a hero. Gene Kelly had been acclaimed for his nonmusical performance in Saroyan's *The Time Of Your Life* [October 25, 1939]; the cynical antiheroine Vera was written for operetta star-turned-comedienne Vivienne Segal. Both roles were well cast, written, and performed. Rodgers and Hart provided a properly cynical score, the one gentler spot being *I Could Write A Book*. Segal was particularly well served with *Bewitched, Take Him, What Is A Man?*, and *Den Of Iniquity*. **PAL JOEY** met with far greater success (and 542 performances) when revived by Jule Styne [January 3, 1952], with Segal making her final Broadway appearance. Kelly, meanwhile, choreographed Abbott and Rodgers' **BEST FOOT FORWARD** [Martin: October 1, 1941] before leaving for Hollywood. He returned only once, to direct Rodgers' **FLOWER DRUM SONG** [December 1, 1958].

BEST FOOT FORWARD
A Modern Musical Comedy

OCTOBER 1, 1941   ETHEL BARRYMORE THEATRE   326 PERFORMANCES

Music and lyrics mostly by Hugh Martin and Ralph Blane (see **Martin: October 1, 1941**)

Book by John Cecil Holm
Choreographed by Gene Kelly
Directed and produced by George Abbott
With Rosemary Lane, Nancy Walker, Gil Stratton, Jr., and June Allyson

Rodgers song recorded:
The Guy Who Brought Me (music by Rodgers, lyric by Rodgers and
    Martin; credited to Martin and Blane)

Larry Hart's deteriorating condition caused Rodgers to be concerned about his
future. Observing George Abbott's success as producer of THE BOYS FROM
SYRACUSE [Novemver 23, 1938], TOO MANY GIRLS [October 18, 1939], and
PAL JOEY [December 25, 1940], Rodgers determined that he, too, might want
to move into production. When Abbott optioned BEST FOOT FORWARD—
composed by Hugh Martin, vocal arranger of SYRACUSE and TOO MANY
GIRLS—Rodgers signed on as coproducer (unbilled). He also contributed this
otherwise forgettable song.

BY JUPITER

JUNE 2, 1942   SHUBERT THEATRE   427 PERFORMANCES

Lyrics by Lorenz Hart
Book by Rodgers and Hart
(Based on *The Warrior's Husband* [play] by Julian F. Thompson)
Directed by Joshua Logan
Produced by Dwight Deere Wiman and Rodgers in association with
Richard Kollmar
With Ray Bolger, Constance Moore, Ronald Graham, and Benay Venuta
NOTE: ALL'S FAIR, pre-Broadway title

Published Songs:
Careless Rhapsody
Ev'rything I've Got
Here's A Hand
Jupiter Forbid
Nobody's Heart (Ride Amazon Ride!)
Wait Till You See Her

Additional songs recorded:
Bottoms Up
The Boy I Left Behind Me
Finale Act One (No, Mother, No)
Fool Meets Fool—cut
For Jupiter And Greece

In The Gateway Of The Temple Of Minerva
Life Was Monotonous—cut
Life With Father
Nothing To Do But Relax—cut
Now That I've Got My Strength

Ray Bolger returned from Hollywood (where he did *not* make the ON YOUR TOES [April 11, 1936] movie—Eddie Albert, of THE BOYS FROM SYRACUSE [November 23, 1938], did) to star in this wartime hit. Bolger's performance was enough to insure success, with Rodgers and Hart providing two very good comedy duets— *Ev'rything I've Got* and *Life With Father*—and the rhapsodic *Careless Rhapsody*. Rodgers here officially began his producing career, although he was also the silent partner of George Abbott on BEST FOOT FORWARD [October 1, 1941] and the forthcoming BEAT THE BAND [October 14, 1942] (written by Johnny Green, conductor of BY JUPITER).

OKLAHOMA!

MARCH 31, 1943   ST. JAMES THEATRE   2,248 PERFORMANCES

Book and lyrics by Oscar Hammerstein 2nd
(Based on *Green Grow the Lilacs* [play] by Lynn Riggs)
Choreography by Agnes de Mille
Directed by Rouben Mamoulian
Produced by The Theatre Guild
With Alfred Drake, Joan Roberts, Celeste Holm, Howard da Silva and Lee Dixon
NOTE: AWAY WE GO!, pre-Broadway title

Published songs:
All 'Er Nothin'—initial publication upon use in 1955 movie version
Boys And Girls Like You And Me—cut
The Farmer And The Cowman—initial publication upon use in movie
    version
I Cain't Say No
Kansas City—initial publication upon use in movie version
Many A New Day
Oh, What A Beautiful Mornin'
Oklahoma!
Out Of My Dreams
People Will Say We're In Love
Pore Jud—initial publication upon use in movie version
The Surrey With The Fringe On Top

Additional songs published in vocal score:
It's A Scandal! It's An Outrage!
Laurey Makes Up Her Mind [ballet]
Lonely Room

Additional song published in "Rodgers and Hammerstein Rediscovered":
When I Go Out Walking With My Baby—cut

The twenty-four-year-old Theatre Guild was foundering, without a hit since the Lunts' *There Shall Be No Night* [April 29, 1940]. Having been surprisingly successful with their first musical (**THE GARRICK GAIETIES [May 17, 1925]**), the Guild asked Rodgers and Hart to adapt a 1931 folk play. The unstable Hart was not interested, so Rodgers convinced the producers to let him collaborate with one of his pre-Hart lyricists: Oscar Hammerstein, author of the landmark **SHOW BOAT [Kern: December 27, 1927]** and nothing but flops since 1932. Rouben Mamoulian directed; he had pioneered the integration of music and dialogue in the 1932 Rodgers and Hart movie "Love Me Tonight" and the Guild's folk opera **PORGY AND BESS [Gershwin: October 10, 1935]**. Choreographer Agnes de Mille had been fired from her first two Broadway jobs; but her successful Ballet Russe 'Rodeo' [October 16, 1942] indicated her suitability for the assignment. With Mamoulian, Rodgers, Hammerstein, and de Mille approaching their creative peaks, the separate elements of **OKLAHOMA!** were highly superior and excellently integrated. **OKLAHOMA!** set new long-run records, not only on Broadway but everywhere.

A CONNECTICUT YANKEE

< Second Version—also see November 3, 1927>

NOVEMBER 17, 1943   MARTIN BECK THEATRE   135 PERFORMANCES

Lyrics by Lorenz Hart
Book by Herbert Fields
(Based on *A Connecticut Yankee in King Arthur's Court* [novel] by Mark Twain)
Directed by John C. Wilson
Produced by Rodgers
With Vivienne Segal, Dick Foran, Julie Warren, Vera-Ellen, and Chester Stratton

New published songs:
Can't You Do A Friend A Favor?
Lunchtime Follies—advertised but not published
Something—advertised but not published (apparently a misprint)

This Is My Night To Howl—advertised but not published; recorded
To Keep My Love Alive
You Always Love The Same Girl

Hoping to get Hart back into working shape, Rodgers produced a new version of the final Rodgers, Hart, and Fields hit. The updated book was not very good, although it did provide another starring role for Vivienne Segal. The new songs included one of Hart's best comedy lyrics, *To Keep My Love Alive*. But the lyricist was beyond saving; during a two-week binge, Larry Hart contracted pneumonia, and died on November 22, 1943.

CAROUSEL

APRIL 19, 1945   MAJESTIC THEATRE   890 PERFORMANCES

Book and lyrics by Oscar Hammerstein 2nd
(Based on *Liliom* [play] by Ferenc Molnar, as adapted by Benjamin F. Glaser)
Choreography by Agnes de Mille
Directed by Rouben Mamoulian
Produced by The Theatre Guild
With John Raitt, Jan Clayton, Murvyn Vye, and Bambi Linn

Published songs:
Carousel Waltz [instrumental]—issued in separate edition
If I Loved You
June Is Bustin' Out All Over
Mister Snow
A Real Nice Clambake
Soliloquy
What's The Use Of Wond'rin'
When The Children Are Asleep
You'll Never Walk Alone

Additional songs published in vocal score:
Ballet [instrumental]
Blow High, Blow Low
Geraniums In The Winder
The Highest Judge Of All
Stonecutters Cut It On The Stone
You're A Queer One, Julie Jordan

As with **PORGY AND BESS** [Gershwin: October 10, 1935] and **OKLAHOMA!** [March 31, 1943], the Theatre Guild had one of their plays musicalized under the supervision of Mamoulian: in this case the 1921 *Liliom* (which was reputedly ghost-translated by Larry Hart). The creators of **Oklahoma!** combined for **Carousel,** one of the very finest American musicals. Rodgers, Hammerstein, and Mamoulian opened with an unconventional, fully staged instrumental prelude (a waltz, naturally); following was a lengthy dramatic scene almost entirely set to music, important segments of which were *You're A Queer One, Julie Jordan, Mister Snow,* and the multi-part *If I Loved You.* Innovations abounded, with an extended, dramatic *Soliloquy* and a highly effective de Mille ballet. **Carousel** was a substantial hit, although the run was far shorter than four other Rodgers and Hammerstein shows. Nevertheless, many agree with Rodgers' personal selection of **Carousel** as his favorite work.

ANNIE GET YOUR GUN

see Berlin

[May 16, 1946]

HAPPY BIRTHDAY

October 31, 1946   Broadhurst Theatre   564 performances

Play by Anita Loos
Lyric by Oscar Hammerstein 2nd
Directed by Joshua Logan
Produced by Rodgers and Hammerstein
With Helen Hayes

Published song:
I Haven't Got A Worry In The World

Rodgers and Hammerstein began their producing partnership with the comedy *I Remember Mama* [October 19, 1944] (see **I Remember Mama** [May 31, 1979]). This was followed by **Annie Get Your Gun** [Berlin: May 16, 1946] and others. After six straight hits came two 1950 failures; thereafter the team only produced their own work.

ALLEGRO

October 10, 1947   Majestic Theatre   315 performances

Book and lyrics by Oscar Hammerstein 2nd
Directed and choreographed by Agnes de Mille
Produced by The Theatre Guild
With John Battles, Roberta Jonay, Annamary Dickey, and Lisa Kirk

Published songs:
Come Home
A Fellow Needs A Girl
The Gentleman Is A Dope
Money Isn't Everything
My Wife—cut; for initial publication see **South Pacific** [April 7, 1949]
So Far
You Are Never Away

Additional songs published in vocal score:
Allegro
A Darn Nice Campus
Finale Act 1 (Wedding Introduction)
I Know It Can Happen Again
It May Be A Good Idea
Joseph Taylor, Jr.
One Foot, Other Foot
Poor Joe
To Have And To Hold
What A Lovely Day For A Wedding—different than *It's A Lovely Day
        For A Murder* from **Higher and Higher** [April 4, 1940]
Wildcats
Wish Them Well
Ya-Ta-Ta

This original folk/morality musical approached pretentiousness, and proved
that even Rodgers and Hammerstein could fail. **Allegro** was inventive, and
contained some good material; it just didn't work. De Mille (with five hit
musicals since **Oklahoma!** [March 31, 1943]) was given her first of three
directing opportunities, each of which failed.

SOUTH PACIFIC

April 7, 1949   Majestic Theatre   1,925 performances

Lyrics by Oscar Hammerstein 2nd
Book by Hammerstein and Joshua Logan
(Based on *Tales of the South Pacific* [stories] by James Michener)
Directed by Logan
Produced by Rodgers and Hammerstein in association with Leland
Hayward and Logan
With Mary Martin, Ezio Pinza, William Tabbert, Myron McCormick,
and Juanita Hall

Published songs:
Bali Ha'i
A Cockeyed Optimist
Dites-Moi
Happy Talk
Honey Bun
I'm Gonna Wash That Man Right Outa My Hair
Loneliness Of Evening—cut, published in separate edition; revised version
    of *Bright Canary Yellow* (cut, unpublished)
My Girl Back Home—cut; initial publication upon reuse in 1958 movie
    version
Some Enchanted Evening
Suddenly Lucky—cut; for initial publication see THE KING AND I [March
    29, 1951]
There Is Nothin' Like A Dame
This Nearly Was Mine
Will You Marry Me?—cut; initial publication upon reuse in PIPE DREAM
    [November 30, 1955]
A Wonderful Guy
You've Got To Be Carefully Taught—initial publication upon use in
    movie version
Younger Than Springtime—new lyric for *My Wife* (cut, unpublished)
    from ALLEGRO [October 10, 1947]

Additional songs published in vocal score:
Bloody Mary
Twin Soliloquies

*Additional Song Published in "Rodgers and Hammerstein
Rediscovered":*
Now Is The Time—cut

Rodgers, Hammerstein, and Logan won the 1950 Pulitzer (for Drama) with
this adaptation of James Michener's 1948 Pulitzer winner (for Fiction). Logan
had directed two Rodgers and Hart hits, as well as ANNIE GET YOUR GUN
[Berlin: May 16, 1946]. Mary Martin, who had turned down the lead in
OKLAHOMA! [March 31, 1943], was well known to the trio for her performance
in the national company [March 10, 1947] of ANNIE GET YOUR GUN. She
was joined by opera star Pinza, who reluctantly agreed to the necessary eight-
performance schedule—but insisted on singing no more than the equivalent
of two operatic appearances a week. Therefore, his SOUTH PACIFIC singing part
consisted of two booming solos and very little else. The score is on a level with
CAROUSEL [April 19, 1945], which is to say near perfection. Hammerstein's
uncompromising statement against racial intolerance—*You've Got To Be*

Carefully Taught—made many 1949 audience members uncomfortable. The song wasn't individually published until a decade later.

THE KING AND I

MARCH 29, 1951   ST. JAMES THEATRE   1,246 PERFORMANCES

Book and lyrics by Oscar Hammerstein 2nd
(Based on *Anna and the King of Siam* [novel] by Margaret Landon)
Choreography by Jerome Robbins
Directed by John van Druten
Produced by Rodgers and Hammerstein
With Gertrude Lawrence, Yul Brynner, Doretta Morrow, and Dorothy Sarnoff

Published songs:
Getting To Know You—new lyric for *Suddenly Lucky* (cut, unpublished)
        from SOUTH PACIFIC [April 7, 1949]
Hello, Young Lovers
I Have Dreamed
I Whistle A Happy Tune
March Of The Siamese Children [instrumental]
My Lord And Master
Shall We Dance?
Something Wonderful
We Kiss In A Shadow

Additional songs published in vocal score:
A Puzzlement
The Royal Bangkok Academy
Shall I Tell You What I Think Of You?
The Small House Of Uncle Thomas [ballet]
The Song Of The King
Western People Funny

The last of the four major Rodgers and Hammerstein musicals. The team had continually tried to explore musical theatre in their methods and choice of material; hereafter they were to be less ambitious (and less successful). Outstanding from the score were *Something Wonderful,* the waltz *Hello, Young Lovers,* and the King's soliloquy *A Puzzlement.* If the score was not up to the calibre of CAROUSEL [April 19, 1945] or SOUTH PACIFIC [April 7, 1949], well—wouldn't that be asking a bit much? Gertrude Lawrence brought the material to Rodgers and Hammerstein, seeing a good role for herself. There was also a role for Alfred Drake, of OKLAHOMA! [March 31, 1943] and KISS ME, KATE [Porter: December 30, 1948]. He wanted too much money, though, so Yul Brynner—whose only credit was opposite Mary Martin in the brief LUTE SONG [February 6, 1946]—became the King and remained so. During the second year of the run, Gertrude Lawrence died of cancer on September 6, 1952.

ME AND JULIET

MAY 28, 1953   MAJESTIC THEATRE   358 PERFORMANCES

Book and lyrics by Oscar Hammerstein 2nd
Choreographed by Robert Alton
Directed by George Abbott
Produced by Rodgers and Hammerstein
With Isabel Bigley, Joan McCracken, Bill Hayes, and Ray Walston

Published songs:
The Big Black Giant
I'm Your Girl
It Feels Good
It's Me
Keep It Gay
Marriage Type Love
No Other Love—revised version of *Beneath The Southern Cross*
    [instrumental] from 1952 TV documentary "Victory at Sea"
That's The Way It Happens
A Very Special Day
We Deserve Each Other

Additional songs published in vocal score:
Intermission Talk (The Theatre Is Dying)
Me, Who Am I?—cut; included (no lyric) in *Opening Of 'Me And Juliet'*
Opening of 'Me And Juliet'

George Abbott's only new work with Rodgers after PAL JOEY [December 25, 1940] was this weak backstage play-within-a-weak-play. Now Rodgers was the producer, and things did not work so well. Rodgers and Hammerstein's two original-book musicals were both problematical, but the popularity of the team helped ME AND JULIET achieve a slightly profitable run. The tango *No Other Love*, the droll *Marriage Type Love*, and *Intermission Talk* stand out from the score.

PIPE DREAM

NOVEMBER 30, 1955   SHUBERT THEATRE   245 PERFORMANCES

Book and lyrics by Oscar Hammerstein 2nd
(Based on *Sweet Thursday* [novel] by John Steinbeck)
Directed by Harold Clurman
Produced by Rodgers and Hammerstein
With Helen Traubel, Bill Johnson, Judy Tyler, and Mike Kellin

Published songs:
All At Once You Love Her
Everybody's Got A Home But Me
The Man I Used To Be
The Next Time It Happens
Suzy Is A Good Thing
Sweet Thursday

Additional songs published in vocal score:
All Kinds Of People
Bum's Opera (You Can't Get Away From A Dumb Tomato)
Dance Fugue [instrumental]
Fauna's Song [1st]—used (no lyric) as *Change Of Scene*— #15
      [instrumental]
Fauna's Song [2nd] (Beguine)
The Happiest House On The Block
How Long?
On A Lopsided Bus
The Party That We're Gonna Have To-Morrow Night
Thinkin'
The Tide Pool
We Are A Gang Of Witches
Will You Marry Me?—originally used (cut) in SOUTH PACIFIC [April 7,
      1949]

Additional song recorded:
Fauna's Song [1st]

What might have made an interesting musical did not work, suffering from
strangely varying points of view. Rodgers provided his most ambitious later
score: tuneful, atmospheric, and full of interesting things. Hammerstein's
close friend Steinbeck had previously written *Burning Bright* [October 19,
1950], Rodgers and Hammerstein's final play production. The protagonist of
"Sweet Thursday" was fashioned after the novelist's friend Henry Fonda.
Fonda's singing audition was weak, though, so the part went to Bill Johnson,

who had played opposite Dolores Gray in the London production [June 7, 1947] of ANNIE GET YOUR GUN [Berlin: May 16, 1946]. Starring as the proprietress of *The Happiest House On The Block* was miscast opera diva Helen Traubel, as in "second-act Traubel."

FLOWER DRUM SONG

DECEMBER 1, 1958   ST. JAMES THEATRE   602 PERFORMANCES

Lyrics by Oscar Hammerstein 2nd
Book by Hammerstein and Joseph Fields
(Based on the novel by C. Y. Lee)
Choreographed by Carol Haney
Directed by Gene Kelly
Produced by Rodgers and Hammerstein in association with Fields
With Miyoshi Umeki, Larry Blyden, Pat Suzuki, and Juanita Hall

Published songs:
Don't Marry Me
Grant Avenue
A Hundred Million Miracles
I Enjoy Being A Girl
Love, Look Away
My Best Love—cut
Sunday
You Are Beautiful—initially published as *She Is Beautiful*

Additional songs published in vocal score:
Chop Suey
Fan Tan Fannie
Gliding Through My Memoree
I Am Going To Like It Here
Like A God
The Other Generation

Rodgers and Hammerstein returned to an Oriental theme, this time the assimilation of Chinese immigrants in San Francisco. Unlike SOUTH PACIFIC [April 7, 1949] and THE KING AND I [March 29, 1951], the conflicts were used for comedic purposes only. The resulting musical was nonexceptional, if moderately successful. Librettist Joseph Fields was number-one son to Lew and brother to Herb, partners-in-crime with Rodgers and Hart on the early Oriental CHEE-CHEE [September 25, 1928]. Gene Kelly (of PAL JOEY [December 25, 1940]) returned from Hollywood to direct. Carol Haney, former Kelly assistant who had been "discovered" in Bob Fosse's THE PAJAMA GAME

[**Adler: May 13, 1954**], choreographed. Her not-so-Chinese husband, Larry Blyden, took over the leading role from Larry Storch during the tryout.

THE SOUND OF MUSIC

NOVEMBER 16, 1959   LUNT-FONTANNE THEATRE   1,433
PERFORMANCES

Lyrics by Oscar Hammerstein 2nd
Book by Howard Lindsay and Russel Crouse
(Based on *The Trapp Family Singers* [biography] by Maria Augusta Trapp)
Choreographed by Joe Layton
Directed by Vincent J. Donehue
Produced by Leland Hayward, Richard Halliday, Rodgers and
Hammerstein
With Mary Martin (Halliday), Theodore Bikel, and Patricia Neway

Published songs:
Climb Ev'ry Mountain
Do-Re-Mi
Edelweiss
I Have Confidence (lyric by Rodgers)—written for 1965 movie version
The Lonely Goatherd
Maria
My Favorite Things
An Ordinary Couple
Sixteen Going On Seventeen
So Long, Farewell—initial individual publication upon use in movie
      version
Something Good (lyric by Rodgers)—written for movie version
The Sound Of Music

Additional songs published in vocal score:
Alleluia
How Can Love Survive
No Way To Stop It
Preludium

A huge hit and ultimately one of Hollywood's all-time greatest successes, despite initial critical carping. Serious subjects which Rodgers and Hammerstein had sensitively handled in the past came out treacly in Lindsay and Crouse's book; Hammerstein was suffering from cancer at the time, and died on August 23, 1960. The high spot of the final Rodgers and Hammerstein score: *My Favorite Things.*

NO STRINGS

MARCH 15, 1962   54TH STREET THEATRE   580 PERFORMANCES

Lyrics by Rodgers
Book by Samuel Taylor
Directed and choreographed by Joe Layton
Produced by Rodgers
With Diahann Carroll, Richard Kiley, Bernice Massi, and Polly Rowles

Published songs:
Be My Host
Eager Beaver
La-La-La
Loads of Love
Look No Further
Love Makes The World Go
Maine
The Man Who Has Everything
No Strings
Nobody Told Me
The Sweetest Sounds
You Don't Tell Me

Additional songs published in vocal score:
How Sad
An Orthodox Fool

Working as his own lyricist, Rodgers again tried something innovative: using on-stage instrumentalists to counterpoint the moods and emotions of the characters. Unfortunately, there was very little plot; just a basic situation, an interesting score, and the dazzling Diahann Carroll. The experiment was successful enough, and NO STRINGS enjoyed a profitable run.

DO I HEAR A WALTZ?

MARCH 18, 1965   46TH STREET THEATRE   220 PERFORMANCES

Lyrics by Stephen Sondheim
Book by Arthur Laurents
(Based on *The Time of the Cuckoo* [play] by Laurents)
Directed by John Dexter
Produced by Rodgers
With Elizabeth Allen, Sergio Franchi, Carol Bruce, and Madeleine Sherwood

Published songs:
Do I Hear A Waltz?
Here We Are Again
Moon In My Window
Perhaps—cut
Someone Like You
Stay
Take The Moment
Thank You So Much
Two By Two (By Two) [1st]—cut; different than song from **Two By Two**
      [November 10, 1970]

Additional songs published in vocal score:
Bargaining
No Understand
Perfectly Lovely Couple
Someone Woke Up
Thinking
This Week Americans
We're Gonna Be All Right
What Do We Do? We Fly!

Additional song recorded:
Everybody Loves Leona

Rodgers and his co-workers—Hammerstein-protégé Sondheim, accomplished librettist Laurents, and English director John Dexter—got along poisonously; the resulting musical romance was misconceived, miscast, misromantic, and mistaken. Rodgers felt that the trio had ganged up against him, and accused them of making changes without his knowledge. (He was, after all, the producer.) Despite all this, much of the Rodgers and Sondheim work—disowned by both sides—is really quite charming. *Moon In My Window, Here We Are Again, Take The Moment,* and *Someone Woke Up* all accomplish what they set out to with charm and grace; and in the title song Rodgers came up with his final sweeping waltz.

TWO BY TWO

November 10, 1970   Imperial Theatre   343 performances

Lyrics by Martin Charnin
Book by Peter Stone
(Based on *The Flowering Peach* [play] by Clifford Odets)
Directed and choreographed by Joe Layton

Produced with Rodgers
With Danny Kaye, Harry Goz, and Joan Copeland

Published songs:
I Do Not Know A Day I Did Not Love You
An Old Man
Something Doesn't Happen
Something, Somewhere
Two By Two [2nd]—different than song (cut) from **Do I Hear A Waltz**
    [March 18, 1965]

Additional songs published in vocal score:
As Far As I'm Concerned
The Covenant
The Gitka's Song [instrumental]
The Golden Ram
Hey, Girlie
Ninety Again
Poppa Knows Best
Put Him Away
When It Dries
Why Me?
You
You Have Got To Have A Rudder On The Ark

In 1970, the sixty-eight-year-old Rodgers suffered a heart attack. He went on to write three more musicals, each without merit. **Two By Two** was an unhappy show and an unhappy experience. There was virtually nothing of interest, including Danny Kaye. The star did what he could to force a run, resulting in a slight profit for producer Rodgers. The best that can be said was that there was one pretty song, *I Do Not Know A Day I Did Not Love You.*

REX

April 25, 1976   Lunt-Fontanne Theatre   48 performances

Lyrics by Sheldon Harnick
Book by Sherman Yellen
Directed by Edwin Sherin
Produced by Richard Adler in association with Roger Berlind and Edward R. Downe
With Nicol Williamson, Penny Fuller, and Tom Aldredge

Published songs:
As Once I Loved You
Away From You

Additional songs recorded:
At The Field Of Cloth Of Gold
The Chase
Christmas At Hampton Court
Elizabeth
From Afar
In Time
No Song More Pleasing
So Much You Loved Me
Te Deum
The Wee Golden Warrior
Where Is My Son?
Why?

REX was poorly conceived and badly produced. Michael Bennett was passed over early in the game (when he was refused a percentage of the profits, he went off to develop **A CHORUS LINE** [**April 15, 1975**] instead). The directorial reins were entrusted to Edwin Sherin, whose musical experience consisted of being fired from **SEESAW** [**Coleman: March 18, 1973**] in Detroit (and being replaced by Michael Bennett). On **REX** it was Harold Prince (who had produced Adler's two hits as composer) who was brought to Boston. But much too late.

I REMEMBER MAMA

MAY 31, 1979   MAJESTIC THEATRE   108 PERFORMANCES

Lyrics mostly by Martin Charnin
Book by Thomas Meehan
(Based on the play by John van Druten and the stories by Kathryn Forbes)
Directed by Cy Feuer
Produced by Alexander H. Cohen and Hildy Parks
With Liv Ullmann, George Hearn, and George S. Irving

Published songs:
Ev'ry Day (Comes Something Beautiful)
It Is Not The End Of The World
Time
You Could Not Please Me More

Additional songs recorded:
Easy Come, Easy Go
I Remember Mama
I Write, You Read (Fair Trade)
It's Going To Be Good To Be Gone
Lars, Lars
A Little Bit More (lyric by Jessel)
Lullaby (The Hardangerfjord)
Mama Always Makes It Better
Most Disagreeable Man
Uncle Chris (lyric by Jessel)
When?
A Writer Writes At Night

Alexander H. Cohen assembled a typical Alexander H. Cohen package: star composer, star actress, and the lyricist, librettist, director, designer, etc. from Broadway's most recent smash hit (the one about the little orphan girl and her dog, Sandy). But Rodgers was seventy-six and in ill health; Liv Ullmann was a musical novice who barely spoke (let alone sang) the language; and the musical-comedy track records of the Messrs. Charnin and Cohen were less than inspiring. Van Druten's *I Remember Mama* had been a wartime hit (produced by Rodgers and Hammerstein) and a popular Fifties television series. Cohen fired Charnin during the tryout and brought in producer Cy Feuer to direct, along with lyricist Raymond Jessel (of Cohen's BAKER STREET [Bock: February 16, 1965]). I REMEMBER MAMA was Richard Rodgers' final work. He died as the decade ended, on December 30, 1979 in New York.

It is impossible to go through the complete work of Richard Rodgers without being overwhelmed by the man's talent. So many wonderful songs! For twenty-five years Rodgers was among the leaders of the field; no one (other than Jerome Kern) was as responsible for the development of the American musical theatre. During a span of less than a decade, Rodgers wrote five innovative, high-quality musicals. ON YOUR TOES [April 11, 1936] introduced real ballet to musical comedy—and used it as a plot element. THE BOYS FROM SYRACUSE [November 23, 1938] was farce musical comedy par excellence. PAL JOEY [December 25, 1940] first brought realistic (if disreputable) characters and subjects onto the musical stage. OKLAHOMA! [March 31, 1943] combined all theatrical elements into a cohesive whole. And all culminated in the stunning CAROUSEL [April 19, 1945], serious, dramatic musical theatre. Consider that all five scores are highly effective almost a half century later; during these nine years Rodgers also wrote *five additional* musical successes, including the hit-filled BABES IN ARMS [April 14, 1937]; and he wrote many of his best songs in the years *before* and *after* this golden period (including the SOUTH PACIFIC [April 7, 1949] score). A close look at the theatre music of Richard Rodgers shows how very important and enduring his accomplishments, innovations, and songs were.

Cole Porter

BORN: June 9, 1891   Peru, Indiana
DIED: October 15, 1964   Santa Monica, California

Cole Porter's father, a druggist, played a very small part in his life: his maternal grandfather, however, was industrial magnate J. O. Cole. While Cole wanted the boy raised to take over his business, Porter's mother cultivated his love of music; she even had an early composition, *Bobolink Waltz*, published in 1902. By his fourteenth birthday Porter was away at Eastern schools, and in 1913 he graduated from Yale (where he'd majored in writing football songs—*Bulldog* is still sung—and varsity shows). His first Tin Pan Alley song was the 1910 *Bridget*. Porter forsook Indiana for high society. A New York patroness was theatrical agent Elisabeth Marbury, creator of the innovative "Princess Theatre Show" series (see NOBODY HOME [Kern: April 20, 1915]). Latching on to the entertaining sophisticate, she went about getting him a Broadway hearing.

[all music and lyrics by Cole Porter unless indicated]

HANDS UP
Musico-Comico-Filmo-Melo-Drama

JULY 22, 1915   44TH STREET THEATRE   52 PERFORMANCES

Music mostly by E. Ray Goetz and Sigmund Romberg
Book and lyrics mostly by Goetz
Directed by J. H. Benrimo
Produced by the Messrs. Shubert

Published song:
Esmeralda

MISS INFORMATION

A Little Play With A Little Music

OCTOBER 5, 1915   GEORGE M. COHAN THEATRE   47 PERFORMANCES

Music mostly by Jerome **Kern**
Lyrics mostly by Elsie Janis
Book by Paul Dickey and Charles W. Goddard
Directed by Robert Milton
Produced by Charles Dillingham
With Elsie Janis and Irene Bordoni

Published song:
Two Big Eyes (lyric by John Golden)

Irene Bordoni was to star in Porter's first Broadway hit, PARIS [October 8, 1928]—thirteen years later!

SEE AMERICA FIRST

A Patriotic Comic Opera

MARCH 28, 1916   MAXINE ELLIOTT THEATRE   15 PERFORMANCES

Book, music and lyrics by T. Lawrason Riggs and Cole Porter
Directed by J. H. Benrimo
Produced by The Marbury-Comstock Company
With Dorothie Bigelow, John H. Goldsworthy, Leonard Joy, and Clifton Webb

Published Porter/Riggs songs:
Buy Her A Box At The Opera
Ever And Ever Yours
I've A Shooting Box In Scotland
I've Got An Awful Lot To Learn
The Language Of Flowers
Lima
Oh, Bright Fair Dream—cut
Pity Me Please—cut
Prithee, Come Crusading
See America First
Slow Sinks The Sun—cut
Something's Got To Be Done
When I Used To Lead The Ballet

Porter's first complete Broadway score was for this vanity production produced by Marbury and her "Princess Theatre Show" partner. Following a highly successful society preview, SEE AMERICA FIRST—made up mostly of material written for fraternity musicals—was viewed as a mediocre college show (with surprisingly adept lyrics) and quickly closed. Of interest in the cast was dancer Clifton Webb, who was to be a feature of Broadway's sophisticated Thirties revues before leaving for Hollywood. For the record, Yale man Riggs was Porter's roommate during the latter's brief visit to Harvard Law School (by order of grandfather Cole, who controlled the millions). Following SEE AMER-ICA FIRST, Riggs became a priest.

VERY GOOD EDDIE

MAY 18, 1918   PALACE THEATRE < LONDON >   46 PERFORMANCES

Music mostly by Jerome **Kern** (see [**December 23, 1915**])
Lyrics mostly by Schuyler Greene and Herbert Reynolds
Book by Philip Bartholomae and Guy Bolton
(Based on *Over Night* [play] by Bartholomae)
Directed by Guy Bragdon
Produced by Alfred Butt and André Charlot
With Nelson Keys

Published song:
Alone With You (by Porter and Melville Gideon)

Porter escaped the World War I draft by going to his beloved France, where he was involved with a society-sponsored food distribution program. He spent the war attending and throwing parties, not in the French Foreign Legion (as reported in later years). Songwriting continued as a hobby, with trips across the Channel to interpolate in London musicals. With the exception of a few attempts at revues, Porter spent the next ten years as a very talented dilettante.

TELLING THE TALE

[CIRCA OCTOBER 1918]   AMBASSADOR'S THEATRE < LONDON >

Book by Sydney Blow and Douglas Hoare
Produced by Gerald Kirby and John Wyndham
With Birdie Courtenay and Kirby

Published song:
Altogether Too Fond Of You (by Melville Gideon, James Heard, and
    Porter)—also used (cut) in BUDDIES [**October 27, 1919**]

HITCHY-KOO 1919

Third Edition

OCTOBER 6, 1919   LIBERTY THEATRE   56 PERFORMANCES

Book by George V. Hobart
Directed by Julian Alfred
Produced by Raymond Hitchcock
With Hitchcock and Joe Cook

Published songs:
Another Sentimental Song—cut
Bring Me Back My Butterfly
I Introduced
In Hitchy's Garden
I've Got Somebody Waiting
My Cozy Little Corner In The Ritz
Old Fashioned Garden
Peter Piper/The Sea Is Calling
That Black And White Baby Of Mine—cut
When I Had A Uniform On

The war over, Porter returned to America. His already growing reputation as a clever sophisticate resulted in this commission. Hitchcock, a fairly successful comic, began his annual revue series in 1917. Although parts of HITCHY-KOO's score displayed Porter's sophisticated lyricism, it was the simple, sentimental *Old Fashioned Garden* that became his first song hit.

BUDDIES

Comedy Of Quaint Brittany

OCTOBER 27, 1919   SELWYN THEATRE   259 PERFORMANCES

Music and lyrics mostly by B. C. Hilliam
Book by George V. Hobart
Produced by Selwyn and Co.
With Donald Brian, Peggy Wood, and Roland Young

Published songs:
Altogether Too Fond Of You (by Melville Gideon, James Heard and
    Porter)—cut before opening; originally used in TELLING THE TALE
    [Circa October 1918]
I Never Realized (music by Gideon, lyric by Porter; issued as by
    Gideon)—cut before opening; also used in THE ECLIPSE [November
    12, 1919]

Washington Square (music by Gideon, lyric by Porter; issued as by
   Gideon)—cut before opening; also see AS YOU WERE [January 27,
   1920] and THE ECLIPSE

THE ECLIPSE

NOVEMBER 12, 1919   GARRICK THEATRE <LONDON>
   117 PERFORMANCES

Music by Herman Darewski and Melville Gideon
Lyrics mostly by Adrian Ross
Book by Fred Thompson and E. Phillips Oppenheim
Produced by Charles B. Cochran
With Nancy Gibbs and F. Pope Stamper

Published songs:
I Never Realized (music by Gideon, lyric by Porter; issued as lyric by
   Adrian Ross)—originally used (cut) in BUDDIES [October 27, 1919]
In Chelsea Somewhere (music by Gideon, lyric by "Col. E. Porter" and
   James Heard)—revised lyric for *Washington Square* (cut) from
   BUDDIES

AS YOU WERE

A Fantastic Revue

JANUARY 27, 1920   CENTRAL THEATRE   143 PERFORMANCES

Music mostly by Herman Darewski
Lyrics mostly by Arthur Wimperis and E. Ray Goetz
Book by Glen MacDonough
(Based on *Plus Ça Change* [revue] by Rip)
Produced by Goetz
With Sam Bernard and Irene Bordoni (Goetz)

Published song:
Washington Square (music by Melville Gideon, lyric by Porter and
   Goetz)—revised lyric for song originally used (cut) in BUDDIES
   [October 27, 1919]; also see THE ECLIPSE [November 12, 1919]

A NIGHT OUT

SEPTEMBER 18, 1920   WINTER GARDEN THEATRE <LONDON>
   311 PERFORMANCES

Music mostly by Willie Redstone (see YOUMANS [September 7, 1925])
Porter lyrics by Clifford Grey

Book by George Grossmith and Arthur Miller
(Based on a farce by Georges Feydeau and Maurice Desvallières)
Directed by Tom Reynolds
Produced by Grossmith and Edward Laurillard
With Leslie Henson and Lily St. John

Published Porter/Grey songs:
Finale (It's A Sad Day At This Hotel)
Look Around
Our Hotel
Why Didn't We Meet Before?

MAYFAIR AND MONTMARTRE

MARCH 9, 1922   NEW OXFORD THEATRE <LONDON>
77 PERFORMANCES

Music mostly by others
Book by John Hastings Turner
Directed and produced by Charles B. Cochran
With Alice Delysia, Evelyn Laye, and Joyce Barbour

Published songs:
The Blue Boy Blues
Cocktail Time
Olga (Come Back To The Volga)

PHI-PHI

AUGUST 16, 1922   PAVILION THEATRE <LONDON>
132 PERFORMANCES

Music mostly by Christiné
Lyrics mostly by Clifford Grey
Book by Fred Thompson and Grey
(From the French by Willemetz and Sollar)
Produced by Charles B. Cochran
With Clifton Webb

Published song:
The Ragtime Pipes of Pan

HITCHY-KOO OF 1922

Fifth Edition

[OCTOBER 10, 1922]   SHUBERT THEATRE < PHILADELPHIA,
   PENNSYLVANIA > ; CLOSED DURING PRE-BROADWAY TRYOUT

Book by Harold Atteridge
Directed by J. C. Huffman
Produced by Messrs. J. J. and Lee Shubert
With Raymond Hitchcock

Published songs:
The American Punch
The Bandit Band
The Harbor Deep Down In My Heart
Love Letter Words
When My Caravan Comes Home

Porter wrote his third complete score for this out-of-town failure. On October 25, 1923, Porter's ballet "Within The Quota"—his only attempt at serious music—premiered in Paris.

GREENWICH VILLAGE FOLLIES

Sixth Annual Production

SEPTEMBER 16, 1924   SHUBERT THEATRE   127 PERFORMANCES

Book by Lew Fields, Irving Caesar, and others
Directed by John Murray Anderson
Produced by The Bohemians, Inc.
With the Dolly Sisters

Published songs:
Brittany
I'm In Love Again—added after opening; also used in UP WITH THE
   LARK [August 25, 1927]
Make Every Day A Holiday
My Long Ago Girl
Two Little Babes In The Wood—initial publication upon reuse in PARIS
   [October 8, 1928]
Wait For The Moon

This series had begun life as an intimate, bohemian, off-Broadway revue in 1919; the Shuberts bought the title in 1921 and undressed it. *I'm In Love Again* and *Two Little Babes In The Wood* both became hits—but not until Porter's first wave of popularity in 1928.

UP WITH THE LARK

August 25, 1927   Adelphi Theatre < London >

Music mostly by Philip Braham
Lyrics mostly by Douglas Furber
Book by Furber and Hartley Carrick
(Based on *Le Zebre* [play] by Armont and Nancy)
Directed by George Grossmith
Produced by Westland Productions (in association with Martin Henry)
With Allen Kearns, Leslie Sarony, and Charles King

Published song:
I'm In Love Again—originally used in Greenwich Village Follies
    (Sixth) [September 16, 1924]

LA REVUE DES AMBASSADEURS

Nightclub Revue

May 10, 1928   Les Ambassadeurs < Paris >

Music and lyrics mostly by Porter
Directed by Bobby Connolly
Produced by Edmond Sayag
With Morton Downey, Evelyn Hoey, Fred Waring, and Frances
Gershwin

Published songs:
Almiro
Hans
Military Maids
Looking at You—cut; initial publication upon reuse in Wake Up and
    Dream [March 27, 1929]
An Old Fashioned Girl
You And Me

Additional songs published in vocal selection:
Alpine Rose
Baby, Let's Dance
Blue Hours
Fish
Fountain Of Youth
In A Moorish Garden
The Lost Liberty Blues
Pilot Me

This nightclub show was presented for expatriate Americans in Paris. Included in the cast was the Gershwins' talented sister, who sang a medley of Gershwin tunes.

PARIS

OCTOBER 8, 1928   MUSIC BOX THEATRE   195 PERFORMANCES

Book by Martin Brown
Directed by W. H. Gilmore
Produced by Gilbert Miller in association with E. Ray Goetz
With Irene Bordoni (Goetz), Louise Closser Hale, and Arthur Margetson

Published songs:
Dizzy Baby—cut; advertised but not published; initial recording upon use
    in London revue COLE [July 2, 1974]
Don't Look At Me That Way!—see LET'S FACE IT [October 29, 1941]
The Heaven Hop
Let's Do It—also used in WAKE UP AND DREAM (London) [March 27,
    1929]
Let's Misbehave—cut
Quelque Chose—cut
Two Little Babes In The Wood—originally used in GREENWICH VILLAGE
    FOLLIES (Sixth) [September 19, 1924]
Vivienne
Which—cut; also used in WAKE UP AND DREAM

Porter's first hit, featuring the saucy Bordoni. The risqué *Let's Do It* was a quick hit, placing Porter in league with Lorenz Hart as Broadway's cleverest and most sophisticated lyricists.

WAKE UP AND DREAM

MARCH 27, 1929   PAVILION THEATRE < LONDON >
    263 PERFORMANCES

DECEMBER 30, 1929   SELWYN THEATRE < NEW YORK >
    136 PERFORMANCES

Music and lyrics mostly by Porter (see **Schwartz** [December 30, 1929])
Book by John Hastings Turner
Choreography (London) by George Balanchine
Directed by Frank Collins
LONDON: Produced by Charles B. Cochran

With Jessie Matthews and Sonny Hale
NEW YORK: Produced by Arch Selwyn in association with Cochran
With Jessie Matthews and Jack Buchanan

Published songs:
Agua Sincopada (Tango) [instrumental]
The Banjo (That Man Joe Plays)
I Dream Of A Girl In A Shawl—advertised but not published; included
    (no lyric) in piano selection
I Loved Him But He Didn't Love Me
I Want To Be Raided By You—advertised but not published
Gigolo
Let's Do It—originally used in PARIS [October 8, 1928]
Looking At You—originally used (cut/unpublished) in LA REVUE DES
    AMBASSADEURS [May 10, 1928]
Wake Up And Dream
What Is This Thing Called Love?
Which—originally used (cut) in PARIS [October 8, 1928]

Additional song published in "The Unpublished Cole Porter":
After All, I'm Only A Schoolgirl

Additional song published (no lyric) in piano selection:
I've Got A Crush On You

Additional songs recorded:
I Want To Be Raided By You
Pills

[NOTE: not all songs used in New York edition]
Cochran had been successful in hiring the Americans Rodgers and Hart for his 1927 LONDON PAVILION REVUE (ONE DAM THING AFTER ANOTHER) [Rodgers: May 20, 1927]; now he tried Porter, with similarly successful results. The New York production of WAKE UP AND DREAM did not do quite as well, hampered by the stock market crash and competition from Porter's just-opened hit FIFTY MILLION FRENCHMEN [November 27, 1929].

FIFTY MILLION FRENCHMEN

A Musical Comedy Tour of Paris

NOVEMBER 27, 1929   LYRIC THEATRE   254 PERFORMANCES

Book by Herbert Fields
Directed by Monty Woolley
Produced by E. Ray Goetz
With William Gaxton, Genevieve Tobin, and Helen Broderick

Published songs:
Find Me A Primitive Man
The Happy Heaven Of Harlem
I Worship You—cut
I'm In Love
I'm Unlucky At Gambling
Let's Step Out—added after opening
Paree, What Did You Do To Me?
Please Don't Make Me Be Good—cut
The Queen Of Terre Haute—cut
You Do Something To Me
You Don't Know Paree
You've Got That Thing

Additional songs published in "The Unpublished Cole Porter":
The Tale Of The Oyster—cut
Why Don't We Try Staying Home?—cut

Additional song recorded:
The Boy Friend Back Home—cut
Where Would You Get Your Coat?

Herbert Fields left his long-time collaborators following the CHEE-CHEE [Rodgers: September 25, 1928] debacle, joining Porter in the first of their seven consecutive hits. Gaxton, whose first important role had been as Fields' CONNECTICUT YANKEE (First Version) [Rodgers: November 3, 1927] now became a star. Porter wrote two more hits for Gaxton and future partner Victor Moore. Directing was Porter's close friend and classmate (turned Yale drama professor) Woolley, making his professional debut; he eventually turned to acting. Porter added to his hit songs with *You Do Something To Me* and *You've Got That Thing*.

THE NEW YORKERS

< Second Version >

DECEMBER 8, 1930   BROADWAY THEATRE   168 PERFORMANCES

Music and lyrics mostly by Porter
Book by Herbert Fields
(Based on a story by Peter Arno and E. Ray Goetz)
Directed by Monty Woolley
Produced by Goetz
With Hope Williams, Ann Pennington, Charles King, and Jimmy
Durante

Published songs:
But He Never Said He Loved Me—cut; initial publication upon reuse in
    NYMPH ERRANT [October 6, 1933] retitled *The Physician*
The Great Indoors
I Happen To Like New York—added after opening
I'm Getting Myself Ready For You
Just One Of Those Things [1st]—cut; different than hit song from
    JUBILEE [October 12, 1935]
Let's Fly Away
Love For Sale
Take Me Back To Manhattan
Where Have You Been?

Another hit for Porter, though not as successful as FIFTY MILLION FRENCH-
MEN [November 27, 1929]. Porter continued to earn a reputation for sophistication: lyrics like *Love For Sale* outraged some (but pleased many more).

GAY DIVORCE

NOVEMBER 29, 1932   ETHEL BARRYMORE THEATRE   248
    PERFORMANCES

Book by Dwight Taylor
Adapted by Kenneth Webb and Samuel Hoffenstein
(Based on an unproduced play by J. Hartley Manners)
Directed by Howard Lindsay
Produced by Dwight Deere Wiman and Tom Weatherly
With Fred Astaire, Claire Luce, and Luella Gear

Published songs:
After You
How's Your Romance

I've Got You On My Mind
Mister and Missus Fitch—initial publication as 1954 nonshow song
Night And Day
You're In Love

Additional songs published (no lyrics) in piano selections (also recorded):
I Love You Only—written for London production [November 2, 1933]
Never Say No
Salt Air

Additional songs recorded:
Fate—cut
I Still Love The Red, White And Blue
A Weekend Affair—cut
Why Marry Them?

Could Fred Astaire make it on his own following Adele's retirement after THE BAND WAGON [Schwartz: June 3, 1931]? He did moderately well in GAY DIVORCE, which was kept alive by the popularity of *Night And Day.* The 1934 movie version "Gay Divorcee"—which threw out Porter's entire score (except *Night And Day*)—teamed Astaire with Ginger Rogers, and that was the end of Astaire and Broadway. Hollywood also cut the score for the 1931 version of FIFTY MILLION FRENCHMEN [November 27, 1928] and the 1937 ROSALIE [Gershwin: January 10, 1928]—for which Porter wrote the replacement. Librettist Taylor, later to collaborate with Porter on OUT OF THIS WORLD [December 21, 1950], was Manners' stepson (and son of actress Laurette).

NYMPH ERRANT

OCTOBER 6, 1933   ADELPHI THEATRE < LONDON >   154
PERFORMANCES

Book and direction by Romney Brent
(Based on the novel by James Laver)
Produced by Charles B. Cochran
With Gertrude Lawrence, Elisabeth Welch, and David Burns

Published songs:
Experiment
How Could We Be Wrong?
I Look At You—cut; initial publication as 1934 nonshow song with new
     lyric, retitled *You're Too Far Away*
It's Bad For Me
Nymph Errant

The Physician—originally used (cut/unpublished) in THE NEW YORKERS
    [December 8, 1930]
Solomon
When Love Comes Your Way—cut; also used in JUBILEE [October 12,
    1935]

Additional songs published (no lyrics) in piano selection (also recorded):
Back To Nature With You
The Castle
The Cocotte
Georgia Sand
Neauville-Sur-Mer

Additional songs recorded:
Cazanova
My Louisa—cut
Plumbing
Si Vous Aimez Les Poitrines
Sweet Nudity—cut
They're Always Entertaining

A suggestive romp about a staid British nymphomaniac, which thrilled Continental society but left the staid British lukewarm.

HI DIDDLE DIDDLE

OCTOBER 3, 1934   COMEDY THEATRE < LONDON >   198
    PERFORMANCES

Play by William Walker and Robert Nesbitt
Produced by André Charlot
With Douglas Byng

Published song:
Miss Otis Regrets

Miss Otis Regrets is one of Porter's Twenties party songs, which was eventually published and achieved considerable popularity.

ANYTHING GOES

NOVEMBER 21, 1934   ALVIN THEATRE   420 PERFORMANCES

Book by Guy Bolton and P. G. Wodehouse
Revised by Howard Lindsay and Russel Crouse
Directed by Howard Lindsay

Produced by Vinton Freedley
With William Gaxton, Ethel Merman, Victor Moore, and Bettina Hall

Published songs:
All Through The Night
Anything Goes
Blow, Gabriel, Blow
Buddie, Beware—cut after opening
The Gypsy In Me
I Get A Kick Out Of You
There'll Always Be A Lady Fair—initial publication upon reuse in 1936
     movie version
Waltz Down The Aisle—cut; see KISS ME, KATE [December 30, 1948]
You're The Top

Additional songs published in vocal score:
Be Like The Bluebird
Bon Voyage
Public Enemy Number One (Opening Act Two)
Where Are The Men?

Additional song published in "Music and Lyrics by Cole Porter, Vol. 2":
Kate The Great—cut

Additional songs recorded:
There's No Cure Like Travel
What A Joy To Be Young

Unquestionably Porter's second best show (after KISS ME, KATE [December 30, 1948]). Freedley, heretofore associated with the Gershwins, was just recovering from his insolvency (see PARDON MY ENGLISH [Gershwin: January 20, 1933]). Gaxton and Moore had worked together in OF THEE I SING [Gershwin: December 25, 1931] and its sequel LET 'EM EAT CAKE [Gershwin: October 21, 1933]; now they established themselves as an ongoing partnership. Ethel Merman, discovered in the final Aarons and Freedley hit GIRL CRAZY [Gershwin: October 14, 1930], took Broadway by storm with her renditions of several sparkling Porter gems. ANYTHING GOES played the Alvin, the house that Aarons, Freedley, and the Gershwins' hits built—except Freedley had to rent it, having lost ownership. The Bolton-Wodehouse libretto about the comic aftermath of a shipwreck was hastily discarded when the Morro Castle sank off the New Jersey coast (with 134 dead). The authors being unavailable for revisions, it fell to director Lindsay (from GAY DIVORCE [November 29, 1932]) to fashion a new book around the existing songs. Theatre Guild press agent Crouse was brought in to help, forming yet another highly successful partnership. Wodehouse, though, retired from the musical theatre. A new libretto was prepared by John Weidman and Timothy (son of Russel) Crouse for the Lincoln Center Theater's popular revival [October 19, 1987; 804 performances].

JUBILEE

OCTOBER 12, 1935   IMPERIAL THEATRE   169 PERFORMANCES

Book by Moss Hart
Book directed by Monty Woolley
Directed by Hassard Short
Produced by Sam H. Harris and Max Gordon
With Mary Boland, Melville Cooper, and June Knight

Published songs:
Begin The Beguine
Just One Of Those Things [2nd]—the hit; different than song from THE
    NEW YORKERS [December 8, 1930]
The Kling-Kling Bird On The Divi-Divi Tree
Me And Marie
A Picture Of Me Without You
When Love Comes Your Way—originally used (cut) in NYMPH ERRANT
    [October 6, 1933]
Why Shouldn't I?

Additional songs recorded:
Entrance of Eric
Ev'rybod-ee Who's Anybod-ee
My Loulou
My Most Intimate Friend
Sunday Morning, Breakfast Time
What A Nice Municipal Park
When Me, Mowgli, Love

Porter rarely needed an excuse to travel; in this case he invited Hart and Woolley along on a five-month world cruise, during which they put together this lavish musical. By the time *Begin The Beguine* and *Just One Of Those Things* caught on, JUBILEE was gone—lasting no longer than the cruise and costing a whole lot more.

RED, HOT AND BLUE!

OCTOBER 29, 1936   ALVIN THEATRE   183 PERFORMANCES

Book by Howard Lindsay and Russel Crouse
Directed by Lindsay
Produced by Vinton Freedley
With Ethel Merman, Jimmy Durante, and Bob Hope

Published songs:
Down In The Depths (On The Ninetieth Floor)
Goodbye, Little Dream, Goodbye—cut; see O MISTRESS MINE [December
    3, 1936]
It's De-Lovely
A Little Skipper From Heaven Above
Ours
The Ozarks Are Calling Me Home
Red, Hot And Blue
Ridin' High
You're A Bad Influence On Me
You've Got Something

Additional songs published in "special edition" vocal selection:
Perennial Debutantes
What A Great Pair We'll Be

Additional song published in "The Unpublished Cole Porter":
When Your Troubles Have Started—cut

Additional songs recorded:
Bertie and Gertie—cut
Who But You?—cut

An uneven successor to ANYTHING GOES [November 20, 1934] which had
some success—not surprisingly, considering the star comedians. William Gaxton withdrew when he learned Merman had been promised equal billing.
Durante, in the Victor Moore role, presented billing problems himself; the
two finally settled on a diagonal criss-cross design. (Merman got first billing
when she met Durante again in STARS IN YOUR EYES [Schwartz: February
9, 1939].) Bob Hope, fresh from Fanny Brice and the ZIEGFELD FOLLIES OF
1936 [Duke: January 30, 1936], didn't bother with billing: he had a line of
his own below the others, undiagonal and considerably more readable. Hope
followed RED, HOT AND BLUE! with Hollywood, never to return. Porter's work
was far below his ANYTHING GOES output, but he did come up with a worthy
successor to *You're the Top* in *It's De-Lovely.* On October 24, 1937, just
months after Gershwin's death, Porter was critically injured in a horseback

riding accident. Amputation was averted but he suffered constant pain for the rest of his life. After twenty years and thirty operations, his right leg was finally amputated.

O MISTRESS MINE

DECEMBER 3, 1936   ST. JAMES THEATRE < LONDON >

Play by Ben Travers
Directed and produced by William Mollison
With Yvonne Printemps and Pierre Fresnay

Published song:
Goodbye, Little Dream, Goodbye—originally cut from RED, HOT AND BLUE! [October 29, 1936]

YOU NEVER KNOW

SEPTEMBER 21, 1938   WINTER GARDEN THEATRE   78 PERFORMANCES

Music and lyrics also by others
Book and direction by Rowland Leigh
(Based on *Candle Light* [play] by Siegfried Geyer)
Produced by John Shubert
With Clifton Webb, Lupe Velez, and Libby Holman

Published songs:
At Long Last Love
For No Rhyme Or Reason
From Alpha To Omega
Maria
What Is That Tune?
What Shall I Do?
You Never Know

Additional songs published in "The Unpublished Cole Porter":
Greek To You—from unproduced musical GREEK TO YOU [circa 1937];
    added to off-Broadway revival [March 12, 1973; 8 performances]
I'm Going In For Love—cut

Writing in his hospital bed (press releases claim a song was written as he lay crushed beneath the horse, waiting for the ambulance), Porter turned out a mediocre score for a poor musical. The Shuberts brought in other songwriters to try to strengthen the show. As the major problem was the book, and the additional songs weren't even as good as Porter's, this didn't help much.

LEAVE IT TO ME!

NOVEMBER 9, 1938   IMPERIAL THEATRE   291 PERFORMANCES

Book by Bella and Samuel Spewack
(Based on *Clear All Wires* [play] by the Spewacks)
Directed by Samuel Spewack
Produced by Vinton Freedley
With William Gaxton, Victor Moore, Sophie Tucker, Tamara, and Mary
Martin

Published songs:
Far Away
From Now On
Get Out Of Town
I Want To Go Home
Most Gentlemen Don't Like Love
My Heart Belongs To Daddy
Taking The Steps To Russia
To-morrow

Additional song published in vocal selection:
Vite, Vite, Vite—initial publication upon reuse in 1982 movie "Evil
    Under the Sun"

Porter bounced back with a string of hits well into the war years—although
the scores were far below the quality of earlier work. The Spewacks had an
enormous success with their George Abbott farce *Boy Meets Girl* [November
27, 1935]; LEAVE IT TO ME! was in the same vein. Victor Moore for once
had a better role than Gaxton (who was getting a little past the age for
romantic leads), and gave one of his funniest performances; red-hot Sophie
Tucker played in her only musical comedy role; and Mary Martin overshadowed them all in her Broadway debut, with the auspicious *My Heart Belongs
To Daddy* striptease.

THE SUN NEVER SETS

JUNE 9, 1939   DRURY LANE THEATRE < LONDON >

Play by Pat Wallace and Guy Bolton
(Based on stories by Edgar Wallace)
Directed by Basil Dean and Richard Llewellyn
With Todd Duncan, Leslie Banks, Adelaide Hall, and Edna Best

Published song:
River God

THE MAN WHO CAME TO DINNER

October 16, 1939   Music Box Theatre   739 performances

Play by Moss Hart and George S. Kaufman
Directed by Kaufman
Produced by Sam H. Harris
With Monty Woolley, Edith Atwater, and David Burns

Song published in acting edition of script:
What Am I To Do?

Hart and Kaufman's play satirized mutual friend Alexander Woollcott. Among the characters was a Cowardish personality who whisked over to the piano and dashed off a little song. Porter, who had brought college professor Woolley to Broadway, supplied *What Am I To Do?*—credited to "Noel Porter."

DUBARRY WAS A LADY

December 6, 1939   46th Street Theatre   408 performances

Book by Herbert Fields and B. G. DeSylva
Directed by Edgar MacGregor
Produced by DeSylva
With Bert Lahr, Ethel Merman, Betty Grable, and Benny Baker

Published songs:
But In The Morning, No
Come On In
Do I Love You?
Ev'ry Day A Holiday
Friendship
Give Him The Oo-La-La
It Was Written In The Stars
Katie Went To Haiti
Well, Did You Evah?
When Love Beckoned (In Fifty-Second Street)

Additional song published in "Music And Lyrics by Cole Porter Vol. 2":
It Ain't Etiquette

Following his 1931 breakup with partners Brown and Henderson, B. G. DeSylva began a highly successful movie producing career. In 1939 he returned to Broadway, producing (and coauthoring librettos for) three major hits in less than a year: two Porter shows and LOUISIANA PURCHASE [Berlin: May 28, 1940]. DeSylva brought Herb Fields back from Hollywood for DuBARRY, and signed Merman (star of his preceding musical, TAKE A CHANCE [Youmans: November 26, 1932]) and Bert Lahr (star of two DeSylva, Brown, and Henderson hits). Also on hand was ingenue Betty Grable, who went right to Hollywood. Porter's score included another classic list song, *Friendship*.

PANAMA HATTIE

OCTOBER 30, 1940   46TH STREET THEATRE   501 PERFORMANCES

Book by Herbert Fields and B. G. DeSylva
Directed by Edgar MacGregor
Produced by DeSylva
With Ethel Merman, James Dunn, and Arthur Treacher

Published songs:
All I've Got To Get Now Is My Man
Fresh As A Daisy
I've Still Got My Health
Let's Be Buddies
Make It Another Old Fashioned, Please
My Mother Would Love You
Visit Panama
Who Would Have Dreamed?

Additional song published in "The Unpublished Cole Porter":
I'm Throwing A Ball Tonight

Additional song recorded:
They Ain't Done Right By Our Nell

Another hit for the DuBARRY WAS A LADY [December 6, 1939] team, although this wartime entertainment was considerably weaker. Following his threefold success, DeSylva was called back to Hollywood to head Paramount Studios.

LET'S FACE IT

OCTOBER 29, 1941   IMPERIAL THEATRE   547 PERFORMANCES

Music and lyrics mostly by Porter
Book by Herbert and Dorothy Fields
(Based on *The Cradle Snatchers* [play] by Norma Mitchell and Russell Medcraft)
Directed by Edgar MacGregor

Produced by Vinton Freedley
With Danny Kaye, Eve Arden, Benny Baker, Edith Meiser, and Mary
Jane Walsh

Published songs:
Ace In The Hole
Ev'rything I Love
Farming
I Hate You Darling
Jerry, My Soldier Boy
Let's Not Talk About Love—revised version of *Don't Look At Me That
      Way!* from PARIS [October 8, 1928]
A Little Rumba Numba
Rub Your Lamp
You Irritate Me So

Additional songs recorded:
Get Yourself A Girl
A Lady Needs A Rest
Pets—cut
What Are Little Husbands Made Of—cut

This wartime hit was bolstered by the starring debut of Danny Kaye (fresh
from LADY IN THE DARK [Weill: January 23, 1941]). Porter and Freedley had
not been getting along well since RED, HOT AND BLUE! [October 29, 1936];
LET'S FACE IT was their final show together—and Freedley's final hit. Fields
began a long-term collaboration with his sister Dorothy; he did most of his
future work teamed with her.

SOMETHING FOR THE BOYS

JANUARY 7, 1943   ALVIN THEATRE   422 PERFORMANCES

Book by Herbert and Dorothy Fields
Directed by Hassard Short and Herbert Fields
Produced by Michael Todd
With Ethel Merman, Bill Johnson, Allen Jenkins, Betty Garrett, and
Paula Laurence

Published songs:
By The Mississinewah
Could It Be You?
He's A Right Guy
Hey, Good Lookin'
I'm In Love With A Soldier Boy

The Leader Of A Big-Time Band
See That You're Born In Texas
Something For The Boys
When My Baby Goes To Town

Additional song recorded:
There's A Happy Land In The Sky

With a new producer, Porter (and Fields) continued their string of hits. The presence of Merman and the wartime atmosphere ensured popularity, even for such inferior material as SOMETHING FOR THE BOYS—a long-run success without even one hit song. Dorothy Fields did her second Merman show; it occured to her that her friend might do well as a musical-comedy Annie Oakley (see ANNIE GET YOUR GUN [Berlin: May 16, 1946]).

MEXICAN HAYRIDE

JANUARY 28, 1944   WINTER GARDEN THEATRE   481 PERFORMANCES

Book by Herbert and Dorothy Fields
Directed by Hassard Short
Produced by Michael Todd
With Bobby Clark, June Havoc, George Givot, and Wilbur Evans

Published songs:
Abracadabra
Carlotta
Count Your Blessings
Girls
The Good-Will Movement
I Love You
It Must Be Fun To Be You—cut
Sing To Me, Guitar
There Must Be Someone For Me

Additional song published in "The Unpublished Cole Porter":
It's Just Yours—cut

Additional songs recorded:
A Humble Hollywood Executive—cut
What A Crazy Way To Spend Sunday

The final success in Porter's string (and the final one with Herb Fields). Bobby Clark carried the show, while Porter came up with the song hit *I Love You.*

SEVEN LIVELY ARTS

December 7, 1944   Ziegfeld Theatre   183 performances

Music also by others
Sketches by Moss Hart, George S. Kaufman, Ben Hecht, and others
Directed by Hassard Short
Produced by Billy Rose
With Beatrice Lillie, Bert Lahr, and Benny Goodman

Published songs:
The Band Started Swinging A Song
Ev'ry Time We Say Goodbye
Frahngee-Pahnee
Hence It Don't Make Sense
Is It The Girl (Or Is It The Gown?)
Only Another Boy And Girl
When I Was A Little Cuckoo
Wow-Ooh-Wolf

Additional songs recorded:
Big Town
Dainty, Quainty Me—cut
I Wrote A Play—cut
Pretty Little Missus Bell—cut

Billy Rose followed his greatest theatre success—Oscar Hammerstein 2nd's CARMEN JONES [December 2, 1943]—by purchasing the Ziegfeld Theatre. He determined to open it with a spectacularly Roseian spectacle, with Lillie and Lahr and Benny Goodman, Salvador Dali scenic conceptions, and a Broadway ballet composed by no less than Igor Stravinsky. All to no avail, and no thanks to Porter's pedestrian score. For the record, Rose's ego was such that his first production (starring then-wife Fanny Brice) was originally called CORNED BEEF AND ROSES; revamped after road disasters, it reached Broadway as SWEET AND LOW [November 17, 1930].

AROUND THE WORLD

May 31, 1946   Adelphi Theatre   75 performances

Book and direction by Orson Welles
(Based on *Around the World in Eighty Days* [novel] by Jules Verne)
Produced by The Mercury Theatre (Welles)
With Arthur Margetson, Julie Warren, and Welles

Published songs:
If You Smile At Me
Look What I Found
Pipe-Dreaming
Should I Tell You I Love You
There He Goes, Mister Phileas Fogg
Wherever They Fly The Flag Of Old England

Welles, who had earned a reputation for being wildly creative and totally uncontrollable, returned to Broadway (see THE CRADLE WILL ROCK [Blitzstein: June 16, 1937]) and ran amuk with this wildly insane extravaganza. AROUND THE WORLD was Porter's biggest flop, losing a record $300,000 in a day when a big musical could be produced for $100,000. (KISS ME, KATE [December 30, 1948], two years later, was mounted for $180,000.) In trying to cover ballooning costs, Welles sold the motion picture rights to former Porter producer Mike Todd; Todd made the highly successful 1958 movie version without Welles (or, for that matter, Porter).

KISS ME, KATE

DECEMBER 30, 1948   NEW CENTURY THEATRE   1,077 PERFORMANCES

Book by Bella and Samuel Spewack
(Based on *The Taming of the Shrew* [play] by William Shakespeare)
Choreographed by Hanya Holm
Directed by John C. Wilson
Produced by Arnold Saint-Subber and Lemuel Ayers
With Alfred Drake, Patricia Morison, Harold Lang, and Lisa Kirk

Published songs:
Always True To You In My Fashion
Another Op'nin', Another Show
Bianca
Brush Up Your Shakespeare
From This Moment On—added to 1953 movie version; originally used
    (cut) in OUT OF THIS WORLD [December 21, 1950]
I Am Ashamed That Women Are So Simple (lyric by Shakespeare)
I Hate Men
I Sing Of Love
I've Come To Wive It Wealthily In Padua
So In Love
Tom, Dick Or Harry
Too Darn Hot
We Open In Venice

Were Thine That Special Face
Where Is The Life That Late I Led?
Why Can't You Behave?
Wunderbar—revised version of *Waltz Down The Aisle* (cut) from
 ANYTHING GOES [November 21, 1934]

Additional song published in vocal score:
Kiss Me, Kate

Additional song published in "The Unpublished Cole Porter":
I'm Afraid, Sweetheart, I Love You—cut

Additional songs recorded:
If Ever Married I'm—cut
It Was Great Fun The First Time—cut
We Shall Never Be Younger—cut
What Does Your Servant Dream About?—cut
A Woman's Career—cut

While Kern, Hammerstein, Rodgers, and others had been working towards integrated musical theatre since the mid-Twenties, Porter never tried for anything more than the best songs he could write at the time—many of them rather good—in whatever framework his librettists happened upon. Following a long creative slump, Porter and the Spewacks (of **LEAVE IT TO ME** [November 9, 1938]) suddenly and unexpectedly came up with one of the very finest musical comedies in Broadway history. The contemporary backstage setting gave the composer an opportunity to have swinging musical fun, with *Too Darn Hot* and *Always True To You In My Fashion*; the Shakespearean farce-musical excerpts gave the adept lyricist a free dramatic reign to rhyme, with *I've Come To Wive It Wealthily In Padua* and *Where Is The Life That Late I Led?*; and the anachronistic combinations of style—*Bianca* and especially *Brush Up Your Shakespeare*—were delightfully perfect. Porter also included one of his highly effective, carefully constructed ballads, *So In Love*. **KISS ME, KATE** was the best, most successful and most personally gratifying show of Porter's career.

OUT OF THIS WORLD

DECEMBER 21, 1950   NEW CENTURY THEATRE   157 PERFORMANCES

Book by Dwight Taylor and Reginald Lawrence
(Based on the *Amphitryon* legend)
Choreographed by Hanya Holm
Directed by Agnes de Mille
Produced by Saint-Subber and Lemuel Ayers

With Charlotte Greenwood, William Eythe, Priscilla Gillette, and David Burns

Published songs:
Cherry Pies Ought To Be You
Climb Up The Mountain
From This Moment On—cut; reused in 1953 motion picture version of
     KISS ME KATE [December 30, 1948]
Hark To The Song Of The Night
I Am Loved
No Lover
Nobody's Chasing Me
Use Your Imagination
Where, Oh Where?
You Don't Remind Me—cut

Additional song published in "The Unpublished Cole Porter":
Oh It Must Be Fun—cut

Additional songs recorded:
Entrance Of Juno (Hail, Hail, Hail)
I Got Beauty
I Jupiter, I Rex
I Sleep Easier Now
Prologue
They Couldn't Compare To You
What Do You Think About Men?
Why Do You Wanta Hurt Me So?—cut

As was generally the case, a major hit was followed up with a similarly conceived, highly awaited major flop. Porter provided some of his most intricate lyrics; but his skill was overshadowed by a labored book, and OUT OF THIS WORLD was roundly attacked for questionable taste (verbal and visual). The uncredited George Abbott took over from de Mille, but the problems needed more than doctoring. Porter provided some uncharacteristically lovely songs—*I Am Loved* and the waltzing *Where, Oh Where*—along with *From This Moment On.* OUT OF THIS WORLD's most striking feature was the most colorful, lavish physical production yet seen on Broadway: coproducer Ayers was an inventive, gifted designer (with OKLAHOMA! [March 31, 1943] and KISS ME, KATE [December 30, 1948] to his credit), who died in 1955 at the age of forty.

CAN-CAN

MAY 7, 1953   SHUBERT THEATRE   892 PERFORMANCES

Book and direction by Abe Burrows
Choreographed by Michael Kidd
Produced by Cy Feuer and Ernest Martin
With Lilo, Peter Cookson, Erik Rhodes, Hans Conried, and Gwen
Verdon

Published songs:
Allez-Vous En
Can-Can
C'est Magnifique
Come Along With Me
I Am In Love
I Love Paris
If You Loved Me Truly
It's All Right With Me
Live And Let Live
Montmart
Never Give Anything Away

Additional songs published in vocal score:
Every Man Is A Stupid Man
Maidens Typical Of France
Never, Never Be An Artist

Additional songs published in "The Unpublished Cole Porter":
To Think That This Could Happen To Me—cut
When Love Comes To Call—cut
Who Said Gay Paree—cut

Additional songs recorded:
The Garden Of Eden Ballet [instrumental]
Her Heart Was In Her Work—cut

Feuer and Martin followed their first two shows—hit Loesser musicals—with Porter's final two works. Porter had been undergoing a rough period, with increasing deterioration of his legs, a 1951 nervous breakdown, and the death of his mother (to whom he was devoted) in 1952. CAN-CAN managed a fair-sized success despite a lukewarm critical reception, and Porter enjoyed his final hit show tune, *I Love Paris.* Stealing the show was dancer Gwen Verdon, in her first major role.

SILK STOCKINGS

FEBRUARY 24, 1955   IMPERIAL THEATRE   478 PERFORMANCES

Book by George S. Kaufman, Leueen MacGrath, and Abe Burrows
(Based on *Ninotchka* [movie] from a story by Melchior Lengyel)
Directed by Cy Feuer
Produced by Feuer and Ernest Martin
With Don Ameche, Hildegarde Neff, and Gretchen Wyler

Published songs:
All Of You
As On Through The Seasons We Sail
Fated To be Mated—written for 1957 movie version
It's A Chemical Reaction, That's All
Josephine
Paris Loves Lovers
Ritz Roll And Rock—written for 1957 movie version
Satin And Silk
Siberia
Silk Stockings
Stereophonic Sound
Without Love

Additional song published in "The Unpublished Cole Porter":
Give Me The Land—unused

Additional songs recorded:
Hail Bibinski
The Red Blues
Too Bad
Under the Dress—cut

Porter's final Broadway show was this painfully assembled, unsatisfying effort.
Facing severe out-of-town troubles, librettist/director Kaufman and wife Mac-
Grath were replaced by Burrows, who had been on GUYS AND DOLLS [Loesser:
November 24, 1950] and CAN-CAN [May 7, 1953]. Feuer himself took over
as director (as he would on the last Richard Rodgers musical, I REMEMBER
MAMA [Rodgers: May 31, 1979]). Porter did some final work in Hollywood,
including *True Love* for the 1956 film "High Society" and the 1958 TV
musical "Aladdin." In April of 1958 he finally lost his long-time medical
battle: his leg had to be amputated. Porter withdrew from public view and
stopped writing. After several years of ill health and severe depression, Cole
Porter died of pneumonia in Santa Monica, California on October 15, 1964.

Following a lackadaisical twelve-year apprenticeship, Cole Porter startled New York and London in 1928 with sharp, dazzling lyrics and tuneful (if less dazzling) music. His work continued fresh and imaginative until 1935, when he seemed to hit a dry spell. Then came his 1937 accident, which seems to have had a permanent effect on his writing—the fun was gone. The next decade contained an impressive number of successful shows—mostly energetic wartime hits—but few of the songs were at all comparable to the earlier work. With the brilliant KISS ME, KATE [December 30, 1948], Porter instantly caught up with his contemporaries and the newcomers who had passed him by. But the creative renaissance proved to be temporary. It is disconcerting (and somewhat surprising) to discover that the majority of Porter's songs are really quite ordinary. But the good music is often very good, and the good lyrics are always superb, more than enough to earn Porter a well-deserved reputation.

Arthur Schwartz

BORN: November 25, 1900   Brooklyn, New York
DIED: September 3, 1984   Kintnersville, Pennsylvania

Despite an early interest in music, Arthur Schwartz entered law (like his father before him). While attending Columbia, he supported himself by teaching high school English. Schwartz continued his hobby of writing songs; his first published work was the 1923 *Baltimore, Md., That's The Only Doctor For Me* (lyric by Eli Dawson). In 1926, lawyer Schwartz got his first big songwriting chance: writing for an intimate, sophisticated revue.

THE GRAND STREET FOLLIES OF 1926
Third Edition

JUNE 15, 1926   NEIGHBORHOOD PLAYHOUSE < OFF-BROADWAY >   55
PERFORMANCES

Music also by Lily Hyland and Randall Thompson
Book, lyrics, and direction by Agnes Morgan
Produced by The Neighborhood Playhouse
With Albert Carroll and Morgan

Published songs:
If You Know What I Mean (lyric by Theodore Goodwin and Carroll)
Little Igloo For Two
Polar Bear Strut

THE GRAND STREET FOLLIES was an intimate revue providing amusing, contemporary competition to the uptown annuals. The Schwartz contributions were entertaining, if not overwhelming.

THE NEW YORKERS

< First Version >

MARCH 10, 1927   EDYTH TOTTEN THEATRE   52 PERFORMANCES

Music also by Edgar Fairchild and Charles M. Schwab
Lyrics by Henry Myers
Book by Jo Swerling
Directed by Milton Bender
Produced by Bender and Myers
NOTE: **1928**, pre-Broadway title

Published song:
Floating Thru The Air

Lorenz Hart had written summer-camp songs with Schwartz and was a firm believer in his talent. THE NEW YORKERS was assembled by his close friend, dentist Milton Bender (see ONE MINUTE PLEASE [**Rodgers: December 29, 1917**]). "Doc" Bender held Machiavellian power over Hart, soon giving up his dental career to become the lyricist's agent; his power increased as Hart brought in friends and coworkers like the Russians Geva, Balanchine, Zorina, and Duke.

GOOD BOY

SEPTEMBER 5, 1928   HAMMERSTEIN'S THEATRE   253 PERFORMANCES

Music mostly by Harry Ruby and Herbert Stothart
Lyrics mostly by Bert Kalmar
Book by Otto Harbach, Oscar Hammerstein 2nd, and Henry Myers
Directed by Reginald Hammerstein
Produced by Arthur Hammerstein
With Eddie Buzzell and Helen Kane

Published song:
You're The One (lyric by Harbach)

This musical comedy featured Helen Kane introducing the Kalmar-Ruby *I Wanna Be Loved By You;* the lyric of that song swept her to fame as the "Boop-Boop-A-Doop" girl.

THE RED ROBE

DECEMBER 25, 1928   SHUBERT THEATRE   167 PERFORMANCES

Music mostly by Jean Gilbert
Book and lyrics mostly by Harry B. Smith
(Based on the novel by Stanley Weyman)
Directed by Stanley Logan
Presented by The Messrs. Shubert
With Walter Woolf and José Ruben

Published song:
Believe In Me

This dreary operetta was one of seven Broadway shows to open on that Christmas Night of 1928, none of them distinguished. Hart, meanwhile, prodded Schwartz into giving up his law practice to concentrate on songwriting.

NED WAYBURN'S GAMBOLS

JANUARY 15, 1929   KNICKERBOCKER THEATRE   31 PERFORMANCES

Music mostly by Walter G. Samuels
Lyrics by Morrie Ryskind
Produced and directed by Ned Wayburn

Published song:
The Sun Will Shine

Ned Wayburn, formerly staff director for Lew Fields, Ziegfeld, and the Shuberts, worked on an impressively large number of early revues and musicals. The totally unknown and neglected *The Sun Will Shine* was the first of Schwartz's beautiful ballads. The lyric was by Morrie Ryskind, who went on to do much better work as a satirical librettist (see STRIKE UP THE BAND (Second Version) [Gershwin: January 14, 1930]).

THE LITTLE SHOW

APRIL 30, 1929   MUSIC BOX THEATRE   321 PERFORMANCES

Music mostly by Arthur Schwartz
Lyrics mostly by Howard Dietz
Sketches by Dietz, George S. Kaufman, and others
Directed by Dwight Deere Wiman and Alexander Leftwich

Produced by William A. Brady, Jr. and Wiman, in association with Tom
Weatherly
With Clifton Webb, Fred Allen, and Libby Holman

Published songs:
I Guess I'll Have To Change My Plan (The Blue Pajama Song)—new
   lyric for *I Love To Lie Awake In Bed* (lyric by Lorenz Hart;
   unpublished)
I've Made A Habit Of You
Song Of The Riveter (lyric by Lew Levinson)—published in nonshow
   edition

Additional songs published (no lyric) in piano selection:
Get Up On A New Routine
The Theme Song

Following the lead of the **Music Box** [Berlin: **September 22, 1921**] and other
intimate revues of the Twenties, **The Little Show** added sophistication and
contemporary comedy to the format. This new-styled revue was to have great
success during the Depression, with Schwartz and Dietz leading the field. For
most of his songwriting career, Howard Dietz was head of publicity at MGM
(where he created that most famous animal actor, Leo the Lion). His first hit
was *Alibi Baby* (music by Stephen Jones) from **Poppy** [September 3, 1923],
although the show's contractual lyricist refused him credit. But publisher Max
Dreyfus was impressed, and sent Dietz to Kern for the unsuccessful **Dear Sir**
[Kern: **September 23, 1924**]. Schwartz recognized something in the lyrics akin
to Hart, and tried to collaborate with Dietz (a Columbia classmate of both
Hart and Hammerstein); Dietz preferred not to go from Kern to an unknown
lawyer, and found very little work (except filling in during Ira Gershwin's
appendicitis on **Oh, Kay!** [Gershwin: **November 8, 1926**]). By 1929 he was
ready to reconsider Schwartz's offer, and the successful collaboration began
with **The Little Show**—although the hit song, *Moanin' Low,* was composed
by Ralph Rainger.

THE GRAND STREET FOLLIES OF 1929
Sixth Edition

May 1, 1929   Booth Theatre   93 performances

Music also by Max Ewing and others
Lyrics mostly by Agnes Morgan
Book and direction by Morgan
Produced by The Actor-Managers, Inc. in association with Paul Moss
With Albert Carroll, Paula Trueman, and James Cagney

Published songs:

I Love You And I Like You (lyric by Max and Nathaniel Lief)—also used in HERE COMES THE BRIDE [February 20, 1930]
I Need You So (lyric by David Goldberg and Howard Dietz)
What Did Della Wear (When Georgie Came Across?) (lyric by Morgan and Carroll)

For the record: *What Did Della Wear* was introduced by Albert Carroll impersonating Fanny Brice, according to the sheet music of this Revolutionary War novelty.

THE HOUSE THAT JACK BUILT

NOVEMBER 8, 1929   ADELPHI THEATRE < LONDON >   270 PERFORMANCES

Music mostly by Ivor Novello
Lyrics mostly by Donovan Parsons
Book by Ronald Jeans and Douglas Furber
Directed and produced by Jack Hulbert
With Cicely Courtneidge (Hulbert) and Hulbert

Published song:

She's Such A Comfort To Me (lyric by Furber and Parsons)—also used in WAKE UP AND DREAM [December 30, 1929]

WAKE UP AND DREAM

DECEMBER 30, 1929   SELWYN THEATRE   136 PERFORMANCES

Music and lyrics mostly by Cole **Porter** [see **March 27, 1929**]
Book by John Hastings Turner
Directed by Frank Collins
Produced by Arch Selwyn in association with Charles B. Cochran
With Jack Buchanan and Jessie Matthews

Published song:

She's Such A Comfort To Me (lyric by Douglas Furber, Max and Nathaniel Lief, and Donovan Parsons)—revised lyric for song originally used in THE HOUSE THAT JACK BUILT [November 8, 1929]

HERE COMES THE BRIDE

A Musical Farcical Comedy

FEBRUARY 20, 1930   PICCADILLY THEATRE < LONDON >   175
   PERFORMANCES

Lyrics mostly by Desmond Carter
Book by R. P. Weston and Bert Lee
(Based on the play by Edgar MacGregor and Otto Harbach)
Produced by Julian Wylie
With Clifford Mollison and Edmund Gwenn

Published songs:
High And Low (lyric by Howard Dietz and Carter)—also used in THE
      BAND WAGON [June 3, 1931]
Hot (lyric by Carter and Lew Levinson)
I Love You And I Like You (lyric by Max and Nathaniel Lief)—originally
      used in GRAND STREET FOLLIES OF 1929 [May 1, 1929]
I'll Always Remember (lyric by Max and Nathaniel Lief and Carter)
I'm Like A Sailor (Home From The Sea) (lyric by Dietz and Carter)
Rose In Your Hair

Schwartz's first successful book show, and the first of three Thirties hits in
London. The lyric to the pretty *High And Low* is probably indeed by Dietz
and Carter, although the latter is not credited on copies of the (identical) song
issued from THE BAND WAGON.

THE CO-OPTIMISTS OF 1930

A Pierrotic Entertainment

APRIL 4, 1930   HIPPODROME < LONDON >

Book and lyrics mostly by Greatrex Newman
Directed by Leslie Henson
With Stanley Holloway, Cyril Ritchard, and Elsie Randolph

Published songs:
Dancing Town
The Moment I Saw You (lyric by Howard Dietz and Newman)—also used
      in THREE'S A CROWD [October 15, 1931]
Steeplejack
Sunday Afternoon

Additional songs published (no lyrics) in piano selections:
Nothing Up Our Sleeves
The Stuff To Give The Troops

The Moment I Saw You was solely credited to Dietz in its American printing.

THE SECOND LITTLE SHOW

SEPTEMBER 2, 1930   ROYALE THEATRE   63 PERFORMANCES

Music mostly by Arthur Schwartz
Lyrics mostly by Howard Dietz
Directed by Dwight Deere Wiman and Monty Woolley
Produced by William A. Brady, Jr. and Wiman, in association with Tom Weatherly
With J. C. Flippen and Gloria Grafton

Published songs:
I Like Your Face—initially issued as *Foolish Face*
Lucky Seven
What A Case I've Got On You!
You're The Sunrise

The producers of THE LITTLE SHOW [April 30, 1929] decided to do a follow-up. Attempting to establish themselves independent of stars, they went ahead without Webb, Allen, and Holman of the first edition. THE SECOND and (non-Schwartz and Dietz) THIRD LITTLE SHOW [Lane: June 1, 1931] did poorly, while Webb, Allen, and Holman went on to immediate success—in a new Schwartz and Dietz revue. Farm-machinery heir Dwight Deere Wiman entered the theatre in 1925, joining veteran producer William A. Brady. Soon going out on his own, Wiman was associated with the late-Thirties successes of Rodgers and Hart (see ON YOUR TOES [Rodgers: April 11, 1936]).

PRINCESS CHARMING

OCTOBER 13, 1930   IMPERIAL THEATRE   56 PERFORMANCES

Music by Albert Sirmay and Arthur Schwartz
Lyrics by Arthur Swanstrom
Book by Jack Donahue
(Based on Arthur Wimperis and Lauri Wylie's British adaptation of the Austrian book by F. Martos)
Directed by Bobby Connolly
Produced by Connolly and Swanstrom
With Evelyn Herbert, George Grossmith, and Victor Moore

Published songs:
I Must Be One Of Those Roses
I'll Be There

I'll Never Leave You
Just A Friend Of Mine
Never Mind How
Trailing A Shooting Star
You

A not-very-good operetta with an undistinguished score. The one hit song was the interpolated *I Love Love* (music by Robert Dolan, lyrics by Walter O'Keefe). Hungarian-born Sirmay went on to become a major behind-the-scenes figure working closely with Cole Porter and others as editor for the music publishing house of Chappell & Co.

THREE'S A CROWD

OCTOBER 15, 1930   SELWYN THEATRE   271 PERFORMANCES

Music mostly by Arthur Schwartz (see **Duke, Lane**)
Lyrics mostly by Howard Dietz
Sketches by Dietz, Groucho Marx, and others
Choreographed by Albertina Rasch
Directed by Hassard Short
Produced by Max Gordon
With Clifton Webb, Fred Allen, Libby Holman, and Tamara Geva

Published songs:
The Moment I Saw You—see THE CO-OPTIMISTS OF 1930 [April 4, 1930]
Right At The Start Of It
Something To Remember You By—new lyric for *I Have No Words (To Say How Much I Love You)* from LITTLE TOMMY TUCKER [November 19, 1930]

With the authors and cast of THE LITTLE SHOW [April 30, 1929] available, the enterprising Max Gordon (heretofore a vaudeville producer) logically concluded that an unofficial sequel with Webb, Allen, and Holman had a better chance than THE SECOND LITTLE SHOW [September 2, 1930]. He was right. Gordon became a major force in the musical theatre through the decade. While *Something To Remember You By* was a hit, it was Holman singing the interpolated *Body And Soul* (music by Johnny Green, lyric by Edward Heyman and Robert Sour), which created a furor.

LITTLE TOMMY TUCKER

NOVEMBER 19, 1930   DALY'S THEATRE < LONDON >

Music mostly by Vivian Ellis
Lyrics by Desmond Carter
Book by Carter, Caswell Garth, Bert Lee, and R. P. Weston
Directed by William Mollison
Produced by Herbert Clayton
With Ivy Tresmand, Rita Pepe, Jane Welsh, and Melville Cooper

Published songs:
I Have No Words—see THREE'S A CROWD [October 15, 1930]
Out Of The Blue (music by Ellis and Schwartz)

Although LITTLE TOMMY TUCKER opened after THREE'S A CROWD, *I Have No Words* was published two weeks before the Dietz lyric for the same music, *Something To Remember You By.*

THE BAND WAGON

JUNE 3, 1931   NEW AMSTERDAM THEATRE   260 PERFORMANCES

Lyrics by Howard Dietz
Sketches by George S. Kaufman and Dietz
Choreographed by Albertina Rasch
Directed by Hassard Short
Produced by Max Gordon
With Fred and Adele Astaire, Helen Broderick, Frank Morgan, and Tilly Losch

Published songs:
Confession
Dancing In The Dark
High And Low (I've Been Waiting For You)—see HERE COMES THE
        BRIDE [February 20, 1930]
Hoops
I Love Louisa
Miserable With You
New Sun In The Sky
Sweet Music
That's Entertainment—written for 1953 movie version
Triplets—added to 1953 movie version; revised version of song
        (unpublished) from BETWEEN THE DEVIL [December 22, 1937]

Additional number published in piano selection:
Beggar's Waltz [instrumental]—subsequently published (1932) as nonshow
    song *Is It All A Dream?* (lyric by Dietz)

Additional songs recorded:
Ballet Music [instrumental]
It Better Be Good (Opening)
Nanette
Where Can He Be?
White Heat

Schwartz and Dietz had realized the advantage of having the fewest possible
writers involved in creating a revue; on THE BAND WAGON they worked solely
with George S. Kaufman, who had contributed important sketches to THE
LITTLE SHOW [April 30, 1929]. Like Dietz, the immensely successful Kaufman
kept a fulltime "real" job—as drama editor of *The New York Times.* Director
Hassard Short, prime force in the MUSIC BOX REVUES [Berlin: September 22,
1921], experimented with moving turntables, mirrors, and novel lighting effects. Songs, sketches, and dances were carefully tailored to the exceptional
cast. The result: what is considered the finest revue in Broadway history. THE
BAND WAGON marked the final professional appearance of Adele Astaire; after
spending most of her first thirty years on the stage, she retired to marry a
British lord. Broadway wondered if her brother—the less charming, weak-
voiced, balding straight man of the team—could succeed on his own.

FLYING COLORS
The Howard Dietz Revue

SEPTEMBER 15, 1932   IMPERIAL THEATRE   188 PERFORMANCES

Lyrics, sketches, and direction by Dietz
Choreographed by Albertina Rasch
Produced by Max Gordon
With Clifton Webb, Charles Butterworth, Tamara Geva, and Patsy Kelly

Published songs:
Alone Together
Fatal Fascination
Louisiana Hayride
A Rainy Day
A Shine On Your Shoes
Smokin' Reefers
Two-Faced Woman—added after opening; published in separate edition

Additional song published (no lyric) in piano selection:
Mein Kleine Acrobat—initial publication upon reuse in FOLLOW THE SUN
      [February 4, 1936]

Additional song recorded:
Mother Told Me So

In their fifth revue together, Schwartz and Dietz had a difficult time coming through with FLYING COLORS. Grave conditions were faced, including the nervous breakdown (and attempted suicide) of producer Max Gordon and the last-minute replacement of novice choreographer Agnes de Mille. The show certainly didn't compare with THE BAND WAGON [June 3, 1931], although the score had three hits (including the *Dancing In The Dark* successor, *Alone Together*).

NICE GOINGS ON

SEPTEMBER 13, 1933   STRAND THEATRE < LONDON >   221
      PERFORMANCES

Lyrics mostly by Frank Eyton
Book by Douglas Furber
Directed by Leslie Henson
Produced by Henson and Firth Shepard
With Henson and Zelma O'Neal

Published songs:
I Know The Kind Of Girl (lyric by Furber)
Sweet One
'Twixt The Devil And The Deep Blue Sea
What A Young Girl Ought To Know
Whatever You Do
With You Here And Me Here

SHE LOVES ME NOT

NOVEMBER 20, 1933   46TH STREET THEATRE   248 PERFORMANCES

Play by Howard Lindsay
(Based on a novel by Edward Hope)
Lyrics by Edward Heyman
Directed by Lindsay
Produced by Dwight Deere Wiman and Tom Weatherly

Published songs:
After All, You're All I'm After
She Loves Me Not

BRING ON THE GIRLS

[OCTOBER 22, 1934]   NATIONAL THEATRE < WASHINGTON, D.C. > ;
CLOSED DURING PRE-BROADWAY TRYOUT

Play by George S. Kaufman and Morrie Ryskind
Directed by Kaufman
Produced by Sam H. Harris
With Jack Benny, Porter Hall, Claire Carleton and Oscar Polk

Published song:
Down On The Old-Time Farm (lyric by Ryskind)

This Kaufman/Ryskind New Deal satire just did not work. Audiences expecting another OF THEE I SING [Gershwin: December 26, 1931] were greatly disappointed: to begin with, BRING ON THE GIRLS wasn't even a musical.

REVENGE WITH MUSIC

NOVEMBER 28, 1934   NEW AMSTERDAM THEATRE   158
PERFORMANCES

Book and lyrics by Howard Dietz
(Based on *The Three-Cornered Hat* [novel] by Pedro de Alarcon)
Directed by Komisarjevsky and others
Produced by Arch Selwyn and Harold B. Franklin
With Charles Winninger, Libby Holman, and Georges Metaxa

Published songs:
If There Is Someone Lovelier Than You
Maria
That Fellow Manuelo
Wand'ring Heart
When You Love Only One
You And The Night And The Music—revised version of *To-Night* (lyric by Desmond Carter) from 1934 movie "The Queen"

Additional song recorded:
In The Noonday Sun

The abundant publicity surrounding Libby Holman's return to the stage after her brief marriage to Zachary Smith Reynolds (which ended with the young tobacco heir's suicide) wasn't enough to salvage this first Schwartz and Dietz book musical. *To-Night* was a sweeping waltz version of what, in Latin tempo, became *You And The Night And The Music.*

AT HOME ABROAD
A Musical Holiday

SEPTEMBER 19, 1935   WINTER GARDEN THEATRE   198 PERFORMANCES

Lyrics by Howard Dietz
Sketches by Dietz and others
Directed by Vincente Minnelli and Thomas Mitchell
Produced by Messrs. Shubert
With Beatrice Lillie, Ethel Waters, Herb Williams, Reginald Gardiner, and Eleanor Powell

Published songs:
Farewell, My Lovely
Got A Bran' New Suit
The Hottentot Potentate
Love Is A Dancing Thing
O Leo
That's Not Cricket
Thief In The Night
What A Wonderful World

Additional songs published in USO/Camp Shows "AT EASE":
Get Away From It All—with revised lyric, retitled *Come Along To Our Show* (Volume 4)
The Lady With The Tap-Tap-Tap—with revised lyric, retitled *The Soldier With The Tap-Tap-Tap* (Volume 3)

Additional songs recorded:
Get Yourself A Geisha
Loadin' Time
Paree

Schwartz and Dietz met Lillie in this first of two hit revues they did together. *Get Yourself A Geisha*—with Lillie at the end of a Japanese chorus line—was classic. Also along on this worldwide travelogue were comics Williams and Gardiner, while Ethel Waters sang and Eleanor Powell tapped her way to Hollywood. Despite their continued Broadway success Dietz remained at MGM, leaving Schwartz a full-time composer with a part-time lyricist. Schwartz began to search for a new collaborator.

FOLLOW THE SUN

February 4, 1936   Adelphi Theatre <London>   204
PERFORMANCES

Lyrics by Howard Dietz and Desmond Carter
Book by Ronald Jeans and John Hastings Turner
Produced by Charles B. Cochran
With Claire Luce and Nick Long, Jr.

Published songs:
Dangerous You (lyric by Carter)
How High Can A Little Bird Fly? (lyric by Dietz)—originally used in
    1934 radio serial "The Gibson Family"
Nicotina (lyric by Carter)
Sleigh Bells (lyric by Dietz)—published in separate edition

Additional songs published (no lyric) in piano selection:
Follow The Sun
Mein Kleine Acrobat—originally used (unpublished) in Flying Colors
    [September 15, 1932]
The Steamboat Whistle

THE SHOW IS ON

December 25, 1936   Winter Garden Theatre   237 performances

Music mostly by Vernon **Duke** (also see **Arlen, Gershwin** and **Rodgers**)
Lyric to Schwartz song by Howard Dietz
Sketches mostly by David Freedman and Moss Hart
Directed by Vincente Minnelli
Produced by Lee Shubert
With Beatrice Lillie and Bert Lahr

Song published in USO/Camp Shows "AT EASE" (Volume 4):
Shakespearean Opening—with revised lyric

VIRGINIA

The American Musical Romance

September 2, 1937   Center Theatre   60 performances

Lyrics by Albert Stillman
Book by Laurence Stallings and Owen Davis
Book directed by Edward Clark Lilley

Staged by Leon Leonidoff
Produced by The Center Theatre
With Anne Booth, Gene Lockhart, Ronald Graham, and Nigel Bruce

Published songs:
Good And Lucky
Good-Bye Jonah
If You Were Someone Else
My Bridal Gown (lyric by Stillman and Stallings)
My Heart Is Dancing
An Old Flame Never Dies (lyric by Stillman and Stallings)
Virginia
You And I Know (lyric by Stillman and Stallings)

The Rockefellers' initial theatrical attraction at their Music Hall twin had been Max Gordon's spectacular production of Strauss's THE GREAT WALTZ [September 22, 1934]. The overwhelming scale of the house made it difficult to come up with suitable future attractions—a fact which was soon to end the theatre's legitimate career. The Colonial operetta VIRGINIA was overblown and represented a major financial loss; but Schwartz's work was good, particularly *If You Were Someone Else* and *You And I Know.*

BETWEEN THE DEVIL

DECEMBER 22, 1937   IMPERIAL THEATRE   93 PERFORMANCES

Book and lyrics by Howard Dietz
Directed by Hassard Short
Produced by Messrs. Shubert
With Jack Buchanan, Evelyn Laye, and Adele Dixon

Published songs:
By Myself
Don't Go Away, Monsieur
Double Trouble—advertised but not published
I Believe In You—issued as professional copy
I See Your Face Before Me
Why Did You Do It?
You Have Everything

Additional song published in USO/Camp Shows "AT EASE" (Volume 3):
The Uniform—with revised lyric

Additional songs recorded:
Imaginist Rhythm
Triplets—initial publication in revised form upon reuse in 1953 movie
      version of THE BAND WAGON [June 3, 1931]

This second Schwartz/Dietz book show attempt was a dated marital farce; Dietz never found Broadway success outside the revue format. Following **BETWEEN THE DEVIL,** the team terminated their collaboration after eight full scores in as many years. Dietz continued his MGM work and entered a wartime collaboration with Vernon Duke; Schwartz worked with a variety of lyricists and embarked on a successful Hollywood career as composer and producer.

STARS IN YOUR EYES

FEBRUARY 9, 1939   MAJESTIC THEATRE   127 PERFORMANCES

Lyrics by Dorothy Fields
Book by J. P. McEvoy
Directed by Joshua Logan
Produced by Dwight Deere Wiman
With Ethel Merman, Jimmy Durante, Tamara Toumanova, and Richard Carlson

Published songs:
All The Time
I'll Pay The Check
It's All Yours
Just A Little Bit More
A Lady Needs A Change
Terribly Attractive
This Is It

What began as a politically tinged satire of the movie industry with Durante as union organizer lost its bite early on. All that remained was Merman and Durante, which was nothing to be sneezed at. This time, incidentally, Merman got first billing without a fight (see **RED, HOT AND BLUE!** [Porter: **October 29, 1936**]). Schwartz's new lyricist was Dorothy Fields, daughter/sister of Lew/Herbert (see **BLACKBIRDS OF 1928** [**PART 4: May 9, 1928**]) and 1936 Oscar winner for *The Way You Look Tonight* (music by Jerome Kern).

AMERICAN JUBILEE

MAY 12, 1940   AMERICAN JUBILEE THEATRE,   NEW YORK WORLD'S
          FAIR

Book and lyrics by Oscar Hammerstein 2nd
Directed by Leon Leonidoff
Produced by Albert Johnson
Presented by New York World's Fair Corporation
With Lucy Monroe (and a cast of 350)

Published songs:
How Can I Ever Be Alone?
My Bicycle Girl
Tennessee Fish Fry
We Like It Over Here

A patriotic pageant. The only item of interest was Schwartz's catchy *Tennessee Fish Fry*, which composer Leroy Anderson appears to have caught. He added sleigh bells and called it *Sleigh Ride*, now a Christmas standard. Following AMERICAN JUBILEE, Schwartz went to Hollywood (not MGM) where he produced two successful movie musicals: the 1944 Kern/Ira Gershwin "Cover Girl" and the 1946 Cole Porter pseudobiography "Night and Day."

PARK AVENUE

NOVEMBER 4, 1946   SHUBERT THEATRE   72 PERFORMANCES

Lyrics by Ira Gershwin
Book by Nunnally Johnson and George S. Kaufman
Directed by Kaufman
Produced by Max Gordon
With Leonora Corbett and Arthur Margetson

Published songs:
For The Life Of Me
Goodbye To All That
There's No Holding Me

Additional song published in "Intimate Songs":
Don't Be A Woman If You Can

A highly disappointing show from a distinguished set of authors. Left behind was the beautiful ballad *Goodbye To All That*. For the fifty-year-old Gershwin, two consecutive flops were enough; he went back home to Hollywood. After several more movies Gershwin permanently retired, but not before writing one last classic, *The Man That Got Away* (music by Harold Arlen), for the 1954 remake of "A Star is Born."

INSIDE U.S.A.

APRIL 30, 1948   NEW CENTURY THEATRE   399 PERFORMANCES

Lyrics by Howard Dietz
Sketches by Arnold Auerbach, Moss Hart, and Arnold Horwitt
(Title suggested by the book by John Gunther)

Directed by Robert H. Gordon
Produced by Schwartz
With Beatrice Lillie, Jack Haley, Herb Shriner, and Valerie Bettis

Published songs:
Blue Grass
First Prize At The Fair
Haunted Heart
My Gal Is Mine Once More
Rhode Island Is Famous For You

Additional songs recorded:
At The Mardi Gras
Atlanta
Come O Come (To Pittsburgh)
Inside U.S.A.
Protect Me

Schwartz, reunited with Dietz, produced this sequel to AT HOME ABROAD [September 19, 1935]. INSIDE U.S.A. was formatted as a stateside travelogue, whereas the earlier show had an international motif. With a fair score, good sketches and the comedy of Lillie and Haley, INSIDE U.S.A. was a moderate hit. Surprisingly, it was to be the final success either writer had (although some of Schwartz's finest work was still to come).

A TREE GROWS IN BROOKLYN

APRIL 19, 1951   ALVIN THEATRE   270 PERFORMANCES

Lyrics by Dorothy Fields
Book by Betty Smith and George Abbott
(Based on the novel by Smith)
Choreographed by Herbert Ross
Directed by George Abbott
Produced by Abbott with Robert Fryer
With Shirley Booth, Johnny Johnston, Marcia Van Dyke, and Nathaniel Frey

Published songs:
Growing Pains
If You Haven't Got A Sweetheart
I'll Buy You A Star
I'm Like A New Broom
Look Who's Dancing
Love Is The Reason
Make The Man Love Me

Additional songs recorded:
Don't Be Afraid Of Anything
Halloween [instrumental]
He Had Refinement
Is That My Prince?
Mine 'Til Monday
Payday
That's How It Goes
Tuscaloosa—cut; see BY THE BEAUTIFUL SEA [April 8, 1954]

One of Schwartz's richest scores and his best book musical. Based on the popular novel, the librettists sought to balance the story's tragic elements by building up the humorous subplot; this proved a fatal mistake, as the casting of Shirley Booth made a star role out of a subordinate character. Booth's fine performance helped the show achieve a respectable, if unprofitable, run. The usually urbane Schwartz revealed a powerful, emotional side in writing for the unsophisticated, uneducated characters. Resulting treasures (adorned by Fields' best work) included *Make The Man Love Me, I'll Buy You A Star,* and *Don't Be Afraid Of Anything.*

BY THE BEAUTIFUL SEA

APRIL 8, 1954   MAJESTIC THEATRE   270 PERFORMANCES

Lyrics by Dorothy Fields
Book by Herbert and Dorothy Fields
Directed by Marshall Jamison
Produced by Robert Fryer and Lawrence Carr
With Shirley Booth, Wilbur Evans, and Mae Barnes

Published songs:
Alone Too Long
Hang Up!
Happy Habit
More Love Than Your Love
The Sea Song (By The Beautiful Sea)

Additional songs recorded:
Coney Island Boat
Good Time Charlie
Hooray For George The Third
I'd Rather Wake Up By Myself
Old Enough To Love—new lyric for *Tuscaloosa* (cut, unpublished) from
        A TREE GROWS IN BROOKLYN [April 19, 1951]
Please Don't Send Me Down A Baby Brother
Throw The Anchor Away

Trying to come up with a more successful venture than **A TREE GROWS IN BROOKLYN** [April 19, 1951], the two Fieldses wrote a more comic vehicle for Booth. But without powerful basic material or the strong hand of George Abbott, the result was little more than an old-fashioned costume piece. The Schwartz/Fields score was merely adequate, but Booth's performance gave the show a run of identical length. *I'd Rather Wake Up By Myself* was superb comedy writing.

THE GAY LIFE

NOVEMBER 18, 1961   SHUBERT THEATRE   114 PERFORMANCES

Lyrics by Howard Dietz
Book by Fay and Michael Kanin
(Based on *Anatol* [play] by Arthur Schnitzler)
Directed by Gerald Freedman
Produced by Kermit Bloomgarden
With Walter Chiari, Barbara Cook, and Jules Munshin

Published songs:
Bloom Is Off The Rose
Come A-Wandering With Me
For The First Time
I'm Glad I'm Single
Magic Moment
Oh Mein Leibchen
Something You Never Had Before—revised version of *Oh, But I Do* (lyric
    by Leo Robin) from 1946 movie "The Time, The Place and The
    Girl"
Who Can? You Can!
Why Go Anywhere At All?

Additional songs recorded:
Bring Your Darling Daughter
I Never Had A Chance
I Wouldn't Marry You
The Label On The Bottle
Now I'm Ready For A Frau
This Kind Of A Girl
What A Charming Couple
You Will Never Be Lonely
You're Not The Type

Dietz retired his vice-presidency at MGM in 1957 and reunited with Schwartz for two final book shows. **THE GAY LIFE** was saddled with a lifeless book and a lifeless star (Chiari), which defeated the attributes: a fine, sweeping Viennese score by Schwartz, a *sacher-torte* physical production—with Tony Award-winning costumes by Lucinda Ballard (Dietz)—and a luscious performance by Barbara Cook. *Magic Moment, Why Go Anywhere At All,* and *Something You Never Had Before* were all absolutely lovely.

JENNIE

OCTOBER 17, 1963   MAJESTIC THEATRE   82 PERFORMANCES

Lyrics by Howard Dietz
Book by Arnold Schulman
(Based on *Laurette* [biography] by Marguerite Taylor Courtney)
Directed by Vincent J. Donehue
Produced by Cheryl Crawford and Richard Halliday
With Mary Martin, George Wallace, and Ethel Shutta

Published songs:
Before I Kiss The World Goodbye
Born Again
High Is Better Than Low
I Believe In Takin' A Chance
I Still Look At You That Way
On The Other Hand—cut
Waitin' For The Evening Train
When You're Far Away From New York Town
Where You Are

Additional songs recorded:
For Better Or Worse
Lonely Nights
The Night May Be Dark
Over Here
Sauce Diable [instrumental]
See Seattle

Mary Martin decided against Fanny Brice—she wasn't really right for **FUNNY GIRL** [Styne: **March 26, 1964**]—and chose the feisty, alcoholic, "Peg O' My Heart" Laurette Taylor instead. Martin also turned down Dolly Levi. Schwartz's final show was an unhappy experience for all. Dietz had engaged in lyric-suitability battles with Merman on **SADIE THOMPSON** [Duke: **November 16, 1944**], resulting in her replacement. The same problems arose with Mary Martin . . . who was married to the coproducer. Martin and the enormous advance sale stayed. **JENNIE** was a shambles, and quickly went the way of all shambles. A 1960 nonmusical dramatization "(Laurette)" of the biography by Taylor's daughter, starring the more suitable Judy Holliday, had closed during tryout; hence the name change. The best element of JENNIE was the music, including the final beautiful Schwartz ballad: *Before I Kiss The World Goodbye,* which was actually written for an unproduced musicalization of the Paul Gallico novel "Mrs. 'Arris Goes To Paris.")" Schwartz and Dietz both went into virtual retirement. Dietz, who suffered from Parkinson's disease, died July 30, 1983; Schwartz, following a stroke, died September 3, 1984 at his home in Kintnersville, Pennsylvania.

Arthur Schwartz wrote some of the finest theatre music of his time—particularly the minor-key ballads of the Thirties (*Dancing In The Dark, Alone Together*) and the later, much warmer ones (*Make The Man Love Me* and *Magic Moment*). His skill also displayed itself in outstanding rhythmic work (*I Guess I'll Have To Change My Plan* and the 1953 movie song *That's Entertainment*). All of which make it difficult to explain Schwartz's record of *no* successful Broadway book musical. Not having Dietz as a full-time collaborator certainly was part of it, although the lyricist's nonrevue work indicates Schwartz would have done better with, say, Dorothy Fields. However—and happily—a good number of glorious Arthur Schwartz songs remain.

Harold Arlen

BORN: February 15, 1905   Buffalo, New York
DIED: April 23, 1986   New York, New York

Harold Arlen was the son of a cantor, whose melodic and colorful improvisatory style was to be a tremendous influence on Arlen's work. With his interest firmly in pop music, Arlen began his career as a bandleader and soon moved to New York as an arranger/singer. His first published piece was the 1926 instrumental *Minor Gaff (Blues Fantasy)* (by Harold Arluck and Dick George). By 1928, he had changed his name to Arlen. His first Broadway experience was as vocalist, rehearsal pianist, and sometime musical secretary to Vincent Youmans for the tryout of **GREAT DAY!** [**Youmans: October 17, 1929**]. When the troubled show went back into rehearsal for a preopening overhaul, Arlen left the cast. Youmans, who had set up his own doomed-to-failure publishing company, bought and issued Arlen's *Rising Moon* (lyric by Jack Ellis) in the summer of 1929.

NINE-FIFTEEN REVUE

FEBRUARY 11, 1930   GEORGE M. COHAN THEATRE   7 PERFORMANCES

Music and lyrics mostly by others (see **Gershwin**)
Lyrics to Arlen songs by Ted Koehler
Sketches by Eddie Cantor, George S. Kaufman, Ring Lardner, Wm. Anthony McGuire, and others
Directed by Alexander Leftwich
Produced by Ruth Selwyn
With Ruth Etting

Published songs:
Get Happy
You Wanted Me, I Wanted You

While accompanying dance rehearsals of **GREAT DAY!** [**Youmans: October 17, 1929**], Arlen improvised a catchy break. He played it for a friend, pop songwriter Harry Warren; Warren suggested Arlen get together with lyricist Ted Koehler and turn it into a song. *Get Happy* was the result, and Arlen switched careers to songwriting (although he remained a remarkable blues singer, making occasional recordings of his songs). NINE-FIFTEEN REVUE featured work by many top composers, but it was Arlen's *Get Happy* which stood out—for the week of the run, anyway. Ruth Etting, who attracted notice with *Love Me Or Leave Me* in WHOOPEE [PART 4: December 4, 1928], sang Arlen's first hit. With NINE-FIFTEEN REVUE quickly closed, Etting rushed across Times Square to join SIMPLE SIMON [Rodgers: February 18, 1930], and introduced her second song classic of the week, *Ten Cents A Dance*.

EARL CARROLL VANITIES

Eighth Edition

America's Greatest Revue

JULY 1, 1930   NEW AMSTERDAM THEATRE   215 PERFORMANCES

Music also by Jay Gorney
Lyrics to Arlen songs by Ted Koehler
Book by Eddie Welch and Eugene Conrad
Directed by Priestly Morrison
Produced by Earl Carroll
With Jack Benny, Jimmy Savo, and Herb Williams

Published songs:
Contagious Rhythm
Hittin' The Bottle
The March Of Time
One Love
Out Of A Clear Blue Sky

Get Happy attracted attention to Arlen and Koehler. They were hired to contribute half the score for this edition of the VANITIES, the weakest of the three major annual revues. The rest of the songs were written by another young team, Jay Gorney and E. Y. Harburg, who soon took Koehler's place as Arlen's collaborator.

BROWN SUGAR

Sweet But Unrefined

Nightclub Revue

[CIRCA DECEMBER 1930]   COTTON CLUB < HARLEM, NEW YORK >

Lyrics by Ted Koehler
Directed by Dan Healy

Produced by The Cotton Club
With Duke Ellington and His Orchestra

Published songs:
Linda
Song Of The Gigolo

Having tried out Arlen and Koehler material at the Silver Slipper nightclub, proprietors Owney Madden and associates—i.e., the Mob—sent the songwriters uptown to replace McHugh and Fields (who had graduated to Broadway with BLACKBIRDS OF 1928 [PART 4: May 9, 1928]). Featuring black performers but catering to an exclusively white clientele, the Cotton Club offered elaborate midnight floor shows to accompany the main business in bootleg liquor. The Arlen/Koehler team did their best work together for the Cotton Club, turning out several blues standards.

YOU SAID IT

The Musicollegiate Comedy Hit

JANUARY 19, 1931   46TH STREET THEATRE   168 PERFORMANCES

Lyrics by Jack Yellen
Book by Yellen and Sid Silvers
Directed by John Harwood
Produced by Yellen and Lou Holtz
With Holtz and Lyda Roberti

Published songs:
If He Really Loves Me
It's Different With Me
Learn To Croon
Sweet And Hot
What Do We Care?
While You Are Young
You Said It
You'll Do

Arlen was signed to write his first book show by Yellen, a successful Tin Pan Alley lyricist and former member of Arlen's father's congregation in Buffalo. Though the show was moderately successful, Arlen's work was undistinguished (except for the sweet and hot *Sweet And Hot*). He returned to Koehler and the revue format.

RHYTH-MANIA

Nightclub Revue

[CIRCA DECEMBER 1931] COTTON CLUB < HARLEM, NEW YORK >

Lyrics by Ted Koehler
Directed by Dan Healy
Produced by The Cotton Club
With Aida Ward and Cab Calloway

Published songs:
Between The Devil And The Deep Blue Sea
Breakfast Dance
Get Up, Get Out, Get Under The Sun
I Love A Parade—issued separately from other songs
Kickin' The Gong Around
'Neath The Pale Cuban Moon
Without Rhythm

Arlen's second Cotton Club show, with another hit song: *Between The Devil And The Deep Blue Sea.*

COTTON CLUB PARADE

Twentieth Edition

Nightclub Revue

[CIRCA APRIL, 1932] COTTON CLUB (HARLEM, NEW YORK)

Lyrics by Ted Koehler
Directed by Dan Healy
Produced by The Cotton Club
With Cab Calloway and His Orchestra

Published songs:
In The Silence Of The Night
Minnie The Moocher's Wedding Day
You Gave Me Everything But Love

Despite the caption, this was actually the first COTTON CLUB PARADE. It was, however, the twentieth of the nightclub revues mounted at the Cotton Club (and the third written by Arlen and Koehler).

EARL CARROLL VANITIES

Tenth Edition

America's Greatest Revue

SEPTEMBER 27, 1932   BROADWAY THEATRE   87 PERFORMANCES

Music also by others
Lyrics to Arlen songs by Ted Koehler
Sketches by Jack McGowan
Directed by Edgar J. McGregor
Produced by Earl Carroll
With Will Fyffe, Milton Berle, and Helen Broderick

Published songs:
I Gotta Right To Sing The Blues
Rockin' In Rhythm

Arlen came up with another treasure—*I Gotta Right To Sing The Blues*—this time for Broadway. Influenced by the improvisatory style of the black jazz underground, Arlen's blues replaced the synthetic-but-popular torch songs of the Twenties for immediate public acceptance.

AMERICANA

Third Edition

A Musical Revue

OCTOBER 5, 1932   SHUBERT THEATRE   77 PERFORMANCES

Music mostly by Jay Gorney
Lyrics mostly by E. Y. Harburg
Book by J. P. McEvoy
Directed by Harold Johnsrud
Produced by J. P. McEvoy
Presented by Lee Shubert

Published song:
Satan's Li'l Lamb (lyric by Harburg and John Mercer)

This short-lived revue, best known for.the Gorney/Harburg *Brother, Can You Spare a Dime?*, was the first time Arlen worked with two of his important future collaborators. Johnny Mercer was, like Arlen, a fine singer. He was then appearing as a Rhythm Boy with Paul Whiteman's Band (Arlen's younger brother Jerry was also in the trio).

COTTON CLUB PARADE

Twenty-First Edition

Nightclub Revue

OCTOBER 23, 1932   COTTON CLUB < HARLEM, NEW YORK >

Lyrics by Ted Koehler
Directed by Dan Healy
Produced by The Cotton Club
With Aida Ward and Cab Calloway

Published songs:
Harlem Holiday
I've Got The World On A String
That's What I Hate About Love
The Wail Of The Reefer Man

GEORGE WHITE'S MUSIC HALL VARIETIES

NOVEMBER 22, 1932   CASINO THEATRE   71 PERFORMANCES

Music mostly by others
Book by George White and William K. Wells
Produced by White
With Harry Richman, Bert Lahr, and Lily Damita

Published song:
Two Feet In Two-Four Time (lyric by Irving Caesar)

THE GREAT MAGOO

DECEMBER 2, 1932   SELWYN THEATRE   11 PERFORMANCES

Play by Ben Hecht and Gene Fowler
Directed by George Abbott
Produced by Billy Rose
With Paul Kelly

Published song:
If You Believed In Me (lyrics by E. Y. Harburg and Rose)—initial
publication upon reuse in CRAZY QUILT OF 1933 [July 28, 1933]
retitled *It's Only A Paper Moon*

Arlen's auspicious hit was born in this inauspicious flop; it found widespread
popularity via interpolation in the 1933 movie version of TAKE A CHANCE

[**Youmans: November 26, 1932**]. Rose, producer of the play, claimed colyricist credit.

COTTON CLUB PARADE

Twenty-Second Edition

Nightclub Revue

April 6, 1933   Cotton Club < Harlem, New York >

Lyrics by Ted Koehler
Directed by Dan Healy
Produced by The Cotton Club
With Ethel Waters, George Dewey Washington, and Duke Ellington and
His Orchestra

Published songs:
Calico Days
Get Yourself A New Broom (And Sweep The Blues Away)
Happy As The Day Is Long
Muggin' Lightly
Raisin' The Rent
Stormy Weather

The most successful edition of the series. Ethel Waters had her first exposure to a predominantly white audience. Her tear-filled rendition of *Stormy Weather* was effective enough to convince Irving Berlin to place her as a lead in his new revue, As Thousands Cheer [Berlin: September 30, 1933].

CRAZY QUILT OF 1933

July 28, 1933   < Albany, New York > ; post-Broadway tour

Music mostly by others
Produced by Billy Rose
With Anita Page

Published song:
It's Only A Paper Moon (lyric by E. Y. Harburg and Rose)—initial
  publication of *If You Believed In Me* (unpublished) from The
  Great Magoo [December 2, 1932]

COTTON CLUB PARADE

Twenty-Fourth Edition

Nightclub Revue

MARCH 23, 1934   COTTON CLUB <HARLEM, NEW YORK>

Lyrics by Ted Koehler
Directed by Dan Healy
Produced by The Cotton Club
With Adelaide Hall and Jimmie Lunceford and His Orchestra

Published songs:
As Long As I Live
Breakfast Ball
Here Goes
Ill Wind
Primitive Prima Donna

Arlen's final Cotton Club show featured sixteen-year-old chorine Lena Horne, singing and dancing *As Long As I Live* with Avon Long.

LIFE BEGINS AT 8:40

A Musical Revue

AUGUST 27, 1934   WINTER GARDEN THEATRE   237 PERFORMANCES

Lyrics by Ira Gershwin and E. Y. Harburg
Sketches mostly by David Freedman
Directed and produced by John Murray Anderson
Presented by Messrs. Shubert
With Ray Bolger, Bert Lahr, Luella Gear, and Frances Williams

Published songs:
Fun To Be Fooled
Let's Take A Walk Around the Block
Shoein' The Mare
What Can You Say In A Love Song?
You're A Builder Upper

Additional songs published in USO/Camp Shows "AT EASE":
I Couldn't Hold My Man—with revised lyric, retitled *I Look Bad In Uniform* (Volume 3)
Life Begins Introduction—with revised lyric (Volume 4)
Spring Fever—(Volume 4)

Additional songs recorded:
C'est La Vie
The Elks And The Masons
I'm Not Myself
Quartet Erotica
Things
Will You Love Me Monday Morning?

Having broken up with Vernon Duke following the ZIEGFELD FOLLIES OF 1934 [DUKE: January 4, 1934], Harburg astutely selected Arlen as his next collaborator. Arlen could not turn down this first major opportunity; the success of LIFE BEGINS AT 8:40 effectively ended the Arlen/Koehler partnership. Veteran Ira Gershwin, influential in placing college classmate Harburg's early work, became colyricist; George was writing PORGY AND BESS [Gershwin: October 10, 1935] with DuBose Heyward (although Ira was soon to join them). Arlen wrote his finest work with Harburg, Gershwin, and Johnny Mercer, songs that Koehler—a decent pop lyricist—could not have kept up with.

THE SHOW IS ON

DECEMBER 25, 1936   WINTER GARDEN THEATER   237 PERFORMANCES

Music mostly by Vernon **Duke** (also see **Gershwin, Rodgers,** and **Schwartz**)
Lyrics to Arlen song by E. Y. Harburg
Sketches by David Freedman and Moss Hart
Directed and designed by Vincente Minnelli
Produced by Lee Shubert
With Beatrice Lillie and Bert Lahr

Song recorded:
Song Of The Woodman

Arlen and Harburg's adeptness at Lahr-ese was to continue with *If I Were King Of The Forest* and *If I Only Had The Nerve* for the 1939 movie "The Wizard of Oz." They also wrote a 1939 Groucho classic, *Lydia, The Tattooed Lady.*

HOORAY FOR WHAT!

DECEMBER 1, 1937   WINTER GARDEN THEATRE   200 PERFORMANCES

Lyrics by E. Y. Harburg
Book by Howard Lindsay and Russel Crouse

(Conceived by Harburg)
Choreographed by Robert Alton
Directed by Lindsay
Supervised by Vincente Minnelli
Produced by the Messrs. Shubert
With Ed Wynn, Jack Whiting, June Clyde, and Vivian Vance

Published songs:
Buds Won't Bud—cut
Down With Love
God's Country
I've Gone Romantic On You
In The Shade Of The New Apple Tree
Life's A Dance
Moanin' In The Mornin'

Additional song published in USO/Camp Shows "AT EASE" (Volume 4):
Hooray For What!—with revised lyric, retitled *Hooray For Us!*

What started out as a strong antiwar satire lost much of its bite, along with choreographer Agnes de Mille and costars Kay Thompson and Hannah Williams (Mrs. Jack Dempsey), during its pre-Broadway tryout. What remained—Ed Wynn and the fine score—was more than enough to make HOORAY FOR WHAT! a moderate hit. The debut of vocal arranger (and backup singer) Hugh Martin made a striking impression on Broadway: Rodgers, Berlin and Porter immediately put him to work (see BEST FOOT FORWARD [Martin: October 1, 1941]). Arlen, who had been writing for the movies since 1934, returned to Hollywood for an extended stay.

SYMPHONY IN BROWN

Nightclub Revue

[CIRCA MARCH, 1942]   TROCADERO

Published song:
Life Could Be A Cakewalk With You (lyric by Ted Koehler)

BLOOMER GIRL

OCTOBER 5, 1944   SHUBERT THEATRE   654 PERFORMANCES

Lyrics by E. Y. Harburg
Book by Sig. Herzig and Fred Saidy
(Based on a play by Dan and Lilith James)

Choreographed by Agnes de Mille
Book directed by William Schorr
Production staged by Harburg
Produced by John C. Wilson (in association with Nat Goldstone)
With Celeste Holm, David Brooks, Joan McCracken, and Dooley Wilson

Published songs:
The Eagle And Me
Evelina
I Got A Song—initial publication of song cut from 1943 movie version of
  CABIN IN THE SKY [Duke: October 25, 1940]
Right As The Rain
T'morra', T'morra'
When The Boys Come Home

Additional songs recorded:
Civil War Ballet
The Farmer's Daughter
It Was Good Enough For Grandma
Liza Crossing The Ice
Lullaby (Satin Gown And Silver Shoe)
Man For Sale
Never Was Born
The Rakish Young Man With The Whiskahs
Sunday In Cicero Falls
Welcome Hinges

Arlen returned to Broadway with this Civil War-period costume musical. Trying to follow the success of OKLAHOMA! [Rodgers: March 31, 1943], BLOOMER GIRL employed the same choreographer, designers, and two of the leading players. Though certainly not in the same league, BLOOMER GIRL was entertaining and nostalgic enough for wartime audiences and flourished. Arlen's score included *The Eagle And Me* and the gentle *Evelina.*

ST. LOUIS WOMAN

MARCH 30, 1946   MARTIN BECK THEATRE   113 PERFORMANCES

Lyrics by Johnny Mercer
Book by Arna Bontemps and Countee Cullen
(Based on *God Sends Sunday* [novel] by Bontemps)
Directed by Rouben Mamoulian
Produced by Edward Gross
With Ruby Hill, Harold Nicholas, June Hawkins, and Pearl Bailey

Published songs:
Any Place I Hang My Hat Is Home
Cakewalk Your Lady
Come Rain Or Come Shine
I Had Myself A True Love
I Wonder What Became of Me—cut
Legalize My Name
Ridin' On The Moon

Additional song published in "Intimate Songs":
A Woman's Prerogative

Additional songs recorded:
Leavin' Time
L'il Augie Is A Natural Man
Lullaby
Sleep Peaceful, Mr. Used-To-Be

Arlen and Mercer had established their unique chemistry with the 1941 movie "Blues in the Night." (Who else could have written that song? *Blues In The Night* is incomparable, two of America's most exciting songwriters combined for their colorful best.) St. Louis Woman was another ambitious Mamoulian musical, saddled with an unfocused script by two first-time librettists—one of whom (Cullen) died before rehearsals. Arlen's theatre music had developed from his early rhythmic tunes and blues—superb and memorable as they were—to art songs with beauty, grace, and the unique Arlen coloring. The exquisite *I Wonder What Became Of Me* was cut, and remains relatively unknown (as does *Sleep Peaceful, Mr. Used-To-Be*); *Come Rain Or Come Shine* and *Any Place I Hang My Hat Is Home* managed to find their way to the public. As with all of Arlen's remaining shows, the scores were overcome by the productions' fatal flaws. Arlen and Mercer reworked the St. Louis Woman material into the 1959 "blues opera" "Free and Easy," which was unsuccessfully performed in Europe.

HOUSE OF FLOWERS

December 30, 1954   Alvin Theatre   165 performances

Lyrics by Truman Capote and Harold Arlen
Book by Capote
(Based on the novella by Capote)
Choreographed by Herbert Ross
Directed by Peter Brook
Produced by Saint-Subber

With Pearl Bailey, Diahann Carroll, Juanita Hall, Ray Walston, and
Geoffrey Holder

Published songs:
House Of Flowers—revised version of *Let's Go, Sailor* (cut, unpublished)
    from 1942 movie "Star Spangled Rhythm" and *I Love A New
    Yorker* from 1950 movie "My Blue Heaven"
I Never Has Seen Snow
A Sleepin' Bee
Smellin' Of Vanilla (Bamboo Cage)
Two Ladies In De Shade Of De Banana Tree

Additional songs published in vocal selections:
Can I Leave Off Wearin' My Shoes?—also recorded as *I'm Gonna Leave
    Off Wearin' My Shoes*
Don't Like Goodbyes
Jump De Broom (lyric by Capote)—written for off-Broadway revival
    [January 28, 1968]
Madame Tango's Particular Tango—written for revival; different than
    Madame Tango's Tango (cut, unpublished) from original version
One Man Ain't Quite Enough
Somethin' Cold To Drink—written for revival
Waitin'
What Is A Friend For?
Woman Never Understan'—written for revival

Additional songs recorded:
Has I Let You Down
Mardi Gras
Slide, Boy, Slide
Turtle Song (One Brave Man Against The Sea)
Waltz [instrumental]—revised version of 1942 piano solo *American
    Minuet*

A legendary failure with a legendary score. A first-time librettist/colyricist and
a very talented director making his musical *and* Broadway debut did not help
the situation, and the very special material suffered. The tryout was one
continuous, many-sided battle with Pearl Bailey—who had stolen the show in
St. Louis Woman [March 30, 1946]—winning most of the backstage bouts.
Diahann Carroll memorably introduced some of Arlen's most beautiful songs
and herself. The gems in Arlen's finest score included *A Sleepin' Bee, I Never
Has Seen Snow,* and the unique *Two Ladies In De Shade Of De Banana Tree.*

JAMAICA

OCTOBER 31, 1957   IMPERIAL THEATRE   557 PERFORMANCES

Lyrics by E. Y. Harburg
Book by Harburg and Fred Saidy
Choreographed by Jack Cole
Directed by Robert Lewis
Produced by David Merrick
With Lena Horne, Ricardo Montalban, and Adelaide Hall

Published songs:
Ain' It De Truth?—originally used (cut) in 1943 movie version of CABIN
    IN THE SKY [Duke: October 25, 1940]
Cocoanut Sweet
I Don't Think I'll End It All Today
Incompatibility
Little Biscuit
Napoleon
Pretty To Walk With (That's How A Man Gets Got)
Push De Button
Savannah
Take It Slow, Joe
What Good Does It Do?

Additional songs recorded:
For Every Fish There's A Little Bigger Fish
Leave De Atom Alone
Monkey In The Mango Tree
Pity De Sunset
Savannah's Wedding Day
Sweet Wind Blowin' My Way—cut
The Yankee Dollar (Hooray For)

When calypso star Harry Belafonte withdrew from this project he was replaced by Lena Horne, who started her career in Arlen's final COTTON CLUB
PARADE (Twenty-fourth Edition) [March 23, 1934] and rode to stardom
singing the title song in the 1943 movie "Stormy Weather." The unorthodox
cast change didn't much matter; JAMAICA in its final state was little more than
Horne singing a string of songs. Ironically, JAMAICA was Arlen's only hit show
after BLOOMER GIRL [October 5, 1944], due to the entrepreneurial finesse of
Merrick. Note that the four Arlen/Harburg shows, as well as their one complete film musical, "The Wizard of Oz," were all successes.

SARATOGA

December 7, 1959   Winter Garden Theatre   80 performances

Lyrics by Johnny Mercer
Book and direction by Morton DaCosta
(Based on *Saratoga Trunk* [novel] by Edna Ferber)
Produced by Robert Fryer
With Howard Keel, Carol Lawrence, Carol Brice, and Edith King

Published songs:
A Game Of Poker
Goose Never Be A Peacock
Love Held Lightly
The Man In My Life
Saratoga

Additional songs published in vocal selection:
Dog Eat Dog
The Parks Of Paris—cut
Petticoat High
You For Me—cut

Additional songs recorded:
Countin' Our Chickens
The Cure
Gettin' A Man (music by Mercer)
Have You Heard (Gossip Song)
I'll Be Respectable
The Men Who Run The Country (music by Mercer)
One Step—Two Step
Why Fight This? (music by Mercer)
You Or No One

A misguided, heavy-handed effort burying some lovely Arlen/Mercer work. **Saratoga** was in the hands of Morton DaCosta, briefly invincible with *No Time For Sergeants* [October 20, 1955], *Auntie Mame* [October 31, 1956] and **The Music Man** [**Willson: December 19, 1957**]. Writing his own libretto as well as directing, DaCosta was clearly influenced by and aspiring to the earlier Ferber-based musical **Show Boat** [**Kern: December 27, 1927**]; things didn't work out. Mercer's musical contributions came about when illness forced the composer away from part of the tryout. **Saratoga** was Arlen's shortest-running—and final—Broadway show. Following some additional motion picture work, the composer went into retirement in the mid-Sixties, but continued to write some fine (although presently unpublished) songs. Harold Arlen died on April 23, 1986.

There are those who place Gershwin and Arlen at the top of the list of American composers, with the slight lead going to Arlen. Gershwin led the way, scattering delightful surprises ("blue notes," catchy rhythms, musical whimsy) throughout his work. The younger composer used these same elements, but not for effect: to Arlen they were *natural*. Gershwin's fascinatin' rhythms were carefully built and marvelously effective; Arlen's—*Get Happy*, for example—were infectious and light as air. Gershwin's blues relied on that "blue note," as in the superb *The Man I Love*; Arlen's blues were ruled only by his limitless imagination. The music of Harold Arlen has remained ageless; the songs—theatre, screen, and all—are filled with never-ending magic.

Vernon Duke

BORN: October 10, 1903   Parafianovo (Minsk), Russia
DIED: January 17, 1969   Santa Monica, California

Born to a White Russian family, Vernon Duke was the son of a civil engineer. A highly musical child, Duke studied with Glière and enrolled in the Kiev Conservatory in 1913. Uprooted by the October Revolution of 1917, Duke—with mother and younger brother—fled the country, reaching America in 1921. Unable to find a musical career here, he moved to Paris; in 1924 he composed the successful ballet "Zephyr et Flore" for Serge Diaghilev's Ballet Russe.

KATJA THE DANCER

FEBRUARY 21, 1925   GAIETY THEATRE < LONDON >   505
    PERFORMANCES

Music mostly by Jean Gilbert
Book by Frederick Lonsdale and Harry Graham
(Based on the Austrian musical)
Produced by George Edwardes
With Lilian Davies and Maida Vale

Published songs:
Back To My Heart (lyric by Percy Greenbank)—added after opening
Try A Little Kiss (lyric by Greenbank and Wimperis)—added after
    opening

Arriving in London with his Ballet Russe success, Duke was hired to add contemporary songs to this long-running operetta. *Try A Little Kiss* was his first published popular song. Duke's real name—Vladimir Dukelsky—was contractually restricted to his concert works; Geroge Gershwin, friend and fan since 1921, came up with the pseudonym.

YVONNE

MAY 22, 1926   DALY'S THEATRE < LONDON >   280 PERFORMANCES

Music also by Jean Gilbert
Book and lyrics by Percy Greenbank
(Based on the Austrian musical)
Directed by Herbert Mason
Produced by George Edwardes
With Ivy Tresmand and Hal Sherman

Published songs:
Day Dreams
It's Nicer To Be Naughty
Lucky
The Magic Of The Moon
We Always Disagree

Additional songs published in vocal score:
All Men Are The Same
Charming Weather (Opening)
Don't Forget The Waiter

Duke added a half-score to this import, which Noël Coward dubbed "Yvonne The Terrible."

TWO LITTLE GIRLS IN BLUE

[CIRCA APRIL 1927] < PORTSMOUTH, ENGLAND > ; CLOSED DURING
     PRE-LONDON TRYOUT

Music mostly by Paul Lannin and Vincent **Youmans** [May 3, 1921]
Lyrics mostly by Ira Gershwin
Book by Fred Jackson
Produced by Norman J. Norman and David Marks
With The Barry Twins and Barrie Oliver

Published song:
Somebody's Sunday (music and lyric by Duke)

THE BOW-WOWS

A Hare-m Scare-m Musical Show

OCTOBER 12, 1927   PRINCE OF WALES'S THEATRE < LONDON >   124
PERFORMANCES

Music and lyrics mostly by others
Directed and produced by Laddie Cliff
With Elsie Gregory and Georges Metaxa

Published song:
For Goodness' Sake (lyric by James Dyrenforth)

THE YELLOW MASK

A Mystery Thriller Musical

FEBRUARY 8, 1928   CARLTON THEATRE < LONDON >   218
PERFORMANCES

Lyrics mostly by Desmond Carter
Book by Edgar Wallace
Directed by Laddie Cliff
Produced by Julian Wylie and Cliff
With Bobby Howes, Phyllis Dare and Leslie Henson

Published songs:
The Bacon And The Egg
Blowing The Blues Away (lyric by Eric Little)
Deep Sea
Half A Kiss (lyric by Little)
I Love You So
I Still Believe In You (lyric by Duke and Carter)
I'm Wonderful
You Do, I Don't

Additional songs published (no lyrics) in piano selection:
Chinese Ballet
Chinese March
March
Opening Chorus Act One
Walking On Air
Yellow Mask

Duke, already attracting notice with his distinctive interpolations in Gershwin-crazy London, wrote his first complete score for this hit. *Blowing The*

Blues Away was in the Gershwin *Sweet And Low Down/Kickin' The Clouds Away* tradition, only with Duke's more complex natural harmonies; *Half A Kiss* was a pleasant enough fox trot.

OPEN YOUR EYES

[CIRCA AUGUST 1929]   EMPIRE THEATRE < EDINBURGH > ; CLOSED
    DURING PRE-LONDON TRYOUT

Lyrics by Collie Knox
Book by Frederick Jackson
Directed by John Harwood
With Ella Logan, Marie Burke, and Geoffrey Gwyther

Published songs:
Happily Ever After
Jack And Jill
Open Your Eyes
Such A Funny Feeling
Too, Too Divine—see GARRICK GAIETIES (Third) [June 4, 1930]
You'd Do For Me—I'd Do For You

Dukelsky's "First Symphony" was introduced by mentor/publisher Serge Koussevitzky and the Boston Symphony on March 15, 1929. Duke permanently moved to America in June—before the OPEN YOUR EYES production—and became a citizen in 1938.

GARRICK GAIETIES
Third Edition

JUNE 4, 1930   GUILD THEATRE   170 PERFORMANCES

"Music and Lyrics By Everybody" (see **Blitzstein**)
Lyrics to Duke songs by E. Y. Harburg
Directed by Philip Loeb
Produced by The Theatre Guild
With Sterling Holloway, Edith Meiser, and Imogene Coca

Published songs:
I Am Only Human After All (lyric by Ira Gershwin and Harburg)
Too, Too Divine—cut after opening; new lyric for song from OPEN YOUR
    EYES [Circa August 1929]; also used with third lyric as *Shavian*
    Shivers (unpublished)

Ira Gershwin teamed former CCNY classmate (turned Depression-bankrupt electrical-appliance salesman) Harburg and George's friend Duke; the three collaborated on Duke's first American song, *I Am Only Human After All.* While looking for Broadway opportunity, Duke found a background music job at the Paramount film studios in Astoria. Duke and Harburg also wrote additional songs (unpublished) for the post-Broadway tour of this final **Garrick Gaieties.**

THREE'S A CROWD

October 15, 1930   Selwyn Theatre   271 performances

Music mostly by Arthur **Schwartz** (see **Lane**)
Lyrics mostly by Howard Dietz
Sketches by Dietz and others
Choreographed by Albertina Rasch
Directed by Hassard Short
Produced by Max Gordon
With Clifton Webb, Fred Allen, Libby Holman, and Tamara Geva

Published songs:
None

Duke contributed Tamara Geva's memorable *Talkative Toes* (unpublished). Geva, wife of Balanchine, was the first of Duke's Ballets Russe group to achieve Broadway success.

SHOOT THE WORKS

July 21, 1931   George M. Cohan Theatre   87 performances

Music and lyrics mostly by others (see **Berlin**)
Sketches by Nunnally Johnson, Heywood Broun, and others
Directed by Ted Hammerstein
Produced by Broun, with Milton Raison
With Broun, George Murphy, and Imogene Coca

Published songs:
Mu-Cha-Cha (music by Duke and Jay Gorney, lyric by E. Y. Harburg)

WALK A LITTLE FASTER

December 7, 1932   St. James Theatre   119 performances

Lyrics by E. Y. Harburg
Sketches by S. J. Perelman
Directed by Monty Woolley
Produced by Courtney Burr

With Beatrice Lillie, Bobby Clark and Paul McCullough, and Evelyn Hoey

Published songs:
April In Paris
Off Again, On Again
A Penny For Your Thoughts
So Nonchalant (lyric by Harburg and Charles Tobias)
Speaking of Love
That's Life
Where Have We Met Before?

Duke wrote his most famous song—*April In Paris*—for his first complete Broadway score. Trained in concert music and jazz ballet, he quickly attracted notice with his advanced-form theatre songs. Duke rarely attracted great popularity, but he found (and maintains) an ardent "highbrow" following.

ZIEGFELD FOLLIES OF 1934

JANUARY 4, 1934   WINTER GARDEN THEATRE   182 PERFORMANCES

Music mostly by Duke
Lyrics mostly by E. Y. Harburg
Directed by Bobby Connolly and John Murray Anderson
Produced by "Mrs. Florenz Ziegfeld" [Messrs. Shubert]
With Fanny Brice, Willie and Eugene Howard, and Jane Froman

Published songs:
I Like The Likes of You
Suddenly (lyric by Billy Rose and Harburg)
This Is Not A Song (lyric by Harburg and E. Hartman)
What Is There To Say?

Additional song recorded:
Water Under The Bridge

Following Ziegfeld's death in 1932, the Shuberts—longtime second-rate competition to the FOLLIES—bought the rights to the title from debt-ridden Billie Burke Ziegfeld. Unbilled but acknowledged, they produced two successful editions with Duke scores (see ZIEGFELD FOLLIES OF 1936 [January 30, 1936]).

THUMBS UP

DECEMBER 27, 1934   ST. JAMES THEATRE   156 PERFORMANCES

Music and lyrics mostly by others
Directed by John Murray Anderson and Edward Clarke Lilley
Produced by Eddie Dowling.
With Bobby Clark and Paul McCullough, Hal LeRoy, and J. Harold Murray

Published song:
Autumn In New York (lyric by Duke)

Duke's one contribution was his followup to *April In Paris* from WALK A LITTLE FASTER [December 7, 1932]. Both shows starred the comedy team of Clark and McCullough (who, of course, did not sing either song).

ZIEGFELD FOLLIES OF 1936

JANUARY 30, 1936   WINTER GARDEN THEATRE   115 PERFORMANCES

Lyrics by Ira Gershwin
Sketches by David Freedman
Choreographed by George Balanchine
Directed by John Murray Anderson
Produced by "Mrs. Florenz Ziegfeld" [Messrs. Shubert]
With Fanny Brice, Bob Hope, Eve Arden and Josephine Baker

Published songs:
The Gazooka
I Can't Get Started
Island In The West Indies
My Red Letter Day
That Moment Of Moments
Words Without Music

Additional songs published in USO/Camp Shows "AT EASE" (Volume 4):
Economic Situation—with revised lyric, retitled *New War Situation*
Fancy, Fancy
She Hasn't A Thing Except Me
Time Marches On
We Hope You'll Soon Be Dancing To Our Score—with revised lyric, retitled *We Somehow Feel That You Enjoyed Our Show*

Duke and Harburg—both volatile and opinionated—broke up over disagreements on the previous FOLLIES. Ira Gershwin was free, as George was busy finishing and orchestrating **PORGY AND BESS** [October 10, **1935**]. Memorable moments: Freedman's creation of the "Baby Snooks" character for Brice, and Hope introducing the immortal *I Can't Get Started.* Also introduced to America was Duke's Ballets Russe pal, George Balanchine.

THE SHOW IS ON

DECEMBER 25, 1936   WINTER GARDEN THEATRE   237 PERFORMANCES

Music mostly by Duke (see **Arlen, Gershwin,** and **Rodgers** and **Schwartz**)
Lyrics mostly by Ted Fetter
Sketches mostly by David Freedman and Moss Hart
Directed by Vincente Minnelli
Produced by Lee Shubert
With Beatrice Lillie and Bert Lahr

Published song:
Now

Additional song published in USO/Camp Shows "AT EASE" (Volume 4):
The Finale Marches On (lyric by E. Y. Harburg and Fetter)

Duke wrote songs and ballet music as well as compiling the interpolations from a number of major composers. Following the shock of Gershwin's death (July 11, 1937), Duke went to Hollywood to complete his friend's final score for the 1938 movie "The Goldwyn Follies."

A VAGABOND HERO

A Dashing Musical Romance

[DECEMBER 26, 1939]   NATIONAL THEATRE < WASHINGTON D.C. > ;
        CLOSED DURING PRE-BROADWAY TRYOUT

Music also by Samuel D. Pokrass
Book and lyrics mostly by Charles O. Locke
(Based on *Cyrano de Bergerac* [play] by Edmond Rostand)
Directed by George Houston
Produced by Messrs. Shubert
With Houston, Ruby Mercer, Hope Emerson, and Bill Johnson
NOTE: **THE WHITE PLUME,** original tryout title

Songs issued as professional copies:
Bonjour, Goodbye
I Cling To You (Roxane's Song) (lyric by Locke and Ted Fetter)
Shadow Of Love (lyric by Locke and Fetter)

Cyrano de Bergerac had toured unsuccessfully in 1932. With the Depression over, the Shuberts decided to remount it (they already had the costumes) and hired Duke to supplement the score. A week in Washington as THE WHITE PLUME, a week in Pittsburgh as A VAGABOND HERO—and that was it. *I Cling To You* is particularly lovely.

KEEP OFF THE GRASS

MAY 23, 1940   BROADHURST THEATRE   44 PERFORMANCES

Music mostly by Jimmy McHugh
Lyrics by Al Dubin and Howard Dietz
Sketches by Parke Levy, Norman Panama and Melvin Frank, and others
Choreographed by George Balanchine
Directed by Fred de Cordova and Edward Duryea Dowling
Produced by the Messrs. Shubert
With Ray Bolger, Jimmy Durante, José Limon, Larry Adler, and Jane Froman

Published song:
None

Duke provided *Raffles* (unpublished), a ballet for Bolger.

IT HAPPENS ON ICE

An Ice Extravaganza

OCTOBER 10, 1940   CENTER THEATRE   180 PERFORMANCES

Music also by others
Lyrics by Al Stillman
Staged and devised by Leon Leonidoff
Produced by Sonja Henie and Arthur Wirtz
With Joe Cook

Published songs:
Don't Blow That Horn, Gabriel (lyric by Stillman and Will Hudson)
Long Ago

CABIN IN THE SKY

OCTOBER 25, 1940   MARTIN BECK THEATRE   156 PERFORMANCES

Lyrics by John Latouche
Book by Lynn Root

Dialogue staged by Albert Lewis
Directed and choreographed by George Balanchine
Produced by Lewis in association with Vinton Freedley
With Ethel Waters, Todd Duncan, Rex Ingram, Dooley Wilson, and
Katherine Dunham

Published songs:
Cabin In The Sky
Do What You Wanna Do
Honey In The Honeycomb
In My Old Virginia Home (On The River Nile)—cut
Livin' It Up (lyric by Duke)—written for revival [January 21, 1964]
Love Me Tomorrow
Love Turned The Light Out
Savannah
Taking A Chance On Love (lyric by Latouche and Ted Fetter)

Additional songs recorded:
Great Day
Make Way
The Man Upstairs
Not So Bad To Be Good
Wade In The Water
We'll Live All Over Again—cut

Duke wrote his best and most successful score for this fantasy musical, with
friend and compatriot Balanchine not only choreographing but directing as
well. Ethel Waters introduced *Taking A Chance On Love* in her greatest
musical role. Also standing out: *Cabin In The Sky, Love Me Tomorrow,* and
In My Old Virginia Home. For the 1943 movie version—made while Duke
was serving in the Coast Guard—Harold Arlen and E. Y. Harburg wrote three
additional songs, including *Happiness Is Just A Thing Called Joe.*

BANJO EYES

DECEMBER 25, 1941   HOLLYWOOD THEATRE   126 PERFORMANCES

Music mostly by Duke
Lyrics mostly by John Latouche
Book by Joe Quillan and Izzy Elinson
(Based on *Three Men on a Horse* [play] by John Cecil Holm and George
Abbott)
Directed by Hassard Short
Produced by Albert Lewis
With Eddie Cantor, Audrey Christie, June Clyde, and Lionel Stander

Published songs:
Banjo Eyes
Don't Let It Happen Again—cut; issued as professional copy
I Always Think of Sally—issued as professional copy
I'll Take The City—issued as professional copy
Make With The Feet (lyric by Harold Adamson)
My Song Without Words
A Nickel To My Name
Not A Care In The World
We're Having A Baby (My Baby and Me) (lyric by Adamson)
Who Made The Rumba?—advertised but not published

Eddie Cantor's only Broadway appearance after **WHOOPEE** [**PART 4**: December 4, 1928] was in this undistinguished wartime hit, the run cut short by the star's illness. The title character, incidentally, was not Cantor but a rumba-ing racehorse (of the two-person variety). A second musical version of the play was the unsuccessful Livingston and Evans' **LET IT RIDE** [October 12, 1961]. George Abbott, no fool, knew enough to stay away from both attempts at altering his classic farce.

THE LADY COMES ACROSS

JANUARY 9, 1942   44TH STREET THEATRE   3 PERFORMANCES

Lyrics by John Latouche
Book by Fred Thompson and Dawn Powell
Choreography by George Balanchine
Book directed by Romney Brent
Under the supervision of Morrie Ryskind
Produced by George Hale
With Evelyn Wyckoff, Joe E. Lewis, Ronald Graham, Gower Champion, and Jeanne Tyler

Songs issued in professional copies:
I'd Like To Talk About The Weather
Lady
Summer Is A-Comin' In—also used in **THE LITTLEST REVUE** [May 25, 1956]
This Is Where I Came In
You Took Me By Surprise

This ill-fated musical started life as the Sammy Fain/Al Dubin **SHE HAD TO SAY YES**, produced and coauthored by (and starring) Dennis King. Duke and Latouche were called in to doctor; when King closed the show on the road, George Hale bought the sets and costumes and assembled **THE LADY COMES**

ACROSS. Then the trouble really started. British musical comedy great Jessie Matthews (see EVER GREEN [Rodgers: December 3, 1930]) came across to star; she played Boston and disappeared, a victim of shell shock. Evelyn Wyckoff bravely took over for the Broadway opening; the show got bombed. Duke entered the Coast Guard.

DANCING IN THE STREETS

[MARCH 22, 1943]   SHUBERT THEATRE < BOSTON, MASSACHUSETTS > ;
CLOSED DURING PRE-BROADWAY TRYOUT

Lyrics by Howard Dietz
Book by John Cecil Holm and Matt Taylor
Directed by Edgar MacGregor
Produced by Vinton Freedley
With Mary Martin, Dudley Digges, and Ernest Cossart

Published songs:
Dancing In The Streets
Got A Bran' New Daddy
Indefinable Charm
Irresistible You

A wartime musical comedy which Duke wrote while serving in Brooklyn. He had collaborated with Dietz before, on *Talkative Toes* from THREE's A CROWD [October 15, 1930]. Mary Martin had been discovered in LEAVE IT TO ME [Porter: November 9, 1938] and signed to a Hollywood contract. She returned East to star in the Ralph Rainger/Leo Robin NICE GOIN' [October 21, 1939], which closed on the road. She turned down the lead in OKLAHOMA! [Rodgers: March 31, 1943] to do DANCING IN THE STREETS. It wasn't till her next try that she came up with a hit, ONE TOUCH OF VENUS [Weill: October 7, 1943].

JACKPOT

JANUARY 13, 1944   ALVIN THEATRE   69 PERFORMANCES

Lyrics by Howard Dietz
Book by Guy Bolton, Sidney Sheldon, and Ben Roberts
Directed by Roy Hargrave
Produced by Vinton Freedley
With Nanette Fabray, Betty Garrett, Allan Jones, and Benny Baker

Published songs:
I've Got A One Track Mind
Sugarfoot

There Are Yanks (From The Banks Of The Wabash)
What Happened?

Another undistinguished wartime musical comedy. Freedley had lost his touch; he had nothing but flops following LET'S FACE IT! [Porter: October 29, 1941]. Retiring in 1950, he spent the rest of his life serving as an officer and ultimately president of the Actors' Fund.

TARS AND SPARS

A Tabloid Recruiting Revue for the United States Coast Guard

MAY 5, 1944   STRAND THEATRE

Music by Lt. Vernon Duke USCGR(T)
Book and lyrics by Howard Dietz
Choreography by Ted Gary and Gower Champion Seaman 1c
Directed and produced by Max Liebman
With Victor Mature CBM, Sidney Caesar Seaman 1c, and Champion

Published songs:
Arm In Arm
Civilian
Farewell For A While
Silver Shield—published in nonshow edition

Additional songs published in vocal selection:
Apprentice Seaman
Palm Beach

The Army had Irving Berlin (THIS IS THE ARMY [July 4, 1942]), Frank Loesser, and Harold Rome; the Coast Guard had Duke, and assigned him to put together a recruiting show. Assembling the cast from enlisted men, Sid Caesar was found playing saxophone in the base's band and given comedy routines. TARS AND SPARS toured the country, keeping Duke, Caesar, and Champion stateside. SPARS, incidentally, were the Coast Guard's equivalent to WACS.

SADIE THOMPSON

NOVEMBER 16, 1944   ALVIN THEATRE   60 PERFORMANCES

Lyrics by Howard Dietz
Book by Dietz and Rouben Mamoulian
(Based on *Rain* [play] by W. Somerset Maugham and John Colton)
Directed by Rouben Mamoulian

Produced by A. P. Waxman
With June Havoc, Lansing Hatfield, and Ralph Dumke

Published songs:
Any Woman Who Is Willing Will Do—advertised but not published
If You Can't Get The Love You Want
Life's A Funny Present From Someone
The Love I Long For
Poor As A Churchmouse
Sailing At Midnight
When You Live On An Island
You—U.S.A.—advertised but not published

An ambitious failure. SADIE THOMPSON's fate was sealed during the first week of rehearsals, when star Ethel Merman found Dietz's lyrics lacking and quit. Her replacement: "Baby June" Havoc. Duke's fine score disappeared, including the lovely *Sailing At Midnight.*

SWEET BYE AND BYE

[OCTOBER 10, 1946]   SHUBERT THEATRE < NEW HAVEN,
      CONNECTICUT > ; CLOSED DURING PRE-BROADWAY TRYOUT

Lyrics by Ogden Nash
Book by S. J. Perelman and Al Hirschfeld
Directed by Curt Conway
Produced by Nat Karson
With Dolores Gray, Erik Rhodes, and Percy Helton

Published songs:
Just Like A Man—also used in TWO'S COMPANY [December 15, 1952]
Low and Lazy
An Old Fashioned Tune
Round About—also used in TWO'S COMPANY
Sweet Bye And Bye

Another out-of-town disaster. Beginning with Eddie Cantor's illness which cut short the run of BANJO EYES [December 26, 1941], Duke wrote ten consecutive flops (four closing on the road). Not surprisingly, it became increasingly difficult for Duke to get productions, despite the continued quality and inventiveness of his work.

TWO'S COMPANY

DECEMBER 15, 1952   ALVIN THEATRE   90 PERFORMANCES

Music mostly by Duke
Lyrics mostly by Ogden Nash
Sketches mostly by Charles Sherman and Peter DeVries
Choreographed by Jerome Robbins
Sketches directed by Jules Dassin
Production supervised by John Murray Anderson
Produced by James Russo and Michael Ellis
With Bette Davis, Hiram Sherman, and Nora Kaye

Published songs:
Good Little Girls (lyric by Sammy Cahn)—cut; also used in THE
    LITTLEST REVUE [May 22, 1956]
It Just Occurred To Me
Just Like A Man—originally used in SWEET BYE AND BYE [October 10,
    1946]
Out Of The Clear Blue Sky
Round About—originally used in SWEET BYE AND BYE

Additional songs recorded:
Esther (lyric by Cahn)
Haunted Hot Spot
Purple Rose
Roll Along Sadie
The Theatre Is A Lady
Turn Me Loose On Broadway

A turmoil-wracked Broadway failure, with Bette Davis in her musical debut;
the not-very-good show had to close when she developed a "sudden illness."
Her second musical, the Broadway-bound MISS MOFFAT [October 7, 1974],
had to close when she developed a "sudden illness."

THE LITTLEST REVUE

MAY 22, 1956   PHOENIX THEATRE   (OFF-BROADWAY)   32
    PERFORMANCES

Music mostly by Duke (also see **Blitzstein** and **Strouse**)
Lyrics mostly by Ogden Nash
Sketches by Nat Hiken, Michael Stewart, and others
Directed by Paul Lammers

Produced by T. Edward Hambleton and Norris Houghton by arrangement
with Ben Bagley
With Charlotte Rae, Tammy Grimes, Joel Grey, and Larry Storch

Published songs:
Born Too Late
Good Little Girls—originally used in **Two's Company** [December 15,
    1952]
Madly In Love
Summer Is A-Comin' In (lyric by John Latouche)—originally used in **The
    Lady Comes Across** [January 9, 1942]
You're Far From Wonderful

Additional songs recorded:
I'm Glad I'm Not A Man
A Little Love, A Little Money
Love Is Still In Town
Second Avenue And Twelfth Street Rag

The Phoenix Theatre had ended its first season with the award-winning
Jerome Moross/John Latouche **Golden Apple** [Part 4: March 11, 1954].
Looking for another musical success, it commissioned Duke for this intimate
revue. Success, however, was not duplicated. Duke's score included the moving and incredible *Born Too Late.*

TIME REMEMBERED

November 2, 1957   Morosco Theatre   248 performances

Play by Jean Anouilh
English version by Patricia Moyes
Incidental music and lyrics by Duke
Directed by Albert Marre (see **April Song** [Leigh: July 9, 1980])
Produced by The Playwrights' Company in association with Milton
Sperling
With Helen Hayes, Richard Burton, and Susan Strasberg

Published songs:
Ages Ago
Time Remembered

This hit drama was Duke's final effort to reach Broadway.

THE PINK JUNGLE

[OCTOBER 14, 1959]   ALCAZAR THEATRE < SAN FRANCISCO,
     CALIFORNIA > ; CLOSED DURING PRE-BROADWAY TRYOUT

Music and lyrics by Duke
Book by Leslie Stevens
Choreographed by Matt Maddox
Directed by Joseph Anthony
Produced by Paul Gregory
With Ginger Rogers, Leif Erickson, and Agnes Moorehead

Published songs:
None

Ginger Rogers' first Broadway musical since GIRL CRAZY [Gershwin: October
14, 1930] was not to be; it closed under a pink cloud of unpaid bills. THE PINK
JUNGLE, for the record, was the cosmetics game.

ZENDA

A Romantic Musical

[AUGUST 5, 1963]   CURRAN THEATRE < SAN FRANCISCO, CALIFORNIA > ;
     CLOSED DURING PRE-BROADWAY TRYOUT

Lyrics mostly by Martin Charnin
Book by Everett Freeman
(Based on *The Prisoner of Zenda* [novel] by Anthony Hope)
Directed by George Schaefer
Produced by Edwin Lester (Civic Light Opera)
With Alfred Drake, Anne Rogers, and Chita Rivera

Published songs:
Let Her Not Be Beautiful (You Are All That's Beautiful)
The Night Is Filled With Wonderful Sounds

Additional songs recorded:
Alive At Last
Alone At Night
Bounce
Enchanting Girls
I Wonder What He Meant By That
Love Is The Worst Possible Thing
The Man Loves Me
My Heart Has Come A 'Tumbling Down

My Royal Majesty
No Ifs! No Ands! No Buts!
No More Love
Now The World Begins Again
A Royal Confession
Words, Words, Words
Yesterday's Forgotten
Zenda

Duke's final show was another road disaster, a costume operetta with many problems and three different lyricists. Inactive through the rest of the Sixties, Vernon Duke died of lung cancer on January 17, 1969, in Santa Monica, California.

Vernon Duke began his Broadway career at the worst possible time—right after the Depression hit the theatre. Harold Arlen and Burton Lane were also 1930 newcomers; they countered by going to Hollywood, not a viable alternative for the musically intricate Dukelsky. Duke's Broadway (and Broadway-bound) record is staggering: fourteen complete scores with only three successes. It had to make for a discouraging career, particularly to a composer who knew that his work was better than most of his contemporaries. And it was. Duke's advanced harmonies and complex forms were—and are—fascinating. George Gershwin discovered Duke in the mid-Twenties and was certainly fascinated: Vernon Duke wrote easily in the style Gershwin aspired to. Gershwin became Duke's biggest fan, started him writing for the theatre and encouraged him to come to America. Duke rarely appealed to the public at large, and his hit songs were few (*April In Paris, I Can't Get Started,* and *Taking A Chance On Love*). But over the years, Duke's brilliance has attracted—and continues to attract—many devotees.

Burton Lane

BORN: February 2, 1912   New York, New York

Burton Lane began his musical career at the age of fifteen, when he left school to work as a pianist at Remick's, where Gershwin and Youmans had started a decade earlier. Lane's expert playing attracted attention—Gershwin was a particular fan—and a Shubert offer to write the 1928 edition of the GREEN-WICH VILLAGE FOLLIES, which was never produced. The sixteen-year-old had to wait another two years before being heard on Broadway.

ARTISTS AND MODELS
Paris-Riviera Edition

JUNE 10, 1930   MAJESTIC THEATRE   65 PERFORMANCES

Music mostly by others
Lane lyrics by Samuel Lerner
(Based on *Dear Love* [British musical])
Directed by Frank Smithson
Produced by Messrs. Shubert
With Aileen Stanley and Phil Baker

Published songs:
My Real Ideal
Two Perfect Lovers

Book troubles were dealt with by throwing out the book and tacking on the name of one of the Shuberts' perennial revues. "Paris-Riviera Edition" explained the sets and costumes. Lane's early songs were bright and tuneful.

THREE'S A CROWD

OCTOBER 15, 1930   SELWYN THEATRE   271 PERFORMANCES

Music mostly by Arthur **Schwartz** (See **Duke**)
Lyrics mostly by Howard Dietz
Sketches by Dietz, Groucho Marx, and others

Directed by Hassard Short
Produced by Max Gordon
With Clifton Webb, Fred Allen, Libby Holman, and Tamara Geva

Published songs:
Forget All Your Books (lyric by Dietz and Samuel Lerner)
Out In The Open Air (lyric by Dietz and Ted Pola)

Howard Dietz was impressed with Lane; he fixed up the lyrics of two songs and inserted them into this first Schwartz and Dietz/Max Gordon revue.

THE THIRD LITTLE SHOW

JUNE 1, 1931   MUSIC BOX THEATRE   136 PERFORMANCES

Music mostly by others
Sketches by Noël Coward, S. J. Perelman, Marc Connelly, and others
Directed by Alexander Leftwich
Produced by Dwight Deere Wiman in association with Tom Weatherly
With Beatrice Lillie, Ernest Truex, and Constance Carpenter

Published song:
Say The Word (lyric by Harold Adamson)

THE SECOND LITTLE SHOW [Schwartz: September 2, 1930]—without Webb, Holman and Allen—had done poorly; this final edition, without even Schwartz and Dietz, fared little better.

EARL CARROLL'S VANITIES

Ninth Edition

AUGUST 27, 1931   EARL CARROLL THEATRE   278 PERFORMANCES

Music also by others
Lyrics to Lane songs by Harold Adamson
Sketches by Ralph Spence and Eddie Welch
Directed by Edgar MacGregor
Produced by Earl Carroll
With Will Mahoney, Lillian Roth, and William Demarest

Published songs:
Goin' To Town
Have A Heart
Love Come Into My Heart

The early years of the Depression were not a good time for teenage songwriters on Broadway. Lane and collaborator Harold Adamson went to Hollywood, quickly coming up with the hit *Everything I Have Is Yours*. Lane worked successfully through the decade with several lyricists, including Frank Loesser.

HOLD ON TO YOUR HATS

SEPTEMBER 11, 1940   SHUBERT THEATRE   158 PERFORMANCES

Lyrics by E. Y. Harburg
Book by Guy Bolton, Matt Brooks, and Eddie Davis
Directed by Edgar MacGregor
Produced by Al Jolson and George Hale
With Jolson, Martha Raye, Jack Whiting, and Bert Gordon

Published songs:
Don't Let It Get You Down (Love Is A Lovely Thing)
Swing Your Calico—cut; issued as professional copy
There's A Great Day Coming Mañana
The World Is In My Arms
Would You Be So Kindly

Additional songs recorded:
Down On The Dude Ranch
Hold On To Your Hats
Life Was Pie For The Pioneer
Old Timer
She Came, She Saw, She Can-Canned
Then You Were Never In Love
Walking Along Minding My Business
Way Out West

Al Jolson returned to Broadway after a decade, bringing along Harburg (who with Harold Arlen had written some fine Jolson songs for the 1936 movie "The Singing Kid"). The star/producer also brought along wife Ruby Keeler, who disappeared from show and marriage during the tryout. The Lane/Harburg score was bright and tuneful—although, curiously, without any Jolson hits. After running a few months, the star decided to close the show and left Broadway for good.

LAFFING ROOM ONLY

DECEMBER 23, 1944   WINTER GARDEN THEATRE   233 PERFORMANCES

Lyrics mostly by Lane
Sketches by Ole Olsen and Chic Johnson and others
Directed by John Murray Anderson

Produced by the Messrs. Shubert and Olsen and Johnson
With Olsen and Johnson and Betty Garrett

Published songs:
Feudin' And Fightin' (lyric by Lane and Al Dubin)—initial publication
    upon reuse as nonshow song
Got That Good Time
Stop That Dancing

HELLZAPOPPIN'! [September 22, 1938], the Olsen and Johnson vaudeville
revue, had run a staggering 1,404 performances; the Shuberts followed it with
a string of duplicates including LAFFING ROOM ONLY. *Feudin' And Fightin'*
resurfaced several years later via radio to become a surprise hit.

FINIAN'S RAINBOW
A Completely Captivating Musical

JANUARY 10, 1947   46TH STREET THEATRE   725 PERFORMANCES

Lyrics by E. Y. Harburg
Book by Harburg and Fred Saidy
Choreographed by Michael Kidd
Directed by Bretaigne Windust
Produced by Lee Sabinson and William R. Katzell
With Ella Logan, David Wayne, Albert Sharpe, Donald Richards, and
Anita Alvarez

Published songs:
The Begat
How Are Things In Glocca Morra?
If This Isn't Love
Look To The Rainbow
Necessity
Old Devil Moon
Something Sort Of Grandish
That Great Come And Get It Day
When I'm Not Near The Girl I Love
When The Idle Poor Become The Idle Rich

Additional songs published in vocal score:
Dance Of The Golden Crock [instrumental]
This Time Of The Year

A perfectly fanciful musical comedy, one of the very few to explore the field
mined by OF THEE I SING [Gershwin: December 26, 1931]. Mixing a little

social significance with some fantasy and lots of entertainment, FINIAN'S RAINBOW got its message across. Lane wrote a superb, highly melodic score (with bits of Irish charm). Harburg did the best work of his career, probably because he was a leprechaun by nature. The songs are gems, with the shifting harmonies of *Old Devil Moon* and the grand, sweeping-but-hesitating waltz *When I'm Not Near The Girl I Love* the enchanting standouts.

JOLLYANNA

(Second Version of FLAHOOLEY [Part 4: May 14, 1951])

[SEPTEMBER 11, 1952]   CURRAN THEATRE (SAN FRANCISCO,
    CALIFORNIA); CLOSED DURING PRE-BROADWAY TRYOUT

Music mostly by Sammy Fain
Lyrics by E. Y. Harburg
Book by Harburg and Fred Saidy
Choreographed by Ruthanna Boris
Directed by Jack Donohue
Produced by Edwin Lester (San Francisco and Los Angeles Civic Light Opera)
With Bobby Clark, Mitzi Gaynor, John Beal, and Biff McGuire

Recorded song:
Santa Claus

West Coast impressario Ed Lester attempted to commercialize the outspoken FLAHOOLEY by removing the social significance (and Yma Sumac). No soap(box), though, despite the presence of Broadway's Bobby Clark and Hollywood's Mitzi Gaynor. The plan was to bring the reconstituted JOLLYANNA back to Broadway in triumph, but in less than a month it was back in the Fascinating Flop File.

ON A CLEAR DAY YOU CAN SEE FOREVER

OCTOBER 17, 1965   MARK HELLINGER THEATRE   280 PERFORMANCES

Book and lyrics by Alan Jay Lerner
Choreographed by Herbert Ross
Directed by Robert Lewis
Produced by Lerner in association with Rogo Productions (Robert Goulet)
With Barbara Harris, John Cullum, Titos Vandis, and William Daniels

Published songs:
Come Back To Me
Go To Sleep—written for 1970 movie version

Hurry! It's Lovely Up Here!
Love With All The Trimmings—written for movie version
Melinda
On A Clear Day (You Can See Forever)
On The S.S. Bernard Cohn
She Wasn't You
Wait Till We're Sixty-Five
What Did I Have That I Don't Have?
When I'm Being Born Again

Additional songs published in vocal score:
Solicitor's Song
When I Come Around Again—new lyric for *When I'm Being Born Again*

Additional songs recorded:
Don't Tamper With My Sister
Tosy And Cosh

Following the 1960 retirement of Frederick Loewe, Alan Jay Lerner had been unsuccessfully searching for a collaborator. He began his ESP project—initially titled "I Picked A Daisy"—with Richard Rodgers; but Rodgers, used to the more disciplined Oscar Hammerstein and Lorenz Hart, found Lerner impossible to work with. (Rodgers next tried Lionel Bart of OLIVER: [PART 5: January 6, 1963]—who was even *more* difficult.) Lerner turned to Lane, with whom he'd written the 1951 movie "Royal Wedding" (including the Oscar nominee *Too Late Now*). The pair wrote an exceedingly fine score, with the popular *On A Clear Day* and *Come Back To Me,* two perfect character songs (*What Did I Have That I Don't Have* and *Hurry! It's Lovely Up Here!*) and the ballads *She Wasn't You* and *Melinda.* All these—plus the performances of Barbara Harris and John Cullum (who replaced Louis Jourdan during the tryout)—weren't enough to carry ON A CLEAR DAY past a contrived book.

CARMELINA

APRIL 8, 1979   ST. JAMES THEATRE   17 PERFORMANCES

Lyrics by Alan Jay Lerner
Book by Lerner and Joseph Stein
(Based on *Buona Sera, Mrs. Campbell* [movie])
Choreographed by Peter Gennaro
Directed by José Ferrer
Produced by Roger L. Stevens, J. W. Fisher, Joan Cullman, and Jujamcyn Productions
With Georgia Brown, Cesare Siepi, John Michael King, Virginia Martin, and Jossie de Guzman

Published songs:
It's Time For A Love Song
One More Walk Around The Garden

Additional songs recorded:
All That He Wants Me To Be
Carmelina
I Must Have Her
I'm A Woman
The Image Of Me
Love Before Breakfast
Prayer
Signora Campbell
Someone In April
Why Him?
Yankee Doodles Are Coming To Town

Lane returned to Broadway again with Lerner. The property was poorly selected and poorly executed, with a book far below Lerner's capabilities. Lane's work was the best of the evening, particularly *I'm A Woman* and *Someone In April*. The latter song featured especially fine work by Lerner.

In a career that spanned fifty years, Burton Lane chose to limit his Broadway output to only four musical comedies. Only one of these shows was successful; another is at least somewhat familiar, due more to its Hollywood incarnation than the superior score. Yet Lane's work is so very good that he maintains and deserves a position of respect in the musical theatre.

PART 2

INTRODUCTION

Most of the top theatre composers of the Twenties spent the bleak Depression in Hollywood. Broadway's only important new voices of the decade were first heard, fittingly, in politically slanted musicals. The already distinguished Kurt Weill arrived from Germany, where his work had been radical both musically and politically. Marc Blitzstein was deeply influenced by Weill, and even more outspoken. Harold Rome, on the other hand, used comedy and charm to make similar points; not surprisingly, he met with far greater popular success. The Depression ended as the nation geared up for war, and Broadway did its share by providing lively, energetic entertainments. Hugh Martin brought in the pop music sound, both as composer and arranger. Leonard Bernstein made the first of his theatre visits with an extra-lively musical comedy (albeit with a large chunk of modern ballet). After the War it was possible to turn to gentle, more thoughtful musicals. A touch of the European returned with Vienna-born Frederick Loewe. The Forties ended with the entrance of two Hollywood songwriters—Jule Styne and Frank Loesser—whose work quickly established them as important composers of "modern musical comedy." Within a few years Loesser was grooming protégés of his own: pop composers Richard Adler and Meredith Willson, who both enjoyed brief but notable Broadway success.

Kurt Weill

BORN: March 2, 1900   Dessau, Germany
DIED: April 3, 1950   New York, New York

The son of a cantor, Kurt Weill was interested in music at an early age. By 1920 he was studying in Berlin with avant-garde composer Ferruccio Busoni; he soon moved from concert to contemporary work and started writing for the theatre. Caught up in Germany's inflammatory political situation, Weill earned a radical reputation. In 1927 he began collaboration with outspoken playwright/lyricist Bertolt Brecht: the pair received international attention with the success of their controversial DIE DREIGROSCHENOPER [August 28, 1928]. Weill's critical views (and Jewish heritage) made it impossible for him to stay in Germany, and he was forced to flee in 1933.

[Note: Weill's German work is not included except for subsequently presented English-language productions]

THE THREEPENNY OPERA
(First Version; see March 10, 1954)

APRIL 13, 1933   EMPIRE THEATRE   12 PERFORMANCES

Original book and lyrics by Bertolt Brecht
English adaptation by Gifford Cochran and Jerrold Krimsky
(Based on *The Beggar's Opera* by John Gay)
Directed by Francesco von Mendelssohn
Produced by John Krimsky and Cochran
With Robert Chisholm, Steffi Duna, Rex Weber, and Burgess Meredith

Published songs:
None

[Complete vocal score of German version is published]
This heavily Germanic translation of DIE DREIGROSCHENOPER was out of place on Broadway in the midst of the Depression; besides, THE BEGGAR'S OPERA had recently been revived in New York. Neither of the authors was

involved in this unsuccessful production. Weill's personal reviews, however, were quite positive.

MARIE GALANTE

DECEMBER 22, 1934   THÉÂTRE DE PARIS < PARIS >

Book and lyrics by Jacques Deval
(Based on his novel)
Directed by Andre Lefour
Produced by Leon Volterra
With Florelle, Inkijinoff, Alcover, Serge Nadoud, and Joé Alex

Published songs:
Les Filles De Bordeaux—revised version of *In Der Jugend Gold'nem
     Schimmer* from HAPPY END [1928]; also revised to *The Trouble
     With Women* from ONE TOUCH OF VENUS [October 7, 1943]
Le Grand Lustucru
J'Attends Un Navire
Marche De L'Armée Paneméenne [instrumental]
Le Roi D'Aquitaine—see A KINGDOM FOR A COW [June 28, 1935]
Scène Au Dancing [instrumental]
Tango—advertised but not published; initial publication as 1946 nonshow
     song *Youkali* (lyric by Roger Fernay)
Le Train Du Ciel

Weill spent his first two years of exile in Paris, where he continued his concert compositions, composed the ballet "The Seven Deadly Sins," and wrote this unsuccessful book musical. *J'Attends Un Navire* is particularly moving.

A KINGDOM FOR A COW

JUNE 28, 1935   SAVOY THEATRE < LONDON >

Lyrics by Desmond Carter
Book by Reginald Arkell and Carter
(Based on *Der Kuhhandel* [musical] by Robert Vambery)
Directed by Ernest Matrai and Felix Weissberger

Published songs:
As Long As I Love
Two Hearts—new lyric for *Le Roi D'Aquitaine* from MARIE GALANTE
     [December 22, 1934]

Unable to get his satirical operetta 'Der Kuhhandel' mounted in Paris or Zurich, Weill arranged a London production. Translated into English as A

Kingdom for a Cow, this satire was poorly received and quickly closed. Trying America next, the composer arrived September 10, 1935; he immediately adopted this country and became a citizen in 1943.

JOHNNY JOHNSON

November 19, 1936   44th Street Theatre   68 performances

Book and lyrics by Paul Green
Directed by Lee Strasberg
Produced by The Group Theatre
With Russell Collins, Phoebe Brand, Paula Miller, Lee J. Cobb, Robert Lewis, Luther Adler, and Elia Kazan

Published songs:
Mon Ami, My Friend
Oh, Heart Of Love
Oh The Rio Grande
To Love You And To Lose You (lyric by Edward Heyman)—nonshow
    lyric for *Listen To My Song (Johnny's Song)*

Additional songs published in vocal score:
Aggie's Song
The Allied High Command
Asylum Chorus
The Ballad Of San Juan Hill
The Battle [instrumental]
Captain Valentine's Song
Democracy's Call
A Hymn To Peace [hymn]
In No Man's Land [instrumental]
In Times Of War and Tumults
Interlude After Scene III [instrumental]
Introduction [instrumental]
Johnny's Dream [instrumental]
Laughing Generals [instrumental]
Listen To My Song (Johnny's Song)
Music Of The Stricken Redeemer [instrumental]
Over In Europe
The Psychiatry Song
The Sea Song
Song Of The Goddess
Song Of The Guns
Song Of The Wounded Frenchmen

The socially conscious Group Theatre (Harold Clurman, Strasberg and Cheryl Crawford) commissioned Weill for this antiwar musical. Paul Green wrote a controversial but muddled book, and the production suffered from unfocused direction. Although JOHNNY JOHNSON was a failure, Weill's work was well received and he attracted Broadway notice.

THE ETERNAL ROAD

JANUARY 7, 1937   MANHATTAN OPERA HOUSE   153 PERFORMANCES

Play and lyrics by Franz Werfel
Adapted by William A. Drake
(From a translation by Ludwig Lewisohn)
Directed by Max Reinhardt
Produced by Meyer W. Weisgal and Crosby Gaige
With Thomas Chalmers, Sam Jaffe, Dickie Van Patten, Katherine Carrington, and Lotte Lenya (Weill)

Songs published in vocal selection:
Dance Of The Golden Calf
David's Psalm
The March To Zion
Promise
Song Of Miriam
Song Of Ruth

Philanthropist Weisgal had brought Weill to America to work with emigrés Reinhardt and Werfel on this eternally-in-preparation Biblical spectacle that illustrated the history of Jewish persecution. Reinhardt had enormous Broadway success in 1924 with his Passion Play *The Miracle;* both productions featured spectacular and massive sets by Norman Bel Geddes. In the cast were Katherine Carrington (Mrs. Arthur Schwartz) and Lotte Lenya, whose career had virtually ended when she joined her husband in exile. Twenty years later, American audiences finally "discovered" her in THE THREEPENNY OPERA (Second Version) [March 10, 1954].

KNICKERBOCKER HOLIDAY

OCTOBER 19, 1938   ETHEL BARRYMORE THEATRE   168 PERFORMANCES

Book and lyrics by Maxwell Anderson
(Based on *Knickerbocker History of New York* [stories] by Washington Irving)
Directed by Joshua Logan
Produced by The Playwrights' Company
With Walter Huston, Jean Madden, Richard Kollmar, and Ray Middleton

Published songs:
It Never Was You
September Song
There's Nowhere To Go But Up
Will You Remember Me?

Additional songs published in vocal selections:
Ballad Of The Robbers
Dirge For A Soldier
How Can You Tell An American?
May And January
The One Indispensable Man
Our Ancient Liberties
The Scars
To War!
Washington Irving's Song
We Are Cut In Twain
Young People Think About Love

Additional songs published in vocal score:
The Algonquins From Harlem [instrumental]
Clickety-Clack
Entrance Of The Council
Hush, Hush
No Ve Vouldn't Gonto Do It
One Touch Of Alchemy (All Hail The Political Honeymoon)
Opening (Introduction To Washington Irving's Song)
Sitting In Jail

Pulitzer Prize-winning playwright Anderson saw the tyrannical Peter Stuyvesant (and his councillors) as perfect counterparts to Franklin Roosevelt (and his cabinet). Choosing Weill on the strength of JOHNNY JOHNSON [November 19, 1936], the two men became close, lifelong friends and neighbors. The Playwrights' Company was an organization formed by five distinguished dramatists (Anderson, S. N. Behrman, Sidney Howard, Elmer Rice, and Robert E. Sherwood) who, dissatisfied with the treatment they were receiving from producers, decided to present their own works by committee. Weill became deeply involved in the The Playwrights' Company, eventually becoming a full member. KNICKERBOCKER HOLIDAY, their first production, just missed being a hit; Anderson's criticism was too bitter. Walter Huston—in his only musical—introduced one of Weill's few popular hits, *September Song.*

RAILROADS ON PARADE

APRIL 30, 1939 NEW YORK WORLD'S FAIR

Pageant by Edward Hungerford
Incidental music by Kurt Weill
Directed by Charles Alan
Produced by Eastern Presidents' Conference

Published song:
Mile After Mile (lyric by Charles Alan and Buddy Bernier)

A spectacle presented by the railroad industry.

LADY IN THE DARK

JANUARY 23, 1941 ALVIN THEATRE 467 PERFORMANCES

Lyrics by Ira Gershwin
Book by Moss Hart
Choreographed by Albertina Rasch
Directed by Hassard Short
Produced by Sam H. Harris
With Gertrude Lawrence, Victor Mature, Macdonald Carey, and Danny
Kaye

Published songs:
Girl Of The Moment
Jenny (The Saga of Jenny)
My Ship
One Life To Live
The Princess Of Pure Delight
This Is New
Tschaikowsky

Additional songs published in vocal score:
The Best Years Of His Life
Dance Of The Tumblers [instrumental]
The Greatest Show On Earth
Huxley
It Looks Like Liza
Mapleton High Chorale
Oh Fabulous One

Additional song recorded:
It's Never Too Late To Mendelssohn—cut; recorded with revisions by
    Sylvia Fine

You Are Unforgettable—cut
Zodiac Song—cut; for initial recording see The Firebrand Of Florence
     [**March 22, 1945**]

Moss Hart's experience with psychoanalysis provided the inspiration for this musical play. The score was made up of three extended dream sequences, with the heroine's dilemma solved in the final song (*My Ship*). Ira Gershwin, in a dazed retirement since George's death, came back with absolutely dazzling lyrics. Sam Harris provided Broadway's most technically complicated production to date, as Hassard Short made novel use of *two* turntables simultaneously. It was the end of Harris' long career; he died on July 3, 1941. The show's very greatest asset was its **Lady**; Gertrude Lawrence sat on an acrobat's swing and bumped-and-ground *The Saga Of Jenny*, topping all else (including young Danny Kaye's startling verbal acrobatics).

LUNCHTIME FOLLIES

June 22, 1942   Todd Shipyards <Brooklyn, New York>

Music and lyrics also by others (see **Blitzstein** and **Rome**)
Sketches by George S. Kaufman and Moss Hart, Maxwell
Anderson, and others
Production supervised by Weill
Produced by The American Theatre Wing

Songs published in "The Unknown Kurt Weill":
Buddy On The Nightshift (lyric by Oscar Hammerstein 2nd)
Schickelgruber (lyric by Howard Dietz)

The **Lunchtime Follies** was a series of forty-five-minute presentations mounted as morale builders at war-materiel production plants. Weill—who was in the process of applying for citizenship—took on the post of production manager for the volunteer project, which featured songs and sketches by well-known writers (performed by "name" actors). The contents varied, based on the available cast. Weill became an American citizen on August 27, 1943.

ONE TOUCH OF VENUS

October 7, 1943   Imperial Theatre   567 performances

Lyrics by Ogden Nash
Book by S. J. Perelman and Nash
(Based on *The Tinted Venus* [story] by F. Anstey)
Choreography by Agnes de Mille
Directed by Elia Kazan

Produced by Cheryl Crawford
With Mary Martin, Kenny Baker, John Boles, Paula Laurence, Teddy Hart, and Sono Osato

Published songs:
Foolish Heart—reused in 1948 movie version *(Don't Look Now, But) My Heart Is Showing* (lyric by Ann Ronell)
Speak Low
That's Him
The Trouble With Women—see *Les Filles De Bordeaux* from **Marie Galante** [December 22, 1934]
West Wind—reused in movie version as *My Week* (lyric by Ronell)

Additional songs published in vocal selections:
How Much I Love You
I'm A Stranger Here Myself
One Touch Of Venus
Wooden Wedding

Additional songs recorded:
Dr. Crippen
Forty Minutes For Lunch [ballet]
Love In The Mist—cut
Venus In Ozone Heights [ballet]
Very, Very, Very
Vive La Difference—cut
Way Out West In Jersey—also known as *The Jersey Plunk*

Weill's two wartime musical comedies were his only Broadway hits. Mary Martin finally achieved stardom (see **Dancing in the Streets** [Duke: March 22, 1943]) in a role intended for Marlene Dietrich. Nash and Perelman's work was witty and funny, as might be expected. The unlikely team of de Mille and Weill successfully collaborated on modernist ballets (featuring Sono Osato); and Weill provided the exceptional *Speak Low.* Former Group Theatre producer Cheryl Crawford brought in Elia Kazan (who had appeared in **Johnny Johnson** [November 19, 1936]) to direct his first of two Weill/Crawford musicals.

THE FIREBRAND OF FLORENCE

March 22, 1945   Alvin Theatre   43 performances

Lyrics by Ira Gershwin
Book by Edwin Justus Mayer
(Based on *The Firebrand* [play] by Mayer)
Directed by John Murray Anderson

Produced by Max Gordon
With Earl Wrightson, Beverly Tyler, Melville Cooper, and Lotte Lenya
(Weill)
NOTE: **MUCH ADO ABOUT LOVE,** pre-Broadway title

Published songs:
A Rhyme For Angela
Sing Me Not A Ballad
There'll Be Life, Love And Laughter
You're Far Too Near Me

Additional songs recorded:
Act One, Scene One
Alessandro The Wise
Come to Florence
Cozy Nook Trio
Dizzily, Busily
Hangman's Song (Under The Gallows Tree)
Just In Case
The Little Naked Boy
Love Is My Enemy
The Nighttime Is No Time For Thinking
When The Duchess Is Away
You Have To Do What You Do Do—revised version of *Zodiac Song*
    (cut) from **LADY IN THE DARK** [January 23, 1941]

This lavish costume operetta resoundingly flopped, burying an interesting score and some fine lyrics. Ira Gershwin, in his "Arthur Francis" days, had contributed *The Voice Of Love* (music by Russell Bennett and Maurice Nitke) to the original 1924 production of Mayer's play. Lenya made her only Broadway appearance in a Weill musical; she was woefully miscast and scathingly reviewed.

A FLAG IS BORN

SEPTEMBER 5, 1946   ALVIN THEATRE   120 PERFORMANCES

Play by Ben Hecht
Incidental music by Kurt Weill
Directed by Luther Adler
Produced by The American League For A Free Palestine
With Paul Muni, Marlon Brando, Quentin Reynolds, and Sidney Lumet

Published songs:
None

A fund-raising propaganda play in support of the establishment of Israel.

STREET SCENE

January 9, 1947   Adelphi Theatre   148 performances

Lyrics by Langston Hughes and Elmer Rice
Book by Rice
(Based on the play by Rice)
Choreographed by Anna Sokolow
Directed by Charles Friedman
Produced by Dwight Deere Wiman in association with The Playwrights'
Company
With Polyna Stoska, Anne Jeffreys, and Norman Cordon

Published songs:
A Boy Like You (lyric by Hughes)
Lonely House (lyric by Hughes)
Moon-Faced, Starry-Eyed (lyric by Hughes)
We'll Go Away Together (lyric by Hughes)
What Good Would The Moon Be? (lyric by Hughes)

Additional songs published in vocal score:
Ain't It Awful, The Heat?
Blues (Marble and A Star)
Catch Me If You Can
Don't Forget The Lilac Bush
Get A Load Of That
I Loved Her Too
Ice Cream Sextet
Let Things Be Like They Was
Lullaby (lyric by Rice)
Remember That I Care (lyric by Hughes)
Somehow I Never Could Believe (lyric by Hughes)
There'll Be Trouble
When A Woman Has A Baby
The Woman Who Lived Up There
Wouldn't You Like To Be On Broadway?
Wrapped In A Ribbon And Tied With A Bow

Additional song recorded:
Italy In Technicolor—cut

Since coming to America, Weill had been hoping to create a new musical
theatre form combining opera and drama. He did not quite succeed with
Street Scene, a quasi-opera which eventually found success in the opera
house. Weill wrote a fine, rich score, and novice lyricists Elmer Rice (the

playwright) and Langston Hughes (the poet) did fairly well. Particularly effective were *Somehow I Never Could Believe, Blues, What Good Would The Moon Be?* and *Lullaby.* But STREET SCENE was overlong and overly melodramatic. Weill was by now a full member (with Rice) of the Playwrights' Company, which coproduced the show.

DOWN IN THE VALLEY

A Folk Opera

JULY 15, 1948   UNIVERSITY AUDITORIUM < BLOOMINGTON, INDIANA >
    1 PERFORMANCE

Libretto by Arnold Sundgaard
Directed by Hans Busch
With Marion Bell, James Welch, and Charles Campbell

Songs published in vocal score:
Brack Weaver, My True Love
Down In The Valley (based on the folk song)
Hoe-Down
Hop Up, My Ladies (based on the folk song)
The Little Black Train (based on the folk song)
The Lonesome Dove (based on the folk song)
Where Is The One Who Will Mourn Me When I'm Gone?

DOWN IN THE VALLEY was commissioned as a twenty-minute ballad opera for radio in 1945. It went unproduced until 1948, when a thirty-five minute version was prepared for production by the opera department at the University of Indiana. (The female lead was sung by Marion Bell of BRIGADOON [Loewe: March 13, 1947], who was married at the time to Alan Jay Lerner, Weill's collaborator on the upcoming LOVE LIFE [October 7, 1948].) DOWN IN THE VALLEY soon became a staple with non-professional choral groups—"wherever a chorus, a few singers, and a few actors are available," per Weill.

LOVE LIFE

A Vaudeville

OCTOBER 7, 1948   46TH STREET THEATRE   252 PERFORMANCES

Book and lyrics by Alan Jay Lerner
Directed by Elia Kazan
Produced by Cheryl Crawford
With Nanette Fabray and Ray Middleton

Published songs:
Economics
Green-Up Time
Here I'll Stay
Is It Him Or Is It Me?
Love Song
Mr. Right
Susan's Dream—cut
This Is The Life

Additional songs recorded:
I Remember It Well—different than song from GIGI [Loewe: November 13, 1973]
Locker Room
My Kind Of Night
What More Do I Want?—cut
You Understand Me So

Crawford's previous musical had been the hit BRIGADOON [March 13, 1947]. Loewe wasn't interested in this new work, so Crawford teamed Lerner with Weill. They attempted an examination of marriage in vaudeville style, illustrated by one family moving through different eras of American history—not unlike the director's 1942 *Skin of Our Teeth*. But the novel set-up didn't work; Lerner went back to Loewe, Weill to Anderson. (A 1990 regional theatre revival of LOVE LIFE—with Weill's original orchestrations—confirmed my rating of the score as the composer's least interesting American work.)

LOST IN THE STARS

OCTOBER 30, 1949   MUSIC BOX THEATRE   281 PERFORMANCES

Book and lyrics by Maxwell Anderson
(Based on *Cry the Beloved Country* [novel] by Alan Paton)
Directed by Rouben Mamoulian
Produced by The Playwrights' Company
With Todd Duncan, Inez Matthews, Leslie Banks, and Julian Mayfield

Published songs:
Big Mole
A Bird Of Passage—issued in choral edition
The Little Gray House—initial use of 1944 song from unproduced musical
        ULYSSES AFRICANUS
Lost In The Stars—initial use of 1942 song from ULYSSES AFRICANUS;
        previously published in 1946 as nonshow song
Stay Well

Thousands Of Miles
Trouble Man—initial use of 1942 song from ULYSSES AFRICANUS;
    previously published in 1946 as nonshow song *Lover Man*

Additional songs included in published vocal score:
Cry The Beloved Country
Fear!
Four O'Clock
The Hills Of Ixopo
Murder In Parkwold
O Tixo, Tixo, Help Me
The Search
Train To Johannesburg
The Wild Justice
Who'll Buy

Additional songs recorded:
Gold—cut

Weill's final work was this serious piece dealing with racial prejudice in South Africa. While Anderson had great success as a dramatic playwright, he displayed a heavy hand with his two musical librettos; this heaviness worked against LOST IN THE STARS' chances for popular success (as it had with KNICKERBOCKER HOLIDAY [October 19, 1938]). Shortly after his fiftieth birthday, Kurt Weill had a sudden heart attack; he died April 3, 1950 in New York.

HUCKLEBERRY FINN

[CIRCA APRIL 1950]; UNPRODUCED MUSICAL

Lyrics by Maxwell Anderson
(Based on the novel by Mark Twain)

Published songs:
Apple Jack
The Catfish Song
Come In, Mornin'
River Chanty
This Time Next Year

Weill, whose deep interest in American themes had been displayed in several of his musicals (as well as the 1948 one-act folk opera DOWN IN THE VALLEY [July 15, 1948]), was collaborating with Anderson and Rouben Mamoulian on this project at the time of his death. The completed songs were published, and an adaptation of the work was seen on German television.

THE THREEPENNY OPERA

(Second Version; see April 13, 1933)

MARCH 10, 1954   THEATRE DE LYS   < OFF-BROADWAY >   2,706 PERFORMANCES

Original book and lyrics by Bertolt Brecht
English adaptation by Marc Blitzstein
(Based on *The Beggar's Opera* by John Gay)
Directed by Carmen Capalbo
Produced by Capalbo and Stanley Chase
With Scott Merrill, Jo Sullivan, Lotte Lenya (Weill), Beatrice Arthur, and Charlotte Rae

Published song:
Mack The Knife

Additional songs published in vocal selection:
Army Song
Ballad Of Dependency
Ballad Of The Easy Life
Barbara Song
Instead-Of Song
Love Song
Pirate Jenny
Solomon Song
Tango Ballad
Useless

Additional songs recorded (in English):
Call From The Grave
Death Message
Finale (Reprieved)
How To Survive
Melodrama
Jealousy Duet
Morning Anthem
The Mounted Messenger
Overture [instrumental]
Polly's Song
Wedding Song
The World Is Mean

Weill's DIE DREIGROSCHENOPER, perhaps his greatest work, remained virtually unknown outside a very small circle. Marc Blitzstein, studying composition in Berlin in 1928, had been deeply influenced by the original production and was a great fan of the piece. In 1950, Blitzstein translated *Pirate Jenny* and called the composer for an opinion, singing over the telephone. Weill enthusiastically suggested they do the entire work; but within the month he was dead. Blitzstein went about the adaptation as a labor of love, without changing a single note of Weill's work. A production scheduled for the spring of 1952 at City Center (where No For An Answer [Blitzstein: January 5, 1941] had led its troubled life) was suddenly cancelled, and one more obstacle was placed in the way. Blitzstein's protégé Leonard Bernstein was arranging an arts festival at Brandeis College (Waltham, Massachusetts); he arranged for the piece to debut there (see Trouble in Tahiti [Bernstein: April 19, 1955]). With Lenya and David Brooks singing, and Bernstein conducting, the adaptation was performed June 14, 1952. Almost two years later The Threepenny Opera finally opened off-Broadway—for a limited ten-week engagement. Popular demand caused it to reopen, and it became a six-year phenomenon. Lotte Lenya, in her original role of Jenny, began her American career as interpreter of Weill. And *Mack The Knife*—Blitzstein's version of the *Moritat*—became Kurt Weill's biggest hit, some thirty years after it was written. New York has seen two other Threepenny translations, one mounted by the New York Shakespeare Festival [May 1, 1976], and the other featuring the pop singer Sting [November 5, 1989]. Both productions sought to improve on Blitzstein, explaining that his '50s adaptation of the '20s musical (set in 1837) was outdated for our modern times; both productions made Blitzstein look very good, indeed.

BRECHT ON BRECHT

JANUARY 3, 1962   THEATRE DE LYS < OFF-BROADWAY >   440
PERFORMANCES

Staged reading from the works of Bertolt Brecht
Arranged and translated by George Tabori
Music mostly by others
Directed by Gene Frankel
Produced by ANTA and Cheryl Crawford
With Lotte Lenya (Weill), Dane Clark, Anne Jackson, Viveca Lindfors, and George Voskovec

Song recorded:
Ballad Of The Nazi Soldier's Wife (translation by Michael Feingold)

THE RISE AND FALL OF THE CITY OF MAHAGONNY

APRIL 28, 1970   PHYLLIS ANDERSON THEATRE < OFF-BROADWAY >
    8 PERFORMANCES

Original book and lyrics by Bertolt Brecht
English adaptation by Arnold Weinstein
Conceived and directed by Carmen Capalbo
Produced by Capalbo and Abe Margolies
With Barbara Harris, Estelle Parsons, and Frank Poretta

Songs recorded (in English):
Alabama Song
As You Make Your Bed
Deep In Alaska
Oh, Heavenly Salvation

A misguided adaptation of the 1929 Berlin piece. Capalbo had produced and
directed THE THREEPENNY OPERA (Second Version) [March 10, 1954]. But
in that case Marc Blitzstein was on hand as Weill's surrogate. This MAHA-
GONNY closed "for revision" during previews, at which point Poretta replaced
Mort Shuman (of JACQUES BRÈL IS ALIVE AND WELL [PART 4: January 22,
1968]) as the male lead.

HAPPY END

MAY 7, 1977   MARTIN BECK THEATRE   75 PERFORMANCES

Original book and lyrics by Bertolt Brecht
(Based on a play by Elisabeth Hauptmann)
English adaptation by Michael Feingold
Directed by Robert Kalfin and Patricia Birch
Produced by Michael Harvey and the Chelsea Theatre Center
With Meryl Streep, Christopher Lloyd, and Tony Azito

Songs recorded (in English):
Bilbao Song
Childhood's Bright Endeavor
Don't Be Afraid
God Bless Rockefeller
Mandalay Song
March Ahead To The Fight
Sailor Tango

Another unsuccessful attempt to retain the magic of the Weill-Brecht agit-
prop style in an American translation. This production was a second Broadway

transfer from Chelsea's home at the Brooklyn Academy of Music; the first had been the artistically successful CANDIDE (Second Version) [Bernstein: March 10, 1974]. But CANDIDE had Hal Prince and Stephen Sondheim. HAPPY END did not.

Kurt Weill was in America less than fifteen years, little more than half of his creative life. During that time he wrote eight complete musicals, only two of which were financially profitable. Similarly, only two songs—*September Song* and *Speak Low*—became best-selling hits. In the forty years since Weill's death, his work has gradually achieved recognition, chiefly through productions of material written during his early career in Germany. DIE DREIGROSCHENOPER [August 28, 1928] brought Weill instant international acclaim; America didn't take to it until the posthumous Second Version made THE THREEPENNY OPERA [March 10, 1954] Weill's biggest success (and *Mack The Knife* his most popular song). The American shows don't lend as easily to revival, saddled with libretto and production problems; but there is fine musical theatre work throughout.

Marc Blitzstein

BORN: March 2, 1905 Philadelphia, Pennsylvania
DIED: January 22, 1964 Martinique, West Indies

Son of a banker, Marc Blitzstein prepared for a career in serious music. He performed as a piano soloist with the Philadelphia Symphony as early as 1920, and entered the Curtis Institute of Music. In the mid-Twenties he went to Europe to study composition with Nadia Boulanger and Arnold Schoenberg—and was fascinated by the exciting theatre work of Weill and Brecht in Berlin (see THE THREEPENNY OPERA (Second Version) [Weill: March 10, 1954]). Blitzstein came to New York in the late Twenties, as a performer and lecturer.

[all music and lyrics by Marc Blitzstein]

GARRICK GAIETIES
Third Edition

JUNE 4, 1930 GUILD THEATRE 170 PERFORMANCES

"Music and Lyrics by Everybody" (see **Duke**)
Directed by Philip Loeb
Produced by The Theatre Guild
With Sterling Holloway, Edith Meiser, and Imogene Coca

Published songs:
Triple Sec [opera] (text by Ronald Jeans)

The first two editions of the GARRICK GAIETIES [May 17, 1926 and May 19, 1926] had included humorous one-act operas. For this last of the series, another was called for. Blitzstein contributed his 1928 'progressive opera' 'Triple Sec,' originally titled 'Theatre For Cabaret,' which was favorably received despite its avant-garde nature.

PARADE

<First Version>

A Social Revue

MAY 20, 1935   GUILD THEATRE   40 PERFORMANCES

Music mostly by Jerome Moross
Lyrics mostly by others
Directed by Philip Loeb
Produced by The Theatre Guild
With Jimmy Savo and Eve Arden

Song recorded:
Send For The Militia

Studying and teaching during the early Depression years, Blitzstein developed strong left-wing tendencies. **PARADE** was produced by a young branch of The Theatre Guild, much as the initial **GARRICK GAIETIES** [Rodgers: May 17, 1925] had been. But **PARADE** was extremely political—much to the embarrassment of the Guild—and received a stormy reception. Blitzstein was developing a strong interest in the potential of music as social message, and contributed the deftly satirical *Send For The Militia*. Principal composer was twenty-one-year-old Jerome Moross, whose one full theatre piece was to be the superlative **GOLDEN APPLE** [PART 4: March 11, 1954].

THE CRADLE WILL ROCK

A Play In Music

JUNE 16, 1937   VENICE (JOLSON) THEATRE   14 PERFORMANCES

DECEMBER 5, 1937   MERCURY THEATRE   5 PERFORMANCES

JANUARY 3, 1938   WINDSOR THEATRE   104 PERFORMANCES

Book by Blitzstein
Directed by Orson Welles
Produced by Welles and John Houseman
With Will Geer, Howard Da Silva, Olive Stanton, and Blitzstein

Published songs:
The Cradle Will Rock
Croon-Spoon
Doctor And Ella
Drugstore Scene
The Freedom Of The Press

Gus And Sadie Love Song—also included in *Drugstore Scene*
Honolulu
Joe Worker
Leaflets! (and *Art For Art's Sake*)
Nickel Under The Foot
The Rich

Additional songs recorded:
Let's Do Something
Moll Song
Mrs. Mister And Reverend Salvation
Oh, What A Filthy Night Court

Kurt Weill and Bertolt Brecht were both now in America. When Blitzstein played a sketch he had written, *Nickel Under the Foot*, (a prostitute's song) for Brecht, the latter suggested that he write a full-length music/theatre piece in song, showing all members of the establishment as prostitutes. This Blitzstein did, choosing as his hero a union organizer in Steeltown, USA (1936 saw armed riots at Flint, Michigan automobile factories). THE CRADLE WILL ROCK was produced by the Federal Theatre Project of the Works Progress Administration, under the supervision of Houseman and twenty-two-year-old director Orson Welles. The government agency—which had approved and funded the project—became nervous after the first preview, and suddenly suspended *all* new WPA activities "to facilitate budget cuts." That night the doors of the sold-out Maxine Elliott Theatre were padlocked; Welles had actor Will Geer perform on the sidewalk to hold the audience while Houseman looked for an empty theatre. Eight hundred people paraded twenty blocks uptown to the Venice, where the performance finally began two hours late. Actors' Equity had forbidden its members to appear; half the cast showed up anyway, delivering their lines from seats in the house while Blitzstein and Welles played and narrated from the stage. THE CRADLE WILL ROCK continued at the Venice for two weeks, retaining the exciting performance style born of necessity. Welles and Houseman left the WPA to begin their Mercury Theatre Company (with Blitzstein as resident composer) and revived the piece for Sunday night performances; in January, THE CRADLE WILL ROCK was finally opened for a commercial run.

JULIUS CAESAR

NOVEMBER 11, 1937   MERCURY THEATRE   157 PERFORMANCES

Play by William Shakespeare
Incidental music by Blitzstein
Directed by Orson Welles

Produced by The Mercury Theatre (Welles and John Houseman)
With Welles, George Coulouris, Joseph Cotten, Hiram Sherman, and Martin Gabel

Published song:
Orpheus (Lucius' Song) (lyric by Shakespeare)

Welles continued to assault the theatre world with a modern-dress version of JULIUS CAESAR (in which he played Brutus). The Mercury Theatre Group was to have a brief but notable life, dying with a spectacularly Wellesian failure (the 1939 Shakespearean omnibus *Five Kings*). Orson went to Hollywood and made "Citizen Kane" (1941).

DANTON'S DEATH

"A Drama In Individual Scenes Vignetted By Spotlight"

NOVEMBER 2, 1938   MERCURY THEATRE   21 PERFORMANCES

Play by Georg Buchner
(Translated by Geoffrey Dunlop)
Songs by Blitzstein
Directed by Orson Welles
Produced by The Mercury Theatre (Welles and John Houseman)
With Welles, Joseph Cotten, Martin Gabel, Arlene Francis, and Ruth Ford

Song recorded:
Ode To Reason

NO FOR AN ANSWER

JANUARY 5, 1941   MECCA THEATRE (CITY CENTER)   3 PERFORMANCES

Book by Blitzstein
Directed by Walter E. Watts
Produced by "A Committee including Bennett Cerf, Lillian Hellman, Arthur Kober and Herman Shumlin"
With Martin Wolfson, Curt Conway, and Carol Channing

Recorded songs:
Dimples
Francie
Fraught
Gina
In The Clear

Make The Heart Be Stone
Mike
Nick
No For An Answer
Penny Candy
The Purest Kind Of Guy
Secret Singing
Song Of The Bat
Take The Book

Unable to arrange a full production of **No For An Answer,** a distinguished group of theatre people sponsored three Sunday-night staged readings. Public reaction was even more stormy than for **The Cradle Will Rock** [June 16, 1937], and the city threatened to close the theatre for "licensing violations." In the earlier work Blitzstein used stereotyped characters to make his point; here he tried to create a contemporary, realistic play with a musical base. The subject matter was again left-wing, dealing with a strike of hotel restaurant workers. Despite the exciting nature of the work—and the overwhelmingly positive critical reaction—it was impossible to find backing for a commercial production. Among the cast was nineteen-year-old Carol Channing, fresh from Bennington. Blitzstein next went to war, serving with the 8th Air Force in London; his assignments included Director of Music for the American Broadcasting Station in Europe, supervision of the 1943 American Negro Troops Choral Concert at Royal Albert Hall, and composition of the 1944 'Airborne Symphony.'

LUNCHTIME FOLLIES

June 22, 1942   Todd Shipyards   < Brooklyn, New York >

Music and lyrics also by others (see **Rome** and **Weill**)
Sketches by George S. Kaufman and Moss Hart, Maxwell Anderson, and others
Production supervised by Weill
Produced by The American Theatre Wing

Song published:
A Quiet Girl

Lunchtime Follies was a morale-building revue mounted for workers at war-materiel production plants, produced under Kurt Weill's direction. Blitzstein contributed this little ditty about a formerly *Quiet Girl* who—now that she's involved in the war effort—wants "to make the bullet that gets Hitler."

ANOTHER PART OF THE FOREST

NOVEMBER 20, 1946   FULTON THEATRE   182 PERFORMANCES

Play by Lillian Hellman
Incidental music by Blitzstein
(Based on characters from *The Little Foxes* [play] by Hellman)
Directed by Hellman
Produced by Kermit Bloomgarden
With Patricia Neal and Mildred Dunnock

Published songs:
None

Blitzstein continued his association with Lillian Hellman, who had cosponsored NO FOR AN ANSWER [January 5, 1941]. ANOTHER PART OF THE FOREST was actually a prequel to THE LITTLE FOXES [WILLSON: February 15, 1939]. Blitzstein became engrossed in the Hubbards; with the help of a grant from the American Academy of Arts and Letters, he began his major music theatre work, REGINA [October 31, 1949].

ANDROCLES AND THE LION

DECEMBER 19, 1946   INTERNATIONAL THEATRE   40 PERFORMANCES

Play by George Bernard Shaw
Incidental music by Blitzstein
Directed by Margaret Webster
Produced by American Repertory Theatre (Eva Le Gallienne, Cheryl Crawford and Webster)
With Ernest Truex, Richard Waring, and Eli Wallach

Published songs:
None

REGINA

OCTOBER 31, 1949   46TH STREET THEATRE   56 PERFORMANCES

Book by Blitzstein
(Based on *The Little Foxes* [play] by Lillian Hellman)
Directed by Robert Lewis
Produced by Cheryl Crawford in association with Clinton Wilder
With Jane Pickens, Priscilla Gillette, Brenda Lewis, and Russell Nype

Published songs:
The Best Thing Of All
Blues
Chinkypin
Greedy Girl
The Rain—published in choral edition
Summer Day—nonshow version of *Two Old Drybones*
What Will It Be?

Additional songs published in vocal score:
Away!
Big Rich
Deedle-Doodle
Finale (Certainly, Lord)
Gallop
Greetings
Horace's Entrance
I Don't Know
I'm Sick Of You (Horace's Last)
Lionnet (Birdie's Aria)
Make A Quiet Day (Rain Quartet)
Music, Music
Regina's Aria
Sing Hubbard
Small Talk (Marshall)
Things (Regina's Waltz)
Transition (Bonds)
Two Old Drybones
The Veranda [instrumental]
Want To Join The Angels

Blitzstein shared Kurt Weill's vision of an opera-inspired American "music drama" form. (Blitzstein was to be responsible for the rediscovery and accessibility of Weill's greatest and most successful work, THE THREEPENNY OPERA (Second Version) [Weill: March 10, 1954].) Following the War, Blitzstein had removed himself from the Brecht-influenced political drama, and with REGINA created a supreme musical theatre achievement. The advantage of being his own lyricist/librettist enabled a free combination of song and speech, the music written in expanded form or fragmented as it followed the thoughts of the characters. Hellman provided the strong and well-written THE LITTLE FOXES [WILLSON: February 15, 1939]; Blitzstein used the orchestra to elaborate on the already highly pitched emotions of the little Hubbards. His two earlier scores had been performed with piano accompaniments, due to economic reasons. In REGINA the beauties and colors of Blitzstein's music (orchestrated by the composer) were first heard: Alexandra's touching *What Will It Be?*, Addie's sympathetic *Blues*, Regina's dangerous *Things*, the *Rain Quartet*, and especially Birdie's defeated *Lionnet*.

KING LEAR

DECEMBER 25, 1950   NATIONAL THEATRE   48 PERFORMANCES

Play by William Shakespeare
Incidental music by Blitzstein
Directed by John Houseman
Produced by Robert L. Joseph and Alexander H. Cohen
With Louis Calhern, Martin Gabel, Nina Foch, Jo Van Fleet, and Edith Atwater

Published songs:
None

THE THREEPENNY OPERA

see Weill [March 10, 1954]

REUBEN REUBEN

[OCTOBER 10, 1955]   SHUBERT THEATRE < BOSTON, MASSACHUSETTS > ;
    CLOSED DURING PRE-BROADWAY TRYOUT

Book by Blitzstein
Choreographed by Hanya Holm
Directed by Robert Lewis
Produced by Cheryl Crawford
With Eddie Albert, Evelyn Lear, Kaye Ballard, and George Gaynes

Published songs:
Be With Me
The Hills Of Amalfi
Miracle Song
Monday Morning Blues
Never Get Lost

Additional songs recorded:
Love At First Sight
Rose Song
Such A Little While

This highly ambitious work suffered from an overall lack of focus and direction. REGINA [October 31, 1949] had been built upon Lillian Hellman's strong

THE LITTLE FOXES [WILLSON: **February 15, 1939**]; REUBEN REUBEN was original material by Blitzstein (with no relation to the popular novel by Peter de Vries). The far-from-ready show that appeared out of town perplexed audiences, critics, and cast, and was quickly withdrawn. What survives of the score is original, highly imaginative, and often incredibly lovely. *Never Get Lost* and *The Hills Of Amalfi* are tender and fascinating. (Close colleague and friend Leonard Bernstein called Blitzstein's work-failures "falling angels," and named his daughter Nina for the REUBEN REUBEN heroine.) Cheryl Crawford, who entered the musical theatre with JOHNNY JOHNSON [Weill: **November 19, 1936**], produced both REGINA and REUBEN REUBEN. The failures of these last two (along with FLAHOOLEY [Part 4: **May 14, 1951**] and PAINT YOUR WAGON [Loewe: **November 12, 1951**]) caused Crawford to temporarily give up her quest for groundbreaking musical theatre—and drop WEST SIDE STORY [Bernstein: **September 26, 1957**].

THE LITTLEST REVUE

MAY 22, 1956   PHOENIX THEATRE < OFF-BROADWAY >   32
    PERFORMANCES

Music mostly by Vernon **Duke** (also see **Strouse**)
Lyrics mostly by Ogden Nash
Sketches by Nat Hiken, Michael Stewart, and others
Directed by Paul Lammers
Produced by T. Edward Hambleton and Norris Houghton by arrangement with Ben Bagley
With Charlotte Rae, Tammy Grimes, Joel Grey, and Larry Storch

Recorded Song:
Modest Maid (I Love Lechery)—initial use of 1944 nonshow song

"Modest Maid" was written as special material for Beatrice Lillie when Blitzstein was stationed in London. Lillie didn't perform it, but Charlotte Rae of THE THREEPENNY OPERA (SECOND VERSION) [WEILL: **March 10, 1954**] used it in her nightclub act and, eventually, in this LITTLEST REVUE.

A MIDSUMMER NIGHT'S DREAM

[JUNE 20, 1958]   AMERICAN SHAKESPEARE FESTIVAL   < STRATFORD, CONNECTICUT >

Play by William Shakespeare
Incidental music by Blitzstein
Choreographed by George Balanchine
Directed by Jack Landau

Produced by American Shakespeare Festival (John Houseman)
With Richard Waring, June Havoc, Barbara Barrie, John Colicos, Hiram Sherman, Morris Carnovsky, Will Geer, and Ellis Rabb

Songs published in "Six Elizabethan Songs":
Court Song (lyric Anonymous)
Lullaby (You Spotted Snakes With Double Tongue) (lyric by Shakespeare)
Sweet Is The Rose (lyric by Amoretti)

THE WINTER'S TALE

[JULY 20, 1958]   AMERICAN SHAKESPEARE FESTIVAL   < STRATFORD, CONNECTICUT >

Play by William Shakespeare
Incidental music by Blitzstein
Choreographed by George Balanchine
Directed by John Houseman and Jack Landau
Produced by American Shakespeare Festival (Houseman)
With John Colicos, Nancy Wickwire, Richard Waring, Hiram Sherman, Will Geer, Inga Swenson, Richard Easton, and Ellis Rabb

Songs published in "Six Elizabethan Songs":
Shepherd's Song (When Daffodils Begin To Peer) (lyric by Shakespeare)
Song Of The Glove (lyric by Ben Jonson)
Vendor's Song (Lawn As White As Driven Snow) (lyric by Shakespeare)

JUNO

MARCH 9, 1959   WINTER GARDEN THEATRE   16 PERFORMANCES

Book by Joseph Stein
(Based on *Juno and the Paycock* [play] by Sean O'Casey)
Choreographed by Agnes de Mille
Directed by José Ferrer
Produced by The Playwrights' Company, Oliver Smith, and Oliver Rea
With Shirley Booth, Melvyn Douglas, Jack MacGowran, Jean Stapleton, and Sada Thompson

Published songs:
I Wish It So
The Liffey Waltz
My True Heart
One Kind Word

Additional songs recorded:
Bird Upon The Tree
Daarlin' Man
Farewell, Me Butty—cut
For Love
From This Out—cut
Hymn
Ireland's Eye—cut
It's Not Irish
Johnny
Music In The House
Old Sayin's
On A Day Like This
Quarrel Song—cut
Song Of The Ma
We Can Be Proud
We're Alive
What Is The Stars? (Life On The Sea)
Where
You Poor Thing
You're The Girl—cut

Blitzstein was perhaps the perfect choice for this adaptation of O'Casey's strong drama of the Irish Revolution. However, the commercial management tried to give the show popular appeal, using box-office stars Shirley Booth (who had appeared on Blitzstein's 1937 radio play 'I've Got the Tune') and Melvyn Douglas. Both were miscast, and the libretto was entrusted not to Blitzstein but Joe Stein (who originated the idea). The entire project was troubled, under the direction first of musical novice Tony Richardson, who was replaced by musical novice Vincent J. Donehue, who was replaced by José Ferrer. The dramatic and volatile score worked well, particularly effective in expressing tragedy through de Mille dance. But the book's attempts at lightness and charm matched neither Blitzstein nor O'Casey, and JUNO suffered a quick death.

TOYS IN THE ATTIC

FEBRUARY 25, 1960   HUDSON THEATRE   556 PERFORMANCES

Play by Lillian Hellman
Incidental music by Blitzstein
Directed by Arthur Penn
Produced by Kermit Bloomgarden
With Maureen Stapleton, Jason Robards, Jr., and Irene Worth

Published songs:
None

Blitzstein's final theatre work came on this fourth association with Lillian Hellman. His next project was the opera "Sacco and Vanzetti," commissioned by the Metropolitan Opera. While working on the score, Marc Blitzstein was attacked and killed on the island of Martinique on January 22, 1964.

Marc Blitzstein's strong commitment and uncompromising artistic viewpoint worked against popular success; surprisingly, his scores usually received the highly enthusiastic reviews they deserved. His one commercial project was the labor-of-love adaptation of the work of another composer (THE THREEPENNY OPERA (Second Version) [Weill: March 10, 1954]); his own work and name are virtually unknown. But Blitzstein's contributions to the serious musical theatre are of great importance, and point in a direction which has not yet been fully realized.

Harold Rome

BORN: May 27, 1908   Hartford, Connecticut

Harold Rome's musical career began as a college sideline, playing in dance bands to help finance his studies. Upon graduation with an architecture degree in 1934, Rome came to New York during the depths of the Depression. With high qualifications and seven years at Yale, the only architectural work he found was a twenty-four-dollar-a-week WPA job measuring roads and mapping the course of the Hudson River. Spare-time money could be earned playing piano, so Rome took advantage of his musical abilities. In the summer of 1935, Rome got a musical summer job at the Green Mansions resort hotel. Assembling amateur shows for the campers to perform, architect Rome began writing songs. He spent three summers at Green Mansions, writing comic character material for nonperformers.

[all music and lyrics by Harold Rome unless indicated]

PINS AND NEEDLES

NOVEMBER 27, 1937   LABOR STAGE   1,108 PERFORMANCES

Music and lyrics mostly by Rome
Sketches by Charles Friedman and others
Directed by Friedman
Produced by ILGWU
With the ILGWU Players

Published songs:
Back To Work
Chain Store Daisy (Vassar Girl Finds Job)
Doing The Reactionary
Four Little Angels Of Peace
The General Unveiled (A Satirical Ballet)
I've Got The Nerve To Be In Love
It's Better With A Union Man (Or Bertha, The Sewing Machine Girl)
Mene, Mene, Tekel—issued in separate edition

Nobody Makes A Pass At Me
Not Cricket To Picket
One Big Union For Two
Papa Don't Love Mama Any More
Sing Me A Song With Social Significance
Stay Out, Sammy!
Sunday In The Park
We Sing America—issued in separate edition
What Good Is Love
When I Grow Up (G-Man Song)—issued in separate edition

Additional songs published in vocal score:
Cream Of Mush Song
I'm Just Nuts About You
Room For One

Additional song recorded:
Status Quo

NOTE: Due to the topical nature of the piece, various songs cut or added after opening

Louis Schaefer, entertainment director of the International Ladies Garment Workers Union, was looking for an extracurricular morale-building activity. Schaefer heard Rome's work at Green Mansions and commissioned PINS AND NEEDLES. The cast was drafted from garment workers; rehearsals were held over a year and a half of evenings and weekends; and the ILGWU renamed the former Princess Theatre "Labor Stage." The nonprofessional show finally opened and attracted Broadway audiences, eventually moving to the larger Windsor Theatre and setting a new record for long-running musicals (the highest mark for the decade had been OF THEE I SING [Gershwin: December 26, 1931] with 441 performances). The show spoke for the former middle class, optimistically coping until better times came along. Rome became the first new voice to have an impact on Broadway since Arlen and Duke in 1930. His breezy, lightly rhythmic musical style and pointed but gentle comic lyrics proved an attractive alternative to other attempts at *Social Significance*. PINS AND NEEDLES flourished, and the WPA lost an architect.

SING OUT THE NEWS

SEPTEMBER 24, 1938   MUSIC BOX THEATRE   105 PERFORMANCES

Sketches by George S. Kaufman and Moss Hart (unbilled)
Directed by Charles Friedman
Produced by Max Gordon in association with Kaufman and Hart

With Philip Loeb, Mary Jane Walsh, Hiram Sherman, Will Geer, and Rex Ingram

Published songs:
F.D.R. Jones
How Long Can Love Keep Laughing?
My Heart Is Unemployed
One Of These Fine Days
Ordinary Guy
Plaza 6-9423—issued as professional copy only
Yip-Ahoy—issued as professional copy only

PINS AND NEEDLES [November 27, 1937] immediately brought Rome to the attention of Broadway. Max Gordon and his usually silent partners Kaufman and Hart were excited by Rome's new voice and sponsored this full-scale revue. Without the ingratiating, non-professional charm of the still-running earlier show, **SING OUT THE NEWS** was unable to compete; but Rome came up with one of his best songs, the joyful *F.D.R. Jones* (later to be heard sung by victorious Allied troops marching into Germany).

SING FOR YOUR SUPPER

APRIL 24, 1939   ADELPHI THEATRE   60 PERFORMANCES

Music mostly by others
Lyrics mostly by Robert Sour
Directed by Robert H. Gordon
Produced by WPA Federal Theatre Project
With Paula Laurence and Sonny Tufts

Published song:
· *Papa's Got A Job* (music by Ned Lehak, lyric by Hector Troy [Harold Rome])

Rome was asked to come up with a lyric in the *F.D.R. Jones* vein: he wrote *Papa's Got A Job*. Not interested in being approached with lyric-only offers, he came up with the Hector Troy (Rome's nickname is "Heckie") pseudonym.

STREETS OF PARIS

JUNE 19, 1939   BROADHURST THEATRE   274 PERFORMANCES

Music mostly by Jimmy McHugh
Lyrics mostly by Al Dubin
Directed by Edward Duryea Dowling and Dennis Murray
Produced by the Shuberts in association with Olsen and Johnson

With Bobby Clark, Abbott and Costello, Luella Gear, and Carmen
Miranda

Published song:
History Is Made At Night

The highlight of this revue was Carmen Miranda, who came out of nowhere
with the McHugh/Dubin *South American Way.*

THE LITTLE DOG LAUGHED

A Modern Music Comedy

[JULY 13, 1940]   GARDEN PIER <ATLANTIC CITY, NEW JERSEY>;
CLOSED DURING PRE-BROADWAY TRYOUT

Book by Joseph Schrank
Produced and directed by Eddie Dowling
With Mili Monti, Philip Loeb, and Augustin Duncan

Published songs:
Easy Does It
I Have A Song
I Want Romance
Of The People Stomp
You're Your Highness To Me

An extravagant, idealistic fantasy. The show was backed by a wealthy society
matron to showcase her singing "discovery" Mili Monti (who did not over-
whelm them in Atlantic City). Rome provided another of his infectiously
energetic songs, *Of The People Stomp.*

LUNCHTIME FOLLIES

JUNE 22, 1942   TODD SHIPYARDS <BROOKLYN, NEW YORK>

Music and lyrics also by others (see **Blitzstein** and **Weill**)
Sketches by George S. Kaufman and Moss Hart, Maxwell Anderson, and
others
Production supervised by Kurt Weill
Produced by The American Theatre Wing

Published songs:
The Ballad Of Sloppy Joe
Dear Joe
The Lady's On The Job
Men Behind The Man Behind The Gun—issued in professional copy

On That Old Production Line
On Time
That's My Pop
Victory Symphony, Eight To The Bar

Rome's **PINS AND NEEDLES** [**November 27, 1937**] experience made him especially well suited to write for this series of volunteer propaganda revues. By year's end, Rome himself was in uniform.

STAR AND GARTER

JUNE 24, 1942   MUSIC BOX THEATRE   605 PERFORMANCES

Music and lyrics mostly by others
Directed by Hassard Short
Produced by Michael Todd
With Bobby Clark and Gypsy Rose Lee

Published song:
Bunny, Bunny, Bunny

Rome had supplied material for Gypsy Rose Lee in his WPA architect/Green Mansions days. Mike Todd's burlesque revue was a popular wartime hit.

LET FREEDOM SING

OCTOBER 5, 1942   LONGACRE THEATRE   8 PERFORMANCES

Music also by others
Sketches by Sam Locke
Directed by Joseph C. Pevney and Robert H. Gordon
Produced by The Youth Theatre
With Mitzi Green, Betty Garrett, and Lee Sullivan

Published songs:
None

An amateurish, poorly done revue with a youthful cast. The only bright spot was the unknown Betty Garrett, unanimously singled out by the critics. Rome moved from Broadway to Fort Hamilton, Brooklyn.

STARS AND GRIPES

Fort Hamilton All-Soldier Show

JULY 13, 1943   WAR DEPARTMENT THEATRE, FT. HAMILTON
    < BROOKLYN, NEW YORK >

Music and lyrics by PFC Harold Rome
Sketches mostly by T4G Ace Goodrich
Directed by PFC Glenn Jordan and PFC Martin Gabel

Published songs:
The Army Service Forces
Hup! Tup! Thrup! Four! (Jack the Sleepy Jeep)
Jumping To The Jukebox—also used in SKIRTS [January 25, 1944]
The Little Brown Suit My Uncle Bought Me—also used in SKIRTS
Love Sometimes Has To Wait
My Pin-Up Girl—also used in SKIRTS

A morale-builder for the Army.

SKIRTS

An All-American Musical Adventure

JANUARY 25, 1944   CAMBRIDGE THEATRE < LONDON >

Music and lyrics mostly by PFC Harold Rome and PFC Frank **Loesser**
Choreography by Wendy Toye
Directed by Lt. Arthur G. Brest
Produced by U.S. 8th Air Force, Special Service Section

Published songs:
The Little Brown Suit My Uncle Bought Me
Jumping To The Juke Box
My Pin-Up Girl

NOTE: songs originally used in STARS AND GRIPES [July 13, 1943]

The Air Force borrowed these songs from the Army for this publicly presented revue.

CALL ME MISTER

APRIL 18, 1946   NATIONAL THEATRE   734 PERFORMANCES

Sketches by Arnold Auerbach with Arnold Horwitt
Directed by Robert H. Gordon
Produced by Melvyn Douglas and Herman Levin
With Betty Garrett, Jules Munshin, and Lawrence Winters

Published songs:
Along With Me
Call Me Mister
The Drugstore Song
The Face On The Dime
Going Home Train
His Old Man
Little Surplus Me
Love Remains
Military Life (The Jerk Song)
The Red Ball Express
South America, Take It Away
Till We Meet Again

Additional song recorded:
Yuletide, Park Avenue

Rome's joy on returning to civilian life was expressed in his infectious *Call Me Mister*—as opposed to "Private"—and provided the basis for this hit revue. Staffed and cast mostly by ex-servicemen and USO women, CALL ME MISTER was a happy and energetic entertainment. Betty Garrett established herself as a first-rate comedienne, and Rome's attorney/agent Herman Levin went into the producing business. The score showed Rome moving away from his socially relevant PINS AND NEEDLES [November 27, 1937] days: while he could still create hapless characters in comedy lyrics (*Poor Little Surplus Me*), he chose broader subjects for lampooning (*South America, Take It Away*). His music had generally served as support for the lyric; with songs like the Roosevelt eulogy *Face On The Dime*, Rome began to develop his gift for dramatic melody.

THAT'S THE TICKET!

[SEPTEMBER 24, 1948]   SHUBERT THEATRE < PHILADELPHIA,
    PENNSYLVANIA > ; CLOSED DURING PRE-BROADWAY TRYOUT

Book by Julius J. and Philip G. Epstein
Choreographed by Paul Godkin
Directed by Jerome Robbins
Produced by Joseph Kipness, John Pransky, and Al Beckman
With Leif Erickson, Loring Smith, and Kaye Ballard

Published songs:
I Shouldn't Love You
The Money Song
Take Off The Coat—also used in **BLESS YOU ALL** [December 14, 1950]
You Never Know What Hit You (When It's Love)—also used in **PRETTY**
    PENNY [June 20, 1940] and **BLESS YOU ALL**

This misguided effort was written by the Hollywood Epstein brothers, authors
of the 1941 "Casablanca." Jerome Robbins made his non-George Abbott
directing debut. After a week, everybody went home. *The Money Song*
managed to achieve some radio popularity.

PRETTY PENNY

[JUNE 20, 1949]   BUCKS COUNTY PLAYHOUSE < NEW HOPE,
    PENNSYLVANIA > ; SUMMER STOCK TRYOUT

Sketches by Jerome Chodorov
Choreographed by Michael Kidd
Directed by George S. Kaufman
Produced by Leonard Field
With David Burns, Lenore Lonergan, Carl Reiner, Onna White, Peter
Gennaro, and Kidd

Published songs:
Pocketful Of Dreams—initial publication upon reuse in **MICHAEL TODD'S**
    PEEP SHOW [June 28, 1950]
You Never Know What Hit You (When It's Love)—originally used in
    THAT'S THE TICKET [September 24, 1948]

Additional songs recorded:
Cry, Baby, Cry—also used in **ALIVE AND KICKING** [January 7, 1950]
French With Tears—also used in **ALIVE AND KICKING**

A recent hit revue with a "looking for investors" motif had been **ANGEL IN**
THE WINGS [December 11, 1947] with Paul and Grace Hartman. The simi-

larly formatted **PRETTY PENNY** played the stock circuit, while actually looking for Broadway investors. David Burns, a thorough professional with an otherwise unblemished reputation, uncharacteristically castigated and assaulted Kaufman. The actor received a reprimand from Actors' Equity, tendered his resignation, and the show did not go on.

ALIVE AND KICKING

JANUARY 17, 1950   WINTER GARDEN THEATRE   46 PERFORMANCES

Music and lyrics mostly by others
Sketches by Joseph Stein and Will Glickman, I.A.L. Diamond, and others
Choreographed by Jack Cole
Directed by Robert H. Gordon
Produced by William R. Katzell and Ray Golden
With Cole, David Burns, Jack Gilford, Carl Reiner, Gwen Verdon, and Jack Cassidy

Published song:
Love, It Hurts So Good

Additional songs recorded:
Cry, Baby, Cry—originally used in **PRETTY PENNY** [June 20, 1949]
French With Tears—originally used in **PRETTY PENNY**

MICHAEL TODD'S PEEP SHOW

JUNE 28, 1950   WINTER GARDEN THEATRE   278 PERFORMANCES

Music and lyrics mostly by others (see **Styne**)
Sketches by Bobby Clark, William K. Wells, and others
Scenes directed by "Mr. R. Edwin Clark, Esq."
Directed by Hassard Short
Produced by Michael Todd
With Lina Romay, Clifford Guest, and Lilly Christine

Published songs:
Gimme The Shimmy
Pocketful Of Dreams—originally used (unpublished) in **PRETTY PENNY**
    [June 20, 1949]

BLESS YOU ALL

DECEMBER 14, 1950   MARK HELLINGER THEATRE   84 PERFORMANCES

Sketches by Arnold Auerbach
Choreographed by Helen Tamiris
Directed by John C. Wilson
Produced by Herman Levin and Oliver Smith
With Mary McCarty, Jules Munshin, Pearl Bailey, Valerie Bettis, and
Donald Saddler

Published songs:
I Can Hear It Now
Little Things (Meant So Much To Me)
Love Letter To Manhattan
A Rose Is A Rose
Summer Dresses
Take Off The Coat—originally used in THAT'S THE TICKET! [September
    24, 1948]
You Never Know What Hit You (When It's Love)—originally used in
    THAT'S THE TICKET!

Additional song recorded:
Don't Wanna Write About The South

The eagerly awaited follow-up to CALL ME MISTER [April 18, 1946] was a
distinct disappointment and struggled through a brief run. The earlier revue
had played the considerably smaller National (Billy Rose/Trafalgar/Neder-
lander); BLESS YOU ALL was not helped by the extra 400 seats.

WISH YOU WERE HERE

JUNE 24, 1952   IMPERIAL THEATRE   598 PERFORMANCES

Book by Arthur Kober and Joshua Logan
(Based on *Having Wonderful Time* [play] by Kober)
Directed by Logan
Produced by Leland Hayward and Logan
With Jack Cassidy, Patricia Marand, Sheila Bond, and Paul Valentine

Published songs:
Could Be
Don José Of Far Rockaway
Everybody Loves Everybody
Flattery
Glimpse Of Love—cut

Relax
Shopping Around
Summer Afternoon
They Won't Know Me
There's Nothing Nicer Than People—added after opening
Tripping The Light Fantastic
Where Did The Night Go?
Wish You Were Here

Additional songs published in vocal score:
Ballad Of A Social Director
Camp Kare-free (Opening Act One)
Certain Individuals
Mix And Mingle
Waiter's Song (Bright College Days)

Additional song recorded:
Good-bye Love—cut after opening

The enormous popularity of the title song—and the novelty of a featured swimming pool—carried WISH YOU WERE HERE past poor reviews to a long, successful run. The 1937 comedy by Kober (one-time husband to Lillian Hellman) took place at an adult summer camp very much like Green Mansions, where Rome began his career. Logan, who had been disappointed with his treatment as director/coauthor/coproducer of SOUTH PACIFIC [Rodgers: April 7, 1949], left his highly successful six-out-of-seven hit association with Rodgers to direct/coauthor/coproduce WISH YOU WERE HERE. For the record, this was not Broadway's first swimming pool: the Majestic had one for the five-performance run of Broadway's first Mexican musical comedy, VIVA O'BRIEN [October 9, 1941], which made a very little splash indeed.

FANNY

NOVEMBER 4, 1954   MAJESTIC THEATRE   888 PERFORMANCES

Book by S. N. Behrman and Joshua Logan
(Based on the trilogy by Marcel Pagnol)
Choreographed by Helen Tamiris
Directed by Logan
Produced by David Merrick and Logan
With Ezio Pinza, Walter Slezak, and Florence Henderson

Published songs:
Be Kind To Your Parents
Fanny

I Have To Tell You
I Like You
Love Is A Very Light Thing
Never Too Late For Love
Octopus
Restless Heart
To My Wife
Welcome Home
Why Be Afraid To Dance

Additional songs published in vocal score:
Cold Cream Jar Song
Hakim's Cellar
Happy Birthday (Nursery Round)
Oysters, Cockles And Mussels
Panisse And Son
The Thought Of You

Attorney/manager/associate producer David Merrick had spent a decade learning the theatre business. Determining to make his musical debut with Pagnol's trilogy, he underwent enormous obstacles before acquiring the rights and hiring Rome. Rome brought in his WISH YOU WERE HERE [June 25, 1952] collaborator Logan as director; Logan took Merrick to Rodgers and Hammerstein, a more obvious choice to write the score. Coming off the unsatisfying ME AND JULIET [Rodgers: May 28, 1953], the pair wanted to do FANNY—but only if they could produce it themselves. Merrick had no intention of withdrawing, and went back to Rome. [On their next project, Rodgers and Hammerstein *were* able to buy out original producers Feuer and Martin (PIPE DREAM [Rodgers: November 30, 1955]).] The slightly uneven FANNY benefited from Merrick's producing and promotional talents to become a long-running hit. Rome departed from his usual musical style to write a moving, highly emotional score. Emphasizing melody, he came up with the soaring title song and *Restless Heart,* as well as the tenderly touching *To My Wife.*

ROMANOFF AND JULIET

OCTOBER 10, 1957   PLYMOUTH THEATRE   389 PERFORMANCES

Play by Peter Ustinov
Incidental music by Harold Rome
Directed by George S. Kaufman
Produced by David Merrick
With Ustinov, Jack Gilford, Henry Lascoe, and Elizabeth Allen

Published songs: ·
None

Rome provided a guitar solo for George S. Kaufman's final show.

DESTRY RIDES AGAIN

April 23, 1959   Imperial Theatre   472 performances

Book by Leonard Gershe
(Based on the story by Max Brand)
Directed and choreographed by Michael Kidd
Produced by David Merrick in association with Max Brown
With Andy Griffith, Dolores Gray, and Scott Brady

Published songs:
Anyone Would Love You
Are You Ready, Gyp Watson?
Every Once In A While
Fair Warning
Hoop De Dingle
I Know Your Kind
I Say Hello
Once Knew A Fella
Ring On The Finger
Rose Lovejoy Of Paradise Alley

Additional songs published in vocal score:
Ballad Of A Gun
Don't Take Me Back To Bottleneck (Opening)
I Hate Him
Ladies
Not Guilty
Only Time Will Tell
Respectability
Tomorrow Morning

Merrick and Rome followed Fanny [November 4, 1954] with a musical version of the 1939 classic western. The lavish production and Michael Kidd's exciting staging helped, but the musical Destry couldn't compete with the memory of James Stewart and Marlene Dietrich.

I CAN GET IT FOR YOU WHOLESALE

MARCH 22, 1962   SHUBERT THEATRE   300 PERFORMANCES

Book by Jerome Weidman
(Based on the novel by Weidman)
Choreographed by Herbert Ross
Directed by Arthur Laurents
Produced by David Merrick
With Elliot Gould, Lillian Roth, Marilyn Cooper, Harold Lang, Bambi
Linn, and Barbra Streisand

Published songs:
A Gift Today (The Bar Mitzvah Song)
Have I Told You Lately
Miss Marmelstein
Momma, Momma
On My Way To Love
The Sound Of Money
Too Soon
What's In It For Me?
Who Knows?

Additional songs published in vocal score:
Ballad Of The Garment Trade
Eat A Little Something
The Family Way
I'm Not A Well Man
The Way Things Are
What Are They Doing To Us Now?
When Gemini Meets Capricorn

Rome was put together with Jerome (**FIORELLO!** [Bock: November 23, 1959])
Weidman for his third consecutive Merrick musical, an adaptation of the
1944 movie "National Velvet." Weidman's successful 1937 novel seemed a
far better idea, and Merrick agreed to go along. Rome returned to his **PINS
AND NEEDLES** [November 27, 1937] terrain, the New York City garment
district during the Depression; but the music was far richer now, reflecting his
melodic experiences with **FANNY** [November 4, 1954]. The combination of
an unsympathetic antihero and downbeat subject matter worked against
WHOLESALE. Bright spots included a young singer from Brooklyn named
Streisand who breezed into auditions and was immediately cast in a very minor
role. Rome went off and fashioned *Miss Marmelstein* (in his **PINS AND NEE-
DLES** vein) and *What Are They Doing To Us Now?* to her talents.

THE ZULU AND THE ZAYDA

NOVEMBER 10, 1965   CORT THEATRE   179 PERFORMANCES

Play by Howard Da Silva and Felix Leon
Directed by Dore Schary
Produced by Theodore Mann and Schary
With Menasha Skulnik, Ossie Davis, and Louis Gossett

Published songs:
How Cold, Cold, Cold An Empty Room
It's Good To Be Alive
Like The Breeze Blows—see GONE WITH THE WIND [May 3, 1972]
May Your Heart Stay Young (L'Chayim)
Out Of This World (Oisgetzaichnet)
Rivers Of Tears
Some Things
Tkambuza (Zulu Hunting Song)
The Water Wears Down The Stone
Zulu Love Song (Wait For Me)

Additional songs published in vocal selection:
Crocodile Wife

This play with songs attempted to deal with prejudice, telling of an unlikely South African friendship between a Yiddish grandfather and a young Zulu. It didn't work; but Rome, a collector and student of African art, provided a fascinating score in the styles of the two cultures. For a good example of creative song reuse, compare *Like The Wind Blows* with *Bonnie Gone.* The worthy original—with its highly idiomatic content—had no life outside THE ZULU AND THE ZAYDA. Several years later, Rome effectively used the music as background dirge for the rousing wake in GONE WITH THE WIND [May 3, 1972].

LA GROSSE VALISE

DECEMBER 14, 1965   54TH STREET THEATRE   7 PERFORMANCES

Music by Gerard Calvi
Lyrics by Harold Rome
Book and direction by Robert Dhery
Produced by Joe Kipness and Arthur Lesser
With Ronald Fraser, Victor Spinetti, and Joyce Jillson

Published songs:
Delilah Done Me Wrong
For You

Slippy Sloppy Shoes
Xanadu

David Merrick and Kipness had imported Dhery's previous revue, LA PLUME DE MA TANTE [November 11, 1958], which ran a staggering 835 performances. Merrick passed on the sequel, which was a quick failure. Rome contributed English versions of the lyrics.

GONE WITH THE WIND
The Epic Musical

MAY 3, 1972   DRURY LANE THEATRE < LONDON >   397 PERFORMANCES

Book by Horton Foote
(Based on the novel by Margaret Mitchell)
Directed and choreographed by Joe Layton
Produced by Harold Fielding
With Harve Presnell and June Ritchie

Published songs:
Gone With The Wind—written for American production
How Often
Lonely Stranger
Strange And Wonderful
We Belong To You

Additional songs published in vocal selection:
Blueberry Eyes
Little Wonders
Scarlett
A Time For Love
Where Is My Soldier Boy?

Additional songs recorded:
Because There's You—cut
Blissful Christmas
Bonnie Blue Flag—cut
Bonnie Gone—revised version of *Like The Breeze Blows* from THE ZULU AND THE ZAYDA [November 10, 1965]
Gambling Man
Goodbye, My Honey—cut
Home Again
It Doesn't Matter Now
Johnny Is My Darling—cut
Marrying For Fun

My Soldier
Newlywed's Song
O'Hara
A Southern Lady
Tara
Today's The Day (He Loves Me)
Tomorrow Is Another Day
Two Of A Kind
What Is Love
Which Way Is Home?
Why Did They Die?—cut

Rome's final musical began very far out of town when the composer and Joe Layton were invited to Tokyo to create SCARLETT [January 1, 1970], successfully produced by the Japanese in Japanese with a Japanese cast. GONE WITH THE WIND jumped across the globe to England, and the burning of Atlanta took London by storm. Troubles were foreseen in America, though, due to the overwhelming familiarity of the 1939 movie version. A less-than-spectacular third production started August 28, 1973 on the nearer side of the Pacific but never made it East—not even to Atlanta. Lesley Ann Warren and Pernell Roberts were the final Scarlett and Rhett.

Harold Rome began his career during the musical theatre drought of the mid-Thirties. He first achieved success with PINS AND NEEDLES [November 27, 1937], using light but pointed political satire. Rome quickly found a place in the revitalized topical revue. His specialty: sparkling comedy lyrics for everyday characters, set to bright and fresh music. But CALL ME MISTER [April 18, 1946] was Broadway's last great revue, television variety shows proving fatal to the form. After a period of adjustment, Rome responded with surprisingly rich, emotional scores for FANNY [November 4, 1954] and I CAN GET IT FOR YOU WHOLESALE [March 22, 1962]. Then came the musical theatre drought of the mid-Sixties, which forced Rome (along with Schwartz, Arlen, and others) into virtual retirement.

Hugh Martin

BORN: August 11, 1914   Birmingham, Alabama

Trained as a pianist, Martin began his Broadway career as a member of Kay Thompson's backup quartet in HOORAY FOR WHAT! [Arlen: December 1, 1937]. By the end of the tryout Thompson had been replaced; Martin remained and attracted immediate notice with his contemporary, jazz-oriented vocal arrangements. He was quickly hired to bring modernized, swinging choral parts to THE BOYS FROM SYRACUSE [Rodgers: November 23, 1938], DUBARRY WAS A LADY [Porter: December 6, 1939] and CABIN IN THE SKY [Duke: October 25, 1940]. Martin formed a quartet (The Martins) which sang his arrangements in LOUISIANA PURCHASE [Berlin: May 28, 1940]. The Martins included fellow songwriter Ralph Blane (born July 26, 1914 in Broken Arrow, Oklahoma).

BEST FOOT FORWARD
A Modern Musical Comedy

OCTOBER 1, 1941   ETHEL BARRYMORE THEATRE   326 PERFORMANCES

Music and lyrics mostly by Hugh Martin and Ralph Blane (see **Rodgers**)
Book by John Cecil Holm
Choreographed by Gene Kelly
Produced and directed by George Abbott
With Rosemary Lane, Nancy Walker, Gil Stratton, Jr., and June Allyson

Published songs:
Buckle Down, Winsocki
Ev'ry Time
I Know You By Heart
Just A Little Joint With A Juke Box
A Raving Beauty—added to 1963 revival; originally used in MEET ME IN
    ST. LOUIS [June 9, 1960]
Shady Lady Bird
That's How I Love The Blues
The Three B's

What Do You Think I Am?
Wish I May—written for 1943 movie version
You Are For Loving—added to revival; originally used in **Meet Me In St. Louis**
You're Lucky—written for movie version

Additional songs recorded:
Alive And Kicking—written for movie version
Don't Sell The Night Short
The Guy Who Brought Me (music by Richard Rodgers, lyric by Rodgers and Martin; credited to Martin and Blane)
Hollywood Story
Three Men On A Date

Abbott was always looking for new talent: Martin worked for him on **Boys From Syracuse** [Rodgers: November 23, 1938] and **Too Many Girls** [Rodgers: October 18, 1939]. For his next youth musical, Abbott gave the assignment to the musically up-to-the-minute Martin and collaborator Blane. Richard Rodgers, relatively inactive due to Larry Hart's deteriorating condition, decided to get involved and silently coproduced (he also ghosted a song). **Best Foot Forward** was a happy success, with the hit football song *Buckle Down, Winsocki* and the poignant *Ev'ry Time*. Abbott discovery Nancy Walker stole the show and went on to a series of Forties Abbott musicals; June Allyson went right to Hollywood—as did Martin and Blane. Work there included three superlative songs (*The Boy Next Door, Have Yourself A Merry Little Christmas,* and *The Trolley Song*) for the 1944 Judy Garland movie "Meet Me in St. Louis" (see **June 9, 1960** and **November 2, 1989**). Garland and director Vincente Minnelli's daughter Liza was to make her New York debut in the off-Broadway revival [April 2, 1963] of **Best Foot Forward**.

LOOK, MA, I'M DANCIN'!

JANUARY 29, 1948   ADELPHI THEATRE   188 PERFORMANCES

Music and lyrics by Hugh Martin
Book by Jerome Lawrence and Robert E. Lee
Conceived and choreographed by Jerome Robbins
Directed by George Abbott and Robbins
Produced by Abbott
With Nancy Walker, Harold Lang, and Sandra Deel

Published songs:
If You'll Be Mine
I'm Not So Bright
I'm Tired Of Texas

The Little Boy Blues
Shauny O'Shay
Tiny Room
The Way It Might Have Been

Additional songs recorded:
Gotta Dance
I'm The First Girl In The Second Row
Mlle. Scandale Ballet [instrumental]

Abbott, Robbins, and Nancy Walker of **On The Town** [**December 28, 1944**] reunited for this comic dance musical. Robbins had his first directing experience here, and Martin worked without a collaborator. The result was entertaining but not quite a hit. Martin provided the delightful *Little Boy Blues* and the lyrically spectacular *I'm The First Girl In The Second Row (Of The Third Scene In The Fourth Number In Fifth Position At Ten O'Clock On The Nose)*.

MAKE A WISH!

APRIL 18, 1951   WINTER GARDEN THEATRE   102 PERFORMANCES

Music and lyrics by Hugh Martin
Book by Preston Sturges
(Based on *The Good Fairy* [play] by Ferenc Molnar)
Choreographed by Gower Champion
Directed by John C. Wilson
Produced by Harry Rigby and Jule Styne with Alexander H. Cohen
With Nanette Fabray, Melville Cooper, Stephen Douglass, Helen Gallagher, and Harold Lang

Published songs:
Over And Over
Paris, France
Suits Me Fine
That Face—advertised but not published
What I Was Warned About
When Does This Feeling Go Away?

Additional songs recorded:
Hello, Hello, Hello
I Wanna Be Good 'N' Bad
I'll Never Make A Frenchman Out Of You
Make A Wish
The Sale [instrumental]

Take Me Back To Texas With You
That Face
Tonight You Are In Paree
The Tour Must Go On
Who Gives A Sou?

Composer Jule Styne, with two straight musical hits, was ready to enter the producing field. Martin had done vocal arrangements for both HIGH BUTTON SHOES [Styne: October 9, 1947] and GENTLEMEN PREFER BLONDES [Styne: December 8, 1949]; he auditioned his MAKE A WISH score (without a libretto) and Styne agreed to mount it. Alexander Cohen also entered the book musical field, with his first of eight (out of eight) disasters.

LOVE FROM JUDY

SEPTEMBER 25, 1952   SAVILLE THEATRE < LONDON >   594
    PERFORMANCES

Lyrics by Hugh Martin and Jack (Timothy) Gray
Book by Eric Maschwitz and Jean Webster
(Based on *Daddy Longlegs* [novel] by Webster)
Choreographed by Pauline Grant
Directed by Charles Hickman
Produced by Emile Littler
With Jeannie Carson, Bill O'Connor, and Adelaide Hall

Published songs:
Daddy Longlegs
Go And Get Your Old Banjo
Love From Judy
My True Love

Additional songs published in vocal score:
Ain't Gonna Marry
Ballet [instrumental]
Dum Dum Dum
Goin' Back To School
Here We Are
I Never Dream When I Sleep
It's Better Rich
It's Great To Be An Orphan
Kind To Animals
Mardi Gras
A Touch Of Voodoo
What Do I See In You?

The failure of MAKE A WISH [April 18, 1951] virtually ended Martin's Broadway career. He went to London and wrote this highly successful hit with his new collaborator, singer Timothy Gray. Strangely enough, both shows were about innocent waiflike orphan girls who find happiness in the world outside the orphanage.

MEET ME IN ST. LOUIS

<First Version—also see November 2, 1989>

[JUNE 9, 1960]   MUNICIPAL OPERA <ST. LOUIS, MISSOURI>

Music and lyrics by Hugh Martin and Ralph Blane
Book by Sally Benson
(Based on *The Kensington Stories* by Benson and the 1944 movie)

Published songs:
Almost
The Boy Next Door—originally used in 1944 movie version
Diamonds In The Starlight
Have Yourself A Merry Little Christmas—originally used in movie version
How Do I Look?
If I Had An Igloo
A Raving Beauty—also used in 1963 revival of BEST FOOT FORWARD
    [**October 1, 1941**]
Skip To My Lou (adapted from traditional)—originally used in movie
    version
The Trolley Song—originally used in movie version
What's-His-Name
You Are For Loving—also used in revival of BEST FOOT FORWARD

Martin and Blane were reunited in Hollywood in the late Fifties. MEET ME IN ST. LOUIS was a stage version of their popular film, aimed at the stock-and-amateur trade. The summer of 1960 saw several summer stock productions. (Robert Goulet starred in one just prior to making his Broadway debut in CAMELOT [Loewe: December 3, 1960].) This adaptation never reached Broadway, but the new songs included the touchingly beautiful *You Are For Loving.*

HIGH SPIRITS

An Improbable Musical Comedy

APRIL 7, 1964   ALVIN THEATRE   375 PERFORMANCES

Book, music and lyrics by Hugh Martin and Timothy Gray
(Based on *Blithe Spirit* [play] by Noël Coward)

Choreographed by Danny Daniels
Directed by Coward
Produced by Lester Osterman, Robert Fletcher, and Richard Horner
With Beatrice Lillie, Tammy Grimes, and Edward Woodward

Published songs:
The Bicycle Song—advertised but not published
Forever And A Day
I Know Your Heart
If I Gave You
Something Tells Me
Was She Prettier Than I?
You'd Better Love Me

Additional song published in "professional vocal selection":
Faster Than Sound

Additional songs recorded:
The Bicycle Song
Go Into Your Trance
Home Sweet Heaven
Something Is Coming To Tea
Talking To You
What In The World Did You Want?
Where Is The Man I Married?

Martin returned to Broadway with this final Bea Lillie vehicle. Coward's five-character farce was out of place in musical comedy, with the addition of an extraneous chorus particularly jarring. This was unfortunate, as an enjoyable score was wasted on the poorly chosen source material.

MEET ME IN ST. LOUIS

< Second Version—also see June 9, 1960 >

NOVEMBER 2, 1989   GERSHWIN THEATRE   253 PERFORMANCES

Music and lyrics by Hugh Martin and Ralph Blane
Book by Hugh Wheeler
(Based on *The Kensington Stories* by Sally Benson and the 1944 movie)
Choreographed by Joan Brickhill
Directed by Louis Burke
Produced by Brickhill-Burke Productions, Christopher Seabrooke, and EPI Products
With George Hearn, Milo O'Shea, Charlotte Moore, Betty Garrett, Donna Kane, and Courtney Peldon

Additional songs published:
Ice (music and lyric by Martin)—originally used in and only published as from the 1958 television musical "Hans Brinker"

New songs recorded:
Banjos
Be Anything But A Girl
The Boy Next Door [extended version]—includes entire refrain of *I Happen To Love You* (by Martin) from *Hans Brinker*
A Day In New York
Ghosties and Ghoulies That Go Bump In The Night
Irish Jig (The Ball)
Paging Mr. Sousa
A Touch Of The Irish
Wasn't It Fun?

Husband-and-wife team Brickhill and Burke, experts at staging American musicals in their native South Africa, decided to show Broadway a thing or two and hang the expense. They chose MEET ME IN ST. LOUIS as their vehicle, and spent an awful lot of money on an awfully amateurish show. (The famous *Trolley Song* featured a big-as-life trolley which, after a flashy entrance, simply turned around and around and around and around but never went anywhere; it was that kind of evening.) One of the new songs, *Banjos,* was quite peppy; the rest were so far below Martin's standards that maybe it's just as well that he's been absent since 1964. (I don't know when these songs were actually written, but Martin and Blane were both seventy-five when ST. LOUIS finally hit Broadway.) The big surprise, for me anyway, was that even Martin's vocal arrangements were boring.

Hugh Martin's writing career has been incredibly spotty. At his best, his distinctive melodic freedom and colorful harmonies made him stand out as a possible successor to Gershwin and Arlen (or, at least, Duke and Lane); it's truly unfortunate that we heard so little from him. Martin also deserves a great deal of credit for revolutionizing the 'sound' of the Broadway musical, with masterful vocal arrangements for the Messrs. Berlin, Rodgers, Arlen, Porter, and Styne.

Leonard Bernstein

BORN: August 25, 1918   Lawrence, Massachusetts
DIED: October 14, 1990   New York, New York

Leonard Bernstein's first theatre experience came when the twenty-one-year-old Harvard music major mounted the 1939 Boston premiere of THE CRADLE WILL ROCK [Blitzstein: June 16, 1937]. Bernstein played the onstage accompaniment; the composer attended, was impressed, and the two began a close friendship. Following graduation, Bernstein entered the Curtis Institute of Music in Philadelphia—where Blitzstein had studied—to train for a career in symphonic music. Three years assisting Serge Koussevitzky and Artur Rodzinski led to the young conductor's break on November 14, 1943: a last-minute illness (and no suitable replacement) resulted in Bernstein conducting a concert by the New York Philharmonic. Being young and *American* brought the event enormous publicity, and Bernstein was suddenly in the serious music spotlight. His first composition was Ballet Theatre's "Fancy Free" [April 18, 1944], choreographed by (and featuring) Jerome Robbins in *his* debut. Robbins had been on Broadway dancing in the unsuccessful musicals GREAT LADY [Loewe: December 1, 1938] and KEEP OFF THE GRASS [Duke: May 23, 1940]. "Fancy Free" took the ballet and music world by storm, as the two twenty-five-year-olds brought contemporary dance and jazz into the Metropolitan Opera House. It seemed obvious to take the piece and turn it into a hit musical comedy; "Fancy Free's" twenty-five-year-old scenic designer Oliver Smith went along as producer.

ON THE TOWN

DECEMBER 28, 1944   ADELPHI THEATRE   463 PERFORMANCES

Book and lyrics by Betty Comden and Adolph Green
(Based on *Fancy Free* [ballet] by Bernstein and Robbins)
Choreographed by Jerome Robbins
Directed by George Abbott
Produced by Oliver Smith and Paul Feigay
With Nancy Walker, Sono Osato, Comden, and Green

Published songs:
I Can Cook Too (lyric by Bernstein; additional lyric by Comden and
    Green)
Lonely Town
Lucky To Be Me
New York, New York
Some Other Time
Ya Got Me

Additional songs published in "Bernstein On Broadway":
Carried Away
I Feel Like I'm Not Out Of Bed Yet
New York, New York (complete version)

Additional songs recorded:
Come Up To My Place
Do-Do-Re-Do
I Understand
I'm Blue
Imaginary Coney Island Ballet [instrumental]
Lonely Town Ballet [instrumental]
Miss Turnstile Variations [instrumental]
Real Coney Island Ballet [instrumental]
She's A Home Loving Girl
So Long, Baby
Times Square Ballet [instrumental]

The producers—designer Oliver Smith and twenty-four-year-old manager Paul
Feigay—brought in nightclub performers Betty Comden and Adolph Green,
who'd never written book or lyrics or appeared in a Broadway show, to write the
book and lyrics and play featured roles. They were also in their twenties; Green
was a former roommate of Bernstein's. *Then*, somebody brought in George
Abbott to direct. ON THE TOWN, of course, was a bit hit. Bernstein's score
mixed a handful of ballets (no "Fancy Free" music was used) with his first songs,
including *New York, New York, Lonely Town,* and some good comedy numbers. Robbins brought along Sono Osato, with whom he'd danced at Ballet
Theatre. She had one Broadway credit, as Agnes de Mille's lead dancer in ONE
TOUCH OF VENUS [Weill: October 7, 1943]. Abbott, for his part, brought along
Nancy Walker from BEST FOOT FORWARD [October 1, 1941]. The veteran's
fast-paced direction was just right for this new-style musical comedy. Robbins's
work was good, Walker and Osato were good, *everything* was good. Comden
and Green made a sparklingly impressive debut as lyricist/librettists and began
a long and healthy Broadway career. But Bernstein, having conquered Broadway, returned to the world of symphonic music.

PETER PAN
< Third Version >

APRIL 24, 1950   IMPERIAL THEATRE   321 PERFORMANCES

Play by James M. Barrie
Incidental music by Alec Wilder
Songs (music and lyrics) by Leonard Bernstein
Directed by John Burrell
Produced by Peter Lawrence and Roger L. Stevens
With Jean Arthur and Boris Karloff

Published songs:
My House
Never-land
Peter, Peter
Pirate Song—issued in choral arrangement only
Plank Round—issued in choral arrangement only
Who Am I?

Additional song recorded:
Dream With Me—cut

Bernstein ended the Forties with an assortment of serious compositions, including the "Jeremiah Symphony." The Fifties began with this half-dozen-song assignment for the Jean Arthur production of the whimsical Barrie play.

WONDERFUL TOWN

FEBRUARY 25, 1953   WINTER GARDEN THEATRE   559 PERFORMANCES

Lyrics by Betty Comden and Adolph Green
Book by Joseph Fields and Jerome Chodorov
(Based on *My Sister Eileen* [play] by Fields and Chodorov from stories by Ruth McKenney)
Choreographed by Donald Saddler
Directed by George Abbott
Produced by Robert Fryer
With Rosalind Russell, Edith Adams, George Gaynes, and Henry Lascoe

Published songs:
It's Love
A Little Bit In Love
My Darlin' Eileen ("based on an Irish Reel")
Ohio

A Quiet Girl
Swing!
The Wrong Note Rag

Additional songs published in "Bernstein On Broadway":
One Hundred Easy Ways
Pass The Football

Additional songs recorded:
Ballet At The Village Vortex (Let It Come Down) [instrumental]
Christopher Street (opening)
Conga!
Conquering The City—cut
Conversation Piece
Lonely Me—cut
The Story Of My Life—cut
What A Waste

Comden and Green had cast about for a new composer since ON THE TOWN [December 28, 1944], trying out Morton Gould (on the Abbott/Robbins BILLION DOLLAR BABY [December 21, 1945], Saul Chaplin (on the Broadway-bound BONANZA BOUND [December 26, 1947], and Jule Styne (Two ON THE AISLE [Styne: July 19, 1951]). The Styne collaboration seemed particularly promising. Meanwhile, Comden and Green went to Hollywood and had just finished the screenplay for the 1952 "Singin' In The Rain" when Abbott called for help. WONDERFUL TOWN was just a month away from rehearsals when "artistic differences" among the authors resulted in the withdrawal of songwriters Leroy Anderson and Arnold Horwitt. Bernstein joined Comden and Green to write his second musical score. ON THE TOWN had been an experiment in musical/ballet comedy; WONDERFUL TOWN was more in the standard musical comedy form, but a well-executed, highly successful example. The score was delightfully evocative of the Thirties period, and in places playfully creative (including *Ohio, Swing!* and the skillful *Wrong Note Rag*). Abbott kept things moving at his usual fast pace, and Rosalind Russell made the whole package immensely enjoyable.

ALL IN ONE
[Including TROUBLE IN TAHITI]

APRIL 19, 1955   PLAYHOUSE THEATRE   49 PERFORMANCES

Opera music and libretto by Bernstein
Directed by David Brooks
Produced by Charles Bowden and Richard Barr
With Alice Ghostley and John Tyers

Opera vocal score published:
Trouble in Tahiti

NOTE: Also see A QUIET PLACE (Second Version) [July 22, 1984]

The one-act opera TROUBLE IN TAHITI was first performed in June 1952 at a Brandeis College [Waltham, Massachusetts] arts festival put together by Bernstein. Also introduced was the Marc Blitzstein translation of THE THREE-PENNY OPERA (Second Version) [Weill: March 10, 1954]. (Bernstein dedicated TROUBLE IN TAHITI to Blitzstein, and named him godfather of his first child.) Bernstein's opera found its way to a limited Broadway run. The composer found his way to Milan in 1953, when he was the first American to ever conduct opera at La Scala.

THE LARK

NOVEMBER 17, 1955   LONGACRE THEATRE   229 PERFORMANCES

Play by Jean Anouilh
Adaptation by Lillian Hellman
Incidental music and lyrics by Bernstein
Directed by Joseph Anthony
Produced by Kermit Bloomgarden
With Julie Harris, Boris Karloff, and Christopher Plummer

Published songs:
Soldier's Song
Spring Song

Additional songs published in "Choruses From The Lark":
Benedictus
Court Song
Gloria
Prelude
Requiem
Sanctus [1st]—different than song from MASS [September 8, 1971]

A QUIET PLACE

<First>

[NOVEMBER 23, 1955]   SHUBERT THEATRE (NEW HAVEN, CONNECTICUT); CLOSED DURING PRE-BROADWAY TRYOUT

Play by Julian Claman
Title song by Leonard Bernstein

Directed by Delbert Mann
Produced by The Playwrights Company
With Tyrone Power and Leora Dana

Published songs:

None

A Quiet Place was an aria from **Trouble In Tahiti** [April 19, 1955]. It was reused as a song in this quick failure. Thirty years later, Bernstein wrote a sequel to **Trouble in Tahiti**—also named **A Quiet Place** (Second) [July 22, 1984].

CANDIDE

A Comic Operetta

<First Version—also see March 10, 1974>

December 1, 1956   Martin Beck Theatre   73 performances

Lyrics mostly by Richard Wilbur
Book by Lillian Hellman
(Based on the satire by Voltaire)
Directed by Tyrone Guthrie
Produced by Ethel Linder Reiner in association with Lester Osterman, Jr.
With Max Adrian, Barbara Cook, Robert Rounseville, and Irra Petina

Published songs:
The Best Of All Possible Worlds—issued in choral edition
Buenos Aires Tango (I Am Easily Assimilated) (lyric by Bernstein)
Glitter And Be Gay—issued in separate edition
It Must Be Me
Make Our Garden Grow—issued in choral edition
What's The Use?

Additional songs published in vocal score:
Ballad Of Eldorado (lyric by Hellman)
Bon Voyage
Dear Boy—cut
Lisbon Sequence (lyric by Bernstein)
My Love (lyric by John Latouche and Wilbur)
Oh, Happy We
Overture [instrumental]
Pilgrims Procession
Quartet Finale
Quiet

Venice Gambling Scene (Money, Money) (lyric by Dorothy Parker)
Wedding Chorale
You Were Dead, You Know (lyric by Latouche and Wilbur)

Additional songs recorded:
Ringaroundarosie—cut; see (**Second Version**)
We Are Women—cut; written for 1959 London production

Bernstein wrote one of Broadway's most glorious scores for this glorious
failure. Misconceived and misguided, Voltaire's satire was played as light
operetta—not what the author had in mind. Not what the composer and his
lyricists seemed to have in mind, either. John Latouche, best known for **Cabin
In The Sky** [Duke: October 25, 1941], was fresh from his artistic triumph
with **The Golden Apple** [**PART 4: March 11, 1954**]; he suffered a heart
attack and died August 7, 1956, at the age of only thirty-eight. Dorothy Parker,
librettist Hellman, and even Bernstein contributed lyrics before poet Richard
Wilbur came in.

WEST SIDE STORY

September 26, 1957   Winter Garden Theatre   734 performances

Lyrics by Stephen Sondheim
Book by Arthur Laurents
(Suggested by *Romeo and Juliet* [play] by William Shakespeare)
Choreographed by Jerome Robbins and Peter Gennaro
Conceived and directed by Robbins
Produced by Robert E. Griffith and Harold S. Prince by arrangement with
Roger L. Stevens
With Larry Kert, Carol Lawrence, Chita Rivera, and Lee Becker
NOTE: Lyrics initially credited to Sondheim and Bernstein

Published songs:
America
Cool
Gee, Officer Krupke—initial publication upon use in return engagement
    [April 27, 1960; 249 performances]
I Feel Pretty
Maria
One Hand, One Heart
Something's Coming (Could Be)
Somewhere
Tonight

Additional songs published in vocal score:
A Boy Like That (and *I Have A Love*)
The Dance At The Gym [instrumental]
Jet Song
Prologue [instrumental]
The Rumble [instrumental]
Somewhere Ballet [instrumental]
Taunting Scene [instrumental]
Tonight (Quintet)

Arthur Laurents entered the theatre with the fine postwar drama *Home of the Brave* [December 27, 1945]. Discussions in 1945 with Jerome Robbins brought about the idea for an EAST SIDE STORY—Romeo and Juliet using an interfaith romance. Bernstein became involved, but the project fell through. When big-city racial gang wars became news in the mid-Fifties, the idea was reborn. Bernstein started the lyrics himself; when help was needed, Laurents brought in Sondheim as colyricist. (During the tryout, Bernstein relinquished his lyric credit. It has been rumored that this was a tradeoff: that Sondheim himself wrote some of the music while Bernstein was off struggling with CANDIDE [December 1, 1956]. Certainly, it would have been uncharacteristic of Bernstein to arbitrarily drop his billing; he carefully retained lyricist credit for miscellaneous contributions to ON THE TOWN and CANDIDE. Surely, no one would have suggested crediting Broadway novice Sondheim for additional music. Whatever the case may be, the WEST SIDE score is unquestionably a classic—with full credit to the Messrs. Bernstein and Sondheim.) Producer Cheryl Crawford, whose three Fifties musicals had been progressive, unconventional flops (FLAHOOLEY [PART 4: May 14, 1951], PAINT YOUR WAGON [Loewe: November 12, 1951] and REUBEN REUBEN [Blitzstein: October 10, 1955]), was unable to come up with the financing and abandoned the production. Sondheim called friend Harold Prince, coproducer with Robert Griffith of three big George Abbott/Bob Fosse musicals (see NEW GIRL IN TOWN [Merrill: May 14, 1957]), and WEST SIDE STORY finally got underway. As with ON THE TOWN [December 28, 1944], WEST SIDE STORY was centered on ballet; but not for musical comedy purposes. The modern use of dance for dramatic/plot purposes first worked with de Mille's symbolic *Laurey Makes Up Her Mind* in OKLAHOMA! [Rodgers: March 31, 1943]; but here, dance was used as part of the everyday language/movement of the characters. As was to be expected, the exceptional WEST SIDE STORY was not a major hit: THE MUSIC MAN [Willson: December 19, 1957] took all the awards except Best Choreographer. The legendary status did not develop until the release of the 1961 movie version. After WEST SIDE STORY opened, Bernstein once again left the theatre, to become music director of the New York Philharmonic.

THE FIRSTBORN

APRIL 29, 1958   CORONET THEATRE   38 PERFORMANCES

Play by Christopher Fry
Songs by Leonard Bernstein
Directed by Anthony Quayle
Produced by Katharine Cornell and Roger L. Stevens
With Cornell, Quayle, and Mildred Natwick

Published songs:
None

Katharine Cornell made one of her final stage appearances in this limited engagement. Bernstein did not return to the theatre until ten years later, when he joined with Sondheim, Robbins, and playwright John Guare for an adaptation of Bertolt Brecht's *The Exception and the Rule*. A PRAY BY BLECHT (starring Zero Mostel) was announced for a February 18, 1969 opening at the Broadhurst, but the authors were unable to finish the piece and it was withdrawn. It resurfaced in the spring of 1987 as a developmental workshop mounted by Lincoln Center Theater, with Josh Mostel in his father's role. Once again, the piece—retitled THE ROAD TO URGA—was withdrawn.

MASS

A Theatre Piece for Singers, Players and Dancers

[SEPTEMBER 8, 1971]   KENNEDY CENTER OPERA HOUSE
    <WASHINGTON, D.C.> ; LIMITED ENGAGEMENT

Text from the Liturgy of the Roman Mass
Additional text by Stephen Schwartz and Leonard Bernstein
Choreographed by Alvin Ailey
Directed by Gordon Davidson
Produced by Roger L. Stevens
With Alan Titus

Published songs:
Almighty Father
Gloria Tibi
Sanctus [2nd]—different than song from THE LARK [November 17, 1955]
A Simple Song
The Word Of The Lord

Additional songs published in vocal score:
Agnus Dei
Alleluia [1st]

Confiteor Alleluia [2nd]
Credo In Unum Deum
De Profundis
Dominus Vobiscum
Easy
Epiphany
Gloria In Excelsis
God Said (And It Was Good)
Half Of The People (partial lyric by Paul Simon)
Hurry
I Believe In God
I Don't Know
I Go On
In Nomine Patris
Kyrie Eleison
Meditation No. 1 [instrumental]
Meditation No. 2 (on a sequence by Beethoven) [instrumental]
Non Credo (Possibly Yes, Probably No)
Our Father
Pax: Communion (Secret Songs)
Prefatory Prayers (Street Chorus)—see 1600 PENNSYLVANIA AVENUE [May 4, 1976]
Thank You
Things Get Broken
World Without End

Bernstein returned to the stage with this spectacular "theatre piece" commissioned for the opening of the John F. Kennedy Center for the Performing Arts. The nature of the work gave the composer freedom to write in all styles, ranging from modal to atonal. Controversy arose over the inclusion of rock music in the religious MASS. Others protested objectionable messages political and philosophical; the piece, after all, was sponsored by the government. Bernstein's score was incredibly rich, well worth the wait since WEST SIDE STORY [September 26, 1957]. The size and scope of MASS—soloists, chorus, dance company, boys' choir, full orchestra, etc.—precluded much of an afterlife. A second production [June 28, 1972] played a month at the Metropolitan Opera House, and Kennedy Center mounted a tenth-anniversary revival. MASS, most fortunately, remains in full glory on the original cast album.

CANDIDE

< Second Version—also see December 1, 1956>

MARCH 10, 1974   BROADWAY THEATRE   740 PERFORMANCES

Lyrics mostly by Richard Wilbur
New lyrics by Stephen Sondheim
Book by Hugh Wheeler
(Based on the satire by Voltaire)
Choreographed by Patricia Birch
Directed by Harold Prince
Produced by Chelsea Theatre Center of Brooklyn in conjunction with
Prince and Ruth Mitchell
With Mark Baker, Lewis J. Stadlen, and Maureen Brennan

Additional songs published in choral arrangements:
Life Is Happiness Indeed (lyric by Sondheim)—new lyric for *Venice
      Gambling Scene*
This World (Candide's Lament) (lyric by Sondheim)—new lyric for
      Quartet Finale

Additional songs published in new vocal score:
Alleluia [2nd]
Auto Da Fe (What A Day) (lyric by Latouche and Sondheim)—revised
      version of *Ringaroundarosie* (cut) from **(First Version)**
Barcarolle [instrumental]
The Best Of All Possible Worlds—new lyric by Sondheim for song of
      same name
Sheep's Song (lyric by Sondheim)

CANDIDE had been unsuccessful in its original production, and a full-scale
revival had also failed. The remarkable score had always cried out for a correct
mounting; so when Harold Prince was asked to direct the piece off-off-
Broadway, he brought in Sondheim and Wheeler from A LITTLE NIGHT
MUSIC [**Sondheim: February 25, 1973**]. They removed the costume operetta
trappings which had smothered the original, and went back to Voltaire.
Success in Brooklyn brought the new CANDIDE triumphantly to Broadway—
where the cost was too high, the capacity too low, and the union musicians
too many. Another failure, but a smashing artistic success . . . and, with the
revised version accessible, CANDIDE now has a much-deserved life. But the
original score is far more glorious.

BY BERNSTEIN

November 23, 1975   Chelsea Westside Theatre
    <(off-Broadway>   17 performances

New lyrics mostly by Bernstein
Conceived and written by Betty Comden and Adolph Green
Directed by Michael Bawtree
Produced by Chelsea Theatre Center of Brooklyn
With Patricia Elliott, Kurt Peterson, and Janie Sell

Recorded songs:
Ain't Got No Tears Left—based on theme from 1949 symphony "Age of
    Anxiety"
Another Love (lyric by Comden and Green)
It's Got To Be Good To Be Bad
Rio Bamba—originally written (unpublished) as 1943 nonshow song

A revue compiled mostly of cuts and never-performed Bernstein material.

1600 PENNSYLVANIA AVENUE

May 4, 1976   Mark Hellinger Theatre   7 performances

Book and lyrics by Alan Jay Lerner
Choreographed by George Faison
Directed by Gilbert Moses
Produced by Roger L. Stevens and Robert Whitehead
With Ken Howard, Patricia Routledge, Emily Yancy, Gilbert Price, and
Reid Shelton

Published songs:
Bright And Black
The President Jefferson Sunday Luncheon Party March—revised version of
    Prefatory Prayers (Street Chorus) from Mass [September 8, 1971]
Take Care Of This House

Additional songs published in vocal selection:
Pity The Poor
The Red White And Blues
Seena
We Must Have A Ball

Additional song recorded:
Lud's Wedding

Bernstein's first Broadway musical since West Side Story [September 26,
1957] was this ill-conceived mistake. The combination of Bernstein, Lerner,

and the Bicentennial was enough to get the Coca-Cola Company to finance the nondevelopable idea. ON THE TOWN [December 28, 1944] and WEST SIDE had been close music/dance collaborations, with Jerome Robbins and well-constructed books; 1600 PENNSYLVANIA AVENUE had an unworkable book and a small army of directors and choreographers. The impossible leading role was impossible to cast; the actor finally settled upon was far from ideal. All the show had going for it was the score (half of which was very good) and Patricia Routledge (who was very good indeed). The Bernstein-Lerner team proved itself highly capable, as well it should have been; but there were long stretches which a strong director or producer or librettist might well have edited, cut, or replaced. Lost but hopefully to reappear in the future were Routledge's perfectly crafted *Duet For One* and the sonata-form *Overture*—also used for an 1812 minioperetta as the British occupied Washington and set fire to the White House. It was that kind of evening.

MADWOMAN OF CENTRAL PARK WEST

JUNE 13, 1979   22 STEPS THEATRE < OFF-BROADWAY >   86 PERFORMANCES

Music mostly by others (also see **Kander**)
Book by Phyllis Newman and Arthur Laurents
Directed by Laurents
Produced by Gladys Rackmil, Fritz Holt, and Barry M. Brown
With Phyllis Newman

Song published in "Bernstein On Broadway":
My New Friends (lyric by Bernstein)

Bernstein contributed this song to Phyllis (Mrs. Adolph Green) Newman's one-woman show.

A QUIET PLACE

< *Second; see November 23, 1955* >

[JULY 22, 1984] KENNEDY CENTER OPERA HOUSE < WASHINGTON, D.C. >

Opera by Leonard Bernstein
Libretto and direction by Stephen Wadsworth
(Based on characters from *Trouble In Tahiti* [opera] by Bernstein)
Produced by Houston Grand Opera, Kennedy Center, and Teatro alla Scala
With Robert Galbraith, Beverly Morgan, and Peter Kazaras

Vocal score published.

A QUIET PLACE [April 19, 1955] was a sequel to Bernstein's earlier TROUBLE IN TAHITI [April 19, 1955]. Following negative reactions to the initial production in Houston, the two operas (about succeeding generations of the same family) were combined for engagements at La Scala and Washington.

Leonard Bernstein took time from his serious music career to write just five book musicals over forty-five busy years. Only two of these are still performed: WEST SIDE STORY [September 26, 1957] and CANDIDE < SECOND VERSION > [March 10, 1974], which has successfully overcome its initial failure. But Bernstein has justly earned a reputation as one of America's leading composers. After a long and perhaps overly-active career as the world's most renowned music man, Bernstein suddenly announced his retirement at the age of 72. He died of a heart attack five days later, on October 14, 1990.

Frederick Loewe

BORN: June 10, 1904   Vienna, Austria
DIED: February 14, 1988   Palm Springs, California

Frederick Loewe was the son of famous tenor Edmund Loewe, who created the role of Prince Danilo in the 1905 world premiere of Lehar's DIE LUSTIGE WITWE (*THE MERRY WIDOW*). At the age of fifteen, Frederick wrote the European pop-hit *Katrina*, which sold over a million copies; but he wanted a career in serious music, and studied piano and composition with Ferruccio Busoni (Kurt Weill's teacher). Arriving in America in 1924, Loewe was unable to succeed in music and went through a string of unlikely occupations, including prospecting, cowpoking, and professional boxing. In the Thirties he turned again to songwriting.

PETTICOAT FEVER

MARCH 4, 1935   RITZ THEATRE   137 PERFORMANCES

Play by Mark Reed
Directed by Alfred DeLiagre, Jr.
Produced by Richard Aldrich and DeLiagre
With Dennis King, Ona Munson, and Leo G. Carroll

Published song:
Love Tiptoed Through My Heart (lyric by Irene Alexander)

Twenties operetta star Dennis King was a Lambs' Club friend of Loewe's. He liked this song and sang it in his next show, giving Loewe his Broadway debut.

THE ILLUSTRATORS' SHOW

JANUARY 22, 1936   48TH STREET THEATRE   5 PERFORMANCES

Music and lyrics mostly by others (see **Loesser**)
Sketches by Max Liebman, Otto Soglow, and others
Directed by Allen Delano
Produced by Tom Weatherly and The Society of Illustrators

Published song:
A Waltz Was Born in Vienna (lyric by Earle Crooker)—also used in
SALUTE TO SPRING [June 12, 1937]

This short-lived production also included Frank Loesser's first Broadway songs. Loesser got a long-term Hollywood contract for his efforts; Loewe and Crooker didn't.

SALUTE TO SPRING

[JUNE 12, 1937]   MUNICIPAL OPERA < ST. LOUIS, MISSOURI >; SUMMER
STOCK TRYOUT

Book and lyrics by Earle Crooker
Directed by Richard H. Berger
Produced by St. Louis Municipal Opera
With Guy Robertson, Berenice Claire, and Olive Olsen

Published songs:
April Day
One Robin—also used in **LIFE OF THE PARTY** [October 8, 1942]
Salute To Spring
Somehow—also used in **LIFE OF THE PARTY**
A Waltz Was Born in Vienna—originally used in **THE ILLUSTRATORS'**
SHOW [January 22, 1936]

Loewe's first full musical score made for a fairly successful summer pageant.

GREAT LADY

DECEMBER 1, 1938   MAJESTIC THEATRE   20 PERFORMANCES

Lyrics by Earl Crooker
Book by Crooker and Lowell Brentano
Directed by Bretaigne Windust
Produced by Dwight Deere Wiman and J. H. Del Bondio by arrangement
with Frank Crumit
With Norma Terris, Irene Bordoni, Helen Ford, and Tullio Carminati

Published songs:
I Have Room In My Heart
May I Suggest Romance?
There Had To Be The Waltz
Why Can't This Night Last Forever?

Wiman, in the midst of his successful series of Rodgers and Hart musicals (see
ON YOUR TOES [Rodgers: April 11, 1936]), produced this operetta failure.

Heading the cast were leading ladies of **Show Boat** [Kern: December 27, 1927], **Paris** [Porter: October 8, 1928], and **Peggy-Ann** [Rodgers: December 27, 1926]—with very little to sing about.

LIFE OF THE PARTY

[OCTOBER 8, 1942]   WILSON THEATRE < DETROIT, MICHIGAN > ;
CLOSED DURING PRE-BROADWAY TRYOUT

Lyrics by Earle Crooker
Book by Alan Jay Lerner
(Based on *The Patsy* [play] by Barry Connors)
Directed by Russell Filmore
Produced by Henry Duffy
With Dorothy Stone, Charles Collins, Charles Ruggles, and Margaret Dumont

Published songs:
One Robin Doesn't Make A Spring—originally used in **Salute To Spring** [June 12, 1937]
Somehow—originally used in **Salute to Spring**

Henry Duffy successfully operated a number of stock companies on the West Coast beginning in the mid-Twenties. Duffy had first presented Fred Stone's dancing daughter Dorothy (with husband Charles Collins) in **Patricia**, a non-Loewe musicalization of *The Patsy.* Loewe's work on **Salute To Spring** [June 12, 1937] got him the assignment for the new version. Radio scriptwriter Lerner was an aspiring lyricist/librettist recently out of Harvard. Loewe and Lerner knew each other's work from Lambs' Club amateur shows. **Life Of The Party** was a rush job, so Loewe invited Lerner along to patch together a book.

WHAT'S UP?

A Merry Musical

NOVEMBER 11, 1943   NATIONAL THEATRE   63 PERFORMANCES

Lyrics by Alan Jay Lerner
Book by Arthur Pierson and Lerner
Staged and choreographed by George Balanchine
Book directed by Robert H. Gordon
Produced by Mark Warnow
With Jimmy Savo, Johnny Morgan, and Gloria Warren

Published songs:
Joshua
My Last Love
You Wash And I'll Dry
You've Got A Hold On Me

Lerner and Loewe's first Broadway effort was this poor wartime musical, surprising among their otherwise tasteful, high-quality body of work. WHAT'S UP? marked Balanchine's second and final directing attempt; the first had been the more successful CABIN IN THE SKY [Duke: October 25, 1940].

THE DAY BEFORE SPRING

NOVEMBER 22, 1945   NATIONAL THEATRE   165 PERFORMANCES

Book and lyrics by Alan Jay Lerner
Book directed by Edward Padula
Staged and produced by John C. Wilson
With Bill Johnson, Irene Manning and Pat Marshall

Published songs:
The Day Before Spring
God's Green World
I Love You This Morning
A Jug Of Wine
My Love Is A Married Man
This Is My Holiday
You Haven't Changed At All

This psychoanalytical fantasy received good reviews and attracted favorable attention to the authors, although the run was disappointingly short. Director Padula was to resurface as producer of the hit BYE BYE BIRDIE [Strouse: April 14, 1960].

BRIGADOON

MARCH 13, 1947   ZIEGFELD THEATRE   581 PERFORMANCES

Book and lyrics by Alan Jay Lerner
Directed by Robert Lewis
Choreography by Agnes de Mille
Produced by Cheryl Crawford
With David Brooks, Marion Bell, Pamela Britton, and James Mitchell

Published songs:
Almost Like Being In Love
Brigadoon
Come To Me, Bend To Me
Down On MacConnachy Square
From This Day On
The Heather On The Hill
I'll Go Home With Bonnie Jean
The Love Of My Life
There But For You Go I
Waitin' For My Dearie

Additional songs published in vocal score:
The Chase
Funeral [instrumental]
Jeannie's Packin' Up
Prologue
Sword Dance
Vendors' Calls
Wedding Dance [instrumental]

Lerner and Loewe's colorful fantasy of the Scottish Highlands was a surprise hit, impeccably produced by Cheryl Crawford. The fine work of de Mille and the colorful trappings helped sustain the magical mood, but it was the score— not only hits *Almost Like Being In Love* and *The Heather On The Hill*, but also the exquisite *From This Day On* and *There But For You Go I* which supported the sentiment of the evening. It should be pointed out that the hit musicals of that postwar season were both fantasies, normally an impossible musical comedy form: the escapist **BRIGADOON,** with its concentrated use of (but not reliance on) dance; and the longer-running (but more quickly dated) **FINIAN'S RAINBOW** [Lane: January 10, 1947], which used elfin charm, a glorious score, and some strong social satire.

PAINT YOUR WAGON

NOVEMBER 12, 1951   SHUBERT THEATRE   289 PERFORMANCES

Book and lyrics by Alan Jay Lerner
Directed by Daniel Mann
Choreography by Agnes de Mille
Produced by Cheryl Crawford
With James Barton, Olga San Juan, Tony Bavaar, and James Mitchell

Published songs:
Another Autumn
Carino Mio

I Still See Elisa
I Talk To The Trees
I'm On My Way
Sh!—cut
They Call The Wind Maria
Wand'rin' Star

Additional songs published in vocal score:
All For Him
Hand Me Down That Can O' Beans
How Can I Wait?
In Between
Lonely Men [instrumental]
Movin'
Rope Dance [instrumental]
Rumson Town
There's A Coach Comin' In
Trio (Mormons' Prayer)
What's Goin' On Here?
Whoop-ti-ay!

An ambitious but leaden saga of the California Gold Rush. The interwoven use of ballet that worked so well in the Highlands was less scenic on the Prairies, and the subject matter was harsh and cold. In spite of the show's failure, Loewe displayed—as in all his major work—an uncanny ability to write scores indigenous to the time and locale of the characters and plots.

MY FAIR LADY

MARCH 15, 1956   MARK HELLINGER THEATRE   2,717 PERFORMANCES

Book and lyrics by Alan Jay Lerner
(Based on *Pygmalion* [play] by George Bernard Shaw)
Directed by Moss Hart
Choreographed by Hanya Holm
Produced by Herman Levin
With Rex Harrison, Julie Andrews, Stanley Holloway, and Robert Coote

Published songs:
Get Me To The Church On Time
I Could Have Danced All Night
I've Grown Accustomed To Her Face
On The Street Where You Live [2nd]—revised version of [1st]
The Rain In Spain [instrumental]
The Rain In Spain [song version]

Say A Prayer For Me Tonight—cut; initial publication upon reuse in 1958
    movie "Gigi"
Show Me
With A Little Bit Of Luck
Wouldn't It Be Loverly?

Additional songs published in vocal score:
Ascot Gavotte
The Embassy Waltz [instrumental]
A Hymn To Him
I'm An Ordinary Man
Just You Wait, Henry Higgins
Servants' Chorus
Why Can't A Woman Be More Like A Man?
Without You
You Did It!

Additional songs recorded:
Come To The Ball—cut
On The Street Where You Live [1st]—original version

Lerner and Loewe's masterpiece broke the OKLAHOMA! [**Rodgers: March 31,
1943**] long-run record at a time when six-year runs were unheard of. Shaw had
ruled all his work off musical limits: he loathed THE CHOCOLATE SOLDIER, the
1909 Oscar Straus operetta of *Arms And The Man.* But Shaw died in 1950,
and *Pygmalion* went through several hands before Lerner and Loewe got the
chance. For the first time (except for LIFE OF THE PARTY [October 8, 1942])
Lerner did an adaptation, re-forming the material but wisely retaining Shaw's
sparkling language. And *matching* that language in his lyrics. The entire
production sparkled, the score contained no less than five ever-popular standards, and everything went exceptionally well. But Shaw would have carped
at the satisfactorily happy ending.

CAMELOT

DECEMBER 3, 1960   MAJESTIC THEATRE   873 PERFORMANCES

Book and lyrics by Alan Jay Lerner
(Based on *The Once and Future King* [book] by T. H. White)
Directed by Moss Hart
Produced by Lerner, Loewe, and Hart
With Richard Burton, Julie Andrews, Roddy McDowall, Robert Goulet,
and John Cullum

Published songs:
Camelot
Follow Me

How To Handle A Woman
I Loved You Once In Silence
If Ever I Would Leave You
The Lusty Month Of May
The Simple Joys Of Maidenhood
What Do The Simple Folk Do?

Additional songs published in vocal score:
Before I Gaze At You Again
C'est Moi
The Enchanted Forest
Guenevere
I Wonder What The King Is Doing Tonight
The Invisible Wall [instrumental]
The Jousts
Madrigal
The Persuasion
The Seven Deadly Virtues
Tent Scene [instrumental]
The Tumblers [instrumental]

Additional songs recorded:
Fie On Goodness—cut after opening
Then You May Take Me To The Fair—cut after opening; published in
score (no lyric) as *Tent Scene* and *The Tumblers*

My Fair Lady [March 15, 1956] was followed by the Oscar-winning 1958
movie "Gigi," after which Loewe suffered a massive heart attack. Lerner,
Loewe and Hart then began work on the ill-fated **Camelot**, during which
Hart had a heart attack—causing his death within the year—and Lerner
suffered a nervous breakdown. **Camelot** was poorly received but did considerably well, thanks to the strong advance sale built on **My Fair Lady**'s success
and the spirit of the title song. Loewe's nearly fatal illness and the stress caused
by extreme personal differences with Lerner were enough to convince him to
retire. In 1971 he briefly worked with Lerner on the score for the unsuccessful
movie "The Little Prince."

GIGI

November 13, 1973   Uris Theatre   103 performances

Book and lyrics by Alan Jay Lerner
(Based on the novel by Colette and the motion picture by Lerner and
Loewe)
Directed by Joseph Hardy

Produced by Saint-Subber and Edwin Lester (for the Los Angeles and San Francisco Light Opera Company)
With Alfred Drake, Agnes Moorehead, Maria Karnilova, and Daniel Massey

Published songs originally used in movie version:
Gigi
I Remember It Well
I'm Glad I'm Not Young Anymore
The Night They Invented Champagne
She Is Not Thinking Of Me (Waltz At Maxim's)
Thank Heaven For Little Girls

New songs published in vocal score:
The Contract—revised version of *À Toujours* (cut) from motion picture
    version
The Earth And Other Minor Things
I Never Want To Go Home Again
In This Wide, Wide World
It's A Bore—originally used (unpublished) in motion picture version
Paris Is Paris Again
The Telephone (Opening Act Two)

Loewe's final score was this partially new stage version of the Oscar-winning 1958 movie. Far inferior to the original, it quickly failed; ironically, inconsistencies in the Tony Award eligibility rules allowed GIGI to win that year's award for best score. Loewe retreated to Palm Springs, where he lived in retirement until his death on February 14, 1988.

Frederick Loewe's musicals were skillfully written, and a number of his songs are deeply moving. All his mature work, from BRIGADOON [March 13, 1947] on, is of consistently high quality and carefully, professionally crafted. Still, something checks my enthusiasm; a lack of personal color, perhaps? By comparing him with 'competitors' Loesser and Styne, I think I can pinpoint what's missing: the music is good, but it simply isn't as much fun.

Jule Styne

BORN: December 31, 1905   London, England

Jule Styne was born in the slums of London, son of a butter-and-egg man (and sometime wrestler). The family moved to Chicago in 1912, where Styne had a short career as a piano prodigy: a drill-press accident desensitized a finger, and the preteen switched from the concert hall to the burlesque hall. By the Twenties, Styne was leading his own band on the South Side of Chicago, writing a few songs including the 1926 pop hit *Sunday* (words and music by Ned Miller, Chester Cohn, Jules Stein—the composer's real name—and Bennie Kruger). In 1934 Styne set up in New York as a vocal coach; four years later he was in Hollywood, working with Shirley Temple and other stars. Opportunity led to assignments writing cowboy songs for B pictures. A short collaboration with lyricist Frank Loesser brought the 1941 hit *I Don't Want To Walk Without You,* and Styne began a highly successful Hollywood career.

ICE CAPADES OF 1943

The Magnificent Ice-travaganza

SEPTEMBER 4, 1942   MADISON SQUARE GARDEN

Music mostly by others
Directed and choreographed by Chester Hale
Produced by Arena Managers Association (John Harris)
With Vera Hruba

Published song:
The Guy With The Polka-Dot Tie (lyric by Sol Meyer)

This ice show featured the Czech refugee, who looked a lot prettier than she skated (and she was good on ice). Styne used a jaunty tune he'd composed during high school days, distant cousin to *It's Enough To Make A Lady Fall In Love* from DARLING OF THE DAY [January 27, 1968].

GLAD TO SEE YOU!

[NOVEMBER 13, 1944]   SHUBERT THEATRE < PHILADELPHIA,
   PENNSYLVANIA > ; CLOSED DURING PRE-BROADWAY TRYOUT

Lyrics by Sammy Cahn
Book by Eddie Davis and Fred Thompson
Directed by Busby Berkeley
Produced by David Wolper
With Eddie Foy, Jr., Jane Withers, and June Knight

Published sons:
Any Fool Can Fall In Love
Guess I'll Have to Hang My Tears Out to Dry
I Don't Love You No More

In 1942, Styne began a hit-filled Hollywood collaboration with Sammy Chan, bolstered by a close association with Frank Sinatra. Styne and Cahn came to Broadway—or, rather, Philadelphia—with the dismal GLAD TO SEE YOU! Then it was quickly back to Hollywood, where they wrote *It's Been A Long, Long Time.*

HIGH BUTTON SHOES

OCTOBER 9, 1947   CENTURY THEATRE   727 PERFORMANCES

Lyrics by Sammy Cahn
Book by Stephen Longstreet
(Based on *The Sisters Liked Them Handsome* [novel] by Longstreet)
Choreographed by Jerome Robbins
Directed by George Abbott
Produced by Monte Proser and Joseph Kipness
With Phil Silvers, Nanette Fabray, Jack McCauley, Joey Faye, Helen Gallagher, and Donald Saddler

Published songs:
Betwixt And Between—cut; for initial publication see GYPSY [May 21, 1959]
Can't You Just See Yourself?
Get Away For A Day In The Country
I Still Get Jealous
On A Sunday By The Sea
Papa, Won't You Dance With Me
There's Nothing Like A Model 'T'
You're My Girl

Additional songs recorded:
Bathing Beauty Ballet [instrumental]
Bird Watcher's Song—cut
Nobody Ever Died For Dear Old Rutgers

Styne and Cahn gave Broadway another try and came up with a long-running hit. The songs were more in the pop than theatre vein, led by Nanette Fabray's hits *I Still Get Jealous* and *Papa, Won't You Dance With Me.* Styne's outstanding contribution was, surprisingly, his spectacular dance music for Jerome Robbins' legendary *Bathing Beauty Ballet.* Choreographer and composer began a profitable association: Robbins was to direct six Broadway musicals, four with Jule Styne scores. George Abbott's fast-paced musical comedy expertise, Phil Silvers' con-man, and the wonderful ballet made High Button Shoes very funny (if also very old-fashioned). Styne—already in his midforties—realized that the theatre was where he wanted to be: not just writing songs, but writing for characters in dramatic situations.

GENTLEMEN PREFER BLONDES

< also see LORELEI [January 27, 1974] >

December 8, 1949   Ziegfeld Theatre   740 performances

Lyrics by Leo Robin
Book by Joseph Fields and Anita Loos
(Based on the novel by Loos)
Choreographed by Agnes de Mille
Directed by John C. Wilson
Produced by Herman Levin and Oliver Smith
With Carol Channing, Yvonne Adair, Jack McCauley, and George S. Irving

Published songs:
Bye, Bye, Baby
Diamonds Are A Girl's Best Friend
It's Delightful Down In Chile
Just A Kiss Apart
A Little Girl From Little Rock
Sunshine
You Say You Care

Additional songs published in vocal selections:
Homesick Blues
I Love What I'm Doing
It's High Time
Mamie Is Mimi

Additional songs recorded:
Button Up With Esmond
Gentlemen Prefer Blondes
I'm A 'Tingle, I'm A 'Glow
Keeping Cool With Coolidge
Scherzo [instrumental]

The bright and lively GENTLEMEN PREFER BLONDES was dominated by Carol Channing proving *Diamonds Are A Girl's Best Friend* as she played *A Little Girl From Little Rock*. Styne also provided *Bye, Bye, Baby* and the very good comedy song *It's Delightful Down In Chile*. Styne's new lyricist was Leo Robin, who had HIT THE DECK [**Youmans: April 25, 1927**] in his pre-Hollywood past; Sammy Cahn chose to stay in movies. With GENTLEMEN PREFER BLONDES a hit, Styne remained in New York and set out to educate himself in the theatre.

MICHAEL TODD'S PEEP SHOW

JUNE 28, 1950   WINTER GARDEN THEATRE   278 PERFORMANCES

Music mostly by others (see **Rome**)
Lyrics to Styne songs by Bob Hilliard
Sketches by Bobby Clark and others
Scenes directed by "Mr. R. Edwin Clark, Esq."
Directed by Hassard Short
Produced by Michael Todd
With Lina Romay, Clifford Guest, and Lilly Christine

Published songs:
Francie—published in nonshow edition
Stay With The Happy People—published in nonshow edition

MAKE A WISH

see Martin [April 18, 1951]

TWO ON THE AISLE

JULY 19, 1951   MARK HELLINGER THEATRE   276 PERFORMANCES

Sketches and lyrics by Betty Comden and Adolph Green
Choreographed by Ted Cappy
Directed by Abe Burrows
Produced by Arthur Lesser
With Bert Lahr, Dolores Gray, Elliot Reid, and Colette Marchand

Published songs:
Everlasting
Give A Little, Get A Little
Hold Me—Hold Me—Hold Me
How Will He Know?
So Far—So Good—cut; issued as professional copy; revised version of
  Give Me A Song With A Beautiful Melody from 1949 movie "It's
  A Great Feeling"
There Never Was Another Baby

Additional songs published in vocal selection:
Catch Our Act At The Met—initial publication upon reuse in **A Party
  With Comden And Green** [December 23, 1958]
If You Hadn't But You Did —initial publication upon reuse in **A Party
  With Comden And Green**

Additional songs recorded:
The Clown
Here She Comes Now
Show Train
Vaudeville Ain't Dead

Styne first collaborated with Comden and Green on this summer revue. The comic potential of their partnership was demonstrated by *If You Hadn't But You Did, Catch Our Act At The Met,* and the patter for *Show Train.* Bert Lahr and some good comedy sketches helped the flimsily produced **Two On The Aisle** to a respectable run.

HAZEL FLAGG

February 11, 1953   Mark Hellinger Theatre   190 performances

Lyrics by Bob Hilliard
Book by Ben Hecht
(Based on *Letter to the Editor* [story] by James Street and *Nothing Sacred* [movie] by Ben Hecht)
Choreographed by Robert Alton
Directed by David Alexander
Produced by Styne in association with Anthony Brady Farrell
With Helen Gallagher, Jack Whiting, Benay Venuta, and Thomas Mitchell

Published songs:
Champagne And Wedding Cake—written for "Living It Up," 1954
  movie version

Ev'ry Street's A Boulevard (In Old New York)—initial publication upon
　　use in movie version
How Do You Speak To An Angel?
I Feel Like I'm Gonna Live Forever
Money Burns A Hole In My Pocket—added after opening; initial
　　publication upon use in movie version
Salomee (With Her Seven Veils)
That's What I Like—written for movie version
Think How Many People Never Find Love—cut
You're Gonna Dance With Me, Willie

Additional songs recorded:
Autograph Chant
Everybody Loves To Take A Bow
Hello, Hazel
I'm Glad I'm Leaving
Laura De Maupassant
A Little More Heart
Rutland Bounce [instrumental]
Who Is The Bravest?
The World Is Beautiful Today

Styne's Broadway producing career began with a major failure (**MAKE A WISH!** [Martin: April 18, 1951]), followed by the highly successful revival [January 3, 1952] of **PAL JOEY** [Rodgers: December 25, 1940]. Producer Styne determined to make a star out of Helen Gallagher, who had been prominently featured in **HIGH BUTTON SHOES** [October 9, 1947], **Make A Wish!** and **PAL JOEY** (with a Tony Award). The show built around her was not good and failed; Gallagher's career suffered, with her next big opportunity coming eighteen years later, when she won another Tony for the revival [January 19, 1971] of **No, No, NANETTE** [September 16, 1925]. The ultimate indignity: for the movie version, Gallagher was passed over, and her part, originally created on film by Carole Lombard, went to Jerry Lewis!

PETER PAN

<Fourth Version>

OCTOBER 20, 1954　WINTER GARDEN THEATRE　149 PERFORMANCES

Music also by Moose Charlap
Lyrics also by Carolyn Leigh
Lyrics to Styne songs by Betty Comden and Adolph Green
(Based on *Peter Pan* [play] by James M. Barrie)

Directed and choreographed by Jerome Robbins
Produced by Richard Halliday and Edwin Lester
With Mary Martin, Cyril Ritchard, Margalo Gilmore, and Sondra Lee

Published Styne songs:
Captain Hook's Waltz
Distant Melody
Never Never Land
Wendy

Additional songs written for (and published in vocal selection of) 1974 "Arena Version":
Hook's Hook (music and lyric by Styne and Tom Adair)
Youth, Joy And Freedom (music and lyric by Styne and Tom Adair)

Additional songs recorded:
Oh My Mysterious Lady
Ugg-A-Wugg

This version of **PETER PAN** began as a Los Angeles Civic Light Opera summer presentation. Mary Martin made her first appearance since **SOUTH PACIFIC** [Rodgers: April 7, 1949], with Jerome Robbins beginning his career as director/choreographer. The score by Charlap and Leigh was weak, so Robbins called in Styne, Comden, and Green to revamp the show for Broadway. They did, contributing the effective theme song (*Never Never Land*) and the felicitous *Wendy*. After only five months, the Mary Martin **PETER PAN** was telecast—and the Broadway run was cut short. The piece has remained a favorite with audiences, though, and a major revival with Sandy Duncan [September 6, 1979] enjoyed a 578-performance run.

MR. WONDERFUL
see Bock [March 22, 1956]

WAKE UP, DARLING

MAY 2, 1956   ETHEL BARRYMORE THEATRE   5 PERFORMANCES

Play by Alec Gottlieb
Directed by Ezra Stone
Produced by Gordon W. Pollock in association with Lee Segall and Richard Cook
With Barry Nelson, Barbara Britton, Russell Nype, and Kay Medford

Published songs:
None

The (bad) playwright in the (bad) play was writing a (bad) musical about the Civil War, so Styne and Leo Robin (of **Gentlemen Prefer Blondes** [December 8, 1949]) provided a parody (good) of Southern songs entitled *L'il Ol' You and Lil Ol' Me.*

BELLS ARE RINGING

November 29, 1956 · Shubert Theatre · 924 performances

Book and lyrics by Betty Comden and Adolph Green
Choreographed by Jerome Robbins and Bob Fosse
Directed by Robbins
Produced by The Theatre Guild
With Judy Holliday, Sydney Chaplin, Jean Stapleton, Eddie Lawrence, and Peter Gennaro

Published songs:
Bells Are Ringing
Better Than A Dream—written for 1960 movie version
Do It Yourself—written for movie version
Drop That Name
Hello, Hello There
I Met A Girl
Independent (On My Own)
Just In Time
Long Before I Knew You
Mu-cha-cha
The Party's Over

Additional songs published in vocal score:
I'm Going Back
Is It A Crime?
It's A Perfect Relationship
It's A Simple Little System
The Midas Touch
Salzburg

Styne's finest musical comedy (not including **Gypsy** [May 21, 1959]). Comden and Green's sometimes wild comic vision was perfect for this vehicle, starring their former nightclub-act partner Judy Holliday. The score was consistently good, with two enormous hits (*Just In Time* and *The Party's Over*). The whole production worked like a well-made George Abbott musical, which—with Abbott alumni Robbins, Fosse, Styne, Comden, and Green on hand—was not exactly surprising. Costarring was Sydney (son of Charles) Chaplin, not much of a singer but charming and handsome enough to star in two more Styne musicals. The composer used his vocal coach knowledge to fashion songs that even Chaplin could sing—like *Just In Time* and *You Are Woman, I Am Man* (in **FUNNY GIRL** [**March 26, 1964**]).

SAY, DARLING

A Play About A Musical

APRIL 3, 1958   ANTA THEATRE   332 PERFORMANCES

Lyrics by Betty Comden and Adolph Green
Book by Richard and Marian Bissell and Abe Burrows
(Based on the novel by Richard Bissell)
Choreographed by Matt Mattox
Directed by Burrows
Produced by Styne and Lester Osterman
With David Wayne, Vivian Blaine, Johnny Desmond, and Robert Morse

Published songs:
Dance Only With Me
It's The Second Time You Meet That Matters
Let The Lower Lights Be Burning
My Little Yellow Dress—cut
Say, Darling—revised version of *Some Other Time* (lyric by Sammy
    Cahn) from 1944 movie "Step Lively"
Something's Always Happening On The River
Try To Love Me Just As I Am

Additional songs recorded:
The Carnival Song
Chief Of Love
The Husking Bee
It's Doom

Richard Bissell was a Dubuque-born, Harvard-educated former steamboat pilot who came to Broadway to adapt his first novel into **THE PAJAMA GAME** [**Adler: May 13, 1954**]. Bissell's "Say, Darling" was a very funny "fictionalized" account of Bissell's adventures in musical comedy, complete with caricatures of Abbott, Adler, and producers Griffith and Prince. But the musical-comedy adaptation of the second novel, about the making of the musical-comedy adaptation of the first novel, wasn't as good as any of 'em. Styne, Comden, and Green's score was pastiche musical comedy of little

interest. The only true bright spot was the boyish Robert Morse playing the
pretentious-but-lovable boyish coproducer.

GYPSY

MAY 21, 1959   BROADWAY THEATRE   702 PERFORMANCES

Lyrics by Stephen Sondheim
Book by Arthur Laurents
(Based on the memoirs by Gypsy Rose Lee)
Directed and choreographed by Jerome Robbins
Produced by David Merrick and Leland Hayward
With Ethel Merman, Jack Klugman, Sandra Church, and Maria Karnilova

Published songs:
All I Need Is The Girl
Everything's Coming Up Roses—revised version of *Betwixt and Between*
        (cut, unpublished) from HIGH BUTTON SHOES [October 9, 1947]
Let Me Entertain You
Little Lamb
Mama's Talkin' Soft—cut
Mr. Goldstone
Small World
Some People
Together Wherever We Go
You'll Never Get Away From Me—revised version of *I'm In Pursuit Of
        Happiness* from 1956 TV musical "Ruggles of Red Gap"

Additional songs published in vocal score:
Baby June And Her Newsboys
Broadway
Extra! Extra!
Farm Sequence (Caroline)
If Momma Was Married
Rose's Turn
You Gotta Get A Gimmick

Arthur Laurents, librettist of WEST SIDE STORY [Bernstein: September 26,
1957], came up with the key to musicalizing Gypsy Rose Lee's autobiography:
concentrating on the character of the mother. David Merrick brought in
Laurents' WEST SIDE STORY collaborators Robbins and Sondheim, the latter
to make his composing debut. Then Ethel Merman became Rose-and she
wanted Jule Styne, who knew how to write for her voice. (Porter and Berlin
were both approached first.) Robbins, of course, had worked very successfully

with Styne; and Merrick—before Laurents and Merman—had initially gone to Styne, Comden, and Green. What Sondheim's score would have been like is unknown; surely interesting, but one has to be glad things developed as they did. Styne's talent and background were particularly suited to the material, and the combined Styne/Sondheim GYPSY ranks high among the theatre's very best, but THE SOUND OF MUSIC [Rodgers: November 16, 1959] won the awards and ran twice as long. On the other hand, GYPSY can boast two smashingly successful revivals—starring Angela Lansbury (1974) and Tyne Daly (1989)—while THE SOUND OF MUSIC, a staple of the stock & amateur circuit, has not been heard on Broadway since.

DO RE MI

DECEMBER 26, 1960   ST. JAMES THEATRE   400 PERFORMANCES

Lyrics by Betty Comden and Adolph Green
Book and direction by Garson Kanin
(Based on the novel by Kanin)
Choreographed by Marc Breaux and Dee Dee Wood
Produced by David Merrick
With Phil Silvers, Nancy Walker, Nancy Dussault, John Reardon, and David Burns

Published songs:
All You Need Is A Quarter
Asking For You
Cry Like The Wind
Fireworks
Make Someone Happy
What's New At The Zoo?

Additional songs published in vocal score:
Adventure
All Of My Life
Ambition
He's A V.I.P.
I Know About Love
It's Legitimate
The Late, Late Show
Take A Job
Venezuela [instrumental with partial lyric]
Waiting
Who Is Mr. Big?

Additional songs recorded:
Don't Be Ashamed Of A Teardrop—cut; music only recorded
Life's Not Simple—cut

Styne reunited with Comden and Green for this comical musical comedy, which—despite clowns Silvers, Walker, and Dussault, good reviews, and the enormously popular *Make Someone Happy*—had a disappointing run. Expressionistic designer Boris Aronson began his drive to change the way Broadway musicals looked. For this pop musical satire, he constructed a spectacular show curtain of stage-to-ceiling jukeboxes, wired for neon and sound.

SUBWAYS ARE FOR SLEEPING

DECEMBER 27, 1961   ST. JAMES THEATRE   205 PERFORMANCES

Book and lyrics by Betty Comden and Adolph Green
(Based on stories by Edmund G. Love)
Directed and choreographed by Michael Kidd
Produced by David Merrick
With Sydney Chaplin, Carol Lawrence, Orson Bean, and Phyllis Newman

Published songs:
Be A Santa
Comes Once In A Lifetime
How Can You Describe A Face?
I'm Just Taking My Time
Who Knows What Might Have Been?

Additional songs recorded:
Getting Married—cut
Girls Like Me
I Just Can't Wait
I Said It And I'm Glad
I Was A Shoo-In
Let's Talk—cut
Now I Have Someone—cut
Ride Through The Night
Strange Duet—see DARLING OF THE DAY [January 27, 1968]
Subway Directions
Subways Are For Sleeping
Swing Your Projects
What Is This Feeling In The Air?

David Merrick pulled the publicity coup of his distinguished publicity career. Using gentlemen with names legitimately identical to the most powerful drama critics of the day, he composed the full-page quote ad of everyone's dreams: "No doubt about it—SUBWAYS ARE FOR SLEEPING is the best musical of the century! . . . John Chapman." In order to pull this off, Merrick first had to wait for Brooks Atkinson to retire—there was only one Brooks Atkinson in the phone book. Then he had to wait for a big-budget show with dismal reviews. "One of the few great musicals of the last thirty years" said Merrick's Howard Taubman. Taubman of the *Times* called SUBWAYS "dull and vapid." Photographs accompanying the seven-out-of-seven raves indicate that in a liberal (for 1961) move, Merrick chose to include a Mr. Richard Watts from Harlem.

ARTURO UI

NOVEMBER 11, 1963   LUNT-FONTANNE THEATRE   8 PERFORMANCES

Play by Bertolt Brecht
Incidental music by Jule Styne
Directed by Tony Richardson
Produced by David Merrick
With Christopher Plummer, Lionel Stander, Murvyn Vye, and Madeleine Sherwood

Published songs:
None

Styne supplied a brilliant barrelhouse jazz accompaniment to this view of Hitler-as-Capone in prohibition Chicago. (In 1927, Capone asked if he could lead Styne's orchestra in 'Rhapsody in Blue'; Styne said okay.)

FUNNY GIRL

MARCH 26, 1964   WINTER GARDEN THEATRE   1,348 PERFORMANCES

Lyrics by Bob Merrill
Book by Isobel Lennart
(Based on a story by Lennart)
Choreographed by Carol Haney
Directed by Garson Kanin
Production supervised by Jerome Robbins
Produced by Ray Stark
With Barbra Streisand, Sydney Chaplin, Kay Medford, and Jean Stapleton

Published songs:
Don't Rain On My Parade
Funny Girl—cut; published in standard edition

His Love Makes Me Beautiful—initial individual publication upon use in
    1968 version
I'm The Greatest Star—initial individual publication upon use in movie
    version
The Music That Makes Me Dance
People
Who Are You Now?
You Are Woman, I Am Man
You're A Funny Girl—written for movie version

Additional songs published in vocal score:
Cornet Man
Downtown Rag [instrumental]
Find Yourself A Man
Henry Street
I Want To Be Seen With You Tonight
If A Girl Isn't Pretty
Private Schwartz
Rat-Tat-Tat-Tat
Sadie, Sadie
Who Taught Her Everything

Additional song subsequently published in vocal selection:
Individual Thing—cut; see **PRETTYBELLE** [February 1, 1971]

Additional songs recorded:
Absent Minded Me—cut
The Baltimore Sun—cut
Do Puppies Go To Heaven?—cut
He's Got Larceny In His Heart—cut
I Did It On Roller Skates—cut
It's Home—cut
My Daughter Fanny, The Star—cut
Racing Form Lullaby—cut
Roller Skate Rag—cut; initial recording upon use in movie version
A Temporary Arrangement—cut

What started as Mary Martin's follow-up to THE SOUND OF MUSIC [Rodgers:
November 16, 1959] traveled a particularly tortuous path before finally arriving as a Broadway hit. Fanny Brice's son-in-law Ray Stark initially brought the
project to David Merrick, his coproducer on the 1958 *The World of Suzie
Wong*. Merrick assembled his GYPSY [May 21, 1959] team of Styne, Sondheim, and Robbins. Mary Martin wasn't exactly particularly quite right for
Fanny Brice; she moved on to Laurette Taylor (JENNIE [Schwartz: October
17, 1963]) instead. By the time Anne Bancroft came in, lyricist Sondheim was

On The Way To The Forum [Sondheim: May 8, 1962]. Bob Merrill (from Merrick's Carnival! [Merrill: April 13, 1964]) became Styne's collaborator. Barbra Streisand (from Merrick's I Can Get It For You Wholesale [Rome: March 22, 1962]) became Fanny Brice, and all was ready. Then Robbins quit. Bob Fosse came in, Bob Fosse went out. Garson Kanin (from Merrick's Do Re Mi [December 26, 1960]) came in and Funny Girl breezed into rehearsal. *Without* David Merrick, who grew tired of it all and withdrew from the show on December 13, 1963, shortly before the beginning of rehearsals. (Besides, he had Hello, Dolly! [Herman, Strouse, Merrill: January 16, 1964] to keep him busy.) Tryout troubles unexpectedly (?) arose, and Stark replaced Kanin with—Jerome Robbins, who managed to pull the show into presentable if unexceptional shape. Styne's score was adequate, though less adventuresome than usual—influenced, no doubt, by the craftsmanlike Merrill. *Don't Rain On My Parade, I'm The Greatest Star,* and *The Music That Makes Me Dance* were particularly effective, both musically and dramatically. And Streisand sang *People,* too.

WONDERWORLD

May 7, 1964   World's Fair Amphitheatre-in-the-Lake   250 performances

Lyrics by Stanley Styne
Choreographed by Michael Kidd
Conceived and directed by Leon Leonidoff
With Chita Rivera and Gretchen Wyler

Published song:
Wonderworld

Additional song recorded:
Welcome

This twenty-eight-show-a-week spectacle—at the old Billy Rose Aquacade arena—closed owing two-and-a-half million dollars. Styne's lyricist was his older son.

FADE OUT—FADE IN

May 26, 1964   Mark Hellinger Theatre   199 performances

Book and lyrics by Betty Comden and Adolph Green
Choreographed by Ernest Flatt
Directed by George Abbott
Produced by Lester Osterman and Styne
With Carol Burnett, Jack Cassidy, Lou Jacobi, and Tiger Haynes

Published songs:
Fade Out—Fade In
I'm With You
You Mustn't Feel Discouraged

Additional songs published in vocal selection:
Call Me Savage—see HALLELUJAH, BABY! [APRIL 26, 1967]
Go Home Train
It's Good To Be Back Home
The Usher From The Mezzanine

Additional songs recorded:
Close Harmony
The Dangerous Age
Fear
The Fiddler And The Fighter
L.Z. In Quest Of His Youth [ballet]
Lila Tremaine
My Fortune Is My Face
My Heart Is Like A Violin
Oh Those Thirties

ABC-Paramount saw fit to invest three million musical-producing dollars with producers Lester Osterman and Jule Styne (with a track record of MR. WONDERFUL [Bock: March 22, 1956], SAY, DARLING [April 3, 1958] and FIRST IMPRESSIONS [March 19, 1959]). The money went to produce HIGH SPIRITS [Martin: April 7, 1964], FADE OUT—FADE IN, and Sammy Fain's SOMETHING MORE [November 5, 1964]—the last directed by Styne himself. After which ABC-Paramount (and Jule Styne) reassessed their Broadway producing careers. FADE OUT—FADE IN featured a live seal and did very well until Carol Burnett became indisposed. At its best, Burnett played Shirley Temple—Styne's vexation in Hollywood vocal coaching days—to Tiger Haynes' Bill Robinson in *You Mustn't Feel Discouraged.*

HALLELUJAH, BABY!

APRIL 26, 1967   MARTIN BECK THEATRE   293 PERFORMANCES

Lyrics by Betty Comden and Adolph Green
Book by Arthur Laurents
Choreographed by Kevin Carlisle
Directed by Burt Shevelove
Produced by Albert W. Selden and Hal James, Jane C. Nusbaum, and Harry Rigby
With Leslie Uggams, Robert Hooks, Allen Case, and Lillian Hayman

Published songs:
Being Good Isn't Good Enough
Hallelujah, Baby!
My Own Morning
Not Mine—see **Bar Mitzvah Boy** [October 31, 1978]
Now's The Time
Talking To Yourself
When The Weather's Better—cut

Additional song published in vocal selection:
I Wanted To Change Him

Additional songs recorded:
Another Day
Big Talk—cut
Feet Do Yo' Stuff
I Don't Know Where She Got It
The Slice
Smile, Smile
Ugly, Ugly Gal—cut; see **One Night Stand** [October 20, 1980]
Watch My Dust
Witches' Brew—revised version of *Call Me Savage* from **Fade**
    Out—Fade In [May 26, 1964]

Styne, composer of **Bells Are Ringing** [November 29, 1956] and **Gypsy** [May 21, 1959], finally received a Tony Award for this unsuccessful musical— which had long since closed. (**Hallelujah, Baby!** opened after the eligibility cut-off date for 1967; it won the following season.) An unclear (or maybe just poorly executed) concept and a jumbled book made for confusion; racial tensions between cast and staff didn't help, and a better-than-average score wasn't enough. Lost in the shuffle: the rhythmic *When The Weather's Better.* Leslie Uggams—in a role intended for Lena Horne—gave a very good performance, and Lillian Hayman was an unforgettable treasure.

DARLING OF THE DAY

January 27, 1968   George Abbott Theatre   32 performances

Lyrics by E. Y. Harburg
Book by Nunnally Johnson (unbilled)
(Based on *The Great Adventure* [play] by Arnold Bennett)
Choreographed by Lee Becker Theodore
Directed by Noel Willman
Produced by The Theatre Guild and Joel Schenker
With Vincent Price, Patricia Routledge, Brenda Forbes, and Teddy Green

Published songs:
I've Got A Rainbow Working For Me
It's Enough To Make A Lady Fall In Love
Let's See What Happens
Not On Your Nellie
Under The Sunset Tree

Additional songs recorded:
A Blushing Bride—cut
Butler In The Abbey
A Gentleman's Gentleman
He's A Genius
Money, Money, Money
Panache
Putney On The Thames—cut; revised version of *Strange Duet* from
    SUBWAYS ARE FOR SLEEPING [December 27, 1961]
That Something Extra Special
That Stranger in Your Arms—cut
To Get Out Of This World Alive
What Makes A Marriage Merry?

It is always a bad sign when a show reaches Broadway with no book writer credited; the disastrously produced DARLING OF THE DAY almost opened without a director, either. Styne wrote a particularly good score, with Harburg's lyrics second only to his FINIAN'S RAINBOW [Lane: March 13, 1947]. Standing out were *That Something Extra Special, Let's See What Happens,* and the schottische *It's Enough To Make A Lady Fall In Love* (with Harburg's "stork of Damocles"). The lack of interest engendered by Vincent Price (playing the title role) ruined the little chance DARLING OF THE DAY might have had under its ill-fated star. Patricia Routledge was superhuman in her efforts, and became the only foreign, unknown-to-Broadway nonstar ever to make her musical debut in a short-run flop and win the Best Actress Tony Award. Arnold Bennett's original novel version of the material was entitled "Buried Alive."

LOOK TO THE LILIES

MARCH 29, 1970   LUNT-FONTANNE THEATRE   25 PERFORMANCES

Lyrics by Sammy Cahn
Book by Leonard Spigelgass
(Based on *Lilies of the Field* [novel] by William Barrett)
Directed by Joshua Logan

Produced by Edgar Lansbury, Max Brown, Richard Lewine, and Ralph Nelson
With Shirley Booth, Al Freeman, Jr., Taina Elg, and Carmen Alvarez

Songs published in vocal selection:
Follow The Lamb!
I! Yes, Me! That's Who!
I'd Sure Like To Give It A Shot
Look To The Lilies
One Little Brick At A Time
Some Kind Of Man
There Comes A Time

Additional song recorded:
First Class Number One Bum
Kick The Door—cut

Sammy Cahn—with two non-Styne Broadway flops since HIGH BUTTON SHOES [October 9, 1947]—reunited with his former partner for this horror. Even the miscast Shirley Booth (in her final musical) was uninteresting.

PRETTYBELLE

[FEBRUARY 1, 1971]   SHUBERT THEATRE < BOSTON, MASSACHUSETTS > ;
    CLOSED DURING PRE-BROADWAY TRYOUT

Book and lyrics by Bob Merrill
(Based on the novel by Jean Arnold)
Directed and choreographed by Gower Champion
Produced by Alexander H. Cohen
With Angela Lansbury, Charlotte Rae, and Joe Morton

Songs issued in professional copies:
How Could I Know?
To A Small Degree

Additional songs published in vocal selections:
I Met A Man
I'm In A Tree
Individual Thing—initial publication of song cut from FUNNY GIRL
    [March 26, 1964]
Prettybelle
When I'm Drunk I'm Beautiful

Additional songs recorded:
Back From The Great Beyond
God's Garden
I Never Did Imagine
In The Japanese Gardens
Manic Depressives
The No-Tell Motel
You Ain't Hurtin' Your Ole Lady None
You Never Looked Better

Alexander H. Cohen followed his Broadway failure **DEAR WORLD** [Herman: February 6, 1969] with **PRETTYBELLE,** which fared even worse. A valiant Angela Lansbury suffered through both. Styne's score was only slightly better than **LOOK TO THE LILIES** [March 29, 1970].

SUGAR

APRIL 9, 1972   MAJESTIC THEATRE   505 PERFORMANCES

Lyrics by Bob Merrill
Book by Peter Stone
(Based on *Some Like It Hot* [movie] by Billy Wilder and I.A.L. Diamond)
Directed and choreographed by Gower Champion
Produced by David Merrick
With Robert Morse, Tony Roberts, Cyril Ritchard, and Elaine Joyce

Published song:
(Doing It For) Sugar

Additional songs recorded:
All You Gotta Do Is Tell Me—cut
Beautiful Through And Through
The Beauty That Drives Men Mad
Hey, Why Not!
It's Always Love
Nice Ways—cut
November Song (Even Dirty Old Men Need Love)
Penniless Bums
The People In Your Life—cut; revised from *Look At You, Look At Me*
    (music by Styne, lyric by Frank Loesser) from 1941 movie "Sis
    Hopkins"
Sun On My Face—different song than *Sun On Your Face* (cut)
Sun On Your Face—cut; different song than *Sun On My Face*
We Could Be Close

What Do You Give To A Man Who's Had Everything?
When You Meet A Man In Chicago

Somehow or other Merrick managed to get a successful run out of this less-than-satisfying show. Not only was a starring role deleted during the tryout—singer Johnny Desmond as the George Raft gangster—they also threw out Jo Mielziner and his entire set! Styne's Twenties Chicago music was actually pretty good, at least in the first act. The authors were locked out of rehearsals by Champion, and the cutting of the Raft character left the second act void of material. Robert Morse managed to succeed against the memory of the brilliant Jack Lemmon original. Morse's performance of *We Could Be Close* alone was well worth the price of admission (**Sugar** opened with a record-high $15 top).

LORELEI

Or "Gentlemen Still Prefer Blondes"

<Also see GENTLEMEN PREFER BLONDES>

December 8, 1949])   January 27, 1974   Palace Theatre   320
    PERFORMANCES

New lyrics by Betty Comden and Adolph Green
New book material by Kenny Solms and Gail Parent
(Based on *Gentlemen Prefer Blondes* [musical])
Choreographed by Ernest Flatt
Directed by Robert Moore
Produced by Lee Guber and Shelly Gross
With Carol Channing, Dody Goodman, Tamara Long, and Peter Palmer

New published songs:
I Won't Let You Get Away
Lorelei [1st]—cut
Men!

Additional songs recorded:
Looking Back
Lorelei [2nd]
Paris, Paris (lyric by Comden, Green, and Robin)—cut; revised version of
    Sunshine from **Gentlemen Prefer Blondes**

With the lack of suitable properties for Carol Channing, an attempt was made to give Lorelei Lee a facelift. Outfitted with new material and a streamlined book, the charming original was destroyed. The same producers did a similar job on **Bring Back Birdie** [Strouse: March 5, 1981] with similarly dismal results. Prior to Broadway LORELEI played a year on the road, initially directed and choreographed by Joe Layton.

HELLZAPOPPIN'!

[NOVEMBER 22, 1976]   MECHANIC THEATRE < BALTIMORE,
     MARYLAND > ; CLOSED DURING PRE-BROADWAY TRYOUT

Music also by Hank Beebe and Cy **Coleman**
Lyrics by Carolyn Leigh and Bill Heyer
Book by Abe Burrows and others
(Based on a format by Olsen and Johnson)
Choreographed by Donald Saddler
Directed by Jerry Adler
Produced by Alexander H. Cohen in association with Maggie and Jerome Minskoff
With Jerry Lewis, Lynn Redgrave, Joey Faye, and Brandon Maggart

Recorded Styne/Leigh songs:
Hellzapoppin'
Only One To A Customer

Cohen's second attempt to honor the 1,404-performance Olsen and Johnson original [September 22, 1938] died aborning. An earlier version, which premiered (and died) at Expo '67 in Montreal, starred Soupy Sales.

BAR MITZVAH BOY

OCTOBER 31, 1978   HER MAJESTY'S THEATRE < LONDON >   77
     PERFORMANCES

Lyrics by Don Black
Book by Jack Rosenthal
(Based on a TV play by Rosenthal)
Choreographed by Peter Gennaro
Directed by Martin Charnin
Produced by Peter Witt
With Joyce Blair, Harry Towb, Vivienne Martin, and Barry Angel

Songs recorded:
The Bar Mitzvah Of Eliot Green
The Harolds Of This World—revised version of *Not Mine* from
     HALLELUJAH, BABY! [April 26, 1967]
I've Just Begun
If Only A Little Bit Sticks

Rita's Request
Simchas
The Sun Shines Out Of Your Eyes
This This Time Tomorrow
Thou Shalt Not
We've Done Alright
Where Is The Music Coming From?
Why
You Wouldn't Be You

DARLING OF THE DAY [January 27, 1968] and BAR MITZVAH BOY are Styne's two best scores since FUNNY GIRL [March 26, 1964]. BAR MITZVAH BOY was a quick failure, with blame going to everyone involved except the songwriters. The score remains unpublished to date, available only on the presently unavailable original cast album. Styne wrote no less than five tender and lovely songs: *Where Is The Music Coming From, The Harolds Of This World, The Sun Shines Out of Your Eyes, You Wouldn't Be You,* and *We've Done Alright.* And then there were good rhythm songs, comedy songs, etc. An American version (adapted by former critic Martin Gottfried) was attempted off-off-Broadway [May 9, 1987], to no avail.

ONE NIGHT STAND

[OCTOBER 20, 1980]   NEDERLANDER THEATRE; CLOSED DURING PREVIEWS

Book and lyrics by Herb Gardner
Choreographed by Peter Gennaro
Directed by John Dexter
Produced by Joseph Kipness, Lester Osterman, Joan Cullman, James M. Nederlander, and Alfred Taubman
With Jack Weston, Charles Kimbrough, and Catherine Cox

Songs recorded:
Don't Kick My Dreams Around
For You
Go Out Big
Here Comes Never
I'm Writing A Love Song For You
Let Me Hear You Love Me
A Little Travellin' Music Please
Long Way From Home
Somebody Stole My Kazoo
Someday Soon—revised version of *Ugly, Ugly Gal* (cut) from
        HALLELUJAH, BABY! [April 26, 1967]

There Was A Time
Too Old To Be So Young

Another haphazardly assembled enterprise. ONE NIGHT STAND was misconceived, and there were no musical theatre professionals involved (except the seventy-five-year-old Styne) capable of even beginning to deal with realities. The composer provided one pretty good song, *Too Old To Be So Young.*

PIECES OF EIGHT

[NOVEMBER 27, 1985]   CITADEL THEATRE < EDMONTON, CANADA > ;
REGIONAL TRYOUT

Lyrics by Susan Birkenhead
Book by Michael Stewart and Mark Bramble
(Based on *Treasure Island* [novel] by Robert Louis Stevenson]
Directed and choreographed by Joe Layton
Produced by Citadel Theatre and the Edmonton *Journal*
With George Hearn, George Lee Andrews, Graeme Campbell, and
Jonathan Ross

Published songs:
None

An old-fashioned "Treasure Island," without that extra-added dimension which made OLIVER! [PART 5: **January 6, 1963**] or Styne's own PETER PAN [**October 20, 1954**] soar. PIECES OF EIGHT—which, as TREASURE ISLAND, had previously been announced for Broadway by both Harry Rigby and David Merrick—disappeared after its six-week Canadian tryout.

Arriving on Broadway in 1947, forty-two-year-old Jule Styne gave up a successful Hollywood career and committed his future to the theatre. (Richard Rodgers, only three years older than Styne, was on Broadway back in 1919.) Styne compensated for his late start by becoming the theatre's most prolific composer of the next twenty-five years. With BELLS ARE RINGING [**November 29, 1956**] he entered the first rank of musical comedy. Then came the classic GYPSY [**May 21, 1959**], which proved him a top musical dramatist as well. The heavy demands of a continuous production schedule—and the occasional selection of less-than-inspired material—resulted in a number of misses. But even the lesser scores have been marked by optimism, warmth, and Styne's exciting musical professionalism. Bright and alert in his mid-80s, Styne continues writing and may give us another score yet.

Frank Loesser

BORN: June 29, 1910   New York, New York
DIED: July 28, 1969   New York, New York

Frank Loesser was the son of a distinguished German-born piano teacher. While his brother Arthur became a renowned concert pianist, Frank was the musical black sheep of the family. Refusing to study the classics, he took up the harmonica and later taught himself piano, playing pop songs on the sly. Dropping out of college early in the Depression, Loesser supported himself with whatever jobs he could get (including a stint as a process server). Always intrigued by word-play, Loesser's first published lyric was the 1931 pop song *In Love With The Memory Of You* (music by William Schuman, who became a serious composer and president of Juilliard). By the mid-Thirties Loesser was singing and playing in nightclubs, as well as writing lyrics for special material.

[NOTE: All music and lyrics by Frank Loesser unless indicated]

THE ILLUSTRATORS' SHOW

JANUARY 22, 1936   48TH STREET THEATRE   5 PERFORMANCES

Music and lyrics mostly by others (see **Loewe**)
Sketches by Max Liebman, Otto Soglow, and others
Directed by Allen Delano
Produced by Tom Weatherly

Published song:
Bang The Bell Rang (music by Irving Actman, lyric by Loesser)

This quick flop had very little to distinguish it—except early contributions of Loesser and Loewe. A Hollywood executive liked the few Loesser/Actman songs enough to sign the pair to a contract. Once in Hollywood, Loesser quickly moved on to some of the top movie composers of the time, successfully collaborating with Hoagy Carmichael, Jule Styne, Burton Lane, and Arthur Schwartz. Then Loesser was drafted. Without a composer on hand, the lyricist started writing his own tunes. The first were quick wartime hits *Praise The Lord And Pass The Ammunition* (1942) and *What Did You Do In The Infantry* (1943).

SKIRTS

An All American Musical Adventure

JANUARY 25, 1944   CAMBRIDGE THEATRE < LONDON >

Music and lyrics mostly by PFC Frank Loesser and PFC Harold **Rome**
Choreography by Wendy Toye
Directed by Lt. Arthur G. Brest
Produced by U.S. 8th Air Force

Published song:
Skirts

Loesser (along with other Broadway and Hollywood professionals) had been assigned to Special Services—the morale-building entertainment branch of the Army—to write material for soldier shows. "Skirts" was borrowed by the Air Force.

ABOUT FACE!

An Army "Blueprint Special"

MAY 26, 1944   CAMP SHANKS, NEW YORK

Music and lyrics by PFC Frank Loesser, PFC Jerry Livingston, and others
Sketches by PFC Arnold Auerbach and others
Directed by Robert H. Gordon
With Jules Munshin and Vincente Gomez

Published songs:
First Class Private Mary Brown—also used in **PFC MARY BROWN** [Circa
     November 1944]
One Little WAC (music by Eddie Dunstedter)
Why Do They Call A Private A Private? (When His Life's A Public
     Event) (lyric by T/Sgt. Peter Lind Hayes)

Additional songs published in script:
Dogface
Gee But It's Great To Be In The Army!
PX Parade (probably by Loesser)
When He Comes Home—also used in (and separately published from)
     OK, U.S.A.! [Circa June 1945]

Special Services decided to put out a series of do-it-yourself soldier shows, complete with script, songs, designs, publicity material, etc. Loesser headed the songwriting branch, and wrote a considerable amount of material over the next two years, his earliest theatre work. *First Class Private Mary Brown* became another wartime pop hit for Loesser.

HI, YANK!

An Army "Blueprint Special"

AUGUST 7, 1944   THEATRE NO. 5, FORT DIX < NEW JERSEY >

Music and lyrics by PFC Frank Loesser, Lt. Alex North, and others
Skits by PFC Arnold Auerbach and others
Choreographed by PFC José Limon
Directed by Cpl. David E. Fitzgibbon
Produced by Capt. Hy Gardner
With David Brooks and Joshua Shelley

Songs published in script:
Classification Blues
Little Red Rooftops
The Most Important Job
My Gal and I (lyric by Lt. Jack Hill)
Saga Of A Sad Sack (lyric by PFC Hy Zaret)
Yank, Yank, Yank

PFC MARY BROWN

A WAC Musical Revue

[CIRCA NOVEMBER 1944]

Music and lyrics mostly by PFC Frank Loesser
Sketches by PFC Arnold Auerbach and others

Published songs:
First Class Private Mary Brown—originally used in ABOUT FACE! [MAY 26, 1944]
The WAC Hymn

Additional songs published in script:
Come On Honey
Lonely M.P.
Lost In A Cloud Of Blue
New Style Bonnet
Something New
Twenty Five Words Or Less

This WAC show was inspired by Loesser's *Mary Brown* hit. Exact authorship of the songs is unknown, but the score was credited as being "mostly by Loesser."

OK, U.S.A.!

An Army "Blueprint Special"

[CIRCA JUNE 1945]

Published song:
When He Comes Home—originally used in ABOUT FACE! [May 26, 1944]

Additional songs published in script:
I Was Down Texas Way
My Chicago
The Tall Pines
Tonight In San Francisco
A Trip Round The U.S.A.
You're OK, U.S.A.!

Again, exact authorship of the songs in the script is unavailable, but probably by Loesser. After the war, Loesser resumed his movie work, writing his own music. When Hollywood executives Cy Feuer and Ernest Martin decided to become Broadway producers, they invited Loesser along as composer/lyricist. He returned to New York, picking up an Oscar for the 1948 *Baby, It's Cold Outside* from "Neptune's Daughter."

WHERE'S CHARLEY?

OCTOBER 11, 1948   ST. JAMES THEATRE   792 PERFORMANCES

Book and direction by George Abbott
(Based on *Charley's Aunt* [play] by Brandon Thomas)
Choreographed by George Balanchine
Produced by Cy Feuer and Ernest Martin in association with Gwen Rickard (Bolger)
With Ray Bolger, Allyn McLerie, and Doretta Morrow

Published songs:
At The Red Rose Cotillion—advertised but not published (except in vocal score)
Lovelier Than Ever
Make A Miracle
My Darling, My Darling
The New Ashmolean Marching Society And Students' Conservatory Band

Once In Love With Amy
Pernambuco
The Train That Brought You To Town—cut; advertised but not published
Where's Charley?
The Years Before Us—issued in choral arrangement

Additional songs published in vocal score:
Better Get Out Of Here
The Gossips
Serenade With Asides
The Woman In His Room

The novice producers had the foresight to hire veteran Abbott to direct and adapt the 1892 farce. Abbott frequently worked with talented newcomers, shepherding through their first important shows Hugh Martin, Leonard Bernstein, Jule Styne, Richard Adler, Jerry Bock, Bob Merrill, Stephen Sondheim, and John Kander. Loesser and Abbott came up with an energetic showcase for Ray Bolger and a big success. The score was more than adequate, with two high-quality, out-of-the-ordinary songs (*Once In Love With Amy* and *Make A Miracle*). And Broadway novice Loesser was about to unquestionably prove that he was more than just a pop-tune writer from Hollywood.

GUYS AND DOLLS

A Musical Fable Of Broadway

NOVEMBER 24, 1950   46TH STREET THEATRE   1,200 PERFORMANCES

Book by Jo Swerling and Abe Burrows
(Based on stories and characters by Damon Runyon)
Choreographed by Michael Kidd
Directed by George S. Kaufman
Produced by Feuer and Martin
With Sam Levene, Isabel Bigley, Robert Alda, and Vivian Blaine

Published songs:
Adelaide—written for 1955 movie version
Adelaide's Lament
A Bushel And A Peck
Follow The Fold
Fugue For Tinhorns
Guys and Dolls
Guys And Dolls Preamble (Roxy)
I'll Know
I've Never Been In Love Before

If I Were A Bell
It Feels Like Forever—cut; advertised but not published
Luck Be A Lady
Marry The Man Today
More I Cannot Wish You
My Time Of Day
The Oldest Established
Pet Me, Poppa—written for movie version
Shango—cut; advertised but not published
Sit Down You're Rockin' The Boat
Sue Me—nonshow version
Sue Me Argument [duet]—show version
Take Back Your Mink
Three Cornered Tune—nonshow version of *Fugue For Tinhorns*
Traveling Light—cut; advertised but not published; recorded
A Woman In Love—written for movie version

One of the finest modern-day musical comedies. Loesser displayed his ability to lovingly (and with dignity) capture his characters and their vernacular. His "Hot-Box Doll" Adelaide is as sympathetic and real as Nellie Forbush; her chronic dilemma, while more humorous than serious to us, is every bit as important to her. Loesser turned out a hit-filled score (and quickly went into the music publishing business); the happy fact that these hits were endemic to the characters not only put Loesser in the top rank of theatre composers, but made GUYS AND DOLLS the classic it is. An important force on the show was director Kaufman, who had won the first musical Pulitzer for OF THEE I SING [Gershwin: December 26, 1931]. Radio writer Abe Burrows was brought in to replace librettist Jo Swerling and provided a fine book in Runyonese; Burrows took Kaufman lessons, and quickly became a musical comedy director himself. It is theorized that the Pulitzer committee was to have selected GUYS AND DOLLS; but Burrows was brought before the House Un-American Activities Committee and the politically sensitive prize administrators declined to present any award that year. Loesser and Burrows received a Pulitzer for their next collaboration.

THE MOST HAPPY FELLA

MAY 3, 1956   IMPERIAL THEATRE   676 PERFORMANCES

Book by Frank Loesser
(Based on *They Knew What They Wanted* [play] by Sidney Howard)
Choreographed by Dania Krupska
Directed by Joseph Anthony
Produced by Kermit Bloomgarden and Lynn Loesser
With Robert Weede, Jo Sullivan, Art Lund, and Susan Johnson

Published songs:
Big D
Don't Cry
I Like Ev'rybody
Joey, Joey, Joey
The Most Happy Fella
My Heart Is So Full Of You
Somebody, Somewhere
Standing On The Corner
Warm All Over

Additional songs published in vocal score:
Abbondanza
Aren't You Glad?
Benvenuta
Fresno Beauties (Cold and Dead)
Goodbye, Darlin'
Happy To Make Your Acquaintance
Hoedown [instrumental]
How Beautiful The Days
I Don't Like This Dame
I Know How It Is
I Love Him
I Made A Fist
The Letter
Love and Kindness
Mama, Mama
Ooh, My Feet
Please Let Me Tell You That I Love You
Plenty Bambini
Rosabella
Seven Million Crumbs
She's Gonna Come Home With Me
Song Of A Summer Night
Soon You Gonna Leave Me, Joe
Special Delivery! (One Bride)
Sposalizio
Tony's Thoughts
Young People Gotta Dance

Loesser confounded everyone by following the raucous GUYS AND DOLLS [November 24, 1950] with this rich, operatic "musical musical." Writing his own libretto, Loesser came up with this heartwarming piece which, unlike PORGY AND BESS [Gershwin: October 10, 1935], STREET SCENE [Weill: January 9, 1947] and REGINA [Blitzstein: October 31, 1949], was a major commercial success. Included were two hit songs, *Standing On The Corner* and *Big D*. Loesser also came up with a new wife, divorcing coproducer Lynn and marrying Jo "Rosabella" Sullivan. (For notes on additional show tunes possibly ghost-written by Loesser, see THE PAJAMA GAME [Adler: May 13, 1954] and THE MUSIC MAN [Willson: December 19, 1957].)

GREENWILLOW

MARCH 8, 1960   ALVIN THEATRE   95 PERFORMANCES

Book by Lesser Samuels and Loesser
(Based on the novel by B. J. Chute)
Choreographed by Joe Layton
Directed by George Roy Hill
Produced by Robert A. Willey in association with Frank (Loesser) Productions, Inc.
With Anthony Perkins, Cecil Kellaway, Pert Kelton, and Ellen McCown

Published songs:
Faraway Boy
Gideon Briggs, I Love You
Greenwillow Christmas
The Music of Home
Never Will I Marry
Summertime Love
Walking Away Whistling

Additional song published in vocal selection:
Clang Dang The Bell

Additional songs recorded:
Bless This Day—cut
Could've Been A Ring
A Day Borrowed From Heaven
Dorrie's Wish
Greenwillow Walk [instrumental]
He Died Good
The Sermon
What A Blessing (To Know There's A Devil)

Throughout his career Loesser demonstrated a reluctance to repeat himself, following each project with a radical change of pace. GREENWILLOW was a pastoral, folksy, tender musical that played whimsical and dull in performance. Loesser's work, while enchanting, had no life outside the theatre (and very little in it). GREENWILLOW's failure was a major disappointment to Loesser.

HOW TO SUCCEED IN BUSINESS WITHOUT REALLY TRYING

OCTOBER 14, 1961   46TH STREET THEATRE   1,417 PERFORMANCES

Book by Abe Burrows, Jack Weinstock and Willie Gilbert
(Based on the book by Shepherd Mead)
Choreographed by Hugh Lambert
Musical staging by Bob Fosse
Directed by Burrows
Produced by Feuer and Martin in association with Frank (Loesser)
Productions, Inc.
With Robert Morse, Rudy Vallee, Bonnie Scott, Virginia Martin, and
Charles Nelson Reilly

Published songs:
Brotherhood of Man
Grand Old Ivy
Happy To Keep His Dinner Warm
How To Succeed
I Believe In You
Love From A Heart Of Gold
Paris Original

Additional songs published in vocal score:
Been A Long Day
Cinderella, Darling
Coffee Break
The Company Way
Finale—Act One [trio]
Rosemary
A Secretary Is Not A Toy
The Yo-Ho-Ho [instrumental]

This Pulitzer Prize-winning musical cartoon remains one of the funniest evenings in Broadway history. All elements seemed to merge, although not easily: Burrows again provided a replacement libretto and directed, while Bob Fosse was brought in and came up with some very funny numbers. The performers, led by Morse, were superb; and tongue-in-cheek Loesser gave his hero the hypocritical *Brotherhood Of Man* and the narcissistic *I Believe In You*—both taken out of context to become popular hits.

PLEASURES AND PALACES

[MARCH 11, 1965]   FISHER THEATRE < DETROIT, MICHIGAN > ; CLOSED
   DURING PRE-BROADWAY TRYOUT

Book by Sam Spewack and Loesser
(Based on *Once There Was A Russian* [play] by Spewack)
Directed and choreographed by Bob Fosse
Produced by Allen B. Whitehead in association with Frank (Loesser)
Productions, Inc.
With Phyllis Newman, Jack Cassidy, Hy Hazell, and Sammy Smith

Songs issued in professional copies:
Barabanchik
Far, Far, Far Away
In Your Eyes
Oh To Be Home Again
Pleasures And Palaces
Thunder And Lightning
Truly Loved

Spewack had been highly successful with his two previous musicals, **LEAVE IT
To ME** [Porter: November 9, 1938] and **KISS ME, KATE** [Porter: December
30, 1948]; but this comic costume-operetta was a full-scale disaster which
quickly shuttered. The 1961 play version, for that matter, had lasted only one
performance on Broadway. It was Loesser's final complete score. (**SEÑOR
DISCRETION**, an adaptation of a Budd Schulberg story Loesser was preparing
at the time of his death, was mounted in 1985 as a developmental workshop,
but nothing ever developed. One song from it has been recorded, *You Understand Me.*) A heavy chain-smoker, Frank Loesser developed lung cancer and
died July 28, 1969 in New York.

Lyricist Frank Loesser came from Hollywood with no theatrical experience
and only a few years of composing credits. In the next thirteen years he wrote
five Broadway scores, two of them good and the other three exceptional. **GUYS
AND DOLLS** [November 24, 1950], **THE MOST HAPPY FELLA** [May 3, 1956]
and **HOW TO SUCCEED IN BUSINESS WITHOUT REALLY TRYING** [October 14,
1961] all remain among the finest of their genre. Quite significantly, all had
first-rate work from librettists, directors, choreographers, designers, and producers: perfectionist Loesser kept a careful eye on all elements of production. His
innate cleverness and ease with words, combined with a deep respect for his
characters, made him the best comedy lyricist of his time; his music, if not
particularly innovative, was tuneful and always highly skillful. Frank Loesser's
songs remain bright and golden.

Richard Adler

BORN: August 3, 1921   New York, New York

Like Frank Loesser, Richard Adler was the son of a concert pianist (Clarence Adler); like Loesser, young Adler stayed away from the piano. Following wartime Navy service, Adler went into advertising. In the early Fifties he began writing pop songs with Jerry Ross (born March 9, 1926 in the Bronx), including the 1953 hit *Rags To Riches*. Loesser had set up as a music publisher following the success of **GUYS AND DOLLS** [**Loesser: November 24, 1950**], and he began looking for writers to supplement his own output. Adler and Ross were put under contract.

JOHN MURRAY ANDERSON'S ALMANAC

DECEMBER 10, 1953   IMPERIAL THEATRE   229 PERFORMANCES

Music and lyrics also by others (see **Coleman**)
Adler music and lyrics by Adler and Jerry Ross
Sketches by Jean Kerr, William K. Wells, and others
Choreographed by Donald Saddler
Directed by John Murray Anderson and Cyril Ritchard
Produced by Michael Grace, Stanley Gilkey, and Harry Rigby
With Hermione Gingold, Billy DeWolfe, Harry Belafonte, and Orson Bean

Published songs:
Acorn In The Meadow
Fini
You're So Much A Part Of Me

Anderson was a veteran revue director with credits including THE GREENWICH VILLAGE FOLLIES [**Porter; September 16, 1924**] and JUMBO [**Rodgers: November 16, 1935**]. Known for his taste and lavish use of color, he had gravitated to spectacles and spent much of the Forties doing pageants and the Ringling Brothers Circus. His career virtually at an end, Leonard Sillman had given him one last opportunity with the highly successful NEW FACES OF 1952 [May 16, 1952]. (Sillman had done the same thing with his first NEW FACES

[March 15, 1934] when he invited the woebegone Charles Dillingham to supervise the production. Sillman was accused in both cases of merely taking advantage of the formerly illustrious names.) Anderson's NEW FACES prompted the far inferior JOHN MURRAY ANDERSON'S ALMANAC; the director died shortly after the opening. But Adler and Ross received their first theatre experience and attracted notice.

THE PAJAMA GAME

MAY 13, 1954   ST. JAMES THEATRE   1,063 PERFORMANCES

Music and lyrics by Richard Adler and Jerry Ross
Book by George Abbott and Richard Bissell
(Based on *7 ½ Cents* [novel] by Bissell)
Choreographed by Bob Fosse
Directed by Abbott and Jerome Robbins
Produced by Frederick Brisson, Robert E. Griffith, and Harold S. Prince
With John Raitt, Janis Paige, Eddie Foy, Jr., and Carol Haney

Published songs:
Hernando's Hideaway
Hey There
I'm Not At All In Love
Small Talk
Steam Heat
There Once Was A Man

Additional songs published in vocal score:
Her Is
I'll Never Be Jealous Again
A New Town Is A Blue Town
Once-A-Year-Day
The Pajama Game (Opening)
Racing With The Clock
Seven-And-A-Half Cents
Sleep-Tite
Think Of The Time I Save

Griffith was a long-time Abbott stage manager, just then on WONDERFUL TOWN [Bernstein: February 25, 1953] with young Prince as his assistant. The newly formed producing team optioned Bissell's best seller and brought it to their mentor. Unconventional musical comedy material (a labor strike in a Midwest garment factory) made it impossible to find established songwriters. An early choice was Loesser, who sent around his fledgling protégés; they were allowed an audition and got the assignment. Robbins, choreographer of most of Abbott's work since ON THE TOWN [Bernstein: December 28, 1944], turned down the dance job but agreed to back up novice Bob Fosse in exchange for codirector billing. Fosse was recommended by wife Joan McCracken, star of Abbott's BILLION DOLLAR BABY [December 21, 1945] and ME AND JULIET [Rodgers: May 28, 1953]. Thus was this Abbott-trained group of future musical theatre directors brought together. Griffith and Prince called in Brisson, husband of Rosalind Russell (of WONDERFUL TOWN) for financing. The gamble on young talents Adler, Ross and Fosse paid off with a staggeringly successful hit with a little help from Loesser and Robbins. A Frank Note on Authorship: it has been rumored that four of the songs were written wholly or partially by Loesser. As publisher of the score and licensor of the rights, Loesser was to make hundreds of thousands of dollars from PAJAMA GAME—reason enough to help out with a few song ideas. I've heard these rumors so often that I suspect they should be repeated here. (Since I was only a year old at the time, I can't vouch for them.) Anyway, the story goes that Adler & Ross went to Frank, unable to come up with the necessary Big Ballad. Frank said something like: "Easy. Just take any old thing"—here he dashed off a bit of Mozart—"and play it in a slow, leisurely 4/4." The main melodic phrase of *Hey There* is, of course, the first two measures of Mozart's *Sonata in C (K. 545)* played in a slow, leisurely four; Mozart didn't think of the dictaphone, though. Also cited in these unverifiable rumors is *A New Town Is A Blue Town*, which does sound to me like a logical Loesserian stepping stone from *My Time Of Day* (from GUYS AND DOLLS [November 24, 1950]) to *Joey, Joey, Joey* (from THE MOST HAPPY FELLA [May 3, 1956]). The other two songs mentioned are the mock-hillbilly ballad *There Once Was A Man*— the sort of novelty Loesser used to play at parties—and the comic duet *Her Is.*

DAMN YANKEES

MAY 5, 1955   46TH STREET THEATRE   1,019 PERFORMANCES

Music and lyrics by Adler and Jerry Ross
Book by George Abbott and Douglas Wallop
(Based on *The Year the Yankees Lost the Pennant* [novel] by Wallop)
Choreographed by Bob Fosse
Directed by Abbott
Produced by Frederick Brisson, Robert E. Griffith, and Harold S. Prince
in association with Albert Taylor
With Gwen Verdon, Stephen Douglass, and Ray Walston

Published songs:
Goodbye, Old Girl
Heart

A Man Doesn't Know
Near To You
Shoeless Joe From Hannibal, Mo.
There's Something About An Empty Chair (music and lyric by
　　Adler)—written for 1958 movie version
Two Lost Souls
Whatever Lola Wants (Lola Gets)
Who's Got The Pain

Additional songs published in vocal score:
The Game
A Little Brains—A Little Talent
Six Months Out Of Every Year
Those Were The Good Old Days

Follow-up to THE PAJAMA GAME [May 13, 1954] was the equally successful—if less well-made—DAMN YANKEES. The same team (less Robbins) took
another popular off-beat novel and turned it into a fast, funny Fifties musical;
even Richard Bissell contributed unbilled book material (jokes). Gwen Verdon, a Jack Cole dancer who stole the show in Michael Kidd's CAN-CAN
[Porter: May 7, 1953] ballets, became Broadway's new musical comedy dancing star in her first of five Fosse shows. Adler and Ross had another two hit
songs, *Heart* and *Whatever Lola Wants.* But on November 11, 1955 Ross died
of leukemia.

THE SIN OF PAT MULDOON

MARCH 13, 1957　　CORT THEATRE　　5 PERFORMANCES

Play by John McLian
Directed by Jack Garfein
Produced by Richard Adler and Roger L. Stevens
With James Barton and Elaine Stritch

Published song:
The Sin Of Pat Muldoon [music by Adler]—nonshow instrumental
　　inspired by play

Adler began his producing career with this quick failure. In the fall of 1957
he wrote and produced two 1957 television musicals, "The Gift of the Magi"
(starring Sally Ann Howes) and "Little Women." Adler married soprano
Howes, Julie Andrews' replacement in MY FAIR LADY [Loewe: March 15,
1956], and began a Broadway project for her.

KWAMINA

<small>OCTOBER 23, 1961   54TH STREET THEATRE   32 PERFORMANCES</small>

Book by Robert Alan Aurthur
Choreographed by Agnes de Mille
Directed by Robert Lewis
Produced by Alfred de Liagre, Jr.
With Sally Ann Howes, Terry Carter, and Brock Peters

Published songs:
Another Time, Another Place
I'm Seeing Rainbows—cut
Nothing More To Look Forward To
Ordinary People
Something Big
What's Wrong With Me?—also revised and used in 1973 revival of THE
    PAJAMA GAME [May 13, 1954] as *Watch Your Heart* (unpublished)

Additional songs recorded:
Cocoa Bean Song
Did You Hear That?
A Man Can Have No Choice
One Wife
Seven Sheep, Four Red Shirts, And A Bottle Of Gin
The Sun Is Beginning To Crow (You Are Home)
Welcome Home
What Happened To Me Tonight?
You're As English As

An unsuccessful yet notable attempt. With all good intentions, the authors
created a contemporary "King And I Goes To Africa." Hammerstein and
Rodgers had carefully handled their racial intolerance theme in Siam and Bali
H'ai; the KWAMINA book was a poor retread, with bits of Eliza Doolittle
thrown in. Adler, though, came up with a fine, serious score. His work—particularly in the African songs—was far more dramatic than the two pop-song
scores with Jerry Ross. Following the failure of KWAMINA, Adler left Broadway. He went back to pop work, wrote the catchy *Let Hertz Put You In The
Driver's Seat* jingle, and produced special events for the Kennedy and Johnson
Administrations.

A MOTHER'S KISSES

[SEPTEMBER 23, 1968]   SHUBERT THEATRE < NEW HAVEN,
    CONNECTICUT > ; CLOSED DURING PRE-BROADWAY TRYOUT

Music and lyrics by Richard Adler
Book by Bruce Jay Friedman
Based on the novel by Friedman)
Choreographed by Onna White
Directed by Gene Saks
Produced by Lester Osterman, Richard Horner, and Lawrence Kasha
With Beatrice Arthur (Saks), Bill Callaway, and Carl Ballantine

Recorded song:
There Goes My Life

This was the year of the Jewish mother. Hoping to mine theatre party business, two similar items were mounted: the Herbert Martin/Michael Leonard
How To Be A Jewish Mother [December 28, 1967], which died after three
weeks on Broadway, and A MOTHER'S KISSES, which played three deadly weeks
on the road. The former was a two-character musical starring the formidable
team of Molly Picon and Godfrey Cambridge. Adler next returned to Broadway in 1973 as producer of the unsuccessful interracial revival of THE PAJAMA
GAME [May 13, 1954].

REX

SEE RODGERS [APRIL 25, 1976]

MUSIC IS

DECEMBER 20, 1976   ST. JAMES THEATRE   8 PERFORMANCES

Music by Richard Adler
Lyrics by Will Holt
Book and direction by George Abbott
(Based on *Twelfth Night* [play] by William Shakespeare)
Choreographed by Patricia Birch
Produced by Adler, Roger Berlind, and Edward R. Downe, Jr.
With Joel Higgins, Catherine Cox, and Christopher Hewett

Published songs:
Should I Speak—issued as professional copy

Adler rejoined Abbott twenty-two years after their initial collaboration with
Abbott attempting to follow his path on THE BOYS FROM SYRACUSE [Novem-

ber 23, 1938]. But *The Comedy of Errors* lent itself to the farcical treatment that *Twelfth Night* didn't; and, after all, Rodgers and Hart and Balanchine weren't along to contribute. Adler wrote a couple of catchy tunes, but they were of little help; the show was dreary, old-fashioned, and of far less interest than the 1968 off-Broadway rock adaptation of the same play, YOUR OWN THING.

Richard Adler came to Broadway with two major musical comedy successes. Then collaborator Jerry Ross died, and Adler's career has never recovered. KWAMINA [October 23, 1961] showed his potential as a composer of serious theatre work, as well as proving he could write alone; but nothing of worth has been attempted since.

Meredith Willson

BORN: May 8, 1902   Mason City, Iowa
DIED: June 15, 1984   Santa Monica, California

As a small-town child, Meredith Willson did not take up the trumpet and lisp (like Winthrop Paroo in THE MUSIC MAN [December 19, 1957]). Rather, he sang barber shop and became proficient on flute and piccolo. His mother gave piano lessons, though. Willson spent the early Twenties in John Philip Sousa's band, then moved over to the New York Philharmonic. After the stock market crash, Willson went to the West Coast and began a profitable career in radio as performer and conductor.

[all music and lyrics by Meredith Willson]

THE LITTLE FOXES

FEBRUARY 15, 1939   NATIONAL THEATRE   410 PERFORMANCES

Play by Lillian Hellman
Incidental music by Meredith Willson
Produced and directed by Herman Shumlin
With Tallulah Bankhead

Published song:
Never Feel Too Weary To Pray—initial publication upon use in 1941 movie version

Willson's career somehow led him to this first of two curious assignments. In 1940, he composed and arranged the score for Charles Chaplin's film "The Great Dictator." His first song hit was the 1941 pop song *You And I. May The Good Lord Bless And Keep You,* theme song for Tallulah Bankhead's 1950 radio show, was an inspirational hit during the Korean War. In 1948 Willson wrote a slight, nostalgic semiautobiography. Frank Loesser, who had just successfully made the Hollywood-to-Broadway trip with WHERE'S CHARLEY? [October 11, 1948], suggested that Willson write a musical comedy based on his youth.

THE MUSIC MAN

DECEMBER 19, 1957   MAJESTIC THEATRE   1,375 PERFORMANCES

Book by Meredith Willson with Franklin Lacey
(Based on *And There I Stood with My Piccolo* [memoir] by Willson)
Choreographed by Onna White
Directed by Morton DaCosta
Produced by Kermit Bloomgarden with Herbert Greene in association
with Frank (Loesser) Productions
With Robert Preston, Barbara Cook, David Burns, and Pert Kelton

Published songs:
Being In Love—written for 1962 movie version
Goodnight, My Someone
It's You
Lida Rose
Seventy-Six Trombones
Till There Was You—revised lyric for 1950 nonshow song *Till I Met You*
Ya Got Trouble—initial individual publication in 1966

Additional songs published in vocal score:
Gary, Indiana
Iowa Stubborn
Marian The Librarian
My White Knight
Piano Lesson (If You Don't Mind My Saying So)
Pick-A-Little, Talk-A-Little
Rock Island (Train Talk)
The Sadder-But-Wiser Girl
Shipoopi
Sincere
The Wells Fargo Wagon
Will I Ever Tell You?

After eight years and dozens of different versions, Willson's nostalgic musical finally made it to Broadway. With no theatre training, the composer used inventiveness and humor to come up with a delightful score. THE MUSIC MAN became the biggest hit of the post-MY FAIR LADY [Loewe: March 15, 1956] Fifties. The heretofore nonsinging Robert Preston was an inspired casting choice; besides, no one else wanted to do it. Barbara Cook graduated from CANDIDE [Bernstein: December 1, 1956] to musical comedy heroine. Frank Loesser, instigator of the project, reaped multiple benefits as associate producer, publisher of the score, and licensor of rights. Another Frank Note on Authorship: Willson's mentor Loesser appears to have ghosted the glorious

My White Knight. (It can be musically traced to two **Most Happy Fella** [**May 3, 1956**] themes, Marie's cut aria *Eyes Like A Stranger* and underscoring developed from the B section of *Somebody, Somewhere.*) When **The Music Man** went to Hollywood, Willson discarded *My White Knight* and replaced it with a pallid ballid—er, ballad—of his own.

THE UNSINKABLE MOLLY BROWN

November 3, 1960   Winter Garden Theatre   532 performances

Book by Richard Morris
Choreographed by Peter Gennaro
Directed by Dore Schary
Produced by The Theatre Guild and Dore Schary
With Tammy Grimes, Harve Presnell, Cameron Prud'homme, and Edith Meiser

Published songs:
Are You Sure?
Bea-u-ti-ful People Of Denver
Belly Up To The Bar Boys
Bon Jour (The Language Song)
Chick-A-Pen
Dolce Far Niente
He's My Friend—written for 1964 movie version
I Ain't Down Yet
I'll Never Say No
I've A'ready Started In
If I Knew
Keep-A-Hoppin'

Additional songs published in vocal score:
Colorado, My Home
Denver Police
Happy Birthday, Mrs. J. J. Brown
Leadville Johnny Brown (Soliloquy)
My Brass Bed

A second homespun hit with much less appeal than **The Music Man** [**December 19, 1957**]. What had been spontaneous inventiveness in 1957 was too calculated here; but Willson's tunefulness and Tammy Grimes' performance carried the show to moderate success.

HERE'S LOVE

OCTOBER 3, 1963   SHUBERT THEATRE   334 PERFORMANCES

Book by Willson
(Based on *Miracle on 34th Street* [story] by Valentine Davies)
Choreographed by Michael Kidd
Directed and produced by Stuart Ostrow
With Janis Paige, Craig Stevens, Laurence Naismith, and Fred Gwynne

Published songs:
Arm In Arm
The Big Clown Balloons
Dear Mister Santa Claus—cut
Expect Things To Happen
Here's Love
Love, Come Take Me Again—cut
My State, My Kansas, My Home
My Wish
Pine Cones And Holly Berries—countermelody to 1951 nonshow song *It's*
    Beginning To Look Like Christmas
That Man Over There
You Don't Know

Additional songs recorded:
The Bugle
Look Little Girl
She Hadda Go Back

A sure-fire family hit based on the Christmas movie classic, **HERE'S LOVE** had no chance: If you can't do something better, don't do it. Director Norman Jewison departed during the tryout; Ostrow, a former Frank Music administrator with no producing *or* directing experience, took over himself. Outside of choreographer Michael Kidd's interesting Thanksgiving Day Parade opening, **HERE'S LOVE** had nothing but a decent-sized advance sale.

1491

A Romantic Speculation

[SEPTEMBER 2, 1969]   DOROTHY CHANDLER PAVILION < LOS ANGELES, CALIFORNIA >; CLOSED DURING PRE-BROADWAY TRYOUT

Book by Willson and Richard Morris
(Based on an idea by Ed Ainsworth)
Choreographed by Danny Daniels

Directed by Morris
Produced by Edwin Lester (Los Angeles Civic Light Opera)
With John Cullum, Chita Rivera, Jean Fenn and Steve Arlen

Published songs:
None

Willson's final attempt for the theatre was this charmless Christopher Columbus operetta, which suffered a severe critical trouncing and quickly expired. Willson went back into retirement and died June 15, 1984 in Santa Monica, California.

Meredith Willson was not really a theatre composer; rather, he was an inventive novelty writer with one great show in him. THE MUSIC MAN [December 19, 1957] will always remain a one-of-a-kind classic. The composer's three other scores, however, are of little interest.

PART 3

INTRODUCTION

The late Fifties and early Sixties saw an influx of new theatre composers. Jerry Bock more or less consistently turned out satisfying, well-
written scores, the only composer since Jule Styne to do so. Bob Merrill,
a nontheatrical pop songwriter, was surprisingly effective. Stephen
Sondheim entered the theatre as an exceptional lyricist, but his composing career didn't meet encouragement until the Seventies. Since
then he has led the field in progressive *and* worthwhile musical theatre;
unfortunately, no one seems capable of following him, except for the
remarkable William Finn (who has thus far eschewed the commercial
musical). Charles Strouse and Cy Coleman were seriously trained musicians who reached Broadway with pop-styled musical comedies. Jerry
Herman was in the Irving Berlin tradition, concentrating on catchy
song hits rather than theatrical technique. The versatile John Kander
began his career with a refreshing originality, while Harvey Schmidt
has shown an individual, experimental style. Mitch Leigh, from the
lower-than-pop field of television jingles, entered the theatre in 1965
with an all-time great musical. In the twenty years since, only one new
composer—Stephen Schwartz—has been active enough to warrant
inclusion here. Current composers with limited theatre output (including Finn) are represented in PART 4: NOTABLE SCORES BY OTHER
COMPOSERS.

Jerry Bock

BORN: November 23, 1928   New Haven, Connecticut

Jerry Bock grew up in Flushing, New York, where his father was a salesman. He began playing the piano at nine, and by high school was writing songs (including an amateur show to help raise money for a Navy hospital ship). In 1945 he went to the University of Wisconsin as a music major.

BIG AS LIFE

University of Wisconsin Golden Jubilee Production

[Circa May 1948]

Music by Jerrold Bock
Lyrics by Jack Royce
Book by Dave Pollard
Produced by The Haresfoot Club

Published songs:
Everybody Loses
Forest In The Sky—advertised but not published
Great Wisconsin
Starway Lullaby
Today—advertised but not published
Why Sing A Love Song?

A struggle between the radio industry and ASCAP over licensing fees caused formation of the competing BMI (Broadcast Music Inc.). For a brief period ASCAP songs were kept from the airwaves, and BMI went searching for substitute material. A scouring of college campuses resulted in the publishing of varsity shows by Bock and Sondheim [PHINNEY'S RAINBOW: Circa 1948], among others. None of this material proved popular, but the college experiment paid off well: while Sondheim quickly moved to ASCAP, Bock remained with BMI and eventually provided them with a strong group of Broadway hits. As for BIG AS LIFE, *Why Sing A Love Song?* is interesting, if ultimately unsatisfying. Following graduation in 1949, Bock teamed with lyricist Larry

Holofcener. They began writing songs and material for television, including the Sid Caesar "Your Show of Shows" series. They also practiced their craft writing revues at Tamiment, a Pennsylvania adult summer resort similar to Green Mansions (where Harold Rome had begun his career).

CATCH A STAR

SEPTEMBER 6, 1955   PLYMOUTH THEATRE   23 PERFORMANCES

Music mostly by Sammy Fain and Philip Charig
Lyrics to Bock songs by Larry Holofcener
Sketches by Danny and Neil Simon
Conceived and supervised by Ray Golden
Produced by Sy Kleinman
With Pat Carroll, David Burns, and Marc Breaux

Published songs:
None

The Simon brothers were television writers who had worked with Bock and Holofcener at Tamiment. They gave Broadway a try, bringing along a few Bock-Holofcener songs. The show closed quickly and the Simons went back to television.

MR. WONDERFUL

MARCH 22, 1956   BROADWAY THEATRE   383 PERFORMANCES

Music and lyrics by Bock, Larry Holofcener, and George Weiss
Book by Joseph Stein and Will Glickman
Directed by Jack Donohue
Produced by Jule Styne and George Gilbert in association with Lester Osterman, Jr.
With Sammy Davis, Jr., Jack Carter, Pat Marshall, and Chita Rivera

Published songs:
Ethel, Baby
Jacques D'Iraque
Mr. Wonderful
There
Too Close For Comfort
Without You I'm Nothing

Additional songs recorded:
Charlie Welch
I'm Available

I've Been Too Busy
Miami
1617 Broadway
Talk To Him

Producer Jule Styne decided to bring Sammy Davis, Jr. to Broadway. Unable to assemble a vehicle, they went ahead without one. . . . Styne was too busy with stage, screen, and television projects to write the score himself. He auditioned songwriters and gambled on Bock and Holofcener (later adding pop composer George Weiss to help). The resulting MR. WONDERFUL was a poor show, but the star presence of Davis and two hit songs—the title number and *Too Close For Comfort*—helped keep it alive.

THE ZIEGFELD FOLLIES OF 1956

[APRIL 16, 1956]   SHUBERT THEATRE < BOSTON, MASSACHUSETTS > ;
        CLOSED DURING PRE-BROADWAY TRYOUT

Music mostly by others
Lyrics to Bock songs by Larry Holofcener
Sketches by Arnold B. Horwitt, Ronny Graham and others
Choreographed by Jack Cole
Directed by Christopher Hewett
Produced by Richard Kollmar and James W. Gardiner by arrangement with Billie Burke Ziegfeld
With Tallulah Bankhead, David Burns, Mae Barnes, Joan Diener, Carol Haney, Lee Becker, and Larry Kert

Published songs:
None

The last successful FOLLIES had been the Shuberts' wartime edition [April 1, 1943]. Since then there have been several unsuccessful attempts, including this disaster which contained the last of the Bock-Holofcener work. At the opening night party for the fabled Harry Warren flop SHANGRI-LA [June 13, 1956], leading man Jack Cassidy introduced Bock to Sheldon Harnick. Harnick had been successfully interpolating music and lyrics for revues, including the classic *Boston Beguine* for Alice Ghostley in NEW FACES OF 1952 [May 16, 1952]. Bock's publisher Tommy Valando went about getting the new team their first assignment.

THE BODY BEAUTIFUL

JANUARY 23, 1958   BROADWAY THEATRE   60 PERFORMANCES

Lyrics by Sheldon Harnick
Book by Joseph Stein and Will Glickman
Choreographed by Herbert Ross
Directed by George Schaefer
Produced by Richard Kollmar and Albert W. Selden
With Jack Warden, Mindy Carson, Steve Forrest, and Barbara McNair

Published songs:
All Of These And More
Hidden In My Heart—cut
Just My Luck
Leave Well Enough Alone
Uh-huh, Oh Yeah

Additional song recorded:
Summer Is

Bock and Harnick's debut came with this quick failure. But the score was better than average, and attracted the notice of producers Robert Griffith and Harold Prince.

FIORELLO!

NOVEMBER 23, 1959   BROADHURST THEATRE   795 PERFORMANCES

Lyrics by Sheldon Harnick
Book by Jerome Weidman and George Abbott
Choreographed by Peter Gennaro
Directed by Abbott
Produced by Robert E. Griffith and Harold S. Prince
With Tom Bosley, Patricia Wilson, Howard DaSilva, Eileen Rodgers, and Pat Stanley

Published songs:
Gentleman Jimmy
I Love A Cop—advertised but not published (except in vocal selection)
Little Tin Box
Politics And Poker
'Til Tomorrow
(I'll Marry) The Very Next Man
When Did I Fall In Love?
Where Do I Go From Here?—cut

Additional songs recorded:
The Bum Won
Home Again
Marie's Law
The Name's La Guardia
On The Side Of The Angels
Unfair

Arthur Penn, director of the hit drama *Two For The Seesaw* [January 16, 1958], came to Griffith and Prince with the idea for his first musical. The producers, whose four hit musicals had been written by veteran Leonard Bernstein and theatrical novices Adler, Ross, Merrill, and Sondheim, selected Bock and Harnick for the score. Novelist Jerome Weidman (**I Can Get It For You Wholesale** [Rome: March 22, 1962]) was put to work on *his* first theatre project. As the La Guardia biography moved further into the musical comedy vein, Penn departed. Griffith/Prince standby George Abbott took over as director and colibrettist. The resulting **Fiorello!** was one of Broadway's finest book musicals, joining **Of Thee I Sing** [Gershwin: December 26, 1931] and **South Pacific** [Rodgers: April 7, 1949] as a Pulitzer Prize winner. The careful integration of the piece avoided inclusion of potential hit songs; but the score displayed Bock and Harnick's great feel for character work, expressing the thoughts and emotions of the more-or-less contemporary common man. This had been glimpsed in parts of **The Body Beautiful** [January 23, 1958] score, and was to be seen consistently in the best of the team's work.

TENDERLOIN

October 17, 1960   46th Street Theatre   216 performances

Lyrics by Sheldon Harnick
Book by George Abbott and Jerome Weidman
(Based on the novel by Samuel Hopkins Adams)
Choreographed by Joe Layton
Directed by Abbott
Produced by Robert E. Griffith and Harold S. Prince
With Maurice Evans, Ron Husmann, Eileen Rodgers, and Margery Gray

Published songs:
Artificial Flowers
Good Clean Fun
I Wonder What It's Like—cut
Lovely Laurie—cut
My Gentle Young Johnny
My Miss Mary
Tommy, Tommy

Additional songs recorded:
The Army Of The Just
Bless This Land
Dear Friend [1st]—different than song from SHE LOVES ME [April 23, 1963]
Dr. Brock
How The Money Changes Hands
Little Old New York
The Picture Of Happiness
Reform
The Trial
What's In It For You?

Once again, the creators of a landmark musical attempted to follow up with a close copy; once again, the attempt failed. TENDERLOIN took place in a little older New York than FIORELLO! [November 23, 1959], and switched from inside politics to inside vice. Harnick, Layton, and company captured the color of the bad guys so well (in numbers like the opening, *Little Old New York*, and the sparkling *Picture Of Happiness*) that the good guys seemed bland and sappy. This included the star role, played by Shakespearean actor Maurice Evans. Dull leading characters are fatal to musical comedies. Bock, for his part, wrote a fine period score for TENDERLOIN, raucously energetic on the one hand and literately sentimental on the other.

NEVER TOO LATE

NOVEMBER 27, 1962   PLAYHOUSE THEATRE   1,007 PERFORMANCES

Play by Sumner Arthur Long
Incidental music mostly by John **Kander**
Directed by George Abbott
Produced by Elliot Martin and Daniel Hollywood
With Paul Ford, Maureen O'Sullivan, and Orson Bean

Published song:
Never Too Late (lyric by Sheldon Harnick)

MAN IN THE MOON

Marionette Show

APRIL 11, 1963   BILTMORE THEATRE   7 PERFORMANCES

Lyrics by Sheldon Harnick
Book by Arthur Burns

(Based on a story by Bil Baird)
Directed by Gerald Freedman
Produced by Arthur Cantor and Joseph Harris
With Bil and Cora Baird's Marionettes

Published songs:
World's Apart

Additional songs recorded:
Ain't You Never Been Afraid?
Itch To Be Rich
Look Where I Am
You Treacherous Man

Bock and Harnick set a new level for marionette-show songs in this fantasy, which followed Broadway with an overseas State Department tour.

SHE LOVES ME

The Happiest Musical

APRIL 23, 1963   EUGENE O'NEILL THEATRE   302 PERFORMANCES

Lyrics by Sheldon Harnick
Book by Joe Masteroff
(Based on *The Shop Around the Corner* [play] by Miklos Laszlo)
Choreographed by Carol Haney
Directed by Harold Prince
Produced by Prince in association with Lawrence J. Kasha and Philip C. McKenna
With Barbara Cook, Daniel Massey, Jack Cassidy, and Barbara Baxley

Published songs:
Days Gone By
Dear Friend [2nd]—different than song from TENDERLOIN [October 17, 1960]
Grand Knowing You
Ilona—advertised but not published (except in vocal selection)
She Loves Me
Tonight At Eight
Will He Like Me?

Additional songs recorded:
Good Morning, Good Day
Good Bye, Georg
I Don't Know His Name

I Resolve
Ice Cream
No More Candy
Perspective
A Romantic Atmosphere
Sounds While Selling
Tango Tragique
Thank You, Madam
Three Letters
A Trip To The Library
Try Me
Twelve Days To Christmas
Where's My Shoe?

Director Harold Prince, whose Broadway debut had been as replacement on A FAMILY AFFAIR [Kander: January 27, 1962], now prepared his first musical from inception. Bock and Harnick wrote their finest score for this romantic/ comic valentine, which was given a cream-puff production and perfectly played. Yet SHE LOVES ME failed, due to unforseeable managerial miscalculations in promotion and booking. The score survives, and remains a joy. Barbara Cook had her best role as the heroine, and Jack Cassidy, who had introduced Bock to Harnick, received a Tony Award for his supporting role. Carol Haney, featured dancer in THE PAJAMA GAME [Adler: May 13, 1954], choreographed.

TO BROADWAY WITH LOVE

APRIL 22, 1964   TEXAS PAVILION MUSIC HALL   < NEW YORK WORLD'S
    FAIR >

Title theme and original material by Jerry Bock
Lyrics to Bock songs by Sheldon Harnick
Choreographed by Donald Saddler
Conceived and directed by Morton DaCosta
Produced by George Schaeffer and Angus G. Wynne, Jr.
With Carmen Alvarez, Patti Karr, Rod Perry, and Sheila Smith

Recorded Songs:
Beautiful Lady
Mata Hari Mine
Popsicles In Paris
Remember Radio
To Broadway With Love

An unsuccessful World's Fair revue made up mostly of old-time Broadway and popular hits.

FIDDLER ON THE ROOF

SEPTEMBER 22, 1964   IMPERIAL THEATRE   3,242 PERFORMANCES

Lyrics by Sheldon Harnick
Book by Joseph Stein
(Based on stories by Sholom Aleichem)
Directed and choreographed by Jerome Robbins
Produced by Harold Prince
With Zero Mostel, Maria Karnilova, and Beatrice Arthur

Published songs:
Anatevka—initial individual publication upon use in 1971 movie version
Do You Love Me?—initial individual publication upon use in movie version
Far From The Home I Love—initial individual publication upon use in movie version
Fiddler On The Roof (Theme)—nonshow lyric
If I Were A Rich Man
Matchmaker, Matchmaker
Miracle Of Miracles—initial individual publication upon use in movie version
Now I Have Everything
Sabbath Prayer—initial individual publication upon use in movie version
Sunrise, Sunset
To Life—initial individual publication upon use in movie version
Tradition—initial individual publication upon use in movie version

Additional songs published in vocal score:
Chava Sequence (Little Chavaleh)
The Dream
The Rumor
Tevye's Monologue (They Gave Each Other A Pledge)
Tevye's Rebuttal
Wedding Dance [instrumental]

Additional songs recorded:
How Much Richer Could One Man Be?—cut
When Messiah Comes—cut

One of the most successful and beloved musicals in Broadway history. Bock and Harnick began work with Joseph Stein, librettist of Bock's first two musicals, following the failure of TENDERLOIN [October 17, 1960]. In late 1963 producer Fred Coe was joined by Harold Prince (Coe was to disappear from the credits during the pre-Broadway tryout). Prince brought along Jerome Robbins, who had just departed the FUNNY GIRL project (see [**Styne:**

March 26, 1964]). FIDDLER's strong theme—as interpreted by Robbins—brought the piece worldwide acclaim. But compared to the overall excellence of the show, the score must be judged slightly disappointing. Robbins' previous WEST SIDE STORY [Bernstein: September 26, 1957] and GYPSY [Styne: May 21, 1959] had music which captured the essence of the material throughout. The same cannot be said for FIDDLER. Much of the score was perfect, especially *Tradition, Sabbath Prayer, If I Were A Rich Man,* and the *Chava Sequence.* Other songs—*Matchmaker, Matchmaker* and *Sunrise, Sunset*—became popular hits. But while FIDDLER ON THE ROOF was certainly Bock and Harnick's best musical, their best score—at least in this man's opinion—was written for SHE LOVES ME [April 23, 1963].

BAKER STREET

FEBRUARY 16, 1965   BROADWAY THEATRE   313 PERFORMANCES

Music and lyrics mostly by Marian Grudeff and Raymond Jessel
Lyrics to Bock songs by Sheldon Harnick
Book by Jerome Coopersmith
(Based on stories by Sir Arthur Conan Doyle)
Choreographed by Lee Becker Theodore
Directed by Harold Prince
Produced by Alexander H. Cohen
With Fritz Weaver, Inga Swenson, and Martin Gabel

Published Bock songs:
Buffalo Belle—cut
Cold, Clear World
I Shall Miss You (Holmes)
I'm In London Again

Alex Cohen equipped BAKER STREET with the most spectacular front-of-house marquee in Broadway history and little else. Bock and Harnick answered Prince's calls for help by interpolating four songs (publicly credited to Grudeff and Jessel). Harnick seized the opportunity by coming up with a nifty pun about "the stately Holmes of England."

GENERATION

OCTOBER 6, 1965   MOROSCO THEATRE   300 PERFORMANCES

Play by William Goodhart
Incidental music by Jerry Bock
Directed by Gene Saks
Produced by Frederick Brisson
With Henry Fonda and Holly Turner

Published songs:
None

Bock wrote a title song to a lyric by the playwright.

THE APPLE TREE

OCTOBER 18, 1966   SHUBERT THEATRE   463 PERFORMANCES

Lyrics by Sheldon Harnick
Book by Bock and Harnick
Additional material by Jerome Coopersmith
(Based on stories by Mark Twain, Frank R. Stockton, and Jules Feiffer)
Choreographed by Lee Becker Theodore and Herbert Ross
Directed by Mike Nichols
Produced by Stuart Ostrow
With Barbara Harris, Larry Blyden, and Alan Alda

Published songs:
The Apple Tree (Forbidden Fruit)
Beautiful, Beautiful World
I'm Lost—cut
I've Got What You Want
What Makes Me Love Him?

Additional songs published in vocal score:
Ai, Ai!
Eve
Feelings
Fish
Forbidden Love (In Gaul)
Friends
Gorgeous
Here In Eden
I Know
I'll Tell You A Truth
Lullaby (Go To Sleep Whatever You Are)
Make Way
Oh, To Be A Movie Star
Prisoner, Choose!
Razor Teeth
Real
Tiger, Tiger
Wealth

Which Door?
Who Is She?

An interesting idea—an evening of three one-act musicals—proved difficult to pull off. Jerome Robbins and Coopersmith left the project early on; musical novice Mike Nichols came in (bringing along 'Passionella' from THE WORLD OF JULES FEIFFER [Sondheim: July 2, 1962]). The three bites of THE APPLE TREE were uneven. Not surprisingly, the third bite brought forth the best of Bock and Harnick, but too late to make up for the pastoral first and dreary second acts.

HER FIRST ROMAN

OCTOBER 20, 1968   LUNT-FONTANNE THEATRE   17 PERFORMANCES

Book, music and lyrics mostly by Ervin Drake
Lyrics to Bock songs by Sheldon Harnick
(Based on *Caesar and Cleopatra* [play] by George Bernard Shaw)
Choreographed by Dania Krupska
Directed by Derek Goldby
Produced by Joseph Cates and Henry Fownes (in association with Warner Brothers-7 Arts)
With Richard Kiley, Leslie Uggams, and Claudia McNeil

Published Bock songs:
None

The producers were successful in securing the closely guarded rights, only the third musical adaptation of Shaw ever authorized. Then the assignment was given to pop composer Ervin Drake, who had done the score for Cates' long-running but unsuccessful WHAT MAKES SAMMY RUN? [February 27, 1964]; Drake's librettist qualifications were even less impressive. The director and choreographer (and their replacements) were replaced on the road. Bock and Harnick came in for last-minute cosmetic surgery and contributed *Caesar Is Wrong, Old Gentleman,* and *Ptolemy* (all unpublished, publicly credited to Drake).

THE ROTHSCHILDS

OCTOBER 19, 1970   LUNT-FONTANNE THEATRE   507 PERFORMANCES

Lyrics by Sheldon Harnick
Book by Sherman Yellen
(Based on the biography by Frederic Morton)
Directed and choreographed by Michael Kidd
Produced by Lester Osterman and Hillard Elkins

With Hal Linden, Leila Martin, Paul Hecht, Keene Curtis, and Jill Clayburgh

Published songs:
I'm In Love! I'm In Love!
In My Own Lifetime
One Room
Valse De Rothschild (Never Again)

Additional songs published in vocal selection:
Everything
Rothschild And Sons
Sons

Additional songs recorded:
Allons
Bonds
Give England Strength
Have You Ever Seen A Prettier Little Congress?
He Tossed A Coin
Pleasure And Privilege
Stability
They Say
This Amazing London Town

A theatre-party special, calculated to please audiences who were still thronging to the six-year-old FIDDLER ON THE ROOF [September 22, 1964]. But Meyer Rothschild and five sons hadn't the charm of Tevye and five daughters. The weak book lacked warmth and interest, Bock and Harnick were a century out of their element, and there was no Robbins or Prince in sight. The producers who assembled the package had a string of poor musicals to their credit. Director Derek Goldby, who had evidently impressed Bock and Harnick when they tried to patch HER FIRST ROMAN [October 20, 1968] together, had no other musical experience and was soon gone. Michael Kidd, on hand all along as choreographer, was eventually asked to take over, but much too late to deal with the problems (some of which were resolved in a reduced-scale off-Broadway revival in 1990).

Following THE ROTHSCHILDS, Bock ended his twelve-year partnership with Sheldon Harnick. The composer then wrote a mystery-musical (with his own lyrics) which was never produced, and nothing since. Bock's reasons for self-imposed retirement are unknown, although his two final shows were criticized for not being as good as FIDDLER ON THE ROOF [September 22, 1964]. (Of course they were not as good as FIDDLER ON THE ROOF; how many shows are?) Jerry Bock is certainly one of today's finest theatre composers. He hasn't been heard from for twenty years, and that's not good for Broadway.

Bob Merrill

BORN: May 17, 1920   Atlantic City, New Jersey

Following military service, Bob Merrill went to Hollywood as an MGM dialogue director before moving to television writing. An interest in songwriting led to a highly profitable pop song career, highlighted by the 1950 *If I Knew You Were Comin' I'd've Baked A Cake* (with Al Hoffman and Clem Watts) and *How Much Is That Doggie In The Window?* in 1953. His success with novelty songs was such that he had difficulty getting a serious hearing.

[all music and lyrics by Bob Merrill]

NEW GIRL IN TOWN

MAY 14, 1957   46TH STREET THEATRE   431 PERFORMANCES

Book and direction by George Abbott
(Based on *Anna Christie* [play] by Eugene O'Neill)
Choreographed by Bob Fosse
Produced by Frederick Brisson, Robert E. Griffith, and Harold S. Prince
With Gwen Verdon, Thelma Ritter, George Wallace, and Cameron Prud'homme

Published songs:
At The Check Apron Ball
Did You Close Your Eyes?
Elegance—cut; for initial publication see **HELLO, DOLLY!** [January 16, 1964]
Flings
Here We Are Again—cut
If That Was Love
It's Good To Be Alive
Look At 'Er
Theme From 'New Girl in Town' [instrumental]—nonlyric version of *Anna Lilla*
Sunshine Girl
You're My Friend, Ain'tcha?

Additional songs recorded:
Anna Lilla
Chess And Checkers
On The Farm
Roll Yer Socks Up
There Ain't No Flies On Me
Ven I Valse

MGM dropped "A Saint She Ain't," their Doris Day musical remake of *Anna Christie*. Griffith, Prince, and Abbott heard the score and brought Merrill to Broadway. Extreme tryout problems resulted in a rift between the producers/authors and the DAMN YANKEES [Adler: May 5, 1955] team of Verdon and Fosse. The result was a moderate hit, thanks chiefly to Verdon and Thelma Ritter (who shared the Tony Award for Best Actress in a Musical). Griffith, Prince, and Abbott went looking for new songwriters (FIORELLO! [Bock: November 23, 1959]); Fosse and Verdon went looking for new producers (REDHEAD [PART 4: February 5, 1959]); and Merrill was called by David Merrick.

TAKE ME ALONG

OCTOBER 22, 1959   SHUBERT THEATRE   448 PERFORMANCES

Book by Joseph Stein and Robert Russell
(Based on *Ah, Wilderness* [play] by Eugene O'Neill)
Choreographed by Onna White
Directed by Peter Glenville
Produced by David Merrick
With Jackie Gleason, Eileen Herlie, Walter Pidgeon, and Robert Morse

Published songs:
But Yours
I Get Embarrassed
I Would Die
Little Green Snake
Nine O'Clock
Promise Me A Rose
Sid, Ol' Kid
Staying Young
Take Me Along

Additional songs recorded:
Oh, Please
The Parade
That's How It Starts

Volunteer Firemen Picnic (Ladies With A Liberal Point Of View)
We're Home
Wint's Song

Merrill tried a second O'Neill adaptation, this time using the playwright's more suitable turn-of-the-century comedy. But the librettists concentrated on the secondary comic couple, and Merrill gave them show-stopping material. This could have worked if the George M. Cohan part had been diminished; but with a star (Walter Pidgeon) cast in the role, the relatively colorless character was given an equivalently sized part. TAKE ME ALONG might have succeeded anyway; it had a charming score, nostalgic physical production, and fine performances from Eileen Herlie and Robert Morse. But off-stage problems developed with TV star Jackie Gleason, who finally withdrew. Merrill's first show had been successful although not very good; TAKE ME ALONG was considerably better but barely managed to break even. A summer stock revival without stars, fixes, or imagination came to Broadway on April 14, 1985 and closed on April 14, 1985.

CARNIVAL!

APRIL 13, 1961   IMPERIAL THEATRE   719 PERFORMANCES

Book by Michael Stewart
(Based on material by Helen Deutsch)
Directed and choreographed by Gower Champion
Produced by David Merrick
With Anna Maria Alberghetti, Jerry Orbach, Kaye Ballard, James Mitchell, and Pierre Olaf

Published songs:
Beautiful Candy
Grand Imperial Cirque De Paris
Her Face
It Was Always You
Mira (Can You Imagine That?)
She's My Love
Theme From Carnival! (Love Makes The World Go Round)
Three Puppet Songs: Golden, Delicious Fish; The Rich;
     Yum-Ticky-Tum-Tum
Yes, My Heart

Additional song published in "Puppet Songs from Carnival":
Fairyland

Additional song published in piano selection:
Direct From Vienna (music only; lyric is recorded)

Additional songs recorded:
Everybody Likes You
Humming
I Hate Him
I've Got To Find A Reason
Sword, Rose and Cape
A Very Nice Man

David Merrick had been particularly successful with Gallic shows, from
FANNY [Rome: November 4, 1954] to the revue LA PLUME DE MA TANTE
[September 29, 1960]. Securing the rights to the popular 1953 movie "Lili"
Merrick wisely put it in the hands of Gower Champion (and librettist Michael
Stewart) of the surprise hit BYE BYE BIRDIE [Strouse: April 14, 1960]. Merrill,
who did well enough on his first Merrick assignment, came up with his best
score. CARNIVAL! was magical: staging, songs and all (including Broadway's
best puppets ever). Merrill even managed to top the movie's hit theme song
(*Hi-Lili, Hi-Lo*) with *Love Makes The World Go Round.*

HELLO, DOLLY!

JANUARY 16, 1964   ST. JAMES THEATRE   2,844 PERFORMANCES

Music and lyrics mostly by Jerry **Herman** (also see **Strouse**)
Books by Michael Stewart
(Based on *The Matchmaker* [play] by Thornton Wilder)
Directed and choreographed by Gower Champion
Produced by David Merrick
With Carol Channing, David Burns, Eileen Brennan, and Charles Nelson
Reilly

Songs published in vocal score:
Elegance (by Merrill and Herman)
Motherhood March (by Merrill and Herman)

Merrill, awaiting the start of rehearsals for his third consecutive Merrick
musical—FUNNY GIRL [Styne: March 26, 1964]—was called to Detroit by
Merrill when DOLLY! displayed tryout troubles. For details, see **Herman:
January 16, 1964.**

FUNNY GIRL
see Styne [March 26, 1964]

BREAKFAST AT TIFFANY'S

[DECEMBER 14, 1966]   MAJESTIC THEATRE; CLOSED DURING PREVIEWS

Book by Abe Burrows
Book revised by Edward Albee
(Based on the novella by Truman Capote)
Choreographed by Michael Kidd
Directed by Joseph Anthony
Produced by David Merrick
With Mary Tyler Moore, Richard Chamberlain, Art Lund, and Sally Kellerman
NOTE: HOLLY GOLIGHTLY, pre-Boradway title

Songs issued in professional copies:
Breakfast At Tiffany's
Ciao, Compare
Holly Golightly
I've Got A Penny—cut
Travellin'—cut
You've Never Kissed Her

Additional songs recorded:
Freddy Chant
Grade 'A' Treatment
Home For Wayward Girls
I'm Not The Girl Who Used To Be
Lament For Ten Men
Same Mistakes
Stay With Me
When Daddy Comes Home
Who Needs Her?

Merrill, in his fourth Merrick assignment, came up with one of Broadway's all-time fiascos. A popular novel, a smash movie, and two major TV stars added up to a record advance sale; but Merrick chose to close what he considered a hopelessly poor show. A satisfactory point of view for the treatment of the prostitute heroine was never found, even with a drastic tryout revision (Abe Burrows—who took over from Nunnally Johnson—to Edward Albee?). Merrill's work, though, had charm in places, particularly in the two title songs.

Mary Tyler Moore's much-heralded musical comedy debut never happened, and she went back to Hollywood to try her luck in her own television series.

HENRY, SWEET HENRY

OCTOBER 23, 1967　PALACE THEATRE　80 PERFORMANCES

Book by Nunnally Johnson
(Based on *The World of Henry Orient* [novel] by Nora Johnson)
Choreographed by Michael Bennett
Directed by George Roy Hill
Produced by Edward Specter Productions and Norman Twain
With Don Ameche, Carol Bruce, Robin Wilson, Louise Lasser, Neva Small, and Alice Playten

Published songs:
Dearest Darling—cut; issued in professional copy
Do You Ever Go To Boston?
Henry, Sweet Henry
Here I Am
I Wonder How It Is To Dance With A Boy
Love Of My Life—cut; issued in professional copy
My Kind Of Person—cut; issued in professional copy
Somebody Someplace—cut; issued in professional copy
Weary Near To Dyin'
You Might Get To Like Me—cut; issued in professional copy; revised
　　version of *We Only Remember* (cut, unpublished) from HELLO,
　　DOLLY! [January 16, 1964]

Additional songs recorded:
Academic Fugue
I'm Blue Too
In Some Little World
Nobody Steps On Kafritz
Pillar To Post
People Watchers
Poor Little Person—revised version of *My Kind of Person* (cut)
To Be Artistic
Woman In Love

Merrill adapted another popular novel/movie, again meeting with failure. *Ah, Wilderness* and "Lili" had been warm, tender stories about innocents; Holly Golightly and Henry Orient were jaded New Yorkers. The sophisticated adults of HENRY, SWEET HENRY were obnoxious and uninteresting; the teenage girls were amusing and sympathetic. Merrill's tender material for the latter (including *Here I Am* and *In Some Little World*) was overpowered by the former, and the show—in a season where it should have been a hit—defeated itself. Hired to choreograph was Michael Bennett, a Michael Kidd dancer in SUB-WAYS ARE FOR SLEEPING [Styne: December 27, 1961] and HERE'S LOVE [Willson: October 3, 1963]. Bennett had made his choreographic debut with the short-lived A JOYFUL NOISE [December 15, 1966].

PRETTYBELLE

see Styne [February 1, 1971]

SUGAR

see Styne [April 9, 1972]

THE PRINCE OF GRAND STREET

[MARCH 7, 1978]   FORREST THEATRE < PHILADELPHIA,
    PENNSYLVANIA > ; CLOSED DURING PRE-BROADWAY TRYOUT

Book by Merrill
Choreographed by Lee Becker Theodore
Directed by Gene Saks
Produced by Robert Whitehead, Roger L. Stevens, and The Shubert Organization
With Robert Preston, Sam Levene, Neva Small, Werner Klemperer, and Bernice Massi

Published songs:
None

Merrill's Broadway career has been virtually ended by the combination of BREAKFAST AT TIFFANY'S [December 14, 1966], PRETTYBELLE [February 1, 1971] and THE PRINCE OF GRAND STREET—three star vehicles with great potential and heavy advance theatre party bookings. Producers and theatre owners hate to give back ticket money. THE PRINCE OF GRAND STREET was patterned after Jacob Adler, patriarch of the Yiddish Theatre. Robert Preston was one of Broadway's finest and most charming actors, equally at home in drama and musical—but *Jacob Adler?* (In the second act, the aging Yiddish Prince portrayed Huckleberry Finn. Seems that Adler was a great chum of Mark Twain.) Preston also closed out of town when Stuart Ostrow cast him as Pancho Villa in WE TAKE THE TOWN [February 19, 1962]. The actors and writers get blamed for these things, and suffer through the painful perform-ances (no matter how few). But what about the producers who choose the material?

HANNAH . . . 1939

MAY 31, 1990   VINEYARD THEATRE < OFF-OFF-BROADWAY >   46
PERFORMANCES

Book by Merrill
Choreographed by Tina Paul
Directed by Douglas Aibel
Produced by The Vineyard Theatre
With Julie Wilson, Leigh Beery, Neva Small, and Tony Carlin

Published songs:
None

HANNAH . . . 1939—cheery title, isn't it?—was the story of a Jewish fashion
designer (apparently even better than Chanel) whose Prague factory is com-
mandeered to manufacture Nazi uniforms. Hannah becomes fond (in a moth-
erly way) of the young lieutenant who oversees the operation, never dreaming
what the Nazis—*Ah, Our Germans,* she sings—are *really* up to. This from
the guy who wrote *How Much Is That Doggie In The Window?* Grisly, man,
real grisly.

Bob Merrill has written seven scores (plus three sets of lyrics to Jule Styne's
music). His best work—CARNIVAL! [April 13, 1961] and sections of TAKE ME
ALONG [October 22, 1959] and HENRY, SWEET HENRY [October 23,
1967]—displays a wistful innocence. His more 'sophisticated' efforts have
been coarse and less appealing. Since 1967 he has written two musicals,
neither of which have added anything to his reputation or our enjoyment.
Perhaps he should try to enchant us once again?

Stephen Sondheim

BORN: March 22, 1930   New York, New York

At the age of ten, Stephen Sondheim moved from Manhattan to Doylestown, Pennsylvania—Doylestown, home of Oscar Hammerstein 2nd. A friendship with the lyricist's son led to a close teacher/student relationship with the man who had set new musical theatre boundaries in his work with Jerome Kern, and who was just then writing OKLAHOMA! [Rodgers: March 31, 1943] and CAROUSEL [Rodgers: April 19, 1945]. There was little question of career choice, and Sondheim was already writing amateur shows during the War. As Hammerstein was struggling through ALLEGRO [Rodgers: October 10, 1947] and future Broadway lyricists were no doubt delighting over E. Y. Harburg's FINIAN'S RAINBOW [Lane: January 10, 1947] conundrums, Sondheim went off to Williams College as a music major.

[all music and lyrics by Stephen Sondheim unless indicated]

PHINNEY'S RAINBOW
Williams College Show

[CIRCA MAY 1948]   ADAMS MEMORIAL THEATRE   < WILLIAMSTOWN, MASSACHUSETTS >

Book by Sondheim and Josiah T. S. Horton
Directed by David C. Bryant
Produced by Cap and Bells, Inc.

Published songs:
How Do I Know?
Phinney's Rainbow
Still Got My Heart

Sondheim's first published theatre work came from this college show, courtesy of the BMI talent search (see BIG AS LIFE [Bock: Circa May 1948]). The title was borrowed from a recent Broadway hit; the songs, though, were far removed from Glocca Morra. As composer Sondheim's first Broadway musical wasn't until fourteen years later, it's interesting to see how advanced his early songs are. The title song has a strong, complex rhythm (which gets *too* complex along the way); the lyric—oddly enough—is upbeat inspirational, closely echoing the less rhythmic *You'll Never Walk Alone. Still Got My Heart* is particularly interesting for its effective harmonic wanderings and a couple of syncopational tricks.

ALL THAT GLITTERS
Williams College Show

[MARCH 19, 1949]   ADAMS MEMORIAL THEATRE   < WILLIAMSTOWN, MASSACHUSETTS >   3 PERFORMANCES

Book by Sondheim
(Based on *Beggar on Horseback* [play] by George S. Kaufman and Marc Connelly)
Directed by David C. Bryant
Produced by Cap and Bells, Inc.
With Ronald Moir, Betty Dissell, Jeanette Forsey, and Donald Rackerby

Songs published in vocal selection:
I Love You Etcetera
I Must Be Dreaming
I Need Love
Let's Not Fall In Love
When I See You

Teacher Hammerstein instructed student Sondheim to take a play he liked and turn it into a musical; ALL THAT GLITTERS was the result. *When I See You* stands out, surely his prettiest ballad until ANYONE CAN WHISTLE [April 4, 1964]. The complexities are striking—nineteen-year-old Sondheim tried things no one else in those days (except Blitzstein or Duke) was doing. One wonders, though, how a 1949 college soprano coped with the key shifts into and throughout the fascinating bridge. *Let's Not Fall In Love* is the best of the others, a light rhythm number. In these first eight songs Sondheim was least adept in lyric and melody; rhythmically, he was often *too* intricate.

GIRLS OF SUMMER

NOVEMBER 19, 1956   LONGACRE THEATRE   56 PERFORMANCES

Play by N. Richard Nash
Incidental music by Sondheim
Directed by Jack Garfein

Produced by Cheryl Crawford
With Shelley Winters, Pat Hingle, and George Peppard

Published song:
Girls Of Summer

Graduating from Williams, Sondheim studied with avant-garde composer Milton Babbitt on a fellowship. He then worked with George Oppenheimer scripting the TV series "Topper." Sondheim's first Broadway assignment came in 1954, writing music and lyrics for the unproduced SATURDAY NIGHT; the show was abandoned when producer/designer Lemuel Ayers (see OUT OF THIS WORLD [Porter: December 21, 1950]) died. By 1956 Sondheim was collaborating on the lyrics to WEST SIDE STORY [Bernstein: September 26, 1957]. The producer (at the time) was Cheryl Crawford; she gave Sondheim his first Broadway hearing with the incidental music assignment on GIRLS OF SUMMER. The title song is Sondheim at his jazziest.

WEST SIDE STORY

see Bernstein [September 26, 1957]

GYPSY

see Styne [May 21, 1959]

INVITATION TO A MARCH

OCTOBER 29, 1960   MUSIC BOX THEATRE   113 PERFORMANCES

Play by Arthur Laurents
Incidental music by Sondheim
Directed by Laurents
Produced by The Theatre Guild
With Celeste Holm, Madeleine Sherwood, Eileen Heckart, Jane Fonda, and James MacArthur

Published songs:
None

Arthur Laurents had been responsible for bringing Sondheim in on WEST SIDE STORY [Bernstein: September 26, 1957]; he had also done the libretto for Sondheim's GYPSY [Styne: May 21, 1959]. The pair were to create one more musical together, ANYONE CAN WHISTLE [April 4, 1964].

A FUNNY THING HAPPENED ON THE WAY TO THE FORUM

MAY 8, 1962   ALVIN THEATRE   964 PERFORMANCES

Book by Burt Shevelove and Larry Gelbart
(Based on plays by Plautus)
Choreographed by Jack Cole
Directed by George Abbott
Produced by Harold Prince
With Zero Mostel, Jack Gilford, David Burns, and John Carradine

Published songs:
Comedy Tonight
Everybody Ought To Have A Maid
I Do Like You—cut
Love, I Hear
Love Is In The Air—cut
Lovely
That'll Show Him
Your Eyes Are Blue—cut

Additional songs published in vocal score:
Bring Me My Bride
Free
Funeral Sequence
The House of Marcus Lycus [2nd]—scene version
I'm Calm
Impossible
Pretty Little Picture
That Dirty Old Man

Additional songs recorded:
Echo Song—cut
The House Of Marcus Lycus [1st]—cut; song version
There's Something About A War

Composer Sondheim—already highly successful as a lyricist-finally was heard on Broadway with this very funny vaudeville farce. Sondheim's fine comedy lyrics were on a level with the lovingly slapdash book by Shevelove and Gelbart; his music was witty but slightly tame (except for the delectable *Everybody Ought To Have A Maid*). It wasn't until COMPANY [April 26, 1970]—a long eight years later—that the composer began to receive recognition. FORUM was producer Harold Prince's first musical on his own, as partner Robert Griffith had died June 7, 1961. George Abbott had his final musical success (with an assist from Jerome Robbins, who had initially been on the project) and Zero Mostel became an unlikely musical comedy hero.

THE WORLD OF JULES FEIFFER

[JULY 2, 1962]   HUNTERDON HILLS PLAYHOUSE <CLINTON, NEW JERSEY >; SUMMER STOCK TRYOUT

Sketches by Jules Feiffer
Music and lyrics by Stephen Sondheim
Directed by Mike Nichols
Produced by Lewis Allen and Harry Rigby
With Ronny Graham, Dorothy Loudon, and Paul Sand

Song published in "All Sondheim, Volume III":
Truly Content

Mike Nichols first tried his hand at legit directing with this comedy revue. Included was a one-act musical version of Feiffer's 'Passionella.' What has surfaced of Sondheim's work—*Truly Content*—compares favorably with the rather good *Oh, To Be A Movie Star* from THE APPLE TREE [Bock: October 18, 1966]. And Dorothy Loudon, who spent the next fifteen years giving life to a string of musical fatalities (until Nichols put her in ANNIE [Strouse: April 21, 1977]), surely must have made an interesting chimney sweep.

HOT SPOT

APRIL 19, 1963   MAJESTIC THEATRE   43 PERFORMANCES

Music mostly by Mary Rodgers
Lyrics mostly by Martin Charnin
Book by Jack Weinstock and Willie Gilbert
Choreographed by Onna White
Directed by Morton DaCosta
Produced by Robert Fryer and Lawrence Carr, in association with John Herman
With Judy Holliday, Joseph Campanella, Joe Bova, Mary Louise Wilson, and George Furth

Recorded song:
Don't Laugh (music and lyrics by Rodgers, Charnin, and Sondheim)—advertised but not published; recorded upon reuse in THE MADWOMAN OF CENTRAL PARK WEST [Bernstein/Kander: June 13, 1979]

Sondheim was helping out Mary Rodgers, whom he knew through his Hammerstein connection, and Martin Charnin, an ex-Jet from WEST SIDE STORY [Bernstein: September 26, 1957]. A FUNNY THING HAPPENED ON THE WAY

To **The Forum** [**May 8, 1962**] was "saved" at the very last minute, they say, when ghost-director Jerome Robbins requisitioned a new opening number; it was called *Comedy Tonight,* and it told the audience precisely what to expect, and the show was a hit. The last minute balm for the tepid **Hot Spot** was called *Don't Laugh,* and it told the audience exactly what to expect. It's actually a well-composed song, which builds excitingly in the manner of *Truly Content* from **The World Of Jules Feiffer** [**July 2, 1962**] and *A Parade In Town* from **Anyone Can Whistle** [**April 4, 1964**]. The lyric, though, has only three good jokes and quite a few lame ones. While the writers shared equal credit, I would guess that Sondheim provided the music and a few snatches of lyric and Charnin did the rest.

ANYONE CAN WHISTLE
A Wild New Musical

April 4, 1964   Majestic Theatre   9 performances

Book and direction by Arthur Laurents
Choreographed by Herbert Ross
Produced by Kermit Bloomgarden and Diana Krasny
With Angela Lansbury, Lee Remick, and Harry Guardino

Published songs:
Anyone Can Whistle
Come Play Wiz Me
Everybody Says Don't
I've Got You To Lean On
A Parade In Town
See What It Gets You
There Won't Be Trumpets—cut
With So Little To Be Sure Of

Additional songs published in vocal score:
A-1 March
Cora's Chase (Lock 'Em Up)
I'm Like The Bluebird
Me And My Town
Miracle Song
Opposites
Run For Your Lives
Simple (A Is One)
Watchcries

This wild new musical was *too* wild and new (and muddled) to compete with **Hello, Dolly!** [**Herman: January 16, 1964**] and **Funny Girl** [**Styne: March**

26, 1964]. Sondheim's score was impressively well developed, with exciting extended musical sequences, intricate choral work, and many surprises. But **Anyone Can Whistle** was complex enough to scare away composing jobs for the rest of the decade. Angela Lansbury soon became an important musical comedy star—but via Jerry Herman.

DO I HEAR A WALTZ?

see Rodgers [March 18, 1965]

THE MAD SHOW

January 9, 1966   New Theatre < off-Broadway >   871 performances

Music by Mary Rodgers
Lyrics mostly by Marshall Barer
Book by Larry Siegel and Stan Hart
(Based on *Mad* magazine)
Directed by Steven Vinaver
Produced by Ivor David Balding
With Linda Lavin, Paul Sand, Dick Libertini, and Jo Anne Worley

Song published in "Hansen Treasury of Stephen Sondheim Songs":
The Boy From (music by Rodgers, lyric by "Esteban Ria Nido")

Sondheim contributed this nonsense lyric in the Ipanema vein to music by Mary Rodgers. Sondheim's only musical activity between **Anyone Can Whistle** [April 4, 1964] and **Company** [April 26, 1970] was for the one-performance TV mini-musical "Evening Primrose" [November 16, 1966].

COMPANY

April 26, 1970   Alvin Theatre   706 performances

Book by George Furth
Choreographed by Michael Bennett
Directed by Harold Prince
Produced by Prince in association with Ruth Mitchell
With Dean Jones, Elaine Stritch, Barbara Barrie, and Donna McKechnie

Published songs:
Another Hundred People
Being Alive
Company

The Ladies Who Lunch
The Little Things You Do Together
Side By Side By Side
Someone Is Waiting
Sorry-Grateful
You Could Drive A Person Crazy

Additional songs published in vocal score:
Barcelona
Getting Married Today
Have I Got A Girl For You
Poor Baby
Tick-Tock [instrumental]
What Would We Do Without You?

Additional songs published in "All Sondheim":
Happily Ever After—cut (in Volume 3)
Marry Me A Little—cut (in Volume 2)

Sondheim returned to Broadway with the most important new musical since FIDDLER ON THE ROOF [Bock: September 22, 1964]. Producer/director Harold Prince had broken new ground with CABARET [Kander: November 20, 1966], despite a score which lagged several paces behind staging and production. In Sondheim, Prince found the perfect collaborator (or was it the other way around?). The pair had been friends for years; when WEST SIDE STORY [Bernstein: September 26, 1957] lost its producer and was about to be shelved, it was Prince whom Sondheim called for help. COMPANY was something new for Broadway, a musical for Our Times. (It should be noted that although Sondheim's work has been hailed and lauded by the sophisticates, the mass audience has consistently preferred lesser competition like APPLAUSE [Strouse: March 30, 1970], PIPPIN [S. Schwartz: October 23, 1972], ANNIE [Strouse: April 21, 1977], CATS [PART 5: October 7, 1982], and LA CAGE AUX FOLLES [Herman: August 21, 1983].) While Sondheim's COMPANY score was filled with contemporary rhythms, it was anything but "pop." Words and music revealed character in a highly personal, self-analytical way. *Being Alive, Sorry-Grateful, Another Hundred People, Company,* and *Getting Married Today* told more about the characters—and the times—than any monologue or book scene could hope to do. There had been exceptional character studies before—Billy Bigelow's *Soliloquy,* the King of Siam's *A Puzzlement,* Tevye's *If I Were A Rich Man*—but these were exceptional exceptions. The age of Sondheim, if you will, has been distinguished by scores-full of analytical, personalized musical portraits. (This very attribute has also spawned lots of bad work from Sondheim-clones.) At any rate, Sondheim and Prince—abetted by a highly-complementary company of coworkers headed by designer Boris

Aronson and orchestrator Jonathan Tunick—undertook six major musicals over the next eleven years: two hits, three failures (financially, that is), and one discordant disaster which ended it all.

FOLLIES

APRIL 4, 1971   WINTER GARDEN THEATRE   522 PERFORMANCES

Book by James Goldman
Choreographed by Michael Bennett
Directed by Harold Prince and Bennett
Produced by Prince in association with Ruth Mitchell
With Alexis Smith, Dorothy Collins, Gene Nelson, and John McMartin

Published songs:
Broadway Baby
Follies (Beautiful Girls)
Losing My Mind
Too Many Mornings

Additional songs published in vocal score:
Ah, Paris!
Buddy's Blues (The God-Why-Don't-You-Love-Me Blues)
Could I Leave You?
Don't Look At Me
Fox-Trot [instrumental]—nonlyric version of *Can That Boy Fox-Trot!* (cut; initial publication in *Hansen Treasury Of Stephen Sondheim Songs*)
I'm Still Here
In Buddy's Eyes
Live, Laugh, Love
Love Will See Us Through
Loveland [1st]
Lucy And Jessie
One More Kiss
Prologue [instrumental]—nonsong version of *All Things Bright And Beautiful* (cut)
Rain On The Roof
The Road You Didn't Take
Vincent And Vanessa Dance [instrumental]—nonsong version of *That Old Piano Roll* (cut)
Waiting For The Girls Upstairs
Who's That Woman?
You're Gonna Love Tomorrow

Additional songs written for 1987 London production and published in vocal selection:
Ah, But Underneath
Country House
Loveland [2nd]
Make The Most Of Your Music

Additional songs published in "All Sondheim (Volume 2)":
All Things Bright And Beautiful—cut; song version of *Prologue*
Little White House—cut
Uptown, Downtown—cut
Who Could Be Blue?—cut

Additional songs recorded:
It Wasn't Meant To Happen—cut
Pleasant Little Kingdom—cut

One of Sondheim's richest scores was overwhelmed by a bloated concept, aiming for surrealism but winding up pretentious. The "layered ghosts" approach intended to illustrate the characters' psychoneuroses—Sally flirting with Young Ben fighting with Phyllis commiserating with Young Buddy mooning over Young Sally, while a couple of Heidis sang soprano—came across as rather silly, capsizing the otherwise adventurous work by all. (The authors had been working on the project for five years; as THE GIRLS UP-STAIRS, it had no ghosts, no flashbacks, and only one set of characters.) The score, staging, and production made FOLLIES a staggering experience by the third viewing, but that wasn't good enough for the bored businessman. For the listener, the rewards were numerous: *Losing My Mind, I'm Still Here, Too Many Mornings, Broadway Baby, Who's That Woman?, One More Kiss,* and on. An all-star charity concert staging in 1985—and the success of the resulting recording—led superproducer Cameron Mackintosh to mount a revised FOLLIES in London in 1987. Things didn't work out much better than in 1971, though. Only one of Sondheim's new songs was of FOLLIES quality, a remarkable duet/battle called *Country House.*

A LITTLE NIGHT MUSIC

FEBRUARY 25, 1973   SHUBERT THEATRE   601 PERFORMANCES

Book by Hugh Wheeler
(Based on *Smiles of a Summer Night* [film] by Ingmar Bergman)
Choreographed by Patricia Birch
Directed by Harold Prince

Produced by Prince in association with Ruth Mitchell
With Glynis Johns, Len Cariou, Hermione Gingold, and Victoria Mallory

Published songs:
A Little Night Music (The Sun Won't Set) [instrumental version]
The Miller's Son
Remember?
Send In The Clowns
You Must Meet My Wife

Additional songs published in vocal score:
Every Day A Little Death
The Glamorous Life (Pack Up The Luggage) [1st]
In Praise Of Women
It Would Have Been Wonderful
Later
Liaisons
Night Waltz II (The Sun Sits Low)
Now
Perpetual Anticipation
Soon
The Sun Won't Set [song version]
A Weekend In The Country

Additional songs published in "All Sondheim":
Bang—cut (in Volume 2)
The Glamorous Life (The Letter Song) [2nd]—written for 1978 movie
    version—(in Volume 2)
Silly People—cut (in Volume 2)
Two Fairy Tales—cut (in Volume 3)

Additional song recorded:
Love Takes Time—written for movie version; new lyric for *The Sun
    Won't Set*

A waltzing operetta hit, with a book only half as tangled as FOLLIES [April 4, 1971]. No harm, as Sondheim did everything so very well and inventively: the duet *Every Day A Little Death*, the trio of soliloquies, the ensemble's *The Glamorous Life*, and the quintet with their *Sun Won't Set*. *A Weekend In The Country* was musical, lyrical, and choral perfection—not only delightful, but covering what would otherwise have been pages and pages and pages of librettical explication. Sondheim also came up with *Send In The Clowns*, his only popular hit (as composer) to date.

CANDIDE

< Second Version >
see Bernstein [March 10, 1974]

THE FROGS

[MAY 20, 1974]   YALE UNIVERSITY SWIMMING POOL < NEW HAVEN,
   CONNECTICUT >   8 PERFORMANCES

Book and direction by Burt Shevelove
(Based on the play by Aristophanes)
Choreographed by Carmen de Lavallade
Produced by the Yale Repertory Theatre
With Larry Blyden, Alvin Epstein, Carmen de Lavallade, Anthony
Holland, Christopher Durang, Meryl Streep, and Sigourney Weaver

Songs published in "All Sondheim (Volume 2)":
Fear No More (lyric by William Shakespeare)
Invocation To The Gods And Instructions To The Audience

This Yale experiment created quite a splash. The built-in obstacles, though,
made it more curious than theatrical. (It was kind of boring, actually.) And
there were severe echo problems.

PACIFIC OVERTURES

JANUARY 11, 1976   WINTER GARDEN THEATRE   193 PERFORMANCES

Book by John Weidman
Additional material by Hugh Wheeler
Choreographed by Patricia Birch
Directed by Harold Prince
Produced by Prince in association with Ruth Mitchell
With Mako, Soon-Teck Oh, Sab Shimono, and Yuki Shimoda

Songs published in vocal score:
The Advantages Of Floating In The Middle Of The Sea
A Bowler Hat
Chrysanthemum Tea
Four Black Dragons
Lion Dance [instrumental]
Next
Please Hello
Poems

Pretty Lady
Someone In A Tree
There Is No Other Way
Welcome to Kanagawa

Sondheim and Prince attempted something different, and they certainly succeeded. Once again, the work was inaccessible due to an uninvolving book (although that wasn't the only problem). Sondheim's score took repeated hearings to enjoy, with *Pretty Lady* and *Someone In A Tree* standing out. *A Bowler Hat* was exceptional writing: a lucid statement of the show's overall theme, with the character himself ironically illustrating the point. Meanwhile, the high point of the evening was a scenic transition devised by Boris Aronson.

SIDE BY SIDE BY SONDHEIM

MAY 4, 1976   MERMAID THEATRE <LONDON>

APRIL 18, 1977   MUSIC BOX THEATRE <NEW YORK>   390
PERFORMANCES

Directed by Ned Sherrin
Produced (London) by H. M. Tennent, Ltd. and Cameron Mackintosh
Produced (New York) by Harold Prince in association with Ruth Mitchell and the Incomes Company, Ltd.
With Millicent Martin, Julia McKenzie, David Kernan, and Sherrin

Published song:
I Never Do Anything Twice (Madam's Song)—published in separate
    edition, originally used in 1976 movie "The Seven Percent Solution"

London, which had only seen productions of half of the Sondheim musicals, mounted this successful anthology revue. The Broadway transfer did quite well, too, until the cast was replaced by—of all people—Kukla, Fran, and Ollie.

SWEENEY TODD

The Demon Barber of Fleet Street

MARCH 1, 1979   URIS THEATRE   558 PERFORMANCES

Book by Hugh Wheeler
(Based on a play by Christopher Bond)
Choreographed by Larry Fuller
Directed by Harold Prince
Produced by Richard Barr, Charles Woodward, Robert Fryer, Mary Lea Johnson, and Martin Richards

With Len Cariou, Angela Lansbury, Victor Garber, Ken Jennings, and Edmund Lyndeck

Published songs:
Johanna
Not While I'm Around
Pretty Women

Additional songs published in vocal score:
Ah, Miss
The Ballad Of Sweeney Todd
The Barber And His Wife
By The Sea
City On Fire!
The Contest
Epiphany
Final Scene
God, That's Good!
Green Finch And Linnet Bird
Kiss Me
Johanna (Turpin Version)—cut
Ladies In Their Sensitivities
The Letter (Quintet)
A Little Priest
My Friends
No Place Like London
Parlor Songs
Pirelli's Miracle Elixir
Poor Thing
Wait
The Worst Pies In London

Sondheim's finest work to date. The other Sondheim/Prince shows had less than ideal books; SWEENEY TODD, with more plot than its predecessors, was constructed of music and worked far better. The composer wrote an extensive and varied score, ranging from moments of tender beauty (*Pretty Women* and *Not While I'm Around*) to moments of madness (*Johanna—Turpin Version*) and suppressed emotion (*The Barber And His Wife*). The *Epiphany* scene is unquestionably one of the most extraordinary segments in musical theatre writing. Len Cariou (of A LITTLE NIGHT MUSIC [February 25, 1973]) and Angela Lansbury (who had followed ANYONE CAN WHISTLE [April 4, 1964] with Tony Award-winning performances in two Jerry Herman musicals) were breathtaking.

MARRY ME A LITTLE

MARCH 12, 1981   ACTORS PLAYHOUSE < OFF-BROADWAY >   96
PERFORMANCES

Conceived and developed by Craig Lucas and Norman René
Directed by René
Produced by Diane de Mailly in association with William B. Young
With Lucas and Suzanne Henry

Song published in "All Sondheim (Volume 2)":
So Many People—written for unproduced 1954 musical SATURDAY NIGHT

Recorded songs (in initial theatrical use):
A Moment With You—written for SATURDAY NIGHT
Pour Le Sport—written for unproduced 1956 musical THE LAST RESORTS;
    see SUNDAY IN THE PARK WITH GEORGE [May 2, 1984]
Saturday Night—written for SATURDAY NIGHT

This revue featured cut and previously unused Sondheim material. (Songs
from produced musicals are listed with the original scores.) THE LAST RESORTS
was a short-lived Griffith and Prince project, with a Jean Kerr book (based on
Cleveland Amory material). Prince produced Sondheim's first musicals as
lyricist and composer, taking both properties over from other producers.
Prince did originate COMPANY [April 26, 1970] but not FOLLIES [April 4,
1971], which began in the mid-Sixties with GYPSY [May 21, 1959] producers
David Merrick and Leland Hayward. Merrick had been maneuvered off of
A FUNNY THING [May 8, 1962]; he was no doubt glad *not* to be waiting
around for the THE GIRLS UPSTAIRS after the curtain came down.

MERRILY WE ROLL ALONG

NOVEMBER 16, 1981   ALVIN THEATRE   16 PERFORMANCES

Book by George Furth
(Based on the play by George S. Kaufman and Moss Hart)
Choreographed by Larry Fuller
Directed by Harold Prince
Produced by Lord Grade, Martin Starger, Robert Fryer, and Prince
With Jim Walton, Ann Morrison, and Lonny Price

Published songs:
Good Thing Going
Not A Day Goes By

Additional songs published in vocal score:
Bobby And Jackie And Jack
Franklin Shepard, Inc.

The Hills Of Tomorrow
It's A Hit
Like It Was
Meet The Blob
Merrily We Roll Along
Now You Know
Old Friends
Opening Doors
Our Time
Rich And Happy

Additional song published in vocal selection:
Honey—cut

The Sondheim/Prince collaboration ran aground on this curious project. The unsuccessful 1934 Kaufman and Hart play had unsolvable problems; its main distinction was the then revolutionary (for Broadway) device of moving backwards in time. In 1981 the same unsolvable problems existed, and the novelty was no longer novel. The use of youthful actors and a jungle-gym production might have seemed workable at first, but something went wrong. Rather than adjusting, Sondheim and Prince appear to have merrily worked along in their own separate vacuums. The songs came off best, of course, Sondheim providing *Not A Day Goes By, Old Friends, Now You Know,* and the amazing quartet *It's A Hit.* The use of *Merrily We Roll Along* to move back through time worked better than the other conceptual choices of the evening. And mention must be made of the composer's choral work and the dazzling jazz orchestrations by Jonathan Tunick.

SUNDAY IN THE PARK WITH GEORGE

MAY 2, 1984   BOOTH THEATRE   604 PERFORMANCES

Book and direction by James Lapine
(Suggested by a painting by Georges Seurat)
Produced by The Shubert Organization and Emanuel Azenberg in
association with Playwrights Horizons (Andre Bishop)
With Mandy Patinkin, Bernadette Peters, Dana Ivey, and Charles
Kimbrough

Songs published in vocal selection:
Beautiful
Children And Art
Finishing The Hat
Move On
Putting It Together—solo version as revised for Barbara Streisand's 'The
        Broadway Album'; issued in nonshow edition
Sunday

Additional songs recorded:
Chromolume #7 [instrumental]
Color And Light
The Day Off—revised version of *Pour le Sport* (see **MARRY ME A LITTLE**
    [**March 12, 1981**])
Everybody Loves Louis
Gossip
It's Hot Up Here
Lesson #8
No Life
Putting It Together—show version
Sunday In The Park With George
We Do Not Belong Together

Working without Harold Prince for the first time since 1970, Sondheim wrote the uneven but special, Pulitzer Prize-winning **SUNDAY IN THE PARK WITH GEORGE**. The score, here, was the thing; and Broadway musicalizing did *not* work in the piece's favor. Minor weaknesses were only magnified by "theatrical" production values thought necessary for commercial success. Taking his cue from the palette of painter Seurat, Sondheim attempted musical pointillism and produced a first act of color and light: *Sunday*, lyric and music, illustrated the *painting* illustrating the *painter*. The people of 1884 on the island in Paris were real and relevant and interesting. Not so the Impressionist's model's grandson, with his laser-beam art and his doddering musical-comedy grandmother. The authors seemed to think they needed 1984 to prove their point, in the same unsuccessful way **PACIFIC OVERTURES** [**January 11, 1976**] jumped the century. But their 1884 was far more relevant to today than their 1984. As for musical *laser*ism, there seems to be no such thing; and practical lasers beamed over the head of the audience bought realism at the expense of imagery. Meanwhile, Sondheim was at the top of his form (make that *anyone*'s form) in *Finishing The Hat*. This was his second perfect hat song, following the *Bowler;* one can only hope for more. (Does anyone still *wear* a hat? . . .)

INTO THE WOODS

NOVEMBER 5, 1987   MARTIN BECK THEATRE   764 PERFORMANCES

Book and direction by James Lapine
Choreographed by Lar Lubovich
Produced by Heidi Landesman, Rocco Landesman, Rick Steiner, M. Anthony Fisher, Frederic H. Mayerson, and Jujamcyn Theatres
With Bernadette Peters, Joanna Gleason, Chip Zien, Tom Aldredge, and Robert Westenberg

Published songs:
No One Is Alone
Stay With Me

Additional songs published in vocal score:
Agony
Any Moment (Anything Can Happen In The Woods)
Children Will Listen
Cinderella At The Grave
Ever After
First Midnight
Giants In The Sky
Greens
Hello, Little Girl
I Guess This Is Goodbye
I Know Things Now
Into The Woods (Prologue Act One)
It Takes Two (You're Different In The Woods)
Lament (Children Won't Listen)
Last Midnight
Maybe They're Magic (Magic Beans)
Moments In The Woods
No More
On The Steps Of The Palace
So Happy (Prologue Act Two)
A Very Nice Prince
Your Fault

Additional song recorded:
Our Little World—added to 1990 London production

Sunday In The Park [May 2, 1984] was worthwhile, in my opinion, despite its conceptual flaws; Into The Woods was disappointing (and annoying), despite its attributes. Once again, Sondheim and Lapine's socially significant second act strived to show us the evils of Our Modern Times; once again, the device was labored and counterproductive. While Sunday attempted to grapple with the weighty theme of Life versus Art, Into The Woods merely took a potentially intriguing idea and spun it out in undistinguished fashion. No Sondheim score is boring, of course; there are always layers of textures, treasures, and tricks to enjoy. But Woods never paid off musically. The twelve-minute prologue (*Into the Woods*) is a perfect example: Sondheim takes us on a musical journey of bits and pieces, building to a glorious choral cacophony as in *A Weekend In The Country* from A Little Night Music [February 25, 1973]. But while *Weekend* went on to a rousingly exciting finish, *Woods* merely ended with a restatement of the refrain. Similar letdowns mute the fleetingly lovely *Any Moment* and *It Takes Two;* Sondheim seems to cut all of his loveliest *Moments In The Woods* short without satisfactory resolution. Presumably he was doing this on purpose, in a Rapunzelish attempt at weaving a continuous musical thread without stopping for individual highspots. (If so, how does he explain *Agony,* an inferior reworking of NIGHT MUSIC's *In Praise Of Women?*) The only exhilirating moments come in the *Your Fault/Last Midnight* segment, which is similar to—though not nearly as effective as—the exceptional *Epiphany* of SWEENEY TODD [March 1, 1979]. Much of the score, in fact, recalls similar but better moments in NIGHT MUSIC and SWEENEY. It's almost as if the composer determined to write a "popular" musical with commercial appeal (unsuccessfully, as it turned out); when the material didn't inspire him to new creative heights, he was forced to look backwards for ideas. Which is not the sort of creativity we've grown accustomed to—and desperately need—from Sondheim.

ASSASSINS

JANUARY 27, 1991   PLAYWRIGHTS HORIZONS
    < OFF-OFF-BROADWAY >   72 PERFORMANCES

Book by John Weidman
Choreographed by D. J. Giagni
Directed by Jerry Zaks
Produced by Playwrights Horizons (Andre Bishop)
With Victor Garber, Terrence Mann, Jonathan Hadary, Eddie Korbich, Annie Golden and Debra Monk

Songs published in vocal score *[*in preparation*]*:
Another National Anthem
The Ballad Of Booth
The Ballad Of Czolgosz
The Ballad Of Guiteau
Everybody's Got The Right
Gun Song
How I Saved Roosevelt
Unworthy Of Your Love

What a wonderful system where a true artist (i.e. Sondheim) can work on whatever he is compelled to work on (ASSASSINS), and can hear it mounted under optimum conditions (like at Playwrights Horizons) without the overpowering commercial and financial pressures of our legitimate theatre. Did ASSASSINS work? No. Was it conceptually flawed? Perhaps. Was it worth Sondheim's time and energy? Absolutely. My own opinion is that this was an interesting idea which didn't quite make it off the page and onto the stage. The collaborators formatted the show as a series of revue sketches, which was probably the best way to do it; but maybe they were writing sketches for two different revue/musicals? I should probably add that I thought the composer was also sabotaged by his librettist in their earlier collaboration, PACIFIC OVERTURES [January 11, 1976]. Had ASSASSINS been brought to Broadway it would, I believe, have been a failure on the grand scale, suffering the same ignominity as ANYONE CAN WHISTLE [April 4, 1964] and MERRILY WE ROLL ALONG [November 16, 1981]—two scores surely appreciated by all of us (except, perhaps, the investors). Mark ASSASSINS an unsuccessful experiment, perhaps; but who among us would want Sondheim to stop experimenting?

Stephen Sondheim has written fourteen shows, music and/or lyrics. Virtually all of his work is exceptional, although half of the shows—and a few of the scores—leave something to be desired. (Of the musicals he composed, only FORUM [May 8, 1962], COMPANY [April 26,1970], and A LITTLE NIGHT MUSIC [February 25, 1973] returned their investments and can be considered "hits"—but that is of little matter.) Sondheim has never settled for the merely adequate; virtually every song is interesting and intriguing. What is somewhat disconcerting is that the scores since SWEENEY TODD [March 1, 1979] have all been problematic. Perhaps he is trying to move us into a new style of musical theatre. Perhaps I just don't get it. Perhaps his next score—and we rely on him to keep toiling away, for he is irreplaceable—will dispel these concerns. Certainly, anything Mr. Sondheim sees fit to expend his efforts on is sure to be expertly crafted—and eagerly awaited!

Charles Strouse

BORN: June 7, 1928   New York, New York

Charles Strouse began his musical career with a training in serious composition. After graduating from the Eastman School of Music, he studied with
Nadia Boulanger in Paris and Aaron Copland before changing over to popular
music. His first theatre composing came in 1953, writing summer amateur
shows at Green Mansions (Harold Rome's training ground); his collaborator
was Lee Adams, a magazine editor. For three years Strouse supported himself
as a rehearsal pianist and accompanist, returning to Green Mansions for
summers of high-pressure songwriting.

SHOESTRING REVUE

FEBRUARY 28, 1955   PRESIDENT THEATRE < OFF-BROADWAY >   100
PERFORMANCES

Music and lyrics mostly by others
Lyrics to Strouse songs by Michael Stewart
Sketches by Stewart, Sheldon Harnick, and others
Directed by Christopher Hewett
Produced by Ben Bagley in association with Mr. and Mrs. Judson S. Todd
With Dorothy Greener, Beatrice Arthur, Dody Goodman, and Chita
Rivera

Recorded songs:
The History Of The World
Man's Inhumanity To Man
Three Loves

Twenty-two-year-old Ben Bagley came to New York and compiled three
memorable (if not overly successful) off-Broadway revues in two seasons;
featured were early songs and sketches by novices Strouse, Stewart, Adams,
Harnick, and Schmidt & Jones. Bagley then left the theatre, eventually alight-
ing in the record business. Strouse was musical director for the first SHOE-
STRING REVUE and placed interpolations in all three Bagley revues, this first
in collaboration with Mike Stewart.

THE LITTLEST REVUE

MAY 22, 1956   PHOENIX THEATRE < OFF-BROADWAY >   32
PERFORMANCES

Music mostly by Vernon **Duke** (also see **Blitzstein**)
Lyrics mostly by Ogden Nash
Sketches by Nat Hiken, Michael Stewart, and others
Directed by Paul Lammers
Produced by T. Edward Hambleton and Norris Houghton, by
arrangement with Ben Bagley
With Tammy Grimes, Charlotte Rae, Joel Grey, and Larry Storch

Recorded songs:
I Lost The Rhythm (lyric by Strouse)
Spring Doth Let Her Colours Fly (lyric by Lee Adams)

Spring Doth Let Her Colours Fly was written for Charlotte Rae as an opera
star doing a nightclub act. It was a very funny cartoon in words and (Wag-
nerian) music, suitable for the first New York work of Adams and Strouse.

SIXTH FINGER IN A FIVE FINGER GLOVE

OCTOBER 8, 1956   LONGACRE THEATRE   2 PERFORMANCES

Play by Scott Michel
Incidental music by Charles Strouse
Directed by John Holden
Produced by Gertrude Caplin and Thelma Fingar
With Jimmie Komack and Salome Jens

Published songs:
None

Strouse made his Broadway debut with this little horror, instantly proclaimed
one of the worst plays of the decade. The critics had virtually nothing favorable
to say—except that Strouse's original music (which included an impressionis-
tic ballet and "a daybed that folds up to music") deserved a better fate.

SHOESTRING '57

NOVEMBER 5, 1956   BARBIZON PLAZA THEATRE
< OFF-BROADWAY >   110 PERFORMANCES

Music mostly by others (see **Schmidt**)
Lyrics by Sheldon Harnick, Michael Stewart, Tom Jones, Carolyn Leigh,
and others

Lyrics to Strouse songs by Lee Adams
Choreographed by Danny Daniels
Directed by Paul Lammers
Produced by Ben Bagley in association with E. H. Morris
With Dody Goodman, Dorothy Greener, and Paul Mazursky

Recorded Song:
The Arts

E. H. Morris was a music publisher, using a new method for arranging interpolations: coproducing (financing) the show himself. While nothing of interest came from SHOESTRING '57, Morris signed three of the important early Sixties composers: Strouse, Carolyn Leigh's new partner Cy Coleman, and Jerry Herman. (Herman remains with the Morris group, now owned by Paul McCartney—who also owns Loesser's Frank Music.)

BYE BYE BIRDIE

APRIL 14, 1960   MARTIN BECK THEATRE   607 PERFORMANCES

Lyrics by Lee Adams
Book by Michael Stewart
Directed and choreographed by Gower Champion
Produced by Edward Padula in association with L. Slade Brown
With Chita Rivera, Dick Van Dyke, Susan Watson, Dick Gautier, and Kay Medford

Published Songs:
Baby, Talk To Me
Bye Bye Birdie—written for 1963 movie version
How Lovely To Be A Woman
Kids!
A Lot Of Livin' To Do
One Boy
One Last Kiss
Put On A Happy Face
Rosie

Additional songs published in vocal score:
An English Teacher
A Healthy, Normal American Boy
Honestly Sincere
Hymn For A Sunday Evening (Ed Sullivan)
One Hundred Ways Ballet [instrumental]
Shriner's Ballet [instrumental]

Spanish Rose
The Telephone Hour
We Love You Conrad
What Did I Ever See In Him?

To the surprise of everyone (including the authors), this cartoon musical was an enormously popular hit. After going through a number of different librettists including nightclub performer Mike Nichols, Michael Stewart—a TV writer for Sid Caesar and Strouse's lyricist for SHOESTRING REVUE [February 28, 1955]—came up with a book that worked. Gower (and Marge) Champion had been approached to star; instead, he directed his first book musical and became a major musical comedy force for a decade. Strouse, doing arrangements for the two-week flop GIRLS AGAINST THE BOYS [November 2, 1959], recommended the show's featured comic; he couldn't dance like Gower, but . . . Dick Van Dyke was joined by SHOESTRING REVUE alumna Chita Rivera, just back from the London production of WEST SIDE STORY [Bernstein: September 26, 1957]. Seriously inclined composer Strouse attempted simple pop tunes and rock lampoons—and found himself with *Put On A Happy Face, A Lot Of Livin' To Do, Rosie,* and the pretty *Baby, Talk To Me.*

ALL AMERICAN

MARCH 19, 1962   WINTER GARDEN THEATRE   80 PERFORMANCES

Lyrics by Lee Adams
Book by Mel Brooks
(Based on *Professor Fodorski* [novel] by Robert Lewis Taylor)
Choreographed by Danny Daniels
Directed by Joshua Logan
Produced by Edward Padula in association with L. Slade Brown
With Ray Bolger, Eileen Herlie, Fritz Weaver, Ron Husmann, and Anita Gillette

Published songs:
The Fight Song
If I Were You
I'm Fascinating
It's Fun To Think
I've Just Seen Her (As Nobody Else Has Seen Her)
Nightlife
Once Upon A Time
Our Children
We Speak The Same Language
What A Country!

Additional songs recorded:
Have A Dream
I Couldn't Have Done It Alone
Melt Us
Physical Fitness
The Real Me
Search Your Heart
Which Way?

The BYE BYE BIRDIE [April 14, 1960] team was quickly split: David Merrick snapped up Gower Champion and Mike Stewart to do, initially, CARNIVAL! [Merrill: April 13, 1961]. Strouse, Adams, and their producers turned to veteran Joshua Logan (directing his first of five musicals since FANNY [Rome: November 4, 1954]—all increasingly disastrous failures). The new librettist was another Sid Caesar comedy writer Strouse had met while composing dance music for "Your Show of Shows." Mel Brooks's one book show had been SHINBONE ALLEY [April 13, 1957], the stage version of "archie and mehitabel." Watching the troubled ALL AMERICAN tryout, Brooks began to wonder what'd happen if someone actually *tried* to produce a sure-fire musical bomb. The result: the 1968 Oscar-winning screen-play for "The Producers." The charm of Ray Bolger and Eileen Herlie wasn't enough to carry this charmless college football musical, which did include the gentle hit *Once Upon A Time* and the feathery soft-shoe *I'm Fascinating.*

HELLO, DOLLY!

JANUARY 16, 1964   ST. JAMES THEATRE   2,844 PERFORMANCES

Music and lyrics mostly by Jerry **Herman** (also see **Merrill**)
Book by Michael Stewart
(Based on *The Matchmaker* [play] by Thornton Wilder)
Directed and choreographed by Gower Champion
Produced by David Merrick
With Carol Channing, David Burns, Eileen Brennan, and Charles Nelson Reilly

When Gower Champion (of BYE BYE BIRDIE [April 14, 1960]) found his new musical ailing on the road, he called in Strouse and Adams for first-aid. For details, see **Herman: January 16, 1964.**

GOLDEN BOY

OCTOBER 20, 1964   MAJESTIC THEATRE   569 PERFORMANCES

Lyrics by Lee Adams
Book by Clifford Odets and William Gibson
(Based on the play by Odets)
Choreographed by Donald McKayle
Directed by Arthur Penn
Produced by Hillard Elkins
With Sammy Davis, Jr., Billy Daniels, and Paula Wayne

Published songs
Can't You See It?
Gimme Some
Golden Boy
I Want To Be With You
Lorna's Here
Night Song
Stick Around
This Is The Life
While The City Sleeps

Additional songs published in vocal selection:
Colorful
Don't Forget 127th Street
Everything's Great
No More

Additional song recorded:
What Became Of Me?—written for 1968 London production; see DANCE
    A LITTLE CLOSER [May 11, 1983]
Workout

The second Sammy Davis, Jr. Broadway vehicle had as many problems as the first (MR. WONDERFUL [Bock: March 22, 1956]); this time, at least, they started with strong basic material. But the 1937 Odets play was already clichéd; and the harried white manager, the young black newcomer who makes it big, etc. were familiar enough from both MR. WONDERFUL and the boxing BODY BEAUTIFUL [Bock: January 23, 1958]. The intent of the librettists (Odets died during the writing; Gibson came in, precipitating the replacement of Peter Coe by Arthur Penn) was admirable enough, but the results were anything but satisfying. Strouse had his first Broadway opportunity to write an emotional, nonlampoon score; what seemed like a complex departure from his BYE BYE BIRDIE [April 14, 1960] success was actually a return to his abstract training. *Night Song, Lorna's Here, I Want To Be With You,* and *Golden Boy* were all highly moving and fascinating in structure; and the seductive *While The City Sleeps* perfectly expressed what should have been the tone of the entire production. With GOLDEN BOY's failure Strouse went back to writing contemporary, pop musicals; his work hasn't shown such inventiveness and texture since.

"IT'S A BIRD, IT'S A PLANE, IT'S SUPERMAN"

MARCH 29, 1966   ALVIN THEATRE   129 PERFORMANCES

Lyrics by Lee Adams
Book by David Newman and Robert Benton
(Based on the comic strip)
Choreographed by Ernest Flatt
Directed by Harold Prince
Produced by Prince in association with Ruth Mitchell
With Jack Cassidy, Patricia Marand, Bob Holiday, Michael O'Sullivan, and Linda Lavin

Published songs:
It's Superman
Love Theme From Superman [instrumental]—nonlyric version of *What
    I've Always Wanted*
Superman March [instrumental]
Superman Theme
What I've Always Wanted
You've Got Possibilities

Additional songs published in vocal selection:
Doing Good
I'm Not Finished Yet
It's Super Nice
Ooh, Do You Love You!
Pow! Bam! Zonk!
Revenge
So Long, Big Guy
The Strongest Man In The World
We Don't Matter At All
We Need Him
The Woman For The Man Who Has Everything
You've Got What I Need, Baby

Strouse turned to comic-strip music for this comic-strip musical, with a particularly fine set of comedy lyrics by the underrated Lee Adams. Librettists Newman and Benton held on to their Superman treatment and successfully duplicated it a decade later in Hollywood—without Strouse, Adams, and Prince. For director/producer Prince it was the end of his standard-musical-comedy days: he determined to move away from the world of Abbott to the progressive world of Prince (via Robbins). First stop: CABARET [Kander: November 20, 1966].

APPLAUSE

MARCH 30, 1970   PALACE THEATRE   896 PERFORMANCES

Lyrics by Lee Adams
Book by Betty Comden and Adolph Green
(Based on *All About Eve* [story] by Mary Orr)
Directed and choreographed by Ron Field
Produced by Joseph Kipness, Lawrence Kasha, James M. Nederlander, and George Steinbrenner III
With Lauren Bacall, Len Cariou, Penny Fuller, and Bonnie Franklin

Published songs:
Applause
Backstage Babble
The Best Night Of My Life
But Alive
Good Friends
Hurry Back
It Was Always You—cut
Love Comes First—cut
One Of A Kind
She's No Longer A Gypsy
Something Greater
Think How It's Gonna Be (When We're Together Again)
Welcome To The Theatre

Additional songs published in vocal score:
Fasten Your Seat Belts
Inner Thoughts
One Hallowe'en
Who's That Girl?

Strouse and Adams had their second hit with this Lauren Bacall vehicle. The star ably carried her first musical, with assists from Len Cariou and the energetic Bonnie Franklin. Ron Field, fresh from two Harold Prince shows, did a fine job; but the score was not very good at all. Comden and Green provided book *without* lyrics for the first time in their career, replacing Sidney Michaels.

SIX

APRIL 12, 1971   CRICKET THEATRE < OFF-BROADWAY >   8
PERFORMANCES

Book and lyrics by Strouse
Directed by Peter Coe
Produced by Slade Brown
With Lee Beery, Gilbert Price, Hal Watters, and Alvin Ing

Published songs:
None

Reestablished on Broadway, Strouse expressed his abstract background with the experimental SIX. Produced on a small scale, the piece baffled audiences and was quickly withdrawn.

I AND ALBERT

NOVEMBER 6, 1972   PICCADILLY THEATRE < LONDON >   120
PERFORMANCES

Lyrics by Lee Adams
Book by Jay Presson Allen
Directed by John Schlesinger
Produced by Lewis M. Allen and Si Litvinoff
With Polly James and Sven-Bertil Taube

Published songs:
I And Albert
Just You And Me—see RAGS **[August 21, 1986]**
This Gentle Land
Victoria
Victoria And Albert Waltz [instrumental]

Additional songs recorded:
All Bless The Genius Of Man
Draw The Blinds
Enough!
Go It, Old Girl!
Hans
His Royal Highness
I've 'Eard The Bloody 'Indoos 'As It Worse
It Has All Begun
Leave It Alone
No One To Call Me Victoria

When You Speak With A Lady
The Widow At Windsor

Strouse and Adams seemed an unlikely pair to write a Victorian British musical about Queen and Consort. London audiences were not amused.

ANNIE

APRIL 21, 1977   ALVIN THEATRE   2,377 PERFORMANCES

Lyrics by Martin Charnin
Book by Thomas Meehan
(Based on "Little Orphan Annie" [comic strip])
Choreographed by Peter Gennaro
Directed by Charnin
Produced by Mike Nichols, Irwin Meyer, Stephen Friedman, and Lewis Allen
With Reid Shelton, Dorothy Loudon, Andrea McArdle, and Robert Fitch

Published songs:
Annie
Easy Street
I Don't Need Anything But You
It's The Hard-Knock Life
Let's Go To The Movies—written for 1982 movie version
Little Girls
Maybe
A New Deal For Christmas
N.Y.C.
Sandy (Dumb Dog)—written for movie version
Sign—written for movie version
Tomorrow
We Got Annie!—cut; initial publication upon reuse in movie version
You're Never Fully Dressed Without A Smile

Additional songs published in vocal score:
I Think I'm Gonna Like It Here
Something Was Missing—revised version of *You Rat, You* from 1968 movie "The Night They Raided Minsky's"
We'd Like To Thank You, Herbert Hoover
You Won't Be An Orphan For Long

An unlikely, impossible-to-get-produced cartoon musical finally got mounted —and was the runaway smash hit of the decade (second only to A CHORUS LINE [PART 4: April 15, 1975]). A 1976 summer-stock tryout at the Goodspeed

Opera House finally got ANNIE on her feet, but just barely. Then Mike Nichols came in to produce, assuring financing and offering helpful suggestions. Like adding a starring role for Dorothy Loudon, his original "Passionella" in THE WORLD OF JULES FEIFFER [Sondheim: July 2, 1962]). For Loudon, ANNIE was reward for consistently outstanding valor on such battlefields as Sidney Lumet's NOWHERE TO GO BUT UP [November 10, 1962], George Abbott's THE FIG LEAVES ARE FALLING [January 2, 1969], and Alan Jay Lerner's LOLITA, MY LOVE [February 16, 1971]. The score was synthetic and banal, although Strouse's work far outclassed the lyrics. The only originality in the piece was the delightfully sassy *We Got Annie.* They cut out the melody, cut out the rhythm, and retained the counter-melody for an insipid title song.

A BROADWAY MUSICAL

DECEMBER 21, 1978   LUNT-FONTANNE THEATRE   1 PERFORMANCE

Lyrics by Lee Adams
Book by William F. Brown
Directed and choreographed by Gower Champion
Produced by Norman Kean and Garth H. Drabinsky
With Warren Berlinger, Larry Marshall, Patti Karr, and Tiger Haynes

Song published in "Beautiful Broadway Melodies":
The 1934 Hot Chocolate Jazz Babies Revue

A poorly produced musical about a poorly produced musical, A BROADWAY MUSICAL played its out-of-town tryout *up* town. Librettist Brown (of THE WIZ [PART 4: January 5, 1975]) and Strouse and Adams (of GOLDEN BOY [October 20, 1964]) prepared a good-natured description of their experiences as white writers on black musicals. Things took on the very racial overtones they were trying to avoid when black director/choreographer George Faison (from the hit WIZ) was replaced by the white Gower Champion (in a slump since 1966). Opening in time for Broadway's big holiday week, A BROADWAY MUSICAL was long gone by Christmas Eve.

FLOWERS FOR ALGERNON

JUNE 14, 1979   QUEEN'S THEATRE < LONDON >   28 PERFORMANCES

CHARLIE AND ALGERNON

SEPTEMBER 14, 1980   HELEN HAYES THEATRE < NEW YORK >   17
PERFORMANCES

Book and lyrics by David Rogers
(Based on "Flowers for Algernon" [story] by Daniel Keyes)
Directed [London] by Peter Coe
Directed [New York] by Louis W. Scheeder
Produced [London] by Michael White in association with Isobel Robins
Konecky
Produced [New York] by Kennedy Center, Konecky, Fisher Theatre
Foundation, and Folger Theatre Group
With [London] Michael Crawford and Cheryl Rogers
With [New York] P. J. Benjamin and Sandy Faison

Published songs:
Charlie
I Got A Friend
Midnight Riding
No Surprises
Whatever Time There Is

Additional songs recorded:
Charlie And Algernon
Dream Safe With Me
His Name Is Charlie Gordon
Hey Look At Me!
I Can't Tell You
I Really Loved You
The Maze
Now
Our Boy Charlie
Reading
Some Bright Morning

Strouse once again departed from the conventional with seemingly impossible-to-handle subject matter. What had been pulled off in the 1968 movie "Charly" was too painful for a live audience. After a tryout in Ontario, the piece was unsuccessfully mounted in London. The production which eventually reached Broadway was of stock-company caliber (except for the sensitive performance by P. J. Benjamin) and an even quicker failure.

BRING BACK BIRDIE

MARCH 5, 1981   MARTIN BECK THEATRE   4 PERFORMANCES

Lyrics by Lee Adams
Book by Michael Stewart
(Based on characters from *Bye Bye Birdie*
Directed and choreographed by Joe Layton
Produced by Lee Guber, Shelly Gross, Slade Brown, and Jim Milford
With Donald O'Connor, Chita Rivera, Maria Karnilova, and Maurice Hines

Songs published in "Beautiful Broadway Melodies":
Middle Age Blues
Young

Additional songs recorded:
Baby, You Can Count On Me
Back In Show Business Again
Bring Back Birdie
Half Of A Couple
I Like What I Do
I Love 'Em All
Inner Peace
A Man Worth Fightin' For
Movin' Out
There's A Brand New Beat In Heaven
Twenty Happy Years
Well, I'm Not
When Will Grown-ups Grow Up?
You Can Never Go Back

BYE BYE BIRDIE [April 14, 1990]'s phenomenal success in the stock and amateur field (i.e., high school and community group production) prompted the authors to write a sequel—for that market. BRING BACK BIRDIE was *not* written or suitable for Broadway, but overenthusiastic stock producers got hold of the piece. They'd have been much better off bringing back BIRDIE.

UPSTAIRS AT O'NEALS

Cabaret Revue

OCTOBER 28, 1982   O'NEAL'S RESTAURANT < OFF-BROADWAY >   308
PERFORMANCES

Music and lyrics mostly by others
Conceived and directed by Martin Charnin
Produced by Charnin and Michael and Patrick O'Neal

Song recorded:
Boy Do We Need It Now (music and lyric by Strouse)

Strouse contributed this song to a revue devised by ANNIE [April 21, 1977] collaborator Charnin.

THE NIGHTINGALE

DECEMBER 18, 1982   LYRIC THEATRE < HAMMERSMITH, ENGLAND >

Book and lyrics by Strouse
Choreographed by Gillian Gregory
Directed by Peter James
Produced by the Lyric Theatre
With Sarah Brightman, Susannah Fellows, and Gordon Sandison

Songs published in vocal score:
Charming
Death Duet
The Emperor Is A Man
I Was Lost
The Mechanical Bird
Never Speak Directly To An Emperor
The Nightingale
Perfect Harmony
Please Don't Make Me Hear That Song Again
Rivers Cannot Flow Upwards
A Singer Must Be Free
Take Us To The Forest
We Are China
Who Are These People?
Why Am I So Happy?

Despite his string of post-ANNIE [April 21, 1977] failures, Strouse continued to get productions of almost everything he turned out. This was an all-Strouse children's opera, initially mounted April 25, 1982 by The First All Children's Theatre (a New York-based amateur group).

DANCE A LITTLE CLOSER

MAY 11, 1983   MINSKOFF THEATRE   1 PERFORMANCE

Book, lyrics and direction by Alan Jay Lerner
(Based on *Idiot's Delight* [play] by Robert E. Sherwood)
Choreography by Billy Wilson
Produced by Frederick Brisson, Jerome Minskoff, James Nederlander, and Kennedy Center
With Len Cariou, Liz Robertson (Lerner), and George Rose

Published songs:
Another Life
Dance A Little Closer—new lyric for *What Became Of Me?* written for
        1968 London production of GOLDEN BOY [October 20, 1964]
I Never Want To See You Again
There's Always One You Can't Forget

Additional song published in "Beautiful Broadway Melodies":
There's Never Been Anything Like Us

Additional songs recorded:
Anyone Who Loves
Auf Wiedersehen
Happy Happy New Year
He Always Comes Home To Me
Homesick
I Don't Know
I Got A New Girl
It Never Would've Worked
Mad
No Man Is Worth It
On Top Of The World
Pas De Deux
What Are You Going To Do About It?
Why Can't The World Go And Leave Us Alone?
A Woman Who Thinks I'm Wonderful

DANCE A LITTLE CLOSER was a total, if momentary, shambles. However, two of the surviving songs—*Another Life* and *There's Always One You Can't Forget*—are particularly worthwhile. Strouse here displayed more emotion and melodic inventiveness than in anything he'd written since GOLDEN BOY [October 20, 1964].

MAYOR

MAY 13, 1985   VILLAGE GATE UPSTAIRS < OFF-BROADWAY >   268
PERFORMANCES

Music and lyrics by Charles Strouse
Book by Warren Leight
(Based on the autobiography by Edward I. Koch)
Choreographed by Barbara Siman (Strouse)
Directed by Jeffrey B. Moss
Produced by Martin Richards, Jerry Kravat, Mary Lea Johnson with the
New York Music Company
With Lenny Wolpe

Published songs:
Good Times
I'll Never Leave You (We Are One)
Mayor
My City

Additional songs published in vocal selection:
Ballad
Hootspa
How'm I Doin'?
I Want To Be The Mayor
The Last 'I Love New York' Song
March Of The Yuppies
What You See Is What You Get
You Can Be A New Yorker, Too!
You're Not The Mayor

Strouse wrote his own lyrics for this harmless, charmless cabaret revue.

RAGS

The New American Musical

AUGUST 21, 1986   MARK HELLINGER THEATRE   4 PERFORMANCES

Lyrics by Stephen Schwartz
Book by Joseph Stein
Choreographed by Ron Field
Directed by Gene Saks
Produced by Lee Guber, Martin Heinfling, and Marvin A. Krauss
With Teresa Stratas, Larry Kert, Dick Latessa, Terrence Mann, Lonny
Price, and Judy Kuhn

Songs recorded:
Blame It On The Summer Night
Brand New World—revised version of *Just You And Me* from I AND
      ALBERT [November 6, 1972]
Bread And Freedom (Sisters We Stand)
The Cherry Street Cafe
Children Of The Wind
Dancing With The Fools
Easy For You
For My Mary
Greenhorns
Hard To Be A Prince
I Remember
Kaddish
Nothing Will Hurt Us Again
Penny A Tune (East Side Melodies)
Rags
The Sound Of Love (Gramophone Sequence)
Three Sunny Rooms
Uptown
Wanting
What's Wrong With That?
Yankee Boy

A new musical from the composer of ANNIE [Strouse: April 21, 1977]!; the lyricist of PIPPIN [S. Schwartz: October 23, 1972]!; the librettist of FIDDLER ON THE ROOF [Bock: September 22, 1964]! Couldn't miss, right? Of course, these same gents were also guilty of the more recent BRING BACK BIRDIE [Strouse: March 5, 1981], WORKING [S. Schwartz: May 14, 1978], and SO LONG, 174TH STREET [May 9, 1976]. More to the point, the three collaborators seemed to have been working in three separate vacuums. RAGS was misguided, misconceived, and misdirected. Don't blame Gene Saks, either; he was only there for the last three weeks. As it happens, Strouse provided his best work since SUPERMAN [March 29, 1966]. The musical concept—taking old world melodies and throwing them into the melting pot of new world ragtime—worked extremely well on four songs: *Brand New World, Greenhorns, Rags,* and the exquisitely bluesy *Blame It On The Summer Night.* The rest of the music ranged from ordinary to n.s.g.; but those lyrics! "Oy!," as the characters in RAGS would say, and did.

ANNIE 2 (MISS HANNIGAN'S REVENGE)

[JANUARY 4, 1990]   KENNEDY CENTER OPERA HOUSE <WASHINGTON, D.C.>; CLOSED DURING PRE-BROADWAY TRYOUT

Lyrics and direction by Martin Charnin
Book by Thomas Meehan
(Based on *Little Orphan Annie* [comic strip] and the musical **Annie**)
Choreographed by Danny Daniels
Produced by Lewis Allen, Roger Berlind, Martin Heinfling and Fifth
Avenue Productions/Margo Lion Ltd.
With Dorothy Loudon, Harve Presnell, Ronny Graham, Lauren Mitchell,
Marian Seldes, and Danielle Findley

Published songs:
When You Smile (I Smile)
A Younger Man

First off, let me say that this entry might be presumptive: it's still possible that an overhauled **ANNIE 2** will make it to Broadway (**ANNIE 2(B)**, perhaps?). If so, it will be dealt with in the next edition of *Show Tunes* in the same manner as other reborn folderoos like **CHU-CHEM** [Leigh: March 17, 1989] and **MEET ME IN ST. LOUIS** [Martin: November 2, 1989]. Secondly, I readily admit that I didn't much like **ANNIE** [April 21, 1977], either. But **ANNIE** was at least humorous, in a simplistic way. **ANNIE 2** was remarkable in that it was one of the most mirthless musicals in memory. (I saw it twice, and counted one good joke.) The major problem stemmed from **ANNIE**'s 1976 summer-stock tryout, in which secondary character Miss Hannigan was found to be a real crowd-pleaser. The role was beefed up for Broadway, with Dorothy Loudon carrying the show; but compared to Annie and Daddy and Sandy, Miss H. was *still* only a secondary character. **ANNIE 2 (MISS HANNIGAN'S REVENGE)** cast the villainess as leading lady. Since the plot made her a fugitive from justice, she couldn't play many scenes with the kid, could she? (As it was, nobody recognized her except the dog.) So you had a musical in which the star and the main characters barely met. To those who say we should be less critical at "family shows" and heed audience reaction instead, I offer this eyewitness report: a sweet little ribboned-and-bowed miss sitting a couple of rows over me threw up in the first act, 'round about the time the lyricist rhymed "squash" with "galoshes."

Charles Strouse's record shows thirteen full-scale musicals, ten of which have been failures. Only two of his scores have been particularly exciting, **BYE BYE BIRDIE** [April 14, 1960] and **GOLDEN BOY** [October 20, 1964]. And then there was **ANNIE** [April 21, 1977], as big a hit as anyone ever needs to be set for life. Annie's *Tomorrow* has brought six quick flops so far, five of them—A Broadway Musical [December 21, 1978], Bring Back Birdie [March 5, 1981], Dance A Little Closer [May 11, 1983], Rags [August 21, 1986], and Annie 2 [January 4, 1990]—lighting the lights of Broadway for a total of only 10 performances *combined.* (How's that for a record??) Nevertheless, bits of Strouse's recent flops demonstrate that he is still capable of writing a highly catchy show tune; and he deserves credit for not throwing in the proverbial sponge, at least. We're sure to hear more Charles Strouse on Broadway: the underfinanced Nick And Nora and the stillborn Annie 2 still threaten to hit the street. Perhaps Mr. Strouse will be lucky once more.

Cy Coleman

BORN: June 14, 1929 Bronx, New York

A piano prodigy, Cy Coleman began his musical training in serious music before turning to pop in the late Forties. Coleman started writing songs with lyricist Joseph McCarthy, Jr. (whose father wrote IRENE [PART 4: November 1, 1919]) while playing in nightclubs.

JOHN MURRAY ANDERSON'S ALMANAC

DECEMBER 10, 1953   IMPERIAL THEATRE   229 PERFORMANCES

Music mostly by Richard **Adler** and Jerry Ross
Sketches by Jean Kerr, William K. Wells, and others
Choreographed by Donald Saddler
Directed by John Murray Anderson and Cyril Ritchard
Produced by Michael Grace, Stanley Gilkey, and Harry Rigby
With Hermione Gingold, Billy DeWolfe, Harry Belafonte, and Orson Bean

Published song:
Tin Pan Alley (lyric by Joseph McCarthy, Jr.)

Coleman interpolated this song, which held its own against the rest of the JOHN MURRAY ANDERSON'S ALMANAC score.

COMPULSION

OCTOBER 24, 1957   AMBASSADOR THEATRE   140 PERFORMANCES

Play by Meyer Levin
Original music by Cy Coleman
Directed by Alex Segal
Produced by Michael Myerberg
With Roddy McDowall and Dean Stockwell

Published song:
Compulsion [instrumental]

Coleman first worked in the theatre as musical director of this drama based on the Leopold and Loeb case. At about the same time, he found a new lyricist: Carolyn Leigh, best known for her work on the Mary Martin **PETER PAN** (Fourth Version) [**Styne: October 20, 1954**]. Their collaboration immediately turned out pop hits like the 1957 *Witchcraft.*

DEMI-DOZEN

Nightclub Revue

OCTOBER 11, 1958   UPSTAIRS AT THE DOWNSTAIRS < OFF-BROADWAY >

Music mostly by Harvey **Schmidt**
Directed by John Heawood
Produced by Julius Monk
With Jane Connell and Gerry Matthews

Published song:
You Fascinate Me So (lyric by Carolyn Leigh)

MEDIUM RARE

An Intimate Musical Revue

JUNE 29, 1960   HAPPY MEDIUM THEATRE < CHICAGO,
        ILLINOIS >   1,210 PERFORMANCES

Music mostly by others
Directed by Bill Penn
Produced by Robert Weiner
With Anne Meara, Jerry Stiller, and Bobo Lewis

Published song:
The Tempo Of The Times (lyric by Carolyn Leigh)

WILDCAT

DECEMBER 16, 1960   ALVIN THEATRE   172 PERFORMANCES

Lyrics by Carolyn Leigh
Book by N. Richard Nash
Directed and choreographed by Michael Kidd
Produced by Kidd and Nash
With Lucille Ball, Keith Andes, Edith King, Paula Stewart, and Swen Swenson

Published songs:
Angelina—cut
Give A Little Whistle
Hey, Look Me Over!
One Day We Dance
Tall Hope
What Takes My Fancy
You're Far Away From Home—cut
You've Come Home

Additional songs published in vocal score:
Corduroy Road
Dancing On My Tippy-Tippy Toes
El Sombrero
Oil!
Wildcat—cut; included (no lyric) in *Overture*, also recorded with lyric
You're A Liar!

Additional song recorded:
That's What I Want For Janie

The successful pop songs of Coleman and Leigh resulted in this assignment, Lucille Ball's Broadway musical debut (and farewell). Manufactured solely for the purpose of cashing in on Ball's television popularity, WILDCAT had little of interest in it; when Ball "became ill," the show quickly closed. Coleman came up with the hit *Hey, Look Me Over!* and the melodic *You've Come Home.*

LITTLE ME

NOVEMBER 17, 1962   LUNT-FONTANNE THEATRE   257 PERFORMANCES

Lyrics by Carolyn Leigh
Book by Neil Simon
(Based on the novel by Patrick Dennis)
Choreographed by Bob Fosse
Directed by Cy Feuer and Fosse
Produced by Feuer and Ernest Martin
With Sid Caesar, Virginia Martin, Nancy Andrews, and Swen Swenson

Published songs:
Deep Down Inside
Dimples
Don't Ask A Lady—written for revival [January 21, 1982; 36
     performances]

Here's To Us
I Wanna Be Yours—written for revival
I've Got Your Number
Le Grand Boom-Boom
Little Me
On The Other Side Of The Tracks
Poor Little Hollywood Star
Real Live Girl
To Be A Performer!—revised lyric for 1958 nonshow song

Additional songs recorded:
Goodbye (The Prince's Farewell)
I Love You
Rich Kids' Rag [instrumental]
The Truth

Feuer and Martin followed **How To Succeed In Business Without Really Trying** [Loesser: October 14, 1961] with another fast-paced, brash musical. Comedienne Virginia Martin was brought along, as well as choreographer Fosse (codirecting with Feuer). Coleman combined his two strongest musical traits—rhythmic jazz and humor—in a gem of a score, to sparkling Leigh lyrics. Neil Simon, whose only musical work had been in television, provided one of the very funniest librettos. And Sid Caesar headed the good cast. Yet, **Little Me** was a disappointing failure—possibly because it had no heart. When the authors tried to "fix" **Little Me** twenty years later, the changes made it pale, weak, and not even funny.

SWEET CHARITY

January 30, 1966   Palace Theatre   608 performances

Lyrics by Dorothy Fields
Book by Neil Simon
(Based on *Nights of Cabiria* [movie] by Federico Fellini, Tullio Pinelli, and Ennio Flaiano)
Conceived, directed and choreographed by Bob Fosse
Produced by Fryer, Carr, and Harris
With Gwen Verdon, John McMartin, Helen Gallagher, and Thelma Oliver

Published songs:
Baby, Dream Your Dream
Big Spender
Gimme A Rain Check—cut
I Love To Cry At Weddings

I'm A Brass Band
I'm The Bravest Individual (I Have Ever Met) [1st]
If My Friends Could See Me Now
It's A Nice Face—written for 1969 movie version
My Personal Property—written for movie version
Poor Everybody Else—cut; also used in SEESAW [March 18, 1973]
The Rhythm Of Life
Sweet Charity [1st] (*Charity's Theme*) [instrumental]
Sweet Charity [2nd]—new lyric for *You Wanna Bet* (cut)
Sweet Charity [3rd]—written for movie version; new music for lyric of
     Sweet Charity [2nd]
There's Gotta Be Something Better Than This
Too Many Tomorrows
Where Am I Going?
You Should See Yourself
You Wanna Bet—cut; used with new lyric as *Sweet Charity* [2nd]

Additional songs published in vocal score:
Charity's Soliloquy
Rich Man's Frug [1st] [instrumental]

Additional songs recorded:
I'm The Bravest Individual (I Have Ever Met) [2nd]—new music for lyric
     of *I'm The Bravest Individual* [1st]; written for revival [April 27,
     1986; 368 performances]
Pompeii Club (Rich Man's Frug [2nd]) [instrumental]—written for movie
     version
Rebirth (Finale) [instrumental]—written for movie version

Since REDHEAD [PART 4: February 5, 1959], Bob Fosse's only success had been
as replacement choreographer on HOW TO SUCCEED IN BUSINESS WITHOUT
REALLY TRYING [Loesser: October 14, 1961]. With SWEET CHARITY, Fosse
entered a new stage in his career. Leaving the confines of the Abbott-in-
fluenced well-made book musical, the director/choreographer began to im-
print his influence on the material more fully than even Robbins did. CHARITY
boasted the return to the stage of Gwen Verdon, who had followed REDHEAD
by marrying Fosse. REDHEAD lyricist Dorothy Fields was partnered with Coleman from LITTLE ME [November 17, 1962]. Facing book problems, Fosse
replaced librettist Bert Lewis (a.k.a. Robert Lewis Fosse) with Neil Simon; the
result was a cartoon musical valentine. Some of the material was uneven, but
Verdon and Fosse kept things moving. In places like the *Big Spender* number,
all theatrical elements blended perfectly.

KEEP IT IN THE FAMILY

SEPTEMBER 27, 1967   PLYMOUTH THEATRE   5 PERFORMANCES

Play by Bill Naughton
Directed by Allan Davis
Produced by David Merrick
With Maureen O'Sullivan, Patrick Magee, and Karen Black

Published song:
Keep It In The Family (lyric by Dorothy Fields)

SEESAW

MARCH 18, 1973   URIS THEATRE   296 PERFORMANCES

Lyrics by Dorothy Fields
Book and direction by Michael Bennett
(Based on *Two for the Seesaw* [play] by William Gibson)
Choreographed by Bennett and Grover Dale (with Tommy Tune)
Produced by Joseph Kipness, Lawrence Kasha, James Nederlander, and
George Steinbrenner III
With Michele Lee, Ken Howard, and Tommy Tune

Published songs:
He's Good For Me
I'm Way Ahead
In Tune
It's Not Where You Start
My City
Nobody Does It Like Me
Poor Everybody Else—originally used in (cut from) SWEET CHARITY
    [January 20, 1966]
Ride Out The Storm
Seesaw
Spanglish
We've Got It
Welcome To Holiday Inn
You're A Lovable Lunatic

Additional song recorded:
Chapter 54, Number 1909

William Gibson's two-character play was blown up into a massive trouble-
ridden production. Star Lainie Kazan and director Edwin Sherin were both
replaced in Detroit. Michael Bennett came in to redirect and replace a good

deal of the choreography; he also took credit for the book after Mike Stewart departed. The best moments: the inventively staged and well-written title song and the finale *I'm Way Ahead.* Seesaw was the final show of Dorothy Fields' long career. She died March 28, 1974.

STRAWS IN THE WIND

February 21, 1975   American Place Theatre
    < off-Broadway >   33 performances

Music mostly by others
Lyrics to Coleman songs by Betty Comden and Adolph Green
Directed by Phyllis Newman
Produced by American Place Theatre
With Tovah Feldshuh, Brandon Maggart, and Josh Mostel

Recorded songs:
The Lost Word
Simplified Language

HELLZAPOPPIN'!

[November 22, 1976]   Mechanic Theatre < Baltimore,
    Maryland > ; closed during pre-Broadway tryout

Music mostly by Hank Beebe and Jule **Styne**
Lyrics by Carolyn Leigh and Bill Heyer
Book by Abe Burrows and others
(Based on a format by Olsen and Johnson)
Choreographed by Donald Saddler
Directed by Jerry Adler
Produced by Alexander H. Cohen in association with Maggie and Jerome Minskoff
With Jerry Lewis, Lynn Redgrave, Joey Faye, and Brandon Maggart

Published songs:
None

I LOVE MY WIFE

April 17, 1977   Ethel Barrymore Theatre   857 performances

Book and lyrics by Michael Stewart
(Based on a play by Luis Rego)
Choreographed by Onna White

Directed by Gene Saks
Produced by Terry Allen Kramer and Harry Rigby by arrangement with
Joseph Kipness
With Lenny Baker, James Naughton, Joanna Gleason, and Ilene Graff

Published songs:
Hey There, Good Times
I Love My Wife
Love Revolution
Someone Wonderful I Missed

Additional songs published in vocal selection:
By Threes
Ev'rybody Today Is Turning On
Lovers On Christmas Eve
Married Couple Seeks Married Couple
Monica
A Mover's Life
Scream
Sexually Free
We're Still Friends

Following the death of Dorothy Fields, Coleman teamed up with Comden
and Green for ON THE TWENTIETH CENTURY [February 19, 1978]. While
that show was in preparation, Mike Stewart (who had worked with Coleman
on SEESAW [March 18, 1973]) found this French comedy and proposed an
intimate musical. Stewart wrote his first lyrics since the SHOESTRING REVUE
[Strouse: November 5, 1955]) and I LOVE MY WIFE was a surprise hit—boast-
ing the charm of Lenny Baker, an on-stage combo wearing Santa Claus suits,
and little else.

ON THE TWENTIETH CENTURY

FEBRUARY 19, 1978   ST. JAMES THEATRE   449 PERFORMANCES

Book and lyrics by Betty Comden and Adolph Green
(Based on *Twentieth Century* [play] by Ben Hecht and Charles
MacArthur)
Choreographed by Larry Fuller
Directed by Harold Prince
Produced by Robert Fryer, Mary Lea Johnson, James Cresson, and Martin
Richards
With John Cullum, Madeline Kahn, Imogene Coca, and Kevin Kline

Published songs:
Never
On The Twentieth Century
Our Private World

Additional songs published in vocal selection:
Five Zeros
I Rise Again
I've Got It All
The Legacy
Life Is Like A Train
Mine
Repent
She's A Nut
Sign, Lily, Sign (Sextet)
Stranded Again
Together
Veronique

Additional song recorded:
Babette
Lily, Oscar

Despite Tony Award-winning performances by John Cullum and Kevin Kline and a lavish art deco production by Robin Wagner, ON THE TWENTIETH CENTURY was top-heavy and ran out of steam. Coleman deserted his normal style for mock operetta, an experiment which didn't work. But Wagner's train, in life-size and miniature, did.

HOME AGAIN, HOME AGAIN

[MARCH 12, 1979]   AMERICAN SHAKESPEARE THEATRE   < STRATFORD, CONNECTICUT > ; CLOSED DURING PRE-BROADWAY TRYOUT

Lyrics by Barbara Fried
Book by Russell Baker
Choreographed by Onna White
Directed by Gene Saks
Produced by Irwin Meyer and Stephen R. Friedman
With Lisa Kirk, Dick Shawn, Anita Morris, and Mike Kellin

Published songs:
None

With a book by *The New York Times* columnist Russell Baker and staging by the I LOVE MY WIFE [April 17, 1977] team, HOME AGAIN, HOME AGAIN held some promise. But the producers—minor cogs from the ANNIE [April 21, 1977] team—ran into severe problems and HOME AGAIN was stranded on the road. Not only did Meyer and Freidman produce three flops in ten months, they also landed in the hoosegow for a coal mining tax shelter fraud. (Their biggest victim was one E. Presley, a former pop singer, who dropped $510,-000.)

BARNUM

APRIL 30, 1980   ST. JAMES THEATRE   854 PERFORMANCES

Lyrics by Michael Stewart
Book by Mark Bramble
Directed and choreographed by Joe Layton
Produced by Coleman, Judy Gordon, and Maurice and Lois F. Rosenfield
With Jim Dale, Glenn Close, and Marianne Tatum

Published songs:
The Colors Of My Life
Come Follow The Band
Join The Circus
One Brick At A Time
There Is A Sucker Born Every Minute

Additional songs published in vocal selection:
Bigger Isn't Better
Black And White
I Like Your Style
Love Makes Such Fools Of Us All
Museum Song
Out There
The Prince of Humbug
Thank God I'm Old

The concept of BARNUM—a circus atmosphere overtaking the theatre space and spilling through the audience—combined with Jim Dale's bravura performance to make for a moderate hit. After less than inspiring management on SEESAW [March 18, 1973] and HOME AGAIN, HOME AGAIN [March 12, 1979], Coleman tried his hand at coproducing, with more satisfactory results.

WELCOME TO THE CLUB

APRIL 13, 1989   MUSIC BOX THEATRE   12 PERFORMANCES

Lyrics by Coleman and A. E. Hotchner
Book by Hotchner
Choreographed by Patricia Birch
Directed by Peter Mark Schifter
Produced by Coleman, Hotchner, William H. Kessler Jr., and Michael M. Weatherly
With Avery Schreiber, Marilyn Sokol, Marcia Mitzman, and Sally Mayes

Published song:
At My Side

Mr. Coleman was to round out the decade on a high note, but not before things got pretty gruesome indeed. WELCOME TO THE CLUB tried out under the title LET 'EM ROT. Enough said?

CITY OF ANGELS

DECEMBER 11, 1989   VIRGINIA THEATRE   647 PERFORMANCES
        [STILL RUNNING AS OF JUNE 30, 1991]

Lyrics by David Zippel
Book by Larry Gelbart
Choreographed by Walter Painter
Directed by Michael Blakemore
Produced by Nick Vanoff, Roger Berlind, Jujamcyn Theatres, Suntory International Corp., and The Shubert Organization
With James Naughton, Gregg Edelman, Randy Graff, Dee Hoty, Kay McClelland, and Rene Auberjonois

Published songs:
Funny
Lost And Found
With Every Breath I Take
You Can Always Count On Me

Additional songs published in vocal selection:
Alaura's Theme—published with cut lyric
Ev'rybody's Gotta Be Somewhere
L.A. Blues—published with cut lyric
Stay With Me
Theme From 'City Of Angels'
What You Don't Know About Women

Additional songs recorded:
All You Have To Do Is Wait
The Buddy System
Double Talk (Stine's Opening)
It Needs Work
The Tennis Song (The Ball Is In Your Court)
You Gotta Look Out For Yourself

Cy Coleman and neophyte lyricist David Zippel ended the Eighties with Broadway's best score of the decade. This is not as complimentary as it might sound, I'm afraid, as a glance at the Chronological Listing of Productions in Appendix One will show. (The best score of the decade—by far—was heard off-Broadway, William Finn's MARCH OF THE FALSETTOS [PART 4: April 1, 1981].) CITY OF ANGELS was brilliant compared to its competition, at least. So what if the lyrics were better than the music, and the book was better than the lyrics. But all is not well when the jokes are more memorable than the songs. Coleman harkened back to his jazz background to create some incredibly liquid melodies, like *Double Talk,* Theme from *'City Of Angels,'* *What You Don't Know About Women,* and *Ev'rybody's Gotta Be Somewhere.* This last song/scene had especially fine work from Zippel, Broadway's most impressive new songwriter since Maury Yeston debuted with NINE [PART 4: May 9, 1982]. But the score eventually suffered from a certain lack of restraint, with perhaps *too* many inventive novelty numbers exploiting the plot's double exposure. (The brilliant vocal arrangements—the best since the heyday of Hugh Martin, thanks to one Yaron Gershovsky—never let down.) Assorted combinations of real and "reel" characters, in and out of disguise, sang with (and against) themselves; but of true emotion there was virtually none. The one ballad, *With Every Breath I Take,* was a little bit *too* torchy (by design) to be taken seriously. The alter-ego duet *You're Nothing Without Me* started out strong and builds entertainingly, but didn't pay off nearly so well as its progenitor *Little Me.* The same can be said of CITY OF ANGELS as a whole: high entertainment, but the best element was the jokebook—and the score just couldn't keep up with that Gelbartian plot packed with purposely contrived contrivances.

THE WILL ROGERS FOLLIES

MAY 1, 1991   PALACE THEATRE   69 PERFORMANCES
     [STILL RUNNING AS OF JUNE 30, 1991]

Lyrics by Betty Comden and Adolph Green
Book by Peter Stone
Directed and choreographed by Tommy Tune
Produced by Pierre Cossette, Martin Richards, Sam Crothers, James M.

Nederlander, Stewart F. Lane, and Max Weitzenhoffer in association with Japan Satellite Broadcasting, Inc.
With Keith Carradine, Dee Hoty, Dick Latessa, and Cady Huffman

Published songs [at present]:
Look Around
Never Met A Man I Didn't Like

Additional songs recorded:
The Big Time
Give A Man Enough Rope
I Got You/First Act Finale
It's A Boy!
Let's Go Flying
Marry Me Now
My Big Mistake
My Unknown Someone
No Man Left For Me
Our Favorite Son
Presents For Mrs. Rogers
So Long Pa
We're Heading For A Wedding
Wild West Show/Dog Act [instrumental]
Will-A-Mania
Without You

I, personally, wasn't wild about BARNUM [April 30, 1980] and quite disliked WOMAN OF THE YEAR [Kander: March 29, 1981] and GRAND HOTEL [PART 4: November 12, 1989]; so perhaps I'm not the person to ask about THE WILL ROGERS FOLLIES? Musically speaking, Cy (*Never Wrote a Song I Didn't Like*) Coleman returned to his pre-CITY OF ANGELS [December 11, 1989] form (remember WELCOME TO THE CLUB [April 13, 1989?]). The lyrics by Comden and Green, who within two days of the opening turned one hundred fifty-one years old, were very tired. Yes, the pair—in tandem with the Messrs. Abbott, Robbins, Bernstein and/or Styne—had played a key role in formulating the post-PAL JOEY [Rodgers: December 25, 1940] *comedy* musical comedy; but their last satisfying set of lyrics had come in 1967. Peter Stone, with the well-crafted 1776 [PART 4: March 16, 1969] to his credit (along with such creaky clunkers as KEAN [November 2, 1961], SKYSCRAPER [November 13, 1965], TWO BY TWO [Rodgers: November 10, 1970], SUGAR [Styne: April 9, 1972], and the aforementioned WOMAN OF THE YEAR), contributed the laughless book. Director/choreographer/magician Tommy Tune appeared once more to have pulled a tip-tapping rabbit out of his top hat, although the WILL ROGERS Tune was at his least inventive. In CITY OF ANGELS, Coleman was forced to write up to the quality of his collaborators; here, as with his other post-**SWEET CHARITY** [January 30, 1966] musicals, this was not the case. The whole of **THE WILL ROGERS FOLLIES**, in sum, seemed to be a rough copy of **BARNUM** without the entertainment value, occassional warmth, and good-natured charm of Coleman's earlier showbiz-life-in-revue biomusical. Yes, the score and the show won Tony Awards; but, then, so did, **WOMAN OF THE YEAR**.

Cy Coleman's early Neil Simon/Bob Fosse collaborations—**LITTLE ME** [November 17, 1962] and **SWEET CHARITY** [January 30, 1966]—had bright, exciting scores. Slightly lacking in heart, perhaps, but well-suited to the material. **CHARITY** was followed by a long inactive period, with only one show over eleven years. His six musicals since 1966 have ranged from disappointingly adequate to bafflingly poor. A capable musician with good ideas, luck and ciîrcumstance always kept him in the shadows of rivals Strouse, Herman, and Kander. Suddenly and unexpectedly, Coleman came through at the age of sixty with his most impressive work, **CITY OF ANGELS** [December 11, 1989]—perhaps the best score written by any of his generation (not including Sondheim and Bock, of course)—and certainly the first exciting work from any of them since the early Seventies.

Jerry Herman

BORN: July 10, 1933   New York, New York

Jerry Herman grew up in Jersey City, son of a summer-camp owner. A self-taught musician, Herman started training as an interior decorator at the Parsons School of Design before switching to drama at the University of Miami.

[all music and lyrics by Jerry Herman unless indicated]

I FEEL WONDERFUL

OCTOBER 18, 1954   THEATRE DE LYS < OFF-BROADWAY >
48 PERFORMANCES

Sketches by Barry Alan Grael
Directed by Herman
Produced by Sidney S. Oshrin
With Phyllis Newman and Richard Tone

Published songs:
None

Herman graduated from Miami and brought back this college show, which was promising if slightly amateurish.

NIGHTCAP

Nightclub Revue

MAY 18, 1958   SHOWPLACE < OFF-BROADWAY >

Choreographed by Phyllis Newman
Directed by Herman
Produced by Jim Paul Eilers
With Kenneth Nelson, Charles Nelson Reilly, Fia Karin, and Estelle Parsons

Published songs:
Show Tune In 2/4—initial publication upon reuse in **PARADE** (**Second**)
    [January 20, 1960]; see **MAME** [May 24, 1966]
Your Good Morning—initial publication upon reuse in **PARADE**

Additional songs recorded:
Confession To A Park Avenue Mother—initial recording upon reuse in
    PARADE
Jolly Theatrical Season—initial recording upon reuse in **PARADE**

Herman, playing piano at the Showplace, talked the owner into putting on this intimate, late-night revue, which ran almost a year. *Show Tune In 2/4* was a lively, catchy show tune in 2/4, and *Jolly Theatrical Season* was cleverly amusing.

PARADE

< Second >

JANUARY 20, 1960   PLAYERS THEATRE < OFF-BROADWAY >   95
    PERFORMANCES

Book and direction by Herman
Choreographed by Richard Tone
Produced by Lawrence N. Kasha
With Dody Goodman, Charles Nelson Reilly, Fia Karin, and Tone

Published songs:
Next Time I Love
Show Tune In 2/4—originally used in **NIGHTCAP** [May 18, 1958]; see
    MAME [May 24, 1966]
The Wonderful World Of The Two-A-Day
Your Good Morning—originally used in **NIGHTCAP**
Your Hand In Mine

Additional songs recorded:
Another Candle
The Antique Man
Confession To A Park Avenue Mother—originally used in **NIGHTCAP**
Jolly Theatrical Season—originally used in **NIGHTCAP**
Just Plain Folks
Maria In Spats
Overture—see **MACK AND MABEL** [October 6, 1974]
Save The Village

PARADE was Herman's first professional show. Charles Nelson Reilly—who repeated his songs from **NIGHTCAP** [May 18, 1958]—left the cast to go to

Broadway with **Bye Bye Birdie** [Strouse: April 14, 1960]; he was to give very good Broadway performances over the next few years in **How To Succeed** ... [**Loesser:** October 14, 1961] and Herman's own **Hello, Dolly!** [January 16, 1964].

FROM A TO Z

April 20, 1960   Brooks Atkinson Theatre   21 performances

Music mostly by others
Lyrics mostly by Fred Ebb and others
Sketches by Woody Allen and others
Directed by Christopher Hewett
Produced by Carroll and Harris Masterson
With Hermione Gingold, Bob Dishy, and Elliot Reid

Published songs:
None

Herman contributed the opening number, *Best Gold,* to this short-lived revue which also introduced Fred Ebb and Woody Allen to Broadway.

MILK AND HONEY

October 10, 1961   Martin Beck Theatre   543 performances

Book by Don Appell
Choreographed by Donald Saddler
Directed by Albert Marre
Produced by Gerard Ostreicher
With Robert Weede, Mimi Benzell, Molly Picon, and Tommy Rall

Published songs:
As Simple As That
Chin Up, Ladies
I Will Follow You
Independence Day Hora
Let's Not Waste A Moment
Milk And Honey
Shalom
That Was Yesterday
There's No Reason In The World

Additional songs published in vocal score:
Hymn To Hymie
Like A Young Man

Sheep Song
The Wedding

An Israel-based musical seemed a safe bet for theatre parties—particularly with Yiddish theatre favorite Molly Picon on hand. The novice producer believed in the novice composer and gave him the assignment; Herman did well enough, attracting attention with the highly melodic, minor-key *Shalom.* MILK AND HONEY became the first Broadway musical to run over five hundred performances and still lose money (now a commonplace occurrence).

MADAME APHRODITE

DECEMBER 29, 1961   ORPHEUM THEATRE <OFF-BROADWAY>   13
    PERFORMANCES

Book by Tad Mosel
Directed by Robert Turoff
Produced by Howard Barker, Cynthia Baer, and Robert Chambers
With Nancy Andrews, Cherry Davis, and Jack Drummond

Published songs:
Beautiful—see LA CAGE AUX FOLLES [August 21, 1983]
The Girls Who Sit And Wait
Only, Only Love
Take A Good Look Around

HELLO, DOLLY!

JANUARY 16, 1964   ST. JAMES THEATRE   2,844 PERFORMANCES

Music and lyrics mostly by Jerry Herman
Book by Michael Stewart
(Based on *The Matchmaker* [play] by Thornton Wilder)
Directed and choreographed by Gower Champion
Produced by David Merrick
With Carol Channing, David Burns, Eileen Brennan, and Charles Nelson Reilly

Published songs:
Before The Parade Passes By (see below)
Dancing
Hello, Dolly!
It Only Takes A Moment
It Takes A Woman—initial individual publication upon use in 1965
    London production

Just Leave Everything To Me—written for 1969 movie version
Love Is Only Love—written for movie version
Love, Look In My Window—added after opening (1970)
Put On Your Sunday Clothes
Ribbons Down My Back
So Long, Dearie
World, Take Me Back—added after opening (1970)

Additional songs published in vocal score:
Elegance—(by Bob Merrill and Herman)
I Put My Hand In
Motherhood March—(by Merrill and Herman)
Waiter's Gallop [instrumental]

Additional song recorded:
Come And Be My Butterfly

HELLO, DOLLY! galloped on to Broadway as the biggest hit of the young decade, and remained so despite competition from the illustrious FIDDLER ON THE ROOF [Bock: September 22, 1964] and MAN OF LA MANCHA [Leigh: November 22, 1965]. Gower Champion's magic, Carol Channing's charisma (in a part nobody wanted and everybody eventually played), David Merrick's showmanship (rejuvenating a fading hit into a sellout simply by adding Pearl Bailey and Cab Calloway), and Jerry Herman's title song did it. Herman paid a $275,000 settlement (without admission of infringement) on a plagiarism claim brought by Mack David, brother of PROMISES, PROMISES [PART 4: December 1, 1968] lyricist Hal David. *Hello, Dolly!* is certainly more than similar to the 1948 pop hit *Sunflower,* but surely an unconscious borrowing on Herman's part. Other parts of the score were of mixed parentage. During the troubled tryout in Detroit, Merrick called in Bob Merrill (from the Champion/Stewart hit CARNIVAL [Merrill: April 13, 1961]) to doctor the score. Champion, meanwhile, brought in Charles Strouse and Lee Adams (from the Champion/Stewart hit BYE BYE BIRDIE [Strouse: April 14, 1960]). Two Merrill offerings (with revisions by Herman) were used, *Motherhood March* and the artful *Elegance.* The latter, in fact, was a discard from NEW GIRL IN TOWN [Merrill: May 14, 1957]. A third Merrill song, the ballad *We Only Remember,* was unused but recycled for HENRY, SWEET HENRY [Merrill: October 23, 1967]. Strouse and Adams came up with a big number to end the first act, *Before the Parade Passes By.* This version was not used, though: instead, Herman wrote a second *Parade.* While Herman received sole public credit for all of these songs, the actual authorship—per Mr. Herman—is as given in the song listings above. (The ASCAP Index of Performed Compositions lists *Parade* as by Adams, Herman, and Strouse, while *Elegance* and *Motherhood March* are credited to Merrill alone.) At any rate, DOLLY!

was immensely entertaining and, after twenty-five years, is still "glowin' and crowin' and goin' strong."

BEN FRANKLIN IN PARIS

OCTOBER 27, 1964   LUNT-FONTANNE THEATRE   215 PERFORMANCES

Music mostly by Mark Sandrich, Jr.
Book and lyrics by Sidney Michaels
Directed and choreographed by Michael Kidd
Produced by George W. George and Harvey Granat
With Robert Preston, Ulla Sallert, and Susan Watson

Published song:
To Be Alone With You

Additional song published in vocal selection:
Too Charming

BEN FRANKLIN IN Boston was having the miseries. Surgeons were called in; but the troubles were terminal. This time Herman was the song doctor; the two songs were publicly credited to Sandrich and Michaels. *To Be Alone With You* is a very pretty ballad, on a level with the best of Herman's work.

MAME

MAY 24, 1966   WINTER GARDEN THEATRE   1,508 PERFORMANCES

Book by Jerome Lawrence and Robert E. Lee
(Based on *Auntie Mame* [novel] by Patrick Dennis)
Choreographed by Onna White
Directed by Gene Saks
Produced by Fryer, Carr, and Harris
With Angela Lansbury, Beatrice Arthur (Saks), Jane Connell, Charles Braswell, and Frankie Michaels

Published songs:
If He Walked Into My Life
It's Today—revised version of *Show Tune In 2/4* from NIGHTCAP [**May 18, 1958**]
Loving You—written for 1974 movie version
Mame
My Best Girl
Open A New Window
That's How Young I Feel
We Need A Little Christmas

Additional songs published in vocal score:
Bosom Buddies
The Fox Hunt (Fall Off, Auntie Mame)
Gooch's Song
The Man In The Moon
St. Bridget

Herman's best show. MAME had great style in every department, thanks to director Gene Saks, who replaced original director/colibrettist Joshua Logan. Angela Lansbury, Jane Connell, and Beatrice Arthur were three clowns with superb material. Herman, needing no last-minute "help," provided a fine score without a weak link. His ballad, *If He Walked Into My Life*, was good, and his comedy numbers *Gooch's Song* and *Bosom Bodies* were perfect. *Mame* joined *Hello, Dolly!* in the popular title-song sweepstakes; and the show had a long and successful run (though not so spectacular as her sister from Yonkers). MAME, incidentally, was produced in tandem with yet another lady, SWEET CHARITY [Coleman: January 30, 1966].

DEAR WORLD

FEBRUARY 6, 1969   MARK HELLINGER THEATRE   132 PERFORMANCES

Book by Jerome Lawrence and Robert E. Lee
(Based on *The Madwoman of Chaillot* [play] by Jean Giradoux)
Directed and choreographed by Joe Layton
Produced by Alexander H. Cohen
With Angela Lansbury, Jane Connell, and Milo O'Shea

Published songs:
And I Was Beautiful
Dear World
Garbage [instrumental]
I Don't Want To Know
I've Never Said I Love You
Kiss Her Now
One Person

Additional songs published in vocal selection:
Dickie
Each Tomorrow Morning
Memories
Pearls
The Spring Of Next Year
Thoughts
Voices

Additional song recorded:
Garbage [song version]

Alexander Cohen assembled the authors and stars of **MAME** [**May 24, 1966**] for this lavishly packaged, sure-fire, misguided failure. Herman's music was actually rather tuneful, but the lyrics were way far below his usual level. (The title song is absolutely frightful, made up for in part by a delightful "Tea Party" trio.) The rest of **DEAR WORLD** suffered from lack of direction. The director was Joe Layton replacing Peter Glenville replacing Lucia Victor.

MACK AND MABEL

OCTOBER 6, 1974   MAJESTIC THEATRE   65 PERFORMANCES

Book by Michael Stewart
(Based on an idea by Leonard Spigelgass)
Directed and choreographed by Gower Champion
Produced by David Merrick
With Robert Preston, Bernadette Peters, Lisa Kirk, and James Mitchell

Published songs:
Hundreds Of Girls
I Promise You A Happy Ending
I Won't Send Roses
Tap Your Troubles Away
Time Heals Everything
Today I'm Gonna Think About Me—cut; issued in separate edition
When Mabel Comes In The Room
Wherever He Ain't

Additional songs published in vocal selection:
Big Time
I Wanna Make The World Laugh—new lyric for unspecified song
        originally used in **PARADE (Second Version)** [**January 20, 1960**]
Look What Happened To Mabel
Movies Were Movies

Additional song recorded:
My Heart Leaps Up

Another poorly conceived, ill-manufactured musical comedy. Herman displayed his ability to write perfect material for the female lead in *Look What Happened To Mabel* and *Time Heals Everything,* but the rest of the score was barren. Gower Champion, meanwhile, had long since lost his touch. His career following **I Do! I Do!** [**December 5, 1966**] was marked by six of the bigger financial disasters of the era, including **THE HAPPY TIME** [**Kander: January**

18, 1968], PRETTYBELLE [Styne: **February 1, 1971**], and the indescribable ROCKABYE HAMLET [February 17, 1976]. Robert Preston gave his usual superb performance, and Bernadette Peters was sympathetic in an unsympathetic role. People keep threatening to revive MACK AND MABEL; they certainly have their work cut out for them.

THE GRAND TOUR

JANUARY 11, 1979 PALACE THEATRE 61 PERFORMANCES

Book by Michael Stewart and Mark Bramble
(Based on *Jacobowsky and the Colonel* [play] by Franz Werfel)
Choreographed by Donald Saddler
Directed by Gerald Freedman
Produced by James Nederlander, Diana Shumlin, and Jack Schlissel
With Joel Grey, Ron Holgate, and Florence Lacey

Published songs:
I'll Be Here Tomorrow
Marianne
You I Like

Additional songs published in vocal selection:
For Poland
I Belong Here
I Think I Think
Mazel Tov
More And More/Less And Less
Mrs. S. L. Jacobowsky
One Extraordinary Thing
We're Almost There

A charmless show, not helped by a miscast star and a poorly directed production. Herman provided a very good opening—*I'll Be Here Tomorrow*—which created sympathy and interest; then things hit bottom and continued to descend. As is the norm in such cases, they fired the choreographer.

A DAY IN HOLLYWOOD/A NIGHT IN THE UKRAINE

MAY 1, 1980 JOHN GOLDEN THEATRE 588 PERFORMANCES

Music mostly by Frank Lazarus
Book and lyrics mostly by Dick Vosburgh
Additional music and lyrics by Herman

Directed and choreographed by Tommy Tune
Produced by Alexander H. Cohen and Hildy Parks
With Priscilla Lopez, David Garrison, and Lazarus

Published song:
The Best In The World

Additional songs published in vocal selection:
Just Go To The Movies
Nelson

This revue needed some beefing up; Herman, at the lowest point in his professional career, contributed three numbers (including the effective *Nelson*).

LA CAGE AUX FOLLES

AUGUST 21, 1983   PALACE THEATRE   1,761 PERFORMANCES

Book by Harvey Fierstein
(Based on the play by Jean Poiret)
Choreographed by Scott Salmon
Directed by Arthur Laurents
Produced by Allan Carr, Kenneth-Mark Productions, Marvin A. Krauss, Stewart F. Lane, James M. Nederlander, Martin Richards, and Fritz Holt and Barry Brown
With George Hearn and Gene Barry

Published songs:
The Best Of Times
La Cage Aux Folles
I Am What I Am
Look Over There
Song On The Sand (La Da Da Da)
With You On My Arm

Additional songs published in vocal selection:
A Little More Mascara—revised version of *Beautiful* from **MADAME
        APHRODITE** [December 29, 1961]
Masculinity
We Are What We Are—alternate lyric for *I Am What I Am*

Additional song recorded:
Cocktail Counterpoint

Herman had been without a hit since **MAME** [**May 24, 1966**]; it was assumed that his "popular touch" was outdated, too old-fashioned. Then came **LA**

Cage Aux Folles, Broadway's biggest hit since Annie [Strouse: April 21, 1977]. Curiously enough, considering the diversity in subject matter, La Cage and Annie were pretty much equally matched in quality of score, book, and direction, which is to say mediocre. The La Cage package was very empty indeed. Herman wrote his blandest score to date, without a single interesting moment. And the book played much better in the movie version, with English subtitles. But audiences loved it, and a hit is a hit. Right?

Jerry Herman wrote one of the most successful musicals of the Sixties, as well as one of the biggest hits of the Eighties. A third show, Mame [May 24, 1966], was also a major hit. Herman's record compares more than favorably with other important theatre composers, yet his work is continually attacked as being banal and derivative. There's a good reason for this. However, it must be remembered that he *has* proven himself highly capable with the score for Mame and a half-dozen fine songs scattered through his other shows. Perhaps Mr. Herman has another hit musical in him?

John Kander

BORN: March 18, 1927   Kansas City, Missouri

John Kander began his musical training at Oberlin College, where he wrote songs with childhood friend James Goldman. Coming to New York to get a Masters Degree from Columbia, Kander began working as an accompanist. His first Broadway assignments came as dance music arranger for GYPSY [Styne: May 21, 1959] and Marguerite Monnot's IRMA LA DOUCE [PART 5: September 29, 1960], two shows with particularly good dance arrangements.

A FAMILY AFFAIR

JANUARY 27, 1962   BILLY ROSE THEATRE   65 PERFORMANCES

Book and lyrics by James and William Goldman
Directed by Harold Prince
Produced by Andrew Siff
With Shelley Berman, Eileen Heckart, Morris Carnovsky, Larry Kert, and Rita Gardner

Published songs:
Beautiful
A Family Affair
Harmony
Mamie In The Afternoon—cut; see THE ACT [October 2, 1977]
There's A Room In My House

Additional songs recorded:
Anything For You
Every Girl Wants To Get Married
Football Game (Marching Songs)
I'm Worse Than Anybody
Kalua Bay
My Son, The Lawyer
Now Morris
Revenge
Right Girls

Summer Is Over
What I Say Goes
Wonderful Party

James Goldman's first play, the 1961 *They Might Be Giants,* closed during its 1961 pre-West End tryout. The producers: Robert Griffith and Harold Prince. Goldman's second effort was **A FAMILY AFFAIR,** written with brother William (best known in theatre circles for his 1969 Broadway chronicle "The Season") and Kander. The intimate musical featured three semi-names, none of whom had ever appeared in a musical. The authors had never done a Broadway show, the producer had never done a Broadway show, even the director—Word Baker of **THE FANTASTICKS** [Schmidt: May 3, 1960]—had never done a Broadway show. Out of town, **A FAMILY AFFAIR** had problems. A call went to Harold Prince, who had never directed *any*thing. Prince helped somewhat, and gained valuable experience. He also kept Kander—whose work came off best—in mind. James Goldman, too, was to work once more with director Prince (on **FOLLIES** [Sondheim: April 4, 1971]).

NEVER TOO LATE

NOVEMBER 27, 1962   PLAYHOUSE THEATRE   1,007 PERFORMANCES

Play by Sumner Arthur Long
Incidental music by John Kander
Song by Jerry **Bock** and Sheldon Harnick
Directed by George Abbott
Produced by Elliot Martin and Daniel Hollywood
With Paul Ford, Maureen O'Sullivan, and Orson Bean

Published songs:
None

Kander provided incidental music for this surprise hit, George Abbott's final smash. The one song used, though, was provided by Bock and Harnick.

FLORA, THE RED MENACE

MAY 11, 1965   ALVIN THEATRE   87 PERFORMANCES

Lyrics by Fred Ebb
Book by George Abbott and Robert Russell
(Based on *Love Is Just Around the Corner* [novel] by Lester Atwell)
Choreographed by Lee Theodore
Directed by Abbott
Produced by Harold Prince

With Liza Minnelli, Bob Dishy, Mary Louise Wilson, Cathryn Damon, and James Cresson

Published songs:
All I Need (Is One Good Break)
Dear Love
Express Yourself
I Believe You—cut
Knock Knock
Not Every Day Of The Week
A Quiet Thing
Sing Happy

Additional songs recorded:
The Flame
Hello Waves
The Joke—written for off-off-Broadway revival [December 6, 1987]
Keepin' It Hot—written for revival
The Kid Herself—cut
Palomino Pal
Sign Here
Street Songs
Unafraid
Where Did Everybody Go?—written for revival
You Are You

Publisher Tommy Valando, who had nurtured Jerry Bock, brought Kander and lyricist Fred Ebb together. Ebb had been contributing undistinguished songs (with music by Norman Martin) to late-Fifties revues. The new team immediately came up with the 1962 pop hit *My Coloring Book*. Harold Prince had been impressed with Kander on **A FAMILY AFFAIR** [January 27, 1962]; he gave the pair their first Broadway assignment. **FLORA, THE RED MENACE** was the last of the Abbott-Prince shows; the old formula was becoming outmoded, and Prince decided to move on without Abbott and direct future shows himself. What was good about **FLORA** was the bright, funny score and Liza Minnelli, who won a Tony Award in her Broadway debut.

CABARET

NOVEMBER 20, 1966   BROADHURST THEATRE   1,165 PERFORMANCES

Lyrics by Fred Ebb
Book by Joe Masteroff
(Based on *I Am a Camera* [play] by John van Druten from stories by Christopher Isherwood)

Choreographed by Ronald Field
Directed by Harold Prince
Produced by Prince in association with Ruth Mitchell
With Jill Haworth, Jack Gilford, Lotte Lenya, and Joel Grey

Published songs:
Cabaret
I Don't Care Much—cut
Married
Maybe This Time—added to 1972 movie version; initial use of 1963
    nonshow song
Meeskite
Mein Herr—written for movie version
Money, Money (Makes The World Go Round)—written for movie version
Tomorrow Belongs To Me
Why Should I Wake Up?
Wilkommen (Welcome)

Additional songs published in vocal score:
Don't Tell Mama
If You Could See Her
It Couldn't Please Me More (The Pineapple Song)
Perfectly Marvelous
Sitting Pretty (Money Song)
So What
Telephone Song
Two Ladies
What Would You Do?

Kander and Ebb's first and biggest hit came with this first of the new-style
Harold Prince musicals. Prince had experimented as director on four musical
comedies; he now successfully moved ahead into a more conceptualized musical theatre (aided by Boris Aronson's striking physical production which drew
the audience into the proceedings). The score was effective, if uneven: the Kit
Kat Club solos (*Wilkommen* and *Cabaret*) and the M.C.'s comic specialties
on the one hand, the bland songs accompanying the weak love story on the
other. The music was highly influenced by Kurt Weill, accentuated by the
presence of Lenya; Kander and Ebb wrote one of their best songs for her,
What Would You Do? Jack Gilford supplied pathos, and the brilliantly
conceived role of the M.C. was well performed by the chilling Joel Grey. The
1972 film version, under the directorial hand of Bob Fosse, solved some of
CABARET's dramaturgical problems; but they went back to the original for a
lacklustre 20th anniversary revival [October 29, 1987; 262 performances]. This
time Joel Grey's M.C. was featured as the "star," throwing things somewhat

off-balance. Kander and Ebb added an indifferent new song, *Don't Go,* and reinstated an indifferent old one, *I Don't Care Much.*

THE HAPPY TIME

JANUARY 18, 1968   BROADWAY THEATRE   286 PERFORMANCES

Lyrics by Fred Ebb
Book by N. Richard Nash
(Based on the novel by Robert L. Fontaine)
Directed and choreographed by Gower Champion
Produced by David Merrick
With Robert Goulet, David Wayne, Mike Rupert, and George S. Irving

Published songs:
A Certain Girl—written for unproduced 1965 musical THE EMPEROR OF
      SAN FRANCISCO (also called GOLDEN GATE)
The Happy Time
I Don't Remember You
The Life Of The Party
Seeing Things
Tomorrow Morning
(Walking) Among My Yesterdays

Additional songs published in vocal selection:
Please Stay
St. Pierre
Without Me

Additional songs recorded:
Catch My Garter
He's Back

Kander and Ebb came up with a charming score for a charming, intimate musical—which was given an overblown, heavy production. When Champion decided to turn THE HAPPY TIME into a multimedia photography show, all was lost. Broadway had its first million-dollar bomb, and Champion received two Tony Awards.

ZORBA

NOVEMBER 17, 1968   IMPERIAL THEATRE   305 PERFORMANCES

Lyrics by Fred Ebb
Book by Joseph Stein
(Based on *Zorba the Greek* [novel] by Nikos Kazantzakis)

Choreographed by Ronald Field
Directed by Harold Prince
Produced by Prince in association with Ruth Mitchell
With Herschel Bernardi, Maria Karnilova, John Cunningham, and
Lorraine Serabian

Published songs:
The First Time
Happy Birthday To Me
No Boom Boom
Only Love
Why Can't I Speak?
Woman—written for revival [October 16, 1983; 362 performances]
Zorba Theme (Life Is) [instrumental]

Additional songs published in vocal selection:
I Am Free
The Top Of The Hill

Additional songs recorded:
The Butterfly
The Crow
Goodbye, Canavaro
Grandpapa (Zorba's Dance)
Life Is [song version]
Y'assou

An attempt to follow a hit—CABARET [November 20, 1966]—with a similarly
assembled, advance-sale blockbuster was once again unsuccessful. There were
also overtones of Prince's longest-running FIDDLER ON THE ROOF [Bock:
September 22, 1964], represented by librettist Stein and stars Bernardi (a
long-time Tevye) and Karnilova. While Kander under the influence of Weill
was right for the earlier show, the manufactured Greek music of ZORBA had
little of the composer's voice in it. After struggling on a while, the stars got
sick—separately—and the show passed away.

70, GIRLS, 70

APRIL 15, 1971   BROADHURST THEATRE   35 PERFORMANCES

Lyrics by Fred Ebb
Book by Ebb and Norman L. Martin
(Based on *Breath of Spring* [play] by Peter Coke)
Choreographed by Onna White
Directed by Paul Aaron

Produced by Arthur Whitelaw
With Mildred Natwick, Lillian Roth, Lillian Hayman, and Hans Conried

Published songs:
The Elephant Song
Yes

Additional songs published in vocal selection:
Believe
Boom Ditty Boom
Broadway, My Street
Coffee (In A Cardboard Cup)
Do We?
Go Visit Your Grandmother
Home
Old Folks
70, Girls, 70

Additional songs recorded:
The Caper
Hit It, Lorraine
See The Light
You And I, Love

Kander and Ebb came back with another charming, if imperfect, score. As with FLORA, THE RED MENACE [May 11, 1965] and THE HAPPY TIME [January 18, 1968], problems in other areas took their toll. 70, GIRLS, 70 also suffered from an unlikely audience identification problem: FOLLIES [Sondheim: April 4, 1971] had recently opened to cautious reviews and poor word-of-mouth among the older, traditional musical comedy fans. The Kander-Ebb/Prince connection, the presence of old-time actors, and the Follies Girls titles confused theatregoers and the intimate musical quickly folded. (The extravaganza died more slowly, painfully.) Ebb wrote the book with Norman Martin, his pre-Kander collaborator. A tragedy of the 70, GIRLS, 70 tryout: veteran David Burns suffered a heart attack doing the *Grandmother* number and died March 12, 1971 in Philadelphia.

CHICAGO

A Musical Vaudeville

JUNE 1, 1975   46TH STREET THEATRE   923 PERFORMANCES

Lyrics by Fred Ebb
Book by Ebb and Bob Fosse
(Based on the play by Maurine Dallas Watkins)

Directed and choreographed by Fosse
Produced by Robert Fryer and James Cresson
With Gwen Verdon, Chita Rivera, Jerry Orbach, and Barney Martin

Published songs:
And All That Jazz
I Can't Do It Alone .
Mr. Cellophane
Me And My Baby
My Own Best Friend
Razzle Dazzle
Roxie

Additional songs published in vocal selection:
All I Care About
Class
Funny Honey
A Little Bit Of Good
Nowadays
When You're Good To Mama

Additional songs recorded:
Cell Block Tango
It—cut
Loopin' De Loop—cut
Ten Percent—cut
We Both Reached For The Gun
When Velma Takes The Stand

Fosse had **CHICAGO** built to order around his concept, as he'd done with **PIPPIN** [S. Schwartz: October 23, 1972]. While the earlier show had at least some effective musical moments, the **CHICAGO** score merely filled Fosse's needs and sounded "authentic." But Fosse, Gwen Verdon (in her first musical since **SWEET CHARITY** [Coleman: January 30, 1966], and Chita Rivera (in her first since **BAJOUR** [November 23, 1964]) provided enough reason to give Kander his second-longest run. I've grown to appreciate this score somewhat more over the years. (I *hated* it in the theatre.) The songs were *supposed* to be genre pastiches, after all; and Kander and Ebb provided quite a few delightful surprises while filling Fosse's needs.

THE ACT

O<small>CTOBER</small> 29, 1977 · M<small>AJESTIC</small> T<small>HEATRE</small>   233 <small>PERFORMANCES</small>

Lyrics by Fred Ebb
Book by George Furth
Choreographed by Ron Lewis
Directed by Martin Scorsese
Produced by The Shubert Organization and Feuer and Martin
With Liza Minnelli and Barry Nelson

Published songs:
City Lights
It's The Strangest Thing
My Own Space
Shine It On

Additional songs recorded:
Arthur In The Afternoon (lyric by Kander, James Goldman, William
    Goldman, and Ebb)—revised lyric for *Mamie In the Afternoon* from
    A F<small>AMILY</small> A<small>FFAIR</small> [January 27, 1962]
Bobo's
Hot Enough For You?
Little Do They Know (Gypsy's Song)
The Money Tree
The Only Game In Town—cut
Please, Sir—cut
There When I Need Him
Turning (Shaker Hymn)
Walking Papers

C<small>HICAGO</small> [June 1, 1975] had Bob Fosse to help triumph over weak components; T<small>HE</small> A<small>CT</small> had weaker material, no Fosse, and one Liza in place of Verdon and Rivera. But Minnelli's popularity at the time made her a sure-fire ticket seller, enabling T<small>HE</small> A<small>CT</small> to get away with a lot on very little. First facing Broadway in F<small>LORA</small>, T<small>HE</small> R<small>ED</small> M<small>ENACE</small> [May 11, 1965], Minnelli became a superstar in Fosse's 1972 movie version of C<small>ABARET</small> [November 20, 1966]. She had subbed for the ailing Verdon in C<small>HICAGO</small>, and Kander and Ebb supplied much of her special material for nightclubs and television. So, Minnelli was closely tied to the songwriters; hence, T<small>HE</small> A<small>CT</small>. Gower Champion replaced Scorsese (without credit); he also made his final stage appearance when he replaced Barry Nelson late in the run.

MADWOMAN OF CENTRAL PARK WEST

June 13, 1979   22 Steps Theatre (off-Broadway)   86
PERFORMANCES

Music mostly by others (also see **Bernstein**)
Lyric to Kander song by Fred Ebb
Book by Phyllis Newman and Arthur Laurents
Directed by Laurents
Produced by Gladys Rackmil, Fritz Holt, and Barry M. Brown
With Phyllis Newman

Song recorded:
Cheerleader

WOMAN OF THE YEAR

March 29, 1981   Palace Theatre   770 performances

Lyrics by Fred Ebb
Book by Peter Stone
(Based on the screenplay by Ring Lardner, Jr. and Michael Kanin)
Choreographed by Tony Charmoli
Directed by Robert Moore
Produced by Lawrence Kasha, David S. Landay, James M. Nederlander,
Warner Communications, Carole J. Shorenstein, and Stewart F. Lane
With Lauren Bacall, Harry Guardino, Roderick Cook, and Rex Everhart

Published songs:
One Of The Girls
See You In The Funny Papers
Sometimes A Day Goes By
We're Gonna Work It Out

Additional songs published in vocal selection:
The Grass Is Always Greener
I Wrote The Book
The Two Of Us
Woman Of The Year

Additional songs recorded:
Happy In The Morning
I Told You So
It Isn't Working
The Poker Game
Shut Up, Gerald

So What Else Is New?
Table Talk
When You're Right, You're Right
Who Would Have Dreamed—cut

Lauren Bacall managed to carry this show for a decent though unprofitable run. The well-written and literate Oscar-winning screenplay was turned into a one-sided comic strip, leaving nothing much to amuse audiences but Marilyn Cooper. Tommy Tune helped out during the tryout and Joe Layton redid the show (with some new material) for the post-Broadway tour. All told, a star vehicle with one of the few stars still capable of carrying a capsized ship.

THE RINK

FEBRUARY 9, 1984   MARTIN BECK THEATRE   204 PERFORMANCES

Lyrics by Fred Ebb
Book by Terrence McNally
Choreographed by Graciela Daniele
Directed by A. J. Antoon
Produced by Jules Fisher, Roger Berlind, Joan Cullman, Milbro Productions, and Kenneth-John Productions in association with Jonathan Farkas
With Chita Rivera and Liza Minnelli

Songs published in vocal selection:
All The Children In A Row
Blue Crystal
Chief Cook And Bottle Washer
Colored Lights
Marry Me
The Rink
Under The Roller-Coaster
Wallflower
We Can Make It

Additional songs recorded:
After All These Years
Angel's Rink And Social Center
The Apple Doesn't Fall
Don't 'Ah, Ma' Me
Mrs. A.
Not Enough Magic
What Happened To The Old Days?
Wine And Peaches—cut

Even Minnelli and Rivera weren't enough to attract any interest to THE RINK, a heartless show (like its predecessors) built around nothing. Attempts to shock the audience were repugnant, and the stars were wasted. A good sign, though: both Kander and Ebb showed more inventiveness and originality than they had in years, particularly in *Colored Lights* and some of the comedy numbers.

KISS OF THE SPIDER WOMAN

[MAY 1, 1990]   PERFORMING ARTS CENTER OF THE STATE UNIVERSITY
    OF NEW YORK AT PURCHASE < PURCHASE, NEW YORK >
    PRE-BROADWAY 'DEVELOPMENTAL WORKSHOP'

Lyrics by Fred Ebb
Book by Terrence McNally
(Based on the novel by Manuel Puig)
Choreographed by Susan Stroman
Directed by Harold Prince
Produced by New Musicals (Marty Bell)
With John Rubinstein, Kevin Gray, Lauren Mitchell, and Harry Goz

Published song:
Kiss of the Spider Woman—see AND THE WORLD GOES 'ROUND [March
    18, 1991]

It has become the norm for new musicals to be mounted in workshops before braving the wilds of Broadway. The theory: see whether or not the material works before spending five or six million dollars. The only trouble with this system is that shows that clearly don't, won't, and shouldn't work—like THE RINK [February 9, 1984], RAGS [Strouse: August 21, 1986], and LEGS DIAMOND [December 26, 1988]—blithely continue on towards sure disaster. How bad does a workshop need to be in order to convince the creators to throw in the towel? What price ego? The New Musicals organization was founded to give still-developing works like KISS OF THE SPIDER WOMAN full-scale mountings; the inevitable failure of their maiden effort was pretty much apparent. A brouhaha arose when the all-powerful New York *Times* decided to cover the show, and the SPIDER WOMAN men were violently swatted with a rolled-up newspaper. They complained vociferously that they weren't "ready"; what made them think this baby ever would be? The *Times* can be credited with saving someone millions of dollars and—more importantly—preventing theatregoers from throwing away their advance sales bucks on another show they're sure to dislike (like THE RINK, RAGS, and LEGS DIAMOND). As for the material: Kander's music was, once again, intelligent and possibly workable, but the efforts of his cohorts were spotty. As for the New Musicals organization, their KISS OF THE SPIDER WOMAN carried the Kiss of Death.

AND THE WORLD GOES 'ROUND
The Songs of Kander & Ebb

MARCH 18, 1991   WESTSIDE THEATRE   < OFF-BROADWAY >   120
    PERFORMANCES [STILL RUNNING AS OF JUNE 30, 1991]

Lyrics by Fred Ebb
Conceived by Scott Ellis, Susan Stroman, and David Thompson
Choreographed by Stroman
Directed by Ellis
Produced by R. Tyler Gatchell, Jr., Peter Neufeld, Patrick J. Patek, and
Gene R. Korf in association with the McCarter Theatre
with Bob Cuccioli, Karen Mason, Brenda Pressley, Jim Walton, and Karen
Ziemba

Published songs (in initial theatrical use):
And The World Goes Round—originally used in 1977 movie "New York,
    New York"
How Lucky Can You Get—originally used in 1975 movie "Funny Lady"
Maybe This Time—see CABARET [November 20, 1966]
Money, Money (Makes the World Go Round—see CABARET
My Coloring Book—published as 1962 popular song
Ring Them Bells—previously used in 1972 tv special "Liza with a Z"
There Goes the Ball Game—originally used in 1977 movie "New York,
    New York"

Additional song published in vocal selection for "Funny Lady":
Isn't This Better?

Additional songs recorded:
Kiss of the Spider Woman—originally used (unpublished) in KISS OF THE
    SPIDER WOMAN [May 1, 1990]
Sara Lee

AND THE WORLD GOES 'ROUND proved to be a friendly, upbeat, and all 'round
pleasant evening in the theatre. This was, in fact, the first Kander & Ebb show
I've left in a content frame of mind since the ill-fated but endearing 70, GIRLS,
70 [April 15, 1971]. Somewhat surprisingly, a good number of the Kander &
Ebb songs worked better here than they had in the shows for which they were
written.

John Kander's first six musicals (through 70, GIRLS, 70 [April 15, 1971]) were
interesting and worthwhile, although only CABARET [November 20, 1966])
was a hit. These were followed by four comparatively ordinary star vehicles
which displayed little of the composer's creativity, and the stillborn KISS OF

THE SPIDER WOMAN [May 1, 1990]. Again, only one of this group was successful. The overall record is less than encouraging, and it is surprising to find only two song hits (*Cabaret* and *Wilkommen*) in the lot. Even so, Kander is one of the more talented composers of his generation. With SPIDER WOMAN he attempted something original; while the experiment was unsuccessful, it was musically a step in the right direction, certainly.

Harvey Schmidt

BORN: September 12, 1929   Dallas, Texas

The son of a Methodist minister, Schmidt was studying art at the University of Texas when he met fellow Texan Tom Jones. A mutual interest in theatre led the pair to a songwriting collaboration on college shows. After serving in the Army, both men came to New York. Jones began directing nightclub revues while Schmidt worked as a commercial artist.

SHOESTRING '57

NOVEMBER 5, 1956   BARBIZON PLAZA
        THEATRE   < OFF-BROADWAY >   110 PERFORMANCES

Music mostly by others (see **Strouse**)
Lyrics by Sheldon Harnick, Michael Stewart, Lee Adams, Carolyn Leigh, and others
Choreographed by Danny Daniels
Directed by Paul Lammers
Produced by Ben Bagley in association with E. H. Morris
With Dody Goodman, Dorothy Greener, and Paul Mazursky

Recorded song:
At Twenty-Two (lyric by Tom Jones)

This revue was a sequel to Ben Bagley's first SHOESTRING REVUE [Strouse: **February 28, 1955**]. Bagley was to leave off-Broadway for a record producing career, specializing in less familiar theatre music; the artist Schmidt was to provide distinctive jacket paintings for the series.

DEMI-DOZEN

Nightclub Revue

OCTOBER 11, 1958   UPSTAIRS AT THE DOWNSTAIRS

Music also by others (see **Coleman**)
Lyrics to Schmidt songs by Tom Jones

Directed by John Heawood
Produced by Julius Monk
With Gerry Matthews and Jane Connell

Recorded songs:
Grand Opening
The Holy Man And The Yankee
Mini Off-Broadway
One And All (lyric by Schmidt)
Race Of The Lexington Avenue Express
A Seasonal Sonatina
Statehood Hula

Jones had been involved as a director with the Julius Monk nightclub revue series. With **DEMI-DOZEN** Jones and Schmidt received their first New York break (and little notice).

THE FANTASTICKS

MAY 3, 1960   SULLIVAN STREET THEATRE < OFF-BROADWAY >
    12,926 PERFORMANCES [STILL RUNNING AS OF JUNE 30, 1991]

Book and lyrics by Tom Jones
(Based on *Les Romantiques* [play] by Edmond Rostand)
Directed by Word Baker
Produced by Lore Noto
With Jerry Orbach, Kenneth Nelson, Rita Gardner, and Thomas Bruce (Jones)

Published songs:
Soon It's Gonna Rain
They Were You
Try To Remember

Additional songs published in vocal score:
Happy Ending
I Can See It
It Depends On What You Pay
Metaphor
Much More
Never Say No
Overture [instrumental]
Plant A Radish
Rape Ballet [instrumental]—lyric for *Abductions (And So Forth)*, song
    version written for 1990 road tour, published in revised edition of
    playscript

'Round And 'Round
This Plum Is Too Ripe

Fellow University of Texas student Word Baker renewed acquaintance with Schmidt and Jones when he served as associate director/producer of DEMI-DOZEN [October 11, 1958]. With the opportunity to mount an original one-act musical at a Barnard College (New York) summer program, Baker asked Schmidt and Jones if they could finish the piece they had been working on; the one-act FANTASTICKS played a week [opening August 3, 1959]. Novice producer Lore Noto optioned it and brought the revised version to Sullivan Street back in 1960. The popularity of *Try To Remember* sustained the show for a dozen years or so, and *Soon It's Gonna Rain* accounted for another decade. The simplicity and theatrical inventiveness (and relatively low operating cost) keep THE FANTASTICKS with us.

110 IN THE SHADE

OCTOBER 24, 1963   BROADHURST THEATRE   330 PERFORMANCES

Lyrics by Tom Jones
Book by N. Richard Nash
(Based on *The Rainmaker* [play] by Nash)
Choreographed by Agnes de Mille
Directed by Joseph Anthony
Produced by David Merrick
With Inga Swenson, Robert Horton, Stephen Douglass, and Lesley Ann Warren

Published songs:
Everything Beautiful Happens At Night
Is It Really Me?
Love, Don't Turn Away
A Man And A Woman
110 In The Shade—written for 1967 London production
Simple Little Things
Too Many People Alone—cut

Additional songs published in vocal score:
Cinderella
Gonna Be Another Hot Day
The Hungry Men
Little Red Hat
Lizzie's Comin' Home
Melisande
Old Maid

Poker Polka
The Rain Song
Raunchy
Wonderful Music
You're Not Fooling Me

Additional song recorded:
Sweet River—cut

David Merrick brought Schmidt and Jones to Broadway and put them together with Nash's 1954 hit *The Rainmaker*. The odd combination came up with a surprisingly effective and well-crafted piece. Particularly impressive: *The Rain Song, Gonna Be Another Hot Day,* and the soliloquy *Old Maid*. By season's end, though, the competition of Merrick's own HELLO, DOLLY! [Herman: January 16, 1964] and FUNNY GIRL [Styne: March 26, 1964] had overwhelmed the intimate 110 IN THE SHADE.

I DO! I DO!

DECEMBER 5, 1966   46TH STREET THEATRE   561 PERFORMANCES

Book and lyrics by Tom Jones
(Based on *The Fourposter* [play] by Jan de Hartog)
Directed and choreographed by Gower Champion
Produced by David Merrick
With Mary Martin and Robert Preston

Published songs:
The Honeymoon Is Over
I Do! I Do!
My Cup Runneth Over
Thousands Of Flowers—cut
Together Forever
What Is A Woman?

Additional songs published in vocal score:
All The Dearly Beloved
The Father Of The Bride
Flaming Agnes
Goodnight
I Love My Wife
Love Isn't Everything
Nobody's Perfect
Roll Up The Ribbons
Someone Needs Me

Something Has Happened
This House
A Well Known Fact
When The Kids Get Married
Where Are The Snows?

Although inventiveness and sparseness were Schmidt and Jones' stock in trade, **I Do! I Do!** was a curious paradox: a plotless, two-character, sweetly sentimental duet *and* a full-scale, big-budget star vehicle. The results were less than inspired, but Merrick and Champion managed to sell the Martin-Preston package to Broadway for a profitable run (cut short by the 1968 Actors' Equity strike).

CELEBRATION

JANUARY 22, 1969   AMBASSADOR THEATRE   110 PERFORMANCES

Book, lyrics, and direction by Tom Jones
Choreographed by Vernon Lusby
Produced by Cheryl Crawford and Richard Chandler
With Keith Charles, Susan Watson, Ted Thurston, and Michael Glenn-Smith

Published songs:
Celebration
I'm Glad To See You've Got What You Want
Love Song
My Garden
Under The Tree

Additional songs published in vocal score:
Beautician Ballet [instrumental]
Bored
Fifty Million Years Ago
It's You Who Makes Me Young
Not My Problem
Orphan In The Storm
Saturnalia [instrumental]
Somebody
Survive
Where Did It Go?
Winter And Summer

After two successful (yet relatively traditional) Merrick musicals, Schmidt and Jones returned to the experimental field of **THE FANTASTICKS [May 3, 1960]**

under the auspices of Cheryl Crawford. Both shows shared a similar theatrical simplicity; but THE FANTASTICKS was slightly metaphoric while CELEBRATION was heavily symbolic. After the show's quick failure, Schmidt and Jones retreated to their off-off-Broadway studio to work on future experiments away from commercial theatre pressures.

COLETTE

< First >

MAY 6, 1970   ELLEN STEWART THEATRE   < OFF-BROADWAY >   101
    PERFORMANCES

Play by Elinor Jones
(Based on *Earthly Paradise* [autobiographical stories] by Colette)
Incidental music by Harvey Schmidt
Lyrics by Tom Jones
Directed by Gerald Freedman
Produced by Cheryl Crawford in association with Mary W. John
With Zoe Caldwell, Mildred Dunnock, Keene Curtis, Barry Bostwick, and Schmidt

Published song:
Earthly Paradise

Additional songs recorded:
The Bouilloux Girls
Femme Du Monde

Tom Jones' wife wrote this rather acclaimed piece. Schmidt performed the on-stage piano accompaniment.

PHILEMON

JANUARY 3, 1975   PORTFOLIO THEATRE   < OFF-OFF-BROADWAY >   60
    PERFORMANCES

Book and lyrics by Tom Jones
Directed by Lester Collins (a.k.a. Tom Jones)
Produced by Jones and Schmidt
With Dick Latessa, Michael Glenn-Smith, Leila Martin, and Kathrin King Segal

Songs recorded:
Antioch Prison
Come With Me

Don't Kiki Me
The Greatest Of These
He's Coming
How Free I Feel
I Love His Face
I Love Order
I'd Do Almost Anything To Get Out Of Here And Go Home
My Secret Dream
Name: Cockian
The Nightmare
Oh, How Easy To Be Scornful!
Sometimes
The Streets of Antioch Stink
Within This Empty Space

Another experiment in the CELEBRATION [January 22, 1969] mode.

COLETTE

< Second >

[FEBRUARY 9, 1982]   FIFTH AVENUE THEATRE < SEATTLE,
     WASHINGTON >; CLOSED DURING PRE-BROADWAY TRYOUT

Book and lyrics by Tom Jones
Choreographed by Carl Jablonski
Directed by Dennis Rosa
Produced by Harry Rigby and The John F. Kennedy Center in association
with the Denver Center and James M. Nederlander
With Diana Rigg, Robert Helpmann, John Reardon, Martin Vidnovic,
and Marta Eggerth

Songs recorded:
Growing Older
Love Is Not A Sentiment Worthy Of Respect
The Room Is Filled With You

Schmidt and Jones returned to the commercial theatre with a full-scale,
full-sized musical that quickly collapsed. This COLETTE, incidentally, was not
based on the < First > [May 6, 1970].

COLETTE COLLAGE

< First Version—also see April 24, 1991 >

MARCH 31, 1983   CHURCH OF THE HEAVENLY REST
   < OFF-OFF-BROADWAY >   20 PERFORMANCES

Book and lyrics by Tom Jones
(Based on *Colette* < *Second* >)
Choreographed by Janet Watson
Directed by Fran Soeder
Produced by York Theatre Company [Janet Hayes Walker]
With Jana Robbins, Timothy Jerome, Steven F. Hall, Joanne Beretta, and
George Hall

Published songs:
None

Schmidt and Jones tried to whittle the top-heavy COLETTE < Second > [February 9, 1982] down to managable size. They would return yet again to the project in 1991.

GROVER'S CORNERS

[JULY 29, 1987]   MARRIOTT'S LINCOLNSHIRE RESORT &
   THEATRE   < LINCOLNSHIRE, ILLINOIS > ; REGIONAL TRYOUT

Book and lyrics by Tom Jones
(Based on *Our Town* [play] by Thornton Wilder)
Directed by Dominic Missimi
Produced by Kary M. Walker in association with the National Alliance of
Musical Theatre Producers
With Deanna Wells, Jones, Michael Bartsch, and Schmidt

Published songs:
None

Sometimes things just don't seem to work out. Jones and Schmidt's adaptation of Thornton Wilder's 1938 classic began as a developmental workshop production in December, 1984, with a Broadway opening slated for May 1, 1985. The producers were unable to attract sufficient backing, though, and the project was dropped. GROVER'S CORNERS made the rounds, eventually coming under the wing of an organization called the National Alliance of Musical Theatre Producers. Instead of braving Broadway, the plan was to mount the show in regional theatres across the country. The premiere production featured Jones himself as the Stage Manager, with Schmidt himself at the piano.

(Ninety minutes of unchecked pathos, according to one local reviewer.) GROVER languished until a full-scale national tour was announced to begin in November 1989, starring Mary Martin as the stage manager. (Well, why not?) But Mary—whose final musical was the boys' **I Do! I Do!** [December 5, 1966]—withdrew due to illness, and the tour was scrubbed. Mary Martin died on November 4, 1990.

COLETTE COLLAGE

Two Musicals about Colette

< Second Version—also see March 31, 1983 >

APRIL 24, 1991   THEATRE AT SAINT PETER'S CHURCH   < OFF
      OFF-BROADWAY >   34 PERFORMANCES

Book and lyrics by Tom Jones
(Based on *Colette* < *Second* >)
Choreographed by Janet Watson and Scott Harris
Directed by Jones and Schmidt
Produced by Musical Theatre Works
With Betsy Joslyn, Kenneth Kantor, James J. Mellon, Joanne Beretta, and Ralston Hill

Schmidt and Jones followed their **GROVER'S CORNERS** [July 29, 1987] disappointment by returning to their long-in-development **COLETTE** [February 0, 1982] project. In its final (?) form, **COLETTE COLLAGE** remained aimlessly puzzling and—ultimately—kind of silly. (**COLETTE COLLAGE** also proved, once and for all, that if your leading lady is nearing forty and slightly chunky and you need her to appear to be a nineteen-year-old slip-of-a-thing, it is not a good idea to ask her to parade around in her underwear.) For the record, there were three exciting songs written in the best Schmidt & Jones manner, all initially used in **COLETTE** < Second > : *Come to Life, I Miss You,* and *Joy.*

Harvey Schmidt and collaborator Tom Jones displayed creativity and inventiveness in their work during the Sixties. Despite two Broadway moneymaking hits, the pair were never comfortable working on the large scale necessary for the mainstem. Now, after many years of self-imposed exile, they find themselves stymied in their attempts to return. Broadway is certainly in great need of creativity and inventiveness just now, and Schmidt and Jones might very well have something more to contribute. (But not **COLETTE**ish, please!) Meanwhile, **THE FANTASTICKS** [May 3, 1960] keeps running.

Mitch Leigh

BORN: January 31, 1928   Brooklyn, New York

Mitch Leigh prepared for his musical career at Yale, studying composition with Paul Hindemith. Upon receiving his Masters, he entered the world of advertising and became an expert at television jingles (his most popular work —after *The Impossible Dream*—remains *Nobody Doesn't Like Sara Lee*). By the mid-Sixties, the highly successful jingle writer was ready to put his musical training to a more creative use.

TOO TRUE TO BE GOOD

MARCH 12, 1963   54TH STREET THEATRE   94 PERFORMANCES

Play by George Bernard Shaw
Incidental music by Mitch Leigh
Directed by Albert Marre
Produced by Paul Vroom, Buff Cobb, and Burry Frederick
With Lillian Gish, Robert Preston, David Wayne, Cedric Hardwicke, Eileen Heckart, Cyril Ritchard, Glynis Johns, and Ray Middleton

Published songs:
None

Leigh began a career-long association with director Albert Marre on this all-star revival. Marre's only musical hit was KISMET [PART 4: December 3, 1953]; more recently, he'd done MILK AND HONEY [Herman: October 10, 1961]. Leigh and Marre began discussing a musical adaptation of Dale Wasserman's 1960 teleplay "I, Don Quixote." The ambitious composer began the adaptation with poet W. H. Auden as lyricist.

NEVER LIVE OVER A PRETZEL FACTORY

MARCH 28, 1964   EUGENE O'NEILL THEATRE   9 PERFORMANCES

Play by Jerry Devine
Incidental music by Mitch Leigh

Directed by Albert Marre
Produced by Paul Vroom, Buff Cobb, and Marre
With Dennis O'Keefe and Martin Sheen

Published songs:
None

Leigh's first Broadway song to be heard—for a week—was *In This Town* (lyric by Jack Wohl).

MAN OF LA MANCHA

NOVEMBER 22, 1965   ANTA WASHINGTON SQUARE THEATRE   2,328
    PERFORMANCES

Lyrics by Joe Darion
Book by Dale Wasserman
(Based on *Don Quixote* [novel] by Miguel de Cervantes)
Choreographed by Jack Cole
Directed by Albert Marre
Produced by Albert W. Selden and Hal James
With Richard Kiley, Joan Diener (Marre), Irving Jacobson, Ray Middleton, and Robert Rounseville

Published songs:
Aldonza
Dulcinea
I Really Like Him
The Impossible Dream (The Quest)
Knight Of The Woeful Countenance (The Dubbing)
Little Bird, Little Bird
A Little Gossip
Man Of La Mancha (I, Don Quixote)
To Each His Dulcinea (To Every Man His Dream)

Additional songs published in vocal score:
Barber's Song
The Combat
Golden Helmet
I'm Only Thinking Of Him
It's All The Same
Knight Of The Mirrors
The Psalm
What Do You Want Of Me?

A summer stock tryout at the Goodspeed Opera House in East Haddam, Connecticut brought forth this monumental worldwide hit (see CHU-CHEM

<FIRST> [November 15, 1966]). Lyricist Joe Darion, W. H. Auden's replacement, had one Broadway musical (SHINBONE ALLEY [April 13, 1957]) to his credit; composer Leigh and librettist Wasserman had none. While the separate elements were not perfect in themselves, everything joined together magically. Leigh's highly theatrical, strongly rhythmic score played an important part in overriding the sometimes saccharine book, with *The Impossible Dream* affecting the public conscience as *Camelot* had five years earlier. Performances by Richard Kiley, Joan Diener and the others; Marre's inventive staging; Howard Bay's dungeon and windmill set—everything worked.

CHU-CHEM

< First Version—also see April 7, 1989>

[NOVEMBER 15, 1966] NEW LOCUST STREET THEATRE   < PHILADELPHIA, PENNSYLVANIA > ; CLOSED DURING PRE-BROADWAY TRYOUT

Lyrics by Jim Haines and Jack Wohl
Book by Ted Allan
Choreographed by Jack Cole
Directed by Albert Marre
Produced by Cheryl Crawford and Mitch Leigh
With Menasha Skulnick and Molly Picon

Published songs:
None

The summer of 1965 saw an ambitious project at the newly restored Goodspeed Opera House in East Haddam, Connecticut: producer Albert Selden and director Albert Marre planned a season of three new musicals with Mitch Leigh scores. Their intention was to move them to Broadway, in turn, for four-week runs. The first opened June 24 at Goodspeed, and took several months to get to New York; but MAN OF LA MANCHA [November 22, 1965] lasted longer than four weeks! The second was a short-lived musical adaptation of Sean O'Casey's 1940 *Purple Dust;* Marre had been trying to mount a production of the play since 1952. The third musical was CHU-CHEM, which was to take more than two decades to reach Broadway.

CRY FOR US ALL

APRIL 8, 1970   BROADHURST THEATRE   9 PERFORMANCES

Lyrics by William Alfred and Phyllis Robinson
Book by Alfred and Albert Marre
(Based on *Hogan's Goat* [play] by Alfred)

Directed by Marre
Produced by Mitch Leigh in association with L. Gerald Goldsmith
With Robert Weede, Joan Diener (Marre), Steve Arlen, Helen Gallagher, and Tommy Rall

Published songs:
Cry For Us All
That Slavery Is Love
The Verandah Waltz

Additional songs recorded:
Aggie, Oh Aggie
The Cruelty Man
The End Of My Race
How Are Ya, Since?
The Leg Of The Duck
The Mayor's Chair
Search Your Heart
Swing Your Bag
This Cornucopian Land
The Wages Of Sin
Who To Love If Not A Stranger

Leigh returned to Broadway with his most serious work. CRY FOR US ALL was a musical drama verging on the operatic; but a muddy book weighed down the already heavy subject matter, and an even heavier set proved far more depressing than the Inquisition prison of MAN OF LA MANCHA [November 22, 1965]. Yet the score was finely written, Leigh working with constantly shifting rhythms for highly emotional effects. CRY FOR US ALL had potential as a serious musical theatre piece. The music was of suitable caliber, but the other elements assembled were lacking.

HALLOWEEN

[MARCH 20, 1972]   BUCKS COUNTY PLAYHOUSE < NEW HOPE,
     PENNSYLVANIA > ; STOCK TRYOUT

Book and lyrics by Sidney Michaels
Directed by Albert Marre
Produced by Albert W. Selden and Jerome Minskoff
With David Wayne, Margot Moser, and Dick Shawn

Published songs:
None

Again working with a collaborator undistinguished in the musical theatre, Leigh turned out the strange, experimental **HALLOWEEN**, which quickly disappeared.

HOME SWEET HOMER

JANUARY 4, 1976   PALACE THEATRE   1 PERFORMANCE

Lyrics by Charles Burr and Forman Brown
Book by Roland Kibbee and Albert Marre
(Based on *The Odyssey* by Homer)
Directed by Marre
Produced by The John F. Kennedy Center
With Yul Brynner and Joan Diener (Marre)
NOTE: **ODYSSEY**, pre-Broadway title

Published songs:
None

A fabled Broadway flop, a rare case of the lyricist/librettist—Erich ("Love Story") Segal—quitting during the tryout tour and pulling his material. Everything worked out splendidly, though: a battery of new writers was brought in, the show was renamed, and **HOME SWEET HOMER** ended its epic odyssey at the Palace Theatre on old Broadway.

SARAVA

FEBRUARY 23, 1979   MARK HELLINGER THEATRE   177 PERFORMANCES

Book and lyrics by N. Richard Nash
(Based on *Dona Flor and Her Two Husbands* [novel] by Jorge Amado)
Directed and choreographed by Rick Atwell
Produced by Eugene V. Wolsk
With Tovah Feldshuh, P. J. Benjamin, and Michael Ingraham

Published song:
Sarava

Additional song recorded:
You Do

Leigh chose yet another amateur lyricist as collaborator. Playwright N. Richard Nash had provided the rather good book for **110 IN THE SHADE** [Schmidt: October 24, 1963] and the less happy **HAPPY TIME** [Kander: January 18, 1968] and **WILDCAT** [Coleman: December 16, 1960]. **SARAVA** was undistinguished, and even a skillfully designed Mitch Leigh advertising campaign didn't help.

APRIL SONG

[JULY 9, 1980]   JOHN DREW THEATRE < EAST HAMPTON, NEW YORK > ;
SUMMER STOCK TRYOUT

Lyrics by Sammy Cahn
Book by Albert Marre
(Based on *Leocadia* [play] by Jean Anouilh)
Directed by Marre
Produced by Marre and Leigh
With Glynis Johns

Published songs:
None

Something impelled Marre to take the Anouilh play—which he had successfully directed in an earlier nonmusical translation (TIME REMEMBERED [Duke:
November 2, 1957])—and turn it into a play with songs. Whatever the
intentions were, they didn't work.

MIKE

[APRIL 6, 1988]   WALNUT STREET THEATRE < PHILADELPHIA,
PENNSYLVANIA > ; REGIONAL TRYOUT

Lyrics by Lee Adams
Book by Thomas Meehan
(Based on the biography *A Valuable Property* by Michael Todd, Jr. and
Susan McCarthy Todd)
Directed by Martin Charnin
Produced by Walnut Street Theatre Company and Cyma Rubin
With Michael Lembeck, Loni Ackerman, Leslie Easterbrook, and Robert
Morse

Published songs:
None

Mike Todd's AS THE GIRLS GO [November 13, 1948], was a star vehicle for
Bobby Clark (with a bland score by Jimmy McHugh and Harold Adamson).
A dismal failure during its tryout, producer Todd threw out most of the book
(about the first lady President, with Bobby as "the First Man") and made it
into a glorified revue. AS THE GIRLS GO came into New York as the first show
with a $7.20 top—SOUTH PACIFIC [Rodgers: April 7, 1949] charged only
$6—unaccountably received a bunch of raves, and ran for 414 performances.
(It closed at a loss, though.) MIKE not only told the story of the making of

As THE GIRLS GO; it also imitated it, up to the part where the show is triumphantly transformed. Mike Todd (1909–1958) wasn't around to fix it, of course, so they brought in Martin Charnin. **MIKE** died in Philadelphia.

CHU CHEM

The 1st Chinese-Jewish Musical

< Second Version—also see November 15, 1966 >

MARCH 17, 1989   RITZ THEATRE   44 PERFORMANCES

Lyrics by Jim Haines and Jack Wohl
Book by Ted Allan
Directed by Albert Marre
Produced by The Mitch Leigh Company and William D. Rollnick
With Mark Zeller, Emily Zacharias, Thom Sesma, and Irving Burton

Published songs:
None

Songs recorded:
Boom!
I Once Believed
It Must Be Good For Me
It's Possible
I'll Talk To Her
Love Is
Orient Yourself
Our Kind Of War
The River
Shame On You
We Dwell In Our Hearts
Welcome
What Happened, What?
You'll Have To Change

Broadway finally got to see **CHU CHEM** (hyphen removed) after twenty-one years, and it was still pretty awful. This from the guy who wrote **MAN OF LA MANCHA** [November 22, 1965]???

Mitch Leigh entered the musical theatre with the instant classic **MAN OF LA MANCHA** [November 22, 1965]. He also wrote the admirable (if flawed) **CRY FOR US ALL** [April 8, 1970]. Otherwise, things have been pretty bleak. Leigh has pretty much controlled the artistic content of his shows, not only as strong-willed author but usually as co-producer as well. If his seven consecutive flops have been the result of poor decisions, the decisions seem to have been made by the composer himself.

Stephen Schwartz

BORN: March 6, 1948   Roslyn Heights, New York

The dearth of musical comedy production since the late Sixties has resulted in the lack of a new generation of theatre writers. Only one composer of the Seventies has shown the ability (and interest) to work principally in the theatre. Stephen Schwartz is a full twenty years younger than the Kander/Bock/Strouse/Schmidt/Coleman group; and no one has come along since Schwartz. After attending Carnegie-Mellon University, the twenty-one-year-old songwriter came to New York to begin his career.

[all music and lyrics by Stephen Schwartz]

BUTTERFLIES ARE FREE

OCTOBER 21, 1969   BOOTH THEATRE   1,128 PERFORMANCES

Play by Leonard Gershe
Directed by Milton Katselas
Produced by Arthur Whitelaw, Max J. Brown, and Byron Goldman
With Keir Dullea, Eileen Heckart, and Blythe Danner

Published song:
Butterflies Are Free

Schwartz got his first New York hearing with this singer-and-guitar title song. The play was a surprise hit; the song pleasant.

GODSPELL

MAY 17, 1971   CHERRY LANE THEATRE < OFF-BROADWAY >
2,124 PERFORMANCES

JUNE 22, 1976   BROADHURST THEATRE   527 PERFORMANCES

Book and direction by John-Michael Tebelak
(Based on *The Gospel According to St. Matthew*)
Produced by Edgar Lansbury, Stuart Duncan, and Joseph Beruh
With Stephen Nathan and David Haskell

Published songs:
All For The Best
All Good Gifts
Day By Day
Finale (Long Live God)
Learn Your Lessons Well
Light Of The World
O Bless The Lord
On The Willows
Prepare Ye The Way Of The Lord
Save The People
Turn Back, O Man
We Beseech Thee

Additional songs published in vocal score:
Alas For You
Prologue
Tower Of Babble

Schwartz's success began with this pop-Biblical revue, the **FANTASTICKS** [**Schmidt: May 3, 1960**] of the Seventies, although **GODSPELL**'s run was far shorter, only six-plus years. The score was easy and tuneful, with *Day By Day* bringing Schwartz to the attention of Broadway.

MASS

see Bernstein [September 8, 1971]

PIPPIN

OCTOBER 23, 1972   IMPERIAL THEATRE   1,944 PERFORMANCES

Book by Roger O. Hirson
Directed and choreographed by Bob Fosse
Produced by Stuart Ostrow
With John Rubinstein, Ben Vereen, Irene Ryan, and Jill Clayburgh

Published songs:
Corner Of The Sky
Goodtime Ladies Rag
I Guess I'll Miss The Man
Just Between The Two Of Us—cut
Morning Glow

Additional songs published in vocal score:
Extraordinary
Glory

Kind Of Woman
Love Song
Magic To Do
No Time At All
On The Right Track
Pippin
Prayer For A Duck
Simple Joys
Spread A Little Sunshine
There He Was
War Is A Science
Welcome Home, Son
With You

With the success of **GODSPELL** [**May 17, 1971**], a college project of Schwartz's found its way to Broadway. Inability to raise money resulted in a drastically cut budget; hence, the imaginative, minimal production (and a skeletal replacement for the intended set). What **PIPPIN** did have was Bob Fosse at his inventive best, more than making up for the less-than-staggering score and more-than-lackluster book. Ben Vereen and designers Tony Walton and Patricia Zipprodt made valuable contributions; and a revolutionary (for the theatre) TV advertising campaign kept **PIPPIN** running for almost five years.

THE MAGIC SHOW

MAY 28, 1974   CORT THEATRE   1,920 PERFORMANCES

Book by Bob Randall
(Based on magic by Doug Henning)
Directed and choreographed by Grover Dale
Produced by Edgar Lansbury, Joseph Beruh, and Ivan Reitman
With Henning, Dale Soules, Anita Morris, and David Ogden Stiers

Published song:
Lion Tamer

Additional songs published in vocal selection:
Before Your Very Eyes
Charmin's Lament
Solid Silver Platform Shoes
Style
Sweet, Sweet, Sweet
Two's Company
Up To His Old Tricks
West End Avenue

The great magic feat here was pulling a long-run hit out of a very empty hat. THE MAGIC SHOW ran 1,920 performances; A LITTLE NIGHT MUSIC [Sondheim: February 25, 1973], in comparison, barely broke 600.

THE BAKER'S WIFE

[MAY 11, 1976]   DOROTHY CHANDLER PAVILION < LOS ANGELES > ;
CLOSED DURING PRE-BROADWAY TRYOUT

Book by Joseph Stein
(Based on *La Femme de Boulanger* [movie] by Marcel Pagnol and Jean Giono)
Choreographed by Robert Tucker
Directed by John Berry
Produced by David Merrick
With Topol (replaced by Paul Sorvino), Patti LuPone, Keene Curtis, Portia Nelson, and David Rounds

Songs published in vocal selection:
If I Have To Live Alone
Meadowlark—cut
Where Is The Warmth?

Additional songs recorded:
Any-Day-Now Day
Bread
Buzz-A-Buzz—added to 1989 British production
Chanson
Endless Delights
Feminine Companionship—added to British production
Gifts Of Love
If It Wasn't For You—added to British production
Look For The Woman
The Luckiest Man In The World
Merci, Madame
Plain And Simple—added to British production
Proud Lady
Romance
Serenade

Stephen Schwartz's track record led to this assignment on the biggest musical of the season. David Merrick brought together Topol, the Israeli-born star of the London and Hollywood FIDDLER ON THE ROOF [Bock: September 22, 1964], and Joe Stein, that musical's librettist, for a big-budget, sure-fire hit . . . like BREAKFAST AT TIFFANY'S [Merrill: December 14, 1966]. Director

Joseph Hardy left midway through the tryout; star Topol lasted till the next-to-last stop. Paul Sorvino could not handle the problematic material nearly so well, and THE BAKER'S WIFE was quickly no more. An "improved" London production [October 27, 1989] also proved to be half-baked.

WORKING

MAY 14, 1978   46TH STREET THEATRE   25 PERFORMANCES

Music and lyrics also by others
Book and direction by Stephen Schwartz
(Based on the book by Studs Terkel)
Choreographed by Onna White
Produced by Stephen R. Friedman and Irwin Meyer (in association with Joseph Harris)
With Lenora Nemetz, Rex Everhart, Bobo Lewis, Patti LuPone, and Arny Freeman

Songs published in vocal selection:
All The Livelong Day (lyric including "I Hear America Singing" by Walt Whitman)
Fathers And Sons
It's An Art
Neat To Be A Newsboy

If Broadway can be said to take retribution for undeserved hits, then Broadway took retribution on composer Schwartz with THE BAKER'S WIFE [May 11, 1976]. Then they did it again, more publicly. Schwartz conceived, directed, and cowrote WORKING, which didn't work at all.

RAGS

See Strouse [August 21, 1986]

CHILDREN OF EDEN

JANUARY 8, 1991   PRINCE EDWARD THEATRE < LONDON > 103 PERFORMANCES

Book by John Caird
(Based on the Old Testament)
Choreographed by Matthew Bourne
Directed by Caird
Produced by William MacDonald and Patricia MacNaughton
With Ken Page, Martin Smith, Shezwae Powell, and Frances Ruffelle

Songs recorded:
Ain't It Good?
Children Of Eden
Civilized Society
Close To Home
Degenerations
The Dove Song
The Expulsion
Generations
The Hardest Part Of Love
In Pursuit Of Excellence
In The Beginning
In Whatever Time We Have
Let There Be
Lost In The Wilderness
The Naming
The Return Of The Animals
Shipshape
The Spark Of Creation
Stranger To The Rain
Wasteland
World Without You

The story of Adam and Eve and the Serpent and Noah, from the guy who wrote **GODSPELL** [**May 17, 1971**] (and the co-director of **LES MISERABLES** [**PART 5: March 12, 1987**]). A fourth consecutive mammoth disaster.

The highpoint of Stephen Schwartz's career was unquestionably **PIPPIN** [**October 23, 1972**]. The low point has been—well—everything since. With three long-running goldmines to his credit, though, Mr. Schwartz will presumably be back one of these days to try anew.

PART 4

INTRODUCTION

The following section contains additional shows which merit discussion. Some were enormous hits and are included for that reason only; others were written by popular or interesting composers who never found Broadway success; and a handful are included because of the high quality of the work. Until the late Sixties, Broadway was virtually dominated by the thirty composers already discussed. Since that time, the increased expenses and complications of musical production have made it difficult for newcomers to get repeated hearings (save one, who will be discussed in **PART 5: NOTABLE IMPORTED MUSICALS**).

Notable Scores by Other Composers

IRENE

NOVEMBER 1, 1919   VANDERBILT THEATRE   675 PERFORMANCES

Music by Harry Tierney
Lyrics by Joseph McCarthy
Book by James Montgomery
Directed by Edward Royce
Produced by Vanderbilt Producing Corp.
With Edith Day

Published songs:
Alice Blue Gown
Castle Of Dreams
The Family Tree (additional lyric by Charles Gaynor)—initial publication
       upon use in 1973 revival
Hobbies
Irene
The Last Part Of Ev'ry Party
The 'Paul Jones'
Skyrocket
Talk Of The Town
To Be Worthy (Worthy Of You)
We're Getting Away With It
You've Got Me Out On A Limb—written for 1940 movie version

Additional songs published in vocal score:
To Love You—countermelody to *To Be Worthy*
Too Much Bowden (Opening Chorus Act 2, Scene 2)

Tin Pan Alley composer Harry Tierney (1895–1965) made occasional Broadway visits. His first and most successful, IRENE, set the mold for the "American Cinderella" musicals. (The Shuberts, ever on the lookout for a catchy title, actually came up with SALLY, IRENE & MARY [September 4, 1922]; SALLY being Kern [December 21, 1920], and MARY [October 18, 1920] being Louis Hirsch's *Love Nest* musical.) IRENE waltzed to a record-length run in her *Alice Blue Gown*, unsurpassed until PINS AND NEEDLES [Rome: November 27, 1937] set a new mark of 1,108. Tierney and McCarthy wrote two other successful shows, both for Ziegfeld: Eddie Cantor's KID BOOTS [December 31, 1923] and RIO RITA [February 2, 1927].

SHUFFLE ALONG

A Musical Melange

MAY 23, 1921   63RD STREET MUSIC HALL   484 PERFORMANCES

Music by Eubie Blake
Lyrics by Noble Sissle
Book by Flournoy Miller and Aubrey Lyles
(Conceived by Miller and Lyles)
Directed by Miller
Produced by Nikko Producing Co.
With Blake, Sissle, Miller, Lyles, and Florence Mills

Published songs:
Aintcha Comin' Back, Mary Ann, To Maryland
Baltimore Buzz
Bandana Days
Daddy Won't You Please Come Home
Everything Reminds Me Of You
Gypsy Blues
Good Night, Angeline (by Jim Europe, Sissle, and Blake)—originally
    issued as 1919 pop song
I'm Craving For That Kind Of Love (Kiss Me)
I'm Just Simply Full Of Jazz
I'm Just Wild About Harry—new melody for lyric revised from 1916
    nonshow song *My Loving Baby*
*If You've Never Been Vamped By A Brown Skin (You've Never Been
    Vamped At All)*
In Honeysuckle Time (When Emaline Said She'd Be Mine)
Kentucky Sue
Love Will Find A Way
Liza Quit Vamping Me—advertised but not published
Low Down Blues
Old Black Joe And Uncle Tom
Oriental Blues
Pickaninny Shoes
Shuffle Along
Sing Me To Sleep, Dear Mammy (With A Hush-A-Bye Pickaninny Tune)
Vision Girl—originally used in MIDNIGHT ROUNDERS [July 12, 1920]
NOTE: Songs cut or added after the opening not so noted

This shoestring revue set a standard for ragtag black musicals. A surprise hit,
SHUFFLE ALONG outran most shows of the time and then toured for years. Two
revised versions [December 26, 1932] and [May 8, 1952]—both headed by

Sissle and Blake—lasted twenty-one performances combined. Eubie Blake (1883–1983) had no success with his other Broadway work. EUBIE! [September 20, 1978], an anthology revue, attempted to cash in on the overflow from the Fats Waller success AIN'T MISBEHAVIN' [May 8, 1978].

GEORGE WHITE'S SCANDALS OF 1926
Eighth Edition

JUNE 14, 1926   APOLLO THEATRE   432 PERFORMANCES

Music by Ray Henderson
Lyrics by B. G. DeSylva and Lew Brown
Sketches by George White and W. K. Wells
Directed and produced by White
With Ann Pennington, Willie and Eugene Howard, and Harry Richman

Published songs:
The Birth Of The Blues
Black Bottom
The Girl Is You And The Boy Is Me
Here I Am—added after opening; published in separate edition
It All Depends On You—added after opening; published in separate
        edition
Lucky Day
Sevilla
Tweet Tweet

Ray Henderson (1896–1970) became a force in the pop music field with hits like *That Old Gang Of Mine* and *Bye Bye Blackbird.* When George Gershwin left the SCANDALS to concentrate on book musicals, White turned to Henderson, pop lyricist Lew Brown, and De Sylva (Gershwin's SCANDALS collaborator). Thus was born the most successful songwriting team of the late Twenties. This edition of the SCANDALS alone had four hits, including *Black Bottom*—which launched a dance craze—and the fine *Birth Of The Blues.* Gershwin's five editions had brought forth only two worthwhile songs, *I'll Build A Stairway To Paradise* and *Somebody Loves Me*—both with DeSylva as collaborator.

GOOD NEWS!
The Collegiate Musical

SEPTEMBER 6, 1927   CHANIN'S 46TH STREET THEATRE   551
PERFORMANCES

Music by Ray Henderson
Lyrics by B. G. DeSylva and Lew Brown
Book by Laurence Schwab and DeSylva
Choreographed by Bobby Connolly
Directed by Edgar MacGregor
Produced by Schwab and Frank Mandel
With Mary Lawlor, John Price Jones, Zelma O'Neal, and George Olsen
and his Orchestra

Published songs:
The Best Things In Life Are Free
A Girl Of The Pi Beta Phi
Good News
Happy Days
He's A Ladies' Man
Just Imagine
Lucky In Love
The Varsity Drag

Additional songs published in vocal score:
Baby! What?
Flaming Youth
In The Meantime
On The Campus
Tait Song
Today's The Day

DeSylva, Brown, and Henderson entered the book musical field with five hits
in a row. Following FLYING HIGH [March 3, 1930], the team went to Hollywood—where DeSylva soon moved on to a producing career (see DUBARRY
WAS A LADY [Porter: December 6, 1939]). Henderson and Brown continued
writing (together and individually) but never equalled the success of their five
great years. GOOD NEWS! was a mindless football musical in the LEAVE IT TO
JANE [Kern: August 28, 1917] tradition; *The Best Things In Life Are Free* and
The Varsity Drag were hits in the DeSylva, Brown, and Henderson tradition.

BLACKBIRDS OF 1928

MAY 9, 1928   LIBERTY THEATRE   519 PERFORMANCES

Music by Jimmy McHugh
Lyrics by Dorothy Fields
Directed and produced by Lew Leslie
With Bill Robinson, Adelaide Hall, and Aida Ward

Published songs:
Baby!
Bandanna Babies
Diga-Diga-Doo
Dixie
Doin' The New Low Down
Here Comes My Blackbird
I Can't Give You Anything But Love
I Must Have That Man!
Porgy
Magnolia's Wedding Day
Shuffle Your Feet And Just Roll Along

Pop songwriter Jimmy McHugh (1894–1969) began contributing material to Harlem's Cotton Club in 1921. In 1927 he found a new lyricist: Dorothy Fields, of the familiar show business family. Cotton Club work got them the assignment for the highly successful **BLACKBIRDS OF 1928**, which, unlike **SHUFFLE ALONG [PART 4: May 23, 1921]**, was a professional, high-caliber production. The score brought McHugh and Fields immediate acclaim, with *I Can't Give You Anything But Love* and *Diga-Diga-Doo* leading the way. The team moved to Hollywood for successful work (including *I'm In The Mood For Love*) until Jerome Kern needed a new lyric for his 1935 movie version of **ROBERTA [November 18, 1933]**. Fields, on staff at RKO, got the chance and wrote *Lovely To Look At.* McHugh, per terms of his contract, shared credit for the lyric; but Kern claimed Fields as his new collaborator. McHugh wrote for another twenty-five years—including a handful of Broadway musicals—but never so well as during his Dorothy Fields days.

WHOOPEE

DECEMBER 4, 1928   NEW AMSTERDAM THEATRE   255 PERFORMANCES

Music mostly by Walter Donaldson
Lyrics mostly by Gus Kahn
Book and direction by Wm. Anthony McGuire
(Based on *The Nervous Wreck* [play] by Owen Davis)

Produced by Florenz Ziegfeld, Jr.
With Eddie Cantor, Ruth Etting, and George Olsen and his Orchestra

Published songs:
Come West, Little Girl, Come West
A Girl Friend Of A Boy Friend Of Mine—written for 1930 movie version
Gypsy Joe
The Gypsy Song (Where Sunset Meets The Sea)
Here's To The Girl Of My Heart!
I'm Bringing A Red, Red Rose
Love Me Or Leave Me
Makin' Whoopee!
My Baby Just Cares For Me—written for movie version
The Song Of The Setting Sun
Until You Get Somebody Else

Walter Donaldson (1893–1947) was a top Tin Pan Alley composer, with hits like *How Ya Gonna Keep 'Em Down On The Farm?*, *My Blue Heaven* and Al Jolson's *My Mammy*. Although he occasionally contributed interpolations, his only full stage score was this Ziegfeld hit for Eddie Cantor. Donaldson's popular touch was evident in *Makin' Whoopee!* and *Love Me Or Leave Me*.

FINE AND DANDY

SEPTEMBER 23, 1930 · ERLANGER THEATRE 255 PERFORMANCES

Music by Kay Swift
Lyrics by Paul James
Book by Donald Ogden Stewart
"Many Nonsensical Moments Created by Joe Cook"
Directed by Morris Green
Produced by Green and Lewis Gensler
With Joe Cook, Nell O'Day, Dave Chasen, and Eleanor Powell

Published songs:
Can This Be Love?
Fine And Dandy
The Jig Hop
Let's Go Eat Worms In The Garden
Nobody Breaks My Heart
Rich Or Poor
Starting At The Bottom

A handful of female lyricists have been successful in the theatre, starting with Anne Caldwell, Dorothy (THE STUDENT PRINCE [Romberg: December 2,

1924]) Donnelly and Dorothy Fields. But for some unaccountable reason, almost no women composers have had Broadway impact. Kay Swift (born 1907) made a promising start with notable interpolations in THE LITTLE SHOW [Schwartz: April 30, 1929] and NINE-FIFTEEN REVUE [Arlen: February 11, 1930]. Her first and only book musical was FINE AND DANDY, with one of the best scores of the season. Swift wrote three extraspecial songs: *Can't We Be Friends?* (from THE LITTLE SHOW), *Can This Be Love?* and the dandy *Fine And Dandy.* She then left her lyricist-husband Paul James (Warburg) and began a professional/personal relationship with George Gershwin. Her only return to Broadway was with songs for Cornelia Otis Skinner's one-woman PARIS '90 [March 4, 1952]. Irene Dunne played Swift in her 1952 movie semi-biography. Other early women composers included Alma Sanders (who wrote a string of unimportant Twenties musicals with lyricist-husband Monte Carlo) and Ann Ronell, another Gershwin protégé best known for her lyric to the 1933 *Who's Afraid Of The Big Bad Wolf?* In more recent times, Mary Rodgers and Carol Hall were both successful with transfers from off-Broadway's old Yiddish Art (Phoenix/Entermedia) Theatre, ONCE UPON A MATTRESS [PART 4: May 11, 1959] and THE BEST LITTLE WHOREHOUSE IN TEXAS [PART 4: April 17, 1978]. And the Nineties began with Lucy Simon's THE SECRET GARDEN [PART 4: April 25, 1991].

WALK WITH MUSIC

JUNE 4, 1940   ETHEL BARRYMORE THEATRE   55 PERFORMANCES

Music mostly by Hoagy Carmichael
Lyrics mostly by Johnny Mercer
Book by Guy Bolton, Parke Levy, and Alan Prescott
(Based on *Three Blind Mice* [play] by Stephen Powys)
Directed by Clarke Lilley
Produced by Ruth Selwyn in association with the Messrs. Shubert
With Kitty Carlisle, Mitzi Green, Jack Whiting and Stepin' Fetchit
NOTE: THREE AFTER THREE, pre-Broadway title

Published songs:
Darn Clever, These Chinee—advertised but not published
Everything Happens To Me—advertised but not published
How Nice For Me—issued in professional copy only
I Walk With Music
Ooh! What You Said
The Rumba Jumps!
Way Back In 1939 A.D.
What'll They Think Of Next

Additional songs published in USO/Camp Shows "AT EASE" (Volume 3):

Break It Up, Cinderella—with revised lyric, retitled *Break It Now, Buck Private*

Wait Till You See Me In The Morning—with revised lyric

Hoagy Carmichael (1899–1981) was one of our premiere American melodists; his credits include such fascinating stunners as *Stardust, Lazy River, Georgia On My Mind,* and *How Little We Know.* A prewar Hollywood collaboration with Frank Loesser turned out hits like *Two Sleepy People* and *Heart And Soul* (second only to *Chopsticks* in popularity with piano duetists). His periodic collaboration with Johnny Mercer resulted in *Lazy Bones* and the 1951 Oscar winner *In The Cool, Cool, Cool Of The Evening.* WALK WITH MUSIC, Carmichael's only complete score, was a quick failure; his one Broadway song hit was *Little Old Lady* (lyric by Stanley Adams), interpolated into THE SHOW IS ON [Arlen, Duke, Gershwin, Rodgers, Schwartz: December 25, 1936]. For the record, Stephen Powys, author of WALK WITH MUSIC's original work, was the pseudonym of Virginia De Lanty (the fourth Mrs. Guy Bolton).

EARLY TO BED

JUNE 17, 1943 · BROADHURST THEATRE · 380 PERFORMANCES

Music by Thomas (Fats) Waller
Book and lyrics by George Marion, Jr.
Choreographed by Robert Alton
Produced by Richard Kollmar and Alfred Bloomingdale
With Kollmar, Muriel Angelus, and Mary Small

Published songs:
The Ladies Who Sing With A Band
Slightly Less Than Wonderful
There's A Man In My Life
This Is So Nice
When The Nylons Bloom Again—issued as professional copy only

Additional songs recorded:
Hi-De-Ho-Hi

Fats Waller (1904–1943) was a jazz pianist/singer with a distinctive style. One of his very few Broadway visits brought *Ain't Misbehavin',* from the revue HOT CHOCOLATES [June 20, 1929]. Waller's second and final complete score was EARLY TO BED, which began a decent wartime run shortly before the composer's death. An anthology revue of Waller's work, AIN'T MISBEHAVIN' [May 8, 1978], was a major success. Collaborator Marion's father was a popular early musical comedy director. Producer/star Kollmar, husband to columnist Dorothy Kilgallen, had been the juvenile in **KNICKERBOCKER HOLIDAY** [Weill: October 19, 1938] and **TOO MANY GIRLS** [Rodgers: October 18, 1939].

BEGGAR'S HOLIDAY

DECEMBER 26, 1946   BROADWAY THEATRE   108 PERFORMANCES

Music by Duke Ellington
Book and lyrics by John Latouche
(Based on *The Beggar's Opera* by John Gay)
Choreographed by Valerie Bettis
Directed by Nicholas Ray
Produced by Perry Watkins and John R. Sheppard, Jr.
With Alfred Drake, Bernice Parks, Marie Bryant, and Zero Mostel

Published songs:
On The Wrong Side Of The Railroad Tracks
Take Love Easy
Tomorrow Mountain
When I Walk With You

Additional songs published in vocal selection:
Brown Penny [instrumental]
I've Got Me—lyric revised for song of same title in **BALLET BALLADS**
    [May 9, 1948] (music by Jerome Moross)
Maybe I Should Change My Ways
Tooth and Claw
Wanna Be Bad
Where Is My Hero?

Additional songs recorded:
In Between
Lullaby for Junior
Ore From A Goldmine
The Scrimmage Of Life

This ambitious musical was the first book show by bandleader/composer Duke Ellington (1899–1974). Based on **THE BEGGAR'S OPERA**—at a time when the Weill/Brecht adaptation was virtually unknown in this country (see **THE THREEPENNY OPERA** (Second Version) [Weill: March 10, 1954])—**BEGGAR'S HOLIDAY** ran into tryout trouble when star Libby Holman quit. Audiences looking for a happy, black revusical from the Duke were confronted by Zero Mostel's perplexing Poppa Peachum. Ellington came back once more with **POUSSE-CAFE** [March 18, 1966], which lasted three performances. The black composer anthology fad of the late Seventies brought forth an Ellington revue, **Sophisticated Ladies** [March 1, 1981].

FLAHOOLEY

May 14, 1951   **Broadhurst Theatre**   40 **performances**

Music mostly by Sammy Fain (also see **Lane: September 11, 1952**)
Lyrics mostly by E. Y. Harburg
Book and direction by Harburg and Fred Saidy
Choreographed by Helen Tamiris
Produced by Cheryl Crawford in association with Harburg and Saidy
With Ernest Truex, Yma Sumac, Barbara Cook, Edith Atwater, and Irwin Corey

Published songs:
Come Back, Little Genie—advertised but not published
Flahooley
He's Only Wonderful
Here's To Your Illusions
How Lucky Can You Get?—written for revised touring production,
         retitled **Jollyanna** [Lane: September 11, 1952]
The Springtime Cometh
Who Says There Ain't No Santa Claus?—advertised but not published
The World Is Your Balloon

Additional songs recorded:
B. G. Bigelow, Inc.
Birds (music and lyric by Moises Vivanco)
Come Back, Little Genie
Jump, Little Chillun!
Najala's Lament (music and lyric by Vivanco)
Najala's Song Of Joy (music and lyric by Vivanco)
Sing The Merry
The Spirit of Capsulanti
Who Says There Ain't No Santa Claus?
You, Too, Can Be A Puppet

Sammy Fain was the only successful movie composer who continually returned to Broadway throughout his career—coming up with eight flops. The unconventional **Flahooley** stands out for its above-average score and very good intentions. In **Finian's Rainbow** [Lane: January 10, 1947] Harburg slyly cloaked his points with humor; but during the witch-hunt days of **Flahooley,** Harburg couldn't laugh. (He could, though, provide the lyrically dazzling *You, Too, Can Be A Puppet.*) Cheryl Crawford once again gambled on an important, uncommercial musical and paid the price.

TOP BANANA

NOVEMBER 1, 1951   WINTER GARDEN THEATRE   350 PERFORMANCES

Music and lyrics by Johnny Mercer
Book by H. S. Kraft
Choreographed by Ron Fletcher
Directed by Jack Donohue
Produced by Paula Stone and Mike Sloane
With Phil Silvers, Rose Marie, Joey Faye, and Bob Scheerer

Published songs:
Be My Guest
My Home Is In My Shoes
O.K. For T.V.
Only If You're In Love
Sans Souci
That's For Sure
Top Banana

Additional songs recorded:
A Dog Is A Man's Best Friend
The Elevator Song (Going Up)
I Fought Every Step Of The Way
The Man Of The Year This Week
Meet Miss Blendo
Slogan Song
A Word A Day
You're So Beautiful That . . .

Exceptional pop lyricist Johnny Mercer (1909–1976) occasionally wrote his own music—including movie song hits *I'm An Old Cowhand* and *Something's Gotta Give*. TOP BANANA was a burlesque musical featuring Phil Silvers, a handful of clowns, and a dog named Ted "Sport" Morgan (who sang an inspired duet with Silvers). The show, which did not quite make it, was coproduced by Paula Stone (of the Stepping Stones—see RIPPLES [Kern: February 11, 1930]).

KISMET

A Musical Arabian Night

DECEMBER 3, 1953   ZIEGFELD THEATRE   583 PERFORMANCES

Music by Alexander Borodin
Musical adaptation and lyrics by Robert Wright and George Forrest
Book by Charles Lederer and Luther Davis

(Based on the play by Edward Knoblock)
Choreographed by Jack Cole
Directed by Albert Marre
Produced by Lederer
With Alfred Drake, Doretta Morrow, Richard Kiley, Joan Diener, and
Henry Calvin

Published songs:
And This Is My Beloved
Baubles, Bangles And Beads
Bored—written for 1955 movie version
He's In Love
Night Of My Nights
Sands Of Time
Stranger In Paradise

Additional songs published in vocal score:
Fate
Gesticulate
Not Since Nineveh
The Olive Tree
Rahadlakum
Rhymes Have I
Was I Wazir?
Zubbediya [instrumental]

Additional songs recorded (music and lyrics by Wright and Forrest):
Golden Land, Golden Life—written for revised version, TIMBUKTU [April
        1, 1978; 243 performances]
In The Beginning, Woman—written for TIMBUKTU
My Magic Lamp—written for TIMBUKTU
Power—written for TIMBUKTU

The Messrs. Wright and Forrest had joined with West Coast impresario
Edwin Lester for a series of operettas "borrowing" tunes from dead composers.
The first, Eddie Grieg's SONG OF NORWAY [August 21, 1944; 860 perform-
ances], moved to Broadway for an enormously successful wartime run. This
was followed by quick flops set to Vic Herbert, Frank Lehar, and that crazy
Brazilian Villa-Lobos (who was alive, but certainly highbrow). Then came
KISMET with tunes by Al Borodin, the only man to win a Tony Award 67 years
after he'd kicked off (thanks to his famous ditty *Stranger In Paradise*, better
known—to him at least—as a section of the *Polovtsian Dances* from "Prince
Igor"). Wright and Forrest then decided it was time to write their own
music—or maybe they just ran out of dead composers?—and penned three
flops of their own, only one of which (the Alfred Drake-starrer KEAN [Novem-

ber 2, 1961]) made it to Broadway. The boys next turned to the works of Serge Rachmaninoff (d. 1943) for one last floperetta, ANYA [November 29, 1965]. And that was that for a quarter of a century—when AT THE GRAND [July 7, 1958], one of their out-of-town mishaps, was dusted off, overhauled, and considerably Tuned up under the title GRAND HOTEL [PART 4: November 12, 1989].

THE GOLDEN APPLE

MARCH 11, 1954   PHOENIX THEATRE < OFF-BROADWAY >   46
  PERFORMANCES

APRIL 20, 1954   ALVIN THEATRE   127 PERFORMANCES

Music by Jerome Moross
Book and lyrics by John Latouche
(Based on *The Odyssey* by Homer)
Choreographed by Hanya Holm
Directed by Norman Lloyd
Produced by The Phoenix Theatre (T. Edward Hambleton and Norris Houghton)
With Priscilla Gillette, Stephen Douglass, Kaye Ballard, Jack Whiting, and Jonathan Lucas

Published songs:
Goona-Goona
It's The Going Home Together
Lazy Afternoon
Store-Bought Suit
Windflowers—initially issued as *When We Were Young*

Additional songs recorded:
Calypso
Circe, Circe
Come Along, Boys (Raise A Ruckus Tonight)
Departure For Rhododendron (1st Act Finale)
Doomed, Doomed, Doomed
Hector's Song (People Like You And Like Me)
Helen Is Always Willing
The Heroes Come Home
It Was A Glad Adventure
Judgement Of Paris
Mother Hare's Prophecy
My Love Is On The Way
My Picture In The Papers

Overture [instrumental]
Scylla And Charybdis
Sewing Bee
The Tirade (Finale)
Ulysses' Soliloquy (Despair Cuts Through Me Like A Knife)

A brilliant musical theatre experiment. Jerome Moross (1913–1983) had been principal composer of the radical PARADE < First > [Blitzstein: May 20, 1935], but most of his career was spent scoring motion pictures. John Latouche's best work had been on CABIN IN THE SKY [Duke: October 25, 1940]. THE GOLDEN APPLE benefited from a perfect blend of theatrical elements, but it was the more-than-glorious score that carried it all the way to Broadway. The musical received the 1954 New York Drama Critics' Circle Award.

PLAIN AND FANCY

JANUARY 27, 1955   MARK HELLINGER THEATRE   461 PERFORMANCES

Music by Albert Hague
Lyrics by Arnold B. Horwitt
Book by Joseph Stein and Will Glickman
Choreographed by Helen Tamiris
Directed by Morton Da Costa
Produced by Richard Kollmar and James W. Gardiner in association with Yvette Schumer
With Richard Derr, Barbara Cook, David Daniels, Shirl Conway, and Nancy Andrews

Published songs:
City Mouse, Country Mouse
Follow Your Heart
It Wonders Me
Plain We Live
Plenty of Pennsylvania
This Is All Very New To Me
Young And Foolish

Additional songs published in vocal score:
How Do You Raise A Barn?
It's A Helluva Way To Run A Love Affair
I'll Show Him
Take Your Time And Take Your Pick
Why Not Katie?
You Can't Miss It

By the mid-Fifties, musical comedy had been Abbottized into slick, well-made, slightly-satirical laugh machines like **WONDERFUL TOWN [Bernstein: February 25, 1953]** and **THE PAJAMA GAME [Adler: May 13, 1954].** Along came **PLAIN AND FANCY,** an old-fashioned, low-pressure alternative set among the Pennsylvania Dutch (Amish); while the material was no more than adequate, it was pleasant and certainly suitable for the family trade. The show was buoyed by the work of first-time composer Albert Hague, providing some of the loveliest melodies of the season (*It Wonders Me, Young and Foolish, Follow Your Heart*). The moderate success of **PLAIN AND FANCY** encouraged the mounting of a second slice of folksy Americana, one that had been kicking around since 1951: Meredith Willson's **THE MUSIC MAN [December 19, 1957],** with director and leading lady from **PLAIN AND FANCY.** And that same basic plot—unmarried big-city couple go to small-town U.S.A., observe quaint customs, suffer romantic discord, and patch things up by the final curtain—was satirically embellished to far greater effect for **BYE BYE BIRDIE [Strouse: April 14, 1960].**

LI'L ABNER

NOVEMBER 15, 1956   ST. JAMES THEATRE   693 PERFORMANCES

Music by Gene de Paul
Lyrics by Johnny Mercer
Book by Norman Panama and Melvin Frank
(Based on the comic strip by Al Capp)
Directed and choreographed by Michael Kidd
Produced by Panama, Frank, and Kidd
With Edith Adams, Peter Palmer, Stubby Kaye, and Charlotte Rae

Published songs:
If I Had My Druthers
It's A Nuisance Having You Around—cut
Jubilation T. Cornpone
Love In A Home
Namely You
Otherwise (I Wish It Could Be)—written for 1959 movie version
Unnecessary Town

Additional songs published in vocal score:
The Country's In The Very Best Of Hands
Dogpatch Dance [instrumental]
It's A Typical Day
The Matrimonial Stomp
Oh, Happy Day

Past My Prime
Progress Is The Root Of All Evil
Put 'Em Back
Rag Off'n The Bush
Sadie Hawkins Ballet [instrumental]
There's Room Enough For Us
What's Good For General Bullmoose

Choreographer Michael Kidd came to Broadway with the magical FINIAN'S RAINBOW [Lane: January 10, 1947], and attained genius status (and three quick Tony Awards) with his work on GUYS AND DOLLS [Loesser: November 24, 1950] and CAN-CAN [Porter: May 7, 1953]. Kidd was in league with Jerome Robbins, setting a new dance style for Broadway. The pair had, incidentally, danced the 1944 premiere of the latter's "Fancy Free" (see ON THE TOWN [Bernstein: December 28, 1944]). Kidd went to MGM for their 1953 version of THE BAND WAGON [Schwartz: June 3, 1931]. This was followed by a second movie musical classic, the 1954 "Seven Brides for Seven Brothers" (with a fine score by pop composer Gene de Paul and Johnny Mercer). Screenwriters Panama and Frank combined with Kidd—here making his directing debut—to produce LI'L ABNER. Al Capp's cartoon characters had been looking for a stage role for several years, but Broadway writers had given up on them. Kidd and company did just fine, with Johnny Mercer's most sparkling stage lyrics and Kidd's extra-special *Sadie Hawkins Ballet.* The choreographer won his fourth Tony, and was to receive another for his next musical (DESTRY RIDES AGAIN [Rome: April 23, 1959]). However, the talented Kidd has had nothing but flops since.

GOLDILOCKS

OCTOBER 11, 1958   LUNT-FONTANNE THEATRE   161 PERFORMANCES

Music by Leroy Anderson
Lyrics by Joan Ford, Walter and Jean Kerr
Book by Walter and Jean Kerr
Choreographed by Agnes de Mille
Directed by Walter Kerr
Produced by The Producers Theatre and Robert Whitehead
With Don Ameche, Elaine Stritch, Russell Nype, Pat Stanley, Nathaniel Frey, and Margaret Hamilton

Published songs:
Guess Who—cut
Heart Of Stone (Pyramid Song)

I Never Know When (To Say When)
Lady In Waiting
Lazy Moon
The Pussy Foot
Save A Kiss
Shall I Take My Heart And Go?

Additional songs recorded:
Bad Companions
Give The Little Lady (A Great Big Hand)
I Can't Be In Love
No One Will Ever Love You (Like You Do)
There Never Was A Woman (Who Couldn't Be Had)
Two Years In The Making
Who's Been Sitting In My Chair?

Pop composer Leroy Anderson (1908–1975) was best known for orchestral compositions like *The Syncopated Clock* and *Sleigh Ride*. The songs from GOLDILOCKS—his only musical—might not be great, but they sure are a lot of fun. Favorites include *I Never Know When (To Say When)*, a stunning torch song; *Who's Been Sitting In My Chair?*, a comic lament; and the infectiously delectable dance specialty *The Pussy Foot*. There are also a bunch of good comedy songs, with especially smart lyrics from the Kerrs and Joan Ford. The show itself had problems; either the book was too silly, os the 1958 audiences didn't appreciate the satire. But I'm mighty glad that the GOLDILOCKS score has been preserved for our listening pleasure.

REDHEAD

FEBRUARY 5, 1959   46TH STREET THEATRE   452 PERFORMANCES

Music by Albert Hague
Lyrics by Dorothy Fields
Book by Herbert and Dorothy Fields, Sidney Sheldon, and David Shaw
Directed and choreographed by Bob Fosse
Produced by Robert Fryer and Lawrence Carr
With Gwen Verdon, Richard Kiley, and Leonard Stone

Published songs:
I Feel Merely Marvelous
I'm Back In Circulation
It Doesn't Take A Minute—cut
Just For Once
Look Who's In Love

My Girl Is Just Enough Woman For Me
The Right Finger Of My Left Hand
Two Faces In The Dark

Additional songs published in vocal score:
Behave Yourself
Chase [instrumental]
Dream Dance [instrumental]
'Erbie Fitch's Dilemma
I'll Try
Pickpocket Tango [instrumental]
The Simpson Sisters
Uncle Sam Rag
We Loves Ya, Jimey

Albert Hague (of PLAIN AND FANCY [PART 4: January 27, 1955]) teamed up with veteran lyricist Dorothy Fields for this Gwen Verdon/Bob Fosse vehicle. While the earlier score had a few pretty tunes, this one was extremely mediocre. REDHEAD nevertheless won the Best Musical Tony Award—with Hague, the librettists, choreographer Fosse, and stars Verdon and Kiley all winning as well. (One can imagine the overall quality of the season!) This was Fosse's third Tony in five years, Verdon's fourth in six; they got married. Fosse's next project was THE CONQUERING HERO [January 16, 1961], from which he was fired out of town; the show finally stumbled in with no director or choreographer credited. Fosse's *next* show as full director/choreographer, PLEASURES AND PALACES [Loesser: March 11, 1965], didn't even make it to Broadway. Seven years after the seven-Tony REDHEAD, Fosse and Verdon finally returned with SWEET CHARITY [Coleman: January 30, 1966]. As for Hague, his Broadway future was hopelessly hapless: CAFE CROWN [April 17, 1964], THE FIG LEAVES ARE FALLING [January 2, 1969], and Bette Davis' out-of-town flop MISS MOFFAT [October 7, 1974].

ONCE UPON A MATTRESS

MAY 11, 1959   PHOENIX THEATRE < OFF-BROADWAY >   216
PERFORMANCES

NOVEMBER 25, 1959   ALVIN THEATRE   244 PERFORMANCES

Music by Mary Rodgers
Lyrics by Marshall Barer
Book by Jay Thompson, Barer, and Dean Fuller
Choreographed by Joe Layton
Directed by George Abbott

Producer by T. Edward Hambleton, Norris Houghton, and William and Jean Eckart
With Carol Burnett, Joe Bova, Jack Gilford, and Jane White

Published songs:
In A Little While
Normandy
Shy
Yesterday I Loved You

Additional songs published in vocal score:
Happily Ever After
Man To Man Talk
Many Moons Ago
An Opening For A Princess
Sensitivity
Song Of Love
Spanish Panic [instrumental]
The Swamp Of Home
Very Soft Shoes

Yet another group of musical comedy novices were shepherded in by Old Man Abbott. The best work came from composer Mary Rodgers, whose father had pioneered the modern musical comedy with Mr. A. (beginning with ON YOUR TOES [Rodgers: April 11, 1936]). Miss Rodgers provided some especially lilting melodies, including *In A Little While* and *Normandy*. Her next musical HOT SPOT [Sondheim: April 19, 1963], was one of those big-budget, big-advance-sale bonanzas which go wrong and turn into highly-public busts. Rodgers returned once more with the long-running off-Broadway hit THE MAD SHOW [Sondheim: January 9, 1966], after which she withdrew from the arena. MATTRESS is best remembered as the launching pad for comedienne Carol Burnett.

JACQUES BREL IS ALIVE AND WELL AND LIVING IN PARIS

JANUARY 22, 1968   VILLAGE GATE < OFF-BROADWAY >   1,847
PERFORMANCES

Music mostly by Jacques Brel
Lyrics by Mort Shuman and Eric Blau, from the French lyrics by Jacques Brel
Production Conception and Additional Material by Blau and Shuman
Directed by Moni Yakim

Produced by 3W Productions (including Blau)
With Elly Stone, Mort Shuman, Shawn Elliott, and Alice Whitfield

NOTE: all music and French lyrics by Brel, all English lyrics by Shuman and Blau unless indicated

Published songs:
Fanette
If We Only Have Love (Quand On N'a Que L'Amour)
Marathon (Les Flamandes) (English lyric by Blau)

Additional songs published in vocal selection(s):
Alone (Seul) (English lyric by Blau)
Amsterdam
Bachelor's Dance (La Bourée du Célibataire) (English lyric by Blau)
Brussels (Bruxelles) (music by Brel and Gerard Jouannest, English lyric by
    Blau)
The Bulls (Les Toros) (music by Brel, Jouannest and Jean Corti)
Carousel (La Valse À Mille Temps) (English lyric by Blau)
The Desperate Ones (Les Déséspéres) (music by Jouannest)
Funeral Tango (La Tango Funebre) (music by Jouannest)
I Loved (J'aimais) (music by Jouannest and François Rauber)
Jackie (La Chanson De Jacky) (music by Jouannest)
Madeleine (music by Brel, Jouannest and Corti, English lyric by Blau)
Marieke (music by Brel and Jouannest, English lyric by Blau)
Mathilde (music by Jouannest)
My Death (La Mort)
Next (Au Suivant)
The Old Folks (Les Vieux) (music by Brel, Jouannest and Corti)
Sons Of (Fils De) (music by Jouannest)
Timid Frieda (Les Timides)
You're Not Alone (Jef)

JACQUES BREL IS ALIVE AND WELL AND LIVING IN PARIS was a string of songs about the human condition which perfectly captured the mood of its time. (While it would be unfair to label it a Vietnam protest piece, that message clearly came across.) BREL was phenomenally successful; this despite the fact that the majority of the audience had never heard of Brel (1929–1978), a Belgian-born singer/songwriter who was at the time alive and well and heading the Paris company of MAN OF LA MANCHA [Leigh: November 22, 1965]. (Despite its foreign authorship, BREL was devised by Americans and is therefore discussed in PART 4.) Someone hearing the score today for the first time might wonder what all the fuss was about; all I can say is that it was magically spellbinding at the time (and remains so, for me at least). The 22-song score touched on just about every emotion. A good part of the credit must be ascribed to the masterful English lyrics by Mort Shuman and Eric Blau; one wonders how literal the translations were, especially in the "gutsy" spellbinders Shuman himself performed (*Amsterdam, Funeral Tango, Next*). Along with the trenchant comments were melodies of exquisite loveliness (*Old Folks, You're Not Alone, My Death, Marieke, Fanette*) and others of outright jubilation (*Carousel, Brussels, Sons Of*). Elly Stone, who headed the cast and sang most of the important songs, became something of a cult favorite.

HAIR

The American Tribal Love-Rock Musical

APRIL 29, 1968   BILTMORE THEATRE   1,742 PERFORMANCES

Music by Galt MacDermot
Book and lyrics by James Rado and Gerome Ragni
Choreographed by Julie Arenal
Directed by Tom O'Horgan
Produced by Michael Butler
With Rado, Ragni, Lynn Kellogg, Melba Moore, and Diane Keaton

Published songs:
Aquarius
Easy To Be Hard
Frank Mills
Good Morning Starshine
Hair
Let The Sunshine In—initially issued as *The Flesh Failures*
Where Do I Go?

Additional songs published in vocal selection(s):
Abie Baby/Fourscore
Ain't Got No
Air
Black Boys
Donna
Electric Blues/Old Fashioned Melody
Hashish
I Got Life
I'm Black
Initials
Manchester England
Somebody To Love—written for 1979 movie version
Three-Five-Zero-Zero
Walking In Space

What A Piece Of Work Is Man (lyric by William Shakespeare)
White Boys

Additional songs recorded:
Be-In
The Bed
Colored Spade
Don't Put It Down
My Conviction
Sodomy

NOTE: additional cut and unused material has been recorded

HAIR had a pre-Broadway tryout of sorts, playing three months at the New York Shakespeare Festival [October 29, 1967] before briefly moving to the Cheetah discotheque. A new production team was then assembled, led by director Tom O'Horgan (replacing Gerald Freedman). Invading the sacred precincts of Broadway, HAIR shocked, insulted, enraged, etc. But the show quickly won over most of the audience, with its strong overall viewpoint (credit director Tom O'Horgan) and a very good, tuneful score: *Where Do I Go, Easy To Be Hard, Aquarius.* Broadway audiences were comfortable enough with the songs, and non-Broadway audiences first discovered theatre courtesy of the American Tribal Love-Rock Musical. Canadian-born composer Galt MacDermot's next project was John Guare's successful pop adaptation of TWO GENTLEMEN OF VERONA [December 1, 1971]. Broadway adventures since have all been imaginative failures.

PROMISES, PROMISES

DECEMBER 1, 1968   SHUBERT THEATRE   1,281 PERFORMANCES

Music by Burt Bacharach
Lyrics by Hal David
Book by Neil Simon
(Based on *The Apartment* [movie] by Billy Wilder and I. A. L. Diamond)
Choreographed by Michael Bennett
Directed by Robert Moore
Produced by David Merrick
With Jerry Orbach, Jill O'Hara, A. Larry Haines, Marian Mercer, and Donna McKechnie

Published songs:
Christmas Day
I'll Never Fall In Love Again

Knowing When To Leave
Promises, Promises
Wanting Things
Whoever You Are I Love You

Additional songs published in vocal score:
A Fact Can Be A Beautiful Thing
Grapes Of Roth [instrumental]
Half As Big As Life
It's Our Little Secret
She Likes Basketball
Turkey Lurkey Time
Upstairs
Where Can You Take A Girl?
You'll Think Of Someone
A Young Pretty Girl Like You

The mid-Sixties saw pop composer Burt Bacharach rise to celebrity status, with a string of hits (*What The World Needs Now, Alfie,* etc.) and a personable personality. David Merrick brought Bacharach and his less-visible collaborator to Broadway, putting them together with Neil Simon and a classic Billy Wilder screenplay. Simon wrote his best libretto to date, Bacharach and David wrote a lively score (bordering on the over-bouncy), and Merrick supplied a good director, Robert Moore. Also hired were choreographer Michael Bennett (who had performed unbilled salvage work on Merrick's unsalvagable How Now, Dow Jones [December 7, 1967]) and designer Robin Wagner (who made his Broadway musical debut with Hair [Part 4: April 29, 1968]). Bennett and Wagner began experimenting with choreographed set changes, with immediately gratifying results. The assignment of adapting Bacharach's pop recording sound to live theatre went to Jonathan Tunick, who began his reign as the musical theatre's finest modern-day orchestrator.

1776

March 16, 1969   46th Street Theatre   1,217 performances

Music and lyrics by Sherman Edwards
Book by Peter Stone
Choreographed by Onna White
Directed by Peter Hunt
Produced by Stuart Ostrow
With William Daniels, Howard Da Silva, Ken Howard, Virginia Vestoff, Paul Hecht, and Ronald Holgate

Published songs:
He Plays The Violin
Is Anybody There?
Momma Look Sharp
Yours, Yours, Yours!

Additional songs published in vocal selection:
But, Mr. Adams
Cool, Cool, Considerate Men
The Egg
The Lees Of Old Virginia
Molasses To Rum
Piddle, Twiddle And Resolve
Sit Down, John
Till Then

Theatrical novice Sherman Edwards (1919–1981) decided to musicalize the suspenseful tale of John Adams, Ben Franklin, and Tom Jefferson writing the Declaration of Independence. Edwards received encouragement and tutelage from Frank Loesser, as had Meredith Willson with THE MUSIC MAN [Willson: December 19, 1957]. Producer Ostrow, a former Frank (Loesser) Music executive, took up the unlikely project. The result was not particularly well made, but an effective (and surprising) hit.

PROMENADE

JUNE 4, 1969   PROMENADE THEATRE < OFF-BROADWAY >   259
PERFORMANCES

Music by Al Carmines
Book and lyrics by Maria Irene Fornes
Directed by Lawrence Kornfeld
Produced by Edgar Lansbury and Joseph Beruh
With Madeline Kahn, George S. Irving, Ty McConnell, Gilbert Price, Shannon Bolin, and Alice Playten

Published song:
Promenade Theme [instrumental]

Additional songs published in vocal selection:
Capricious And Fickle
The Cigarette Song
A Flower
I Saw A Man
The Moment Has Passed
Unrequited Love

Additional songs recorded:
All Is Well In The City
Chicken Is He
Clothes Make The Man (Who Could Marry A Gigolo?)
Crown Me
Four (Naked Ladies)
Isn't That Clear?
Listen, I Feel
Little Fool
The Passing Of Time
A Poor Man
Two Little Angels

PROMENADE was avant garde, experimental, unconventional, and pretty strange—which is no doubt how 1928 Berliners described DIE DREIGROSCHENOPER [Weill: April 13, 1933]. Not that it belongs in the same class as the Weill-Brecht masterwork; PROMENADE has quickly dated, and the book and lyrics by Maria Irene Fornes were closer in style to Gert Stein than Bert Brecht. But Al Carmines' music was vibrant, alive, and exciting (and different). Carmines, pastor of the Judson Memorial Church in Greenwich Village, has written dozens of off- and off off-Broadway musicals since 1964, usually with gay themes. PROMENADE has been his only "commercial" success; his only Broadway stab was W.C., a Bill Fields stage bio starring Mickey Rooney and Bernadette Peters which closed during its 1971 summer-stock tryout. PROMENADE, incidentally, seems to be the only musical in history which actually had a theatre named after it.

PURLIE

MARCH 15, 1970   BROADWAY THEATRE   689 PERFORMANCES

Music by Gary Geld
Lyrics by Peter Udell
Book by Ossie Davis, Philip Rose and Udell
(Based on *Purlie Victorious* [play] by Davis]
Choreographed by Louis Johnson
Directed and produced by Rose
With Cleavon Little, Melba Moore, John Heffernan, Sherman Hemsley, and Novella Nelson

Published songs:
He Can Do It
I Got Love
Purlie
Walk Him Up The Stairs

Additional songs published in vocal selection:
Big Fish, Little Fish
Down Home
First Thing Monday Mornin'
New Fangled Preacher Man
World Is Comin' To A Start, The

Additional songs recorded:
Barrels Of War, The
God's Alive
Great White Father (Of The Year)
Harder They Fall, The
Skinnin' A Cat
Unborn Love, The

PURLIE had a lot going for it, including a quartet of good songs (*I Got Love, Purlie, Walk Him Up The Stairs, and Down Home*) from popwriters Gary Geld and Peter Udell, and Tony-caliber performances by Cleavon Little and Melba Moore. But the unheralded PURLIE faced a series of struggles. The plot tells of the fast-talking, Harold Hill-like Purlie, who is Victorious over white plantation owner "Ol' Cap'n"; the opening number, in fact, is a jubilant spiritual celebrating his death. PURLIE was the first Broadway show to attract a substantial black audience, which—believe it or not—made some older white theatregoers uncomfortable. (These were the days before TV's 'All in the Family' came along and began battering away at bigotry.) Perhaps PURLIE's biggest problem was that it was an independently-produced show with no financial backing from the Broadway establishment. Forced into three expensive theatre moves (to make way for "more desirable" bookings), PURLIE finally gave up and closed at a loss.

MINNIE'S BOYS

A Rollicking New Marx Brothers Musical

MARCH 26, 1970   IMPERIAL THEATRE   80 PERFORMANCES

Music by Larry Grossman
Lyrics by Hal Hackaday
Book by Arthur Marx and Robert Fisher
(Based upon the lives of the Marx Brothers)
Choreographed by Marc Breaux
Directed by Stanley Prager
Produced by Arthur Whitelaw, Max Brown, and Byron Goldman
With Shelley Winters, Arny Freeman, Mort Marshall, Julie Kurnitz, Lewis J. Stadlen and Daniel Fortus

Published songs:
Be Happy
Empty—cut
Mama, A Rainbow
Minnie's Boys
Rich Is
Theme From Minnie's Boys (Ninety-Third Street) [instrumental]
They Give Me Love—published as *He Gives Me Love*
Where Was I When They Passed Out Luck?

Additional songs published in vocal selection:
You Don't Have To Do It For Me
You Remind Me Of You

Additional songs recorded:
The Act
Five Growing Boys
The Four Nightingales
Underneath It All

If they could make Gypsy Rose Lee's mom a star, why not Groucho's? (Perhaps Laurents and Styne and Sondheim could have, but not this group—which included Minnie's grandson.) Whenever MINNIE's BOYS got funny—which was fairly frequently—their Mom, in the shape of Shelley Winters, would come in and Gummo up the works. Larry Grossman's melodies were bright, perky, and promising—qualities notably absent from his future work, the dismal GOODTIME CHARLEY [March 3, 1975] and two conceptually overblown (Hal) Princicals, A DOLL's LIFE [September 23, 1982] and GRIND [April 16, 1985].

GREASE

FEBRUARY 14, 1972   EDEN THEATRE < OFF-BROADWAY >   128
    PERFORMANCES

JUNE 7, 1972   BROADHURST THEATRE   3,388 PERFORMANCES

Book, music and lyrics by Jim Jacobs and Warren Casey
Choreographed by Patricia Birch
Directed by Tom Moore
Produced by Kenneth Waissman and Maxine Fox
With Barry Bostwick, Carole Demas, and Adrienne Barbeau

Published songs:
Freddy, My Love
Summer Nights

There Are Worse Things I Could Do
Those Magic Changes

Additional songs published in vocal score:
All Choked Up
Alone At A Drive-In Movie
Beauty School Dropout
Born To Hand Jive
Greased Lightnin'
It's Raining On Prom Night
Look At Me, I'm Sandra Dee
Mooning
Rock 'n Roll Party Queen
Rydell Alma Mater
Rydell's Fight Song
Shakin' At The High School Hop
We Go Together

Like **HAIR** [**PART 4: April 29, 1968**]—but without its quality or charm—**GREASE** moved from off-Broadway and attracted many, many theatregoers for many years. Most of them left **GREASE** satisfied; a significant number returned again and again.

THE WIZ

JANUARY 5, 1975   MAJESTIC THEATRE   1,672 PERFORMANCES

Music and lyrics by Charlie Smalls
Book by William F. Brown
(Based on *The Wizard of Oz* [novel] by L. Frank Baum)
Choreographed by George Faison
Directed by Geoffrey Holder
Produced by Ken Harper
With Stephanie Mills, Tiger Haynes, Hinton Battle, and DeeDee Bridgewater

Published songs:
Be A Lion
Don't Cry Girl
Ease On Down The Road
Everybody Rejoice
He's The Wizard
Home
If You Believe
A Rested Body Is A Rested Mind

Additional songs published in vocal selections:
Don't Nobody Bring Me No Bad News
The Feeling We Once Had
I Was Born On The Day Before Yesterday
I'm A Mean Ole Lion
Slide Some Oil To Me
So You Want To See The Wizard
Soon As I Get Home
Tornado
What Would I Do If I Could Feel
Who, Who Do You Think You Are?
Y'all Got It
You Can't Win—initial publication upon use in 1978 movie version

Another negligible but highly successful musical. *Ease On Down The Road* became the first blockbuster Broadway song hit of the Seventies and helped pull THE WIZ past a dismal initial reception.

SHENANDOAH

JANUARY 7, 1975   ALVIN THEATRE   1,050 PERFORMANCES

Music by Gary Geld
Lyrics by Peter Udell
Book by James Lee Barrett, Philip Rose and Udell
(Based on the screenplay by Barrett)
Choreographed by Robert Tucker
Directed by Rose
Produced by Rose, and Gloria and Louis K. Sher
With John Cullum, Donna Theodore, Joel Higgins, and Penelope Milford

Published songs:
Freedom
Pass The Cross
We Make A Beautiful Pair

Additional songs published in vocal score:
I've Heard It All Before
It's A Boy
Meditation (This Land Don't Belong To Virginia)
Next To Lovin' (I Like Fightin' Best)
The Only Home I Know
Over The Hill
Papa's Gonna Make It Alright
The Pickers Are Comin'

Raise The Flag
Violets And Silverbells
Why Am I Me?

Gary Geld, Peter Udell and Philip Rose returned with a second musical which—unlike their superior PURLIE [**Part 4: March 15, 1970**]—managed to run two and a half years and make a little money. (*Very* little money.) John Cullum carried the show with his strong performance in a heavy singing/ acting role, written for Robert Ryan (who died before rehearsals). The property had potential as a serious musical in the CAROUSEL [**Rodgers: April 19, 1945**] vein; but no Hammerstein, Mamoulian, or Rodgers was on hand. Don Walker, skillful orchestrator of CAROUSEL and other classics, *was* on hand; you could tell. The final Geld, Udell, and Rose musical was the Thomas Wolfe-based ANGEL [May 10, 1978], which played five performances before giving up the ghost.

A CHORUS LINE

APRIL 15, 1975   PUBLIC THEATRE < OFF-BROADWAY >   101
      PERFORMANCES

JULY 25, 1975   SHUBERT THEATRE   6,137 PERFORMANCES

Music by Marvin Hamlisch
Lyrics by Edward Kleban
Book by James Kirkwood and Nicholas Dante
Choreographed by Michael Bennett and Bob Avian
Directed and conceived by Bennett
Produced by New York Shakespeare Festival (Joseph Papp)
With Donna McKechnie, Priscilla Lopez, Carole (Kelly) Bishop, Sammy Williams and Pamela Blair

Published songs:
Dance: Ten, Looks: Three
I Can Do That
The Music And the Mirror
One
What I Did For Love

Additional songs published in vocal score:
And . . .
At The Ballet
Hello Twelve, Hello Thirteen, Hello Love
I Hope I Get It
Nothing
Sing!

Michael Bennett, codirector of FOLLIES [Sondheim: April 4, 1971], had an idea for a musical. Rather than placing it in the hands of writers, he assembled a group of dancers and developed the idea in workshop. Marvin Hamlisch, Bennett's dance arranger on HENRY, SWEET HENRY [Merrill: October 23, 1967], came in to compose. Hamlisch was the Burt Bacharach of the Seventies, achieving fame and acclaim with a burst of recording and movie work. Bennett's idea was brilliantly realized, and A CHORUS LINE went on to become Broadway's long-run champ. (OKLAHOMA! [March 31, 1943] held the record for fifteen years. Nowadays, the title changes frequently. Nothing on the horizon seems likely to surpass A CHORUS LINE, but that's what they said about FIDDLER ON THE ROOF [September 22, 1964].)

THE ROBBER BRIDEGROOM

OCTOBER 9, 1976   BILTMORE THEATRE   145 PERFORMANCES

Music by Robert Waldman
Book and lyrics by Alfred Uhry
(Based on the novella by Eudora Welty)
Choreographed by Donald Saddler
Directed by Gerald Freedman
Produced by John Houseman, Margot Harley, and Michael B. Kapon
With Barry Bostwick, Rhonda Coullet, and Barbara Lang

Published songs:
Deeper In The Woods
Nothin' Up
Sleepy Man

Additional songs published in vocal selection:
Goodbye Salome
Love Stolen
Once Upon The Natchez Trace
The Pricklepear Bloom
Poor Tied Up Darlin'
Riches
Rosamund's Dream
Steal With Style
Two Heads
Where Oh Where

An inventive but uncommercial musical. THE ROBBER BRIDEGROOM never reached the proper audience, and died with a struggle. Robert Waldman and Alfred Uhry have had two other short-lived opportunities, the "East of Eden" musical HERE'S WHERE I BELONG [March 3, 1968] and Stuart Ostrow's out-of-town fiasco Swing [February 25, 1980]. Uhry was infinitely more suc-cessful when he tried his hand at playwriting, with the 1987 *Driving Miss Daisy*. The Robber Bridegroom was initially presented for a limited engage-ment at the Harkness Theatre [October 7, 1975] by John Houseman's Acting Company (from Juilliard). Playing the bridegroom and bride: Kevin Kline and Patti LuPone.

THE BEST LITTLE WHOREHOUSE IN TEXAS

April 17, 1978   Entermedia Theatre   85 performances

June 19, 1978   46th Street Theatre   1,584 performances

Music and lyrics by Carol Hall
Book by Larry L. King and Peter Masterson
(Based on an article by King)
Choreographed by Tommy Tune
Directed by Masterson and Tune
Produced by Universal Pictures
With Carlin Glynn, Henderson Forsythe, Pamela Blair, Delores Hall, and Jay Garner

Songs published in vocal selection:
The Aggie Song
Bus From Amarillo
Doatsy Mae
Girl, You're A Woman
Good Old Girl
Hard Candy Christmas
A Li'l Ole Bitty Pissant Country Place
No Lies
The Sidestep
Texas Has A Whorehouse In It
Twenty Fans
Twenty-Four Hours Of Lovin'
Watch Dog Theme

A potentially good musical settled for being just a crowd-pleasing li'l ole hit. Theatrical novices Carol Hall and Larry King did well enough, although the effectiveness of their material was diminished by pre-opening "improvements" from the experienced hands on hand.

MARCH OF THE FALSETTOS

APRIL 1, 1981   PLAYWRIGHTS
   HORIZONS   < OFF-OFF-BROADWAY >   170 PERFORMANCES
NOVEMBER 9, 1981   WESTSIDE ARTS
   CENTER   < OFF-BROADWAY >   128 PERFORMANCES

Music and lyrics by William Finn
Directed by James Lapine
Produced by Mary Lea Johnson, Francine Lefrak, Martin Richards,
Warner Theatre Productions, Inc., and Playwrights Horizons (Andre
Bishop)
With Michael Rupert, Alison Fraser, Chip Zien, Stephen Bogardus, and
James Kushner

Recorded songs:
The Chess Game
Everyone Tells Jason To See A Psychiatrist
Father To Son
Four Jews In A Room Bitching
The Games I Play
I Never Wanted To Love You
Jason's Therapy
Love Is Blind
Making A Home
March Of The Falsettos
A Marriage Proposal
Marvin At The Psychiatrist (A 3-Part Mini-Opera)
Marvin Hits Trina
My Father's A Homo
Please Come To My House
This Had Better Come To A Stop
The Thrill Of First Love
A Tight-Knit Family
Trina's Song

The best score of the Eighties, a highly original, highly exciting piece which—surprisingly—was immediately recognized and enthusiastically supported. William Finn adhered to no structure: music and lyrics just went where they needed to go, forming a tapestry of strong, emotional musical themes. The author displayed a keen ability at drawing his characters in *Four Jews In A Room Bitching, Trina's Song,* and *The Games I Play.* Particularly stunning were the intricately written musical conversations for combinations of the five characters: *This Had Better Come To A Stop, Love Is Blind, The Chess Game,* and *I Never Wanted To Love You.* A very special theatre work! (Also see In Trousers [Part 4; March 26, 1985] and Falsettoland [Part 4: June 28, 1990]).

DREAMGIRLS

December 20, 1981   Imperial Theatre   1,522 performances

Music by Henry Krieger
Book and lyrics by Tom Eyen
Choreographed by Michael Bennett and Michael Peters
Directed by Bennett
Produced by Bennett, Bob Avian, Geffen Records, and the Shubert Organization
With Jennifer Holliday, Loretta Devine, Sheryl Lee Ralph, Cleavant Derricks, Obba Babatunde, and Ben Harney

Songs published in vocal selection:
Ain't No Party
And I Am Telling You I'm Not Going
Cadillac Car
Dreamgirls
Fake Your Way To The Top
Family
Hard To Say Goodbye, My Love
I Am Changing
Move (You're Steppin' On My Heart)
One Night Only
Steppin' To The Bad Side
When I First Saw You

Additional songs recorded:
Firing Of Jimmy
I Meant You No Harm
I Miss You Old Friend
Press Conference
The Rap

Michael Bennett and Bob Fosse perfected the concept musical, built on plenty of concept and (often) little else. Talent freed them from relying on book, music, lyrics: instead of assembling a production around written material, they seemed to start with *movement* and add on songs, plot, etc. Jerome Robbins worked in the same way, but he insisted on first-rate material—which explains his absence since Fiddler On The Roof [Bock: September 22, 1964]. Bennett and designer Robin Wagner began experimenting with "choreographed sets" with **PROMISES, PROMISES** [**PART 4: December 1, 1968**] and **SEESAW** [**Coleman: March 18, 1973**]. While Wagner scenery has been known to overpower weak material (i.e., **ON THE TWENTIETH CENTURY** [**Coleman: February 19, 1978**]), the **DREAMGIRLS** set enhanced and carried the show. Bennett's work as *director* was particularly impressive, with the six principal actors—singer/dancers with little dramatic experience—each giving fine performances. The score of **DREAMGIRLS** was slightly more than adequate, with a puzzling tendency to switch from high-gear Motown to decidedly non-Motown quasi-*recitative*. Composer Henry Krieger's second musical, **THE TAP DANCE KID** [December 21, 1983], was of little interest.

NINE

MAY 9, 1982   46TH STREET THEATRE   739 PERFORMANCES

Music and lyrics by Maury Yeston
Book by Arthur Kopit
(Based on Mario Fratti's adaptation of *8½* [movie] by Federico Fellini, Tullio Pinelli, and Ennio Flaiano)
Choreographed by Thommie Walsh
Directed by Tommy Tune
Produced by Michel Stuart, Harvey J. Klaris, Roger S. Berlind, James M. Nederlander, Francine Lefrak and Kenneth D. Greenblatt
With Raul Julia, Liliane Montevecchi, Karen Akers, Anita Morris, Taina Elg, and Shelly Burch

Published songs:
Be Italian
Be On Your Own
Only With You
Simple
Unusual Way

Additional songs published in vocal selection:
A Call From The Vatican
Folies Bergère
Getting Tall
Guido's Song
My Husband Makes Movies
Nine

Additional songs recorded:
The Bells Of St. Sebastian
The Germans At The Spa
Grand Canal Sequence

A Man Like You
Not Since Chaplin
Overture Delle Donne
Ti Voglio Bene

Yale professor Maury Yeston arrived on Broadway with good music and an interesting musical—which only partially survived its libretto and production. A parade of fine supporting performances helped alleviate one-gimmick-concept problems, while the dazzling costumes by William Ivey Long took advantage of the strictures. Yeston's inventive and highly melodic score suffered in spots from lower-grade lyrics; but he certainly can write music. After NINE came a score for LA CAGE AUX FOLLES [Herman: August 21, 1983]; but Yeston's version was not used. Then came a Yeston-Kopit musicalization of "The Phantom of the Opera"; Andrew Lloyd Webber got his on first, though. (Yeston's version was finally mounted in 1991, in Atlanta.) Yeston finally made it back to Broadway with GRAND HOTEL [PART 4: November 12, 1989].

BABY

DECEMBER 4, 1983   ETHEL BARRYMORE THEATRE   241
        PERFORMANCES

Music by David Shire
Lyrics by Richard Maltby, Jr.
Book by Sybille Pearson
(Based on a story by Susan Yankowitz)
Choreographed by Wayne Cilento
Directed by Maltby
Produced by James B. Freydberg and Ivan Bloch, Kenneth-John
Productions, and Suzanne J. Schwartz
With Liz Callaway, James Congdon, Catherine Cox, Beth Fowler, Todd
Graff, and Martin Vidnovic

Published song:
I Want It All

Additional songs published in vocal selection:
And What If We Had Loved Like That?
At Night She Comes Home To Me
Baby, Baby, Baby
Easier To Love
Fatherhood Blues
I Chose Right—song version of unpublished theme from 1981 movie
    "Only When I Laugh"
Patterns—cut

The Story Goes On
Two People In Love
With You

Additional songs recorded:
The Birth
The Ladies Singing Their Song
Opening
The Plaza Song
Romance
We Start Today
What Could Be Better Than That?

A very special musical which Broadway audiences just never discovered. A more creative promotional campaign might have helped; but it wasn't, and it didn't. BABY was warm, pink and tender, with a better score than Broadway had heard in a long while: *Baby, Baby, Baby, And What If We Had Loved Like That,* the especially moving *The Story Goes On,* and more. BABY was slightly weakened, though, by the lack of Broadway experience among director, librettist, and producers. David Shire and Richard Maltby had been around since the off-Broadway SAP OF LIFE [October 2, 1961]. The cabaret revue STARTING HERE, STARTING NOW [March 7, 1977] was far more successful, but their one previous Broadway attempt (LOVE MATCH [November 3, 1968]) closed during its tryout. Maltby had reached Broadway a few years earlier, as director of the off-Broadway transfer AIN'T MISBEHAVIN' [May 8, 1978]. Maltby also found work as a colyricist on Cameron Mackintosh musicals, beginning with SONG AND DANCE [PART 5: September 18, 1985]. Maltby and Shire's next theatre piece was a pleasant but non-exceptional off-Broadway revue, CLOSER THAN EVER [November 6, 1989].

IN TROUSERS

MARCH 26, 1985   PROMENADE THEATRE < OFF-BROADWAY >   16
    PERFORMANCES

Music and lyrics by William Finn
Directed by Matt Casella
Produced by Roger Berlind, Franklin R. Levy and Gregory Harrison
With Catherine Cox, Tony Cummings, Kathy Garrick, and Sherry Hursey

Published songs:
None

Recorded songs:
Another Sleepless Night
Breakfast Over Sugar

High School Ladies At Five O'Clock
How Marvin Eats His Breakfast
How The Body Falls Apart
I Am Wearing A Hat (Marvin Takes A Wife)—cut
In Trousers (The Dream)
Love Me For What I Am
Marvin Takes A Victory Shower—cut
Marvin's Giddy Seizures
My Chance To Survive The Night—cut
My High School Sweetheart
The Nausea Before The Game—cut
The Rape of Miss Goldberg
Set Those Sails
Whizzer Going Down
Your Lips And Me—cut

IN TROUSERS began life as a developmental workshop at Playwrights Horizons [December 8, 1978; 8 performances]. Then came a sequel, the brilliant MARCH OF THE FALSETTOS [PART 4: April 1, 1981]. A revised version of IN TROUSERS was belatedly mounted off-Broadway, imported from Los Angeles. Finn's earlier score was exciting and highly impressive, although not up to the level of FALSETTOS. The piece was hampered by structural problems, dramatic immaturity, and (in the case of this production) poor direction. Musical highspots: *Love Me For What I Am*, a beautiful, soaring ballad, and the rambunctious Whizzer Going Down. Finn's *Marvin Trilogy* was brought to an exuberant close with FALSETTOLAND [PART 4: June 28, 1990].

BIG RIVER

APRIL 25, 1985   EUGENE O'NEILL THEATRE   1,005 PERFORMANCES

Music and lyrics by Roger Miller
Book by William Hauptman
(Based on *Huckleberry Finn* [novel] by Mark Twain)
Directed by Des McAnuff
Produced by Rocco Landesman, Heidi Landesman, Rick Steiner, M. Anthony Fisher, and Dodger Productions
With Daniel H. Jenkins, Ron Richardson, Bob Gunton, and Rene Auberjonois

Published songs:
River In The Rain
Muddy Water
Waitin' For The Light To Shine
Worlds Apart

Additional songs published in vocal selection:
Arkansas/How Blest We Are
The Boys
The Crossing
Do Ya Wanna Go To Heaven?
Free At Last
Guv'ment
Hand For The Hog
I, Huckleberry, Me
Leavin's Not The Only Way To Go
The Royal Nonesuch
When The Sun Goes Down In The South
You Oughta Be Here With Me

BIG RIVER was the best musical of the worst (?) season for Broadway musicals in seventy years. The score by country songwriter Roger Miller was dramatically ineffective and the book was weak, but Mark Twain and the lack of competition—with an assist from director McAnuff—managed to give BIG RIVER some life.

GRAND HOTEL
The Musical

NOVEMBER 12, 1989   MARTIN BECK THEATRE   681 PERFORMANCES
    [STILL RUNNING AS OF JUNE 30, 1991]

Music and lyrics by Robert Wright and George Forrest
Additional music and lyrics by Maury Yeston
Book by Luther Davis
(Based on the novel by Vicki Baum and *At the Grand* [musical] by Wright, Forrest, and Davis)
Directed and Choreographed by Tommy Tune
Produced by Martin Richards, Mary Lea Johnson, Sam Crothers, Sander Jacobs, Kenneth D. Greenblatt, Paramount Pictures, and Jujamcyn Theaters
With David [James] Carroll, Liliane Montevecchi, Jane Krakowski, Michael Jeter, Timothy Jerome, and Karen Akers

NOTE: music and lyrics by Wright and Forrest unless otherwise indicated; "preliminary version" indicates published Wright/Forrest songs which were performed in the show with revisions (unpublished) by Yeston

Songs published in vocal selection(s):
As It Should Be—preliminary version
At The Grand Hotel (by Yeston)

Bonjour, Amour (by Yeston)
The Grand Charleston (H-A-P-P-Y)
The Grand Fox-Trot (Trottin' The Fox/Who Couldn't Dance With You?)
     (by Wright and Forrest "with Wally Harper")
Grand Parade (Theme from 'Grand Hotel') (by Yeston)
Grand Tango (Table With A View)—preliminary version
I Waltz Alone—preliminary version
I Want To Go To Hollywood (by Yeston)
Love Can't Happen (by Yeston)
Maybe My Baby Loves Me
Roses At The Station (by Yeston)
Villa On A Hill
We'll Take A Glass Together—preliminary version
What You Need—preliminary version of *What She Needs*

At The Grand, a lugubrious operetta from the Kismet [Part 4: December 3, 1953] boys, opened in Los Angeles on July 7, 1958. Paul Muni starred in the Lionel Barrymore role, with the director's wife Joan Diener Marre as Greta Garbo. Two months later the Grand closed its doors—but not forever. The piece unaccountably resurfaced twenty-one years later. Not surprisingly, half the score was summarily discarded in the alley of the Colonial Theatre in Boston; surprisingly, the replacements by Maury (Nine [Part 4: May 9, 1982]) Yeston were just as dreary. (The book was similarly overhauled, without credit, by Peter Stone.) Director/choreographer Tommy Tune dressed up the material with some dynamically stylish staging, although vestiges of Follies [Sondheim: April 4, 1971] and Cabaret [Kander: November 20, 1966] abounded; but why purposely choose to build a grand show around bad tunes? The producers proclaimed Grand Hotel "The Mega-Hit of the '90s!," but somehow I don't think so.

FALSETTOLAND

June 28, 1990   Playwrights Horizons < off-off-Broadway >
     75 performances

September 16, 1990   Lucille Lortel Theatre
     < off-Broadway >   165 performances

Music and lyrics by William Finn
Conceived by Finn and James Lapine
Directed by Lapine
Produced by Maurice Rosenfield & Lois F. Rosenfield, Inc. with Steven Suskin, in association with Playwrights Horizons (Andre Bishop)
With Michael Rupert, Stephen Bogardus, Faith Prince, Lonny Price, Danny Gerard, Heather MacRae, and Janet Metz

Songs published in vocal selection:
The Baseball Song
A Day In Falsettoland
Everyone Hates His Parents
Holding To The Ground (Trina's Song)
Something Bad Is Happening
Unlikely Lovers
What More Can I Say?
What Would I Do?
You Gotta Die Sometime

Additional songs recorded:
Another Miracle of Judaism
Cancelling The Bar Mitzvah
Days Like This
Do You Know How Great My Life Is?
Falsettoland
I Don't Get It
Jason's Bar Mitzvah
Miracle of Judaism
More Racquetball
Planning A Bar Mitzvah (Round Tables, Square Tables)
Racquetball
Trina Works It Out
Year Of The Child

William Finn, composer/lyricist/author of **MARCH OF THE FALSETTOS** [**PART 4: April 1, 1981**] and **IN TROUSERS** [**PART 4: March 26, 1985**], concluded his "Marvin Trilogy" with **FALSETTOLAND**. Rather than sound biased, let me just say that I went to see **FALSETTOLAND** during its limited engagement at Playwrights Horizons in order to include it in this book—and immediately determined that it simply had to be moved for an open-ended run. It is certainly one of the very best musicals *I* have ever seen (and I'm kind of hard to please).

THE SECRET GARDEN

APRIL 25, 1991   ST. JAMES THEATRE   77 PERFORMANCES
    [STILL RUNNING AS OF JUNE 30, 1991]

Music by Lucy Simon
Book and lyrics by Marsha Norman
(Based on the novel by Frances Hodgson Burnett)
Choreographed by Michael Lichtefeld
Directed by Susan H. Schulman

Produced by Heidi Landesman, Rick Steiner, Frederic H. Mayerson,
Elizabeth Williams, Jujamcyn Theatres [Rocco Landesman]/TV ASAHI,
and Dodger Productions
With Daisy Eagen, Mandy Patinkin, Rebecca Luker, Alison Fraser, and
Robert Westenberg

Published songs:
None [at present]

From rather unlikely visitors to the musical theatre—pop songwriter Lucy
Simon and first-class dramatist Marsha Norman—came an admirable and
intriguing musical drama. Imperfect, perhaps; unconventional, certainly; but
a breath of fresh wind in a Broadway garden grown stale. In one of those
surprises that our commercial theatre continually springs upon us, quite a
number of people—including, but not limited to, some of the more important
critics—simply did not enjoy THE SECRET GARDEN. It is to be hoped that the
piece can withstand the odds against it (which at this writing appear rather
formidable) and enjoy the long and healthy life it deserves.

PART 5

INTRODUCTION

During the early years of the century, musical theatre in America was dominated by British and Continental imports (as can be seen in our discussion of the early career of Jerome Kern). It wasn't until World War I—when imports ceased—that the American musical began to emerge. By the time imports resumed after the War, Broadway firmly belonged to Kern, Friml, Berlin, Gershwin, and friends. Important Twenties offerings included two influential revues for the intelligentsia: the White Russian CHAUVE-SOURIS [February 4, 1922] and the fabled CHARLOT'S REVUE [January 9, 1924], which introduced Beatrice Lillie and Gertrude Lawrence to Broadway. There was also a stream of mostly second-rate Continental operettas, produced (mostly) by the Shuberts; these included the blockbuster BLOSSOM TIME [September 28, 1921], a highly-Americanized adaptation of Schubert by Shubert house composer Sigmund Romberg, and Emmerich Kalman's COUNTESS MARITZA [September 18, 1926]. The final import of the decade was Florenz Ziegfeld's production of Noel Coward's BITTER SWEET [November 5, 1929]—which had the misfortune to open the week the stock market crashed. Broadway was to see only three British book musicals over the next twenty-five years, all short-lived flops. There were also a handful of Continental imports, including Ralph Benatzky's long-running WHITE HORSE INN [August 20, 1936] and a notable failure, THE THREEPENNY OPERA < FIRST VERSION > [Weill: April 13, 1933]. The Second World War put a virtual halt to all musical imports until 1954, when producers Feuer and Martin—on a hit-streak with WHERE'S CHARLEY? [Loesser: October 11, 1948], GUYS AND DOLLS [Loesser: November 24, 1950], and CAN-CAN [Porter: May 7, 1953]—found a light-hearted musical spoof in London and determined to bring it across the ocean.

Notable Imported Scores

THE BOY FRIEND
A New Musical Comedy of the 1920's

SEPTEMBER 30, 1954   ROYALE THEATRE   485 PERFORMANCES

Book, music and lyrics by Sandy Wilson
Choreographed by John Heawood
Directed by Vida Hope
Produced by Cy Feuer and Ernest Martin
With Julie Andrews, Ann Wakefield, John Hewer, Bob Scheerer, and
Ruth Altman

Published songs:
Fancy Forgetting
I Could Be Happy With You
It's Never Too Late To Fall In Love
A Room In Bloomsbury
Won't You Charleston With Me?—initial individual publication upon use
in revival [April 14, 1970; 119 performances]

Additional songs published in vocal score:
The Boy Friend
Carnival Tango [instrumental]
Perfect Young Ladies
Poor Little Pierrette
The Riviera [1st]—cut
Safety In Numbers
Sur La Plage
The You Don't Want To Play With Me Blues

Additional song recorded:
The Riviera [2nd]

Sandy Wilson's affectionate spoof of musicals of the 20's began life in a
"private theatre club" on April 14, 1953. An expanded BOY FRIEND moved
to the West End on January 14, 1954, where it enjoyed an unprecedented run
of 2,084 performances. But would it work in America, land of the well-made,
modern musical comedy? Absolutely! THE BOY FRIEND received an ecstatic
reception, being precisely the right thing at the right time. (It's still a pretty

good show, actually.) It also brought to our shores Miss Julie Andrews, who turned nineteen the day after the Broadway opening.

IRMA LA DOUCE

SEPTEMBER 29, 1960   PLYMOUTH THEATRE   524 PERFORMANCES

Music by Marguerite Monnot
Original book and lyrics by Alexandre Breffort
English book and lyrics by Julian More, David Heneker, and Monty Norman
Choreographed by Onna White
Directed by Peter Brook
Produced by David Merrick in association with Donald Albery and H. M. Tennent, Ltd.
With Elizabeth Seal, Keith Michell, and Clive Revill

Published songs:
Bravo!—cut; published in U.K. only
Christmas Child
Dis-Donc, Dis-Donc
From A Prison Cell
Irma La Douce
Our Language Of Love
She's Got The Lot
There Is Only One Paris For That

Additional song published (no lyric) in piano selection:
Bridge of Caulaincourt

Additional songs recorded:
But
Le Grisbi Is Le Root of Le Evil In Man
Sons Of France
That's A Crime
Valse Milieu
The Wreck Of A Mec

Ah, dis-donc! what a delectable little musical! IRMA LA DOUCE, a fairy tale of the backstreets of Pigalle, began a four-year Paris run on November 12, 1956. An English-language adaptation was prepared under the magical hand of Peter Brook, opening in London on July 17, 1958 [1,712 performances]. David Merrick, who had brought Broadway six imports in less than two years (including the smash musical revue LA PLUME DE MA TANTE [November 11, 1958; 835 performances]), outbid the competition for IRMA and set her up on

West 45th Street. The three stars came along—none of that alien actor nonsense in those days—and Elizabeth Seal became the first "overnight discovery" to win a Best Actress/Actor Tony Award. IRMA's infectious music was the work of Marguerite Monnot (1903–1961), best known for *The Poor People Of Paris* and other songs written for Edith Piaf. IRMA was Monnot's only musical comedy score—and what a score it is!

STOP THE WORLD—I WANT TO GET OFF

OCTOBER 3, 1962   SHUBERT THEATRE   556 PERFORMANCES

Book, music and lyrics by Leslie Bricusse and Anthony Newley
Directed by Newley
Produced by David Merrick in association with Bernard Delfont
With Newley, Anna Quayle, and Jennifer and Susan Baker

Published songs:
Gonna Build A Mountain
Once In A Lifetime
Someone Nice Like You
What Kind Of Fool Am I?

Additional songs published in vocal selection:
Lumbered
Meilinki Meilchik
Typically English

Additional songs recorded:
All American—alternate lyric for *Typically English*
The A.B.C. Song
Family Fugue
Glorious Russian—alternate lyric for *Typically English*
I Wanna Be Rich
Mumbo Jumbo
Nag! Nag! Nag!
Typische Deutsche—alternate lyric for *Typically English*

Having done well with IRMA LA DOUCE [Part 5: September 29, 1960], David Merrick bought STOP THE WORLD—I WANT TO GET OFF [London: July, 20, 1961; 478 performances] and brought it to town, complete with star/co-author Anthony Newley and the international song hit *What Kind Of Fool Am I?* STOP THE WORLD was a conversation piece; you either loved it or loathed it, but you simply had to see it. (The *Times* critic loathed it. Merrick complained that the review was so poorly written as to be incomprehensible, and reprinted it as an ad—translated into Greek!) At any rate, audiences thronged to the

Shubert; Newley became a Big Star; and **Stop The World** became one of Merrick's all-time biggest money makers.

OLIVER!

January 6, 1963   Imperial Theatre   774 performances

Book, music and lyrics by Lionel Bart
Directed by Peter Coe
Produced by David Merrick and Donald Albery
With Clive Revill, Georgia Brown, Danny Sewell, David Jones, and Bruce Prochnik

Published songs:
As Long As He Needs Me
Consider Yourself
Food, Glorious Food
I'd Do Anything
It's A Fine Life
Oom-Pah-Pah
Where Is Love?
Who Will Buy?

Additional songs published in vocal score:
Be Back Soon
Boy For Sale
I Shall Scream
My Name
Oliver
Pick A Pocket Or Two
Reviewing The Situation
That's Your Funeral

Irma La Douce [Part 5: September 29, 1960] and **Stop The World** [Part 5: October 3, 1962] had been "special" attractions for "sophisticated audiences." For his next musical import, David Merrick latched onto the biggest international smash to come out of Britain since **Florodora** [November 10, 1900]. **Oliver!**—which began its record-breaking London run of 2,618 performances on June 30, 1960—was a family show in a class with **The Music Man** [Willson: December 19, 1957], **The Sound Of Music** [Rodgers: November 16, 1959], and **Annie** [Strouse: April 21, 1977]. It's not perfect, being somewhat ragtag in construction; but **Oliver!** works splendidly. Especially helpful are two infectiously energetic rousers (*Food, Glorious Food* and *Consider Yourself*) and a pair of highly effective ballads (*Where Is Love?* and *As Long As He Needs Me*). Composer Lionel Bart—who's been called "the welfare state Noel Coward"—began his career writing for (and singing with) Tommy Steele, England's top rock 'n roll star of the late '50s. He brought contemporary sounds to the long-dormant British musical, becoming the first of only two composers to have three West End musicals running simultaneous. (He remains the only British composer to win a Tony Award for Best Musical, Mr. Lloyd Webber notwithstanding.) Bart's other hits—**Fings Ain't Wot They Used T' Be** [February 11, 1960], **Blitz** [May 8, 1962] and **Maggie May** [September 22, 1964]—were considered too British for export. He did write one musical for Broadway, an adaptation of Fellini's **La Strada** [December 14, 1969] which starred Bernadette Peters. The score contained some beautiful work, but the show was a one-performance fiasco. Bart disappeared during the tryout: carted off to the loony bin, it has been said. All but three of his songs were summarily chucked out and replaced with feeble hackwork—which Bart himself was generally credited/blamed for. (I'm not going to mention any names, not even Martin Charnin.) By 1972, Bart had squandered the several million pounds earned by **Oliver!** and his other hits and was forced into bankruptcy.

THE ROAR OF THE GREASEPAINT—THE SMELL OF THE CROWD

May 16, 1965   Shubert Theatre   232 performances

Book, music and lyrics by Leslie Bricusse and Anthony Newley
Choreographed by Gillian Lynne
Directed by Newley
Produced by David Merrick in association with Bernard Delfont
With Newley, Cyril Ritchard, Sally Smith, Gilbert Price, and Joyce Jillson

Published songs:
Feeling Good
The Joker
Look At That Face
Nothing Can Stop Me Now!
On A Wonderful Day Like Today
This Dream
Who Can I Turn To? (When Nobody Needs Me)

Additional songs published in vocal selection:
The Beautiful Land
It Isn't Enough
My First Love Song
My Way
Put It In The Book

Sweet Beginning
That's What It Is To Be Young
Things To Remember
What A Man!
Where Would You Be Without Me?
With All Due Respect

Newley and Bricusse's follow-up to Stop The World [Part 5: October 3, 1962] was no world-beater, closing in the provinces before making it to London. This didn't faze Mr. Merrick, who owned the American rights and figured he could put Greasepaint over anyway. He did (just barely), thanks to the popularity of his star, a second major song hit (*Who Can I Turn To?*), and a whole bucketful of tuneful ditties. But that was the end of the age of Newley, who hasn't been heard from in these parts since. The London The Good Old Bad Old Days [December 20, 1977] never made it to these shores, while Chaplin [August 13, 1983]—written without Bricusse and starring guess who—quickly flickered out after its Los Angeles tryout.

JESUS CHRIST SUPERSTAR

October 12, 1971   Mark Hellinger Theatre   711 performances

Music by Andrew Lloyd Webber
Lyrics by Tim Rice
Conceived for the stage and directed by Tom O'Horgan
Produced by Robert Stigwood in association with MCA, Inc., by arrangement with David Land
With Jeff Fenholt, Ben Vereen, and Yvonne Elliman

Published songs:
Everything's Alright
Heaven On Their Minds
Hosanna
I Don't Know How To Love Him—new lyric for nonshow song *Kansas Morning*
I Only Want To Say (Gethsemane)
King Herod's Song
Superstar

Additional songs published in vocal selection:
The Last Supper
Pilate's Dream

Additional songs recorded:
The Arrest
Blood Money

Could We Start Again, Please?
The Crucifixion
Damned For All Time
John 19:41
Judas' Death
Peter's Denial
Pilate And Christ
Poor Jerusalem
Simon Zealotes
Strange Thing Mystifying
The Temple
Then We Are Decided
This Jesus Must Die
Trial Before Pilate
What's The Buzz?

Andrew Lloyd Webber (born 1948) and Tim Rice had first attracted attention with a twenty-minute oratorio for school children entitled JOSEPH AND THE AMAZING TECHNICOLOR DREAMCOAT [Part 5: December 30, 1976]. Their next piece, also with a religious theme, was initially recorded as a pop record album. JESUS CHRIST SUPERSTAR proved especially popular in the United States, so a stage version was mounted on Broadway. HAIR [Part 4: April 29, 1968] had aroused controversy due to nudity and a non-patriotic use of the American flag; SUPERSTAR was roundly attacked for sacrilege. Both shows—directed by Tom O'Horgan—were highly successful, bringing many non-theatregoers into the theatre for the first time; SUPERSTAR, though, was far inferior to HAIR. The score included the first of Lloyd Webber's surprisingly few song hits, *I Don't Know How To Love Him.*

JOSEPH AND THE AMAZING TECHNICOLOR DREAMCOAT

DECEMBER 30, 1976   BROOKLYN ACADEMY OF MUSIC OPERA HOUSE
     < BROOKLYN, NEW YORK >   22 PERFORMANCES

Music by Andrew Lloyd Webber
Lyrics by Tim Rice
Choreographed by Graciela Daniele
Directed by Frank Dunlop
With David-James Carroll and Cleavon Little

Songs published in vocal selection(s):
Any Dream Will Do
Benjamin Calypso
Close Ev'ry Door To Me

The Coat Of Many Colours
Hang On Now Joseph
Jacob And Sons
Joseph's Dreams
One More Angel In Heaven
Pharaoh's Number Two (Egypt Looks To You)
Poor, Poor Joseph
Seven Years
Song Of The King

Additional songs recorded:
The Brothers Came To Egypt
Grovel, Grovel
Jacob In Egypt
Joseph All The Time
May I Return To The Beginning
Pharaoh's Dream Explained
Pharaoh's Story
Potiphar
Stone The Crows
Those Canaan Days
Who's The Thief?

JOSEPH AND THE AMAZING TECHNICOLOR DREAMCOAT was written as a twenty-minute oratorio to be performed by the children of the Colet Court School in London, where it was first presented on March 1, 1968. Lloyd Webber and Rice expanded it into a successful recording, which led to a full-scale production at the 1972 Edinburgh Festival by director Frank Dunlop's Young Vic Company. This production was taken to London for a seven-month run. When Dunlop was named to head a (short-lived) resident theatre company at the Brooklyn (N.Y.) Academy of Music, he mounted an American JOSEPH as his initial offering. A second New York production opened off-Broadway at the Entermedia on November 18, 1981, quickly transferred to the Royale, and cashed in on the hot Lloyd Webber name for an impressive 824 performances.

EVITA

SEPTEMBER 25, 1979   BROADWAY THEATRE   1,568 PERFORMANCES

Music by Andrew Lloyd Webber
Lyrics by Tim Rice
Choreographed by Larry Fuller
Directed by Harold Prince

Produced by Robert Stigwood in association with David Land
With Patti LuPone, Mandy Patinkin, and Bob Gunton

Published songs:
Another Suitcase In Another Hall—individually published in U.K. only
Don't Cry For Me Argentina
On This Night Of A Thousand Stars—individually published in U.K. only

Additional songs published in vocal selection:
And The Money Kept Rolling In (And Out)
Buenos Aires (What's New?)
Eva, Beware Of The City
High Flying, Adored
I'd Be Surprisingly Good For You
Rainbow High
She Is A Diamond
Waltz For Eva And Che

Additional songs recorded:
The Actress Hasn't Learned (The Lines You'd Like To Hear)
The Art Of The Possible
Dice Are Rolling
Goodnight And Thank You
Lament
A New Argentina
Oh What A Circus
On The Balcony Of The Casa Rosada
Peron's Latest Flame
Rainbow Tour
Requiem For Evita
Santa Evita

While most detractors of Lloyd Webber claim that he is unable to write anything finer than derivative pablum, EVITA—another record-album-adapted-for-the-stage—offers evidence that the man *can* write an effective, exciting score. The presence of Harold Prince certainly helped make EVITA the smashing theatrical event it was, but the songs were impressive in their own right. Lloyd Webber's music was often exciting (*Rainbow High, Buenos Aires*) and in some cases quite lovely (*Another Suitcase In Another Hall, I'd Be Surprisingly Good For You*). There were also a couple of highly inventive novelties, *Peron's Latest Flame* and *The Art Of The Possible*. Perhaps the over-abundant music began to sound repetitive after a while; perhaps the lyrics tended towards the simplistic. Still, the overall effect of the piece more than made up for any weaknesses.

CATS

OCTOBER 7, 1982   WINTER GARDEN THEATRE   3,645 PERFORMANCES
[STILL RUNNING AS OF JUNE 30, 1991]

Music by Andrew Lloyd Webber
Lyrics by T.S. Eliot; additional lyrics by Trevor Nunn and Richard Stilgoe
(Based on *Old Possum's Book of Practical Cats* by T.S. Eliot)
Choreographed by Gillian Lynne
Directed by Trevor Nunn
Produced by Cameron Mackintosh, The Really Useful Company
(Webber), David Geffen and The Shubert Organization
With Betty Buckley

Published song:
Memory (lyric by Nunn, after Eliot)

Additional songs published in vocal score:
The Ad-dressing Of Cats
The Ballad Of Billy M'Gaw
Bustopher Jones
Grizabella
Grizabella, The Glamour Cat
Growltiger's Last Stand
Gus: The Theatre Cat
The Invitation To The Jellicle Ball
The Jellicle Ball
Jellicle Songs For Jellicle Cats (lyric by Nunn and Richard Stilgoe, after
     Eliot)
The Journey To The Heaviside Layer
Macavity
Mr. Mistoffolees
Mungojerrie And Rumpleteazer
The Naming Of The Cats
Old Deuteronomy
The Old Gumbie Cat
The Rum Tum Tigger
Skimbleshanks: The Railroad Cat

Having terminated his partnership with Tim Rice, Andrew Lloyd Webber
took a bunch of T. S. Eliot poems and musicalized them into the most
lucrative theatrical goldmine ever. CATS didn't fare especially well with critics
or sophisticates, but the Great Ticket-Buying Public adored it with frenzied
adulation—not only in England and America but across the world. (As Ezio
Pinza once said, "Who can explain it, who can tell you why?" *Memory* became

Webber's biggest song hit, a blockbuster on the level of *Ease On Down The Road* and *Tomorrow.*

SONG AND DANCE

SEPTEMBER 18, 1985   ROYALE THEATRE   474 PERFORMANCES

Music by Andrew Lloyd Webber
Lyrics by Don Black
American adaptation and additional lyrics by Richard Maltby, Jr.
Choreographed by Peter Martins
Directed by Maltby
Produced by Cameron Mackintosh Inc., The Shubert Organization, and FWM Producing Group by arrangement with The Really Useful Company (Webber)
With Bernadette Peters, Christopher d'Amboise, and Gregg Burge

Published songs:
Tell Me On A Sunday—individually published in U.K. only
Unexpected Song—song version of a theme from 'Variations'

Additional songs published in vocal selection:
Capped Teeth And Caesar Salad
Come Back With That Same Look In Your Eyes
English Girls
First Letter Home
I Love New York
Let Me Finish
Married Man
Nothing Like You've Ever Known—cut
Second Letter Home
So Much To Do In New York (3 Versions)
Take That Look Off Your Face
Third Letter Home
What Have I Done?
You Made Me Think You Were In Love

Additional song recorded:
I'm Very You, You're Very Me—cut

SONG AND DANCE combined a 1980 one-act TV musical, "Tell Me On A Sunday," with a ballet based on Lloyd Webber's 1979 'Variations' on Paganini's 'A Minor Caprice.' Bernadette Peters did a marvelous job of making the one-person minimusical work, but she had some pretty good material to work with (like *Unexpected Song* and *Tell Me On A Sunday*). As with

Evita [Part 5: **September 25, 1979**], things ultimately got a little too repetitious for comfort, and Song And Dance's Emma didn't have the innate box office lure of Eva Peron. Still, Song And Dance was well worth a trip to the theatre.

LES MISERABLES

March 12, 1987   Broadway Theatre   1,733 performances
[still running as of June 30, 1991]

Music by Claude-Michel Schonberg
Lyrics by Herbert Kretzmer
Book by Alain Boublil and Schonberg
(Based on the novel by Victor Hugo)
Directed and adapted by Trevor Nunn and John Caird
Produced by Cameron Mackintosh
With Colm Wilkinson, Terrence Mann, Randy Graff, Judy Kuhn, Michael Maguire, and Frances Ruffelle

Published song:
I Dreamed A Dream
Little People—individually published in U.K. only
Love Montage—individually published in U.K. only

Additional songs published in vocal selection(s):
At The End Of The Day
Bring Him Home
Castle On A Cloud
Do You Hear The People Sing?
Drink With Me To Days Gone By
Empty Chairs At Empty Tables
A Heart Full Of Love
In My Life
A Little Fall Of Rain
Master Of The House
On My Own
Stars
Who Am I?

Additional songs recorded:
Beggars At The Feast
Come To Me
Dog Eats Dog
Look Down
Lovely Ladies
One Day More

Prologue
Red And Black
Soliloquy
Thenardier Waltz
Turning
Wedding Chorale

Another epochal hit from producer Cameron Mackintosh and director Trevor Nunn (this time *not* accompanied by Andrew Lloyd Webber). I bow in admiration to the high standards of the adaptors, and acknowledge the almost universal acclaim of the score; I am unable, however, to appreciate the thing myself. Yes, this musicalization has brought "Les Miserables" to literally millions of people who would surely never have bothered with the book; yes, it provides some rousing theatrical entertainment. But I've seen the show twice now, on two continents, and it just doesn't work for me. Maybe I never should have read the (remarkable) novel?

STARLIGHT EXPRESS

MARCH 15, 1987   GERSHWIN THEATRE   761 PERFORMANCES

Music by Andrew Lloyd Webber
Lyrics by Richard Stilgoe
Choreographed by Arlene Phillips
Directed by Trevor Nunn
Produced by Martin Starger and Lord Grade
With Andrea McArdle

Songs published in vocal selection:
Engine Of Love
I Am The Starlight
Light At The End Of The Tunnel
Make Up My Heart
One Rock And Roll Too Many
Only You
Pumping Iron
The Race Is On [instrumental; song version is recorded]
Starlight Express
There's Me

Additional songs recorded:
AC/DC
Lotta Locomotion

There seems little point in commenting on Lloyd Webber's roller skate musical. I barely got through the first act; a lot of people seem to have liked it,

though, thronging to Broadway's largest theatre for almost two years. STAR-
LIGHT ultimately closed at a loss, only the second of Lloyd Webber's Broadway
ventures to do so. Still, it did rack up a lot of mileage. The score was remarkably unpalatable, even by Lloyd Webber's standards.

THE PHANTOM OF THE OPERA

JANUARY 26, 1988   MAJESTIC THEATRE   1,432 PERFORMANCES
    [STILL RUNNING AS OF JUNE 30, 1991]

Music by Andrew Lloyd Webber
Lyrics by Charles Hart
Book and additional lyrics by Richard Stilgoe
(Based on the novel by Gaston Leroux)
Choreographed by Gillian Lynne
Directed by Harold Prince
Produced by Cameron Mackintosh and The Really Useful Theatre
Company (Webber)
With Michael Crawford, Sarah Brightman, Steve Barton, and Judy Kaye

Published song:
All I Ask Of You
The Phantom Of The Opera (lyric by Hart, Stilgoe and Mike
    Batt)—individually published in U.K. only

Additional songs published in vocal selection:
Angel of Music
Masquerade
The Music Of The Night
The Point Of No Return
Prima Donna
Think Of Me
Wishing You Were Somehow Here Again

Additional songs recorded:
Bravo, Bravo
Down Once More
I Remember
Little Lotte
Magical Lasso
The Mirror
Notes
Poor Fool, He Makes Me Laugh
Raoul, I've Been There
Stranger Than You Dreamt It

Track Down This Murderer
Twisted Every Way
Wandering Child
Why Have You Brought Me Here?
Why So Silent?

Producers Mackintosh and Lloyd Webber combined Harold Prince's visually-arresting staging with a highly effective physical production to make PHANTOM yet another worldwide superhit. Lloyd Webber's music was far less interesting than EVITA [Part 5: September 25, 1979] or SONG AND DANCE [Part 5: September 18, 1985]. Eschewing his accustomed "contemporary" sound, the composer settled on an ersatz romanticism—thus becoming a kind of Phantom of the Operetta. Material weaknesses didn't matter in the least, as the overall spectacle made THE PHANTOM spectacular indeed.

ASPECTS OF LOVE

APRIL 8, 1990   BROADHURST THEATRE   377 PERFORMANCES

Music by Andrew Lloyd Webber
Lyrics by Don Black and Charles Hart
Book by Webber
(Based on the novel by David Garnett)
Choreographed by Gillian Lynne
Directed by Trevor Nunn
Produced by The Really Useful Theatre Company (Webber)
With Ann Crumb, Michael Ball, Kevin Colson, and Kathleen Rowe McAllen

Published song:
Love Changes Everything

Additional songs published in vocal selection(s):
Anything But Lonely
Chanson d'Enfance
Everybody Loves A Hero
Falling
The First Man You Remember
Hand Me The Wine And The Dice
Journey Of A Lifetime
Leading Lady
A Memory Of A Happy Moment
Mermaid Song
Other Pleasures
Parlez-vous Francais?

Seeing Is Believing
She'd Be Far Better Off With You
Stop, Wait, Please
There Is More To Love

The Broadway production of ASPECTS OF LOVE amassed a whopping advance sale, as was usual with Lloyd Webber musicals. The critics didn't like it much, as was usual with Lloyd Webber musicals. The audiences didn't seem to either, as was *not* usual with Lloyd Webber musicals. While the British musicals keep bombarding Broadway, the mere fact that they *are* British supermusicals no longer insures that they will be hits; witness the commercial failure of Lloyd Webber's SONG AND DANCE [Part 5: September 18, 1985], STARLIGHT EXPRESS [Part 5: March 15, 1987], Rice's CHESS [April 28, 1988], and ASPECTS. The enormous advance and the magical aura were simply not enough to override audience apathy—Lloyd Webber's name no longer a sure thing, poor thing. So what's an eight million dollar loss, as long as you're Really Useful (Ltd.)?

MISS SAIGON

APRIL 11, 1991   BROADWAY THEATRE   92 PERFORMANCES
    [STILL RUNNING AS OF JUNE 30, 1991]

Music by Claude-Michel Schönberg
Lyrics by Richard Maltby, Jr. and Alain Boublil (from the original lyrics by Boublil, with additional material by Maltby)
Book by Boublil and Schönberg
(Suggested by *Madame Butterfly* [play] by John Luther Long and David Belasco and the opera by Giacomo Puccini)
Choreographed by Bob Avian
Directed by Nicholas Hynter
Produced by Cameron Mackintosh
With Jonathan Pryce, Lea Salonga, Hinton Battle, Willy Falk, and Liz Callaway

Songs published in vocal selection:
The American Dream
Bui-Doi
The Heat Is On In Saigon
I Still Believe
I'd Give My Life For You
If You Want To Die In Bed
The Last Night Of The World
The Movie In My Mind

Now That I've Seen Her—new lyric for *Her Or Me*
Sun And Moon
Why, God, Why?

Additional songs recorded:
Back In Town
The Ceremony
The Confrontation
The Guilt Inside Your Head
Her Or Me—original lyric for *Now That I've Seen Her*
Little God Of My Heart
The Morning Of The Dragon
Please
Room 317
The Telephone
The Transaction
What A Waste
You Will Not Touch Him

In LES MISERABLES [Part 5: **March 12, 1987**], the Messrs. Schönberg and Boublil made a noble attempt at scaling down Victor Hugo's massive treatise on the human condition. With MISS SAIGON, though, they were merely building up John Luther Long and David Belasco's turn-of-the-century tear-jerker. (Long was a Philadelphia lawyer. When he suffered a nervous break-down, his doctor ordered him to forgo his strenuous practice—so he sat down and concocted "Madame Butterfly.") In my view, MISS SAIGON was not so bad as its critics claimed; more entertaining than its Broadway competitor THE WILL ROGERS FOLLIES [Coleman: **May 1, 1991**], certainly. Musically, though, it was—shall we say—familiar? And the less said about the lyrics (with Richard Maltby translating and expanding from Boublil's original French) the better. Puccini's operatic version was first heard stateside in 1906 in English; within three months they were singing it in Italian. Perhaps MISS SAIGON would sound better in some foreign language or other? Or maybe they should have just gone back to Long's original, from which I quote:

> *Rog-a-bye-bebby,*
> *Off in Japan,*
> *You just a picture*
> *Off of a fan.*

Schönberg could have come up with a real snappy tune for this, I'll bet.

Appendix 1

All productions discussed are listed below in chronological order.

Dates represent the official New York or London <L> opening. Brackets represent date of first performance of productions which did not play New York or London. Approximate dates are given as [c. month] (c. standing for "circa").

Where more than one composer contributed to the same production, each is named. Song listings will be found in the respective chapters.

The page number in the final column represents the *primary* discussion(s) of each production; for further mention of the show, see the index.

Chronological Listing of Productions

1908

January 27	A WALTZ DREAM	Kern	11
September 2	THE GIRLS OF GOTTENBERG	Kern	11
September 7	FLUFFY RUFFLES	Kern	12
November 2	THE BOYS AND BETTY	Berlin	67

1909

January 25	KITTIE GREY	Kern	12
July 29	THE GAY HUSSARS	Kern	12–13
September 6	THE DOLLAR PRINCESS	Kern	13
September 27	THE GIRL AND THE WIZARD	Berlin/ Kern	68–69 13
[October 26]	THE GOLDEN WIDOW	Kern	14

1910

January 6	THE JOLLY BACHELORS	Berlin	68
January 10	KING OF CADONIA	Kern	14
[c. April]	ARE YOU A MASON?	Berlin	68
June 20	ZIEGFELD FOLLIES OF 1910	Berlin	68–69
July 18	UP AND DOWN BROADWAY	Berlin	69
August 17	THE ECHO	Kern	14–15
August 29	OUR MISS GIBBS	Kern	15
[c. August]	THE GIRL AND THE DRUMMER	Berlin/ Kern	67–68 15
September 21	HE CAME FROM MILWAUKEE	Berlin	70
November 7	GETTING A POLISH	Berlin	70
[c. December]	TWO MEN AND A GIRL	Berlin	70–71

1911

February 4	THE HENPECKS	Kern	15–16
March 6	JUMPING JUPITER	Berlin	71
March 20	LA BELLE PAREE	Kern	16
April 3	LITTLE MISS FIX-IT	Kern	16
April 27	GABY (FOLIES BERGÈRE)	Berlin	71
May 28	FRIARS' FROLIC OF 1911	Berlin	72

June 26	ZIEGFELD FOLLIES OF 1911	Berlin/ Kern	72 17
August 28	THE SIREN	Kern	17
September 11	THE FASCINATING WIDOW	Berlin	72–73
September 18	THE KISS WALTZ	Kern	17–18
September 25	THE LITTLE MILLIONAIRE	Berlin	73
October 5	THE NEVER HOMES	Berlin	73
[c. October]	A REAL GIRL	Berlin	74
[c. November]	WINTER GARDEN VAUDEVILLE	Berlin	74

1912

[January 15]	SHE KNOWS BETTER NOW	Berlin	74
February 8	HOKEY-POKEY	Berlin	74
February 12	THE OPERA BALL	Kern	18
March 5	THE WHIRL OF SOCIETY	Berlin	75
April 11	A WINSOME WIDOW	Kern	18
[c. April]	COHAN AND HARRIS MINSTRELS	Berlin	76
July 22	PASSING SHOW OF 1912	Berlin	76
August 5	THE GIRL FROM MONTMARTRE	Kern	19
August 5	HANKY PANKY	Berlin	76
[August 31]	A POLISH WEDDING	Kern	19
September 9	THE "MIND-THE-PAINT" GIRL	Kern	20
September 12	MY BEST GIRL	Berlin	76–77
October 7	THE WOMAN HATERS	Kern	20
October 21	ZIEGFELD FOLLIES OF 1912	Berlin	77
November 13	THE RED PETTICOAT	Kern	20–21
November 30	THE SUN DODGERS	Berlin	77
December 23 <L>	HULLO, RAGTIME!	Berlin	78

1913

February 3	THE SUNSHINE GIRL	Kern	21
April 28	THE AMAZONS	Kern	21
June 5	ALL ABOARD!	Berlin	78

May 29	STEP THIS WAY	Berlin	82
June 12	ZIEGFELD FOLLIES OF 1916	Berlin/ Kern	31–32 82
June 22	PASSING SHOW OF 1916	Gershwin	104
September 19 <L>	THEODORE AND CO.	Kern	32
September 25	MISS SPRINGTIME	Kern	32–33
October 24	GO TO IT	Kern	33
November 6	THE CENTURY GIRL	Berlin	83

1917

January 11	HAVE A HEART	Kern	33–34
January 15	LOVE O' MIKE	Kern	34–35
February 20	OH, BOY	Kern	35–36
[c. April]	DANCE AND GROW THIN	Berlin	83
June 12	ZIEGFELD FOLLIES OF 1917	Kern	36
August 28	LEAVE IT TO JANE	Kern	36–37
September 10	RAMBLER ROSE	Berlin	83–84
September 24	THE RIVIERA GIRL	Kern	37
October 16	JACK O'LANTERN	Berlin	84
November 5	MISS 1917	Kern	37–38
December 25	GOING UP	Berlin	84
December 29	ONE MINUTE PLEASE	Rodgers	152–153
December 31	THE COHAN REVUE OF 1918	Berlin	84–85

1918

February 1	OH LADY! LADY!!	Kern	41
March 11	TOOT-TOOT!	Kern	39
May 18 <L>	VERY GOOD EDDIE	Porter	204
May 22	ROCK-A-BYE BABY	Kern	39–40
June 6	HITCHY-KOO OF 1918	Gershwin	105
June 18	ZIEGFELD FOLLIES OF 1918	Berlin	85
August 19	YIP-YIP-YAPHANK	Berlin	85–86
August 22	EVERYTHING	Berlin	86
August 29	HEAD OVER HEELS	Kern	40–41
October 24	LADIES FIRST	Gershwin	105
[c. October] <L>	TELLING THE TALE	Porter	204
November 4	THE CANARY	Berlin/ Kern	86–87 41

| November 27 | OH, MY DEAR | Kern | 41 |
| [December 9] | HALF-PAST EIGHT | Gershwin | 106 |

1919

February 6	GOOD MORNING JUDGE	Gershwin	106
February 17	THE ROYAL VAGABOND	Berlin	87
March 8	UP STAGE AND DOWN	Rodgers	153
May 5	SHE'S A GOOD FELLOW	Kern	41–42
May 12	THE LADY IN RED	Gershwin/ Kern	106–07 42
May 26	LA, LA LUCILLE	Gershwin	107
June 10	A LONELY ROMEO	Rodgers	153–154
June 23	ZIEGFELD FOLLIES OF 1919	Berlin	87–88
October 2	ZIEGFELD MIDNIGHT FROLIC	Berlin	88
October 6	HITCHY-KOO 1919	Porter	205
October 24	CAPITOL REVUE	Gershwin	108
October 27	BUDDIES	Porter	205–06
November 1	IRENE	PART 4	545
November 12 <L>	THE ECLIPSE	Porter	206
[December 8]	ZIP, GOES A MILLION	Kern	42–43
December 27	MORRIS GEST'S MIDNIGHT WHIRL	Gershwin	108
[c. December]	SINBAD	Gershwin	108–09

1920

January 13	THE PASSION FLOWER	Berlin	88
January 27	AS YOU WERE	Porter	206
February 2	THE NIGHT BOAT	Kern	43–44
[February 2]	DERE MABLE	Gershwin	109
March 6	YOU'D BE SURPRISED	Rodgers	154–55
March 8	ZIEGFELD GIRLS OF 1920	Berlin	88
March 24	FLY WITH ME	Rodgers	155–56
April 5	THE ED WYNN CARNIVAL	Gershwin	109
June 7	GEORGE WHITE'S SCANDALS 1920	Gershwin	109–10

October 23	MUSIC BOX REVUE < second >	Berlin	90–91
November 28	THE BUNCH AND JUDY	Kern	48
December 4	OUR NELL	Gershwin	116
December 25	ROSE BRIAR	Kern	48

1923

January 24	THE DANCING GIRL	Gershwin	116
February 7	WILDFLOWER	Youmans	140
April 3 < L >	THE RAINBOW	Gershwin	116
June 18	GEORGE WHITE'S SCANDALS 1923	Gershwin	117
August 28	LITTLE MISS BLUEBEARD	Gershwin	117
September 5 < L >	THE BEAUTY PRIZE	Kern	49
September 22	MUSIC BOX REVUE < third >	Berlin	91
September 25	NIFTIES OF 1923	Gershwin	117–18
October 4	HAMMERSTEIN'S NINE O'CLOCK REVUE	Youmans	141
November 6	THE STEPPING STONES	Kern	49–50
December 25	MARY JANE McKANE	Youmans	141

1924

January 21	LOLLIPOP	Youmans	141–42
January 21	SWEET LITTLE DEVIL	Gershwin	118
April 8	SITTING PRETTY	Kern	50–51
May 13	THE MELODY MAN	Rodgers	157–58
May 21 < L >	THE PUNCH BOWL	Berlin	92
June 30	GEORGE WHITE'S SCANDALS 1924	Gershwin	118–19
September 11 < L >	PRIMROSE	Gershwin	119–20
September 16	GREENWICH VILLAGE FOLLIES 1924	Porter	208
September 23 < L >	CHARLOT'S REVUE	Youmans	142
September 23	DEAR SIR	Kern	51–52
November 6	PETER PAN < second >	Kern	52
December 1	LADY, BE GOOD!	Gershwin	120–21
December 1	MUSIC BOX REVUE < fourth >	Berlin	92–93

1925

February 21 <L>	KATJA THE DANCER	Duke	270
April 13	TELL ME MORE	Gershwin	121–22
May 17	GARRICK GAIETIES <first>	Rodgers	158–59
August 6	JUNE DAYS	Rodgers	159
[September 7]	A NIGHT OUT	Youmans	142–43
September 16	NO, NO, NANETTE	Youmans	143–44
September 18	DEAREST ENEMY	Rodgers	159–60
September 22	SUNNY	Kern	52–53
October 26	THE CITY CHAP	Kern	53–54
December 8	THE COCOANUTS	Berlin	93–94
December 28	TIP-TOES	Gershwin	122
December 30	SONG OF THE FLAME	Gershwin	123

1926

[c. January]	FIFTH AVENUE FOLLIES	Rodgers	160
March 17	THE GIRL FRIEND	Rodgers	160–61
April 29 <L>	COCHRAN'S 1926 REVUE	Rodgers	161
May 10	GARRICK GAIETIES <second>	Rodgers	161–62
May 22 <L>	YVONNE	Duke	271
June 14	GEORGE WHITE'S SCANDALS <eighth>	PART 4	547
June 15	GRAND STREET FOLLIES OF 1926	Schwartz	232
July 26	AMERICANA <first>	Gershwin	123
October 12	CRISS-CROSS	Kern	54
November 8	OH, KAY!	Gershwin	124
December 1 <L>	LIDO LADY	Rodgers	162–63
December 17	OH, PLEASE!	Youmans	144
December 27	PEGGY-ANN	Rodgers	163–64
December 28	BETSY	Berlin/	94
		Rodgers	164

1927

March 10	THE NEW YORKERS <first>	Schwartz	233
March 22	LUCKY	Kern	54–55

April 25	HIT THE DECK	Youmans	145
April 27 <L>	LADY LUCK	Rodgers	164–65
[c. April] <L>	TWO LITTLE GIRLS IN BLUE	Duke	139
May 20 <L>	LONDON PAVILION REVUE	Rodgers	165
August 16	ZIEGFELD FOLLIES OF 1927	Berlin	94–95
August 25 <L>	UP WITH THE LARK	Porter	209
[August 29]	STRIKE UP THE BAND <first>	Gershwin	125
September 6	GOOD NEWS!	PART 4	548
October 12 <L>	THE BOW-WOWS	Duke	272
November 3	A CONNECTICUT YANKEE <first>	Rodgers	166
November 22	FUNNY FACE	Gershwin	125–26
December 27	SHOW BOAT	Kern	55–57

1928

January 3	SHE'S MY BABY	Rodgers	167
January 10	ROSALIE	Gershwin	126–27
February 8 <L>	THE YELLOW MASK	Duke	272–73
February 23 <L>	LADY MARY	Kern	57
April 26	PRESENT ARMS!	Rodgers	167–68
April 27 <L>	BLUE EYES	Kern	57–58
May 9	BLACKBIRDS OF 1928	PART 4	549
[May 10]	LA REVUE DES AMBASSADEURS	Porter	209–10
September 5	GOOD BOY	Schwartz	233
September 25	CHEE-CHEE	Rodgers	168
October 8	PARIS	Porter	203
November 8	TREASURE GIRL	Gershwin	127
November 21	RAINBOW	Youmans	146
December 4	WHOOPEE	PART 4	549–50
December 25	THE RED ROBE	Schwartz	234

1929

January 15	NED WAYBURN'S GAMBOLS	Schwartz	234
January 31	LADY FINGERS	Rodgers	169
March 11	SPRING IS HERE	Rodgers	169
March 27 <L>	WAKE UP AND DREAM	Porter	210–11

1933

January 20	PARDON MY ENGLISH	Gershwin	132
April 6	COTTON CLUB PARADE < twenty-second >	Arlen	260
April 13	THREEPENNY OPERA < first >	Weill	297–98
[July 28]	CRAZY QUILT OF 1933	Arlen	260
September 13 < L >	NICE GOINGS ON	Schwartz	242
September 30	AS THOUSANDS CHEER	Berlin	96–97
October 6 < L >	NYMPH ERRANT	Porter	214–15
October 21	LET 'EM EAT CAKE	Gershwin	132–33
November 16 < L >	PLEASE!	Rodgers	173
November 18	ROBERTA	Kern	62
November 20	SHE LOVES ME NOT	Schwartz	242–43

1934

January 4	ZIEGFELD FOLLIES OF 1934	Duke	275
March 23	COTTON CLUB PARADE < twenty-fourth >	Arlen	261
April 19 < L >	THREE SISTERS	Kern	63
August 27	LIFE BEGINS AT 8:40	Arlen	261–62
October 3 < L >	HI DIDDLE DIDDLE	Porter	215
[October 22]	BRING ON THE GIRLS	Schwartz	243
November 21	ANYTHING GOES	Porter	215–17
November 28	REVENGE WITH MUSIC	Schwartz	243–44
[December 22]	MARIE GALANTE	Weill	298
December 27	THUMBS UP!	Duke	276

1935

March 4	PETTICOAT FEVER	Loewe	364
April 29	SOMETHING GAY	Rodgers	173–74
May 20	PARADE < first >	Blitzstein	315
June 28 < L >	A KINGDOM FOR A COW	Weill	298–99
September 19	AT HOME ABROAD	Schwartz	244
October 10	PORGY AND BESS	Gershwin	133–35
October 12	JUBILEE	Porter	217
November 16	JUMBO	Rodgers	174

1936

January 22	THE ILLUSTRATORS' SHOW	Loesser/ Loewe	397 364–65
January 30	ZIEGFELD FOLLIES <OF 1936>	Duke	276–77
February 4 <L>	FOLLOW THE SUN	Schwartz	245
April 11	ON YOUR TOES	Rodgers	175
October 29	RED, HOT AND BLUE!	Porter	218–19
November 19	JOHNNY JOHNSON	Weill	299–300
December 3 <L>	O MISTRESS MINE	Porter	219
December 25	THE SHOW IS ON	Duke/ Arlen/ Gershwin/ Rodgers/ Schwartz	277 262 135 176 245

1937

January 7	THE ETERNAL ROAD	Weill	300
April 14	BABES IN ARMS	Rodgers	176–77
[June 12]	SALUTE TO SPRING	Loewe	365
June 16	THE CRADLE WILL ROCK	Blitzstein	315–16
September 2	VIRGINIA	Schwartz	245–46
November 2	I'D RATHER BE RIGHT	Rodgers	177–78
November 11	JULIUS CAESAR	Blitzstein	316–17
November 27	PINS AND NEEDLES	Rome	326–27
December 1	HOORAY FOR WHAT!	Arlen	262–63
December 22	BETWEEN THE DEVIL	Schwartz	246–47

1938

May 11	I MARRIED AN ANGEL	Rodgers	178
[June 3]	GENTLEMEN UNAFRAID	Kern	63–64
September 21	YOU NEVER KNOW	Porter	219
September 24	SING OUT THE NEWS	Rome	327–28
October 19	KNICKERBOCKER HOLIDAY	Weill	300–301
November 2	DANTON'S DEATH	Blitzstein	317
November 9	LEAVE IT TO ME!	Porter	220
November 23	THE BOYS FROM SYRACUSE	Rodgers	179
December 1	GREAT LADY	Loewe	365–66

1939

January 3	MAMBA'S DAUGHTERS	Kern	64
February 9	STARS IN YOUR EYES	Schwartz	247
February 15	THE LITTLE FOXES	Willson	414
April 24	SING FOR YOUR SUPPER	Rome	328
April 30	RAILROADS ON PARADE	Weill	302
June 9 <L>	THE SUN NEVER SETS	Porter	220
June 19	STREETS OF PARIS	Rome	328–29
October 16	THE MAN WHO CAME TO DINNER	Porter	221
October 18	TOO MANY GIRLS	Rodgers	180
November 17	VERY WARM FOR MAY	Kern	64–65
December 6	DUBARRY WAS A LADY	Porter	221–22
[December 26]	A VAGABOND HERO	Duke	277–78

1940

April 4	HIGHER AND HIGHER	Rodgers	181
May 12	AMERICAN JUBILEE	Schwartz	247–48
May 23	KEEP OFF THE GRASS	Duke	278
May 28	LOUISIANA PURCHASE	Berlin	97
June 4	WALK WITH MUSIC	PART 4	551–52
[June 24]	TWO WEEKS WITH PAY	Rodgers	182
[July 13]	THE LITTLE DOG LAUGHED	Rome	329
September 11	HOLD ON TO YOUR HATS	Lane	290
October 10	IT HAPPENS ON ICE	Duke	278
October 25	CABIN IN THE SKY	Duke	278–79
October 30	PANAMA HATTIE	Porter	222
December 25	PAL JOEY	Rodgers	182–83

1941

January 5	NO FOR AN ANSWER	Blitzstein	317–18
January 23	LADY IN THE DARK	Weill	302–03
October 1	BEST FOOT FORWARD	Martin/ Rodgers	343–44 183–84
October 29	LET'S FACE IT	Porter	222–23
December 25	BANJO EYES	Duke	279–80

1942

January 9	THE LADY COMES ACROSS	Duke	280–81
[c. March]	SYMPHONY IN BROWN	Arlen	263
June 2	BY JUPITER	Rodgers	184–85
June 22	LUNCHTIME FOLLIES	Blitzstein/	318
		Rome/	329–30
		Weill	303
June 24	STAR AND GARTER	Rome	330
July 4	THIS IS THE ARMY	Berlin	98–99
September 4	ICE CAPADES OF 1943	Styne	373
October 5	LET FREEDOM SING	Rome	330
[October 8]	LIFE OF THE PARTY	Loewe	366

1943

January 7	SOMETHING FOR THE BOYS	Porter	223–24
[March 22]	DANCING IN THE STREETS	Duke	281
March 31	OKLAHOMA!	Rodgers	185–86
June 17	EARLY TO BED	PART 4	552–53
[July 13]	STARS AND GRIPES	Rome	331
October 7	ONE TOUCH OF VENUS	Weill	303–04
November 11	WHAT'S UP?	Loewe	366–67
November 17	A CONNECTICUT YANKEE < second >	Rodgers	186–87

1944

January 13	JACKPOT	Duke	281–82
January 25	SKIRTS	Loesser/	398
		Rome	331
[January 27]	VINCENT YOUMANS' BALLET REVUE	Youmans	150
January 28	MEXICAN HAYRIDE	Porter	224
[c. April]	TARS AND SPARS	Duke	282
[May 26]	ABOUT FACE!	Loesser	398–99
[August 7]	HI, YANK!	Loesser	399
October 5	BLOOMER GIRL	Arlen	263–64
[November 13]	GLAD TO SEE YOU!	Styne	374
November 16	SADIE THOMPSON	Duke	282–83
[c. November]	PFC MARY BROWN	Loesser	399–400

| September 25 <L> | LOVE FROM JUDY | Martin | 346–47 |
| December 15 | TWO'S COMPANY | Duke | 284 |

1953

February 11	HAZEL FLAGG	Styne	377–78
February 25	WONDERFUL TOWN	Bernstein	352–53
May 7	CAN-CAN	Porter	229
May 28	ME AND JULIET	Rodgers	192
December 3	KISMET	PART 4	555–57
December 10	JOHN MURRAY ANDERSON'S ALMANAC	Adler/ Coleman	407–08 481

1954

March 10	THREEPENNY OPERA < second >	Weill	310–11
March 11	THE GOLDEN APPLE	PART 4	557–58
April 8	BY THE BEAUTIFUL SEA	Schwartz	250–51
May 13	THE PAJAMA GAME	Adler	408–09
September 30	THE BOY FRIEND	PART 5	589–90
October 18	I FEEL WONDERFUL	Herman	495
October 20	PETER PAN < fourth >	Styne	378–79
November 4	FANNY	Rome	336–37
December 30	HOUSE OF FLOWERS	Arlen	295–96

1955

January 27	PLAIN AND FANCY	PART 4	558–59
February 24	SILK STOCKINGS	Porter	230
February 28	SHOESTRING REVUE	Strouse	462
April 19	ALL IN ONE	Bernstein	353–54
May 5	DAMN YANKEES	Adler	409–10
September 6	CATCH A STAR	Bock	422
[October 10]	REUBEN REUBEN	Blitzstein	321–22
November 17	THE LARK	Bernstein	354
[November 23]	A QUIET PLACE < first >	Bernstein	354–55
November 30	PIPE DREAM	Rodgers	193–94

1956

| March 15 | MY FAIR LADY | Loewe | 369–70 |
| March 22 | MR. WONDERFUL | Bock | 422–23 |

[April 16]	ZIEGFELD FOLLIES OF 1956	Bock	423
May 2	WAKE UP, DARLING	Styne	379–80
May 3	THE MOST HAPPY FELLA	Loesser	402–04
May 22	THE LITTLEST REVUE	Blitzstein/	322
		Duke/	284–85
		Strouse	463
October 8	SIXTH FINGER IN A FIVE FINGER GLOVE	Strouse	463
November 5	SHOESTRING '57	Schmidt/	520
		Strouse	463–64
November 15	LI'L ABNER	PART 4	559–60
November 19	GIRLS OF SUMMER	Sondheim	443–44
November 29	BELLS ARE RINGING	Styne	380–81
December 1	CANDIDE < first >	Bernstein	355–56

1957

March 13	THE SIN OF PAT MULDOON	Adler	410
May 14	NEW GIRL IN TOWN	Merrill	434–35
September 26	WEST SIDE STORY	Bernstein	356–57
October 10	ROMANOFF AND JULIET	Rome	337–38
October 24	COMPULSION	Coleman	481–82
October 31	JAMAICA	Arlen	267
November 2	TIME REMEMBERED	Duke	285
December 19	THE MUSIC MAN	Willson	415–16

1958

January 23	THE BODY BEAUTIFUL	Bock	424
April 3	SAY, DARLING	Styne	381–82
April 29	THE FIRSTBORN	Bernstein	358
May 18	NIGHTCAP	Herman	495–96
June 20	A MIDSUMMER NIGHT'S DREAM	Blitzstein	322–23
July 20	THE WINTER'S TALE	Blitzstein	323
October 11	DEMI-DOZEN	Coleman/	482
		Schmidt	520–21
October 11	GOLDILOCKS	PART 4	560–61
December 1	FLOWER DRUM SONG	Rodgers	194–95

1959

1960

1961

1962

January 3	BRECHT ON BRECHT	Weill	311
January 27	A FAMILY AFFAIR	Kander	506–07
March 15	NO STRINGS	Rodgers	196
March 19	ALL AMERICAN	Strouse	465–66
March 22	I CAN GET IT FOR YOU WHOLESALE	Rome	339
May 8	A FUNNY THING . . .	Sondheim	445–47
[July 2]	WORLD OF JULES FEIFFER	Sondheim	446
October 3	STOP THE WORLD . . .	PART 5	591–92
October 20	MR. PRESIDENT	Berlin	101–02
November 17	LITTLE ME	Coleman	483–84
November 27	NEVER TOO LATE	Bock/	426
		Kander	507

1963

January 6	OLIVER!	PART 5	592–93
March 12	TOO TRUE TO BE GOOD	Leigh	529
April 11	MAN IN THE MOON	Bock	426–27
April 19	HOT SPOT	Sondheim	446–47
April 23	SHE LOVES ME	Bock	427–28
[August 5]	ZENDA	Duke	286–87
October 3	HERE'S LOVE	Willson	417
October 17	JENNIE	Schwartz	252–53
October 24	110 IN THE SHADE	Schmidt	522–23
November 11	ARTURO UI	Styne	385

1964

January 16	HELLO, DOLLY!	Herman/	498–500
		Merrill/	437
		Strouse	466
March 26	FUNNY GIRL	Styne	385–87
March 28	NEVER LIVE OVER A PRETZEL FACTORY	Leigh	529–30
April 4	ANYONE CAN WHISTLE	Sondheim	447–48
April 7	HIGH SPIRITS	Martin	347–48
April 22	TO BROADWAY WITH LOVE	Bock	428

1968

January 18	THE HAPPY TIME	Kander	510
January 22	JACQUES BREL IS ALIVE	PART 4	563–65
January 27	DARLING OF THE DAY	Styne	389–90
April 29	HAIR	PART 4	565–66
[September 23]	A MOTHER'S KISSES	Adler	412
October 20	HER FIRST ROMAN	Bock	432
November 17	ZORBA	Kander	510–11
December 1	PROMISES, PROMISES	PART 4	566–67

1969

January 22	CELEBRATION	Schmidt	524–25
February 6	DEAR WORLD	Herman	501–02
March 16	1776	PART 4	567–68
June 4	PROMENADE	PART 4	568–69
[September 2]	1491	Willson	417–18
October 21	BUTTERFLIES ARE FREE	S. Schwartz	537

1970

March 15	PURLIE	PART 4	569–70
March 26	MINNIE'S BOYS	PART 4	570–71
March 29	LOOK TO THE LILIES	Styne	390–91
March 30	APPLAUSE	Strouse	469
April 8	CRY FOR US ALL	Leigh	531–32
April 26	COMPANY	Sondheim	448–50
April 28	RISE AND FALL OF . . . MAHAGONNY	Weill	312
May 6	COLETTE < first >	Schmidt	525
October 19	THE ROTHSCHILDS	Bock	432–33
November 10	TWO BY TWO	Rodgers	197–98

1971

[February 1]	PRETTYBELLE	Styne	391–92
April 4	FOLLIES	Sondheim	450–51
April 12	SIX	Strouse	470
April 15	70, GIRLS, 70	Kander	511–12
May 17	GODSPELL	S. Schwartz	537–38
[September 8]	MASS	Bernstein	358–59
October 12	JESUS CHRIST SUPERSTAR	PART 5	594–95

1972

February 14	GREASE	PART 4	571–72
[March 20]	HALLOWEEN	Leigh	532–33
April 9	SUGAR	Styne	392–93
May 3 <L>	GONE WITH THE WIND	Rome	341–42
October 23	PIPPIN	S. Schwartz	538–39
November 6 <L>	I AND ALBERT	Strouse	470–71

1973

February 25	A LITTLE NIGHT MUSIC	Sondheim	451–52
March 18	SEESAW	Coleman	486–87
November 13	GIGI	Loewe	371–72

1974

January 27	LORELEI	Styne	393–94
March 10	CANDIDE <second>	Bernstein	360
[May 20]	THE FROGS	Sondheim	453
May 28	THE MAGIC SHOW	S. Schwartz	539–40
October 6	MACK AND MABEL	Herman	502–03

1975

January 3	PHILOMEN	Schmidt	525–26
January 5	THE WIZ	PART 4	572–73
January 7	SHENANDOAH	PART 4	573–74
February 21	STRAWS IN THE WIND	Coleman	487
April 15	A CHORUS LINE	PART 4	574–75
June 1	CHICAGO	Kander	512–13
November 23	BY BERNSTEIN	Bernstein	361

1976

January 4	HOME SWEET HOMER	Leigh	533
January 11	PACIFIC OVERTURES	Sondheim	453–54
April 25	REX	Rodgers	198–99
May 4	1600 PENNSYLVANIA AVENUE	Bernstein	361–62
May 4 <L>	SIDE BY SIDE BY SONDHEIM	Sondheim	454
[May 11]	THE BAKER'S WIFE	S. Schwartz	540–41

October 9	THE ROBBER BRIDEGROOM	PART 4	575–76
[November 22]	HELLZAPOPPIN'!	Coleman/	487
		Styne	394
December 20	MUSIC IS	Adler	412–13
December 30	JOSEPH AND THE . . . DREAMCOAT	PART 5	595–96

1977

April 17	I LOVE MY WIFE	Coleman	487–88
April 21	ANNIE	Strouse	471–72
May 7	HAPPY END	Weill	312–13
October 29	THE ACT	Kander	514

1978

February 19	ON THE TWENTIETH CENTURY	Coleman	488–89
[March 7]	PRINCE OF GRAND STREET	Merrill	440
April 17	BEST LITTLE WHOREHOUSE . . .	PART 4	576
May 14	WORKING	S. Schwartz	541
October 31 <L>	BAR MITZVAH BOY	Styne	395
December 21	A BROADWAY MUSICAL	Strouse	472

1979

January 11	THE GRAND TOUR	Herman	503
February 23	SARAVA	Leigh	533
March 1	SWEENEY TODD	Sondheim	454–55
[March 12]	HOME AGAIN, HOME AGAIN	Coleman	489–90
April 8	CARMELINA	Lane	293–94
May 31	I REMEMBER MAMA	Rodgers	199–200
June 13	MADWOMAN OF CENTRAL PARK WEST	Bernstein/ Kander	362 515
June 14 <L>	FLOWERS FOR ALGERNON	Strouse	473
September 25	EVITA	PART 5	596–97

1980

April 30	BARNUM	Coleman	490
May 1	A DAY IN HOLLYWOOD	Herman	503–04
[July 9]	APRIL SONG	Leigh	534
[October 20]	ONE NIGHT STAND	Styne	395–96

1981

March 5	BRING BACK BIRDIE	Strouse	474
March 12	MARRY ME A LITTLE	Sondheim	456
March 29	WOMAN OF THE YEAR	Kander	515–16
April 1	MARCH OF THE FALSETTOS	PART 4	577–78
November 16	MERRILY WE ROLL ALONG	Sondheim	456–57
December 20	DREAMGIRLS	PART 4	578–79

1982

[February 9]	COLETTE < second >	Schmidt	526
May 9	NINE	PART 4	579–80
October 7	CATS	PART 5	604–05
October 28	UPSTAIRS AT O'NEALS	Strouse	475
[December 18]	NIGHTINGALE	Strouse	475–76

1983

March 31	COLETTE COLLAGE < first >	Schmidt	527
May 11	DANCE A LITTLE CLOSER	Strouse	476
August 21	LA CAGE AUX FOLLES	Herman	504–05
December 4	BABY	PART 4	580–81

1984

February 9	THE RINK	Kander	516–17
May 2	SUNDAY IN THE PARK WITH GEORGE	Sondheim	457–58
July 22	A QUIET PLACE < second >	Bernstein	362–63

1985

March 26	IN TROUSERS	PART 4	581–82
April 25	BIG RIVER	PART 4	582–83
May 13	MAYOR	Strouse	477
September 18	SONG AND DANCE	PART 5	599–600
[November 27]	PIECES OF EIGHT	Styne	396

1986

August 21	RAGS	Strouse	477–78

1987

March 12	LES MISERABLES	PART 5	600–01
March 15	STARLIGHT EXPRESS	PART 5	601–02
[July 29]	GROVER'S CORNERS	Schmidt	527–28
November 5	INTO THE WOODS	Sondheim	458–60

1988

January 26	PHANTOM OF THE OPERA	PART 5	602–03
[April 6]	MIKE	Leigh	534–35

1989

March 17	CHU CHEM < second >	Leigh	535
April 13	WELCOME TO THE CLUB	Coleman	491
November 2	MEET ME IN ST. LOUIS < second >	Martin	348–49
November 12	GRAND HOTEL: THE MUSICAL	PART 4	583–84
December 11	CITY OF ANGELS	Coleman	491–92

1990

[January 4]	ANNIE 2	Strouse	479
April 8	ASPECTS OF LOVE	PART 5	603–04
[May 1]	KISS OF THE SPIDER WOMAN	Kander	517
May 31	HANNAH . . . 1939	Merrill	441
June 28	FALSETTOLAND	PART 4	584–85

1991

Appendix 2

The reader will have noted certain collaborators regularly mentioned throughout this book. There was a core of lyricists, librettists, directors, choreographers and producers who shared responsibility for the better shows and more important innovations.

The lyricists, of course, were especial contributors to the musical theatre. Many of them have been praised far too little (or not at all) in this book; that's not to say they are unappreciated.

As an added reference, more than forty of these collaborators have been selected for this appendix. Productions they collaborated on are listed, giving a partial view of their careers. (Only shows discussed in this book are listed.) Included are unofficial credits: where they were unbilled "helpers," replaced during the tryout, etc. Acting credits are not included.

The usual function(s) performed are mentioned. The collaborator did not necessarily serve in all capacities on each production.

The format remains as elsewhere, except that the dates given do not reflect shows which closed out of town.

This reference guide can serve as just that: a guide. The work of the collaborators has been discussed only as it affected the composers; most are worthy of separate study.

Collaborator Reference Listing

ALEXANDER A. AARONS
Producer

BORN: [Circa 1891]   Philadelphia, Pennsylvania
DIED: March 14, 1943   Beverly Hills, California

May 26, 1919	Gershwin	LA, LA LUCILLE
May 3, 1921	Youmans	TWO LITTLE GIRLS IN BLUE
February 20, 1922	Gershwin	FOR GOODNESS SAKE
December 1, 1924	Gershwin	LADY, BE GOOD!
December 28, 1925	Gershwin	TIP-TOES
November 8, 1926	Gershwin	OH, KAY!
November 22, 1927	Gershwin	FUNNY FACE
November 8, 1928	Gershwin	TREASURE GIRL
March 11, 1929	Rodgers	SPRING IS HERE
November 11, 1929	Rodgers	HEADS UP!
October 14, 1930	Gershwin	GIRL CRAZY
January 20, 1933	Gershwin	PARDON MY ENGLISH

GEORGE ABBOTT
Librettist, Director, Producer

BORN: June 25, 1887   Forrestville, New York

December 2, 1932	Arlen	THE GREAT MAGOO
November 16, 1935	Rodgers	JUMBO
April 11, 1936	Rodgers	ON YOUR TOES
November 23, 1938	Rodgers	THE BOYS FROM SYRACUSE
October 18, 1939	Rodgers	TOO MANY GIRLS
December 25, 1940	Rodgers	PAL JOEY
October 1, 1941	Martin	BEST FOOT FORWARD
December 28, 1944	Bernstein	ON THE TOWN
October 9, 1947	Styne	HIGH BUTTON SHOES
January 29, 1948	Martin	LOOK, MA, I'M DANCIN'!

October 11, 1948	Loesser	WHERE'S CHARLEY?
October 12, 1950	Berlin	CALL ME MADAM
December 21, 1950	Porter	OUT OF THIS WORLD
April 19, 1951	Schwartz	A TREE GROWS IN BROOKLYN
February 25, 1953	Bernstein	WONDERFUL TOWN
May 28, 1953	Rodgers	ME AND JULIET
May 13, 1954	Adler	THE PAJAMA GAME
May 5, 1955	Adler	DAMN YANKEES
May 14, 1957	Merrill	NEW GIRL IN TOWN
May 11, 1959	[PART 4]	ONCE UPON A MATTRESS
November 23, 1959	Bock	FIORELLO!
October 17, 1960	Bock	TENDERLOIN
May 8, 1962	Sondheim	A FUNNY THING
November 27, 1962	Bock/Kander	NEVER TOO LATE
May 26, 1964	Styne	FADE OUT—FADE IN
May 11, 1965	Kander	FLORA, THE RED MENACE
December 20, 1976	Adler	MUSIC IS

LEE ADAMS
Lyricist

BORN: August 14, 1924   Mansfield, Ohio

May 22, 1956	Strouse	THE LITTLEST REVUE
November 5, 1956	Strouse	SHOESTRING '57
April 14, 1960	Strouse	BYE BYE BIRDIE
March 19, 1962	Strouse	ALL AMERICAN
January 16, 1964	Strouse	HELLO, DOLLY!
October 20, 1964	Strouse	GOLDEN BOY
March 29, 1966	Strouse	"IT'S . . . SUPERMAN"
March 30, 1970	Strouse	APPLAUSE
November 6, 1972 <L>	Strouse	I AND ALBERT
December 21, 1978	Strouse	A BROADWAY MUSICAL
March 5, 1981	Strouse	BRING BACK BIRDIE
April 6, 1988	Leigh	MIKE

GEORGE BALANCHINE
Choreographer, Director

BORN: January 9, 1904   St. Petersburg, Russia
DIED: April 30, 1983   New York, New York

March 27, 1929 <L>	Porter	WAKE UP AND DREAM
January 30, 1936	Duke	ZIEGFELD FOLLIES OF 1936
April 11, 1936	Rodgers	ON YOUR TOES
April 14, 1937	Rodgers	BABES IN ARMS
May 11, 1938	Rodgers	I MARRIED AN ANGEL
November 23, 1938	Rodgers	THE BOYS FROM SYRACUSE
May 23, 1940	Duke	KEEP OFF THE GRASS
May 28, 1940	Berlin	LOUISIANA PURCHASE
October 25, 1940	Duke	CABIN IN THE SKY
January 9, 1942	Duke	THE LADY COMES ACROSS
November 11, 1943	Loewe	WHAT'S UP
October 11, 1948	Loesser	WHERE'S CHARLEY?
June 20, 1958	Blitzstein	A MIDSUMMER NIGHT'S DREAM
July 20, 1958	Blitzstein	THE WINTER'S TALE

MICHAEL BENNETT
Director, Choreographer

BORN: April 8, 1943 Buffalo, New York
DIED: July 2, 1987 Tucson, Arizona

October 23, 1967	Merrill	HENRY SWEET HENRY
December 1, 1968	[PART 4]	PROMISES, PROMISES
April 26, 1970	Sondheim	COMPANY
April 4, 1971	Sondheim	FOLLIES
March 18, 1973	Coleman	SEESAW
April 15, 1975	[PART 4]	A CHORUS LINE
December 20, 1981	[PART 4]	DREAMGIRLS

GUY BOLTON
Librettist

BORN: November 23, 1884 Broxbourne, England
DIED: September 5, 1979 London, England

January 25, 1915	Kern	NINETY IN THE SHADE
April 20, 1915	Kern	NOBODY HOME
December 23, 1915	Kern	VERY GOOD EDDIE
September 25, 1916	Kern	MISS SPRINGTIME
January 11, 1917	Kern	HAVE A HEART

February 20, 1917	Kern	OH, BOY!
August 28, 1917	Kern	LEAVE IT TO JANE
September 24, 1917	Kern	THE RIVIERA GIRL
November 5, 1917	Kern	MISS 1917
February 1, 1918	Kern	OH LADY! LADY!!
May 18, 1918 <L>	Porter	VERY GOOD EDDIE
November 27, 1918	Kern	OH, MY DEAR!
February 21, 1920	Kern	SALLY
April 8, 1924	Kern	SITTING PRETTY
September 11, 1924 <L>	Gershwin	PRIMROSE
December 1, 1924	Gershwin	LADY BE GOOD
December 28, 1925	Gershwin	TIP-TOES
November 8, 1926	Gershwin	OH, KAY!
January 3, 1928	Rodgers	SHE'S MY BABY
January 10, 1928	Gershwin	ROSALIE
April 27, 1928 <L>	Kern	BLUE EYES
February 18, 1930	Rodgers	SIMPLE SIMON
October 14, 1930	Gershwin	GIRL CRAZY
November 21, 1934	Porter	ANYTHING GOES
June 9, 1939 <L>	Porter	THE SUN NEVER SETS
June 4, 1940	[PART 4]	WALK WITH MUSIC
January 13, 1944	Duke	JACKPOT

ANNE CALDWELL
Lyricist, Librettist

BORN: August 30, 1867   Boston, Massachusetts
DIED: October 22, 1936   Beverly Hills, California

February 2, 1914	Kern	WHEN CLAUDIA SMILES
May 5, 1919	Kern	SHE'S A GOOD FELLOW
May 12, 1919	Gershwin/Kern	THE LADY IN RED
February 2, 1920	Kern	THE NIGHT BOAT
August 31, 1920	Gershwin	THE SWEETHEART SHOP
October 19, 1920	Kern	HITCHY-KOO 1920
November 1, 1921	Kern	GOOD MORNING DEARIE
November 28, 1922	Kern	THE BUNCH AND JUDY
November 6, 1923	Kern	THE STEPPING STONES
October 26, 1925	Kern	THE CITY CHAP

| October 12, 1926 | Kern | CRISS-CROSS |
| December 17, 1926 | Youmans | OH, PLEASE! |

GOWER CHAMPION
Director, Choreographer

BORN: June 22, 1920   Geneva, Illinois
DIED: August 25, 1980   New York, New York

[c. April 1944]	Duke	TARS AND SPARS
April 18, 1951	Martin	MAKE A WISH
April 14, 1960	Strouse	BYE BYE BIRDIE
April 13, 1961	Merrill	CARNIVAL!
January 16, 1964	Herman/Merrill/ Strouse	HELLO, DOLLY!
December 5, 1966	Schmidt	I DO! I DO!
January 18, 1968	Kander	THE HAPPY TIME
February 1, 1971	Styne	PRETTYBELLE
April 9, 1972	Styne	SUGAR
October 6, 1974	Herman	MACK AND MABEL
October 29, 1979	Kander	THE ACT
December 21, 1978	Strouse	A BROADWAY MUSICAL

BETTY COMDEN   /   ADOLPH GREEN
Lyricist, Librettist   *Lyricist, Librettist*

BORN: May 3, 1915   BORN: December 2, 1915
Brooklyn, New York   Bronx, New York

December 28, 1944	Bernstein	ON THE TOWN
July 19, 1951	Styne	TWO ON THE AISLE
February 25, 1953	Bernstein	WONDERFUL TOWN
October 20, 1954	Styne	PETER PAN < fourth >
November 29, 1956	Styne	BELLS ARE RINGING
April 3, 1958	Styne	SAY, DARLING
December 26, 1960	Styne	DO RE MI
December 27, 1961	Styne	SUBWAYS ARE FOR SLEEPING
May 26, 1964	Styne	FADE OUT—FADE IN
April 26, 1967	Styne	HALLELUJAH, BABY!
March 30, 1970	Strouse	APPLAUSE
January 27, 1974	Styne	LORELEI
February 21, 1975	Coleman	STRAWS IN THE WIND
November 23, 1975	Bernstein	BY BERNSTEIN

| February 19, 1978 | Coleman | ON THE TWENTIETH CENTURY |
| May 1, 1991 | Coleman | THE WILL ROGERS FOLLIES |

CHERYL CRAWFORD
Producer

BORN: September 24, 1902   Akron, Ohio
DIED: October 7, 1986   New York, New York

November 19, 1936	Weill	JOHNNY JOHNSON
October 7, 1943	Weill	ONE TOUCH OF VENUS
December 19, 1946	Blitzstein	ANDROCLES AND THE LION
March 13, 1947	Loewe	BRIGADOON
October 7, 1948	Weill	LOVE LIFE
October 31, 1949	Blitzstein	REGINA
May 14, 1951	[PART 4]	FLAHOOLEY
November 12, 1951	Loewe	PAINT YOUR WAGON
October 10, 1955	Blitzstein	REUBEN REUBEN
November 19, 1956	Sondheim	THE GIRLS OF SUMMER
October 17, 1963	Schwartz	JENNIE
November 15, 1966	Leigh	CHU-CHEM < first >
January 22, 1969	Schmidt	CELEBRATION
May 6, 1970	Schmidt	COLETTE < first >

AGNES DE MILLE
Choreographer, Director

BORN: September 18, 1905   New York, New York

September 15, 1932	Schwartz	FLYING COLORS
October 6, 1933 < L >	Porter	NYMPH ERRANT
December 1, 1937	Arlen	HOORAY FOR WHAT!
March 31, 1943	Rodgers	OKLAHOMA!
October 7, 1943	Weill	ONE TOUCH OF VENUS
October 5, 1944	Arlen	BLOOMER GIRL
April 19, 1945	Rodgers	CAROUSEL
March 13, 1947	Loewe	BRIGADOON
October 10, 1947	Rodgers	ALLEGRO
December 8, 1949	Styne	GENTLEMEN PREFER BLONDES

December 21, 1950	Porter	OUT OF THIS WORLD
November 12, 1951	Loewe	PAINT YOUR WAGON
October 11, 1958	[PART 4]	GOLDILOCKS
March 9, 1959	Blitzstein	JUNO
October 23, 1961	Adler	KWAMINA
October 24, 1963	Schmidt	110 IN THE SHADE

B. G. DESYLVA
Lyricist, Librettist, Producer

BORN: January 27, 1895 New York, New York
DIED: July 11, 1950 Los Angeles, California

May 26, 1919	Gershwin	LA, LA LUCILLE
December 8, 1919	Kern	ZIP, GOES A MILLION
December 27, 1919	Gershwin	MORRIS GEST'S MIDNIGHT WHIRL
[c. December 1919]	Gershwin	SINBAD
December 21, 1920	Kern	SALLY
June 21, 1921	Kern	ZIEGFELD FOLLIES OF 1921
November 7, 1921	Gershwin	THE PERFECT FOOL
February 20, 1922	Gershwin	THE FRENCH DOLL
July 6, 1922	Gershwin	SPICE OF 1922
August 28, 1922	Gershwin	GEO. WHITE'S SCANDALS < fourth >
June 18, 1923	Gershwin	GEO. WHITE'S SCANDALS < fifth >
August 28, 1923	Gershwin	LITTLE MISS BLUEBEARD
January 21, 1924	Gershwin	SWEET LITTLE DEVIL
June 30, 1924	Gershwin	GEO. WHITE'S SCANDALS < sixth >
September 11, 1924 < L >	Gershwin	PRIMROSE
November 6, 1924	Kern	PETER PAN < second >
April 13, 1925	Gershwin	TELL ME MORE
June 14, 1926	[PART 4]	GEO. WHITE'S SCANDALS < eighth >
September 6, 1927	[PART 4]	GOOD NEWS!
November 26, 1932	Youmans	TAKE A CHANCE
December 6, 1939	Porter	DUBARRY WAS A LADY
May 28, 1940	Berlin	LOUISIANA PURCHASE
October 30, 1940	Porter	PANAMA HATTIE

HOWARD DIETZ
Lyricist, Librettist

BORN: September 8, 1896   New York, New York
DIED: July 30, 1983   New York, New York

September 23, 1924	Kern	DEAR SIR
November 8, 1926	Gershwin	OH, KAY!
April 30, 1929	Schwartz	THE LITTLE SHOW
May 1, 1929	Schwartz	GRAND STREET FOLLIES < sixth >
February 20, 1930 <L>	Schwartz	HERE COMES THE BRIDE
April 4, 1930 <L>	Schwartz	CO-OPTIMISTS OF 1930
September 2, 1930	Schwartz	SECOND LITTLE SHOW
October 15, 1930	Schwartz/Duke/Lane	THREE'S A CROWD
June 3, 1931	Schwartz	THE BAND WAGON
September 15, 1932	Schwartz	FLYING COLORS
November 28, 1934	Schwartz	REVENGE WITH MUSIC
September 19, 1935	Schwartz	AT HOME ABROAD
February 4, 1936 <L>	Schwartz	FOLLOW THE SUN
December 25, 1936	Schwartz	THE SHOW IS ON
December 22, 1937	Schwartz	BETWEEN THE DEVIL
May 23, 1940	Duke	KEEP OFF THE GRASS
June 22, 1942	Weill	LUNCHTIME FOLLIES
March 22, 1943	Duke	DANCING IN THE STREETS
January 13, 1944	Duke	JACKPOT
[c. April 1944]	Duke	TARS AND SPARS
November 16, 1944	Duke	SADIE THOMPSON
April 30, 1948	Schwartz	INSIDE U.S.A.
November 18, 1961	Schwartz	THE GAY LIFE
October 17, 1963	Schwartz	JENNIE

CHARLES B. DILLINGHAM
Producer

BORN: May 30, 1868   Hartford, Connecticut
DIED: August 30, 1934   New York, New York

August 17, 1910	Kern	THE ECHO
December 8, 1914	Berlin	WATCH YOUR STEP
October 5, 1915	Kern/Porter	MISS INFORMATION
December 25, 1915	Berlin	STOP! LOOK! LISTEN!

May 10, 1926	Rodgers	GARRICK GAIETIES <second>
December 27, 1926	Rodgers	PEGGY-ANN
April 25, 1927	Youmans	HIT THE DECK
November 3, 1927	Rodgers	A CONNECTICUT YANKEE <first>
April 26, 1928	Rodgers	PRESENT ARMS!
September 25, 1928	Rodgers	CHEE-CHEE
November 27, 1929	Porter	FIFTY MILLION FRENCHMEN
December 8, 1930	Porter	THE NEW YORKERS
February 10, 1931	Rodgers	AMERICA'S SWEETHEART
January 20, 1933	Gershwin	PARDON MY ENGLISH
December 6, 1939	Porter	DUBARRY WAS A LADY
October 30, 1940	Porter	PANAMA HATTIE
October 29, 1941	Porter	LET'S FACE IT!
January 7, 1943	Porter	SOMETHING FOR THE BOYS
November 17, 1943	Rodgers	A CONNECTICUT YANKEE <second>
January 28, 1944	Porter	MEXICAN HAYRIDE
May 16, 1946	Berlin	ANNIE GET YOUR GUN
April 8, 1954	Schwartz	BY THE BEAUTIFUL SEA
February 5, 1959	[PART 4]	REDHEAD

BOB FOSSE
Director, Choreographer

BORN: June 23, 1927   Chicago, Illinois
DIED: September 23, 1987   Washington, D.C.

May 13, 1954	Adler	THE PAJAMA GAME
May 5, 1955	Adler	DAMN YANKEES
November 29, 1956	Styne	BELLS ARE RINGING
May 14, 1957	Merrill	NEW GIRL IN TOWN
February 5, 1959	[PART 4]	REDHEAD
October 14, 1961	Loesser	HOW TO SUCCEED . . .
November 17, 1962	Coleman	LITTLE ME
March 11, 1965	Loesser	PLEASURES AND PALACES
January 30, 1966	Coleman	SWEET CHARITY

October 23, 1972	Schwartz	PIPPIN
June 1, 1975	Kander	CHICAGO

VINTON FREEDLEY
Producer

BORN: November 5, 1891   Philadelphia, Pennsylvania
DIED: June 5, 1969   New York, New York

December 1, 1924	Gershwin	LADY, BE GOOD!
December 28, 1925	Gershwin	TIP-TOES
November 8, 1926	Gershwin	OH, KAY!
November 22, 1927	Gershwin	FUNNY FACE
November 8, 1928	Gershwin	TREASURE GIRL
March 11, 1929	Rodgers	SPRING IS HERE
November 11, 1929	Rodgers	HEADS UP!
October 14, 1930	Gershwin	GIRL CRAZY
January 20, 1933	Gershwin	PARDON MY ENGLISH
November 21, 1934	Porter	ANYTHING GOES
October 29, 1936	Porter	RED, HOT AND BLUE!
November 9, 1938	Porter	LEAVE IT TO ME
October 24, 1940	Duke	CABIN IN THE SKY
October 29, 1941	Porter	LET'S FACE IT
March 22, 1943	Duke	DANCING IN THE STREETS
January 13, 1944	Duke	JACKPOT

IRA GERSHWIN
Lyricist

BORN: December 6, 1896   New York, New York
DIED: August 17, 1983   Beverly Hills, California

October 24, 1918	Gershwin	LADIES FIRST
August 31, 1920	Gershwin	THE SWEETHEART SHOP
September 27, 1920	Youmans	PICCADILLY TO BROADWAY
March 21, 1921	Gershwin	A DANGEROUS MAID
May 3, 1921	Youmans	TWO LITTLE GIRLS IN BLUE
February 20, 1922	Gershwin	FOR GOODNESS SAKE
August 28, 1922	Gershwin	GEO. WHITE'S SCANDALS < fourth >

| August 28, 1923 | Gershwin | LITTLE MISS BLUEBEARD |
| | | |

NOTE: above lyrics credited to "Arthur Francis"

September 11, 1924 <L>	Gershwin	PRIMROSE
December 1, 1924	Gershwin	LADY, BE GOOD!
April 13, 1925	Gershwin	TELL ME MORE
September 7, 1925	Youmans	A NIGHT OUT
December 28, 1925	Gershwin	TIP-TOES
July 26, 1926	Gershwin	AMERICANA <first>
November 8, 1926	Gershwin	OH, KAY!
[c. April 1927] <L>	Duke	TWO LITTLE GIRLS IN BLUE
August 29, 1927	Gershwin	STRIKE UP THE BAND <first>
November 22, 1927	Gershwin	FUNNY FACE
January 10, 1928	Gershwin	ROSALIE
November 8, 1928	Gershwin	TREASURE GIRL
July 2, 1929	Gershwin	SHOW GIRL
January 14, 1930	Gershwin	STRIKE UP THE BAND <second>
February 11, 1930	Gershwin	NINE-FIFTEEN REVUE
June 4, 1930	Duke	GARRICK GAIETIES <third>
October 14, 1930	Gershwin	GIRL CRAZY
December 26, 1931	Gershwin	OF THEE I SING
January 20, 1933	Gershwin	PARDON MY ENGLISH
October 21, 1933	Gershwin	LET 'EM EAT CAKE
August 27, 1934	Arlen	LIFE BEGINS AT 8:40
October 10, 1935	Gershwin	PORGY AND BESS
January 30, 1936	Duke	ZIEGFELD FOLLIES <OF 1936>
December 25, 1936	Gershwin	THE SHOW IS ON
January 23, 1941	Weill	LADY IN THE DARK
March 22, 1945	Weill	THE FIREBRAND OF FLORENCE
November 4, 1946	Schwartz	PARK AVENUE
March 9, 1951	Gershwin	LET ME HEAR THE MELODY

MAX GORDON
Producer

BORN: June 28, 1892   New York, New York
DIED: November 2, 1978   New York, New York

October 15, 1930	Schwartz	THREE'S A CROWD
June 3, 1931	Schwartz	THE BAND WAGON
October 15, 1931	Kern	THE CAT AND THE FIDDLE
September 15, 1932	Schwartz	FLYING COLORS
November 18, 1933	Kern	ROBERTA
October 12, 1935	Porter	JUBILEE
September 24, 1938	Rome	SING OUT THE NEWS
November 17, 1939	Kern	VERY WARM FOR MAY
March 22, 1945	Weill	FIREBRAND OF FLORENCE
November 4, 1946	Schwartz	PARK AVENUE

OSCAR HAMMERSTEIN 2ND
Lyricist, Librettist, Producer

BORN: July 12, 1895   New York, New York
DIED: August 23, 1960   Doylestown, Pennsylvania

[c. March 1919]	Rodgers	UP STAGE AND DOWN
March 24, 1920	Rodgers	FLY WITH ME
February 7, 1923	Youmans	WILDFLOWER
December 25, 1923	Youmans	MARY JANE McKANE
September 22, 1925	Kern	SUNNY
December 30, 1925	Gershwin	SONG OF THE FLAME
December 27, 1927	Kern	SHOW BOAT
September 5, 1928	Schwartz	GOOD BOY
November 21, 1928	Youmans	RAINBOW
September 2, 1929	Kern	SWEET ADELINE
November 8, 1932	Kern	MUSIC IN THE AIR
April 9, 1934 <L>	Kern	THREE SISTERS
June 3, 1938	Kern	GENTLEMEN UNAFRAID
November 17, 1939	Kern	VERY WARM FOR MAY
May 12, 1940	Schwartz	AMERICAN JUBILEE
June 22, 1944	Weill	LUNCHTIME FOLLIES
March 31, 1943	Rodgers	OKLAHOMA!

April 19, 1945	Rodgers	CAROUSEL
May 16, 1946	Berlin	ANNIE GET YOUR GUN
October 31, 1946	Rodgers	HAPPY BIRTHDAY
October 10, 1947	Rodgers	ALLEGRO
April 7, 1949	Rodgers	SOUTH PACIFIC
March 29, 1951	Rodgers	THE KING AND I
May 28, 1953	Rodgers	ME AND JULIET
November 30, 1955	Rodgers	PIPE DREAM
December 1, 1958	Rodgers	FLOWER DRUM SONG
November 16, 1959	Rodgers	THE SOUND OF MUSIC

OTTO HARBACH
Lyricist, Librettist

BORN: August 18, 1873 Salt Lake City, Utah
DIED: January 24, 1963 New York, New York

September 11, 1911	Berlin	THE FASCINATING WIDOW
December 25, 1917	Berlin	GOING UP
February 7, 1923	Youmans	WILDFLOWER
September 16, 1925	Youmans	NO, NO, NANETTE
September 22, 1925	Kern	SUNNY
December 30, 1925	Gershwin	SONG OF THE FLAME
October 12, 1926	Kern	CRISS-CROSS
December 17, 1926	Youmans	OH, PLEASE!
March 22, 1927	Kern	LUCKY
September 5, 1928	Schwartz	GOOD BOY
February 20, 1930	Schwartz	HERE COMES THE BRIDE
October 15, 1931	Kern	THE CAT AND THE FIDDLE
November 18, 1933	Kern	ROBERTA
June 3, 1938	Kern	GENTLEMEN UNAFRAID

E. Y. HARBURG
Lyricist, Librettist

BORN: April 8, 1898 New York, New York
DIED: March 5, 1981 Los Angeles, California

June 4, 1930	Duke	GARRICK GAIETIES < third >

July 1, 1930	Arlen	EARL CARROLL VANITIES < eighth >
October 5, 1932	Arlen	AMERICANA < third >
December 2, 1932	Arlen	THE GREAT MAGOO
December 7, 1932	Duke	WALK A LITTLE FASTER
July 28, 1933	Arlen	CRAZY QUILT OF 1933
January 4, 1934	Duke	ZIEGFELD FOLLIES OF 1934
August 27, 1934	Arlen	LIFE BEGINS AT 8:40
December 25, 1936	Arlen	THE SHOW IS ON
December 1, 1937	Arlen	HOORAY FOR WHAT!
September 11, 1940	Lane	HOLD ON TO YOUR HATS
October 5, 1944	Arlen	BLOOMER GIRL
January 10, 1947	Lane	FINIAN'S RAINBOW
May 14, 1951	[PART 4]	FLAHOOLEY
September 11, 1952	Lane	JOLLYANNA
October 31, 1957	Arlen	JAMAICA
January 27, 1968	Styne	DARLING OF THE DAY

SHELDON HARNICK
Lyricist

BORN: December 27, 1924   Chicago, Illinois

February 28, 1955	Strouse	SHOESTRING REVUE
November 5, 1956	Strouse	SHOESTRING '57
January 23, 1958	Bock	THE BODY BEAUTIFUL
November 23, 1959	Bock	FIORELLO!
October 17, 1960	Bock	TENDERLOIN
November 27, 1962	Bock	NEVER TOO LATE
April 11, 1963	Bock	MAN IN THE MOON
April 23, 1963	Bock	SHE LOVES ME
April 22, 1964	Bock	TO BROADWAY WITH LOVE
September 22, 1964	Bock	FIDDLER ON THE ROOF
February 16, 1965	Bock	BAKER STREET
October 18, 1966	Bock	THE APPLE TREE
October 20, 1968	Bock	HER FIRST ROMAN
October 19, 1970	Bock	THE ROTHSCHILDS
April 25, 1976	Rodgers	REX

SAM H. HARRIS
Producer

BORN: February 3, 1872   New York, New York
DIED: July 3, 1941   New York, New York

September 25, 1911	Berlin	THE LITTLE MILLIONAIRE
[c. April 1912]	Berlin	COHAN AND HARRIS MINSTRELS
August 31, 1912	Kern	A POLISH WEDDING
May 28, 1916	Berlin	FRIARS' FROLIC OF 1916
December 25, 1917	Berlin	GOING UP
December 31, 1917	Berlin	THE COHAN REVUE OF 1918
February 17, 1919	Berlin	THE ROYAL VAGABOND
September 22, 1921	Berlin	MUSIC BOX REVUE < first >
October 23, 1922	Berlin	MUSIC BOX REVUE < second >
September 22, 1923	Berlin	MUSIC BOX REVUE < third >
December 1, 1924	Berlin	MUSIC BOX REVUE < fourth >
December 8, 1925	Berlin	THE COCOANUTS
December 26, 1931	Gershwin	OF THEE I SING
February 17, 1932	Berlin	FACE THE MUSIC
September 30, 1933	Berlin	AS THOUSANDS CHEER
October 21, 1933	Gershwin	LET 'EM EAT CAKE
October 12, 1935	Porter	JUBILEE
November 2, 1937	Rodgers	I'D RATHER BE RIGHT
January 23, 1941	Weill	LADY IN THE DARK

LORENZ HART
Lyricist, Librettist

BORN: May 2, 1895   New York, New York
DIED: November 22, 1943   New York, New York

June 10, 1919	Rodgers	A LONELY ROMEO
March 6, 1920	Rodgers	YOU'D BE SURPRISED
March 24, 1920	Rodgers	FLY WITH ME
July 28, 1920	Rodgers	POOR LITTLE RITZ GIRL

April 20, 1921	Rodgers	YOU'LL NEVER KNOW
May 13, 1924	Rodgers	THE MELODY MAN
May 17, 1925	Rodgers	GARRICK GAIETIES < first >
August 6, 1925	Rodgers	JUNE DAYS
September 18, 1925	Rodgers	DEAREST ENEMY
[c. January 1926]	Rodgers	FIFTH AVENUE FOLLIES
March 17, 1926	Rodgers	THE GIRL FRIEND
April 29, 1926 <L>	Rodgers	COCHRAN'S 1926 REVUE
May 10, 1926	Rodgers	GARRICK GAIETIES < second >
December 1, 1926 <L>	Rodgers	LIDO LADY
December 27, 1926	Rodgers	PEGGY-ANN
December 28, 1926	Rodgers	BETSY
April 27, 1927 <L>	Rodgers	LADY LUCK
May 20, 1927 <L>	Rodgers	LONDON PAVILION REVUE
November 3, 1927	Rodgers	A CONNECTICUT YANKEE <first>
January 3, 1928	Rodgers	SHE'S MY BABY
April 26, 1928	Rodgers	PRESENT ARMS!
September 25, 1928	Rodgers	CHEE-CHEE
January 31, 1929	Rodgers	LADY FINGERS
March 11, 1929	Rodgers	SPRING IS HERE
November 11, 1929	Rodgers	HEADS UP!
February 18, 1930	Rodgers	SIMPLE SIMON
December 3, 1930 <L>	Rodgers	EVER GREEN
February 10, 1931	Rodgers	AMERICA'S SWEETHEART
May 19, 1931	Rodgers	CRAZY QUILT
November 16, 1933 <L>	Rodgers	PLEASE!
April 29, 1935	Rodgers	SOMETHING GAY
November 16, 1935	Rodgers	JUMBO
April 11, 1936	Rodgers	ON YOUR TOES
December 25, 1936	Rodgers	THE SHOW IS ON
April 14, 1937	Rodgers	BABES IN ARMS
November 2, 1937	Rodgers	I'D RATHER BE RIGHT
May 11, 1938	Rodgers	I MARRIED AN ANGEL
November 23, 1938	Rodgers	THE BOYS FROM SYRACUSE

October 18, 1939	Rodgers	TOO MANY GIRLS
April 4, 1940	Rodgers	HIGHER AND HIGHER
June 24, 1940	Rodgers	TWO WEEKS WITH PAY
December 25, 1940	Rodgers	PAL JOEY
June 2, 1942	Rodgers	BY JUPITER
November 17, 1943	Rodgers	A CONNECTICUT YANKEE < second >

MOSS HART
Librettist, Director, Producer

BORN: October 24, 1904   New York, New York
DIED: December 20, 1961   Palm Springs, California

February 17, 1932	Berlin	FACE THE MUSIC
September 30, 1933	Berlin	AS THOUSANDS CHEER
October 12, 1935	Porter	JUBILEE
December 25, 1936	Duke	THE SHOW IS ON
November 2, 1937	Rodgers	I'D RATHER BE RIGHT
September 24, 1938	Rome	SING OUT THE NEWS
October 16, 1939	Porter	THE MAN WHO CAME TO DINNER
January 23, 1941	Weill	LADY IN THE DARK
June 22, 1942	Weill	LUNCHTIME FOLLIES
December 7, 1944	Porter	SEVEN LIVELY ARTS
April 30, 1948	Schwartz	INSIDE U.S.A.
July 15, 1949	Berlin	MISS LIBERTY
March 15, 1956	Loewe	MY FAIR LADY
December 3, 1960	Loewe	CAMELOT

TOM JONES
Lyricist, Librettist

BORN: February 17, 1928   Littlefield, Texas

November 5, 1956	Schmidt	SHOESTRING '57
October 11, 1958	Schmidt	DEMI-DOZEN
May 3, 1960	Schmidt	THE FANTASTICKS
October 24, 1963	Schmidt	110 IN THE SHADE
December 5, 1966	Schmidt	I DO! I DO!
January 22, 1969	Schmidt	CELEBRATION
May 6, 1970	Schmidt	COLETTE < first >
April 8, 1975	Schmidt	PHILEMON

February 9, 1982	Schmidt	COLETTE < second >
March 31, 1983	Schimdt	COLETTE COLLAGE < first >
July 29, 1987	Schmidt	GROVER'S CORNERS
April 24, 1991	Schmidt	COLETTE COLLAGE < second >

GEORGE S. KAUFMAN
Lyricist, Librettist, Director, Producer

BORN: November 14, 1889   Pittsburgh, Pennsylvania
DIED: June 2, 1961   New York, New York

September 22, 1923	Berlin	MUSIC BOX REVUE < third >
December 8, 1925	Berlin	THE COCOANUTS
August 29, 1927	Gershwin	STRIKE UP THE BAND < first >
April 30, 1929	Schwartz	THE LITTLE SHOW
January 14, 1930	Gershwin	STRIKE UP THE BAND < second >
February 11, 1930	Arlen	NINE-FIFTEEN REVUE
June 3, 1931	Schwartz	THE BAND WAGON
December 26, 1931	Gershwin	OF THEE I SING
February 17, 1932	Berlin	FACE THE MUSIC
October 21, 1933	Gershwin	LET 'EM EAT CAKE
October 22, 1934	Schwartz	BRING ON THE GIRLS
December 25, 1936	Duke	THE SHOW IS ON
September 24, 1938	Rome	SING OUT THE NEWS
October 16, 1939	Porter	THE MAN WHO CAME TO DINNER
June 22, 1942	Weill	LUNCHTIME FOLLIES
December 7, 1944	Porter	SEVEN LIVELY ARTS
November 4, 1946	Schwartz	PARK AVENUE
June 20, 1949	Rome	PRETTY PENNY
November 24, 1950	Loesser	GUYS AND DOLLS
February 24, 1955	Porter	SILK STOCKINGS
October 10, 1957	Rome	ROMANOFF AND JULIET

MICHAEL KIDD
Director, Choreographer

BORN: August 12, 1919   New York, New York

| January 10, 1947 | Lane | FINIAN'S RAINBOW |
| June 20, 1949 | Rome | PRETTY PENNY |

November 24, 1950	Loesser	GUYS AND DOLLS
May 7, 1953	Porter	CAN-CAN
November 15, 1956	[PART 4]	LI'L ABNER
April 23, 1959	Rome	DESTRY RIDES AGAIN
December 16, 1960	Coleman	WILDCAT
December 27, 1961	Styne	SUBWAYS ARE FOR SLEEPING
October 3, 1963	Willson	HERE'S LOVE
May 7, 1964	Styne	WONDERWORLD
October 27, 1964	Herman	BEN FRANKLIN IN PARIS
December 14, 1966	Merrill	BREAKFAST AT TIFFANY'S
October 19, 1970	Bock	THE ROTHSCHILDS

ALAN JAY LERNER
Lyricist, Librettist

BORN: August 31, 1918   New York, New York
DIED: June 14, 1986   New York, New York

October 8, 1942	Loewe	LIFE OF THE PARTY
November 11, 1943	Loewe	WHAT'S UP
November 22, 1945	Loewe	THE DAY BEFORE SPRING
March 13, 1947	Loewe	BRIGADOON
October 7, 1948	Weill	LOVE LIFE
November 12, 1951	Loewe	PAINT YOUR WAGON
March 15, 1956	Loewe	MY FAIR LADY
December 3, 1960	Loewe	CAMELOT
October 17, 1965	Lane	ON A CLEAR DAY YOU CAN SEE FOREVER
May 4, 1976	Bernstein	1600 PENNSYLVANIA AVENUE
April 8, 1979	Lane	CARMELINA
May 11, 1983	Strouse	DANCE A LITTLE CLOSER

JOSHUA LOGAN
Director, Librettist, Producer

BORN: October 5, 1908   Texarkana, Texas
DIED: July 12, 1988   New York, New York

| May 11, 1938 | Rodgers | I MARRIED AN ANGEL |
| December 19, 1938 | Weill | KNICKERBOCKER HOLIDAY |

February 9, 1939	Schwartz	STARS IN YOUR EYES
April 4, 1940	Rodgers	HIGHER AND HIGHER
June 3, 1942	Rodgers	BY JUPITER
July 4, 1942	Berlin	THIS IS THE ARMY
May 16, 1946	Berlin	ANNIE GET YOUR GUN
October 3, 1946	Rodgers	HAPPY BIRTHDAY
April 7, 1949	Rodgers	SOUTH PACIFIC
June 25, 1952	Rome	WISH YOU WERE HERE
November 4, 1954	Rome	FANNY
March 19, 1962	Strouse	ALL AMERICAN
October 20, 1962	Berlin	MR. PRESIDENT
May 24, 1966	Herman	MAME
March 29, 1970	Styne	LOOK TO THE LILIES

ROUBEN MAMOULIAN
Director

BORN: October 8, 1898   Tiflis, Russia
DIED: December 4, 1987   Woodland Hills, California

October 10, 1935	Gershwin	PORGY AND BESS
March 31, 1943	Rodgers	OKLAHOMA!
November 16, 1944	Duke	SADIE THOMPSON
April 19, 1945	Rodgers	CAROUSEL
March 30, 1946	Arlen	ST. LOUIS WOMAN
October 30, 1949	Weill	LOST IN THE STARS
[c. April 1950]	Weill	HUCKLEBERRY FINN

DAVID MERRICK
Producer

BORN: November 27, 1911   St. Louis, Missouri

November 4, 1954	Rome	FANNY
October 10, 1957	Rome	ROMANOFF AND JULIET
October 31, 1957	Arlen	JAMAICA
April 23, 1959	Rome	DESTRY RIDES AGAIN
May 21, 1959	Styne	GYPSY
October 22, 1959	Merrill	TAKE ME ALONG
December 26, 1960	Styne	DO RE MI
April 13, 1961	Merrill	CARNIVAL!
December 27, 1961	Styne	SUBWAYS ARE FOR SLEEPING

March 22, 1962	Rome	I Can Get It for You Wholesale
October 24, 1963	Schmidt	110 in the Shade
November 11, 1963	Styne	Arturo Ui
January 16, 1964	Herman/Merrill/ Strouse	Hello, Dolly!
December 5, 1966	Schmidt	I Do! I Do!
December 14, 1966	Merrill	Breakfast at Tiffany's
September 27, 1967	Coleman	Keep It in the Family
January 18, 1968	Kander	The Happy Time
December 1, 1968	[PART 4]	Promises, Promises
April 9, 1972	Styne	Sugar
October 6, 1974	Herman	Mack and Mabel
May 11, 1974	S. Schwartz	The Baker's Wife

HAROLD PRINCE
Producer, Director

BORN: January 30, 1928   New York, New York

May 13, 1954	Adler	The Pajama Game
May 5, 1955	Adler	Damn Yankees
May 14, 1957	Merrill	New Girl in Town
September 26, 1957	Bernstein	West Side Story
November 23, 1959	Bock	Fiorello!
October 17, 1960	Bock	Tenderloin
January 27, 1962	Kander	A Family Affair
May 8, 1962	Sondheim	A Funny Thing . . .
April 23, 1963	Bock	She Loves Me
September 22, 1964	Bock	Fiddler on the Roof
February 16, 1965	Bock	Baker Street
May 11, 1965	Kander	Flora, the Red Menace
March 29, 1966	Strouse	"Its . . . Superman"
November 20, 1966	Kander	Cabaret
November 17, 1968	Kander	Zorba
April 26, 1970	Sondheim	Company
April 4, 1971	Sondheim	Follies
February 25, 1973	Sondheim	A Little Night Music
March 10, 1974	Bernstein	Candide < second >

January 11, 1976	Sondheim	PACIFIC OVERTURES
April 25, 1976	Rodgers	REX
February 19, 1978	Coleman	ON THE TWENTIETH CENTURY
March 1, 1979	Sondheim	SWEENEY TODD
November 16, 1981	Sondheim	MERRILY WE ROLL ALONG
September 25, 1979	[PART 5]	EVITA
January 26, 1988	[PART 5]	PHANTOM OF THE OPERA
May 1, 1990	Kander	KISS OF THE SPIDERWOMAN

JEROME ROBBINS
Director, Choreographer

BORN: October 11, 1918   New York, New York

December 28, 1944	Bernstein	ON THE TOWN
October 9, 1947	Styne	HIGH BUTTON SHOES
January 29, 1948	Martin	LOOK, MA, I'M DANCIN!
September 24, 1948	Rome	THAT'S THE TICKET!
July 15, 1949	Berlin	MISS LIBERTY
October 12, 1950	Berlin	CALL ME MADAM
March 29, 1951	Rodgers	THE KING AND I
December 15, 1952	Duke	TWO'S COMPANY
May 13, 1954	Adler	THE PAJAMA GAME
October 20, 1954	Styne	PETER PAN < fourth >
November 29, 1956	Styne	BELLS ARE RINGING
September 26, 1957	Bernstein	WEST SIDE STORY
May 21, 1959	Styne	GYPSY
May 8, 1962	Sondheim	A FUNNY THING . . .
March 26, 1964	Styne	FUNNY GIRL
September 22, 1964	Bock	FIDDLER ON THE ROOF

HASSARD SHORT
Director

BORN: October 15, 1877   Edlington, Lincs, England
DIED: October 9, 1956   Nice, France

September 22, 1921	Berlin	MUSIC BOX REVUE < first >

October 23, 1922	Berlin	MUSIC BOX REVUE < second >
September 22, 1923	Berlin	MUSIC BOX REVUE < third >
September 22, 1925	Kern	SUNNY
December 17, 1926	Youmans	OH, PLEASE!
March 22, 1927	Kern	LUCKY
October 15, 1930	Schwartz	THREE'S A CROWD
June 3, 1931	Schwartz	THE BAND WAGON
February 17, 1932	Berlin	FACE THE MUSIC
September 30, 1933	Berlin	AS THOUSANDS CHEER
November 18, 1933	Kern	ROBERTA
October 12, 1935	Porter	JUBILEE
December 22, 1937	Schwartz	BETWEEN THE DEVIL
November 17, 1939	Kern	VERY WARM FOR MAY
January 23, 1941	Weill	LADY IN THE DARK
December 25, 1941	Duke	BANJO EYES
June 24, 1942	Rome	STAR AND GARTER
January 7, 1943	Porter	SOMETHING FOR THE BOYS
January 28, 1944	Porter	MEXICAN HAYRIDE
December 7, 1944	Porter	SEVEN LIVELY ARTS
June 28, 1950	Rome	MICHAEL TODD'S PEEP SHOW

MICHAEL STEWART
Librettist, Lyricist

BORN: August 1, 1929   New York, New York
DIED: September 20, 1987   New York, New York

February 28, 1955	Strouse	SHOESTRING REVUE
May 22, 1956	Strouse	THE LITTLEST REVUE
November 5, 1956	Strouse	SHOESTRING '57
April 14, 1960	Strouse	BYE BYE BIRDIE
April 13, 1961	Merrill	CARNIVAL!
January 16, 1964	Herman/Merrill/ Strouse	HELLO, DOLLY!
March 18, 1973	Coleman	SEESAW
October 6, 1974	Herman	MACK AND MABEL
April 17, 1977	Coleman	I LOVE MY WIFE
January 11, 1979	Herman	THE GRAND TOUR

April 30, 1980	Coleman	BARNUM
March 5, 1981	Strouse	BRING BACK BIRDIE
November 27, 1985	Styne	PIECES OF EIGHT

TOMMY TUNE
Director, Choreographer

BORN: February 28, 1939   Wichita Falls, Texas

March 18, 1973	Coleman	SEESAW
April 17, 1978	[PART 4]	THE BEST LITTLE WHOREHOUSE IN TEXAS
May 1, 1980	Herman	A DAY IN HOLLYWOOD/A NIGHT IN THE UKRAINE
May 9, 1982	[PART 4]	NINE
November 12, 1989	[PART 4]	GRAND HOTEL: THE MUSICAL
May 1, 1991	Coleman	THE WILL ROGERS FOLLIES

DWIGHT DEERE WIMAN
Producer

BORN: August 8, 1895   Moline, Illinois
DIED: January 20, 1951   Hudson, New York

April 30, 1929	Schwartz	THE LITTLE SHOW
September 2, 1930	Schwartz	THE SECOND LITTLE SHOW
June 1, 1931	Lane	THE THIRD LITTLE SHOW
November 29, 1932	Porter	THE GAY DIVORCE
November 20, 1933	Schwartz	SHE LOVES ME NOT
April 11, 1936	Rodgers	ON YOUR TOES
April 14, 1937	Rodgers	BABES IN ARMS
May 11, 1938	Rodgers	I MARRIED AN ANGEL
December 1, 1938	Loewe	GREAT LADY
February 9, 1939	Schwartz	STARS IN YOUR EYES
April 4, 1940	Rodgers	HIGHER AND HIGHER
June 2, 1942	Rodgers	BY JUPITER
January 9, 1947	Weill	STREET SCENE

P. G. WODEHOUSE
Librettist, Lyricist

BORN: October 15, 1881 Guildford, England
DIED: February 14, 1975 Southampton, New York

March 19, 1906 <L>	Kern	THE BEAUTY OF BATH
September 25, 1916	Kern	MISS SPRINGTIME
January 11, 1917	Kern	HAVE A HEART
February 20, 1917	Kern	OH, BOY!
August 28, 1917	Kern	LEAVE IT TO JANE
September 24, 1917	Kern	THE RIVIERA GIRL
November 5, 1917	Kern	MISS 1917
February 1, 1918	Kern	OH LADY! LADY!!
November 27, 1918	Kern	OH, MY DEAR!
February 21, 1920	Kern	SALLY
September 19, 1921 <L>	Kern	THE CABARET GIRL
September 5, 1923 <L>	Kern	THE BEAUTY PRIZE
April 8, 1924	Kern	SITTING PRETTY
November 8, 1926	Gershwin	OH, KAY!
December 27, 1927	Kern	SHOW BOAT
January 10, 1928	Gershwin	ROSALIE
November 21, 1934	Porter	ANYTHING GOES

FLORENZ ZIEGFELD, JR.
Producer

BORN: March 15, 1867 Chicago, Illinois
DIED: July 22, 1932 Los Angeles, California

June 20, 1910	Berlin	ZIEGFELD FOLLIES OF 1910
June 26, 1911	Berlin/Kern	ZIEGFELD FOLLIES OF 1911
April 11, 1912	Kern	A WINSOME WIDOW
October 21, 1912	Berlin	ZIEGFELD FOLLIES OF 1912
June 12, 1916	Berlin/Kern	ZIEGFELD FOLLIES OF 1916
November 6, 1916	Berlin	THE CENTURY GIRL
[c. April 1917]	Berlin	DANCE AND GROW THIN

June 12, 1917	Kern	ZIEGFELD FOLLIES OF 1917
November 5, 1917	Kern	MISS 1917
June 18, 1918	Berlin	ZIEGFELD FOLLIES OF 1918
June 23, 1919	Berlin	ZIEGFELD FOLLIES OF 1919
October 2, 1919	Berlin	ZIEGFELD MIDNIGHT FROLIC
March 8, 1920	Berlin	ZIEGFELD GIRLS OF 1920
June 22, 1920	Berlin	ZIEGFELD FOLLIES OF 1920
December 21, 1920	Kern	SALLY
June 21, 1921	Kern	ZIEGFELD FOLLIES OF 1921
December 25, 1922	Kern	ROSE BRIAR
December 28, 1926	Rodgers/Berlin	BETSY
August 16, 1927	Berlin	ZIEGFELD FOLLIES OF 1927
December 27, 1927	Kern	SHOW BOAT
January 10, 1928	Gershwin	ROSALIE
December 4, 1928	[PART 4]	WHOOPEE
July 2, 1929	Gershwin/Youmans	SHOW GIRL
February 18, 1930	Rodgers	SIMPLE SIMON
November 18, 1930	Youmans	SMILES

Appendix 3

Bibliography and a Word About Finding Music

Bibliography

This section lists the more helpful sources used in the preparation of this book. The most important material has been the songs, over 6,000 of them: for obvious reasons, printed music, scores, and collections are not included below. Neither are newspaper reviews and articles, theatre programs, souvenir programs, record album notes, etc.

Abbott, George. *Mister Abbott.* New York: Random House, 1963.

ASCAP Index of Performed Compositions (Four Editions). New York: American Society Of Composers, Authors And Publishers, 1952 through 1978.

Astaire, Fred. *Steps In Time.* New York: Harper & Brothers, 1959.

Bernstein, Leonard. *Findings.* New York: Simon And Schuster, 1982.

Bloom, Ken. *American Song.* New York: Facts on File Publications, 1985.

Blum, Daniel, editor. *Theatre World, Vols. 1–4.* New York: Daniel C. Blum/Theatre World, 1945–1948; *Vols. 5–13.* New York: Greenberg Publisher, 1949–1957; *Vols. 14–20.* Philadelphia: Chilton Books, 1958–1964.

Bordman, Gerald. *American Musical Theatre.* New York: Oxford University Press, 1978.

Bordman, Gerald. *Days To Be Happy, Years To Be Sad.* New York: Oxford University Press, 1982.

Bordman, Gerald. *Jerome Kern.* New York, Oxford University Press, 1980.

Burrows, Abe. *Honest Abe.* Boston: Little, Brown & Co., 1980.

Cantor, Eddie. *My Life Is In Your Hands.* New York: Blue Ribbon Books, 1932.

Chapman, John, editor. *The Best Play Series, Vols. 1947–1948* through *1951–1952.* New York: Dodd, Mead & Company, 1948–1952.

[Chappell Group]. *Comprehensive Catalogue of Vocal Solos.* New York: Chappell Group, [Circa 1953].

Crawford, Cheryl. *One Naked Individual.* Indianapolis: Bobbs-Merrill Co., 1977.

de Mille, Agnes. *Dance To The Piper.* Boston: Little, Brown and Co., 1952.

Dietz, Howard. *Dancing In The Dark.* New York: Quadrangle, 1974.

Drew, David. *Kurt Weill: A Handbook.* Berkeley, Cal.: University of California Press, 1987.

Duke, Vernon. *Passport To Paris.* Boston: Little, Brown & Co., 1955.

Ewen, David. *New Complete Book Of The American Musical Theatre.* Holt, Rinehart and Winston, 1970.

Ewen, David. *Popular American Composers.* New York: H. W. Wilson Co., 1962. *First Supplement,* 1972.

Fordin, Hugh. *Getting To Know Him.* New York: Random House, 1977.

Freedland, Michael. *Irving Berlin.* New York: Stein & Day, 1974.

Gershwin, Ira. *Lyrics On Several Occasions.* New York: Alfred A. Knopf, 1959.

Goldberg, Isaac, supplemented by Garson, Edith. *George Gershwin: A Study In American Music.* New York: Frederick Ungar Publishing Co., 1958.

Gordon, Eric A. *Mark the Music: The Life And Work of Marc Blitzstein.* New York: St. Martin's Press, 1989.

Gordon, Max and Funke, Lewis. *Max Gordon Presents.* New York: Bernard Geis, 1963.

Green, Stanley. *Encyclopedia Of The Musical Theatre.* New York: Dodd, Mead & Co., 1976.

Green, Stanley. *Ring Bells! Sing Songs!* New York: Arlington House, 1971.

Green, Stanley, editor. *Rodgers And Hammerstein Fact Book.* New York: Rodgers And Hammerstein, 1955. *Supplement,* 1961.

Green, Stanley. *The World Of Musical Comedy (Revised And Enlarged Fourth Edition).* San Diego: A. S. Barnes & Co., 1980.

Guernsey, Jr., Otis L., editor. *The Best Plays Series, Vols. 1964–1965* through *1982–1983.* New York: Dodd, Mead & Company, 1965–1983.

Hart, Dorothy. *Thou Swell, Thou Witty.* New York: Harper & Row, 1976.

Hellman, Lillian. *Pentimento: A Book Of Portraits.* Boston: Little, Brown and Company, 1973.

Hewes, Henry, editor. *The Best Plays Series, Vols. 1961–1962* through *1963–1964.* New York: Dodd, Mead & Co., 1962–1964.

Higham, Charles. *Ziegfeld.* Chicago: Henry Regnery, 1972.

Hughes, Elinor. *Passing Through To Broadway.* Boston: Waverly House, 1948.

Hummel, David. *The Collector's Guide To The Musical Theatre.* Metuchen, N.J.: Scarecrow Press, 1984.

Jablonski, Edward and Stewart, Lawrence D. *The Gershwin Years.* Garden City, N.Y.: Doubleday and Company, Inc., 1973.

Jablonski, Edward. *Harold Arlen: Happy With The Blues.* New York: Doubleday & Co., 1961.

Jay, Dave. *The Irving Berlin Songography.* New Rochelle: Arlington House, 1969.

Kimball, Robert, editor. *Cole.* New York: Holt, Rinehart and Winston, 1971.

Kimball, Robert, editor. *The Complete Lyrics Of Cole Porter.* New York: Alfred A. Knopf, 1983.

Kimball, Robert, and Simon, Alfred. *The Gershwins.* New York: Atheneum, 1973.

Kronenberger, Louis, editor. *The Best Plays Series, Vols. 1952–1953* through *1960–1961.* New York: Dodd, Mead & Co., 1953–1961.

Lamb, Andrew. *Jerome Kern In Edwardian London.* East Preston, West Sussex, England: Andrew Lamb, 1981.

Leonard, William Torbert. *Broadway Bound.* Metuchen, N.J.: Scarecrow Press, 1983.

Lerner, Alan Jay. *The Street Where I Live.* New York: W. W. Norton & Co., 1978.

Lewine, Richard, and Simon, Alfred. *Encyclopedia Of Theatre Music.* New York: Random House, 1961.

Lewine, Richard, and Simon, Alfred. *Songs Of The American Theatre.* New York: Dodd, Mead and Company, 1973.

Logan, Joshua. *Josh.* New York: Delacorte Press, 1976.

Lynch, Richard Chigley. *Broadway On Record.* New York: Greenwood Press, 1987.

Mantle, Burns, editor. *The Best Plays Series, Vols. 1919–1920* through *1923–1924.* Boston: Small, Maynard & Co., 1920–1924; *Vols. 1924–1925* through *1946–1947.* New York: Dodd, Mead & Co., 1925–1947.

Mantle, Burns, and Sherwood, Garrison P., editors. *The Best Plays of 1899–1909; The Best Plays of 1909–1919.* New York: Dodd, Mead & Co., 1944; 1933.

Marx, Samuel and Clayton, Jan. *Rodgers & Hart: Bewitched, Bothered And Bedeviled.* New York: G. P. Putnam's Sons, 1976.

McNamara, Daniel, editor. *The ASCAP Biographical Dictionary Of Composers, Authors & Publishers.* New York: Thomas Y. Crowell Co., 1948.

Meredith, Scott. *George S. Kaufman And His Friends.* Garden City: Doubleday & Co., 1974.

Nathan, George Jean. *The Theatre Book Of The Year, Vols. 1941–1942* through *1950–1951.* New York: Alfred A. Knopf, 1943–1951.

New York Theatre Critics Reviews, Vols. 1 through *30.* New York: Critics' Theatre Reviews, Inc., 1940–1970.

The New York Times Directory Of The Film. New York: Arno Press, 1971.

The New York Times Directory Of the Theatre. New York: Arno Press, 1973.

Nolan, Frederick. *The Sound Of Their Music.* New York: Walker & Co., 1978.

Parker, John, editor. *Who's Who In The Theatre, 1st* through *16th Editions.* London: Sir Isaac Pitman & Sons, 1912 through 1977.

Prince, Hal. *Contradictions: Notes On Twenty-Six Years In The Theatre.* New York: Dodd, Mead & Company, 1974.

Rigdon, Walter, editor. *Biographical Encyclopedia And Who's Who Of The American Theatre.* New York: Heineman, 1966.

Rodgers, Richard. *Musical Stages.* New York: Random House, 1975.

Sanders, Ronald. *The Days Grow Short: The Life And Music Of Kurt Weill.* New York: Holt, Rinehart & Winston, 1980.

Schwartz, Charles. *Cole Porter.* New York: Dial Press, 1977.

Schwartz, Charles. *Gershwin: His Life And Music.* New York: Bobbs-Merrill, 1973.

Stagg, Jerry. *The Brothers Shubert.* New York: Random House, 1968.

Stone, Fred. *Rolling Stone.* New York: Whittlesey House, 1945.

Stott, William, with Fehl, Fred and Stott, Jane. *On Broadway.* Austin: University of Texas Press, 1978.

Suskin, Steven. *Berlin, Kern, Rodgers, Hart and Hammerstein: A Complete Song Catalogue.* Jefferson, N.C.: McFarland & Co., 1990.

Taylor, Theodore. *Jule: The Story Of Composer Jule Styne.* New York: Random House, 1979.

Teichmann, Howard. *George S. Kaufman: An Intimate Portrait.* New York: Atheneum, 1972.

Toohey, John L. *A History Of The Pulitzer Prize Plays.* New York: Citadel Press, 1967.

[U.S. Army Service Forces]. *About Face!* New York: Special Services Division, [Circa 1944].

[U.S. Army Service Forces]. *Hi, Yank!* New York: Special Services Division, [Circa 1944].

[U.S. Army Service Forces]. *OK, U.S.A.!* New York: Special Services Division, [Circa 1945].

[U.S. Army Service Forces]. *PFC Mary Brown.* New York: Special Services Division, [Circa 1944].

Wharton, John. *Life Among The Playwrights.* New York: Quadrangle, 1974.

Willis, John, editor. *Theatre World, Vols. 21* through *44.* New York: Crown Publishers, 1965–1988.

Wintergreen, John P. *Diary Of An Ex-President.* New York: Minton, Balch and Company, 1932.

[Writers and Material Committee for Soldier Shows]. *At Ease, Vols. III and IV.* USO-Camp Shows, Inc., 1943.

Zadan, Craig. *Sondheim & Co.* New York: Macmillan and Co., Inc. 1974.

A Word About Finding Music

Recently issued songs and still-popular standards can best be found in local music stores. Many vocal scores and selections are still in print. During the last ten years, publishers have begun reissuing long-out-of-print songs in new vocal selections and composer anthologies; in some cases these include previously unpublished work. Chain stores which sell only standard hits won't be of much help; but any place which carries instruction books, classical music, etc. will have (or gladly order) these items. Publishers can be contacted directly for in-print material. Some long-established music stores still have out-of-print material in stock.

An increasing number of stores now carry out-of-print music, especially dealers in used and rare books and antiques. If they don't handle music, they will generally know of others who do. There are dozens of mail-order dealers specializing in music; they advertise in newspapers and journals for antique dealers and collectors. Flea markets and antique shows can also be good places to find music.

The best place to find specific out-of-print songs is in one of several libraries with specialized collections. Those listed below are especially recommended. (Other collections also exist; check with your local library or university library.) Individual policies vary, but some of these facilities allow photocopying of out-of-print material for noncommercial use.

Library of Congress
Music Division—Room 113
Madison Building
1st Avenue and Independence, S.E.
Washington, DC 20540
(202) 707-5504

New York Public Library
Performing Arts Research Center
Music Division—Third Floor
111 Amsterdam Avenue
New York, NY 10023
(212) 870-1650

New York Public Library
General Library of the Performing Arts
Music Circulation—First Floor
111 Amsterdam Avenue
New York, NY 10023
(212) 870-1625

Brown University
John Hay Collection
Box A
20 Prospect Street
Providence, RI 02912
(401) 863-2146

Buffalo and Erie County Public Library
Lafayette Square
Buffalo, NY 14203
(716) 858-7121

Chicago Public Library
Music Section, Fine Arts Division
78 East Washington
Chicago, IL 60602
(312) 269-2886

Indiana University
Lilly Library
Bloomington, IN 47405
(812) 855-2452

UCLA Archive of Popular American Music
1102 Schoenberg Hall
405 Hilgard Avenue
Los Angeles, CA 90024-1490
(213) 825-1665

The majority of the recorded songs mentioned are included on original cast albums. The *Schwann Catalog* lists those presently in print, which any dealer can order. Labels specializing in reissues and rarities are no doubt familiar to collectors of records. Any of several books cataloguing record albums can be consulted for further information.

Song Title Index

Show Index

This index includes all musicals and plays as well as basic property material, motion pictures, etc. The principal listings for productions written by the major composers (or included as Notable Scores) are denoted by boldface page numbers.

People Index

This index contains many, but not all, of the persons mentioned in this book. Those who worked importantly or primarily in musical theatre are included. Demands of space, time, and interest have limited the inclusion of some only tangentially associated with the songs, shows, and careers of the major composers. For ease of usage, page numbers of the primary discussion of each of the major composers and collaborators are in boldface.